ALAN ROGERS
GOOD CAMPS GUIDE

BRITAIN and IRELAND
2000

Quality Camping and Caravanning Parks

THE ALAN ROGERS'
Good camps guide

Compiled by: Deneway Guides & Travel Ltd

Cover design: Design Section, Frome

Cover photography: 'Dawn Sky over England' by Tony Ord
Telegraph Colour Library

Maps created by Customised Mapping (01985 844092)
contain background data provided by GisDATA Ltd.
Maps are © Customised Mapping and GisDATA Ltd. 1999.

Clive Edwards, Lois Edwards & Sue Smart have asserted
their rights to be identified as the authors of this work.

First published in this format 1999

© Haynes Publishing & Deneway Guides & Travel Ltd 1999

Published by: Haynes Publishing, Sparkford, Nr Yeovil, Somerset BA22 7JJ
in association with
Deneway Guides & Travel Ltd, West Bexington, Dorchester, Dorset DT2 9DG

British Library Cataloguing-in-Publication Data:
A catalogue record for this book is available from the British Library.

ISBN: 0 901586 71 4

Printed in Great Britain by J H Haynes & Co Ltd

Contents

Foreword 4
How to use the Guide 5

Selected and Inspected Campsites
England 9
Wales 160
Scotland 177
Northern Ireland 200
Irish Republic 206
Channel Islands 230

Open All Year 234
Parks for Adults Only 235
No Dogs! 236
Fishing 237
Bicycle Hire 238
Golf 239
Horse Riding 239
Boat Launching 239
Camping for People with Disabilities . . . 240
Alan Rogers' Travel Service 242
Reports by Readers 244
Town and Village Index 245
Campsite Index 248
Maps 253

Introduction

There are many officially recognised campsites, or parks as they prefer to be called in both mainland Britain and in Ireland, which vary significantly in terms of the quality of their facilities and in respect of the standard of maintenance and in the way they are run. This guide features a selection of those sites which, as a result of our own inspection system, we are satisfied provide good quality facilities, and are well maintained and well run.

After a thorough inspection and a detailed report by one of our own professional Site Assessors, a decision is made as to whether or not to include a site in this guide. A fully detailed and objective description of each site selected is then written, designed to help you to choose those sites which meet your own and your family's needs. Our selection of sites includes not just the most expensive ones, but also a range of sites designed to cater for a wide variety of preferences, from those seeking a small peaceful campsite in the heart of the countryside, to those looking for an 'all singing, all dancing' site in a popular seaside resort, and for those with more specific needs such as sports facilities, cultural or historical attractions, even sites for naturism.

The Alan Rogers' Approach to Selecting Sites

A few words about our approach to selecting the parks to be featured in our guides may be helpful. Firstly, and most importantly, our selection is based entirely on our own rigorous inspection. Parks cannot buy their way into our guides – indeed the extensive Site Report which is written by us, not by the site owner, is provided free of charge so we are free to say what we think and to provide an honest description.

The criteria which we use when selecting sites are numerous, but the most important by far is the question of good quality and standards. Whatever the size of the site, whether it's part of a campsite chain, or even a local authority site, makes no difference in terms of it being required to meet our exacting standards in terms of its quality. In other words, irrespective of the size of the site, or the number of facilities offered, the essentials (the welcome, the pitches, the sanitary facilities the cleanliness and the general maintenance) must all be of a good standard.

Since none of the campsites have to pay to be featured in our guides, we are free to select exactly those which we think our readers will enjoy, and to reject any that don't meet our standards. This is an on-going process and depends on sites not only meeting our standards when they are initially selected, but also on their continuing to do so year after year. Circumstances can and sometimes do change, of course. Parks can change hands or standards can fall for a variety of reasons, all of which requires that the parks are revisited and that the guide is substantially up-dated every year, so it really is important to make sure you have an up-to-date edition!

We rely on our small, dedicated team of Site Assessors, all of whom are experienced campers, caravanners or motorcaravanners, to visit and recommend parks, following which our Sites Director makes the final decision on those to be included in the following year's guide. Once a park is included, it will be regularly inspected to ensure that standards are being maintained. We also appreciate the feedback we receive from many of our readers, and we always make a point of following up complaints, suggestions or recommendations for possible new sites. However, should you have a specific complaint about a park this should be addressed to the Park Operator at the time, preferably in person. Please bear in mind that although we are interested to hear about any complaints, we have no contractual relationship with the sites featured in our guides and are therefore not in a position to intervene in any dispute between a reader and a park.

Hints on using the Alan Rogers Guides

As you will see, and hopefully appreciate, unlike most other guides we don't rely on 'icons' or symbols to describe the sites featured in our guides. This is partly because we prefer to write our descriptions in plain English and partly because it is virtually impossible to express an opinion about the quality or the ambience, for example, by means of symbols, and those descriptions and opinions are what makes the Alan Rogers Guides unique.

Being written in plain English, our guides are exceptionally easy to use, but a few words of explanation regarding the layout, etc. may be helpful.

Regions and counties

For England we have used official Tourist Board Regions and the counties. For Wales and Scotland, where there are many official regions, we have adopted our own regional structure based on the needs of the average holidaymaker. For Ireland (North and South) we use the counties.

Index

Not one, but two – on pages 248-253 you will find each campsite indexed by its number, and on pages 245-247 you will find an index of the villages or towns nearest to where the sites are situated.

Maps

These appear on pages 253-256. The approximate position of each campsite is indicated on the map by a * next to which is the site number. The maps incorporate a simple grid system which is used to cross-reference the Site Report to the relevant square in which it's situated on the map. The maps are intended to help you find the approximate location of campsites, not to navigate by! Each Site Report includes succinct directions as to how to find the site, based on the assumption that you will be using a proper road map, such as those produced by the Ordnance Survey, the AA or RAC, etc. and for convenience we have also included an Ordnance Survey Grid Reference in our Site Report in respect of sites in mainland Britain.

The Site Reports

These are really self-explanatory, but please remember that all prices shown are per night, and all telephone numbers assume that you are 'phoning from within the country where the site is situated - thus if you want to telephone a site from abroad you will need to prefix the number with the appropriate International Dialling Code.

Example of an entry:

---

number park name, nearest village, town

These details should identify the park's location to within a mile or so on any medium scale map - finer details are given in the directions section at the foot of the main report.

summary line

main text	**Charges**

A description of the park in which we try to give an idea of the general features of the park - its size, its situation, its strengths and weaknesses, the quality and adequacy of the toilet block, special amenities and any special local attractions. Some things may be assumed unless the report **Open** *states otherwise: that the toilet block has free hot showers, hot water in washbasins, mirrors, some razor points and chemical toilet disposal, and that dogs are accepted on leads. Throughout the reports the word `site' is* **Address** *used in the sense of park or campsite itself, not your individual place on the park, which we have called a 'pitch'. Practically all our parks now have electrical connections to some pitches and we include details of the amperage available. We try to tell you if the park does not take any* **Tel** *particular type of normal touring unit - caravans, motorcaravans and* **Fax** *tents - however, if you have an unusual unit (e.g. American motorhome or* **E-mail** *commercial vehicle) it is advisable to check with the park first to make* (*if available*) *sure that there are no special restrictions.*

Directions: **Reservations**
Given last, separated from the main text in order that they may be read *General adminis-* *and assimilated more easily by a navigator en route. It is possible that a* *trative detail is* *few may have changed due to road improvement schemes, etc. since we* *given in the right* *visited the park. If this has happened we trust that any delay caused is or* *hand column* *was of only minor proportions. The 6-figure Ordnance Survey Grid* *- see below.* *Reference (O.S.GR:) point is provided by the park for those wishing to locate a site by this means.*

General information:

Grouped under the headings of charges, opening dates, address, telephone and reservations.

Charges are the latest provided by the parks. In those few cases where 1999 or 2000 prices are not given, we try to give a general guide. The pricing structures vary considerably and we try to be as uniform and succinct as possible in what is included since some parks have a simple tariff, while others have a vast complex of possibilities. The same is true of reservations and what is written cannot wholly replace the official park tariff and reservation form.

Please note that the opening dates are those advised to us during the early autumn of the previous year - park operators can, and sometimes do, alter these dates before the start of the following season - often for good reasons - so if you intend to visit a park shortly after its published opening date, or shortly before its closing date, it really is wise to check that it will actually be open at the time required. Similarly some parks operate a restricted service during the low season, only opening some of their facilities (e.g.

swimming pools) during the main season - where we know about this, and have the relevant dates, we indicate it, but if you are at all doubtful again it is wise to check.

We note an ever increasing number of 'special' pitches under a variety of fancy names (for example, Executive, Panorama, Super). These provide a range of extra facilities such as waste water disposal, TV and phone connections, patios, etc. and they are often booked up well in advance. We would suggest that readers interested is such pitches should contact the park concerned to check exactly what is provided and to pre-book if that is what they want. Disabled readers are also advised to telephone the park of their choice before turning up to ensure that facilities are appropriate to their particular needs.

Quick Reference Sections

Our Guide includes several Quick Reference Sections, (see pages 235-239) which should enable you to quickly identify those parks that are open all year, those which welcome dogs, and those which don't, parks where fishing facilities are available, those where there are facilities for launching small boats, those where there are bicycles for hire, those with riding stables or golf courses nearby, and those which are strictly '**adults only**'.

Discount Vouchers

We have been able to negotiate special 'Alan Rogers' discounts with some of the parks featured in this Guide, and with a number of tourist attractions and with Irish Ferries, whereby on presentation of a valid discount card, to be found between pages 192-193 of this guide, readers will be able to enjoy a reduction compared with the normal public price. Full details are shown on the relevant discount card.

 Where a park offers a discount to our readers this is indicated in the Site Report by a small Alan Rogers Logo, and a brief description of the discount available.

Our Site Assessors

And finally, thank you to our Site Assessors for all their efforts and hard work:

Rosemary and George Boyce   Lorraine Houghton
Thelma and Jack Mitchell   Gordon and Joyce Pearce
Steve and Jacqui Perritt

We are, of course, also out and about ourselves. We wish all our readers thoroughly enjoyable Camping and Caravanning in the new Millennium.

Lois Edwards MA, FTS
Clive Edwards BEd, FTS
Sue Smart   Directors

ALAN ROGERS' Good Camps Guide
BRITAIN & IRELAND 2000 - DISCOUNT VOUCHERS

Inside this Guide you will find several different Discount Vouchers which will provide you with potential savings of much more than the cost of the Guide itself!

Voucher A – Use to claim your Alan Rogers Exclusive Offer at those sites featured in this guide which have a small Alan Rogers Logo beneath the Site Report, alongside which you will find details of the special offer applying to that particular site. This voucher should be kept in the Guide, and shown to the site staff on arrival to claim the relevant special offer

Voucher B – Use when applying for the special Alan Rogers Heritage Breakdown and/or Personal Travel Insurance Discount. It should be sent with your insurance application, or if you are applying for insurance by telephone or fax (only for travel during the coming week) you must quote the Discount Card number in order to claim your discount *(see colour pages opposite page 161).*

Voucher C – Use to claim your special Alan Rogers Discount on Irish Ferries. Send to Irish Ferries at the time of booking, or if booking by telephone quote the Discount Card number when phoning, and send the card to them when confirming your booking *(see advert opposite page 224).*

Voucher D – Use to claim your Alan Rogers Discount at the Aviation Museum *(see page between pages 160/161).*

Voucher E – Used to claim your Alan Rogers Discount at the National Maritime Museum *(see advert between pages 160/161).*

Voucher F – Use to claim your Alan Rogers Discount at Haynes Motor Museum *(see colour advert between pages 160/161).*

New for 2000

The Alan Rogers Travel Service
First-timers escorted trip to France

Many readers of our Britain & Ireland Guide have expressed an interest in the idea of taking their caravan or motorcaravan to France (we also publish the highly respected and best-selling **Alan Rogers Good Camps Guide – France**) but are put off by the thought of getting on and off a ferry, having to drive on the 'wrong' side of the road, not being able to speak the language, different customs and food, and continental campsites.

For the year 2000 we have established the Alan Rogers Travel Service, and have also engaged the services of Four Seasons Touring, a small company run by well-known and very experienced caravanners Dave and Liz King, who are freelance writers and contributors to a well-known caravan magazine. We are therefore delighted to announce that Dave and Liz will be organising a special Alan Rogers 'First Time Abroad' holiday to Northern France. This is aimed specifically at those of our readers who are tempted to visit what is arguably the best camping and caravanning country in Europe but have previously been reluctant to undertake such a venture without any readily available advice and guidance.

Essentially the Alan Rogers 'First Time Abroad' holiday will consist of a fully escorted one week trip to France, staying at one of our selected sites in the grounds of a French Château near St Omer in the Pas de Calais, less than an hour's drive from the Channel ports of Calais and Boulogne. The trip will start with a night at one of our selected sites in Kent, close to Dover and Folkestone, where clients will meet up with Dave and Liz, who will accompany you on the ferry and throughout the holiday, including the return ferry crossing! Not only that, the trip will also offer participants a number of 'flavour of France' excursions and experiences designed to provide an insight into just how easy and enjoyable a caravanning holiday abroad can be! In association with the Motorcaravanners Club we are also planning to offer a similar 'First Time Abroad' holiday for motorcaravanners. More details of these exciting initiatives are on page 242-243 and on the colour page opposite page 160.

Camping Cheques arrive in Britain

Europe's hottest idea for making camping better for off-season customers is here at last!

Throughout Europe it is being hailed as the most exciting development the camping and caravanning business has seen for more than a decade. "It" is Camping Cheques – a simple scheme which makes good sites even better and more affordable for campers, caravanners and motorcaravanners who can use them in the quieter low seasons

The scheme is simplicity itself. The camper – to use the European term which also includes caravanners and motorcaravanners – buys Cheques in advance which they can exchange for a pitch on any Camping Cheque site.

The sites selected to join the scheme are among the best in Europe, but the Cheques are priced at the sort of cost more usually associated with a sparse site with minimal facilities. In France they say that Camping Cheque customers enjoy four-star sites at two-star prices!

As a requirement to join the Camping Cheques scheme the sites have to make a commitment to keep most of their facilities open even during the low season – Now, after an exhaustive selection process, the first three British parks have been selected to join the 150 or so European sites which are already part of the scheme. At Alan Rogers we are delighted that not only are all three of the British Parks invited to join the Camping Cheques scheme ones that are featured in our Britain & Ireland Guide, but over 90% of the Camping Cheques Europe sites are ones that are featured in our France or Europe Guides

With Camping Cheques it's now possible to book an off-peak holiday in Britain, France and several other European countries knowing that you're getting the best sites at the best possible price.

UK Camping Cheque Sites
Polmanter Tourist Park (No 005, page 9)
Pentewan Sands Holiday Park (No 025, page 23)
Newlands Caravan Park (No 181, page 66)

To find out more, and to reserve your copy of the Year 2000 Camping Cheques Programme 'phone 01606 787655 now!

The New Star Rating Scheme

For the year 2000, the British Graded Holiday Parks 'Q' Tick Scheme for caravan and camping parks has been replaced by new STAR ratings. It is a completely new scheme and we have received the following description from the English Tourism Council:

'The Star rating reflects the overall quality of the park and the highest rating of Five Stars is reserved for those parks of exceptional quality which also provide specific key facilities and services. It is a new scheme with a new symbol and new ratings reflecting the ever-higher standards which holiday touring caravan and camping parks have to offer in the new millennium.

The new Star (★) ratings demand an even higher standard than the previous Tick (✓) ratings and should not be compared with them'.

Star Quality   ★★★★★'Exceptional' Quality,   ★★★★'Excellent' Quality

★★★'Very Good' Quality, ★★'Good' Quality, ★'Acceptable' Quality

Whilst we welcome the new scheme, we continue to believe that our detailed site reports provide a better guide to the quality and character of a park than any grading scheme, however sophisticated.

Millennium Thoughts

You would not be campers or caravanners if you did not appreciate the countryside and want to enjoy it in all its many shapes and forms.

The countryside of the British Isles is the unique product of physical development providing re-sources on which man's activities and interference have played a part in the shaping and character of the land. The standing stones and circles, the ruins of castles and monasteries, the pattern of the fields, the patches of woodland, the hedgerows of the south, the walls of the north, the hamlets and villages, the windmills and water wheels and the stately mansions, are all outward visible signs of man's impact on the natural landscape.

This is the tourism heritage which we want to enjoy as we travel around the country and hope our children will do the same. It is perhaps a timely reminder as we move into a new millennium that we have a crucial role to play in conserving the earth's natural resources for future generations. Travel and tourism cannot continue unchecked without having an adverse impact on the environment, and both wildlife and wild places continue to be threatened as a result of man's activities.

Professor David Bellamy has done much to raise awareness of these issues among park owners. Parks that make a positive contribution to conser-vation and the environment, such as landscaping, recycling and waste management, or are involved with any small or large project which encourages wildlife to flourish, can be eligible for an award. These awards are jointly organised by David Bellamy and the British Holiday & Home Parks Association and some exciting projects are in hand, such as the reed bed development at Oakdown Park in Devon.

We have tried within the limits of our quality process to select sites which provide a wide enough geographical range to allow readers to enjoy and explore our heritage. We have also provided the addresses of the regional tourist boards to follow up for further detailed information.

We hope you enjoy your travels this millennium year whether you get to visit the Dome or not; but please wherever you go and whatever you do, enjoy yourselves but remember that we all have a respon-sibility to preserve our heritage.

ENGLAND

West Country Tourist Board

West Dorset, Devon, Cornwall,
Somerset, Wiltshire and the City of Bristol

Address: 60 St. David's Hill, Exeter, Devon EX4 4SY
Tel: (01392) 425426 Fax: (01392) 420891
E-mail: post@wctb.co.uk Internet: http://www.wctb.co.uk

No other part of Britain can match the West Country for its diversity of scenery, its warm summers and mild winters making it one of the premier holiday regions covering the six counties of **Cornwall, Devon, Dorset, Wiltshire, Somerset** and the **City of Bristol**.

Its main gateway is the county of **Wiltshire**, less than an hour from London characterised by the rolling downlands of Salisbury Plain in the centre and the Marlborough Downs to the north with giant figures, mostly of horses carved into the chalky hillsides while Avebury and Stonehenge remind us of the area's prehistoric significance.

Dorset

The western part of Dorset covers the seaside side resort of Weymouth made famous by George III, the fossil rich cliffs of Lyme Regis and the rustic Thomas Hardy countryside.

Somerset

Somerset ranges from sleepy backwaters, golden stoned market towns, grand Elizabethan country houses and lush gardens to the unusual Somerset Levels, mystical Glastonbury Tor, and the caves and gorges of the Mendips to the moorland of Exmoor.

The new county and city of **Bristol** covers the busy cities and ports of Bristol and Bath with its Roman connections and Georgian architecture.

Devon

Devon is the largest and most scenically varied of the six counties including a chunk of Exmoor edged by the Golden Coast of Woolacombe and Ilfracombe fame, with marvellous thatched cottages, and narrow lanes. Dartmoor must be one of the last great wild places of southern England hence all the 'outward ' bound courses which take place there.

The southern resorts of Torquay, Paignton and Brixham are known as the English Riviera – 22 miles of palm fringed beaches whilst Dartmouth and Kingsbridge estuaries are yachting meccas. The cities of Exeter with its lovely cathedral and Plymouth with the Hoe and its nautical history are well worth visiting.

Cornwall

Cornwall is the land of Arthurian legend and Celtic tradition whilst the remnants of deserted mines and quarries recall the once important copper, tin and china clay industries. Now the 300 miles of coastline ensures that tourism rules. The Atlantic coast from Bude to Land's End features towering cliffs, hardy little ports like Boscastle and Port Isaac, marvellous sandy beaches and well known family and surf-orientated resorts of Newquay and St Ives now boasting a Tate Gallery. The south coast, calmed by the Gulf Stream becomes more sheltered and lush as it progresses east ward. Little craft moored in wooded creeks and colourful harbours like Falmouth and Fowey and pretty fishing villages interspersed with sandy coves overflow with character and old world atmosphere.

---

005 Polmanter Tourist Park, Halestown, nr. St. Ives

Family owned farm park with pool, just outside St. Ives.

Polmanter is a good example of a sympathetic conversion of a farm from agricultural to leisure use and the Osborne family have developed the park well. The converted farm buildings provide a cosy bar lounge overlooking the heated swimming pool, toddler's pool and sunbathing area. Bar meals are served (good value) and there is a family area with high chairs, an upstairs games room with pool and table tennis and the new conservatory between the bar and the pool provides extra space for families (open all day). Occasional entertainment is organised in season. The 240 tourist pitches (no statics) are well spaced in several fields with growing shrubs and hedges and connecting tarmac roadways. There are 16 hardstandings, 190 electric hook-ups (16A) and 80 deluxe pitches with electricity, water and waste water. The toilet blocks vary - as the park has grown, so extra blocks have been added. There are now four, the latest being modern and good, the others refurbished and tiled. All still incorporate the ideas of the first block, which include a wall cupboard for clothes in each shower to keep them dry. Heating is available, showers are free and there are two fully equipped en-suite family shower rooms, plus a baby changing room. There are hair dryers, chemical disposal, extra dishwashing sinks in the new block and good laundry provision including free irons. Activities include two full size tennis courts, two children's play areas with large wooden climbing frame on a sand base, a sports field and a games room with two pool tables, table tennis and games machines. Well stocked, self service shop (bar, shop and pool Whitsun - mid Sept). It is a busy park with a happy atmosphere within 1½ miles of St Ives - a footpath leads from the park (20 minutes downhill) or there is a bus service from the park in high season hourly, 10 am. - midnight. Golf 1 mile, fishing, riding, bicycle hire and boat launching facilities within 2 miles. Dogs are accepted on leads (but not on the St. Ives beaches in high season) with a large exercise field provided and there are walks from the park. The park gates are closed midnight - 6.30 am. with outside parking. A member of the Best of British group.

Charges 2000:
-- Per unit incl. 2 adults, car and awning £9.00 - £14.00; extra adult £3.00 - £4.50; child (3-15 yrs) £2.00 - £3.50; electricity (16A) £2.00; multi-service pitch £3.00; dog £1.00; extra car or pup tent £1.00.
-- VAT included.
-- Credit cards accepted.
Open:
Easter - 31 October (full facilities to 10 Sept)
Address:
Halestown, St. Ives, Cornwall TR26 3LX.
Tel:
(01736) 795640.
FAX: as phone.
E-mail: phillip_ osborne@hotmail.com.
Reservations:
Made with £30 deposit. For 15/7-26/8 only: multiples of 7 nights with arrival on Fri, Sat or Sunday for electric pitches, multiples of 7 nights but any day arrival for non-electric pitches.

Directions: Take B3074 to St. Ives from the A30 and then first left at a mini-roundabout taking 'Holiday Route' (B3311) to St. Ives (Halestown). At T-junction turn right for Halestown, right again at the Halestown Inn then first left. O.S.GR: SW509392.

Cornwall

002 Cardinney Camping Park, Crows an Wra, Penzance

Well kept, personally run small park near Lands End beauty spots.

A friendly Geordie welcome awaits from the owners, Liz and Kevin Lindley, when you visit Cardinney, which is perfectly situated for visiting the famous Lands End beauty spots and attractions and also within easy driving distance of small Cornish beaches and coves. The level field is semi-divided into three camping areas and is neatly kept with some landscaping. Bushes and a central Cornish stone wall give privacy and shelter, allowing for 105 marked, level pitches, 50 with electricity and some with hardstanding. Facilities are limited compared to many of the more sophisticated sites in Devon and Cornwall, the toilet block originally built over 30 years ago but adapted over the years to provide three metered showers and six washbasins for each sex. Razor points, hair dryers, a baby cubicle and chemical disposal, plus laundry facilities and a dishwashing sink with hot water. The combined café and bar acts as a social point providing breakfasts, takeaway at most times and good evening cheer. Games room with TV, pool table and video games. Fishing 3 miles, bicycle hire 5 miles. Coastal, cliff-top walks, surfing beaches and the Minnack Open Air Theatre near.

Directions: Park is signed at Crows an Wra on main Penzance - Lands End A30 road, 5 miles west of Penzance. O.S.GR: SW426285.

Charges 2000:
-- Per unit incl. 2 adults £5.00 - £7.50; extra adult £2.00; child (2-15 yrs)£1.00; electricity (10A) £1.75; pets free.
-- Less for over 2 weeks.
-- Credit cards accepted.
Open:
1 February - 30 Nov.
Address:
Crows an Wra,
St Buryan,
Cornwall TR19 6HX.
Tel:
(01736) 810880.
FAX: (01736) 810998.
Reservations:
Made with £10 per week deposit.

003 Ayr Holiday Park, St. Ives

Family park with holiday homes within walking distance of St. Ives, with superb views.

On first arrival Ayr Park seems to be all caravan holiday homes but behind them is a series of naturally sloping fields, with marvellous views over St. Ives Bay and Porthmeor beach, providing 40 touring pitches. Level, hard-core, terraced areas also provide places for motorhomes and vans with 35 electrical connections (16A). The toilet block, consisting of various parts, is modern and well maintained with free, hot, controllable showers (some accessed direct from the outside and some with toilet), hot water to washbasins, vanity style, hairdryer, three dishwashing sinks with hot water under cover and good laundry facilities. With the extra tent field open in July/Aug, the facilities may be a little hard-pressed, but were coping well when we visited in August. Amenities include a games room with pool table and TV, hot drinks and snack machines and an adventure play area and football field. A milkman calls daily except Weds, a newspaper shop is near. St. Ives centre and supermarkets are an easy walk, also the new Tate Gallery. Direct access to the coastal footpath. One dog per pitch, up to medium size, is permitted but dogs are not allowed on St. Ives beaches in high season.

Directions: 300 yds after leaving the A30 turn left at mini-roundabout following signs for St. Ives for heavy vehicles and day visitors which, after approx. 2 miles, joins B3311 and then B3306 1 mile from St. Ives (octagonal building on left). Still heading for St Ives, left at mini-roundabout following camp signs through residential areas. Park entrance is 600 yds at Ayr Terrace. O.S.GR: SW515388.

Charges guide:
-- Per adult £2.15 - £3.35; child (5 -16 yrs) £1.05 - £1.65; caravan or tent £4.00 - £6.60; car £1.20; motorcaravan £4.50 - £6.90; large tent £4.40 - £8.75; awning £1.80 - £3.50; dog £1.00; electricity £2.10.
-- VAT included.
-- Credit cards accepted.
Open:
Easter/1 April - 31 Oct.
Address:
Higher Ayr, St. Ives,
Cornwall TR26 1EJ.
Tel:
(01736) 795855.
FAX: (01736) 798797.
Reservations:
Made with £25 deposit.

004 Trevalgan Holiday Farm, St Ives

Friendly, smallish, 'no frills' site.

We have two very different sites in the St Ives area and Trevalgan is different yet again. Based on a working farm on the cliffs 1½ miles west of St Ives, it provides 120 clearly marked pitches in a level stone walled field, which vary in size (the park is popular with walkers). A purpose built toilet block has curtained basins, controllable hot showers with seat and curtain, plus baby room, laundry and washing up, chemical disposal and even a hot drinks machine. Reception has a small shop (June - mid Sept). Farm House Kitchen with takeaway (end June-end Aug), popular for breakfast or evening meals. Games field, play area and pets corner with baby chickens, two donkeys, etc. A games room in an original barn has table tennis, pool, fruit machines and a comfortable upstairs TV room. Gas supplies. There is direct access to the coastal path and it is a 25 minutes walk to St. Ives. Bus service at top of road. Fishing 3 miles, bicycle hire, riding, golf, all within 2 miles. With tractor rides (high season), plus farm and hill trails it is, in all, quite an original type of park. A member of the Countryside Discovery group.

Directions: Approach site down a narrow Cornish lane from the B3306 St. Ives - Lands End road, following sign. O.S.GR: SW490400.

Charges 1999:
-- Per adult £3.00 - £5.00; child 3-14 yrs £2.00 - £4.00, under 3 yrs £1.50; electricity £2.50.
-- Credit cards accepted.
Open:
1 May - 30 September.
Address:
Trevalgan Farm, St Ives,
Cornwall TR26 3BJ.
Tel:
(01736) 796433.
FAX: as phone.
Reservations:
Contact park.

001 Chacewater Park, Chacewater, Truro

Quiet, value-for-money park for adults over 30 only.

Chacewater has a pleasant rural situation and has now made the decision to go 'adults only'. For those who want to be away from the hectic coastal resorts and to take advantage of the peace and quiet of an 'adults only' park, this will be an excellent value for money choice. The site is run with care and attention by Richard Peterken and his daughters Debbie and Mandy, providing 94 level touring pitches in two large field areas (with a slight slope) edged with young trees or in smaller bays formed by hedging. There arc 9 fully serviced pitches with electricity, water, drainage and sewage connections. The main toilet block provides free hot water throughout, vanity style washbasins, well equipped showers and two en-suite units, along with covered washing up sinks, a laundry room and chemical disposal facilities. This block has now been supplemented by a new one providing similar facilities near reception. Reception is not at the entrance but through the park to one side in a pleasant courtyard area. Truro is only 5 miles and there is a good choice of beaches north or south within 5-10 miles. Six caravan holiday homes are situated to one side of the park and available to let.

Directions: Chacewater can be approached either from the A390 road or from the A30. Park is ½ mile west of the village - follow signs. O.S.GR: SW742439.

Charges 2000:
-- Per unit incl. 2 adults from £9.00; extra person £4.00; electricity 95p; dog 50p; extra car £1.50.
-- Weekly rates for pre-booked pitches.
-- Less for senior citizens excl. 19/7-31/8.
-- VAT included.
-- Credit cards accepted.

Open:
1 May - 30 September.

Address:
Cox Hill, Chacewater, Truro TR4 8LY.

Tel:
(01209) 820762.
FAX: (01209) 820544.

Reservations:
Any length, £15 deposit, balance on arrival.

Alan Rogers' Discount

Less 10% off standard tarrif only

010 Leverton Place Caravan Park, Truro

Neat, well kept park with swimming pool and other amenities, just west of Truro.

About 6 miles from the northern coast of Cornwall and not much more from the southern, Leverton Place has been well designed and laid out along continental lines and is now part of the Caravan Club 'managed under contract' scheme although non-members are very welcome. The pitches are attractively arranged in groups in a series of secluded bays with neat, well drained lawns divided up by access roads, hedges and shrubs. There is provision for 107 touring units of any type with 7 chalets and 15 caravans to let. Pitches are marked, 100 with electrical connections (10A), 39 with hardstanding and 8 fully serviced with their own water, waste drainage, full hardstanding and picnic bench. There are four toilet blocks serving the touring section, a central one providing 15 individual en-suite shower rooms, heated in winter, including one specifically designed for disabled people. It is a good, well maintained provision with two excellent dishwashing and laundry kitchens. The newest block near reception has a 'state of the art' chemical disposal and boot washing facility. Motorcaravan service point. An attractive walled patio area, complete with palm trees, provides a 18 m. long pool (heated mid May - mid Sept), a paddling pool, lounge bar and bistro (mid May - mid Sept) with terraced sitting out area overlooking the pool. The bar opens each evening and perhaps at other times, but is sufficient distance from the pitch areas so as not to be intrusive. Shop with gas beside reception, open all day, all year. Two children's playgrounds and two games rooms, both with pool, one with table tennis. First aid room. Bicycles, roller skates and skate boards not allowed. Winter caravan storage. Two well stocked fishing lakes are 400 yds, riding or golf 2 miles.

Directions: Park is 3 miles west of Truro, signed from A390 road ½ mile from village of Threemilestone on road to Chacewater. O.S.GR: SW770451.

Charges 1999:
-- Per pitch 24 July - 31 Aug. £10.00, otherwise £1.00; adult £3.25 - £4.00; child (5-16 yrs) £1.10 - £1.20; dog free - £1.00; electricity £1.45 - £2.20; fully serviced pitch plus £2.00.
-- VAT included.
-- Credit cards accepted.

Open:
All year.

Address:
Truro,
Cornwall TR4 8QW.

Tel:
(01872) 560462.
FAX: (01872) 560668.

Reservations:
Made with deposit of £20 per week or part for high season, £5 at other times.

Cornwall

006 River Valley Caravan Park, Relubbus, Penzance

Quiet touring park for caravans and a few tents, east of Penzance.

A spacious park in the natural environment of a pleasant river valley and run by Brian and Eileen Milson, River Valley provides 150 touring pitches. Mainly around the perimeters of small meadows or in natural clearings, most have electrical connections (15A), some have hardstanding and there are special sections for families, couples, tents, dogs, etc. Three good quality, tiled toilet blocks are large enough, clean and well maintained. Hot water is free in the washbasins, showers and the 12 covered dishwashing sinks. Two male and two female family shower rooms have been added in the top block, there are a few private cabins for ladies and a special make-up room with hair dryers, also providing tourist information, plus separate laundry facilities and baby bath. Water points around the park, chemical disposal and motorcaravan service point (fresh water top up and waste water emptying). There are now 39 caravan holiday homes in a more or less separate area, beside the river at the far end of the park (27 to rent). Shop (limited hours and closed from Oct). Public phone. There is no children's playground, but lots of very tame ducks on the river. Working windmill and waterwheel. A good pub serving meals is 20/30 minutes walk along the river walk to St Earth, and St Michael's Mount is only 3 miles and can be reached by footpath. Trout fishing is free on the site and there are walks. Much of the valley is a protected nature reserve and the park encourages wildlife by not using weedkillers and by leaving parts un-cut - badgers, foxes, herons, kingfishers and glow-worms are regular visitors. Bicycle hire 5 miles, riding or golf 3 miles. A member of the Best of British group.

Directions: Park approach leads off B3280 at east end of Relubbus village, northeast of Marazion. O.S.GR: SW566320.

Charges guide:
-- Per pitch (incl. vehicle) £3.50; adult £1.50 - £3.25; child 50p - £1.25; awning/pup tent £1.00; dog £1.00; electricity £1.50.
-- Min. charge 2 adults per vehicle; large motor-caravans add £1.00.
-- VAT included.
-- Credit cards accepted.

Open:
All year except Jan. and Feb.

Address:
Relubbus, Penzance, Cornwall TR20 9ER.

Tel:
(01736) 763398
FAX: as phone.
E-mail: rivervalley@surfbay.dircon.co.uk.

Reservations:
Any period with deposit (£20) and fee (£1).

See colour feature for 'BEST of BRITISH' between pages 96/97

011 Calloose Caravan Park, Leedstown, Hayle

Friendly, family rural touring park with swimming pool and a few holiday caravans.

This park is quietly situated in an inland valley, about 4 miles from Hayle, with an extra ½ mile to the beaches beyond, 9 to St. Ives on the north coast and 6 to Helston and Praa Sands on the south. Attractively landscaped with almost a tropical feel, units are personally sited. The terrain is mainly flat but is dry, with two slightly raised areas on terraces. There are 120 tourist pitches (99 with 16A electricity, 8 with water and 28 gravel hardstandings) with individual markers, and 17 caravan holiday homes. In the main meadow areas, pitches are arranged round the perimeter with free space in the middle. Both toilet blocks have been refurbished and they provide washbasins in cubicles, free hot showers, a family shower room, baby room, a unit for disabled visitors, dishwashing up sinks under cover and chemical disposal. A heated swimming pool (40 x 20 ft. open from early May) with separate paddling pool, is neatly landscaped with sunbathing terrace and access for disabled people. The shop is well stocked (including gas) and a large, recreation block with themed bar and family room adjoins. Bar meals are served (daily in the main season, slightly restricted in early season), with takeaway, and entertainment is organised most evenings in the main season including weekly barbecues. Activities include a TV lounge, pool table, games room with skittle alley, all-weather tennis court, crazy golf (floodlit), table tennis and an adventure playground. Four acres of recreation fields include dog exercise fields, a full size football pitch and mountain bike scramble track. Laundry room, first aid room and public phones. Sun loungers and mountain bike hire and extensive local information in reception. All public areas have wheel chair access. The village is within walking distance. Golf 4 miles, fishing 2 miles, riding 5 miles. A popular park, booking is essential.

Directions: From crossroads of B3280 and B3302 in Leedstown take the B3302 towards Hayle. First right, then left on ½ mile access road to park. O.S.GR: SW599353.

Charges 1999:
-- Per unit incl. 2 persons £6.50 - £12.50; awning free; extra person (over 3 yrs) 75p - £2.00; pup tent 75p - £1.50; dog 75p - £2.00; electricity (10A) £2.00; 'super' pitch plus £2.00.
-- VAT included.
-- Credit cards accepted.

Open:
1 April - 30 September.

Address:
Leedstown, Hayle, Cornwall TR27 5ET.

Tel:
(01736) 850431.
FAX: as phone.

Reservations:
Made with £20 deposit per pitch, balance on arrival.

013 Liskey Touring Park, nr. Truro

Quiet, family run park centrally situated for touring central Cornwall.

Liskey is pleasantly landscaped with rockery plants and well manicured grass and first impressions of loving care are carried all through the park. The first small building is a room for TV, tourist information and a library. It can also be used by families for board games should the weather turn inclement. Next comes reception, a large informal room with settee and chairs, where milk, bread, newspapers and gas are also sold (Truro supermarkets are only 3 miles). The main, slightly sloping camping area is beautifully landscaped with trees, shrubs and heathers and the level, well spaced pitches have good views across the countryside. A strictly touring site, 46 of the 60 pitches have 10A electricity and 12 are fully serviced with level hardstanding and a gravel area for awnings. There are all weather pea-gravel pitches for tents (a new venture which has proved very popular with tenters). There is a great feeling of spaciousness, mainly because the owners do not try to fit in too many units. Breathable groundsheets are welcome on the grassy pitches. The central toilet block is very clean, well maintained and can be heated. There is free hot water, some washbasins in cubicles, push-button showers, a family bathroom (50p) and chemical disposal. Everywhere is tiled and there are free hairdryers, hand-dryers and soap. The laundry room is also well equipped and dishwashing sinks are under cover, also with free hot water. Motorcaravan service point. An adventure playground and playing field with volleyball and basketball nets should keep older children out of mischief and, should it be wet, there is a barn with pea-gravel base with more equipment and table tennis. For under 5s there is a fenced play area with a large selection of equipment. No bikes, skateboards or roller-blades are allowed. A boules pitch has been added. Dogs are accepted on short leads with a good dog walk provided. Winter caravan storage. A pub with good food and real ale is only 600 yds. and buses to Truro pass the gate. Coarse fishing ¼ mile, bicycle hire 3 mile, riding 2 miles, golf 1 mile. Within 5 miles are beaches and facilities for tennis and boat launching. Liskey is a good place for the family that can amuse itself without the need for discos and gaming machines.

Directions: From the A30 take A390 to Truro. At the next roundabout turn right (signed Threemilestone) and, immediately at mini-roundabout, right again towards Chacewater. Park is 600 yds on right past Leverton Place. O.S.GR: SW772452.

Charges 2000:
-- Per unit incl. 2 persons £6.50 - £10.50; extra adult £2.50 - £3.50, teenager (13-17 yrs) £1.50 - £2.00, child (3-12 yrs) £1.20 - £1.50; first dog free - £1.00, extra dog £1.00; electricity (10A) £1.70; tent power unit incl. electricity £2.70; serviced pitch £2.20 - £3.20.
-- Low season discounts for over 55s, fully retired.
-- Credit cards accepted.

Open:
1 April - 22 September.

Address:
Greenbottom, Truro, Cornwall TR4 8QN.

Tel:
(01872) 560274.
FAX: as phone.
E-mail:
enquiries@liskey.co.uk.

Reservations:
Made with £3 deposit per night booked or payment in full if less than 5 days.

Alan Rogers' Discount

Apply to park for details

Cornwall

007 Silver Sands Holiday Park, Kennack Sands, nr. Helston

Small, 'away-from-it-all', peaceful park in a remote part of the Lizard.

On a corner of the Lizard peninsula, the most southerly part of mainland Britain and an area of outstanding natural beauty, and only reached after passing Culdrose Naval Base and the Goonhilly Earth Station down a single track road, one finds Silver Sands – tucked away behind two other parks with static holiday homes with very little else. A ½ mile footpath leads down through a small valley to the twin beaches of Kennack Sands (one is dog free) divided by a small headland. This is generally an unspoilt walking area with the coastal path passing through and under the care of English Nature. The park has 16 caravan holiday homes for hire, along with 14 touring pitches with 5A electricity for caravans and motorcaravans which are large, nicely situated and divided into bays by flowering shrubs. An adjoining tent field has similar pitches (4 with electricity) but the shrubs are younger and the pitches in bays are slightly sloping. Another, undeveloped 3-acre field can be used for walking, kite flying, etc. The sanitary block is old and quite quaint, but seemed well maintained. It has showers, a laundry room, chemical disposal, hair drying area and dishwashing sinks (H&C). Reception in an elderly static van has good tourist information. Play equipment for under 6's opposite reception, with swings and a sand pit in other areas. Shop 20 yds on the next site and a pub within walking distance. Fishing 1 mile, bicycle hire or riding 5 miles, golf 6 miles. A member of the Countryside Discovery group.

Directions: From Helston take A3038 Lizard road. After Culdrose turn left on B3293 passing Goonhilly after 4 miles. At the next crossroads turn right (signed Kennack Sands, continue for 1½ miles then left to Gwendreath on single track road - site is 1 mile. O.S.GR: SW732170.

Charges 2000:
-- Per touring unit incl. 2 persons £5.75 - £7.50; extra adult £2.00; child (3-13 yrs) £1.60; awning or extra pup tent 80p; dog £1.60; extra car or boat £1.00; electricity £1.60 - £1.80.
-- Less £2 for cyclists or hikers with pup tent.
-- Reductions for some bookings.
-- No credit cards.

Open:
1 May - 30 September.

Address:
Kennack Sands,
Ruan Minor, Helston,
Cornwall TR12 7LZ.

Tel:
(01326) 290631.
FAX: as phone.

Reservations:
Made with 25% deposit, min. £15; balance on arrival.

039 Trelowarren Touring Caravan and Camping Park, Mawgan

Delightful park in grounds of Cornish Manor with Craft and Countryside Centre.

There is a sense of timelessness about Trelowarren - perhaps it is the mature parkland or the mellow manor house, home to the Vyvyan family since 1427. Whatever, it is a beautiful, tranquil park set on the eastern side of the Lizard Peninsula, close to the banks of the Helford river. Access from the main road is via a single track road for one mile but it is well worth it. Set in 20 acres, there are three distinctive areas for camping all with neatly cut grass and providing 125 places for caravans and motorcaravans and 75 for tents. First is the walled gardens with some pitches on a slight slope and with its own if basic, small sanitary block with toilets, washbasins and chemical disposal point. Second is the apple orchard edged by the woods with a secluded area known as the quarry at the lower end, with some level but mainly sloping pitches. The third area is more open, with views across the valley and running parallel to the orchard, separated by Cornish stone walls. It has some mature trees and the main toilet block. There are 25 level hardstandings in this area which fit even large motorhomes. Sanitary facilities in original stone buildings are modern and attractively equipped with free, comfortably sized showers with good curtain dividers, some washbasins in cubicles for ladies, and a bath. Five dishwashing sinks are under cover, and a laundry room, with stone walls and floor, provides three sinks, a washing machine and dryer. Motorcaravan service point. There is a en-suite facility for disabled visitors, and reception, a small shop, takeaway and a little Inn complete the amenities. However, through a small door just past the walled garden, is the stable courtyard with a delightful 'bistro' which is licensed and open at lunchtimes and some evenings (with jazz and folk music). A Countryside Centre charts the development of the Lizard from pre-history to the present day and is a must to try and understand this unique area, which is now home to the Goonhilly Earth Station. The Pottery and Weaving Centre and the various exhibitions organised by the Cornwall Craft Association, not to mention the house and gardens (being rebuilt to the original design but incorporating 20th century techniques, plants and architectural incident) and the woodland walks, make this a most attractive place to spend some time in a most relaxing, yet interesting, setting.

Directions: From Helston take A3083 for the Lizard. Just after Culdrose Naval Air Station turn left on B3293. Avoid turnings to Gweek and Mawgan and watch for Trelowarren signs on left before reaching Goonhilly. O.S.GR: SW719239.

Charges guide:
--Per person £3.00 - £4.00; child (3-16 yrs) £1.45 - £1.80; dog, extra car or boat £1.00; electricity £1.60.
-- Pitch and awning incl.

Open:
1 April/Easter - 30 Sept, (as are all other facilities on the park which are open to the public).

Address:
Mawgan, Nr. Helston
Cornwall TR12 6AF.

Tel:
(01326) 221637.

Reservations:
Made with deposit (£10 for electric hook-up, £5 without).

008 Maen Valley Holiday Park, Falmouth

Long established park in sheltered valley with a relaxed atmosphere.

Maen Valley has two beaches within a mile, a range of activities nearby from sailing, windsurfing, fishing and diving to tennis coaching, access to the coastal path and many well known Cornish gardens near by. In a south facing, sheltered valley, a clear stream runs through the park and the mature woods provide walks. Its principal interest is in caravan holiday homes (many privately owned, 70 to let) but there are also 80 places for touring units, mostly informally arranged on sloping hedged fields, 60 with electricity. A separate level area with views at the top of the park near the second entrance is useful for caravans and motorhomes. The refurbished toilet facilities provide free hot showers with folding seat and curtain, basins, with a small additional unit in the top area. Laundry facilities, no dishwashing sinks except in the top area (more planned). A club (evenings plus weekend lunches) provides social life and food. The bar, club and shop open Whitsun - 30 Sept. (shop 8.30-11am. and 4-7 pm). Crazy golf and skittles. Local village pub. Falmouth is 2 miles; there is an hourly bus service.

Directions: From Truro, follow signs for Falmouth on A39. At first roundabout pass Asda then turn right at next roundabout signed Maenporth and industrial estates (on Bickland Water Road). Park is on right after 1½ miles. The first turning leads to the bottom of the valley and reception and is steep and narrow. The second entrance 100 yds further is easier for caravans. O.S.GR: SW789311.

Charges guide:
-- Per adult £4.00 - £7.00; child (3-16 yrs) £1.00 - £2.50; dog £1.00; electricity £2.00.
-- Special saver offers available.
-- Credit cards accepted.

Open:
Easter - 31 October.

Address:
Falmouth,
Cornwall TR11 5BJ.

Tel:
(01326) 312190.
FAX: (01326) 211120.

Reservations:
Made with £20 deposit.

Maen Valley HOLIDAY PARK

**Situated in a tranquil, sheltered, well wooded valley.
Ideal touring centre and within walking distance to
safe sandy beaches. Sailing, golf & other amenities.**

**Modern holiday caravans and chalets for hire
Caravan rallies welcome
Holiday camping areas with electrical hook-ups**

• CARAVANS • CHALETS • CAMPING •

TELEPHONE 01326 312190 FOR FREE COLOUR BROCHURE

018 Carnon Downs Caravan and Camping Park, Truro

Quiet, quality, family park centrally situated for touring Cornwall.

This is a thoughtfully laid out, level park with attractive hedging and flowering shrubs providing some pleasant bays for caravans, run personally by Tony and Sarah Birch. Gravel roads connect 135 pitches, 120 with 10-16A electricity, 15 with hardstanding (13 fully serviced). Tent pitches, some with electricity, are well spaced around two level fields, the centre of one left for play equipment, the other containing the reception and shop (for basics, gas and papers) where you receive a warm welcome, a neat park plan and tourist information pack. Two well cared for toilet blocks can be heated and provide good facilities including vanity style washbasins - for ladies, three in one block are in cubicles. Showers are unisex, with stool, shelf and curtain and, once you have got used to the idea, it works well. A well-refurbished block includes three very good family bath/shower rooms, one suitable for use by disabled people. Two good laundries, one in each block, and a toddler room (heated), including two baby sinks and a full sized bath, is to be found in the round-house next to the TV room. The round-house housed donkeys who turned the mill which used to be on the site! Although one side of the park is next to the A39 road, it is well screened with mature woodland so noise should be minimal. The woodland and two fields provide walks for dogs. A pub is 100 yds. Fishing 3 miles, riding or bicycle hire 2 miles, golf 1 mile. The park is well situated to explore the tip of Cornwall. Caravan storage.

Directions: From Truro take A39 Falmouth road. There is direct access from Carnon Downs roundabout after 3 miles. O.S.GR: SW805406.

Charges 1999:
Per unit incl. 2 persons £7.00 - £12.00; extra adult £2.00; child (5-14 yrs) £1.70; electricity (10/15A) £2.00; small 2 man tent plus car less £1.00, walker or cyclist (single) less £3.00.
-- Credit cards accepted.
-- VAT included.

Open:
Easter/1 April - 31 Oct.

Address:
Carnon Downs, Truro,
Cornwall TR3 6JJ.

Tel:
(01872) 862283.
FAX: (01872) 862800.
E-mail: acbirch@
aol.com.

Reservations:
Made with £10 deposit - contact park.

Cornwall

012 Silverbow Park, Goonhavern, nr Perranporth

Select, quiet and spacious, well kept park with pool, 2½ miles back from the sea.

Silverbow has been developed by the Taylor family over many years and they are justifiably proud of their efforts. Particularly seeking to encourage couples and quiet families with young children, they believe Silverbow is a way of life and staying is an experience - they have certainly created a relaxed and tranquil atmosphere. Hard work, planting and landscaping has provided a beautiful 14 acre park which now takes part in the well known 'Gardens Scheme'. There are 90 tourist pitches which are all of good size and include 56 'super pitches' in a newly developed area, with electricity, water and drainaway, which are even larger. Many are on a slight slope with some attractive views. There is much free space not used for camping, including an excellent sports area with 2 all weather and 2 grass tennis courts, with free coaching in season, 3 outdoor badminton courts, short mat bowls, a children's adventure playground on sand and a general play field, as well as wild meadow and wooded areas ideal for walks. An attractive, kidney shaped, heated swimming pool and small paddling pool (open mid-May - mid-Sept) sheltered by high surrounding garden walls is a real tropical sun trap. There are 15 park-owned, high quality leisure homes in a separate part. The park is 2½ miles from the long sandy beach at Perranporth (30 mins. walk away from traffic) and 6 miles from Newquay. Three toilet blocks, all of excellent quality with private cabins for each sex, fully controllable free hot showers, four family shower/toilet rooms, two of which are accessible for wheelchairs, and one bath on payment for each sex. Six enclosed washing-up sinks by touring field. Laundry room. Room for reading or quiet games. Recycling bins. Free freezer service. Shop (mid May-mid Sept). Pub within walking distance. Concessionary green fees are available at Perranporth golf club. Gliding, riding and fishing are nearby. Mountain biking from the park (but no bikes on site).

Charges guide:
-- Per unit incl. 2 adults £6.00 - £13.50; extra person 2-12 yrs or over 50 yrs £2.00 - £3.10, 13-50 yrs £3.00 - £5.30; dog free - £1.50; fully serviced pitch incl. electricity £2.00 - £2.50.
-- Discounts available
-- VAT included.

Open:
2 May - 10 October.

Address:
Goonhavern, nr Truro, Cornwall TR4 9NX.

Tel:
(01872) 572347.

Reservations:
Made with £20 p/week deposit (Sat. - Sat. only 18/7-22/8).

Directions: Entrance is directly off the main A3075 road ½ mile south of Goonhavern. O.S.GR: SW781531.

014 Penrose Farm Touring Park, Goonhavern, nr. Truro

Well cared for, quality, family park in popular area.

Penrose Farm is a level, sheltered, touring only park on the edge of the village of Goonhavern. The 100 pitches are spread over five fields, with flower beds and bushes set amongst them. These flowers and all those at the entrance to the park are very colourful and give the park a neat, orderly and well cared for feel. The very enthusiastic owners, Colin and Joanne, take great delight in getting to know their customers, many of whom come every year, and pride in the facilities they provide. The refurbished toilet block is tiled throughout and kept spotless by Joanne. It provides vanity style washbasins, adjustable showers with stool and four excellent family rooms containing an adjustable shower, washbasin, WC and hairdryer. One room is also accessible for wheelchairs. All these amenities are enhanced with beautiful pot plants and flowers like a 'mini Kew Gardens'. Children have an excellent adventure playground and an indoor animal centre with guinea pigs, rabbits and miniature goats for all to stroke and cuddle and fish, terrapins and birds to admire. The reception area has tourist information and a small shop sells gas and basic needs (Easter, then May - Sept). The laundry is well equipped and dishwashing sinks are provided, all with free hot water. Chemical disposal. Dogs accepted on leads with a large exercise field provided. Colin is constantly re-appraising the pitches, always trying to ensure that each unit has plenty of space and doesn't feel overcrowded. There are 50 pitches with 16A electricity and 8 pitches with hardstanding (4 with electricity). It really is a very neat and tidy well run park. Caravan storage available. It is only a short walk to the village and its popular pub, and buses to Newquay stop in the village. The superb beach at Perranporth is only 2½ miles away. Bicycle hire can be arranged, fishing or riding ½ mile, golf 1 mile. To retain its quiet family image, there are no plans for bars or entertainment and only couples and families are admitted.

Charges 2000:
-- Per unit incl. 2 persons £7.00 - £11.00; extra person (5 yrs and over) £3.00; awning, extra car, dog free; electricity (16A) £2.00.
-- Families and couples only.
-- Less 50p for over 60s if booked.
-- VAT included.
-- Credit cards accepted.

Open:
1 April - 30 September.

Address:
Goonhavern, nr. Truro, Cornwall TR4 9QF.

Tel:
(01872) 573185.
E-mail: col@penrose99 .freeserve.co.uk.

Reservations:
Made with £30 deposit.

Alan Rogers' Discount

Less £1 p/night excl. 15/7-31/8

Directions: Take A30 from Exeter past Bodmin and Indian Queens. Just after wind farm take B3285 to Perranporth. Park is on the left as you enter Goonhavern village. O.S.GR: SW790535.

031 Trekenning Tourist Park, Newquay

Inland family park with an attractive garden pool.

Trekenning is owned by John Fynn, his daughter Tracey and son-in-law Dave and they have succeeded in developing a popular park with good facilities. Easy access just off the A39 roundabout at St Columb Major leads to a large sloping field with all the facilities in the opposite corner. In total there are 75 pitches, 68 with 10A electricity. Some have been levelled, others are tucked away at a lower level shaded by tall trees and a well hidden tent field with just a water point is edged by a wooded small stream. There are two sanitary blocks, one providing normal showers and vanity style washbasins, the other with two en-suite bathrooms and six large family showers. It is a nice provision also with a laundry room, covered dishwashing sinks and chemical disposal. The star of the show is undoubtedly the kidney shaped pool and paddling pool which are in a garden-like setting with gazebos and sun loungers, with a terraced lawn and patio at the top. This leads to the games room and cosy upstairs bar. 'Eatery' and takeaway facilities (all July/Aug). Entertainment is provided every night in the main season (ie. singers, quiz nights, connect-4 nights, discos on Fridays). Barbecue areas and a sand based children's play area with Wendy House, contained within a low stone wall in the main field complete the facilities. Fishing 1 mile, riding and golf 2 miles, bicycle hire 6 miles. The A39 runs parallel to one side of the site, so possible road noise.

Directions: Take the A3059 turning to Newquay from St Columb Major then turn immediately left; park is signed (this was the old road). O.S.GR: SW907625.

Charges guide:
-- Per adult £3.75 - £5.40; child (3-13 yrs) £2.55 - £3.90; electricity £2.90.
-- No pitch charges.
-- Less 5% for booked stays paid 6 weeks in advance.
-- VAT included.
-- Credit cards accepted.
Open:
Easter/1 April - 30 Sept.
Address:
Newquay,
Cornwall TR8 4JF.
Tel:
(01637) 880462.
FAX: (01637) 880500.
E-mail: trekenning @aol.com.
Reservations:
Made with £20 deposit.

Cornwall

017 Trevella Caravan and Camping Park, Crantock, Newquay

Orderly touring park close to sea, with pool and fishing lakes; some caravans for hire.

One of the best known and most respected of Cornish parks with its colourful flower-beds and a regular winner of a 'Newquay in Bloom' award, Trevella is also one of the first to fill up and has a longer season than most. Well organised, the pitches are in a number of adjoining meadows, most of which are on a slight slope. Of the 350 pitches for touring units (any type), some 200 can be reserved and these are marked-out individual ones; elsewhere pitches are in rows but not marked. Over 100 pitches have electricity connections (10A), with 28 `premium' serviced pitches (with hardstanding, electricity and TV hook-ups, water, waste water, sewage). A small, free heated swimming pool with sunbathing area is centrally positioned, open like the shop, etc. from Easter-Oct, weather permitting. The nearest beach is ½ mile on foot, 1 mile by car and Newquay is 2 miles. There are pubs and restaurants at Crantock, 1 mile. Trevella is essentially a quiet family touring park with an accent on orderliness and cleanliness; site evening activities are limited. The sanitary facilities are kept very clean, the three blocks providing sufficient coverage with individual washbasins with shelf, in private cabins for ladies, free hot water to plentiful washing-up sinks and controllable showers, hair drying and dressing room, baby room and launderette. Well stocked supermarket. Post box and telephone. Freezer pack service. Nicky's Kitchen offers hot dishes and snacks to take away or eat there, open late. Games room with pool tables and table tennis, and separate TV room. Crazy golf. Large adventure playground, separate play and sports area and pets corner. There is free access to three fishing lakes, two on site (permits from reception); some fishing instruction, and wildlife talks for youngsters in season. A pleasant walk is possible around the lakes, a protected nature reserve, and it is also possible to walk to Crantock beach but the tides must be checked first. Shuttle bus service to Newquay and Crantock. Riding 1 mile, golf 3 miles. A member of the Best of British group.

Charges 1999:
-- Per adult £3.00 - £5.50; child (3-15 yrs) £1.50 - £2.75; car 60p - 80p; dog 50p - £1.20; electricity £2.40; full services incl. electricity £5.50.
-- Min. charge 31/7-21/8 £15.00.
-- Families and couples only.
-- Credit cards accepted.
-- VAT included.
Open:
Easter - 31 October.
Address:
Crantock, Newquay, Cornwall TR8 5EW.
Tel:
(01637) 830308 (24 hr). FAX: (01872) 571254. E-mail: trevella@ compuserve.com.
Reservations:
Made with £20 deposit and £2 booking fee (16/7-27/8: Fri/Fri or Sat/Sat only).

Directions: To avoid Newquay leave A30 or A392 at Indian Queens, straight over crossroads with A39 and A3058, left at A3075 junction and first right at camp sign. O.S.GR: SW802598.

016 Newperran Tourist Park, Rejerrah, nr. Newquay

Large capacity, open touring-only park, with pool and close to popular beaches.

This is a level park in rural Cornish countryside and on high ground making it quite open but also giving excellent views of the coast and surrounding district. Although it has its own manager, it is under the same family direction and ownership as Trevella Park, with the same sort of standards and is also a member of the Best of British group. Newperran is a little further back from the sea, but only 2½ miles from Perranporth beach, and there is a free heated swimming pool on site. Those who prefer traditional camping to a holiday camp atmosphere should appreciate this park. This is not to say that it is without facilities; it certainly has its full share of amenities, but it is a quiet park used mainly by families and with few evening activities. It consists of a number of flat, well drained, hedged meadows divided into 250 individual pitches. Some fields have larger and reservable plots, with more free space in the middle. There are 113 electrical connections (10A) including 13 'all-service' pitches. Sanitary facilities consist of four clean, permanent blocks with free hot water in washbasins (some in cabins) and hot showers. There are two bathrooms, hair drying and dressing room, a unit for disabled visitors, washing up sinks and a launderette. Good self-service shop. Cafe with hot snacks to eat there or take away. TV room with some children's video shows. Actvities for children include an adventure playground, crazy golf, a children's room and an activity programme in season. Free fishing at Trevella. Riding or golf 2 miles. Goonhavern village is within walking distance with pubs and post office. A member of the Best of British group.

Charges 1999:
-- Per adult £3.00 - £5.50; child (3-16 yrs) £1.50 - £2.40; dog 50p - £1.00; electricity (10A) £2.30; full services incl. electricity £5.50.
-- Min. charge 31/7-21/8 £15.00.
-- VAT included.
-- Credit cards accepted.
Open:
Mid-May - mid-Sept.
Address:
Rejerrah, Newquay, Cornwall TR8 5QJ.
Tel:
(01872) 572407. (1/10-1/5: (01637) 830308). FAX: (01872) 571254.
Reservations:
Advised in high season; made with £20 p/w deposit and £2 fee.

Directions: Turn off A3075 to west at camp sign 7 miles south of Newquay and just north of Goonhavern village. O.S.GR: SW794546.

Trevella & Newperran

CARAVAN AND CAMPING PARK **TOURIST PARK**

Both parks have spotless facilities including modern toilet and shower blocks with individual wash cubicles, razor points, babies room, hairdressing room, hairdriers, launderette, crazy golf, games room, TV room, cafe, shop and off licence, free heated swimming pools and adventure play areas.

THE FAMILY RUN HOLIDAY PARKS

Our reputation for cleanliness, friendly and courteous service have earned each park the highest AA rating of 5 pennants and the Top AA Assessment of "Excellent" for Sanitary installations.

• Concessionary green fees at Perranporth's excellent links golf course.

• The well stocked lake at Trevella offers Free Fishing (no closed season).

VOTED TWO OF THE TOP 10 TOURING PARKS IN CORNWALL

TREVELLA PARK
22 CRANTOCK, NEWQUAY, CORNWALL
TR8 5EW.   TEL: 01637 830308
Trevella just outside Newquay and its seven golden beaches. A breathtakingly beautiful secluded family park. As well as touring pitches there are holiday caravans for hire with toilet, shower and colour Satellite TV.

NEWPERRAN TOURIST PARK
22 REJERRAH, NEWQUAY, CORNWALL
TR8 5QJ.   TEL: 01872 572407
Newperran has been developed from a small Cornish farm in a picturesque, beautifully cared for setting. It is a level park with perimeter pitching ideal for caravans, tents, motor homes and the perfect family holiday.

TELEPHONE FOR COLOUR BROCHURES
01637 830308 (24 HOURS)
OR WRITE FOR BROCHURE TO THE SITE OF YOUR CHOICE.

Cornwall

022 Trevornick Holiday Park, Holywell Bay, Newquay

Large, busy, family complex for all units near sandy beach, with wide-ranging amenities.

Trevornick has been converted from a working farm and has grown to provide caravanners and campers (no holiday caravans) with 450 grass pitches (386 with electricity) in five level fields and two terraced areas (few trees, but some good views), providing `all singing, all dancing' facilities for family holidays. The five toilet blocks of a standard modern design provide washbasins in vanity style, toilets, coin operated showers including a family shower room, baby bath, dishwashing and laundry facilities, and chemical disposal. The farm buildings now provide the setting for the farm club (recently refurbished) with licensed facilities and food, children's rooms, games room, cafeteria, chip bar and take-away, plus much entertainment in season. The Trawlers' Bar serves meals and drinks for families (with TV). Activities include a good sized pool (all season) with slide, sauna, tennis courts, an adventure playground, crazy golf and indoor adventure play area (supervised for 2-8 yr olds at a small fee). Dogs are accepted in one field only with a walk provided. A good sized farm shop reminds one of the park's background. The rest of the development has provided an 18 hole golf course, pitch and putt, a small, quiet club with bar meals and lovely views out to sea, Holywell leisure `fun' park next door (site fun pass gives reduced rates) and recently much improved coarse fishing with three lakes. The sandy beach is 5 minutes by car or 20 minutes walk through the sand dunes past the Holywell. Bicycle hire and boat launching 4 miles, riding within 1 mile. The park offers 60 'Eurotents' to hire (pre-erected, fully equipped tents sleeping 6; cot and TV hire available).

Charges 1999:
-- Per adult £2.90 - £5.50; child (4-16 yrs) free - £3.60; car 80p; electricity £2.75 - £3.00; dog £1.75.
-- Families and couples only.
-- VAT included.
-- Credit cards accepted.

Open:
Easter -mid September.

Address:
Holywell Bay, Newquay, Cornwall TR8 5PW.

Tel:
(01637) 830531.
FAX: (01637) 831000.
E-mail: enquiries@ trevornick.co.uk.

Reservations:
Made with £20 deposit per week (Sat. to Sat. only July/Aug).

Directions: From A3075 approach to Newquay - Perranporth road, turn towards Cubert and Holywell Bay. Continue through Cubert to park on the right. O.S.GR: SW776586.

021 Hendra Holiday Park, Newquay

Holiday park with comprehensive entertainment programme.

Hendra is a long-established holiday park for the family which likes to be entertained, as the entertainment programme here is very comprehensive. There are comedians, show bands, cabaret, dancing, bingo, discos, plus entertainment and clubs for children. The 600 pitches, on various fields, are on well mown, slightly sloping grass with country views and mature trees, some more sheltered, There are tarmac roads and lighting and 200 pitches have electrical connections (16A). Some landscaped hardstanding 'super' pitches have individual water, electricity, light, sewer drainage and satellite TV connections (dogs not accepted on these pitches). Many pitches have water, drainage and hardstanding also. There are caravan holiday homes for hire but they are separated from the tourers. The entrance and reception are very attractive with a mass of well tended flower beds which, along with the other facilities, form an attractive, village-like centre to the park. The heated outdoor pool, with a giant slide and sunbathing area, is supervised and there is also a small pool for toddlers, a sauna and solarium. This area is to be refurbished for 2000 and will include a new indoor pool with three flumes. The well stocked shop, various bars and restaurants open all season (limited hours in early season), even for breakfast, including a fish and chip bar and Mario's, which is only open in the main season. The three toilet blocks are being refurbished to provide vanity style washbasins, free showers and some facilities for babies and disabled visitors. Large launderette, chemical disposal and motorcaravan services, plus gas supplies. Activities are well catered for with large playing fields, tennis court, minigolf, adventure play area, table tennis, pool tables and also a very large array of slot machines. Fishing or riding 1 mile, bicycle hire or golf 2 miles. Dogs accepted in some areas of the park (dog walk provided). The park is only 1½ miles from Newquay and its fabulous surfing beaches and a bus to the town passes the gate.

Directions: Park is on the left side of A392 Indian Queens - Newquay road at Newquay side of Quintrell Downs. O.S.GR: SW833601.

Charges 1999:
-- Per adult £3.30 - £5.15; child (3-14 yrs) free - £3.40; vehicle £1.00; awning free; 'super' pitch (electricity, water, chemical disposal, TV point, hardstanding, no dogs) £7.50; hardstanding pitch (electricity, water and drainage) £3.85; electricity only £2.80; dog £1.50.
-- Families and mixed couples only.
-- Various special offers.
-- VAT included.
-- Credit cards accepted.

Open:
1 April - end October.

Address:
Newquay,
Cornwall TR8 4NY.

Tel:
(01637) 875778.
FAX: (01637) 879017.
E-mail: hendra.uk@
dial.pipex.com.

Reservations:
Made with deposit (£20) and fee (£3).

NEW FOR 2000
Indoor Fun Pool with 3 Sensational Water Flumes

NEWQUAY
CORNWALL
Excellent Camping & Touring Facilities
Luxury Static Caravans

Free Entertainment • Cabaret • Licensed Bars
Marios Bar • Fish & Chip Shop • Sauna • Supermarket
Games Fields • Food Bar • Amusements • Train Rides
Pitch n Putt • Heated Swimming Pools & Waterslide
Toddlers Pirate Den • Children's Hippo Club

To ensure everyones enjoyment, Hendra Holiday Park caters exclusively for families and couples only!

Freephone Brochure
0500 242523

Hendra Holiday Park, Newquay,
Cornwall TR8 4NY Tel: 01637 875778
e.mail: hendra.uk@dial.pipex.com
www.hendra-holidays.com

HOLIDAY PARK

ROSE AWARD

Cornwall

020 Newquay Holiday Park, Newquay

Well run park with swimming pools and other amenities near town.

This park lies peacefully on a terraced hillside only just outside the town, 2 miles from the beaches and town centre. The main feature of the park is an attractively laid out group of three heated swimming pools with giant water slide (lifeguards in attendance) and surrounding 'green' sunbathing areas. Mainly a touring park, it has 340 marked pitches for any type of unit in a series of hedged fields, some sloping, with some fields just for caravans and others for tents, plus 138 caravan holiday homes (for hire). Most pitches are individual ones marked out by lines on ground but with nothing between them. Electricity points (16A) are provided for caravans and tents, plus 10 special 'star' pitches with hardstanding, water and drainage. The sanitary installations include two good-sized, modern blocks with washbasins set in flat surfaces with free hot water and fairly basic free hot showers with pre-mixed hot water which runs for four minutes and stops, with an extra block for the main season when they may be under pressure. There is a baby bath, covered external dishwashing sinks with hot water and chemical disposal points. Gas is available. Entertainment each night with live music, discos etc. is provided in the site's Fiesta Club which also has a bar, TV lounge and games room with pool and snooker tables (all open when the site is open). Amusement arcade. Well stocked self-service shop and takeaway food bar (both all season, and good value). Full launderette with free ironing. Activities include a pitch and putt course, crazy golf, a good children's playground, children's club and recreation field for football and volleyball. Fishing and bicycle hire 2 miles, golf 200 yds, riding 2½ miles. Bus service to Newquay from site. No dogs or pets are taken.

Directions: Park is east of Newquay on A3059 road 1 mile east of junction with A3058. O.S.GR: SW853626.

Charges 2000:
-- Per adult £3.10 - £5.70; child (3-15 yrs) free - £3.60; vehicle 80p; electricity (16A) free - £2.50; star pitch supplement £3.50.
-- Min. charge per night in high season £12.20.
-- Many special offers.
-- VAT included.
-- Credit cards accepted.

Open:
Mid May - mid Sept.

Address:
Newquay,
Cornwall TR8 4HS.

Tel:
(01637) 871111.
FAX: (01637) 850818.
E-mail: bookings@ newquay-hol-park. demon.co.uk.

Reservations:
Advised for peak season; made with £18 deposit per week plus £9 cancellation insurance (peak weeks Sat. - Sat. only).

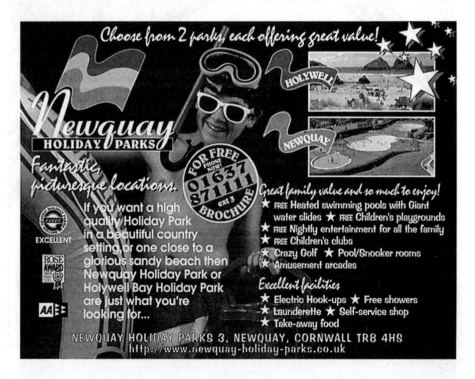

025 Pentewan Sands Holiday Park, Mevagissey

Family park with private beach and swimming pool; some hire caravans and chalets.

Pentewan Sands is a popular park with an ideal position right beside a wide sandy beach, managed by the park, which offers safe bathing and direct flat access with no roads to cross. There is carefully monitored public access to the beach through the park. A busy, 32 acre park with lots going on, there are 480 individual touring pitches, 380 with electricity, and 112 caravan holiday homes for hire. The pitches are of reasonable size on level grass with nothing between them, and are marked by frontage stones, mostly in rows adjoining access roads. The three main toilet blocks serve their purpose well, receiving heavy use in peak season. There is free hot water in nearly all washbasins, many in vanity style, a few for ladies in semi-private cabins, free hot showers, two bathrooms and a baby room, plus facilities for disabled people, a well equipped laundry room, washing up sinks and chemical disposal. A good sized free heated swimming pool (about 72 x 26 ft) with small children's pool (supervised and open Whitsun - mid Sept) is adjacent to the Clubhouse and bowling centre. Open all season, the Clubhouse contains two licensed bar lounges upstairs and a further one downstairs opening on to the pool area, open all day and serving a variety of good value food. A full entertainment programme, beach activities, water sports and a children's club are organised, and there is a small water sports centre on the beach. Other activities include an adventure playground, tennis courts (one full size, one compact) and bicycle hire. Riding or golf 2 miles. The sailing club adjoining offers membership to campers, scuba diving, windsurfing courses, etc. Slipway and boat launching service (Whit - mid Sept). No jet-skis are permitted and no 4WD vehicles allowed on the beach. The site has a large, self-service shop (from Easter but hours may be limited), a bistro, bar meals and fast food (Whitsun - mid-Sept). Freezer service for ice packs, battery charging service, gas, public phones and motorcaravan service point. Caravan and boat storage available. Dogs are not accepted. There is access to the Pentewan Valley Trail, a six mile route for cycling or walking following the old carriageway to Mevagissey with its throngs of tourists (only two miles by the main road). The park has been owned by the Tremayne family for 60 years, along with the beach, and there are links with the award winning Lost Gardens of Heligan nearby.

Directions: From St. Austell ring road take B3273 for Mevagissey. Park is 3½ miles, where the road meets the sea. O.S.GR: SX018468.

Charges 1999:
-- Per unit incl. 2 adults £6.00 - £15.50; extra adult £1.50 - £3.30; child (3-15 yrs) £1.00 - £2.50; awning free; extra small tent or car £1.70; boat £1.70; electricity (10A) £2.60.
-- Sea front pitch plus 10-20%.
-- VAT included.
-- Credit cards accepted.
Open:
Easter/1 April - 31 Oct.
Address:
Pentewan, nr. St. Austell, Cornwall PL26 6BT.
Tel:
(01726) 843485.
FAX: (01726) 844142.
E-mail: pentewansands @btinternet.com.
Reservations:
Made Sat - Sat or Wed - Wed with deposit (£35-£75, acc. to season), £4 booking fee and compulsory cancellation insurance (£3-£6).

see colour advert between pages 32/33

041 Pengrugla Park, Mevagissey

Peaceful park in mature garden setting.

Pengrugla is now under the ownership of Pentewan Sands and the Tremayne family, and we are happy to feature the park to complement the Pentewan Site with its busy beach life and many activities. Part of Pengrugla's boundary actually edges The Lost Gardens of Heligan although nothing can be seen. At some time the land used to develop Pengrugla must have been part of the Gardens and one can enjoy the mature trees and flowering shrubs which have been further landscaped to provide an attractive situation for a number of privately owned holiday homes. These face out over a part of the 'lost valley' of Heligan fame and are interspersed with touring pitches, with some below on sloping grass and others in a more level situation amongst trees and shrubs. In all, there are 100 good sized touring pitches, all with 16A electricity. A modern, heated and tiled toilet block is central and it provides vanity style washbasins and comfortably sized pre-set showers with divider and seat. A heated unisex bathroom is also available, plus three dishwashing sinks under cover, a laundry room with two washing machines, two dryers, iron and board, but no hand washing sinks, and chemical disposal. Reception at the entrance also has a small shop for basics with some tourist gifts and coffee also available. A good adventure playground completes the on-site amenities and the many facilities of Pentewan Sands are available to Pengrugla visitors - see above. Dogs are welcome. There is access to the Pentewan Trail to ride or cycle into Mevagissey or Pentewan.

Directions: Continue past Pentewan Sands up the hill and turn right following site signs. Park on left just before reaching the Gardens. OSGR: SW999464.

Charges 1999:
-- Per pitch incl. 2 adults, caravan/tent and car £6.00 - £14.00; extra adult £2.00 - £3.00; extra child £1.00 - £2.00; extra tent £1.50; extra car or boat £1.00; dog £1.00; electricity £2.00.
Open:
Easter - end October.
Address:
St. Ewe, St Austell, Cornwall PL26 6ER.
Tel:
(01726) 842714.
FAX: (01726) 844414.
Reservations:
Made with £45 deposit £45; write to Pentewan Sands (see above).

Cornwall

009 Trethem Mill Touring Park, St Just-in-Roseland, nr. St Mawes

Peaceful, rural family park on the Roseland Peninsula.

St Mawes is a very popular, pretty village on the Roseland peninsula, which is itself an `area of outstanding natural beauty'. Being only three miles away, Trethem Mill is well placed for either sailing, walking the coastal path around the peninsula, visiting the gardens of Trelissick or Heligan, or simply lazing on the nearby beaches. The Akeroyd family continue to work hard to turn Trethem Mill into a park of which to be proud. The centrally located toilet block has been refurbished to a very high standard and it is kept spotlessly clean. Centrally heated in cooler weather, there is an ample supply of hot water, vanity style washbasins, push-button, free showers, soap and hand-dryers and a baby room. The laundry is well equipped and dishwashing sinks are provided, plus chemical disposal. Also in the central area is reception and shop, which is only small but very well stocked and licensed. Trethem is a strictly touring park and 50 of its 84 pitches have 16A electricity, with several now classified as 'all-weather'. Most are on slightly sloping ground, with tarmac access roads. At the busiest times an extra field, also with tarmac access, is brought into use. Children have a games room, TV room and a well equipped, fenced playground (closed at 9 pm). Skateboards and roller-blades are banned for the safety of everyone. Hire of wet suits and canoes. Freezer for ice packs (free). Public telephone. The park has been carefully landscaped and is a mass of colour, the area around reception being particularly pretty where a small watermill has been built amongst the flowers - the sound of gently flowing water is very relaxing - and there are pet animals (do not feed). A large field alongside the park is used as a recreation area, with a separate dog walk. Fishing 1½ miles, boat launching 2 miles, bicycle hire 4 miles, riding 8 miles, golf 6 miles. Trethem Mill aims to attract couples and families who seek peace and tranquillity, and can manage without a bar and on site entertainment.

Charges 1999:
-- Per unit incl. 2 adults £6.50 - £10.00; per person, hiker or cyclist £3.50 - £5.00; extra adult £2.00 - £2.50; child (4-16 yrs) £1.50 - £2.00; electricity £2.00; dog £1.00; extra car or pup tent £1.00.
-- Credit cards accepted.
Open:
1 April - 18 October.
Address:
St Just-in-Roseland, nr. St Mawes, Truro, Cornwall TR2 5JF.
Tel:
(01872) 580504.
FAX: (01872) 580968.
Reservations:
Made with £30 deposit.

Directions: From Tregony take A3078 to St Mawes. About 2 miles after passing through Trewithian, watch for caravan and camping sign. O.S.GR: SW862364.

024N Southleigh Manor Naturist Holiday Club, St. Columb Major

Welcoming family naturist site in the mature grounds of a large house with heated pool.

For those who have ventured to try the naturist sites in our French guide and who also may appreciate that special ambience at home, we are happy to include Southleigh Manor where Richard and Ann Rowe provide a warm welcome. The respect that the naturist has for the environment and for fellow beings provides a very special, caring atmosphere and this can be truly experienced on this site. The 50 pitches have been developed in the south facing, sheltered, lawned garden and orchard with mature trees. There are 2 hardstandings and 48 electrical connections (5/10A), plus 10 touring vans to let. The purpose built toilet block has identical, well equipped, unisex units at each end, well maintained, with a laundry room in the middle. Chemical disposal. Small shop - bread, milk, papers and tourist information (late May - 31 Aug). A sun room and leisure suite including sauna, spa bath and exercise equipment, are in the house. The small open air swimming pool is heated and can therefore be used all season. Other facilities include boules, croquet (in the walled garden), volleyball, minigolf and a children's play area with tree house and gaily painted train. Dogs are permitted on leads. Fishing 4 miles, bicycle hire 7 miles, riding 2 miles, golf 5 miles. You will be encouraged to get involved, with barbecues and social evenings and the opportunity to enjoy Cornwall's naturist beaches and many tourist attractions, which combine to provide a relaxed holiday atmosphere.

Charges 1999:
-- Per unit incl. 2 adults £11.50 - £12.50; extra adult £2.30 - £2.40; child (13 yrs and under) £1.10 - £1.35; extra pup tent £1.10; electricity £1.95; dog 95p.
-- Club membership £2.50 per couple/family for stay.
-- No credit cards.
-- VAT included.
Open:
April - 20 September.
Address:
St. Columb Major, Cornwall TR9 6HY.
Tel:
(01637) 880938.
FAX: as phone.
E-mail: richard.rowe@saqnet.co.uk.
Reservations:
Made with £40 deposit.

Directions: From north on A30 Bodmin - Truro road, after village of Victoria pass crossroad (Roche Cross) and go under iron railway bridge and then first right on A3059 towards St Mawgan and St Columb. Site is on left in 3 miles. From A39, take A3059 at Newquay/St Columb roundabout and site is on right, almost immediately. O.S.GR: SW904622.

A DISCOVERY ON THE UNEXPLORED ROSELAND

TRETHEM MILL
TOURING PARK

● HIGHEST GRADED FACILITIES ON THE PENINSULA (ETB)
● FAMILY OWNED & RUN OFFERING A RELAXING
ATMOSPHERE IN A TRANQUIL COUNTRYSIDE SETTING
● IDEAL LOCATION FOR WALKING, BEACHES, GARDENS
AND TOURING CORNWALL

ST. JUST-IN-ROSELAND, CORNWALL TR2 5JF TEL: 01872 580504 FAX: 01872 580968

015 Sea View International, Gorran, nr. Mevagissey

First class, quality park with landscaped pool area and near safe beaches.

Sea View is one of the best examples of a well cared for, quality park and this is reflected in the number of awards it has won in the last 20 years. Now in the hands of the third generation of the Michell family, the park is constantly being improved with the aim of providing quality camping for the discerning camper. Although somewhat exposed, the park is a mass of colour with flower beds full of colourful bedding plants and flowering shrubs and has well manicured grass of exceptional quality. The area around the swimming pool is particularly attractive, with sunbathing areas with free sun-beds on tiled terraces surrounded by flowers creating private little areas, all with magnificent views of the sea and the distant headland (the pool is open all season, heated end May-mid Sept). The toilet blocks are excellent - centrally positioned, well maintained, with good quality fittings and central heating. The large showers are free and there are vanity style washbasins, baby baths, facilities for disabled visitors (two showers and WCs), a hairdressing area with free hairdryers, plus bathrooms (on payment). The toilet and washbasin block has been extended recently to provide an enlarged dishwashing area with two small campers' kitchens (one with a microwave, one with a mini-grill and hob), a well equipped laundry and excellent chemical disposal facilities, all fully tiled. A covered, flowered walkway connects these excellent facilities which are topped by a handsome clock tower. A motorcaravan service point with car washing facilities is nearby.

A shop (May-end Sept) and takeaway (Whit-early Sept) are near the park entrance and reception provides plenty of tourist information, plus gas. There are no bars, restaurant or evening entertainment which seems to be the main reason many of the customers come year after year. Booking for July/Aug. is advisable. Many of the 165 large, level pitches have views, all have 16A electricity and 47 are fully serviced, including hardstandings suitable for large motorhomes. There are 38 caravan holiday homes for hire. The excellent large playing field has plenty of room for leisure activities including tennis, volleyball, badminton, football, putting, table tennis, crazy golf and an adventure playground (all free). A barbecue area with tables and seats and a nice touch is a very descriptive weather map which is updated daily. Dogs are accepted and a large exercise field provided. Public phones. Anyone not restricted by school holidays will find May and June a particularly good time to visit, the gardens of Heligan and Trelissick and Lanhydrock House being at their best at that time. The area is full of places to visit from theme parks to the seal sanctuary, not forgetting the safe beaches, one of which is only a ½ mile walk from the park. Fishing ½ mile, bicycle hire 6 miles, boat launching 2 miles, riding 1 mile, golf 9 miles. A member of the Best of British group.

Directions: From St Austell take the B3273 towards Mevagissey; 1 mile before Mevagissey village turn right at Gorran and camp sign and continue towards Gorran for 5 miles. Fork right at camp sign and follow signs to park. O.S.GR: SW991412.

Charges 1999:
-- Per unit incl. 2 persons and awning £6.90 - £16.90; extra adult £2.50 - £4.00; child (3-14 yrs) £1.50 - £2.75; pup tent (outside 18/7-27/8) free - £2.00; electricity £2.50; dog (limited breeds and numbers) free - £2.00; extra car free - £1.00; special facility pitch £2.00 - £3.50.
-- VAT included.
-- Credit cards accepted.

Open:
1 April - 3 October.

Address:
Boswinger, Gorran,
St Austell,
Cornwall PL26 6LL.

Tel:
(01726) 843425.
FAX: (01726) 843358.
E-mail: gary@gmichell.
freeserve.co.uk.

Reservations:
Min 7 nights, w/e - w/e, 27/7-1/9. other times, any length, with £30 deposit and £2 fee.

See colour feature for `BEST of BRITISH' between pages 96/97

Cornwall

026 Penhaven Touring Park, Pentewan, Mevagissey

Family owned touring park with swimming pool, one mile from sandy beach.

Penhaven is a grassy, level 13 acre park, with the road on one side (this can be a little noisy on busy Saturdays) and a river on the other. There is a bridge from the site giving access to the Pentewan Valley Trail, a two mile walk or cycle ride to Pentewan village and beach along this quiet, traffic free track, with links to Mevagissey via Heligan. Owned and developed by the Hackwell family for over 10 years, the park comprises three fields with 105 good sized pitches which are numbered, 80 with 10A electricity and 5 with hardstanding. The North field is used for rallies and has a refurbished 'portacabin' style unit near with washbasins, toilets and a shower. The South field is used as a ball game area, for caravan storage and as a tent area for 35 tents on a 28 day licence (no tarmac road and no lighting). The Middle field has all the main facilities which include a heated swimming pool (mid-May-early Sept), unsupervised and with a paved sunbathing surround and loungers. There is a small fenced play area for children on sand and grass. Reception also incorporates the shop which has a wide variety of goods for sale. The tiled toilet block can be heated and provides washbasins, toilets and showers (a little cramped). There are also four family shower rooms (key on request with deposit) and one is equipped for use by disabled visitors. All hot water is free, there are dishwashing sinks under cover and a well equipped laundry with washing lines provided. Chemical disposal and motorcaravan services. Dogs are welcome on a lead and exercised off site (there is a wood over the river). During high season a van on site sells takeaway snacks and there is a restaurant in the nearby village of London Apprentice. Buses pass the gate for St Austell and Mevagissey. Fishing, bicycle hire and boat launching 1 mile, golf 3 miles, riding 8 miles. The park adjoins the cycle trail to Mevagissy. A busy park, but away from the hectic coastal sites, Penhaven will probably appeal to people who don't want a bar and evening entertainment.

Directions: From St Austell on A390, take B3273 to Mevagissey and park is on left, 1 mile from London Apprentice before the village of Pentewan. O.S.GR: SX008481.

Charges 1999:
-- Per unit incl. 2 persons £8.40 - £17.50; extra adult £3.20 - £4.25; child (5-17 yrs) £1.50; extra car, boat or trailer £1.00; electricity (10A) £2.00; dog 70p.
-- VAT included.
-- Credit cards accepted.

Open:
Easter/1 April - 31 Oct.

Address:
Pentewan, St Austell, Cornwall PL26 6DL.

Tel:
(01726) 843687.
FAX: (01726) 843870.
E-mail:
penhaven.cornwall @virgin.net.

Reservations:
Min. 3 days with £20 deposit per week.

019 Polruan Holiday Centre, Polruan, nr. Fowey

Quiet rural site in elevated situation not far from Fowey.

With 11 holiday homes for hire and 32 touring pitches, this is a very pleasant little site in an elevated situation with sea views. The holiday homes are arranged in a neat circle, with a central area for some tourers, including 7 pitches with gravel hardstanding and electricity. The remaining touring pitches are in an adjacent field with 4 electricity hook-ups, which is part level for motorcaravans and part on a gentle slope for tents. There are marvellous sea views, but it could be a little exposed when the wind blows off the sea. A raised picnic area, with table, gives more views across the estuary to Fowey. A small, old-fashioned sanitary block is centrally situated and provides one controllable hot shower for each sex, washbasins with H&C, plenty of hooks and mirrors, a washing-up and a laundry sink (H&C), plus a washing machine – in the ladies. There are chemical disposal and motorcaravan service facilities, two fresh water taps and waste water points. Reception (with a small terrace) doubles as a small shop for basics and gas, and provides a freezer for ice packs, plenty of local tourist information and bus timetables (for Looe, etc). Recycling bins, a public telephone and a large, sloping field for children's play with swings and seat. Riding or bicycle hire 3 miles, fishing ½ mile, golf 10 miles. This is a nice little park in a popular tourist area, within walking distance (down-hill all the way, and vice-versa!) of the village, where there are various hostelries and a passenger ferry to Fowey. A member of the Countryside Discovery group.

Directions: From main A390 at East Taphouse take B3359 towards Looe. After 5 miles fork right signed Bodinnick and ferry. Watch for signs for Polruan and site to left. Follow these carefully along narrow Cornish lanes to site on right just before village. O.S.GR: SX133509.

Charges 2000:
-- Per unit £6.50 - £10.00; tent £4.50 - 10.00; electricity £2.00.
-- No credit cards.

Open:
Easter - October.

Address:
Polruan-by-Fowey, Cornwall PL23 1QH.

Tel:
(01726) 870263.
FAX: as phone.
E-mail:
polholiday@aol.com.

Reservations:
Advised for July/Aug. - contact park.

029 Carlyon Bay Caravan & Camping Park, Bethesda, Carlyon Bay

Spacious, tranquil, family owned park, 5 minutes walk from busy sandy beach.

Open meadows edged by mature woodland, well cared for by the Taylor family, provide a beautiful holiday setting with a blue flag beach 5 minutes walk from the top gate at this park. The original farm buildings have been converted and added to, providing an attractive centre to the park, also home for the owners, with a certain individuality of design which is very pleasing, particularly in the three modern, impressively tiled toilet blocks. These are now a feature of the park, being of excellent quality and design and providing a mix of facilities from vanity style washbasins to en-suite toilets and washbasins, comfortable, roomy, pre-set showers with divider, shelf, etc, facilities for hair-care and make-up and thoughtful provision for babies - almost 'home from home'! Dishwashing sinks with hot water are under cover at all the blocks. Fully equipped laundry room (hot water metered) with free irons and a well hidden chemical disposal point. The 180 pitches in five areas are spacious and allow for a family meadow, a dog free meadow, and an area for couples, etc. All are on flat, terraced or gently sloping grass with flowers and shrubs in some areas. The 104 pitches with electricity (5/10A) are marked. There is even a 'discreet' area, well screened and hidden, for naturists. The only official naturist beach in Cornwall, Polgaver Bay, at the far end of Carlyon Bay can be reached by walking over the cliff tops. The attractive kidney shaped, heated pool (Easter-Sept) with children's paddling pool, is walled and paved for sunbathing and is part of the central area, along with a canopied entertainment area, TV lounge, crazy golf, table tennis, pool table and barbecue area. Two children's play areas, one adventure type. Modern reception with a good little shop and takeaway (May-mid Sept). Socially the park provides entertainment in high season for families and children but those who wish for more can choose between the Cornish Leisure World complex on the beach, with its pool, bars and discos, or the social club near the park entrance which welcomes campers. For the more active, there is also a golf course opposite the entrance and the coastal footpath passes near. All Cornwall's attractions are within touring distance. Buses to St. Austell and Fowey run from the park entrance.

Directions: From Plymouth direction on A390, pass Lostwithiel and 1 mile after village of St Blazey, turn left at roundabout beside Britannia Inn. After 400 yds turn right on a concrete road and right again at site sign. O.S.GR: SX053526.

Charges 1999:
-- Per unit incl. 2 persons and car £7.00 - £16.00; extra adult £3.00 - £3.50; child (3-17 yrs incl.) £1.50 - £2.50; awning or small pup tent free - £1.00; extra car £1.00; dog £1.00 - £1.50; electricity £2.00.
-- Motorcaravan less £1.00, hiker/tent less £2.00 per night.
-- VAT included.
-- Credit cards accepted.

Open:
April - October.

Address:
Bethesda, Carlyon Bay, St. Austell, Cornwall PL25 3RE.

Tel:
(01726) 812735. FAX: (01726) 815496. E-mail: jeffst@globalnet.co.uk.

Reservations:
Made with £30 deposit and £2 fee (min. 6 nights 19/7-17/8).

Carlyon Bay
CARAVAN & CAMPING PARK

AA CAMPSITE OF THE YEAR 1999 - SOUTH WEST

◆ Award winning family park
◆ Set in over 30 acres of meadows and mature woodlands.
◆ Up to 180 touring pitches (no statics)
◆ Footpath to large sandy beach.
◆ Close to championship Golf Course.

◆ Heated Swimming and paddling pool.
◆ Ben's Play World for kids nearby.
◆ Badminton, Pool, Table-tennis and crazy-golf.

For colour brochure ring: **01726 812735**
www.chycor.co.uk/camping/carlyon-bay **E-mail:** Jeff@globalnet.co.uk

CARLYON BAY CARAVAN & CAMPING PARK, ST. AUSTELL, CORNWALL

For a list of parks which do not accept dogs, or where certain restrictions apply - see page 236

Dogs are banned from many beaches, either all year round or in the summer months. Ask for details from local authorities or the park of your choice.

Cornwall

028 Powderham Castle Tourist Park, Lanlivery, nr. Lostwithiel

Tranquil, sheltered family touring park well situated for exploring Cornwall.

This is a most pleasant, peaceful park with plenty of 'green' space and a natural, uncommercialised atmosphere which has been enhanced by careful planting of trees and shrubs to form a series of linked paddocks with a small stream running through. The nearest beach at Par is some 4 miles. The park has 38 private caravan holiday homes in a separate field and 75 numbered touring pitches, all with electricity connections (5/10A) and 7 with hardstanding, spread round the perimeter of the paddocks, each with 10-15 pitches (awning groundsheets to be lifted alternate days). Dustbin and water points around the park are well hidden by trees and bushes. The single central toilet block is a good one with free hot water in the washbasins (with shelf and mirror), heated shower areas with hot showers on payment, curtained cubicles in the ladies, hairdryers and a family washroom with shower, basin, WC, etc. Separate dishwashing area with five sinks (free hot water), fully equipped laundry room and chemical disposal. It is quite a walk from some pitches and a torch would be useful. Activities include a badminton court, games room with table tennis and pool, TV room and a putting green. A large, well equipped children's activity play area with a super range of adventure type equipment on grass is in one of the hedged paddocks with a fenced paddling pool. Motorcaravan service point. Seasonal pitches and caravan storage available. Telephone. Dogs are allowed on leads. The village pub is within walking distance. Fresh water fishing 1½ miles or sea fishing 3 miles, bicycle hire 4 miles, riding 2 miles, golf 1½ miles. Indoor tennis courts (Bodmin) and a swimming pool are close. There are several good local restaurants.

Charges 1999:
-- Per unit £3.50 - £4.80; adult £1.70 - £2.50; child (3-16 yrs) 60p - £1.25; electricity £1.75; awnings (without groundsheet), extra small tent, car free.
-- No single sex groups (excl. bona fide organisations).
-- No credit cards.
-- VAT included.
Open:
Easter/1 April - 31 Oct.
Address:
Lanlivery, nr. Lostwithiel, Cornwall PL30 5BU.
Tel:
(01208) 872277
Reservations:
Made with £10 deposit.

Alan Rogers' Discount

Less 10%
(with guide)

Directions: Park approach road leads off A390 road, 1½ miles southwest of Lostwithiel. Follow white or brown camping signs. No other approach roads are advised. O.S.GR: SX083592.

040 Trelay Farmpark, Pelynt, by Looe

Small, quietly situated park with lovely views and some caravan holiday homes.

Situated a little back from the coast, just over three miles from Looe and Polperro in a rural situation, this is a neat, tidy and quiet park (there is no farm adjacent). On your right as you drive in, and quite attractively arranged amongst herbaceous shrubs, are caravan holiday homes (13 privately owned, 6 to let by the park). The touring area is behind and slightly above, on level to gently sloping, neatly cut grass. An oval hard-core road connects the good sized, numbered pitches which border the site and back onto hedges, the majority with rural views. Outside the main season the central area is kept for ball games, together with a water/refuse point. An excellent chalet-type, purpose built toilet block is to one side. Light, airy, spacious and insulated, it is a good facility. Well equipped and maintained, it provides semi-private washbasins (H&C) and large comfortable, pre-set showers. In this building, but in separate smaller rooms, are two dishwashing sinks and a laundry sink (all H&C), washing machine and a dryer. Separate chemical disposal. For those with disabilities a complete en-suite unit (with ramp) is accessed by key from reception. A public phone, tourist information, gas supplies and free use of a fridge/freezer complete the provision. You will receive a good welcome from the enthusiastic owners, Heather and Graham Veale, who live in the chalet bungalow near the entrance where the small reception is located. The village with pub and shops is within ½ mile. Fishing or riding 3 miles.

Charges 2000:
-- Per unit incl. 2 persons £7.00 - £8.50; extra person under 5 yrs £1.00, over 5 yrs £2.00; electricity £1.60; dog 50p.
-- No credit cards.
Open:
1 April - end October.
Address:
Pelynt, by Looe, Cornwall PL13 2JX.
Tel:
(01503) 220900.
FAX: as phone.
Reservations:
Made with non refundable deposit of £15 up to £35 total or £20 over £35 total.

Directions: From A390 Lostwithiel road take B3359 south at Middle or East Taphouse towards Looe and Polperro. Site is signed ½ mile past Pelynt on the left. From Looe take A387 towards Polperro and after 2 miles turn right onto B3359 towards Pelynt. Site is signed 1 mile on right. O.S.GR: SX210545.

042 Looe Valley Holiday Park, nr. Looe

Large touring park near sea, with live entertainment and heated outdoor pool.

This park is between the two picturesque fishing villages of Looe and Polperro. Covering 63 acres, there is space for 573 units, with 30 pitches used for caravan holiday homes for letting and 40 for seasonal lets, plus some for 'Eurotents' to hire. The touring pitches are all numbered and marked in three spacious, gently sloping fields, well mown and with 280 electric hook-ups (10A). The pitches are of good size in alternating rows on marker lines - it could be crowded in peak season, although pitch size is conducive to some privacy. Off peak there would be plenty of room. Four toilet blocks serve the whole area and are more than sufficient for peak periods. One modernised block can be heated and they provide all expected facilities. Hot water is free, dishwashing facilities are adequate and there is a launderette. The park has a wide range of facilities - it is a self-contained holiday park with an extensive entertainment centre and live entertainment during the season. The clubhouse has a ballroom, large bar, disco room, three TV rooms, games and amusement rooms and a full restaurant with breakfast as well (Whit - mid Sept) and takeaway. A large self-service, licensed shop is open from late May. Outdoor heated swimming pool, 18 hole crazy golf course, two children's play areas and a children's club in season. Public phone and dog exercise area. Caravan storage. The nearest beach, of sand and rocks, is 1½ miles at Talland.

Charges 1999:
-- Per pitch incl. all persons, awning £7.00 - £10.90; boat, trailer or extra car £1.50; dog £1.50; electricity £2.00.
-- Various special offers.
-- VAT included.
Open:
Easter - end September.
Address:
Polperro Road, Looe, Cornwall PL13 2JS.
Tel:
(01503) 262425.
FAX: as phone.
Reservations:
Contact park.

see colour advert between pages 32/33

Directions: Park entrance is off the north side of the A387, 2 miles west of Looe. O.S.GR: SX228536.

033 Killigarth Manor Caravan Park, Polperro, nr. Looe

Busy park for all units with much on site entertainment and holiday caravans to hire.

A substantial part of Killigarth Estate is occupied by caravan holiday homes but a separate part is allocated to touring units. Approached by a tree lined drive, this provides 202 marked, level or gently sloping grass pitches, of which 75 are taken by seasonal units. There are 73 electric hook-ups (16A) for tourers, plus strategically placed bins and water points. One large, spacious toilet block has pre-set hot showers (no divider, bench outside), vanity style washbasins, dryers, soap, hairdryers, washing up facilities under cover and a chemical disposal point. In peak season the block is supplemented by `portacabin' style toilet facilities. Facilities for disabled visitors are in the main block and a very well equipped laundry with free hot water for sinks. The heart of the site is the Talland Suite, recently enlarged. It provides a large bar and entertainment hall with family room, amusements and games areas, a new restaurant, takeaway and bar snacks, heated indoor pool (adult £2, child £1), fitness centre, sauna and sun bed, and a sun terrace with beautiful views. Early evening `young entertainment' is followed by live shows, discos or groups and a programme of competitions, quizes or family films in a big screen cinema. A children's playground is beside the pool area (plus another in the camping area). Well stocked mini-market (all season) and an information room. Activities include a tennis court (£3 per hour), bicycle hire, a skittle alley, croquet, draughts, badminton and crazy golf. Fishing and boat launching approx. 1 mile. Bus service in high season. Dogs are accepted but not in the leisure areas. This park is popular with families with children of all ages.

Charges 1999:
-- Per pitch £2.80 - £6.00; adult £3.00 - £3.60; child (3-16 yrs) £1.50 - £1.80; electricity £1.90.
-- Pup tents not permitted to share a pitch with another unit.
-- Special offers available.
-- VAT included.
-- Credit cards accepted.
Open:
4 April - 25 October.
Address:
Polperro, Looe, Cornwall PL13 2JQ.
Tel:
(01503) 272216.
FAX: (01503) 272065.
Reservations:
Made (Sat. - Sat. in main season) with £30 deposit.

Directions: On A387 Looe towards Polperro, after 3½ miles, fork left immediately past bus shelter and phone box at sign to site (¼ mile). O.S.GR: SX213519.

Cornwall

032 Polborder House Caravan and Camping Park, Looe

Small, neat touring park just back from sea with good views, personally run by the owners.

Polborder House may appeal to those who prefer a quiet, well kept little family site to the larger ones with many on-site activities. With good countryside views up to 31 touring units can be taken on well tended grass. Pitches are marked with some hedging and there are 28 electrical connections (10A). The sanitary block is well kept, of ample size for the park and provides free hot water in vanity style washbasins with curtained hot showers on payment. There is a baby room, a laundry room (H&C) with washing machine, spin and tumble dryers and iron, and three covered sinks outside for dishwashing (free hot water). An en-suite toilet unit for disabled visitors has a ramped approach. Rubbish is recycled and there are chemical disposal and motorcaravan service facilities. Shop (all season) for gas and basics, including off licence and tourist information, public phone and a toddler's play area, but no other special amenities. The owners live on the park and there are five caravan holiday homes for hire, plus two holiday bungalows (to let Jan-Nov). Fishing, golf and boat launching within 2 miles, riding 8 miles. Seaton is 2 miles, Looe 2½ and the nearest beach 20-25 minutes walk from a gate in the corner of the park.

Directions: Park is ¾ mile south of B3253; turn off 2 miles east of Looe following signs to park and Monkey Sanctuary. O.S.GR: SX283555.

Charges 1999:
-- Per unit incl. 2 persons £6.00 - £9.50; extra person £1.50 - £2.00; child (4-15 yrs) 75p - £1.00; awning £1.00; dog 75p; electricity £1.80.
-- Credit cards accepted.
-- VAT included.
Open:
1 April - 31 October.
Address:
Bucklawren Road, St Martin's-by-Looe, Cornwall PL13 1QR.
Tel:
(01503) 240265.
FAX: (01503) 240700.
E-mail: rlf.polborder @virgin.net.
Reservations:
Any period, £15 deposit.

Alan Rogers' Discount

Less 50p per pitch, per night

043 Trerethern Touring Park, Padstow

Spacious park with marvellous views within walking distance of Padstow.

Trerethern is a traditional park of wide open fields, although there have been attempts to divide it up with hedging which is developing nicely in places despite the rabbits and the elements. There is room for 300 units but only 100 are taken so there is plenty of open space and the views across Bodmin Moor and the estuary are marvellous. The grass is neatly cut and the pitches mostly level, although there is a gentle slope in parts. Electricity (10A) is available on 65 pitches, there are 10 water points and 7 hardstanding places for motorcaravans, 5 of these with electricity plus an emptying point. A unique feature of the site is the four individual en-suite washrooms for use with the 'Kernow' pitches (which also have water and facilities for waste water and TV reception). These come with their own key and are for private use while on site, plus a pass key for the shower room. There are also two sanitary blocks with controllable free hot showers, two washbasins in cabins in the smaller block, otherwise in open rows; they are simple but clean and tidy. A toilet/washbasin with ramp access is at the back of the main toilet block at the far side of the park. A dishwashing and laundry facility has two washing machines and a dryer. The small block which also houses the private units is locked at night so if you need the loo it could be a little walk! A children's play area and the reception cum shop (gas and basic needs) are near the entrance. The owners live on site and ensure a well run park. Padstow is a mile, either by public footpath from the site through the fields (20-30 mins) downhill or for bicycles by the road. A bus service passes (request stop) and reception holds timetables. The nearest beach is at Padstow, others are within 5 miles. Rick Steine has opened a 'bistro' alongside his restaurant - you may just get a reservation!

Directions: Park is signed from the A389, SSW of Padstow. O.S.GR: SW912739.

Charges 1999:
-- Per unit £3.00 - £4.00; adult £1.50 - £2.50; child (under 15 yrs) £1.00 - £1.50; awning £1.00; extra tent £1.00; dog 40p; extra vehicle £2.00 - £3.00; electricity £2.00; 'Kernow' pitch incl. electricity plus £2.00.
-- No credit cards.
Open:
Easter/1 April - 5 Oct.
Address:
Padstow, Cornwall PL28 8LE.
Tel:
(01841) 532061.
FAX: as phone.
Reservations:
Made with deposit (£10 p/week).

023 Glenmorris Park, St Mabyn

Family run, quiet park in north Cornwall.

The beaches of north Cornwall and the wilds of Bodmin Moor are all an easy drive away from Glenmorris Park and the Camel Trail for either cycling or walking all the way to Bodmin, Wadebridge or Padstow is only 2 miles. The amenities at the park include a heated, outdoor swimming pool and paddling pool (late May - early Sept), surrounded by sheltered, paved and grass sunbathing areas. Alongside is an excellent adventure playground which is fenced, with a bark safety base. Reception includes a small shop (from late May) which caters for basic needs and, in the same building, is a games room for teenagers. Bodmin and Wadebridge are only 5 or 6 miles for supermarket shopping. There is no bar but the local village inn has a good reputation for food. A quiet, family run park, Glenmorris has fairly modern sanitary facilities which are kept clean and well maintained. Washbasins are in vanity style units with hairdryers, all hot water is free and showers are pre-set. They do feel a little cramped, but planned improvements should rectify that. There are dishwashing sinks, a laundry with washing machine, dryer and iron and chemical disposal. Of the 75 pitches, 52 have 16A electricity and all are reasonably level and well drained on well mown grass. Dogs are allowed on a lead and a good dog walk is provided (a large, well mown field). Fishing, riding or golf 3 miles, bicycle hire 5 miles. Caravan storage. All in all, this is a pleasant park in which to relax or to use as a base to explore the towns and beaches of Cornwall. A member of the Countryside Discovery group.

Directions: From Bodmin or Wadebridge on the A389, take the B3266 north signed Camelford. At village of Longstone turn left signed St Mabyn and brown camping sign. Site is 400 yds. on the right. Ignore all other signs to St Mabyn. O.S.GR: SX053735.

Charges 2000:
-- Per unit incl. 2 adults and awning £5.00 - £7.50; extra adult £1.00 - £1.75; child (2-16 yrs) free - £1.25; extra vehicle or pup tent free - £1.00; electricity (16A) £2.00; hiker or cyclist's tent (2 adults, no car) £5.00 - £6.50.
-- Weekly rate available.
-- Credit cards accepted.

Open:
Easter - 31 October.

Address:
Longstone Road,
St Mabyn,
Cornwall PL30 3BY.

Tel:
(01208) 841677.
FAX: as phone.
E-mail: glenmorris.
cornwall@virgin.net.

Reservations:
Made with £15 deposit - contact park for details.

038 Wooda Farm Park, Bude

Spacious, relaxed, family run farm park with views of sea and countryside.

This well organised and cared for park with some nice touches is part of a working farm, 1¾ miles from the sandy, surfing beaches of Bude, in peaceful farmland with plenty of open spaces (and some up and down walking). The 200 pitches are spread over four meadows on level or gently sloping grass, 160 with electricity connections (10A), 21 with hardstanding and 21 grass, hedged 'premium' pitches (electricity, water, waste water). There are 55 holiday letting units situated beside the shop and reception at the entrance. Three well maintained toilet blocks, one heated, have free hot water. They provide fully tiled showers with seat and hooks, washbasins in vanity style with shelf and hand dryer, a unit suitable for disabled people, baby room with small bath and new private washroom facilities including shower and bath. Six washing up sinks (H&C) are under cover and two laundry rooms have washing machines, tumble dryers, sinks with hot water and irons. A comprehensive range of facilities is provided from Spr. B.H - Sept. These include a self-service shop with off-licence (8.30 - 8.30 in main season), a licensed courtyard bar with bar meals and a pleasant restaurant, Linney's Larder, with home cooking (closed Mon. and Sat. outside main season). A children's play area is in a separate field on grass, with plenty of room for ball games, a 9 hole 'fun' golf course (clubs provided), plus a woodland walk (where the pixies can be found) and an orchard walk. There is a small farm museum and friendly farm animals – children (and adults) are welcome to assist at feeding time! Tractor and trailer rides, pony riding and trekking, archery and clay pigeon shooting with tuition are provided according to season and demand, likewise barn dances. Games room with TV, table tennis and pool. Coarse fishing is available in a 1½ acre lake (permits from reception, £1.50 per half day, £2.50 per day). Dogs are accepted (not certain breeds) with a large dog exercise field. Public telephone. Caravan storage. The local village inn is five minutes walk. There is much to do in the area - the Leisure Centre and Splash Pool in Bude itself, sandy beaches with coastal walks and Tintagel with King Arthur's Castle and Clovelly nearby. A new member of the Best of British group.

Directions: Park is north of Bude at Poughill; turn off A39 on north side of Stratton on minor road for Coombe Valley, following camp signs at junctions. O.S.GR: SS225080.

Charges 1999:
-- Per unit incl. 2 persons £7.00 - £10.50; extra adult £1.50 - £2.50; child (3-15 yrs) £1.00 - £1.50; awning/pup tent £1.00 - £1.50; dog £1.00 - £1.50; electricity (10A) £2.00; fully serviced pitch (incl. electricity) plus £3.50 - £4.50, with TV point £4.50 - £6.00.
-- VAT included.
-- Credit cards accepted.

Open:
Easter/1 April - October.

Address:
Poughill, Bude,
Cornwall EX23 9HJ

Tel:
(01288) 352069.
FAX: (01288) 355258.

Reservations:
Made with £20 p/week deposit.

Cornwall

030 Colliford Tavern Campsite, Colliford Lake, nr. St. Neot

Quality 'tavern' site on Bodmin Moor.

Colliford Tavern must be unique, quietly situated high on the moor near Colliford Lake but hidden and protected by tall pines. The project has been developed over the last 8 years by the Edwards family with much care and attention and offers a family run free house with excellent, home cooked food and ale in an old world atmosphere complete with 90 year old well and en-suite accommodation. There is a dining room, family room with outside terrace, garden, water wheel and a good fenced play area with Wendy House. For family get-togethers this is an ideal venue 'away from it all' with some original suggestions for food which can be quite special or very simple - ask for the mix and match bar menu or the 'thatched trout'! The camping area, however, is quiet and simple and has been kept very natural with short grass (helped by the rabbits) and sheltered from the moor by tall pines. The main field provides 40 fairly level pitches with 19 electric hook-ups (16A) and 6 hardstandings backing on to the pine trees. The smaller, lower area is nearer to all the facilities. The modern, pine fitted toilet block is well equipped and carefully maintained with free hot water, baby room, unit for disabled people (no shower), laundry sink and spin dryer, two washing up sinks and a good chemical disposal facility. Service wash and tumble dry available Monday to Friday. No barbecues are allowed. A dog exercise area is at far end of the site. Reception is in the 'Tavern' building and emergency bread and milk is available, but grocery orders can be supplied by the local village store at Mount. The gate is closed at night but there is a 24 hour bell. Ideally situated for Colliford Lake and the Moor with its rich history, flora and fauna, be it for walking, fly fishing or birdwatching, the park is also suitable for excursions to the north or south coast. Occasionally some family entertainment is provided.

Directions: Approaching on the A30 travelling south, pass the Jamaica Inn on the right and site is signed a further 1-1½ miles on the left. Follow for ½ mile and site is signed beside Colliford Lake Park. O.S.GR: SX168730.

Charges 1999:
-- Per unit incl. 1 adult £6.00 - £6.75, 2 adults £8.00 - £10.00; extra person (over 4 yrs) £2.00 - £2.75; electricity £1.95; dog 50p.
-- VAT included.
-- Credit cards accepted.

Open:
Easter - end September.

Address:
Colliford Lake,
nr. St. Neot, Liskeard,
Cornwall PL14 6PZ.

Tel:
(01208) 821335.
FAX: as phone.

Reservations:
Advised for high season and made with £10 deposit, plus £5 for electric hook-up.

036 Lakefield Caravan Park and Equestrian Centre, Camelford

Small touring park with BHS and RDA approved equestrian centre.

Lakefield was previously a working farm and, with only 40 pitches, well spaced and in sight of the small lake and its feathered inhabitants, it is no wonder that the owners, Maureen and Dennis Perring, know all the campers. The pitches are all on level grass with 24 electric hook-ups (16A). The toilet block is clean and bright, providing the shelves, hooks, stools etc. which make life easier, washing machine and dryer in the ladies', dishwashing and laundry sinks outside, but under cover and chemical disposal. Hot water is free except in showers where it is metered (no facilities for visitors with disabilities). The white-washed shop/ reception, converted from one of the old barns and including a fascinating picture gallery, is open all day and all season which impressed us for such a small site. It provides all necessary basics, plus sometimes home made cakes, and a new tea room offers cream teas, cakes and sandwiches. A dozen picnic tables are dotted about the site, and a children's play area on grass, a separate dog walking field, gas supplies and a pay phone complete the facilities. Some animals still remain from the park's days as a farm and 'Wabbit World' is fascinating. A BHS approved riding school on site offers lessons and hacks with qualified supervision and instruction and 25 horses, from miniature Shetlands to thoroughbreds. All abilities are catered for (sand menage, show jumping paddock, beginners cross country course and pony rides) and it is the Riding for the Disabled (RDA) Centre for north Cornwall. Pony days and activity days are organised. Mountain bike hire. Fishing (sea 4 miles, coarse 5 miles), golf 2 miles. Tintagel, Boscastle, Bodmin Moor and the many beaches and coves of the north Cornwall coast wait to be explored. Cornwall's first wind farm watches over the site.

Directions: Follow B3266 north from Camelford. Park access is directly from this road on left just before turn to Tintagel, clearly signed. O.S.GR: SX097852.

Charges 2000:
-- Per unit incl. 2 adults £6.00 - £10.50; extra adult or child (5 yrs or over) 50p; dog, awning or extra car 50p; electricity £1.90.
-- No credit cards.

Open:
1 April - 31 October.

Address:
Lower Pendavey Farm,
Camelford,
Cornwall PL32 9TX.

Tel:
(01840) 213279.
FAX: as phone.

Reservations:
Made with £20 deposit per week.

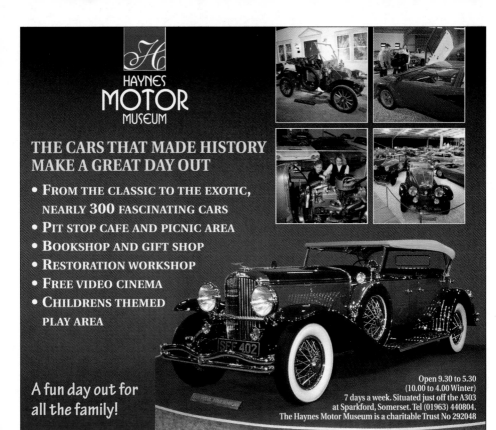

037 Budemeadows Touring Holiday Park, Poundstock, nr. Bude

Touring park with swimming pool, south of Bude, 1 mile from beach.

Budemeadows is maturing well with growing hedging and trees and though close to the A39 through road, offers a good, quiet option being only about a mile from the sandy surfing beaches at Widemouth Bay and 3 miles from Bude with all its amenities. It has been thoughtfully planned and provides large, clearly defined pitches, some slightly sloping but with panoramic rural views, others more sheltered and nearer the facilities. Some 146 units of any type are taken and there is plenty of room for these numbers with 80 electrical connections (10A) and 26 hardstandings. A centrally situated, attractive, fenced pool area has a comfortably heated pool and toddlers pool (also heated), patio and grass sunbathing area. The pine clad toilet block can be heated and is of good quality with free hot water in all the washbasins, good controllable showers and six washing up sinks under cover; six private cabins for ladies with basin and WC, one for men. There are three family shower units, a family bathroom, a baby bathing and changing room, laundry room with tourist information, chemical disposal and motorcaravan service facilities. This has now been supplemented by a new block of similar design, with toilets and washbasins en-suite and full facilities for disabled visitors. Shop (Spr. B.H.-mid Sept). Gas supplies. Large adventure playground. Picnic tables and brick built barbecues provided. Mobile 'Catch a Snack' van calls evenings in high season. Public phone. TV and games room with pool table and board games. Large scale chess set, outdoor table tennis and skittles. Boat launching in Bude, lake fishing 5 miles, riding 3 miles, golf 4 miles. Caravan storage. Holiday chalet for rent. The owners live on site.

Charges 1999:
-- Per adult £4.20 - £5.78; child (5-14 yrs) £2.10 - £2.95; dog 75p - £1.15; electricity £1.95.
-- Pitch and awning included.
-- VAT included.
-- Credit cards accepted.
Open:
All year.
Address:
Poundstock, Bude, Cornwall EX23 0NA.
Tel:
(01288) 361646. FAX: as phone.
E-mail: wendyjo@ globalnet.co.uk.
Reservations:
Made with deposit (£5 p/night or £35 p/week); contact park.

Directions: Park entrance is from a lay-by to the east off A39 road just north of a turning to Widemouth Bay. O.S.GR: SS216017.

044 Dolbeare Caravan and Camping Park, Landrake, nr. Saltash

Neat and tidy site close to Plymouth, open all year.

Bob and Ruth Mahy will make you very welcome at their small, but well kept park. In a rural setting, but very easily accessible from the main A38, the park consists of a large rectangular field of neatly cut grass edged with trees and sloping slightly at the top, connected by a gravel roadway. Caravans and motorcaravans go around the edge, with some terraced pitches with hardstanding, and tents tend to go in the central area where there is also play equipment and water and refuse points. All 60 pitches are numbered and of comfortable size, 51 with electricity (16A). An extra field doubles as a rally and games field and part is set aside for a dog exercise area. The well kept heated sanitary block to one side of the field provides vanity style washbasins with hot and cold water, pre-set showers with curtain and seat, plus two outside, but covered washing up sinks. A chemical toilet point is carefully sited behind a door with bolt. The laundry is next to reception at the entrance and provides a sink (H&C), washing machine, dryer, iron and board. Reception doubles as a small shop for basics including gas (limited hours out of the main season). The Mahys have thoughtfully provided leaflets on 'Where to Eat', 'Where to Walk', and 'Suggestions for what to do' with a good supply of tourist information with maps in a caravan near the caravan storage area. A boules pitch is opposite reception (a set of boules can be hired). The site barrier is closed 11 pm. to 7.30 am. A final comment - dog kennels nearby can provide day care from £3.50, but the drawback is that there could be some noise depending on season and wind direction. A very usefully situated park said to be 20 minutes from everywhere - Plymouth, beaches, National Trust properties, Dartmoor and Bodmin Moor, etc.

Charges 1999:
-- Per unit incl. 2 adults and car £7.50 - £8.00; extra adult £2.00; child (5-16 yrs) £1.00; electricity £1.50; awning £1.00; small tent per person £2.50 - £3.00.
Open:
All year.
Address:
St. Ive Road, Landrake, Saltash, Cornwall PL12 5AF.
Tel:
(01752) 851332.
Reservations:
Contact park.

Directions: After crossing the Tamar Bridge into Cornwall, continue on A38 for a further 4 miles. In village of Landrake turn right following signs and site is ¾ mile on right. O.S.GR: SX366616.

Devon

079 Harford Bridge Park, Peter Tavy, nr. Tavistock

Attractive, mature park on west Dartmoor bordering the delightful River Tavy.

Harford Bridge has an interesting history – originally the Wheal Union tin mine until 1850, then used as a farm campsite from 1930 and taken over by the Royal Engineers in 1939, it is now a quiet, rural park inside the Dartmoor National Park. It is bounded by the River Tavy on one side and the lane from the main road to the village of Peter Tavy on the other, with Harford Bridge, a classic granite moorland bridge, at the corner. With 16½ acres, the park provides 120 touring pitches well spaced on a level grassy meadow with some shade from mature trees and others recently planted; 40 pitches have electrical hook-ups and 8 have 'multi services'. Out of season or by booking in advance you may get one of the delightful spots bordering the river (no hook-ups). Holiday caravans (13) and chalets (7) for hire are neatly landscaped in a discrete area. The single toilet block is older in style but has been refurbished, It is kept clean, well decorated and properly maintained, and hot water is free. Facilities include hand and hair dryers (free), baby room, washing up sinks, a good launderette and drying room, freezer pack facility and chemical disposal. At the entrance, a grassy area is left free for games, which is also used by the town band, village fete, etc. It is overlooked by the site shop which is well stocked and reasonably priced. While the river will inevitably mesmerise youngsters and the ducks and chickens attract their interest, a super central adventure play area on a hilly knoll will claim them. Two restored Wickstead stainless steel slides, a 45 year old carnival carousel roundabout, tunnels and model chimney like the original are just part of a well presented, safe and marvellous provision. Games room with campers' information, table tennis and separate TV room. Tennis court (free). Fly fishing (by licence, £2.80 p/day, £10 p/week). Bicycle hire, riding and golf, all within 2½ miles. Two barbecue areas. Well behaved dogs are accepted with a 4 acre exercise field. With its own and the local history, plus its situation, this is a super place to stay.

Charges 1999:
-- Per unit, incl. 2 persons £6.00 - £10.00; extra adult £2.00 - £2.50; child £1.00 - £1.50; dog 90p; electricity £2.00; awning £1.00; extra car 50p.
-- Less 10% for stays over 7 days (not electricity or fishing).
-- Credit cards accepted.
-- VAT included.

Open:
Late March - early Nov.

Address:
Peter Tavy, Tavistock, Devon PL19 9LS.

Tel:
(01822) 810349.
FAX: (01822) 810028.
E-mail: enquiry@harford-bridge.co.uk.

Reservations:
Made for any length with first night's fees.

Alan Rogers' Discount

 Less 50p p/night off total bill

Directions: Two miles north of Tavistock, off A386 Tavistock - Okehampton road, take the road to Peter Tavy. O.S.GR: SX504768.

080 Higher Longford Farm, Moorshop, nr. Tavistock

Quiet, small, family run park, ideal for staying on lower slopes of Dartmoor.

Situated within the National Park boundaries, this small park has views up to the higher slopes of the moor. The site has a sheltered touring field where 40 level pitches are arranged on each side of a circular access road, two smaller touring areas for 12 units and a seasonal camping field for a further 80. Facilities include 49 electrical hook-ups and an area of hardstanding for poor weather. Residential caravans and chalets for hire are in a separate area adjacent and some attractive converted cottages also for hire form a courtyard area with the farmhouse, reception and bar. The main toilet block is alongside the touring field providing roomy showers, smallish washbasins and one en-suite cabin for ladies, hand and hair dryers and dishwashing, all with plentiful, free hot water. This is supple-mented by extra heated facilities in the courtyard, which include showers with a communal dressing area. Extra smart chemical disposal (like a wishing well), full laundry facilities and a washing line, motorcaravan service point. Within the 14th century farmhouse is a small licensed shop, open on demand, with gas and some fresh farm produce. It adjoins a pleasant, cosy bar and restaurant with open fire and TV, where takeaway or full meals are offered (all April-Nov), and a spacious conservatory, useful in poor weather. Tourist information and public phone. Caravan storage. Dogs are welcome but must be kept under strict control (exercise field provided). This enables the site to keep small animals and lambs (in season) – a delight for youngsters. Higher Longford is an ideal centre for touring Dartmoor, either by car, on foot, or astride a local pony (riding stables nearby). The site is sometimes used as a base by groups of youngsters for trips onto the moor. Game or coarse fishing 3 miles, Tavistock golf course 1 miles, bicycle hire or riding 3 miles. Plymouth and the cross channel ferries are 30 minutes' drive, Tavistock is 3 miles, with a good market and Goose Fair in the autumn.

Charges 1999:
-- Per unit incl. 1 person £6.50 - £7.50, 2 persons £7.50 - £8.50, family (2 adults, 2 children) £9.00 - £10.00; extra adult £2.00; extra child (over 3 yrs) £1.00; electricity £1.75.
-- Less 50p per night for booked stays over 7 nights.
-- No credit cards.
-- VAT included.

Open:
All year.

Address:
Moorshop, Tavistock, Devon PL19 9JU.

Tel:
(01822) 613360.
FAX: (01822) 618722.

Reservations:
Made with £5 deposit.

Directions: Park is clearly signed from B3357, 2 miles from Tavistock. O.S.GR: SX520747.

34

081 Riverside Caravan Park, Plymouth

Good sized touring park with heated outdoor pool, close to main holiday routes.

Riverside is well placed for those visiting Plymouth, the maritime capital of the southwest, using the car ferries or en-route to Cornwall. It is also ideally situated for touring Dartmoor and south Devon. Although under 4 miles from the city centre, its location on the banks of the River Plym in a wooded valley is a quiet one. Attractive shrubs and trees, flower beds, well kept grass and tarmac roads give a neat, park-like appearance. Over 220 units of any type are taken on flat, numbered pitches, including 170 with 10A electrical connections and 40 with hardstandings. There is a separate area for tents and a large, hard area is retained for late arrivals. In the centre of the park arranged around a patio are a lounge bar (fully open from July with nightly entertainment), coffee bar and restaurant with takeaway meals (6-10 pm), games and TV rooms and a play area. A free, sheltered and heated swimming pool (60 x 30 ft), with children's paddling pool, is open from Spr. B.H. to mid-Sept. The two sanitary blocks, one subdivided into two, are of different construction and have been modernised and decorated somewhat haphazardly. They have free hot water in the washbasins (some in private cabins with toilets for ladies in one block), showers (some with two taps and pre-set, but giving adequate flow) and indoor dishwashing sinks. Hair dryers, shaver points and hand dryers. Laundry facilities and irons available on loan. A shop at the entrance is open to all (Spr. B.H. - mid-Sept). Public phones and post box. Fishing on site, riverside walks up to Dartmoor. Bicycle hire (3 miles), boat slipway (2 miles). An added advantage is that the site is security patrolled at night.

Charges guide:
-- Per adult £2.50 - £3.00; child (3-10 yrs) £1.10 - £1.25; pitch £1.50 - £3.50; electricity £2.00 - £2.50; awning free - 50p; dog, extra car or boat £1.00.
-- Special breaks for the over-50s.
-- Credit cards accepted.
Open:
All year.
Address:
Longbridge Road, Marshmills, Plymouth, Devon PL6 8LD.
Tel:
(01752) 344122.
Reservations:
Made with £15 deposit per week or part week.

Directions: From A38 dual-carriageway from Exeter, take Marsh Mill exit (the first signed to Plymouth city centre). Follow good camp site signs to third exit, turning left after a few yards. O.S.GR: SX518576.

104 Old Cotmore Farm, Stokenham, nr. Kingsbridge

Charming, small and secluded park two miles from Start Point.

Sue and John Bradney recently acquired Old Cotmore Farm - that is the farmhouse, two cottages and a small touring site. The only livestock to be seen now are a few chickens and ducks, including a curious pair of black pilot ducks who patrol the site, and maybe some horses. They have worked hard to improve the facilities and now provide 30 pitches, all with electric hook-up, on neatly cut grass. Partly in an orchard situation with some pitches sloping, and partly on a level field with children's play equipment in the centre, Pitches here tend to be used for families with children, with those on the other side of the drive kept for adults only. A small stream runs along one side with a pretty pond area and bridge near the entrance. Reception is past the pitches towards the farmhouse and adjoining the toilet block which has been converted from original buildings. The blocks have been refurbished with a degree of individuality to provide modern vanity style washbasins (H&C) and pre-set hot showers in individual cubicles (stools, no divider and non slip floor). A shower/toilet room can be used by familes or disabled visitors and there is a washbasin and changing area for babies in the ladies' along with tourist information. Dishwashing sinks (H&C) under cover, telephone and small laundry room with three washing machines and two dryers. Chemical toilet and waste water disposal are tucked away behind reception. A separate field with a 28 day licence has water points, two extra sinks (H&C) and two toilets, but it may put pressure on the main block when in use. Mountain bike hire and table tennis. Dog exercise field. Mrs Bradney holds a children's club once a week in high season. Reception stocks gas and basic necessities - warm baguettes can be ordered and helpful wardens will help you pitch. The site is in an area of Outstanding Natural Coastal Beauty, with Slapton Sands, Salcombe and Kingsbridge near and Dartmouth just a little further. It is an ideal area for walking, boating, diving, windsurfing and safe bathing Riding 4 miles, golf 8 miles. Two pubs are within one mile either way. Three cottages to let.

Charges 2000:
-- Per unit incl. 2 persons £7.00 - £9.00; tent incl. 2 persons £6.50; extra adult £2,00; child (3-12 yrs) £1.00; car, extra car or boat £1.00; dog £1.00; electricity £2.00.
-- Less £1.00 per pitch in low seasons.
-- Credit cards accepted
Open:
14 March - 15 November.
Address:
Stokenham, nr. Kingsbridge, South Devon TQ7 2LR.
Tel:
(01548) 580240.
FAX: (01548) 580875.
Reservations:
Made with 25% deposit; contact park.

Directions: From Kingsbridge on A379 Dartmouth road, go through Frogmore and Chillington to Carehouse Cross mini-roundabout at Stokenham. Turn right towards Beesands and follow signs for 1 mile. Site entrance is on left just past post box - look for the churns! Roads narrow in places. O.S.GR: SX804417.

Devon

082 Moor View Touring Park, Modbury

Pleasant, maturing park with magnificent views of Dartmoor.

Purpose designed Moor View has a gently sloping position with terraced, individual fairly level grass pitches connected by hard core roads with marvellous views across to the Dartmoor Tors. It provides 68 pitches of varying size, all with 10A electricity and 12 with hardstanding. Trees and shrubs have been planted which are beginning to mature. A two acre field provides space for children and a dog walk, or for the odd rally. There is also a small play area on grass which is to be modernised. The facilities have been designed in one block near the entrance, not too far from the furthest pitches and providing a reception cum shop with basic food and some camping accessories. There is a comfortable TV room with tourist information, a games room with pool table, table tennis and video machines. Sanitary facilities are modern and kept clean, providing all necessary items with hot water, a laundry room and chemical disposal. Good takeaway facilities to order (6.30-7.30 pm). Public phone. Golf 5 miles, riding and fishing 6 miles. A local country pub is within walking distance. Burgh Island and Bigbury Bay are nearby, Dartmoor is within striking distance. A park which is now maturing, in a lovely corner of Devon, with enthusiastic new owners. A member of the Countryside Discovery group.

Charges 1999:
-- Per pitch incl. 2 adults £7.00 - £12.00; extra adult £2.00; child (3-14 yrs) £1.50; small tent less £1.00; dog free; electricity (10A) £1.75; water hook-up 50p.
-- Credit cards accepted.
Open:
Easter - end October
Address:
California Cross, nr. Modbury, Devon PL21 0SG
Tel:
(01548) 821485.
FAX: as phone.
Reservations:
Made with £10 deposit.

Directions: On A38 from Exeter, pass exit for A385 (Totnes) and continue for a further 2 miles. Just past Woodpecker Inn at Wrangaton Cross turn left and follow straight on at crossroads for 3 miles. Leave garage on left and follow Modbury (B3207). Park is ½ mile on left. O.S.GR: SX705533.

083 Camping and Caravanning Club Site Slapton, nr. Kingsbridge

Well kept site overlooking the sea and freshwater nature reserve, close to Dartmouth; caravans limited.

Slapton is a charming village with tiny lanes and cottages, a shop and two historic pubs, one dominated by the ruined tower of an old monastery. The village (unsuitable for camping traffic) is about ½ mile inland from the shingle beach of Slapton Sands and the freshwater Ley which is administered as a nature reserve by the Field Studies Council. The Camping and Caravanning Club site is situated on the road which leads from the Sands, on a well kept meadow overlooking the bay - the sea views are panoramic from most areas of the site, with shelter provided by some large bushes and the surrounding hedge. There are 115 grass pitches, some with a slight slope, and electrical connections (16A) are available for 25. Motorcaravans, trailer tents and tents are accepted without problems but the planners will only permit 8 caravans (make sure to check with the warden on pitch availability). The modern toilet block is central, can be heated and is kept very clean, providing toilets, washbasins, all in private cabins, and good hot showers (free). Dishwashing facilities, laundry sinks, washing machine and dryer, plus chemical disposal and motorcaravan service point. Other than a small children's play area, there are no other on-site facilities but the village is a pleasant stroll and the milkman calls daily with bread, eggs, etc. A fish and chip van calls on Fridays and reception has sweets for children, a small library, gas and a freezer for ice blocks. Dog walk available. The Field Studies Centre arrange guided walks and short study courses on a wide variety of interests and can issue fishing permits for the Ley (perch and pike, of legendary size, in the summer months). Beach fishing is also popular. Riding ½ mile. This area was used for rehearsals for the WW2 Normandy landings, when the whole population was evacuated - there are memorials, including a tank, in the village of Torcross. The quaint port of Dartmouth is 7 miles, Kingsbridge 8 miles and there is a variety of beaches and coves around the beautiful South Hams coastline, all within easy reach.

Charges 2000:
-- Per 2 adults £7.50 - £10.60; child (6-18 yrs) £1.65; non-member pitch fee £4.30; electricity £1.55.
-- VAT included.
-- Credit cards accepted.
Open:
March - November.
Address:
Middle Grounds, Slapton, Kingsbridge, Devon TQ7 1QW.
Tel:
(01548) 580538
(no calls after 8 pm).
Reservations:
Necessary and made with deposit; contact the wardens.

Directions: From A38 Exeter - Plymouth road, take A384 to Totnes. Just before town, turn right on A381 to Kingsbridge, then A379 through Stokenham and Torcross to Slapton Sands. Half way along the beach road turn left to Slapton village and site is 200 yds on right. Note: Avoid the very narrow Five Mile Lane from the A381 which is signed Slapton (just after a filling station) 6 miles from Kingsbridge. O.S.GR: SX825450.

084 Woodlands Leisure Park, Blackawton, nr. Dartmouth

Well planned touring site forming part of family run, countryside leisure park.

Woodlands is a surprise, a nice one - from the road you have no idea of just what is hidden away deep in the Devon countryside. To achieve this, there has been sympathetic development of farm and woodland to provide a leisure centre, open to the public and with a range of activities appealing to all ages. Children (and many energetic parents too!) are entertained for hours by a variety of imaginative adventure play equipment and amazing water coasters hidden amongst the trees and many farm animals, birds and boats, while those more peacefully inclined can follow woodland walks around the attractive ponds. A Falconry Centre gives opportunities to watch displays (or for the birds to watch you!) There is plenty of play equipment for younger children too, including an indoor play barn with a circus theme. With two nights stay, campers on the touring park are admitted free of charge.

The camping and caravan site which overlooks woodland and part of the leisure park, takes 200 units on two sloping, grassy fields which have been fully terraced to provide groups of 4-8 flat, very spacious pitches, 90% with electrical connections (10A) and a shared water tap, drain and rubbish bin. The terraces are divided by young hedging and shrubs. There are two modern, heated toilet blocks which are well maintained and kept very clean, providing free hot water in pre-set showers and washbasins (with dividers and curtains). New facilities include private bathrooms (coin operated) and 7 family shower cubicles. Each block is fitted with hair dryers, a well equipped laundry room, dishwashing area and a freezer for ice packs. There are also baby changing facilities. The newly constructed Falcons View block also includes a fully equipped TV and games room. Dogs are accepted on the campsite but not in the leisure park (kennels available). The leisure park café, with an outdoor rose terrace, provides good value meals and cream teas with entertainment (music, Morris men, etc.) at busy times, and a takeaway service for campers. The opening hours of the café and adjoining gift shop, where gas and a few basic food supplies are kept, vary according to season and demand. A popular park, reservation is advisable. The charming town of Dartmouth and the South Hams beaches are near. Fishing 3 miles, golf ½ miles, riding 5 miles. Caravan storage.

Charges 1999:
-- Per unit, incl. 2 persons £7.50 - £13.95; extra person (over 2 yrs) £2.75; awning or extra small pup tent £2.50; large tent or trailer tent (120 sq.ft. plus) plus £2.00; extra car, boat or trailer £1.00; dog £2.50; electricity £1.95.
-- Free entry to leisure park for stays 2 nights or more.
-- VAT included.
-- Credit cards accepted.

Open:
15 March - 15 November.

Address:
Blackawton, Totnes, Devon TQ9 7DQ.

Tel:
(01803) 712598.
FAX: (01803) 712680.
E-mail: fun@woodlands-leisure-park.co.uk.

Reservations:
Accepted for min. 3 nights with £35 deposit, except July/Aug. when min. 7 days and £50 deposit. Balance 14 days before arrival.

Directions: From A38 at Buckfastleigh, take A384 to Totnes. Before town turn right on A381 Kingsbridge road. After Halwell turn left at Totnes Cross garage, on A3122 to Dartmouth. Park is on right after 2½ miles. O.S.GR: SX825456.

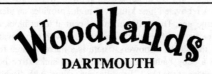

Devon

085 Galmpton Touring Park, Galmpton, nr. Brixham

Quiet touring park close to Torbay, with wonderful views over the River Dart estuary.

Within a few miles of the lively amenities of Torbay, Galmpton Park lies peacefully just outside the village of Galmpton, overlooking the beautiful Dart estuary just upstream of Dartmouth and Kingswear. Some 120 pitches, 60 marked for caravans, are arranged on a wide sweep of grassy, terraced meadow, each pitch with its own view of the river. Situated on the hillside, some parts have quite a slope, but there are flatter areas (the owners will advise and assist). There are 95 electrical connections (10A) and 20 pitches have full services. American motorhomes not accepted. A central, substantial looking sanitary block provides clean facilities including washbasins in flat surfaces with mirrors, with three private cabins, free hot showers, baby unit and hair care areas; also chemical disposal and a dishwashing room (free hot water) with washing machine, iron and ironing board available. Milk, bread, papers and gas are available from reception. There is good adventure play equipment for children. Dogs (max. 2 per unit) are accepted only outside the school summer holidays with an exercise area provided. Two holiday cottages to rent. Galmpton is a quiet and simple park (with the gates closed 11.30 pm - 7.30 am) in a most picturesque setting, within easy reach of all the attractions of South Devon. Under new ownership.

Directions: Take A380 Paignton ring road towards Brixham until junction with the Paignton - Brixham coast road. Turn right towards Brixham, then second right into Manor Vale Road. Continue through the village, past the school and site is 100 yds on the right. O.S.GR: SX885558.

Charges 2000:
-- Per unit incl. 2 persons and awning £6.00 - £10.50, `de-luxe' pitch plus £1.00 - £1.50; extra adult £2.00; extra child £1.00; electricity £1.70; extra car or boat £1.50; dog (off peak only) 50p.
-- Credit cards accepted (from 4/00).
-- VAT included.

Open:
Easter - 31 October.

Address:
Greenway Road, Galmpton. Brixham, Devon TQ5 0EP.

Tel:
(01803) 842066.

Reservations:
Made with £20 deposit p/week booked.

086 Ramslade Touring Park, Stoke Gabriel, Paignton

Well kept, quiet, quality park in attractive rural location, 3 miles from sea at Paignton.

Personally run by the owners, Ramslade is a smaller, rural park and provides a quiet, peaceful alternative to the many larger holiday parks in and around Paignton itself. A member of the Caravan Club's `managed under contract' scheme, non-members are also very welcome. The attractively landscaped park takes 135 touring units of all types. Pitches are neatly arranged in two areas which are planted with attractive young trees which are now rapidly maturing. The larger area slopes towards the centre of the park but has been gently terraced and most pitches are level or very slightly sloping. Tarmac access roads give good access and all but two pitches have electrical hook-ups. There are 32 `all-service' pitches with shared picnic tables, 21 hardstandings for motorhomes and a drive-on service area for caravans and motorcaravans. No groundsheets allowed in awnings and inner tents to be lifted daily. A renovated lime kiln, lit at night, provides an ideal place for semi-communal barbecues. The well maintained central toilet block is heated for cooler weather. Hot water is free for the washbasins, with two private cabins for each sex, and for the plentiful showers. There is a make-up area for ladies and hair dryers, with a baby bathroom and washing-up sinks (free hot water) in a covered area at the rear of the block. Facilities for visitors with disabilities, laundry room with microwave and a super luxury, family bathroom (£2 charge) complete the facilities. A range of recycling bins is provided and four chemical disposal points are enclosed in gazebo form with attractive roof and sides. Small shop for essentials (Easter - mid Sept). TV room and games room with pool and table tennis. Play area set away from the pitches, plus a small, central area for younger children next to an attractive splash pool with fountain feature and jacuzzi (from Spr. B.H.) which is walled with locking gate and a paved area for parents to relax or sunbathe. Weather station with daily forecasts. No dogs or pets are accepted in the peak six weeks, no bicycles on the park. Indoor and outdoor caravan storage available with servicing. Fishing or bicycle hire 3 miles, golf 6 miles. A member of the Best of British group.

Directions: Park is south of A385 (Paignton - Totnes) and is well signed. Turn off A385 to south alongside 'Parkers Arms' pub (½ mile west of Paignton ring road), then follow road for 1½ miles. O.S.GR: SX857583.

Charges 1999:
-- Per unit incl. 2 persons and awning: standard pitch £8.80 - £12.80; electricity £1.45 - £2.20; water and awning 50p - £2.00; extra adult £3.25 - £4.00; child (5-16 yrs) £1.10 - £1.20; extra car or boat £1.00.
-- Credit cards accepted.
-- VAT included.

Open:
1 April - 22 October.

Address:
Paignton Road, Stoke Gabriel, Paignton, Devon TQ9 6QB.

Tel:
(01803) 782575.
FAX: (01803) 782828.
E-mail: ramslade@ compuserve.com.

Reservations:
Any length stay, £15 deposit per week booked.

See colour feature for `BEST of BRITISH' between pages 96/97

087 Beverley Holidays, Paignton

Popular Torbay park tastefully integrated with holiday homes, with many facilities and evening entertainment.

Beverley Park is a holiday centre, attractively sited with views over Torbay. With swimming pools and a large dance hall, with bars and entertainment, etc. - all is run in an efficient and orderly manner. The holiday caravan park has 215 caravan holiday homes, mainly around the central complex. The 194 touring pitches are all reasonably sheltered, mainly in the lower areas of the park and some on slightly sloping ground. All pitches can take awnings and have 16A electricity (15 m. cable), 38 have hardstanding, 21 are fully serviced. Tents are accepted and a limited number of tent pitches have electrical connections. The park has a long season and reservations are essential for caravans. American motorhomes are accepted (max. 20 ft). There are toilet blocks adjacent to the pitches. They are good (particularly the new ones) and, although they can receive heavy use and need regular attention, they are well maintained and heated. Hot water is free for washbasins and showers, baths are on payment and there is a unit for people with disabilities. There are water points around park, a range of recycling bins, laundry, gas supples, chemical disposal points and motorcaravan service facilities. Large general shop, 'express diner', garden bar and takeaway service (all Easter - 31 Oct). Dance hall with bars - entertainment at Easter and from the beginning of May in the Starlight Cabaret bar. There are indoor and outdoor pools, each one heated and supervised. The adult pools are generous in size and the Oasis fitness centre provides a steam room, jacuzzi, sun bed, excellent fitness room, swimming lessons, etc. Other activities include a tennis court, crazy golf, children's playground, nature trail and an amusement centre with pool, table tennis and amusement machines. No dogs are accepted. Fishing, bicycle hire, riding and golf all within 2 miles. The park is in the heart of residential Torbay, with views across the bay to Brixham and Torquay, and sandy beaches less than a mile away. A regular minibus service runs to Paignton (timetable at reception) or normal services from outside the park. A new member of the Best of British group.

Directions: Park is south of Paignton in Goodrington Road between A379 coast road and B3203 ring road and is well signed on both. O.S.GR: SX882584.

Charges 2000:
-- Per unit incl. 2 persons: serviced pitch £9.00 - £20.00, electric pitch £11.00 - £22.00; tent electricity plus £1.50; extra adult £4.00, child (4-14 yrs) £3.00; awning or extra pup tent £3.00.
-- Max. 6 persons per reservation.
-- VAT included.
-- Credit cards accepted.

Open:
28 February - 21 Nov; Tents 13 April - 31 Oct.

Address:
Goodrington Road, Paignton, Devon TQ4 7JE.

Tel:
(01803) 843887.
FAX: (01803) 845427.

Reservations:
Made with £25 deposit (7, 14 or 21 days 17/7-3/9, min. 2 nights all other times); balance payable more than 28 days before arrival.

Devon

089 Grange Court Holiday Centre, Paignton

Busy holiday caravan park with excellent entertainment and recreation facilities; touring sections for caravans only.

Situated to the south of central Paignton, with a short, signed walk to the sea and some views of Torbay, Grange Court's major interest is a complex of 513 holiday homes (to let) which totally dominate the higher of the two touring sites. However there are 157 touring pitches (no tents) in two sections, each with its own resident wardens. One, probably the quieter of the two, is on flat grass by the entrance, with two modern toilet blocks (washbasins with free hot water, shelf and mirror, and free pre-set hot showers with push- button). The other is on higher ground, through the holiday homes at the top of the park with the site shops close by. It is on a gentle slope with some views, and has a larger, but older, tiled block. Pitches are of reasonable size, though with some variation, and all have electricity. For those who like entertainment, the central complex is the park's best feature, with a good sized free outdoor, heated pool (80 x 40 ft. open May - Sept) and a super indoor pool with views across the bay is complete with flume, spa, sauna, steam room (all free), plus a sun-bed. The clubhouse has a large bar lounge and separate room with dance floor - entertainment almost nightly from Spr. B.H. to end Sept. and at Easter. Supermarket and other shops, takeaway and fast food bar (all 1/3-31/10). Games rooms with two pool tables and full size snooker table, and amusement arcade, playground and large adventure play area. Large launderette, recycling bins and chemical disposal. Up to 30 American motorhomes accepted (30 ft. max). No dogs or pets are accepted. Fishing and boat slipway 3 miles, golf 7 miles. Reception is busy, but efficient. Part of the Hoburne group.

Directions: Park is signed (not the normal camp site signs) from outer Paignton ring road. Turn off Goodrington Road into Grange Road. 150 yds from A379 coast road at signs for camp and Marine Park. O.S.GR: SX890585.

Charges 2000:
-- Per unit £8.00 - £23.00, incl. electricity and awning, acc. to season (no tents, trailer tents or pup tents allowed).
-- Weekend breaks available.
-- VAT included.
-- Credit cards accepted.
Open:
All year excl. 15/1-15/2.
Address:
Goodrington, Paignton, Devon TQ4 7JP.
Tel:
(01803) 558010.
FAX: (01803) 663336.
E-mail: enquiries@ hoburne.co.uk.
Reservations:
Advised for July/Aug. For 1-6 nights, full payment in advance required; for 7 nights and over £50 deposit per week (min. 7 days in Jul/Aug and B.H. weeks).

HOBURNE

GRANGE COURT
Award Winning Holiday Park
HOLIDAY CARAVANS • TOURING PITCHES
Exciting indoor leisure complex compliments this already striking family Park in the heart of the English Riviera overlooking Torbay. Close to sandy beaches and Dartmoor.
For FREE colour brochure or credit card bookings please contact:

GRANGE COURT HOLIDAY CENTRE, RG1, Grange Road, Goodrington Paignton, Devon TQ4 7JP.
Telephone: 01803 558010
e-mail - enquiries@hoburne.co.uk   www.hoburne.co.uk

ROSE AWARD

090 Widdicombe Farm Tourist Park, Paignton

Well situated park on fringes of Torquay, yet with rural outlook.

Widdicombe Farm, just 3 miles from Torquay with easy access, offers 200 numbered pitches (156 for touring units). Electricity (10A) is available on 140 and 10 are fully serviced. Surrounded by farmland, the pitches are on gently sloping grass terraces giving a very rural feel. Trees and shrubs have been planted and there are tarmac roads. A few pitches are fairly close to the A380 with some traffic noise. Touring areas are in sections for families, couples or tents. On site are a shop and a restaurant for evening meals, breakfasts, cream teas and takeaway (Easter - mid Oct). A large comfortable bar offers family entertainment and opposite is a 'DIY' barbecue area with large gas barbecues, (£2 per session). Games room with video games and pool tables, children's play area and a field for games. There are three sanitary blocks, one of older construction near the main reception/shop, and two newer blocks, one at the top of the site with provision for disabled visitors and the other in the new lower section. All have good facilities. Baby room, dishwashing under cover, chemical disposal and a small laundry with two machines and dryers. The proprietors live on site. Caravan holiday homes for hire (3). Dogs are permitted in the touring section (no dangerous breeds). Fishing, bicycle hire, riding and golf, all within 2 miles. Caravan storage.

Directions: From Newton Abbot take A380 south for approx. 5 miles; site is well signed off this road. O.S.GR: SX874641.

Charges 2000:
-- Per unit incl. 2 persons £6.00 - £10.00; extra adult £2.00 - £2.50; child (3-16 yrs) £1.00 - £1.50; awning, dog £1.00 - £1.50; electricity £1.80.
-- Credit cards accepted.
Open:
March - November.
Address:
The Ring Road, Compton, Paignton, Devon TQ3 1ST.
Tel:
(01803) 558325.
FAX: (01803) 559526.
Reservations:
Advised for July/Aug. (min. 4 days) and made with deposit (£20 per week) and fee (£2).

091 Ross Park, Ipplepen, nr. Newton Abbot

Excellent, friendly, relaxed park in attractive landscaped surroundings.

Ross Park has to be seen to appreciate its amazing floral displays with their dramatic colours, which are a feature of the park. These are complemented by the use of a wide variety of shrubs which form hedging for most pitches providing your own special plot, very much as on the continent. For those who prefer the more open style, one small area has been left unhedged. There are views over the surrounding countryside but as the foliage has developed these are not as extensive but there is more protection on a windy day. The owners, Mark and Helen Lowe, constantly strive to provide quality facilities, re-tiling and re-fitting sanitary facilities to high standards but including personal touches as seen in the utility room with the beautiful photographs of the countryside and suggestions for visits. Another individual touch is the impressive, heated conservatory with yet more named exotic plants. It is linked to the New Barn which has a comfortable lounge, mezzanine bar and restaurant with a la carte menu or bar snacks (all limited hours in low seasons, closed Nov - March excl. Xmas and New Year). The touring area is divided into bays or groups by the hedging and shrubs and provides 110 pitches all with electricity (10/16A), 82 with a hardened surface. The main toilet facilities next to the New Barn open under a veranda style roof, colourful with hanging baskets. They comprise six nicely equipped en-suite units, one with baby facilities, one suitable for disabled people. At the rear are further separate shower, washbasin and toilet facilities. Below the New Barn are more toilets and washbasins in a well kept 'portacabin' style unit. Hot water is free and shaver points and hairdryers are provided. Separate fully equipped laundry room and utility room with dishwashing sinks, freezer and battery charging facilities. Chemical disposal facilities. Games room and billiards room. Comfortable reception with shop area, fresh bread, etc. according to season and gas supplies. Tourist information chalet with herbs for barbecues nearby. A 4 acre recreation area has bowling and croquet greens and well equipped adventure playground. A conservation area with information on wild flowers and butterflies and extended views completes these environmentally considered amenities. Dogs are welcome with a variety of walks in fields and orchards and they even have shower and grooming facilities, hot water included! Barn dances with barbecue are organised on Sundays in high season. Dainton Park golf course is adjacent. Fishing 3 miles, riding 1 mile. Winter caravan storage. A park well worth consideration.

Charges 1999:
-- Per unit incl. 2 persons £6.80 - £10.90; extra adult £3.00 - £3.50; child (3-16 yrs) £1.50 - £1.75; electricity (16A) £1.70 - £2.20.
-- Christmas packages available.
-- VAT included.
-- No credit cards.
Open:
All year except January.
Address:
Park Hill Farm, Ipplepen, Newton Abbot, Devon TQ12 5TT.
Tel:
(01803) 812983.
FAX: as phone.
Reservations:
Made with £20 deposit.

Directions: From A381 Newton Abbot - Totnes road, park is signed towards Woodland at Park Hill crossroads and Jet filling station. O.S.GR: SX845671.

Devon

088 Dornafield, Two Mile Oak, Newton Abbot

Family run, rural touring park with all modern facilities including luxury pitches.

A quiet, superbly appointed and well maintained park, Dornafield is an idyllic retreat for those who prefer small, quiet, family run parks a little away from the coast and without evening activities. A member of the Caravan Club's 'managed under contract' scheme, members and non-members are all made very welcome. In a sheltered situation away from main roads, the entrance leads into the courtyard of a charming old farmhouse where stone outbuildings have been sympathetically converted into the reception, shop and games room (the old milking parlour, complete with stalls). Well tended flowers and shrubs decorate the park. The original part, the Butter Meadow and the Orchard, offers 75 individual, numbered pitches on flat grass, separated by grassy ridges and in some places, wild rose hedges. They are of good size, all with electricity (10A). Rules require lifting of awning groundsheets every day and re-pitching of tents for stays in excess of a week. An excellent, attractively designed, modern toilet block serves these pitches. Heated in cool weather, it has washbasins (two in private cabins) set in vanity style units and showers with free hot water, with a babies' section and make-up area in the ladies' and a good unit for disabled people. All is kept spotlessly clean. Four dishwashing sinks are under cover with a microwave for campers use and a laundry room. A further 60 extra large, luxury pitches have been added in Blackrock Copse with electricity (10A), water, drainage and TV connections, all cleverly concealed and with 33 hardstandings. A new sanitary block has outstanding features such as under-floor heating, automatic air fresheners and facilities for disabled visitors. The ladies' section has several private cubicles. A separate wooden chalet of attractive design houses dishwashing facilities and a microwave oven. Again many flowers and shrubs have been planted including herbs (useful when barbecuing). Chemical disposal and motorcaravan service points. Gas supplies. Attractive features are woodland play areas with adventure play equipment and Wendy houses, for little ones. Games room with table tennis and TV. All-weather hard tennis court. Pub with meals ½ mile. Fishing 2½ miles, golf 1 mile. Dog exercise area. All year caravan storage.

Directions: Park is northwest of the A381 Newton Abbot - Totnes road. Leave A381 at Two Mile Oak Inn, opposite garage, and turn left at crossroads after about ½ mile. Park entrance is on the right. O.S.GR: SX848683.

Charges 1999:
-- Per pitch £1.50 - £4.50; adult £3.25 - £4.10; child (5-16 yrs) £1.10 - £1.35; awning free - £1.00; pup tent or porch awning free - 50p; tents over 100 sq.ft. charged awning rate; electricity (10A) £1.45 (£2.20 before 31/3 and Oct); extra car or trailer £1.00; dog 70p.
-- Credit cards accepted.
-- VAT included.

Open:
20 March - 31 October.

Address:
Two Mile Oak,
Newton Abbot,
Devon TQ12 6DD.

Tel:
(01803) 812732.
FAX: (01803) 812032.

Reservations:
Any length, £10 p.w. low season, £25 p/week high season.

093 Ashburton Caravan Park, Ashburton

Small secluded park with new, enthusiastic owners; for tents and motorcaravans only.

The 4 acres of Ashburton Park nestle in a hidden valley below Dartmoor, bordered by mature woodland. The Ashburn, a shallow stream with rocky pools, evenly divides and screens the two acres of holiday homes from the 2 acre camping area. Sheltered and south facing, the park is a tranquil retreat but for the energetic a half mile steep uphill walk brings you to the moor or 1½ miles by Devon lanes to Ashburton village. There are 35 level or gently sloping pitches, 8 with electricity connections (16A), either side of a tarmac road which culminates in a small field area. First class, purpose built sanitary facilities provide free hot showers and vanity style washbasins in cabins for ladies. The washing machine and tumble dryer are coin operated but a spin dryer and iron are provided free. The unit also has a public phone and chemical disposal facilities. The reception/information centre provides gas, a freezer pack service, tourist information, maps and walks and a daily weather report. Each visitor receives a copy of the 'Dartmoor Visitor', the information paper supplied by the Dartmoor National Park authorities - the site is within the boundaries of the Park. Shops, banks, post office, a small heated swimming pool and pubs, etc. are in Ashburton, with limited bus services to Newton Abbot, Exeter or Plymouth. Discover the cult of letter boxing on Dartmoor (maps on loan with the walks shown). Fishing 2 miles, bicycle hire 1 mile, riding and golf 3 miles. Dogs (limited breeds) are welcome if exercised off the park. Torches useful. A well maintained, tranquil small park for nature lovers.

Directions: In centre of Ashburton turn northwest into North Street. As built-up area thins out bear right before bridge following signs for 'Waterleat' (tent symbol) for approx. 1½ miles. Park is on the left. O.S.GR: SX752721.

Charges 1999:
-- Per unit incl. 2 persons £7.50 - £10.00; extra person (over 1 yr) £1.50 - £2.25; dog 70p; electricity £1.25.
-- No credit cards.

Open:
Easter - mid October.

Address:
Waterleat, Ashburton,
Devon TQ13 7HU.

Tel:
(01364) 652552.
FAX: as phone.

Reservations:
Made for min. 3 nights with £15 deposit.

092 Finlake Holiday Park, Chudleigh

Large, lively park, with entertainment complex and leisure facilities.

This extensive 130 acre park on the edge of Dartmoor has been purpose built as a modern touring park and leisure complex. Approached by a long, sweeping drive, with views up to the moor, the park is on well landscaped, undulating ground surrounded by woodland. There are 318 flat, numbered pitches in two main areas, with some terracing on the higher parts. The pitches in the area around the central complex may well be affected by noise from the bars, etc. - for a quieter place, ask for a pitch further away (Lakeside or Deer Park). The pitches are of varying size, all with hardstanding and electric point (10A), 51 with water also. A separate, enclosed field is retained for tents and there is a special area for dog owners, with dog walks available. The six modern toilet blocks set around the park are being progressively refurbished, with two new blocks now open. Heated and of good quality, they have washbasins set in flat surfaces and free, pre-set hot showers, family shower rooms, a bathroom for ladies, suitable toilet/washrooms for disabled people and washing-up sinks outside, under cover. With additional 'portacabin' style units for busy times, the provision is acceptable. There are additional facilities in the pool complex. Chemical disposal, motorcaravan service points and gas supplies are provided. Also open to the public, the park offers extensive leisure activities including a 9-hole pitch and putt course, two fishing lakes, fitness track, tennis courts, quad bikes and track for children and walks in the woodland around the park with pony riding at a centre 100 m. from the entrance. The modern, attractively designed, central complex provides three bars around a pool terrace, with one specifically for children with soft drinks, snacks and games. There is a lively, free organised entertainment programme over a long season and food is available in the bars with takeaway also. A fitness suite (open all year) has a beauty treatment room and qualified instructors. The indoor and outdoor pools (with slide) are supervised in high season but are also easily observed from the bar areas and terrace. Supermarket (Easter-Oct, limited opening early and late season). Launderette with ironing room. A bar, open in high season and for adults only, overlooks the fishing lake. Bicycle hire 6 miles, golf 3 miles. For rent are 40 caravan holiday homes and, well hidden in woodland, 41 luxury log cabins. Caravan storage all year.

Charges 1999
-- Per unit incl. 2 persons: caravan, trailer tent or motorcaravan £7.50 - £16.50; electricity £1.80; tent £5.00 - £12.00; extra person (from 3 yrs) £1.50 - £2.50; water and drainage £1.00 - £2.00; awning free; pup tent £1.00 - £2.00; dog £1.00 - £2.00; extra car/boat £1.00.
-- Special themed weekends - details from park.
-- Bookings from young groups not accepted.
-- VAT included.
-- Credit cards accepted.

Open:
All year.

Address:
Chudleigh,
Devon TQ13 0EJ.

Tel:
(01626) 853833.
FAX: (01626) 854031.

Reservations:
Made with 25% deposit, balance 28 days before arrival.

see colour advert between pages 65/65

Directions: Park is signed on A38 dual carriageway; take exit for Chudleigh Knighton, Kingsteignton, Teign Valley. O.S.GR: SX850778.

094 Holmans Wood Caravan and Camping Park, Chudleigh

Neat, attractive family touring park adjacent to main Exeter - Plymouth road.

Close to the main A38 Exeter - Plymouth road, with easy access, this attractive, peaceful park makes a sheltered base for touring south Devon and Dartmoor. The hedged park is arranged on well kept grass surrounding a shallow depression, the floor of which makes a safe, grassy play area for children. Many attractive trees have been planted and the park is decorated with flowers. In two main areas, the 115 level pitches, 109 with electrical hook-ups (10A), are accessed by tarmac roadways. There are 70 with hardstanding, electricity, TV aerial hook up, water and drainage. Grassy areas are provided for tents. The single toilet block is of good quality with washbasins set in flat surfaces, roomy, fully controllable free hot showers, a dishwashing room, laundry room and facilities for babies and the disabled. The reception building at the entrance also houses a small licensed shop. Adventure play equipment is provided for children, with badminton and tennis nets and a recreation meadow. Public phone. Tourist information and advice. A pub/restaurant is nearby in Chudleigh village. The beach or Dartmoor are 7 miles and Haldon Forest for walks is 2 miles. Sunday market at Exeter Racecourse 2 miles. Fishing 1 mile. There may be some traffic noise on pitches to the west of the park. Caravan storage. This is a pleasant, well run park and with no other on-site amenities would suit couples or families who prefer a peaceful stay.

Charges 1999:
-- Per unit incl. 2 persons £6.20 - £8.60, deluxe pitch £7.50 - £10.05; extra adult £1.60 - £2.15; child (4-14 yrs) £1.30 - £1.60; awning or child's tent £1.60; porch awning 85p; dog 80p; extra car or boat £1.00; electricity £1.90; barrier card £1.00 per stay plus £5.00 deposit.
-- Credit cards accepted.
-- VAT included.

Open:
Mid-March - end Oct.

Address:
Chudleigh,
Devon TQ13 0DZ.

Tel:
(01626) 853785.

Reservations:
Any length, £20 deposit per week.

Directions: From Exeter on A38 Plymouth road, ½ mile after the racecourse and just after a garage, take Chudleigh exit (signed). Park is immediately on the left. From Plymouth turn off A38 for Chudleigh/Teign Valley, then right for Chudleigh. Continue through the town and park is 1 mile. O.S.GR: SX882811.

Devon

095 The River Dart Country Park, Ashburton

Good quality, family touring site in country park on Dartmoor, with outdoor activities.

With its mature park and woodland, once part of a Victorian estate, this interesting and unusual park could appeal to many, particularly those with children. Very close to Dartmoor, in the beautiful Dart valley, the park is open to the general public on payment. It features a variety of unusual adventure play equipment (eg. giant spider's web) arranged amongst and below the trees, 'Lilliput Land' for toddlers, woodland streams and a lake with raft for swimming and inflatables, fly fishing and marked nature and forest trails - all free to campers except fishing. It can become busy at weekends and school holidays. Supervised courses in caving, canoeing, archery or climbing are also arranged in school holiday periods (contact the park for details). The camping and caravanning area is in the more open parkland overlooking the woods and is mainly on a slight slope with some shade from mature trees. There are now 170 individual pitches of very reasonable size, marked by lines on the grass with 85 electrical connections (10A). The original toilet block for campers is of very good quality and can be heated. There is free hot water in the washbasins (with flat surface, hook and mirror, plus hair dryers), in the good hot showers and the washing-up sinks. A baby room, a shower for disabled visitors, chemical disposal and a launderette are also provided. A second block has been added to serve the 50 new pitches. Motorcaravan service point. Shop (all season). Restaurant and adjoining snack bar with takeaway (July/Aug). Small, heated swimming pool, tennis courts. Bar (July/Aug, plus Easter and B.Hs) with TV and games room with pool and amusement machines. Some self catering accommodation for rent. The entire estate is kept very clean and tidy. Dogs (up to two per pitch) are allowed on leads. American motorhomes are only accepted in dry periods (no hardstanding). Bicycle hire or riding 4 miles, golf 6 miles.

Charges 1999:
-- Per adult £4.50 - £6.25; child (over 5 yrs) £3.75 - £4.95; electricity £1.70.
-- VAT included.
-- Credit cards accepted.
Open:
Easter - mid September.
Address:
Holne Park, Ashburton, Devon TQ13 7NP.
Tel:
(01364) 652511.
FAX: (01364) 652020.
Reservations:
Low or mid season, any length with £3 fee; high season (strongly recommended), £20 deposit plus £3 fee for 7 days or less; £40 + £3 for longer.

Directions: Signed from the A38, park is about 2 miles west of Ashburton, on the road to Two Bridges. Note: disregard advisory signs stating `no caravans' as access to the park is prior to narrow bridge. O.S.GR: SX734701.

098 Lemonford Caravan Park, Bickington, nr. Newton Abbot

Attractive, family run park nestling in river valley, close to Dartmoor.

Lemonford, now under new management, has the look and atmosphere of the 'cultivated' caravan park. Well mown grass and trimmed, smart hedges bordered by the pretty River Lemon create the tranquil, attractive atmosphere the owners work hard to maintain. Despite its quite close proximity to the main road, this is a peaceful and relaxing site for all ages and families on the southern edge of the National Park, some 3 miles from both Ashburton and Newton Abbot. There are 96 touring pitches (62 with 10A electricity, 40 with hardstanding) on well kept, level grass and grouped in four areas according to whether they are to be used by families, couples or individuals. Some 14 holiday homes in a separate area and a cottage are for rent. The single, modern sanitary block is tiled, can be heated and has free, roomy, pre-set hot showers, free hairdryers and washbasins. Ladies have some private cabins, plus a bathroom (£1 payment). Hot water is free to the dishwashing area which is under cover. Amenities include a reception area and shop, gas, laundry facilities and clothes drying area, ice pack service, a children's play area, putting green, public phone, dog exercise area and a chalet with tourist information. Well located for excursions, the site also provides discount vouchers for many nearby tourist attractions. Two good pubs are within walking distance and there is a leisure pool in Newton Abbot. Fishing 4 miles, riding and bicycle hire 3 miles, golf 2 miles. No commercial vehicles are accepted.

Charges 1999:
-- Per unit incl. 2 persons £5.00 - £9.00; extra person £1.50; child (3-15) £1.10; awning £1.00; electricity £1.70; extra small tent, car or boat £1.00; dog 70p.
-- Special low season offers.
-- VAT included.
-- Credit cards accepted (Visa).
Open:
Easter - 31 October.
Address:
Bickington, Newton Abbot, Devon TQ12 6JR.
Tel:
(01626) 821242.
FAX: as phone.
E-mail: lemonford@ dartmoor.co.uk.
Reservations:
Advised for July/Aug. and made with £15 deposit (min. 4 nights Jul/Aug).

Directions: Turn off A38 Exeter - Plymouth road at A382 (Drumbridges) exit signed Newton Abbot, Bovey Tracey, Mortonhampstead. At roundabout take third exit to Bickington. Continue for 1 mile to Toby Jug Inn in the village and park is on left at the bottom of the hill. O.S.GR: SX793723.

096 Parker's Farm Holiday Park, nr. Ashburton

Modern touring site on working farm at the foot of Dartmoor, close to A38.

Well situated with fine views towards the moor, Parker's Farm shows the trappings of a working farm. Close inspection reveals a chance to experience Devon country life at first hand, with pigs, sheep, goats, calves and rabbits, etc. in pens. Not only can visitors take part in the workings of a farm, but now they can taste it too! The Parker family have added a family bar (open Whitsun - mid Sept) and games room with table tennis and pool and the building and theme are in context with their `country life' programme, including a play area for children with trampoline, made-safe farm implements and a working fire engine. The bar area provides entertainment in season (quiz night, bingo, guitars) and a restaurant has been added. Farm walks are tremendously popular and take place four evenings a week in season, on request at other times. The 60 touring pitches, with electricity (12A), are set directly above the farm buildings on terraces giving broad, flat groups of pitches, all with good views across the valley (to the A38 which may give some road noise). Young trees and hedges are maturing nicely. There are now two shower and toilet blocks. Modern, clean and tiled throughout, they provide good facilities with free hot water, a family shower room and baby bathroom. Dishwashing, laundry and chemical disposal facilities are provided. A small shop is next to reception (Whit - mid Sept) and a TV/games room has been added. Dogs are welcome on leads with 400 acres for walks. Public phone. American motorhomes accepted by prior arrangement. Caravan storage. Holiday homes and barn conversion cottages for hire. Bicycle hire 5 miles, golf 2 miles, riding 1 mile. Parker's Farm will suit those who don't seek the sophisticated amenities of more developed parks and a warm welcome awaits - in the words of one camper, `You come here and feel you belong'.

Charges 1999:
-- Per unit incl. 2 persons £4.50 - £8.50; backpacker tent £3.50 - £7.00; extra adult £1.30; child (3-15 yrs) £1.10; awning £1.30; pup tent £1.20; electricity £1.80; dog 60p.
-- VAT included.
-- Credit cards accepted.

Open:
Easter - 31 October.

Address:
Higher Mead Farm, Ashburton, Newton Abbot, Devon TQ13 7LJ.

Tel:
(01364) 652598.
FAX: (01364) 654004.
E-mail: parkersfarm @hotmail.com.

Reservations:
Made with £10 deposit

Directions: From Exeter on A38, 26 miles from Plymouth, turn left at Alston Cross signed `Woodland Denbury ¼ mile'. Site is ½ mile. O.S.GR: SX757702.

Parkers Farm Holiday Park

Enjoy a relaxing holiday on a 400 acre real working farm on the edge of Dartmoor National Park. Barn converted cottages and holiday caravans and a level, terraced touring site with fully tiled and spotlessly clean shower and toilet blocks. ALL FREE. Park Shop. Restaurant. Take Away. Family Bar. A warm welcome awaits you.

Phone resident owners: Roger or Rhona.
Tel: 01364 652598. Fax: 01364 654004.
Higher Mead Farm, Ashburton,
Newton Abbot, S. Devon TQ13 7LJ

SILVER

Int. Caravan & Camping 99
Gold Award for Quality & Service

076 Bundu Camping and Caravan Park, Okehampton

Simple, small park by main A30 on edge of Dartmoor.

This small park is under new management and is useful as an overnight stop, but it also has access to the moor and to the Sustran cycle route 3. A central hard-core road has level grass pitches of a good size on both sides. All have 16A electricity and water and refuse points. The sanitary block at one end of the site is a bit like a maze with 'add ons' - it is old, but just acceptable and it has been carefully lightened with white paint. Showers require tokens (30p) but are new, good and controllable, washbasins and toilets are adequate. Hair care area, laundry with washing machine and dryer, chemical disposal and a motorcaravan service point. Dogs are welcome with an area at the opposite end of site equipped with dog 'loos'. A chalet style reception with useful tourist information, public telephone and a colourful children's play area in front of you as you drive in, complete the facilities. A further area is for tents. Fishing 5 miles, bicycle hire, riding or golf 4 miles. Bundu (which means 'far from inhabited place') is on the edge of Sourton Tor, ideally situated for 'letter-boxing', exploring Dartmoor National Park and touring Devon and Cornwall - it is a really superb setting. Possible road noise.

Charges 1999:
-- Per unit incl. 2 adults £7.00; tents from £5.00; extra adult £1.00; child (under 14 yrs) 50p; awning £1.00; electricity £1.80.
-- No credit cards.

Open:
15 March - 15 November.

Address:
Sourton Cross, Okehampton, Devon EX20 4HT.

Tel:
(01837) 861611.

Reservations:
Contact park.

Directions: From A30 west, 4 miles after Okehampton, take A386 road towards Tavistock/Plymouth, site is signed to left after ½ mile. O.S.GR: SX546916.

Devon

077 Clifford Bridge Park, Clifford, nr. Drewsteignton

Riverside touring park in beautiful, country location within the Dartmoor National Park.

This 8 acre park provides peace and tranquillity within the National Park and 3 miles from the nearest village with any facilities. In a wooded valley, on the banks of the River Teign, it can only be approached on narrow lanes (single track for the last mile). A site for staying a while rather than overnight, there is plenty to do for those who like country pursuits 'away from it all'. Fingle Bridge is 3½ miles and Castle Drogo (National Trust) 5 miles. It is licensed for 24 touring caravans or motorcaravans and 40 tents. Pitches are of a good size on a flat grassy meadow, mainly around the perimeter of the site with some backing onto the river. Plenty of grassy space is left free for recreation and there is a free swimming pool (54 x 24 ft. open 1/5-1/9, heated from Spr. B.H). There are 3 hardstandings and 25 electrical connections (6A). The toilet block, near the entrance to the park, is not large or modern but is satisfactory and kept clean, with free hot water in smallish washbasins and showers. Hand and hair dryers. Chemical disposal. An adjacent 'portacabin' style unit provides extra facilities in high season. Dishwashing sinks outside, under cover. The farm outbuildings house a shop (Spr. B.H - 1 Sept), gas supplies, games room with pool, amusement machine and tourist information, and a small laundry around a courtyard. Public phone. There are first class walks from the site and game fishing on permit. Riding or golf 6 miles, bicycle hire 3 miles.

Directions: To avoid much single-track road approach via the A30, turning off 11 miles west of Exeter to Cheriton Bishop. Left there (at Old Thatch Inn), 2 miles to crossroads where right for Clifford Bridge, 1 mile of single track, over crossroads and bridge and left to park. O.S.GR: SX782897.

Charges 1999:
-- Per unit incl. 2 persons £7.40 - £12.60; small motorcaravan £6.60 - £10.70; backpacker £2.70 - £4.10; extra adult £2.50; child 8-16 yrs free - £2.10, 4-7 free - £1.35; awning £1.60; dog free - 50p; electricity £1.80.
-- No credit cards.
-- VAT included.

Open:
Easter - 30 September

Address:
Clifford,
nr. Drewsteignton,
Devon, EX6 6QE.

Tel:
(01647) 24226.
FAX: (01647) 24116.
E-mail: info@
clifford-bridge.co.uk.

Reservations:
Advised for school holidays; any length with £20 deposit.

OS REF. SX782897

Heated swimming pool • Small shop Electric hook-ups • Flush toilets & free showers • Fly fishing on Park Golf at nearby Moretonhampstead

Attractive, small and level family-run park, in a Dartmoor National Park woodland valley. Bordered by the River Teign, with just 24 touring pitches and 40 camping pitches. 5 acres set in an area of outstanding natural beauty, this is a holiday setting you won't forget.

Magnificent walks along woodland tracks - up stream through the Teign Gorge to Fingle Bridge or Castle Drogo (NT) - or down stream through Dunsford Nature Reserve.

AA 3 PENNANT FAMILY PARK. QUALITY ✓✓✓ GRADED. RAC.

Free colour brochure: Clifford Bridge Park,
Nr. Drewsteignton, Devon EX6 6QE
Tel: 01647 24226 Web: www.clifford-bridge.co.uk

078 Dartmoor View Holiday Park, Whiddon Down, nr. Okehampton

Medium size park on north Dartmoor touring route with easy access.

Dartmoor View is well situated, just off the main A30 which marks the northern edge of Dartmoor. With new, enthusiastic owners who continue to develop the park, it would be suitable for a base from which to explore Devon and Cornwall or as an overnight stop on the way west. Easily accessible, it offers 72 touring pitches, 40 with electricity (10A) and 14 with other services, 8 with hardstanding, arranged around a flat grass meadow, with stone/gravel access roads. Trees have been planted to break up the rather open nature of the field and 32 caravan holiday homes, 15 for hire, are arranged around the perimeter. The brick-built toilet block is modern and clean, with showers (20p), washbasins (two in cabins), family room with baby bath, dishwashing sinks, laundry equipment and rotary dryers, plus chemical disposal. A friendly site, there is a cosy bar with meals, and barbecue nights are arranged fortnightly on Saturdays in July/Aug. Other amenities include a shop (all season), a games/TV room with tourist information and a takeaway including breakfast in high season (limited in low season). Good quality play equipment and a heated swimming pool (10 x 5 m.) with children's pool, fenced with paved surrounds and open Whit - end Sept. Bicycle hire and 9 hole putting green. No kite flying. Public phone. First aid caravan. Small dog exercise area. Caravan storage. Fishing or riding 5 miles, golf 3 miles. The site is close to the Dartmoor 'letter-boxing' area. Ask to see the journal of the globe-trotting gnome!

Directions: From the Merrymeet roundabout, on the A30 dual-carriageway, take the Whiddon Down road. Park is ½ mile on the right. O.S.GR: SX685928.

Charges 1999:
-- Per unit, incl. 2 adults £6.75 - £9.25; small one person tent £4.50; extra person £1.90; child (3-11 yrs) £1.35; dog £1.00; electricity £2.25; all service pitch £3.60; hardstanding plus 75p; awning or pup tent £1.00.
-- VAT included.
-- Credit cards accepted.

Open:
March - November.

Address:
Whiddon Down,
Okehampton,
Devon EX20 2QL.

Tel:
(01647) 231545.
FAX: (01647) 231654.
E-mail: dartmoorview
@btinternet.com.

Reservations:
Any length, with deposit £25 p/week or £4 p/night.

074 Zeacombe House Caravan Park, East Anstey, nr. Tiverton

Delightful, smallish park on edge of Exmoor.

In a rural situation with views northwards over Exmoor, Zeacombe House is a well cared for park providing 60 pitches for caravans or motorcaravans and 10 for tents. The main field, with a circular tarmac road, has views, whilst the smaller field is more secluded, and both have neatly mown grass (groundsheets must be lifted). Pitches are not allocated - choose from those available - all have 10/16A electricity hook-ups, with water and rubbish bin points in the field centre. The heated toilet block has been redesigned with a comfortable feel. Showers are well equipped, with one adapted for the walking disabled, washbasins are vanity style, two in individual cubicles for ladies, complete with an area for hair drying and make-up. Hair dryers are provided free for both ladies and men. A separate room provides two dishwashing sinks, a laundry sink (all H&C), washing machine, dryer and a baby changing unit. Chemical disposal facilities are in the main field. The shop cum reception provides tourist information, general groceries with gas and caravan accessories (open limited hours out of main season). Food is available 6 - 8 pm. daily and a nice facility is provided whereby plated meals can be ordered by 4.30 each day from a quite extensive menu to be collected to eat in your own van or tent. A dog walk is opposite the site. There is no children's play area. All that Exmoor has to offer is at hand. Fishing 3 miles, bicycle hire 5 miles. Seasonal and all year storage and special offers. Ring for details.

Directions: From M5 junction 27 take A361 signed Tiverton and Barnstaple. At roundabout on outskirts of Tiverton turn right on A396 signed Minehead and Dulverton. In 6¾ miles turn left at Exeter Inn on B3227 signed South Moulton. After 5 miles turn left for Knowstone and park is almost immediately on the right. O.S.GR: SS862241.

Charges 1999:
-- Per unit incl. 2 persons £11.50 - £14.00; extra person £4.00; child (5-16 yrs) £1.20; electricity £1.50.
-- Credit cards accepted.
Open:
15 March - 31 October.
Address:
Blackerton Cross, East Anstey, Tiverton, Devon EX16 9JU.
Tel:
(01398) 341279.
Reservations:
Contact park.

075 Minnows Camping & Caravan Park, Sampford Peverell, Tiverton

Small, neat, rural park for all units, close to M5 motorway with pleasant views.

Minnows is an attractive park with views across the Devon countryside, separated from the Grand Western canal by hedging, yet easily accessible from the M5 and suitable as an ideal touring centre for Devon and Somerset or simply for breaking a long journey. Part of the Caravan Club's 'managed under contract' scheme, non-members are also very welcome. Open for nine months of the year, it provides 45 level pitches of which 34 are all weather (grass and gravel) and 3 are fully serviced for motorcaravans. All pitches will have 16A electricity for the 2000 season. A further 3½ acres have been added to the park recently providing space for more pitches, a new children's playground and a large area for ball games, etc. The heated toilet block is well maintained with all modern facilities, constant hot water, facilities for disabled people, chemical disposal, covered dishwashing sinks and one for laundry, plus a spin dryer. Motorcaravan service point. Gas is available and newspaper delivery can be arranged. The village of Sampford Peverell, with pub and general store, is only a ½ mile walk via the towpath, with Tiverton 7½ miles. In fact, there are 12 miles of level walking on the towpath. The site is also on the Sustran cycle route (route 3). Tiverton Parkway station (BR) is 1 mile, an hourly bus service runs to Tiverton stopping ½ mile from the site. Pay phone. Golf driving range near, full course 4 miles. Riding 6 miles, bicycle hire 5 miles. Coarse fishing permits (from 1 June) for the canal are available from reception. A horse drawn barge makes trips on the winding 11 miles of the canal. Latest arrival: 10 pm. All year caravan storage.

Directions: From M5 junction 27 take A361 signed Tiverton. After about 600 yds leave on the first exit signed Sampford Peverell. After about 200 yds turn right at roundabout and cross bridge over A361 to a second roundabout. Go straight ahead and park immediately ahead. O.S.GR: ST042148.

Charges 2000:
-- Per caravan, motor-caravan or trailer tent £3.00; small tent and car £2.00; adult £2.60 - £3.90; child (5-17 yrs) £1.10 - £1.20; dog free; awning (breathable groundsheets on grass), extra tent or extra car £1.00; electricity £1.50 - £2.25; serviced pitch plus £2.00.
-- Credit cards accepted.
Open:
6 March - 13 November.
Address:
Sampford Peverell, nr. Tiverton Devon EX16 7EN.
Tel:
(01884) 821770.
FAX: as phone.
Reservations:
Made with £10 deposit.

47

Devon

099 Kennford Caravan Park, Kennford, nr. Exeter

Good touring park near historic city, on a main route to the southwest.

A comfortable park attracting a range of visitors, Kennford is within easy reach of the cathedral city of Exeter for shopping or sightseeing, only 5 miles from the estuary at Starcross and 8 miles from the beach at Dawlish. A well run park, it is attractive for longer stays, although most conveniently situated for travellers to and from South Devon and Cornwall beside the main A38 near the end of the M5 motorway (therefore a little road noise should be expected). It takes up to 120 units of any type with 106 electrical connections and 16 hardstandings for caravans, plus connection to mains drainage possible on a few pitches. The way the park was designed has led to the development of a more continental type of site with hedged individual pitches, however the lower, later part provides larger, more open, but still individual, pitches with marvellous rural views. The two log clad toilet blocks with inside pine cladding are less austere than brick built blocks. They provide washbasins with shelf, mirror, 17 individual cabins for ladies with normal basin taps and WC also, free hairdryers, free controllable hot showers and two baths on payment (but free for disabled people). There are also family shower units with external access, covered washing-up sinks, a well equipped laundry room with tourist information, chemical disposal and motorcaravan services. A small, cosy bar and tropical style family café (closed Sept-March) provides good value meals including breakfast and takeaway in high season. Games room. Patio with open fire. Public phone. Gas supplies available. Adventure type children's play equipment on grass and dog exercise field. There is an excellent village shop nearby and supermarkets within a 10 minute drive. Powderham Castle, the racecourse and Sunday market, a leisure centre and bird sanctuary are close. Fishing ½ mile or 2 miles, riding 1 mile, golf 2 miles. Bungalows (3) and mobile homes (3) to hire. A member of the Best of British group.

Directions: From north follow Torbay/Plymouth signs from M5 and take exit for Kennford services and park (signed from both sides of the dual-carriageway). O.S.GR: SX911856.

Charges 2000:
-- Per unit incl. 2 persons £10.50; extra person (over 5 yrs) £1.50; awning or extra small tent £1.50; dog or porch awning £1.00; electricity £2.20 - £2.40.
-- Less 10% for 10 nights or more.
-- VAT included.
-- Credit cards accepted.

Open:
All year (reduced facilities mid-Sept - March).

Address:
Kennford, nr. Exeter, Devon EX6 7YN.

Tel:
(01392) 833046. FAX: as phone.

Reservations:
Made for any length with £15 deposit; balance one month before arrival.

Alan Rogers' Discount

 Less £1 per stay

See colour feature for `BEST of BRITISH' between pages 96/97

105 Springfield Holiday Park, Tedburn St. Mary, nr. Exeter

Quietly situated park with marvellous rural views, all facilities and holiday homes to let.

Well situated to explore both Dartmoor and Exmoor, yet easily accessible, Springfield has room for 88 units on its 9 acres, mainly on level, grass terraces with views across the Devon countryside. Over 50 of these have 10A electricity. There are some seasonal units and 14 mobile homes which are to be found at the lower part of the park with 5 to hire. The reception cum shop is on the right as you drop down into the park and gravel access roads radiate out from here along the terraces and link up at the bottom where a new family 'terrace bar' has been built (open Easter, then May - Sept) with a grass terrace making the most of the rural views. Good value meals are also provided to eat in or takeaway, even cream teas and the odd musical evening. Near reception is a small heated swimming pool, naturally sheltered (unsupervised). Children's play area and games room. Two toilet blocks of older design provide washbasins with curtains, pre-set showers (20p) with curtain and stool, a family bathroom and baby changing facilities. Washing up and laundry sinks (H&C), three washing machines and two dryers, plus two chemical toilet disposal points. In all, it is a satisfactory provision which may be a little stretched when the field below the terrace bar is being used for camping. Martin and Eileen Johnson, the owners, are keen to help everyone enjoy their stay and can provide plenty of local information on Dartmoor walks and where to find the best fishing lakes, etc. Fishing 6 miles, bicycle hire 8 miles, riding 10 miles, golf 2 miles. They encourage local produce in the licensed shop which is quite well stocked. Gas supplies.

Directions: From M5 junction 31 take A30 towards Okehampton. Tedburn is signed at the second exit (8 miles). Turn left at roundabout and follow Springfield signs through the village and site is on the right past the village. You can use the third exit from the A30 which avoids the village. O.S.GR: SX788936.

Charges 1999:
-- Per caravan or tent £6.50 - £10.00; motor-caravan £6.50 - £12.00, acc. to season and size; walker or cyclist £3.00 - £5.00; extra person (over 3 yrs) £1.50; full or half awning £1.60; dog £1.50; extra car, boat or trailer £1.00; electricity £1.50.

Open:
15 March - 15 November.

Address:
Tedburn Road, Tedburn St. Mary, Exeter, Devon EX6 6EW.

Tel:
(01647) 24242. FAX: (01647) 24131.

Reservations:
Made with deposit (£20 per unit per week or £5 per night with electricity).

109 Peppermint Park, Dawlish, nr. Exeter

Family run touring park close to Exeter and large, sandy beaches.

First impressions of this extensive park are perhaps a lack of ambience. However this is quickly dispelled by the friendly reception, plenty of flowers and the constructive way the large pitches have been incorporated into the slightly sloping ground. There are 250 pitches, each with electricity connections (10A), and there at least another 60 hook-ups available for tent campers. Tarmac roads thread through the site giving easy access to all areas, each pitch being marked and numbered. There are two modern sanitary blocks comprising open style washbasins and free pre-set hot showers. They are kept in spotless condition. Two units (WC, washbasin and shower) are provided for disabled visitors. Other facilities include a fully equipped mother and baby room, laundry (washing machines, dryers and free irons) and dishwashing. Two chemical disposal points are clearly marked at each block and there are adequate water taps, fire points and refuse facilities. A shop stocking the usual foods and gas is open end May - end Aug, as are the restaurant, bar and takeaway. In low season Peppermint Park guests can use the full facilities at the adjacent sister site (Golden Sands) which include a large indoor pool. From late May to late August, Peppermint Park's own pool complex is open. Also within the park are a children's playground, field for ball games and a small coarse fishing lake £2.50 for adult day ticket). Nightly entertainment is staged in the Peppermint Club in high season and at Golden Sands at other times. This site's `jewel in the crown' is the walking distance (700 yds) to the large, safe beaches of Dawlish Warren and its pleasure complex.- ideal for families. For others, there is the coastal footpath or the city of Exeter (7 miles) with its cathedral, museums and historic Quay. A passenger ferry operates from Starcross (2 miles) across the estuary to Exmouth during high season. Dawlish Warren nature reserve is adjacent and includes an 18 hole links golf course. Caravan holiday homes to rent are in paddocks to the south of the park.

Directions: Leave M5 at junction 30 and take A379 Dawlish road. After passing through Starcross (7 miles) turn left to Dawlish Warren just before Dawlish. Continue 1½ miles downhill and park is on left in 300 yds. O.S. GR: SX978788.

Charges 1999:
-- Per unit incl. all persons £5.50 - £11.00; tent incl. 2 persons and car £5.50 - £9.00; extra adult £1.00 - £2.20; child (2-13 yrs) £1.00 - £2.00; awning or pup tent £1.00 - £2.20; electricity £2.00; dog £1.00 - £2.00.
-- Credit cards accepted.
-- VAT included.
Open:
1 April - 31 October.
Address:
Warren Road,
Dawlish Warren,
Dawlish,
Devon EX7 0PQ
Tel:
01626 863436.
Reservations:
Made with £15 deposit (Sat. - Sat. only 24 July - 28 Aug).

101 Lady's Mile Touring and Camping Park, Dawlish

Popular, spacious, family touring park with indoor and outdoor pools.

A large, open park, Lady's Mile has extensive grassy fields (with some trees for shade), in addition to the main, landscaped camping area which is arranged in broad terraces. In July and August caravans and tents normally go in separate sections, at other times they are grouped together in the main part. The park has 486 pitches, mostly marked by lines but with nothing between them, and 450 with electrical connections (10A). It is a 20 minute walk to a good sandy beach at Dawlish Warren and also has its own good sized, free swimming pool with 200 ft. plus slide, children's pool and a paved surround (open Easter - Oct with lifeguard in high season), plus an indoor pool (20 x 10 m.) with 100 ft. slide and separate paddling pool. In spite of its size, the park is fully booked over a long season, with reservation necessary. There are four toilet blocks, of various ages and styles, well spaced around the main areas of the park. They are of a good standard, with free hot water and, with an additional shower block (with some basins also), there should be an adequate provision overall. Facilities for disabled people and four family bathrooms (50p). Dishwashing sinks are under cover with free hot water. Two launderettes. Mini market and fish and chip takeaway (both Easter - mid Sept). A bar complex with family area overlooking the indoor pool has food available with a spacious games room below including pool tables and video games. Sloping recreation field, ideal for kite flying and large fenced children's adventure playground with safe, sand surface. Nine hole golf course on site (free but with small charge for hire of clubs). The park reports a new disco and bar, and a multi-sports pitch. Tarmac area at reception for late arrivals. Dog walk. Public phones and post box. Holiday accommodation to rent. Winter caravan storage. Riding and bicycle hire 1 mile, fishing 3 miles.

Directions: Park is 1 mile north of Dawlish with access off the A379 (Exeter - Teignmouth) road. O.S. GR: SX969778.

Charges 1998:
-- Per unit incl. 2 adults £7.00 - £11.50; 2-man tent (no car) £6.00 - £10.00; awning £1.00 - £2.50; child's tent £1.20 - £2.50; extra adult £1.20 - £2.50; child (under 14 yrs) £1.00 - £2.30; boat, dog or extra car £1.00 - £2.50; electricity £2.00.
-- Low season special offers and discounts for OAPs.
-- VAT included.
-- Credit cards accepted
Open:
13 March - 31 October.
Address:
Dawlish,
Devon EX7 0LX.
Tel:
(01626) 863411.
FAX: (01626) 888689.
Reservations:
Made for Sat to Sat only in peak seasons, with £15 deposit.

see colour advert between pages 65/65

Devon

097 Cofton Country Holiday Park, Starcross, nr. Dawlish

Large touring park with fishing, swimming pools, bar and beautiful country views.

About 1½ miles from a sandy beach at Dawlish Warren this popular, family site takes over 400 touring units on a variety of fields and meadows. Although not individually marked, there is never a feeling of overcrowding. The smaller, more mature fields, including a pleasant old orchard for tents only, are well terraced. While there are terraces on most of the slopes of the larger, more open fields, there are still some quite steep gradients to climb. There are some 300 electrical connections (10A). One area has 62 park-owned holiday homes to rent, including a special one for disabled visitors. There are five attractive holiday cottages on the park, plus three others a short drive away in secluded countryside (available all year). A well designed, central complex is decorated with flowers and hanging baskets and houses reception, a shop and off-licence (21 April - 30 Sept) and a bar lounge, the `Cofton Swan', where bar meals are usually available. A family room and bar are on the first floor of this building and there is an outdoor terrace and some light entertainment in season. The adjacent supervised kidney-shaped heated pool (overall length 100 ft. open Spr. B.H - mid Sept), with paddling pool and slide, has lots of grassy space for sunbathing. Other facilities include a fish and chip shop, two launderettes and a games room (busy in high season). A small, but good, adventure playground in an elevated position in the woods overlooks the swimming pools and there is further children's play equipment in two areas - one being modern, the other older and with some concrete bases. Coarse fishing is available in three lakes on the park (from £16.50 per rod for 7 days, discount for senior citizens outside July) and there is a woodland trail towards Dawlish Warren. Sanitary facilities consist of three blocks, one on each side of the road dividing the park for the touring pitches and the third near the holiday home area. The newest, at the top of the larger fields is first rate, with laundry and facilities for the disabled. The blocks have free hot water throughout, well equipped and controllable showers, basins set in rows in flat surfaces with two in cubicles, hair dryers, and dishwashing facilities under cover. In addition four `portacabin' style units with basic toilet facilities are provided for the peak season. Chemical disposal. Gas available. Public phones. Post box. Ice pack hire service. Golf 3 miles. Winter storage available.

Charges 1999:
-- Per unit incl. 2 persons £6.00 - £10.50; extra adult £1.00 - £2.20; child (2-13 yrs) £1.00 - £2.00; awning or child's tent £1.00 - £2.20; boat, dog or extra car £1.00 - £2.00; electricity £2.00.
-- Small discount for Senior Citizens outside July/Aug.
-- VAT included.
-- Credit cards accepted.

Open:
14 April - 28 October.

Address:
Starcross, nr. Dawlish, Devon EX6 8RP.

Tel:
(01626) 890111.
FAX: (01626) 891572.

Reservations:
Made for min. 4 nights, 7 nights in peak season with £15 deposit.

see colour advert between pages 65/65

Directions: Access to the park is off the A379 road 3 miles north of Dawlish, just after Cockwood harbour village. O.S.GR: SX965797.

108 Coast View Holiday Park, Shaldon, nr. Teignmouth

Family run holiday park with magnificent views over Lyme Bay.

On the coast road between Teignmouth and Torquay, this park has a section of caravan holiday homes and chalets. However, the touring area of 100 pitches is quite separate. On terraced grass, some pitches are part sloping. At present, due to recent reconstruction of the park, there is little or no shelter but as the site is terraced into the hillside, there is adequate protection from the prevailing southwest winds. The new sanitary block is spacious with free hot showers and open washbasins, and it includes a baby room. Dishwashing and laundry facilities are separate and there are two chemical disposal points. To the right of the park entrance is an attractive indoor swimming pool, children's pool and an entertainment area comprising a clubroom with bar (bar meals and snacks), takeaway, TV room and games room. A licensed shop also stocks gas. All these facilities are open all season. Entertainment is organised each night and also activities in the mornings for children, who also have an adventure playground and indoor soft play area. The park is convenient for the beach (1½ miles) and the coastal footpath is adjacent. Torbay is 5 miles. A bus service stops at the gates. Good for holidaymakers of all ages, this park offers superb views with excellent facilities.

Charges 1999:
-- Per caravan incl. up to 8 persons £7.00 - £16.00; motorcaravan or tent (up to 8 persons) £7.00 - £14.00; tent incl. 2 persons £6.00 - £8.00; electricity £1.75; dog free - £3.00.
-- 7th night free if pre-booked and paid.

Open:
26 April - 31 October.

Address:
Torquay Road, Shaldon, Teignmouth, Devon TQ14 0BG.

Tel:
(01626)872392.
FAX: (01626) 872719.

Reservations:
Contact park.

Directions: From A380 Exeter - Newton Abbot road, take A381 to Teignmouth. In town turn right over Shaldon Bridge on B3199 for Torquay. Park is on right in approx. 1½ miles. O.S.GR: SX932714.

100 Forest Glade Int. Caravan and Camping Park, nr. Cullompton

Country park with small swimming pool and some holiday homes.

Set in the Blackdown Hills (designated an area of outstanding natural beauty), Forest Glade is owned and run by the Wellard family, deep in wooded Devon away from the hectic life on the coast. A sheltered site set amongst woodland with extensive walking without using your car, there are 80 touring pitches, 70 of which have 16A electricity connections and 24 hardstanding. The pitches are all level, mostly backing onto the forest, and there is also a rally field. There is one main toilet block, heated in cold weather and with free hot water in washbasins (some in cubicles), showers and washing up sinks. The laundry with washing machine, dryer and spin dryer has metered hot water. There are extra facilities of `portacabin' style with toilets, washbasins and showers, at the swimming pool, but this is only available when the pool is open. This is a small heated, covered pool with a paddling pool and a patio area outside. Other amenities include an adventure playground, games room with table tennis, video games and two pool tables, plus an all weather tennis court. The shop (open all season) is quite well stocked including gas and locally made bread and pastries and there is a takeaway (open evenings except Sunday). Chemical disposal and motorcaravan service facilities. Mobile homes to rent. Caravan storage available. Public phone. Dogs are accepted and the surrounding forest makes this a dog lovers paradise. Fishing or riding 1½ miles, golf 6 miles, bicycle hire 5 miles. Touring caravans must book in advance and the easiest route for them will be explained then (phone bookings accepted). Although set in the country, the beaches of East Devon are a fairly easy drive away. A member of the Best of British group.

Directions: Park is 5½ miles from M5 exit 28. Take A373 for 3 miles, turning left at camp sign towards Sheldon. Park is on left after approx. 2½ miles. This access is not suitable for touring caravans owing to a steep hill - phone park for alternative route details. O.S.GR: ST101073.

Charges 2000:
-- Per unit incl. 2 adults £6.00 - £11.50; child (5-9 yrs) £1.00 ; student (10 yrs - end of study) £2.00; awning free; backpacker or cyclist £2.50 per person; dog 50p; electricity £1.90.
-- VAT included.
-- Credit cards accepted.

Open:
26 March - 31 October.

Address:
Cullompton,
Devon EX15 2DT.

Tel:
(01404) 841381.
FAX: (01404) 841593.
E-mail: forestglade@mcmail.com.

Reservations:
Any length with deposit of £4 p/day or £20 p/wk, (£15 for B.H. w/ends). Essential for B.Hs and school holidays.

Alan Rogers' Discount

Less £1 per night off mid or high season rates

See colour feature for `BEST of BRITISH' between pages 96/97

110 Webbers Farm Caravan Park, Woodbury, nr. Exmouth

Family run park in rural, non-commercialised setting.

Over the past twenty years this park has been gradually enlarged from an initial open field site to one that can boast modern facilities, yet retaining its essentially rural character. The 115 marked pitches are large, on grass, with the majority level and a few gently sloping. All have electricity connections. Three modern sanitary blocks provide free hot showers and in the newest block (built in '99), full bathroom facilities (£1). There is a baby room and two units for disabled visitors (WC, shower and washbasin). Hot water is free throughout and the usual dishwashing and laundry facilities are provided. Unusual in terms of number, are seven chemical disposal points, located at each water point (and adequately separated). Amenities on the park include a small shop (limited cold food only) a children's play area, games field and two dog walks. Gas is available and caravan storage. Although essentially a farm site, there is no problem with animal noise - this is a sheep farm and children are encouraged to participate in a hands-on experience. Woodbury village is within walking distance with an excellent pub/restaurant, post office, etc. A short drive takes you to the two miles of glorious sand at Exmouth, with Woodbury Common (excellent heathland walks) just over a mile away. Exeter is 6 miles. This is a mature, friendly and modern park in a lovely situation. A member of the Countryside Discovery group.

Directions: Leave M5 at junction 30 and follow A376 Exmouth road. At second roundabout take B317a (Budleigh Salterton and Woodbury). In village centre follow brown signs to park on right. O.S.GR: SY017874.

Charges 1999:
-- Per pitch incl. 2 persons £7.10 - £9.90; extra person (over 5 yrs) £1.75; awning or extra tent £1.75; electricity £2.00; dog free.

Open:
Easter - 30 September.

Address:
Castle Lane, Woodbury, Exeter, Devon EX5 1EA.

Tel:
(01395) 232276.
FAX: (01395) 233389.

Reservations:
Essential for peak periods and made with £20 deposit.

Devon

102 Oakdown Touring and Holiday Home Park, Weston, Sidmouth

Award winning, exceptionally well kept and environmentally conscious park.

Always a neat and tidy park, we continue to note developments at Oakdown under the special care, guidance and attention of Mr and Mrs Franks, who now provide one of the most comfortable, well equipped and attractively laid out family parks we know, complete with welcoming staff who help pitch your unit (and live on site). The park has a spacious, uncrowded feel with large pitches semi-screened in small bays or groves and edged with trees. There is a marvellous range of trees (all 70 types are named) providing variety, privacy and home for wildlife. A circular concrete road links the 120 pitches, all of which have electricity (16A), 26 with water, waste water and drainage and over 70 with hardstanding. The central amenity block with piped music provides good, fully tiled, heated sanitary facilities, all well maintained. These include controllable showers, washbasins set in flat surfaces (one private cabin for ladies) and sinks for dishwashing, all with free hot water, hairdryers and shaver points. Two unisex family bathrooms (with bath, shower, toilet, washbasin and coin operated entry) also double as useful units for disabled people. There are laundry facilities, plus free use of a freezer and a microwave. Tourist information is provided on a wall board, together with the history of the park. This is interesting as it was within the boundaries of a secret wartime radar station which accounts for the very solid construction of the amenity block. TV room. Other services include a motorcaravan service point for fresh and waste water, chemical disposal, recycling point (glass, paper, cans), public phones and a fax service. A well equipped, grass based children's play area with adventure style equipment and play castle is in the centre of the park. No cycling, skate-boarding or kite flying is permitted. Dogs are accepted but not certain breeds. An interesting footpath edged with wild flowers leads through the fields to the nearby Donkey Sanctuary and one can walk further to the beach and sea (2 miles, steep in parts). There are, in fact, over 113 varieties of wild flower to be seen and 45 varieties of wild bird. A family of Lesser Spotted woodpeckers have caused interest and skylarks and goldfinches are regular visitors. Badgers also visit (after 10.30 pm), and trees and bushes have been planted to encourage butterflies and more birds. It is the care of and attention to all things natural that makes this park rather special. The 'reed bed' development is progressing well and is now complete with a bird-hide. Adjoining is Oak Grove, with 46 holiday homes, 16 for hire (under the same ownership). Riding 6 miles, golf 2 miles. Secure, alarmed caravan storage facilities, also closed circuit TV. A new member of the Best of British group.

Directions: Turn off A3052 (Colyford - Sidford) road to south 2½ miles east of junction with A375 and park is on left. O.S.GR: SY167902.

Charges 1999:
-- Per unit incl. 2 persons: standard pitch £7.25 - £11.00; super pitch (incl. water and drainage services and awning) £10.90 - £14.65; extra person (5 yrs and over) £1.70; dog £1.00; awning £1.70; porch awning £1.00; child's pup tent £1.00; extra car (by arrangement) £1.70; electricity £2.00.
-- Less 70p for senior citizens in low season.
-- VAT included.
-- Credit cards accepted.

Open:
28 March - 1 November.

Address:
Weston, Sidmouth, Devon EX10 0PH.

Tel:
(01297) 680387.
FAX: (01297) 680541.
E-mail: oakdown@btinternet.com.

Reservations:
Made with £20 p/w deposit, min. 3 days at B.Hs. and 3/4 Aug. (Sidmouth Folk Festival).

For a list of parks which are open all year - see page 234

52

072 Easewell Farm Holiday Park, Mortehoe, nr. Woolacombe

Family run park on working sheep farm, with golf course, overlooking Bristol Channel.

Easewell Farm is near to the sandy beaches of Woolacombe and is a family run site run with families in mind. The largest of the camping fields is sloping with superb views across to the sea. Two smaller fields are terraced and one area has hardstandings. Together they provide 250 pitches, 90 with electricity (15A) and 14 with TV and water. The central toilet block can be heated. Washbasins are in vanity style, controllable showers are free and there is a small area with baby facilities, hairdryers, mirrors and seats. Dishwashing sinks are under cover with free hot water and the laundry has sinks, machines, dryers and irons. Well equipped unit for disabled people, chemical disposal and motorcaravan service point. The shop is well stocked (gas available), there is a takeaway and restaurant and an attractive bar with patio overlooking a small duck pond. A small heated indoor swimming pool is well used, as are games/TV rooms. The well equipped, fenced play area has a bark base. The popular well maintained 9 hole golf course has reduced fees for campers. A huge redundant farm building provides table tennis, pool, a skittle alley and flat green bowling. In high season only one dog per pitch is allowed - with an exercise field. Fishing or riding 1 mile, bicycle hire 3 miles. Walks to the local village and along the coastal path are easy from the site and a bus to Ilfracombe and Barnstaple stops 100 yds. from the entrance.

Directions: From Barnstaple, take A361 Ilfracombe road through Braunton. Turn left at Mullacott Cross roundabout on B3343 to Woolacombe, turning right after 2-3 miles to Mortehoe. Park is on right before village. O.S.GR: SS465455.

Charges 1999:
-- Per caravan incl. 2 persons £6.00 - £11.00; tent or motorcaravan incl. 2 persons £5.50 - £9.00; extra person incl. children £1.00; extra car £1.00; electricity £2.00; `supersite' incl. electricity plus £4.00; awning or pup tent free.
-- VAT included.
-- Credit cards accepted.

Open:
Easter - 30 September.

Address:
Mortehoe, Woolacombe, N. Devon EX34 7EH.

Tel:
(01271) 870225.
FAX: as phone.

Reservations:
Made with £20 deposit per week booked.

073 Twitchen Park, Mortehoe, nr. Woolacombe

Holiday park with areas for tourers and tents, with extensive family entertainment.

Set in the grounds of an Edwardian country house, Twitchen Park's main concern lies in holiday caravans and flats. However, it also provides 90 marked pitches for tourers at the top of the park, with some views over the rolling hills to the sea. The 50 formal touring pitches with hardstanding and electricity, are arranged around an oval road in a hedged area. Behind are two open, unmarked fields which are sloping (blocks are provided), with 90 electrical connections (16A) . Two good sanitary blocks are on the sloping field, the larger one of an unusual design with different levels and rather narrow corridors. Both have free, pre-set, hot showers, washbasins in rows and WCs. Dishwashing is under cover at each block with laundry facilities in each, plus a good launderette at the central complex. The touring areas are cared for by wardens who live on site. A smart, modern entertainment complex incorporates a licensed club and family lounge with snacks, restaurant, adults only bar, teenage disco room, and cartoon lounge, together with games rooms for table tennis, pool, snooker and arcade games, and entertainment day and evening. Shop and takeaway. Outside is a swimming pool (heated mid-May - mid-Sept) and paddling pool with free lessons in high season. An excellent indoor pool has a sauna and a paddling pool with fountain. A super adventure play area (on bark), putting green and games field complete the popular family facilities. No dogs or pets permitted. Part of the Hoburne group.

Directions: From Barnstaple take A361 (Ilfracombe) through Braunton. Turn left at Mullacott Cross roundabout towards Woolacombe and then right towards Mortehoe. Park is on the left before village. O.S.GR: SS466456.

Charges 2000:
-- Per touring pitch, incl. electricity, awning and up to 6 persons £9.50 - £23.00; tent pitch (no electricity available) £7.00 - £20.00; pup tent (camping field only) £3.00.
-- VAT included.
-- Credit cards accepted.

Open:
1 April/Easter - end Oct.

Address:
Mortehoe, Woolacombe, N. Devon EX34 7ES.

Tel:
(01271) 870476.
FAX: (01271) 870498.
E-mail: enquiries@ hoburne.co.uk.

Reservations:
Made with £50 deposit for tourers, payment in full for tent pitches.

Devon

071 Hidden Valley Touring & Camping Park, West Down, Ilfracombe

Delightful, family run park in countryside between Barnstaple and Ilfracombe.

Aptly named, this award winning park has been carefully developed by the owners in keeping with its lovely setting. In the valley beside a small stream and lake (with ducks), it is most attractive and is also convenient for several resorts, beaches and the surrounding countryside. The original part of the park offers some 74 level pitches of good size on three sheltered terraces. All have hardstanding and 73 have electricity (16A) and free TV connections, with a water point between each pitch. Kingfisher Meadow, a little way from the main facilities and reached by an unsurfaced road, provides a further 60 pitches entirely on grass (so suitable for campers with tents) of which 50 have electricity, water, waste water and TV hook-ups. Two modern sanitary blocks (one heated), are tiled and have non-slip floors. They provide free hot showers, washbasins in cubicles, some en-suite with toilets in the Kingfisher Meadow block, hand and hairdryers (free), WCs, baby changing room, laundry facilities including washing machine, dryer and iron, and dishwashing sinks under cover, plus complete facilities for disabled people. There are supplementary clean 'portacabin' style facilities in the original area. Chemical disposal and motorcaravan service facilities are provided. There are two good children's adventure play areas with wooden equipment and safe bark surface (one near a fast flowing stream), a dog exercise field, a small shop with off-licence, takeaway and a lounge bar and restaurant serving a range of home cooked meals in attractive surroundings and also a games room. Caravan storage. Gas supples. Fishing or golf 2 miles, bicycle hire 4 miles, riding 5 miles. This is essentially a park for those seeking good quality facilities in very attractive, natural surroundings, without too many man-made distractions - apart from some slight traffic noise during the day time. It provides a really peaceful setting in beautiful surroundings.

Charges 1999:
-- Per unit incl. up to 3 persons £3.50 - £11.80; extra person over 5 yrs £1.00; extra car £1.00; dog free - £1.00; electricity (16A) £1.30 - £2.00.
-- VAT included.
-- Credit cards accepted.

Open:
14 March - 6 November.

Address:
West Down, Ilfracombe, N. Devon EX34 8NU.

Tel:
(01271) 813837.
FAX: (01271) 814041.

Reservations:
Accepted with £25 deposit.

see colour advert between pages 32/33

Directions: Park is on the A361 Barnstaple - Ilfracombe road, 3½ miles after Braunton. O.S.GR: SS499408.

107 Woolacombe Bay Holiday Park, Woolacombe

Newly developed touring park overlooking Woolacombe Bay and part of a holiday park with all its many facilities, for motorcaravans, tents and trailer tents.

Woolacombe Bay, and its sister site Golden Coast nearby, are well known holiday parks providing a range of on site holiday accommodation from caravan holiday homes to chalets and apartments, with many on site amenities including pools, restaurants and bars, and providing a wide range of entertainment. A brand new touring section has now been developed at the Woolacombe Bay park, whereby touring visitors can enjoy all the activities and entertainment of both parks. Partly terraced out of the hillside and partly on the hill top with some existing pine trees but many more new trees planted for landscaping, the site has magnificent views across the bay. A super new central toilet block has excellent facilities, including en-suite shower and washrooms and separate toilets; also included is a sauna and steam room - unusual but nice. Separate dishwashing room and laundry room. Marked and numbered touring pitches have been provided on grass for 146 units, 94 with electricity (10/16A). All should be level, having been terraced where necessary and they are connected at present by gravel roadways. Water and refuse points are well spaced. Some up and down walking is needed for the toilet block. When seen in August '99, some teething problems were being addressed, but the site has much potential, with access to indoor and outdoor pools with slides, sauna, gym, tennis courts to mention just a few of the facilities including supermarkets on both sites. A shuttle bus service runs between the two parks and the beach during the high season, although there is a footpath to the beach from Woolacombe Bay. Both parks have varied entertainment programmes and children's clubs and Woolacombe Bay also boasts a health spa and beauty suite. Dogs are welcome at Woolacombe Bay (not at Golden Coast). At present touring caravans are not accepted - this may change so contact the park.

Charges 1999:
-- Per person £3.95 - £10.65; child (5-16yrs) £1.95 - £5.35; dog £1.42; electricity included.

Open:
Easter - end October.

Address:
Woolacombe Bay Holiday Parcs, Woolacombe, Devon EX34 7HW.

Tel:
(01271) 870343.
FAX: (01271) 870089.
E-mail: goodtimes@ woolacombe-bay.co.uk.

Reservations:
Advised for peak season.

see colour advert between pages 32/33

Directions: Take A361 Barnstaple - Ilfracombe road through Braunton. Turn left at Mullacott Cross roundabout towards Woolacombe then right towards Mortehoe. Park on left before village. O.S.GR: SS463445.

069 Stowford Farm Meadows, Combe Martin, nr. Ilfracombe

Large, pleasant family run farm park with much to do, set in North Devon valley.

Stowford Farm dates from the 15th century and is set in 450 acres of rolling countryside all of which is available for recreation and walking. This large touring park has been developed in the fields and farm buildings surrounding the attractive old farm house. There are 570 pitches on four slightly sloping meadows for all units. Unseparated, they are numbered and marked, most pitches have electricity (10A) and there are well placed water points. Awnings are free in low seasons if breathable groundsheets are used, and cheaper in high season. The four identical toilet blocks are kept clean and provide good, functional facilities with free hot water to the washbasins, which are in rows and set in flat surfaces, and to the dishwashing sinks. Showers are on payment and each block has laundry facilities including irons and boards. The old farm buildings have been converted into a well stocked shop (with holiday goods, gas and camping accessories) and a takeaway service with a restaurant area. There is a new reception area with toilet facilities adjacent which include private washrooms and facilities for disabled visitors. The original stables have become the Old Stable Bars, refurbished recently to a high standard and entertainment in high season includes barn dances, discos, karaoke and other musical evenings. A barn houses a good, 22 x 10 m. swimming pool (heated Easter - end-Sept) at a small charge (60p) and the park has its own riding stables. Other activities available include an 18-hole pitch and putt golf course, games room (with pool tables, table tennis and amusement machines), snooker room, crazy golf, bicycle hire, 'kiddies kar' track (all charged for) and a large children's play area. Children will also be entertained by the under cover mini-zoo (Petorama) where they can handle many sorts of animals (on payment). Games and activities organised in high season. Dogs are welcome in one section (max. 2 per pitch) with an exercise area. Public phone and tourist information at reception. Fishing and boat launching 4 miles. Summer parking and winter caravan storage. In low season some facilities may only open for limited hours. Stowford provides plenty to keep families occupied without leaving the park, including a three mile woodland walk with cream teas possible on the way home. It is a friendly, countryside base for exploring the North Devon coast and Exmoor. The park has a series of discount offers for local attractions.

Charges 1999:
-- Per unit and car incl. 2 persons £4.50 - £9.40; extra person (over 5 yrs) free - £2.00; awning with groundsheet £2.00 - £2.50, without free - £1.50; extra car or small tent £2.00; dog 60p - £1.00; electricity £1.00 - £1.50.
-- Reduced fees for over-50s in low and mid seasons.
-- VAT included.
-- Credit cards accepted.
Open:
Easter - end October.
Address:
Combe Martin,
Ilfracombe,
N. Devon EX34 0PW.
Tel:
(01271) 882476.
FAX: (01271) 883053.
E-mail: enquiries@
stowford.co.uk.
Reservations:
Any length, deposit £2 per night, £12 per week, £20 per fortnight.
Balance due 28 days before arrival.

see colour advert between pages 32/33

Directions: From Barnstaple take A39 towards Lynton. After 1 mile turn left on B3230 and right at garage on A3123 to park 1½ miles. O.S.GR: SS560427.

070 Greenacres Touring Caravan Park, Bratton Fleming

Neat, quiet, small park near Barnstaple, on edge of Exmoor; no tents.

A nice compact, rural park on the edge of Exmoor, Greenacres is managed and run alongside, but separately from, the working farm owned by the family. Drive through the farm access to the park (clearly signed) - you will need to go back and call at the house to book in. There are 30 good sized pitches (no tents), well drained with connecting gravel paths to the road - in theory you can get to your unit without stepping on the grass; 22 electric hook-ups (16A). The top area is level, the lower part next to the beech woods is semi-terraced to provide six hardstandings and three hedged places. There are marvellous views outside the beech hedge which shelters the site. The toilet block, in the centre of the horseshoe layout has been well designed. It has vanity style washbasins with plenty of room, showers (20p) and an en-suite room for disabled people which doubles as a baby room. Laundry room, with spin dryer, iron and board, and dishwashing room, both with free hot water to sinks. Chemical disposal. Gas supplies. An area for children with net and swings is separated by a Devon bank from the 2 acre dog field. Fishing 3 miles, riding 5 miles, golf 12 miles. To the west of Exmoor, the park is very suitable for the coast at Ilfracombe and Combe Martin, or for exploring the moor. A walk across fields to a secluded valley picnic area beside a stream takes advantage of the marvellous views and surroundings.

Charges 1999:
-- Per unit incl. 2 persons £3.50 - £7.00; extra person 50p - £1.00; child (under 7 yrs) free; awning £1.00 - £1.50; dog free; electricity £1.50.
-- No credit cards.
-- VAT included.
Open:
Easter/1 April - 31 Oct.
Address:
Bratton Fleming,
Barnstaple,
Devon EX31 4SG.
Tel:
(01598) 763334.
Reservations:
Made with £5 deposit - contact park.

Directions: From North Devon link road (M5, exit 27) turn north at South Molton on to the A399. Continue for 9 miles, past turning for Exmoor Steam Centre and on to Stowford Cross. Turn left towards Exmoor Zoological Park and Greenacres is on the left. O.S.GR: SS663404.

Somerset

146 Lakeside Touring Caravan Park, Exebridge, nr. Dulverton

Attractively situated park with hillside views, for caravans or motorcaravans only.

Lakeside is a modern park in a rural situation with panoramic views across the valley to wooded hills (very special in the autumn) and within walking distance of the small village of Exebridge. The sloping, neatly mown grass field provides 50 pitches, all with 15A electricity and 9 with level hardstanding. Water and rubbish bin points are central. The top of the next field provides room for ball games, whilst the rest grows naturally. While the grass and wild flowers are growing, paths are mown to provide a 1¼ mile dog walk. Below the main field is the modern, heated, very well equipped toilet block which is light and airy with roomy showers, vanity style washbasins (H&C) and chemical disposal. A separate room, also heated, has a dishwashing and laundry sink, washing machine and dryer, also a small freezer and a good supply of tourist information. A rather unusual, very nice and useful feature is the 'Starlight Express' - an old, but rather splendid railway carriage which has been adapted as a small licensed restaurant with tables in individual compartments overlooking the lake (open Tues-Sat. evenings and for Sunday lunches). The menu, although not extensive, is rather special, but if your pocket is suffering you can always have a bar snack or takeaway. You can also walk beside the fishing lake (tickets from the local garage) to the local pub which has riverside gardens. The village shop (also the garage) makes a nice walk for the morning papers and milk. The owners say this is a site for 'relaxing, reading, sleeping or fishing!' and it certainly is peaceful with perhaps the odd buzzard overhead. However, Exmoor awaits to be explored - Tarr Steps, Dunkery Beacon, Wimbleball Lake (ideal for fishing or walking) and Doone Valley. Riding 1 miles, golf 10 miles. Winter caravan storage. A member of the Countryside Discovery group.

Charges 2000:
-- Per unit incl. 2 adults £7.00 - £9.00; extra adult £2.00; child (3-16 yrs) £1.50; full awning, pup tent or extra vehicle £1.00; porch awning 75p; dog £1.00; electricity £1.90.
-- VAT included.
-- No credit cards.
Open:
1 March - 31 October.
Address:
Higher Grants, Exebridge, Dulverton, Somerset TA22 9BE.
Tel:
(01398) 324068.
Reservations:
Made with deposit (£2 p/night, min. £10); contact park..

Directions: From M5 junction 27 take A361 towards Barnstaple. At the first roundabout turn right on A396 for Dulverton. Turn left at next roundabout by the Exeter Inn. After 2 miles at the Black Cat, there is an unusual junction - taking care go straight on, still on the A396 signed Dulverton. Site is 3 miles further on the left, just past Exebridge village sign. O.S.GR: SS932242.

136 Halse Farm Caravan and Camping Park, Winsford, Minehead

Small park adjacent to moor on Exmoor.

A really rural park with beautiful, moorland views, you may be lucky here and glimpse the red deer across the valley or be able to see Exmoor ponies and foals graze outside the main gate on one of the highest points on Exmoor Two open, neatly cut fields which are level at the top back onto traditional hedging and slope gently to the middle and bottom where wild flowers predominate. One provides electricity points (10A) and is used for motorcaravans and caravans, the other is for tents. The central, heated toilet block is of good quality. Well equipped and maintained, it has free hot water and hairdryers, a toilet, washbasin and shower for visitors with disabilities, washing machine, dryer and iron, chemical disposal facilities, telephone and tourist information. There is no reception - you leave your unit by the toilet block and walk down to the farm kitchen to book in (gas available). Play equipment. The pretty village of Winsford is 1 mile (footpath from farm) with a post office, shop, pub and restaurant. Mrs Brown has encapsulated maps available (at a small cost) detailing six walks of varying distances, starting and finishing at the farm. Also available is a list of the wild birds, flowers, etc. to be found on the site. Fishing 4 miles, bicycle hire 5 miles, riding 6 miles. Tarr Steps and Barle Valley only 3 miles. A member of the Countryside Discovery group.

Charges 2000:
-- Per unit incl. 2 adults £5.50 - £8.00; 1 person tent and car £2.75 - £4.00; extra adult £2.00 - £3.00; child 0-5 yrs 50p, 5-16 yrs £1.00 - £1.25; extra vehicle £1.00; awning £1.00; electricity £1.70 - £1.85.
-- Less 10% for 7 days paid in advance 10 days before arrival.
-- No credit cards.
Open:
25 March - 29 October.
Address:
Winsford, Minehead, Somerset TA24 7JL.
Tel:
(01643) 851259.
FAX: (01643) 851592.
E-mail: andrew_milner_brown_@msn.com.
Reservations:
Made with £5 deposit.

Directions: Turn off A396 (Tiverton - Minehead) for Winsford. In Winsford village turn left in front of the Royal Oak (not over ford) and keep on uphill for 1 mile (go slowly round the sharp bend at the bottom). Cross cattle grid onto moor and turn immediately left to farm. Caravans should avoid Dulverton - keep to the A396 from Bridgetown (signed). O.S.GR: SS898342.

137 Burrowhayes Farm Caravan & Camping Site, West Luccombe

Delightful park with riding stables on site, on the edge of Exmoor.

The stone packhorse bridge over Horner Water beside the farm entrance sets the tone of this park, which the Dascombe family have created over the last thirty years having previous farmed the land. The farm buildings have been converted into riding stables with escorted rides available. Mature trees, neat grass, partly sloping with marvellous views, or level nearer the clear, bubbling river, allows for 20 caravan holiday homes in their own area, 66 tents and 54 touring caravans or motorhomes. Electrical hook-ups are available (10A). The sanitary facilities, in the reception and stable block area, are well maintained providing free hot showers with curtain, vanity style washbasins, a fully equipped laundry room and inside dishwashing. A well stocked shop, doubling with reception, opens 8.30 am.- 6 pm. in the main season. With walking, birdwatching, plenty of wild life to observe, pretty Exmoor villages and Lorna Doone country nearby there is much to do, not forgetting Minehead, 5 miles, and the local pub only 20 minutes walk. Limited trout fishing is available in Horner Water (NT permit) alongside the park. Bicycle hire or golf 5 miles.

Directions: From A39, 5 miles west of Minehead, take first left past Allerford to Horner and West Luccombe. Site is on right after ¼ mile. O.S.GR: SS897460.

Charges 1999:
-- Per unit incl. 1 or 2 persons £5.50 - £7.50; extra person £2.00; child (3-15 yrs) £1.00; 1-man tent £4.00 - £5.00; awning 75p - £1.00; extra car or pup tent 50p; electricity £1.50.
-- Credit cards accepted.
Open:
15 March - 31 October.
Address:
West Luccombe, Porlock, Minehead, Somerset TA24 8HT.
Tel:
(01643) 862463.
Reservations:
Made with £10 deposit per pitch.

138 Blue Anchor Park, Blue Anchor, nr. Minehead

Beach-side site, for caravans and motorhomes only, with views across Bristol Channel.

Although mainly a holiday park, with 300 caravan holiday homes, Blue Anchor nevertheless offers good facilities for tourers (trailer tents accepted but not other tents), providing 103 level touring pitches with hardstanding. All have 16A electricity and are virtually in a separate touring area. Facilities on the park include a good size, irregularly shaped indoor swimming pool with an area for small children, complete with a mushroom shaped fountain. With views of the sea from the pool, it is heated and supervised, with a coffee shop. Crazy golf and an excellent, attractive children's play area in the wood. Small supermarket/shop (open 8 am - 9 pm in high season, less at other times). Sanitary facilities include large, free hot showers with push-button, vanity style washbasins, a launderette and chemical disposal facilities, in a single, modern block serving just the touring area. Although not actually within the park itself, there are both restaurants and takeaway food facilities within easy walking distance. Riding 5 miles, golf 4½ miles. The park's situation, across the small road from the beach, is unusual and gives some beautiful views across the Bristol Channel to South Wales. Dunster Castle, Exmoor, the Quantocks and Minehead are close and the West Somerset Steam Railway runs along one side of the park. No dogs are allowed. American motorhomes are accepted (max. 36 ft). Part of the Hoburne Group.

Directions: From M5 junction 25, take A358 signed Minehead. After approx. 12 miles turn left on A39 at Williton. After 4 miles right on B3191 at Carhampton signed Blue Anchor. Park is 1½ miles on right. O.S.GR: ST025434.

Charges 2000:
-- Per unit, incl. up to 6 persons, electricity and awning £6.50 - £16.00.
-- Weekend breaks available.
-- VAT included.
-- Credit cards accepted.
Open:
1 March - 31 October.
Address:
Blue Anchor Bay, nr. Minehead, Somerset TA24 6JT.
Tel:
(01643) 821360.
FAX: (01643) 821572.
E-mail: enquiries@ hoburne.co.uk.
Reservations:
For stays of 1-6 days, payment required in full at time of booking; for 7 nights or more £50 deposit. Min. bookings at B.Hs.

Somerset

134 Minehead and Exmoor Caravan Park, Minehead

Attractive small park, close to Minehead and Exmoor.

Very conveniently situated in a rural setting on the edge of Exmoor, yet only a mile from the resort of Minehead, this is a small, family run park providing 50 level pitches of reasonable size, 28 of which have electricity. The park is arranged in four small bays, separated by mature trees and hedges and terraced down to a small stream, each with around 8 pitches, and one slightly larger field. Apart from being attractive the hedges and trees help to screen the main road running past the entrance, although some traffic noise is still evident - the traffic dies down during the evening. There are few on-site facilities but it is close to the town with shops, restaurant and a pool within 1 mile. Gas supplies. Sanitary facilities in one main block can be heated and provide hot showers (20p), washbasins with hand dryers, dishwashing under cover and laundry sink (20p), spin dryer, iron and hairdryer (all 20p), plus facilities for disabled people (by key). Chemical disposal and motorcaravan services. Swing, slide and Wendy house for children. Fishing, bicycle hire, boat slipway, riding and golf, all 1 mile. Caravan storage.

Charges 2000:
-- Per adult £4.00; child (over 3 yrs) £2.00; awning £1.00; electricity £1.50.
-- No credit cards.

Open:
1 March - 31 October.

Address:
Porlock Road, Minehead, Somerset TA24 8SN.

Tel:
(01643) 703074.

Reservations:
Made for any length, details from site with SAE.

Directions: By A39 Minehead-Porlock, 1 mile west of town. O.S.GR: SS950457.

135 Quantock Orchard Caravan Park, Crowcombe, nr. Williton

Small, attractive, well cared for park with heated pool.

The old adage 'small is beautiful' certainly fits Quantock Orchard, nestling at the foot of the Quantocks in quiet countryside, yet close to many of the attractions of the area. Crowcombe Station on the West Somerset Steam Railway is only a short walk. The Brendon and Exmoor hills, Minehead, Dunster Castle and Taunton are within 10-15 miles. The park has been most attractively developed by the owners, Mr and Mrs Biggs. Mature apple trees, recently planted trees, shrubs and pretty flower beds with a nice use of heathers, make a very pleasant environment. Accessed by gravel roadways are 54 touring pitches, part separated by shrubs and hedging, and 20 for tents. Of various sizes, 55 have 10A electrical hook ups, 20 with hardstanding, 4 have TV hook-up and 2 are fully serviced, one large with patio and TV (only 'air-flo' groundsheets on grass pitches). The central, heated sanitary block with its clock tower complements the surroundings, has some nice touches and is very well maintained. Hot water is free to ample vanity style washbasins (three in cubicles for ladies) and free hot showers with good screens. An excellent family bathroom and separate baby room are well equipped. Good dishwashing , a microwave, laundry facilities and a new 'state of the art' chemical disposal unit. Other facilities include a games room, Sky TV, fenced safe based children's play area and a heated swimming pool, walled with paved sunbathing surrounds (40 x 20 ft, open May - Sept). Children must be accompanied. A leisure suite is planned for 2000 with sauna, steam room, jacuzzi, spa and min-gym (membership optional). Four barbecues and picnic tables are set in the central grass area. Mountain bikes, some with buggies for children, may be hired. The well stocked licensed shop includes camping accessories and tourist information is in the TV room. A fish and chip van visits (twice weekly in summer). B&B is possible. The Carew Arms serving meals is within walking distance in the mellow village of Crowcombe. Caravan storage Oct. - March.

Charges 2000:
-- Per unit incl. 2 adults and children under 3 yrs £7.00 - £10.45; medium or small tent £6.90 - £8.95; extra adult £2.50; child 3-5 yrs 75p, 5-16 yrs £1.75; child's pup tent with caravan £1.00; electricity £2.00 - £2.20; backpacker or cyclist £3.30 - £4.20 per person.
-- Winter weekend special rates.
-- VAT included.

Open:
All year.

Address:
Flaxpool, Crowcombe, Taunton, Somerset TA4 4AW.

Tel:
(01984) 618618.
FAX: as phone.

Reservations:
Made with £10 per week deposit, per booking (non-returnable).

Directions: Park is west off A358 road (Taunton - Minehead), about 1 mile south of Crowcombe village. O.S.GR: ST140363.

148 Home Farm Holiday Park and Country Club, Burnham-on-Sea

Large, well run park with a wide range of facilities.

Home Farm is impressive - neatly and attractively laid out, well organised and professionally run. Over 500 pitches are regularly laid out on level mown grass, all clearly marked, 160 with hardstanding, accessed by hard-core roadways and divided into various sections (i.e. an area for those with pets or a tenting area, etc). Electrical connections (16A) are available everywhere (fewer in the tenting area) with plenty of water points in all sections, but one central refuse area. Toilet blocks, five in total, are good, heated and well situated for all parts of the park. Free hot showers in the newest block are family size minus dividers, there are vanity style washbasins and also some bathrooms (key with £5 deposit). A baby bath is in one block. Dishwashing facilities are under cover at two blocks and a very well equipped laundry room is in the block nearest the pool. Chemical disposal facilities. A large, modern pool with paved surrounds and a paddling section is neatly walled and overlooked by a pool-side terraced restaurant and takeaway. A sun-bed is also available. Other facilities include a shop with general groceries, camping accessories and camping gaz. Reception holds a good supply of tourist information. There are two playgrounds for children. One a rather unusual adventure type with interesting tunnels and places to hide, the other equipped with more traditional pieces. A children's club for 4- 10 year olds runs in the school holidays. Amusement machines and pool hall for those interested. The club house is a feature of the site providing carvery meals, a range of entertainment, a function room and a wide screen TV. Outside is a very attractive barbecue area, partly under cover formed by using old bricks and tiles which gives a distinctly `olde worlde' look. Other on site amenities include fishing and boating lakes (paddle and bumper boats to hire), BMX and go-karting tracks. In all, it is an excellent provision and Burnham-on-Sea is only a mile away. There is a footpath from the site but you must cross the railway line. With Berrow Sands and Brean Down there is over seven miles of beach to choose from!

Directions: Home Farm is ¼ mile from M5 junction 22 and the A38. It is signed from the B3140 into Burnham-on-Sea. O.S.GR: ST327493.

Charges guide:
-- Per pitch incl. 2 adults, electricity and awning £7.50 - £16.50; small tent incl. 2 persons and car £6.00 - £14.50; extra person over 11 yrs £2.00 - £4.00, 4-10 yrs £1.00 - £2.00; extra car £2.00 - £3.00; dog 50p - £1.00; hardstanding £2.00.
-- Reductions for over 50s in low seasons.
-- Special breaks available.
-- VAT included.
-- Credit cards accepted.
Open:
All year.
Address:
Edithmead, Burnham-on-Sea, Somerset TA9 4HD.
Tel:
(01278) 788888.
FAX: (01278) 780113.
E-mail: homefarm holidaypark@ compuserve.com.
Reservations:
Contact park for details.

149 Greenacres Camping, North Wootton, nr. Shepton Mallet

Rural site in Somerset countryside for tents, trailer tents and motorcaravans only.

Hidden away below the Mendips and almost at the start of the 'Levels', Greenacres is a simple green site - a haven of peace and quiet. The grass is neatly trimmed over the 4.5 acres and hedged with mature trees, though there is a view of Glastonbury Tor in one direction and of Barrow Hill in the other. Thirty perimeter pitches are well spaced and allow central space for ball games, whilst the narrower neck end is ideal for 'adults only' and bird watchers. Wild life abounds. The central wooden toilet block is simple but perfectly acceptable, with free hot showers accessed direct from the outside, H&C water to washbasins and two dishwashing sinks, and all is kept nice and clean. Some children's play equipment with a caravan to use as a play house completes the provision on site but across the lane (gate is always keep shut), at the owner's bungalow where the office is situated, you can find a fridge, freezer, library, tourist information and bicycle hire. Batteries may be charged or borrowed and you may find the 'Turf Rider' which tows the cart used to give children an evening ride (a speciality of the park). In North Wootton itself, ¾ mile walk, is a large pub/restaurant and a vineyard. Fishing and riding are available nearby. There are many nearby attractions should you tire of the peace and quiet, such as Wookey Hole, Cheddar Caves and Gorge, Longleat, the beautiful small city of Wells (with leisure centre), Clarks Village, etc. You can cycle into both Wells and Glastonbury using Sustran Route 3. Dogs are not accepted.

Directions: From A39 Glastonbury - Wells road turn east at Brownes Garden Centre and follow camping signs. From A361 Glastonbury - Shepton Mallet road follow camp signs from Pilton or Steanbow. O.S.GR: ST553416.

Charges 2000:
-- Per adult £5.00; child (4-16 yrs) £1.50.
-- No credit cards.
Open:
March - October incl. plus Carnival Fortnight in Nov.
Address:
Barrow Lane, North Wootton, nr. Shepton Mallet, Somerset BA4 4HL.
Tel:
(01749) 890497.
Reservations:
Made with £2 deposit.

Somerset

139 The Old Oaks Touring Park, Wick, nr. Glastonbury

Excellent family park with extra large pitches in a rural situation.

Tucked below and hidden from the 'Tor', The Old Oaks has a lovely secluded setting with views across to the Mendips. Developed on a working farm over the last 10 years, there are 40 spacious pitches in a series of paddocks, most with 10A electricity and 18 with hardstanding; four are fully serviced (including sewage). Mainly backing on to hedges, they are attractively arranged, interspersed with shrubs and flowers in a circular development or terraced with increasing views. A quiet orchard area or a separated hedged paddock for camping and a larger field with chemical disposal facilities and plenty of space for ball games complete the provision. Mature trees and hedging combine with the mellow farm buildings to give a sense of timelessness, tranquillity and peace. The heated toilet block, converted from the old stables, is of excellent quality with fully equipped, controllable showers and some basins in cubicles, the others vanity style. It is nicely tiled and finished, with free hot water except for the thoughtfully provided bathroom (£1). Disabled visitors have a toilet and basin, together with a shower, toilet and basin next door, with level access. A baby room, well equipped laundry room and covered dishwashing complete the block which is neatly paved outside and has digital security locks (a public footpath from the Tor passes through the farm). Chemical disposal and motorcaravan service facilities are provided, plus two recycling points, a freezer for ice packs (free) and a useful dog wash. An interesting new development features reed beds to deal with waste water, a traditional method which is now coming into its own again as we have seen at Oakdown Touring Park (no. 102). The reception/shop is modern, yet in keeping, providing tourist information and basic food supplies including off licence (limited hours). Off the old farm courtyard a converted family games room with table tennis, and an extra room with two pool tables and fenced play area for younger children are useful provisions. The fishing pond (coarse) costs £2 per half day for adults, £1 per child. Whether you fish or not, the pond is worth a visit with its view of the Tor or just to see the ducks and chickens on your way there. Bicycle hire 3 miles, riding 5 miles and golf 6 miles. Market day is Tuesday. In an area steeped in history and legend, this is a very well equipped and maintained park which should meet the needs of the discerning family camper or caravanner.

Charges 2000:
-- Per unit incl. 2 adults £9.00; extra adult £3.00; child (3-15 yrs) £2.00; awning with breathing groundsheet only £1.00; porch awning 50p; dog 50p - 75p electricity £1.75; `all service pitch £1.00.
-- Walker, cyclist or single person less 75p per pitch.
-- Reduction for O.A.Ps in low season.
-- Credit cards accepted.
-- VAT included.

Open:
1 March - 31 October.

Address:
Wick Farm, Wick, Glastonbury, Somerset BA6 8JS.

Tel:
(01458) 831437.
FAX: (01458) 835108.

Reservations:
Recommended for high season and made with £15 deposit.

Directions: Park is north off A361 Shepton Mallet - Glastonbury road, 2 miles from Glastonbury. Take unclassified road signed Wick for approx. 1 mile and the park is on the left. O.S.GR: ST521394.

140 The Isle of Avalon Touring Caravan Park, Glastonbury

Well planned, modern park with excellent facilities, 10 minutes walk from town centre.

This pleasant, modern park, owned by Mike and Sharon Webb, has a friendly atmosphere. Developed on flat, grassy ground, the park has been landscaped, part with trees and shrubs, part open, to provide 70 individual pitches. Well spaced out and connected by hard roads, they have hardstanding with adjacent grass for awning and electrical points (5/10A). A further 50 tent spaces are on the adjoining, level field. Water and refuse points are well spaced around and attractively surrounded by trees and shrubs. All units are personally seen to their pitches. A single, excellent, tiled toilet block is comfortable and spacious, and can be heated. It provides large, controllable hot showers, basins in cubicles for women and excellent units for disabled visitors (plus ramps to the shop and reception). Large laundry room and dishwashing area. Chemical toilet and motorcaravan disposal point. American motorhomes are welcome. A well stocked shop and reception with gas and tourist information is at the entrance with a well cared for, attractive and spacious feel with beautiful hanging baskets. The top corner of the tenting field is left clear as a playing area for children and parents and bicycle hire is available. Riding or golf 2 miles, fishing 200 yds. Glastonbury centre, with shops, restaurants and cafés, and the Abbey are a short walk and there are indoor and outdoor swimming pools at Street. The nearby town of Street is famous for its shoes and the 'Clark's Village' development with many factory outlets for well known high street names. Winter caravan storage.

Charges 1999:
-- Per unit £4.95 - £5.95 (American style motorhomes +£1.00); hiker or car with small tent £3.95 - £4.95; adult £1.95; child (3-14 yrs) £1.50; awning £1.50; pup tent £1.75; electricity £1.85; dog 75p; extra car 75p.
-- VAT included.
-- No credit cards.

Open:
All year.

Address:
Godney Road, Glastonbury, Somerset BA6 9AF.

Tel:
(01458) 833618.
FAX: as phone.

Reservations:
Any length with £10 deposit.

Directions: Park is on west side of the town bypass (A39), just off B3151 (Wedmore Road) with good signs from the bypass. O.S.GR: ST495397.

141 Broadway House Holiday Caravan and Camping Park, Cheddar

Family owned, characterful touring park with some holiday caravans and activities for all ages, beside Cheddar Gorge.

An interesting and well maintained park offering a range of facilities on continental lines, Broadway has been developed by the Moore family with 'T.L.C'. over a period of 30 years. On a gently sloping area at the foot of the Mendips, the park takes 250 touring units of all types. From the entrance, after the neat caravan holiday home area, a series of touring areas graduates upwards, culminating in a tent and overflow rally field. The central access avenue is lined by trees with the groups of pitches on either side separated by ranch style fencing or hedging and landscaped with trees and shrubs and interesting `bygones'. Most of the 150 pitches have electrical connections (16A) and 10 have water and drainage. This park aims to cater for the normal active family - single sex groups are actively discouraged. The large, purpose built, tiled toilet block at the start of the touring area has a good provision of showers, with seat and hooks, vanity style washbasins and eight private cabins. Behind it are 10 family shower units with shower, bidet and washbasin, two of which are `disabled friendly'. Extra facilities, newly refurbished with bathroom (coin operated) and a unit for the disabled are available near reception, with a `portacabin' type unit in the top tenting field. Other facilities include a babies' room, coin operated hairdryers, washing up sinks and a new, well equipped launderette. There is a secluded heated pool (60 x 25 ft.) and children's pool (Easter - Sept.) with grass sunbathing area and shade from silver birches, but a sun bed is also available! The range of activities now organised from the park is wide and includes abseiling, canoeing, hill-walking, archery, shooting, caving, mountain biking (bicycles for hire), windsurfing can also be arranged and there is a dry ski slope nearby. Fishing ½ and 5 miles. On site is an adventure playground, football field, indoor table tennis, barbecue area, target golf, boules pitch, skateboard ramp, croquet, games/amusements room, family room and large screen TV and tourist information room. Dogs (not dangerous breeds) are accepted and there is a dog exercise field. Two animal enclosures have a variety of interesting animals and Sonny the parrot is a character with a history! A nature trail leads from the park. The shop has a wide range of goods and there is a bar and café with an extensive, reasonably priced menu available at peak periods. Motorcaravan service point. Electronic barrier security. This is really a park to be experienced - there is always something to see and do from the moment you turn in the gates and everything is well signed.

Charges guide:
-- Per adult £2.00 - £4.00; child (3-14 yrs) £1.00 - £2.00; caravan or tent and car £1.00 - £6.00; motorcaravan £1.00 - £2.50; premier pitch (incl. 3 services) plus £2.00; electricity (16A) £1.50; awning, pup tent or extra car free - £1.00; dog £1.00, 2 small dogs £1.50.
-- Special discounts for longer stays and for O.A.P.s.
-- Min. charge £3.50.
-- VAT included.
-- Credit cards accepted (5% surcharge).
Open:
1 March - 30 November.
Address:
Cheddar,
Somerset BS27 3DB.
Tel:
(01934) 742610.
FAX: (01934) 744950.
E-mail: broadway.house
@btinternet.com.
Reservations:
Advisable in high season, with £5 deposit per night. Sat. - Sat. preferred for Spr. B.H. and 20/7-31/8 and essential for electric pitches.

Directions: Park entrance is on the A371 towards Axbridge, about 1 mile northwest of Cheddar. O.S.GR: ST449547.

142 Southfork Caravan Park, Parrett Works, nr. Martock

Personally run small park in pretty surroundings.

Don't be put off by the address, which is historic - it was once a 17th century flax mill, now no more. Mr and Mrs Metcalfe own and run this excellent, modern site (30 pitches on grass with gravel access road, 20 with 10A electrical hook-ups) just outside the lovely village of Martock. This orderly, quiet park is on two acres of flat, tree lined meadow near the River Parrett. All the facilities are close to the entrance. Most things are available, including an NCC approved caravan repair centre (not open Christmas and New Year). The heated, well maintained toilet block has free hot water to the washbasins and showers and there is a laundry room and chemical disposal. Children's play area. Shop with gas and limited off licence (also not Christmas and New Year). Despite the rural setting, the A303 trunk road is just ten minutes away. This area of South Somerset contains so much of interest, including historic houses and sites, the Fleet Air Arm Museum, Haynes Motor Museum and Cricket St Thomas Country Park. As the owners live on the premises, the well drained park is open all year. Three good caravans for hire. Dogs must be on leads, with a walk provided. Fishing is available (and licences) on the River Parrett a few yards from the park. Golf 3 miles

Charges 2000:
-- Per unit incl. 2 persons £6.00 - £9.00; extra person over 5 yrs £1.00; awning £1.00; porch awning 50p; dog 50p; electricity £1.80 - £2.30.
-- Credit cards accepted.
Open:
All year.
Address:
Parrett Works, Martock, Somerset TA12 6AE.
Tel:
(01935) 825661.
FAX: (01935) 825122.
Reservations:
Advisable for B.Hs. and peak season and made with £10 deposit.

Directions: From A303 between Ilchester and Ilminster take signs for South Petherton or Martock; park is mid-way on the road between the two villages (follow signs). O.S.GR: ST447187.

Alan Rogers' Discount

Less £1 per night
(max. 7)

Somerset

150 Long Hazel Caravan and Camping Park, Sparkford, nr. Yeovil

Neat, small site, well situated to explore Somerset.

Pamela and Alan Walton, who live at the park, are really enthusiastic about their park in the Somerset village of Sparkford and will make you most welcome. With neat and level grass, attractive beech hedging, silver birches and many newly planted trees, the park has a comfortable feel and provides 75 pitches for all types of units, 20 with hardstanding (with more planned). At present there are 48 electrical hook-ups (16A) and again more are planned. The heated toilet block is kept immaculate and provides well equipped free hot showers, washbasins (H&C), separate washing up sinks (H&C) and chemical disposal. Motorcaravan discharge point. New, well planned en-suite facilities are available for visitors with disabilities, with level, easily accessible pitches. A laundry is planned for 2000. Play equipment is centrally situated and a badminton net, goal nets and a 9-hole putting green are available. The entrance has been widened for easier access. Gas is available from reception. There is a post office/shop in the village selling bread baked on the premises and the Sparkford Inn provides good food. Sparkford is also home to the famous Haynes Motor Museum (½ mile), a must for those interested in the history of the world's motor industry, and the Fleet Air Arm Museum is near at Yeovilton (3 miles). You will also find several National Trust properties and gardens in the area and the park is the midway site for the Leland Trail. Riding or fishing 8 miles, golf 5 miles. Two holiday caravans to let. Note: the park edges the A303 bypass so there could be some road noise at times.

Charges 2000:
-- Per unit incl. 2 persons £8.00 - £10.00; extra person (over 5 yrs) £1.50 - £2.00; awning £2.00 - £2.50; extra vehicle £1.00; extra single tent £6.00; electricity £2.00 - £2.50.
Open:
1 March - 31 December.
Address:
Sparkford, Yeovil, Somerset BA22 7JH.
Tel:
(01963) 440002. FAX: as phone.
Reservations:
Contact park.

Directions: From Yeovil direction on A303 take road into village of Sparkford and park is signed on the left 100 yds before the Inn. O.S.GR: ST604263.

143 Mendip Heights Camping and Caravan Park, Priddy, nr. Wells

Well kept, family run park in the peaceful Mendip Hills.

Historic Priddy is the highest village in the Mendips and is famed for its annual Sheep Fair in August. Nearby are extensive Roman lead-workings, Bronze Age burial mounds, the Priddy Circle and access to Swildons Hole, one of the popular cave systems in the Mendips. The park is half a mile from the village with tranquil views across the Mendip fields characterised by dry stone walling. It has a simple charm with field margins left natural to encourage wildlife and nest boxes in the mature trees edging the three fields which comprise the site. They provide space for 90 units on mostly level short grass with 21 electric hook-ups (8 at 10A,13 at 16A) and 8 with hardstanding available. The toilet block, although of older design, is bright and cheerful, spotlessly clean and heated, with well equipped showers (coin operated), open washbasins (H&C) and a baby changing area. Chemical disposal facilities are separately situated. Separate dish-washing and laundry facilities are fully equipped and well maintained. There are water points in each field. The reception/shop doubles as the village shop and is therefore open all season selling groceries, calor gas, etc. with an off licence and tourist information. Wendy house and table tennis for children. A range of activities can also be arranged covering canoeing, abseiling, archery, caving, mountain biking and others, with equipment provided. Free guided walks are also usually available at 2 pm. on Sundays during B.Hs and the summer holidays. The park is also on the Padstow-Bristol Sustran Route 3. Fishing 6 miles, riding 2 miles, Two traditional village pubs with very different characters stand by the village green within walking distance (½ mile). Other than all that activity, places like Cheddar Gorge, Wookey Hole, Glastonbury with the Tor, Wells, Bath and Weston-super-Mare are all within a 20 mile radius. Holiday caravan to rent (6 berth). Caravan storage. A member of the Countryside Discovery group.

Charges 1999:
-- Per adult £3.25 - £3.75; child (3-15 yrs) £1.25; electricity £1.80.
-- No charge for awning, extra car or pets.
-- No credit cards.
Open:
1 March - 15 November.
Address:
Priddy, nr. Wells, Somerset BA5 3BP.
Tel:
(01749) 870241. FAX: (01749) 870368..
Reservations:
Made with £10 deposit (min. 3 nights for electricity at B.Hs).

Alan Rogers' Discount

Less 10% over 7 nights if paid in advance

Directions: From M5 exit 21 (Weston-super-Mare) take A371 to Banwell. Turn left on A368, right on B3134 and right on B3135. After 2 miles turn left at camp sign. From M4 westbound exit 18, A46 to Bath, then A4 towards Bristol. Take A39 for Wells and right at Green Ore traffic lights on B3135; after 5 miles turn left at camp sign. From Shepton Mallet, follow A37 north to junction of B3135 and turn left. Continue on B3135 to traffic lights at Green Ore. Straight on and after 5 miles turn left at camp sign. O.S.GR: ST522518.

151 Chew Valley Caravan Park, Bishop Sutton, nr. Bath

Adults only, small, secluded garden site for caravans, motorhomes and trailer tents only.

Chew Valley is run with much tender love and care by Ray and Val Belton. The result is that you pitch on neat lawns amongst colourful beds of flowers and shrubs with your car tucked away on the car park, providing a tranquil and restful atmosphere. For adults only, the park will particularly appeal to garden lovers and has actually been featured on BBC TV's Gardeners' World. A very nice touch is the small nursery 'Gone to Pot' where Val (the garden expert) does all her growing and where those staying on site can purchase some of the plants found in the garden. The same care and attention is evident in all the facilities. The sanitary block is attractively wallpapered giving a 'home from home' feel, also heated with cubicled washbasins and all the other fittings which make life comfortable. Two separate en-suite units ensure that there is an adequate provision for the 31 large pitches. Six pitches have neatly planned hardstanding and Ray will place your van for you levelling it if necessary. No groundsheets are allowed. A useful utility room is for dish or hand washing with spin drier and washing machine for service washes only. Chemical disposal and refuse points and two water points are all clearly marked, neat and well maintained including reception where a warm welcome awaits. Tourist information and a small library with coffee are next door. Animals are welcome with a dog walk provided. The village is only 100 yds up the road with a useful general store, newsagent, two pubs and a post office. Supermarkets are within 15 minutes drive. Chew Valley lake is a walk of about half a mile with trout fishing available and Blagdon lake is popular for birdwatching. Bristol and Bath are within an easy distance and Cheddar Gorge or Longleat make excellent days out. A new member of the Best of British group.

Charges 1999:
-- Per pitch incl. electricity, awning, pets and TV hook-up £7.00; adult £4.00.
Open:
All year.
Address:
Ham Lane,
Bishop Sutton,
North Somerset
BS39 5TZ.
Tel:
(01275) 332127.
FAX: (01275) 332664.
Reservation:
Advisable for B.Hs.

Directions: From Bath direction on A368 turn right opposite the Red Lion pub. Road appears a little narrow but continue past a small track to the left (50 yds) for a further 50 yds. Park entrance appears on your left with neat, clear entrance. O.S.GR: ST584599.

144 Baltic Wharf Caravan Club Site, Bristol

Excellent, small, city centre site, open all year, operated by the Caravan Club.

This gem of a little site in Bristol's re-developed dockland is well laid out and maintained with access via a lockable gate to the Baltic Wharf dockside. It is screened from the road by a high wall with a boatyard on one side and residential apartments on the other, and is well designed with a good use of trees. The view across the dock towards Clifton village and Bristol is unique and you can even glimpse the suspension bridge (lit up at night - quite effective). The 58 pitches are accessed by a circular tarmac road - the central nine are on grass (these are not used in the winter), the rest on stone chippings and ideal for all year round use (steel pegs are provided). All are supplied with 16A electricity. Two neat bin compounds have waste and fresh water points and a motorcaravan service point. The toilet block (with coded access) is heated for winter use and provides good clean facilities including controllable showers and, for ladies, washbasins in cubicles well equipped with hooks, mirrors, etc. Good new facilities are provided for visitors with disabilities, plus toilets for the walking disabled and showers in the main block. Dishwashing under cover, good fully equipped laundry room and enclosed chemical toilet disposal. Overall, it is an excellent provision and there is also a tourist information room and a public phone (card or cash). Reception is manned 8 am.- 8 pm. and the helpful wardens live on the site. A small general store with off licence and newsagent is 200 yds. Dogs are welcome but there is no dog walk. It is a 30 minute walk to the city centre, a ferry is available (weekends only in winter) or a regular bus service (every 30 mins, 7.30 am.- 6 pm). An extra ferry runs from the SS Great Britain. TV reception is poor but a booster may be hired for 55p per night with cable on free loan. Golf 2 miles. The Sustran cycle route 3 ends here. All in all, this is a well serviced situation complete with a pub nearly next door. It is a very popular site so advance booking is necessary. Arrive by 8 pm.

Charges 1999:
-- Per pitch £6.00 - £7.00; person £3.25 - £4.00; child (5-16 yrs) £1.10 - £1.20; electricity £1.45 - £2.20.
-- Credit cards accepted.
Open:
All year.
Address:
Cumberland Road,
Bristol BS1 6XG.
Tel:
0117 926 8030 (8 am. - 8 pm. only).
Reservations:
Always advised, essential in high seasons, and made with £5 deposit; contact the Wardens with SAE for confirmation.

Directions: Easiest access is to follow signs for the `Historic Harbour' and SS Great Britain. Site is just west of SS Great Britain, on right behind a high wall - look carefully for the club sign (no brown signs to follow). O.S.GR: ST572718.

145 Bath Marina and Caravan Park, Bath

Good, purpose-designed touring park for caravans and motorhomes only.

Bath Caravan Park (formerly Newbridge) is under the same ownership as the next door Marina and is a useful, well run park from which to visit historic Bath or Bristol. Indeed, there is a park-and-ride facility for Bath outside the entrance, and the Bath to Bristol cycle path is nearby. Originally developed by Bath City Council (one can still see signs of this in the design) but now run by John and Gail Churchill, it provides 89 pitches for caravans or motorcaravans (no tents). With hardstanding and 16A electricity, they are pleasantly interspersed with grass and flowering trees and bushes. A newer circular area near reception has landscaped hardstanding for the van only with extra, separate hardstanding for the car. One `super' pitch has full services (electricity, water, drain and TV aerial). A reader tells us that TV reception is not good. The two toilet blocks are heated, have plenty of free hot water and are quite well done out. Showers lack shelf space but there are plenty of hooks and stools outside, vanity style washbasins are in semi-cubicles and hair dryers are provided. Both blocks have digital locks. En-suite facilities for disabled people, fully equipped laundry room, outside, under cover dishwashing and chemical disposal at each block. The reception/shop (for essentials and gas) has tourist information as well as necessities for the Marina. A gate provides access to the `Boathouse', a bar with a terrace fronting the River Avon and useful for snacks. Children's play park next door. Public phone (card). Fishing on site, bicycle hire, riding, golf, boat launching within 2 miles. A useful park.

Charges 1999:
-- Per pitch £9.00; adult £2.00; child (5-15 yrs) £1.00; electricity (16A) £2.00; awning free; extra car £1.00; dog free.
-- Winter special (1/11-28/2): £12 per unit inclusive.
-- VAT included.
-- Credit cards accepted.
Open:
All year.
Address:
Brassmill Lane,
Bath BA1 3JT.
Tel:
(01225) 424301 or
428778.
FAX: as phone.
Reservations:
Any length with £10 deposit.

Directions: From M4 exit 18 take A46 for Bath for 8 miles to A4 T-junction. Turn right following signs for Bath city centre to main traffic lights at A36 intersection. Turn left on A36 signed Bristol. After 2 miles, just after Little Chef on right, turn right at traffic lights crossing over river to Newbridge. Immediately turn right next to petrol station into Brassmill Lane. Park is 100 yds on right. O.S.GR: ST720655.

166 Piccadilly Caravan Park, Lacock, Chippenham

Attractive, small, quiet park, family owned and run.

Piccadilly is set in open countryside close to several attractions in northern Wessex, notably Longleat, Bath, Salisbury Plain, Stourhead, and Lacock itself. The park is neat and tidy and the landscaped shrubs and trees are maturing, giving the impression of three separate areas. There are 40 well spaced, clearly marked pitches, 11 of which have hardstanding. Electricity (10A) is available on 34 pitches. The one heated toilet block is exceptionally well maintained with free controllable hot showers in large cubicles, with excellent seat, and washbasins with ample shelving, hooks and mirrors, shaving sockets and hairdryers. It should be adequate for peak period use. A dishwashing area within the block provides four sinks, and there is a laundry room and chemical disposal. Public phone. Dog exercise walks from park. Limited gas supplies and papers can be ordered. There are no other on-site facilities save a small, bark-based children's playground and a large, grassed ball play area. Fishing 1 mile, bicycle hire 6 miles, riding 4 miles, golf 3 miles. Bus service from Lacock village to Chippenham.

Charges 2000:
-- Per unit incl. 2 persons £8.00; extra person over 5 yrs 50p; electricity £1.50.
-- VAT included.
-- No credit cards.
Open:
Easter/1 April - October.
Address:
Folly Lane West,
Lacock, Chippenham,
Wiltshire SN15 2LP.
Tel:
(01249) 730260.
Reservations:
Any length; deposit of 1 nights fee.

Directions: Park is signed west off A350 Chippenham - Melksham road (turn to Gastard) by Lacock village. 300 yds. to park. O.S.GR: ST911682.

A great place for the great outdoors.

If you're looking for a holiday that gives you everything you could want, look no further than Sandy Balls - the only holiday Park twice voted winner of the coveted 'England for Excellence Caravan Holiday Park of the Year Award'.

- Spectacular New Forest setting
- Spacious pitches with electricity, water and satellite TV hook-up
- Indoor and outdoor pools, sauna, solarium, fitness suite and more
- Adventure playground, games room and large screen video
- Spar store, launderettes and gift shop
- Woodside Inn family pub
- Pizza/pasta bar and grill

For a free colour brochure phone

01425 653042

quoting ref: AROG

Sandy Balls

New Forest Country Holidays

OPEN ALL YEAR ROUND

Sandford
in Dorset

beautiful spaces
in breathtaking places!

Sandford Holiday Park is situated in an area of outstanding natural beauty near the New Forest, Bournemouth & Poole.

★ Choose a spacious pitch with super or electric hook-up for your touring caravan, motorcaravan or tent.

★ Enjoy a relaxing break by the indoor or outdoor pools or join in all the fun in one of the entertainment venues.

★ All the convenience of a restaurant, takeaway, bars, supermarket & launderette.

★ Eurotents, holiday homes and lodges are also available.

★ Rallies and group bookings welcome.

South Coast & New Forest

With two high quality destinations to choose from, Shorefield Country Parks offers you the best of both worlds in touring locations

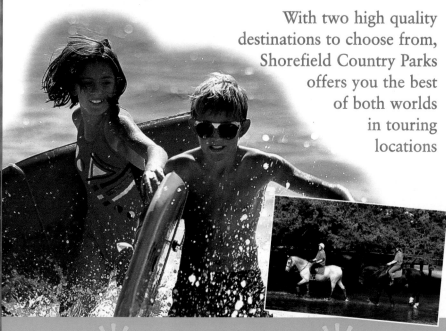

LYTTON LAWN

Set in beautiful natural parkland close to Milford beach and the historic New Forest with views to the Isle of Wight. Peaceful, unspoilt and relaxing. Electricity hook-up, showers, laundrette, shop, 'Premier Pitches' and a children's area. Free Leisure Club facilities 2¹/₂ miles away, at Shorefield.

OAKDENE
FOREST PARK

Over 55 acres of beautiful parkland giving direct access to the Avon Forest, and only 9 miles from Bournemouth's sandy beaches. Brand new indoor and outdoor pools from Easter 2000, riding stables, adventure playground, sauna, solarium, gym, club with entertainment, cafeteria, takeaway, general store and launderette.

SHOREFIELD
COUNTRY PARKS

RALLIES WELCOME AT BOTH SITES

For further details telephone

01590 648331 Ref. A.R.

ENGLAND FOR EXCELLENCE
THE ENGLISH TOURIST BOARD
AWARDS FOR TOURISM

Oakdene Forest Park, St. Leonards, Ringwood, Hants BH24 2RZ
Lytton Lawn, Lymore Lane, Milford on Sea, Hants SO41 0TX
e-mail: holidays@shorefield.co.uk   Fax: 01590 645610   http//www.shorefield.co.uk

Countryside Discovery

Our peace and quiet is worth shouting about

Experience the Peace & Tranquility of Britain's most beautiful countryside

COUNTRYSIDE
DISCOVERY

For a **FREE** brochure with full details of all our parks and types of
accommodation, please telephone our brochure line on –
01986 788646

Britain's best rural holiday parks

168 Plough Lane Caravan Site, Kington Langley, nr. Chippenham

New touring site in north Wiltshire, for adults only.

Opening for its first season in '98, this is a good example of a well designed modern touring site. The 35 pitches all have electricity (16A) with gravel access roads and borders stocked with newly planted shrubs and trees. By the 2000 season, 25 pitches will be half hardstanding, half grass and the remaining 10 will have level hardstanding wheel bases for caravans, The sanitary building is heated, spacious, light and airy, and has all the usual facilities including roomy showers, washbasins (some in cubicles), with a hairdressing area for the ladies. The separate room for disabled visitors has WC, washbasin and a pre-mix hot shower, with a ramped access. Hot water is free throughout. Dishwashing sinks are under cover at the front of the building and the laundry has two further dishwashing sinks, laundry sinks, a free spin dryer, a washing machine and dryer (tokens from reception) and ironing facilities. Chemical disposal. Public telephone kiosk. Tourist information is available in reception. Local facilities include a supermarket, two public houses, and two garages - both of which stock Calor and Camping Gaz. Golf less than 1 mile. This site is an ideal base for visiting Bath, Westonbirt Arboretum and the many attractive villages of north Wiltshire and south Gloucestershire. This park is for adults only.

Charges 1999:
-- Per unit incl. 2 adults and electricity £10.00; extra adult £3.00; extra car £2.00.
-- VAT included.
-- No credit cards.
Open:
1 March - 31 October.
Address:
Plough Lane,
Kington Langley,
nr. Chippenham,
Wiltshire SN15 5PS.
Tel:
(01249) 750795.
FAX: as phone.
Reservations:
Made with £10 deposit..

Directions: From M4 junction 17 turn south on A350 for 2 miles, then turn left at traffic lights where site is signed. From Chippenham head north on A350 (towards M4), approaching traffic lights (signed for site and Kington Langley) you will need the right hand lane. O.S.GR: ST915765.

169 Longleat Caravan Club Site, Longleat, Warminster

Rural park in amazing situation for caravans, motorcaravans and trailer tents only.

What a magnificent situation in which to find a caravan park, amidst all the wonders of the Longleat Estate including the Elizabethan House, Safari Park, the collection of Mazes (including the world's largest), not to mention Doctor Who and the Daleks and the Adventure castle! These are just some of the attractions to be found here to suit all ages amidst a beautiful rural parkland setting. Visitors can roam the woodlands (leaflets are available on a range of walks) and enjoy the views, watch the wildlife and marvel at the azaleas, bluebells, etc. according to the season or listen to the occupants of the Safari Park.

Charges 1999:
-- Per pitch £6.00 - £7.00; adult £2.60 - £4.00; child (5-16 yrs) £1.10 - £1.20; electricity £1.45 - £2.20; extra car, boat or trailer £1.00.
Open:
26 March - 1 November.
Address:
Warminster,
Wiltshire BA12 7NL.
Tel:
(01985) 844663.
Reservations:
Advisable for B.Hs and school holidays and made with £5 deposit.

The site itself, well managed by Caravan Club wardens, is situated in 10 acres of lightly wooded, level grassland within walking distance of the house and gardens. There are 151 spacious pitches, a few with gravel hardstanding for motorhomes, connected by circular tarmac roadways and with 16A electricity available on all, including the late arrivals area. The centrally situated, heated toilet block is well equipped with curtained wash cubicles for ladies, non-slip bases to controllable showers and a vanity section with shelf, mirrors and hairdryers. A separate laundry room, covered dishwashing, chemical toilet disposal and motorcaravan service point are provided. Water points and re-cycling bins are neatly walled with low night lighting. Children's play area and dogs welcome on a lead. The office is manned 8.30 am - 6 pm and stocks basic food items. Papers can be ordered, gas is available and a nice touch - a paperback exchange library. A fresh fruit and vegetable van drives around the site and a fish and chip van calls. A separate wooden chalet houses all the tourist information but the wardens will help you to get the best out of your stay at Longleat.

Directions: The main entrance to Longleat which caravans must use is signed from the A362 Frome-Warminster road near to where it joins the A36 Warminster bypass. Turn into the estate and follow the Longleat House route through the toll booths for 2 miles then follow caravan club signs for 1 mile. There are shorter ways to leave the site. O.S.GR: ST806434.

Wiltshire / West Dorset

167 Alderbury Caravan and Camping Park, Whaddon, nr. Salisbury

New touring park, convenient for visiting Salisbury and the New Forest.

Located at the southern end of Alderbury/Whaddon village, this recently developed park is on level ground, with a gravel access road to the 39 numbered pitches; 26 have access to electricity (16A). The park has some mature trees for shade, plus younger trees, shrubs and flowers. Developments continue with more hardstandings, extra chemical disposal and waste water points, site lighting, more shrubs and trees, and a rally field. The centrally located toilet block is practical, clean and well maintained. It provides hot showers in cubicles with curtain and seat, washbasins set in vanity units, WCs, a separate unit for disabled visitors, a dishwashing sink also in a separate room and chemical disposal. All hot water is free and there are water points around the site. The village shop and post office, a pub serving meals, public phone and a bus stop are within easy level walking distance of the entrance. There are hourly bus services to Salisbury, Southampton and Romsey. Good coarse fishing is available within 1 mile and the country lanes around the area are good for cycling and walking. Fishing 1 mile, bicycle hire 3 miles, riding 2 miles, golf 5 miles. The Cathedral and its Close are well worth a visit. There is some road noise, most noticeable at the far end of the park.

Charges 1999:
-- Per unit incl. 2 adults £7.50; extra adult £2.00; child (under 14 yrs) £1.00; awning £1.00; electricity £1.90.
-- No credit cards.
-- VAT included.
Open:
All year.
Address:
Southampton Road, Whaddon, Salisbury, Wiltshire SP5 3HB.
Tel:
(01722) 710125.
Reservations:
Write or phone park for details.

Directions: From Salisbury take A36 towards Southampton and, after 3 miles (at far end of dual-carriageway section), turn left at sign to Alderbury and Whaddon, then right, over bridge, and left for park entrance. From Southampton on A36 towards Salisbury, continue past A27 (Romsey) junction and over Pepperbox Hill. At end of a downhill straight, left onto slip road marked Alderbury, park is signed. O.S.GR: SU198263.

181 Newlands Caravan Park, Charmouth, nr. Lyme Regis

Family park with range of facilities including indoor and outdoor pools.

This family owned park occupies a prominent position beside the road into Charmouth village with marvellous views southwards to the hills across the valley. By nature of the terrain the pitches are terraced providing over 200 well spaced for touring units, some seasonal, and 86 caravan holiday homes, 50 for hire. The tenting field of mainly sloping grass also has super views towards the sea and Lyme Regis. Electric hook ups (10A) are provided on 144 pitches and 30 of these have hardstanding, water and waste water. Other accommodation on site consists of 9 new, smart pine lodges, 15 apartments and 12 motel rooms (double and family). The lower toilet block is modern and light with roomy showers, WCs and vanity style washbasins, and has an adjoining washing up area. The other block is traditional in design with rather psychedelic tiles, but it is clean, neat and tidy. A laundry room adjoins, plus dishwashing sinks (under cover) and two chemical disposal points. Reception, the well stocked shop, restaurant including takeaway (all March - Nov), a licensed club bar (limited hours Nov-March), and swimming pools are located in a main building to one side of the wide tarmac entrance. Membership of the club is automatic and the bar is open every evening and lunch times to suit. A range of family entertainment includes a children's club during school holidays with Dino Dan (the dinosaur). Out of the main season opening hours of the facilities may vary. A 9 pin bowling alley can be hired at £5 per half hour. The smaller indoor pool and jacuzzi is open when the site is open. The adjacent outdoor pool and paddling pool is walled, paved and sheltered and the outside entrance is key coded; neither are supervised. Both pools are heated, the indoor one is charged for. The large children's play area in the field below the tent field is open dawn to dusk! I was tempted to try the maypole swing and bobsleigh ride. A comfortable site for families with the beach and village an easy walk and for those who enjoy some evening and family activity. Fishing 1 mile, riding 3 miles, golf 2 miles. Charmouth is known for its fossil finds and its connection with Jane Austen. Newlands is connected with a smaller site in the village - Seadown - which has direct access to the beach with 60 touring pitches on level grass and a number of caravan holiday homes and perhaps would be enjoyed by families looking for a quiet holiday.

Charges 1999:
-- Per pitch incl. up to 6 persons and awning £8.00 - £16.00; extra pup tent £3.00; dog (max. 2) £1.00; electricity £2.00.
-- Only one van or tent per pitch.
-- VAT included.
-- Credit cards accepted.

One of the first UK members of the French 'Camping Cheque' scheme for low season budget holidays: Contact park for details.

Open:
All year.
Address:
Charmouth, Dorset DT6 6RB.
Tel:
(01297) 560259.
FAX: (01297) 560787.
Reservations:
Made with £30 deposit per week.

see colour advert between pages 65/65

Directions: Approaching from Bridport leave A35 at first sign for Charmouth at start of the bypass and site almost directly on your left. O.S.GR: SY373935.

176 Wood Farm Caravan Park, Charmouth, nr. Lyme Regis

Excellent family run park maintained to a high standard for all units, with indoor pool.

Wood Farm is a very well kept park on the western side of Charmouth beside the A35 (some road noise may be expected), and only a mile or two from Lyme Regis and its beaches. Part of the Caravan Club's `managed under contract' scheme (non-members are also very welcome) and a member of the Best of British group. On sloping, well landscaped ground, it has open views across the countryside. There are 216 pitches for touring units of which 180 are neat, level all-weather pitches with hardstanding, electricity (10A) and TV connections, and provision for awnings. These are divided by neat, box-like leylandii hedging which has almost become a feature of the park. Water hook-ups are also available. One grassy terraced field takes about 25 tents and there are 80 caravan holiday homes in their own areas. American motorhomes are not accepted. Four modern, heated toilet blocks provide free hot water to the washbasins (some in curtained cubicles for ladies) and well equipped, pre-set hot showers. The lower block has been completely refurbished to a very high standard providing roomy, well equipped showers, wash cubicles, toilets, baby room and en-suite facilities for disabled people. Chemical disposal facilities are in each block. All visitors are offered temporary membership of the good on-site heated indoor swimming pool (27 x 54 ft.) on payment of £1.50 per session. A recreation hall provides a snooker room and family games area with table tennis, also an outdoor tennis court. Laundry room, shop by reception, and a children's play field (equipment on safety surface). Bikes can be ridden on site, but helmets must be worn. A fish and chip van opens 2-4 times a week (acc. to season). Dogs are accepted and there is an enclosed 2 acre dog field. A small coarse fishing lake (carp, rudd, roach, tench) is adjacent - day and weekly tickets (rod licence required, also available from park). Golf 1 mile, riding 4 miles, beaches and shops ¾ and 2 miles. Motorcaravan service point. Winter caravan storage. Caravan holiday homes to rent and two bed S.C. accommodation for visitors with disabilities.

Directions: Park is ½ mile west of Charmouth village with access near roundabout at junction of A35 with A3052 (Lyme Regis) road. O.S.GR: SY356940.

Charges 1999:
-- Per unit incl. side awning £2.00 - £5.00; adult £3.25 - £4.00; child (5-16 yrs) £1.10 - £1.20; electricity (10A) £2.00 - £2.20; mains water £1.00; dog, extra car, trailer or pup tent £1.00.
-- Special senior citizens low season discounts.
-- Credit cards accepted.
-- VAT included.

Open:
30 March - 27 October.

Address:
Axminster Road, Charmouth, Dorset DT6 6BT.

Tel:
(01297) 560697.
FAX: as phone.
E-mail: i.pointing@zetnet.co.uk.

Reservations:
Made with £30 deposit (non-returnable), min. 5 nights in high season, 3 nights other times.

173 Monkton Wylde Farm Touring Caravan Park, nr. Charmouth

Small, relaxed, family run park attached to a working farm.

Opened in 1991 by Simon and Joanna Kewley as part of a working sheep farm, Monkton Wylde is maturing nicely. Planting of flowering shrubs and trees continues (hydrangea and lavender) making an attractive, peaceful park, and a woodland walk have been created in 80 acres of the beautiful countryside surrounding the park. There is an abundance of mature trees around the perimeter providing shade and plenty of space between the 60 pitches gives a feeling of spaciousness. Most pitches have 16A electricity and around 25 have hardstanding. The modern, well maintained sanitary block has a fully equipped family room including baby facilities and which is also accessible by wheelchair. Individual showers with folding screen are very spacious, there are vanity style washbasins and all hot water is free. A small laundry has a washing machine and tumble dryer, washing up is under cover and chemical disposal facilities are provided. On site facilities are limited but an area at the top of the park has been turned into a children's play area, with a good area for ball games, climbing frame, trampoline, etc. Bread, milk and papers available in the main season. There is no reception as such, however a wooden chalet near the entrance provides information regarding pitch vacancies and the owners or the resident wardens (high season) are never far away. The gate is locked at 11 pm. A separate paddock along the lane has been set aside as a dog walk. Caravan storage. Fishing or riding 2 miles, bicycle hire, golf and boat launching 3 miles. Shops and local pubs are within a mile's walking distance and Charmouth and Lyme Regis are only 3 miles (buses leave from just along the road to both towns). A separate new site has been developed next to the existing park for Camping and Caravanning Club members, managed by the Club.

Directions: Park is signed on A35 between Charmouth and Axminster, approx. 1½ miles west of Charmouth. Turn right at Greenway Head (B3165 signed Marshwood) and park is 600 yds on the left past new Club site. Don't go to Monkton Wylde hamlet - the road is very steep. O.S.GR: SY329966.

Charges 1999:
-- Per unit incl. 2 adults £6.25 - £11.00; extra adult £1.50; child (5-16 yrs) 50p - £1.00; electricity £2.00; dog free - 75p; pup tent free - £1.00; no extra charge for awnings, 2nd car, boats or visitors.
-- No credit cards.
-- VAT included.

Open:
26 March - 31 October.

Address:
Monkton Wylde Farm, Charmouth, Dorset DT6 6DB.

Tel:
(01297) 34525.
Warden (May - Sept) (01297) 631131.
FAX: (01297) 33594.

Reservations:
Made with deposit of £3 per night booked.

West Dorset

174 Golden Cap Holiday Park, Chideock, nr. Bridport

Good beach-side touring park with holiday caravans in beautiful rural situation.

Golden Cap, named after the adjacent highest cliff in southern England which overlooks Lyme Bay, is only 150 yards from a shingle beach at Seatown and is surrounded by National Trust countryside and the Heritage Coastline. The park is arranged over several fields on the valley floor, sloping down gently towards the sea. It is in two main areas, having once been two parks, each separated into fields with marvellous views around and providing 108 tourist pitches, 104 with electricity and 28 with hardstandings with drainaway, electricity and gravelled awning area, and an extra sloping tent field for peak season (torch useful). There are 211 caravan holiday homes in their own areas. American motorhomes are not accepted. The main toilet block is modern and of very good quality, with free hot water in the washbasins and spacious shower cubicles (some with toilet and washbasin), good facilities for visitors with disabilities and a baby room. There are two other smaller blocks around the park, plus a laundry room, motorcaravan service point and chemical disposal facilities. Gas is available. Useful and well stocked shop (8.30-10.30 am. and 2-6 pm) and a takeaway service each evening in peak season. Caravan sales information and tourist information rooms. A pub with food is close. The most attractive indoor swimming pool at Highlands End (same ownership) is 3 miles away and open for campers on payment. Public telephone. Dogs are accepted (poop-scoops provided). Beaches, sea fishing, boat launching, riding, fossil hunting and good walks are near, with access to the coastal path. A well run park and a member of the Best of British group.

Directions: Turn off A35 road at Chideock, (a bigger village with shops and restaurants) 3 miles west of Bridport, at sign to Seatown opposite church. Park is less than 1 mile down narrow lane. O.S.GR: SY423919.

Charges 1999:
-- Per unit incl. 2 persons and awning £7.50 - £11.75; extra adult £2.50 - £2.75; child (3-17 yrs) £1.25 - £1.40; dog £1.25 - £1.40; extra car £1.00; electricity £1.75 - £1.50; all service pitch £1.00.
-- VAT included.
-- Credit cards accepted.

Open:
20 March - 1 November.

Address:
Park: Seatown, Chideock, nr. Bridport;
Booking: West Dorset Leisure Holidays, Eype, Bridport, Dorset DT6 6AR.

Tel:
(01308) 422139.
FAX: (01308) 425672.
E-mail: highlands@wdlh.co.uk.

Reservations:
Essential in high season and made with £20 deposit (min. 4 days in high season).

175 Highlands End Farm Holiday Park, Eype, nr. Bridport

Good, well kept park on cliffs by sea, with holiday caravan and touring sections.

On slightly sloping ground with superb open views, both coastal and inland, Highlands End is quietly situated on the Dorset Heritage Coastline. With access to the coastal path, a path in front of the park runs along the cliff top and then leads down to a shingle beach a little further along. There are 180 caravan holiday homes which are mostly privately occupied but 17 are for letting. The 195 touring pitches are in two areas nearest to the sea - one has to travel through the holiday homes to reach them. All have electricity (10A) and 45 also offer water, drainage, hardstanding and a gravel awning area. A further area is used for tents in high season. The two toilet blocks, plus a good separate shower block near the tourist sections, are well kept like the rest of the park and can be heated. They provide washbasins (some in cubicles with toilets), free, pre-set hot showers and covered washing-up sinks. There is a laundry room, facilities for disabled visitors, a baby room and chemical disposal. Water points around and a motorcaravan service point. A modern, attractive building houses a lounge bar, good value restaurant with takeaway facility, family room and games room (open Spr. B.H.- late Sept.) with some musical evenings in high season. There is an excellent air-conditioned indoor heated swimming pool with attendant (20 x 9 m. and charged £1.60 per session, 90p for children), a gym room, sun beds, sauna, tennis court (all charged), snooker room, games room and tourist information room. Good children's adventure playground. A well stocked shop is beside reception (opening times vary with the season). Gas is available. Public phones. The owners are long time enthusiastic supporters of the fire brigade and an historic fire engine (1936 Leyland Pump Escape) along with memorabilia make an interesting display. Dogs are accepted (poop-scoops provided). The park was used to film scenes for Nick Berry's TV series based on nearby West Bay harbour. A well run park and a member of the Best of British group.

Directions: Follow Bridport bypass on A35 around the town and park is signed to south (Eype turning), down narrow lane. O.S.GR: SY452914.

Charges 1999:
-- Per unit incl. 2 persons and awning £7.50 - £12.00; extra adult £2.50 - £2.75; child (3-17 yrs) £1.25 - £1.40; dog £1.25 - £1.40; extra car £1.00; electricity £1.50; all service pitch (hardstanding, water and drainage, excl. electricity) £1.00.
-- VAT included.
-- Credit cards accepted.

Open:
20 March - 1 November.

Address:
West Dorset Leisure Holidays, Eype, nr. Bridport, Dorset DT6 6AR.

Tel:
(01308) 422139.
FAX: (01308) 425672.
E-mail: highlands@wdlh.co.uk.

Reservations:
Essential in high season and made with £20 deposit (min. 4 days in high season).

See colour feature for 'BEST of BRITISH' between pages 96/97

178 Freshwater Beach Holiday Park, Burton Bradstock, Bridport

Busy holiday and touring park with direct access to private beach.

Family run parks for families with direct access to a beach are rare in Britain and this one has the added advantage of being in beautiful coastal countryside in West Dorset. It is an ideal situation to explore the 'Hidden County' and the resort of Weymouth (17 miles) and is next to the sea and a beach of fine pebbles, sheltered from the wind by pebble banks. The River Bride edges the park and joins the sea here. Approached by a fairly steep access road, the park itself is on level, open ground. The 500 plus touring pitches, over 300 with 10A electricity, are on an open, undulating grass field. Caravan pitches (10 x 11 m.) are now marked, evenly spaced in lines. Some tent pitches are in the main field, with others well spaced around the edge of a slightly sloping extra field. In separate areas there are 230 caravan holiday homes, plus 60 for hire. This lively holiday park has an extensive range of facilities which include a licensed restaurant (weekends only in late season) and three bars with an evening entertainment programme in season. A range of daytime entertainment caters for all ages – don't miss the donkey derby! Also a good value supermarket and takeaway, launderette, heated and supervised outdoor swimming pool and children's pool (Whitsun - end Sept), adventure play area, pets corner, bicycle hire and pony trekking (own stables on site). A golf course is adjacent, fishing is possible from the Chesil Bank and there is a good connection to footpaths to the attractive, thatched village of Burton Bradstock or West Bay. Sanitary facilities are in two fully refurbished blocks, plus another with washbasins and toilets only, all with free hot water. They are a good provision for a busy beach park. The main blocks have facilities for disabled people, chemical disposal and a baby changing room (key system), and cleaning and maintenance seem good. Laundry and washing up sinks cope well at peak times. The overall impression is of a large, busy holiday park with a friendly reception and happy atmosphere.

Directions: Park is immediately west of the village of Burton Bradstock, on the Weymouth - Bridport coast road (B3157). O.S.GR: SY980898.

Charges 1999:
-- Per unit incl. up to 6 persons, car and awning £8.00 - £18.00; extra person £1.50; dog £2.50; electricity £2.00; small tent incl. 2 persons walking or cycling £6.00 - £11.00.
-- Single sex groups not admitted.
-- VAT included.
-- Credit cards accepted.

Open:
19 March - 7 November.

Address:
Burton Bradstock, nr. Bridport, Dorset DT6 4PT.

Tel:
(01308) 897317.
FAX: (01308) 897336.
E-mail: enquiries@fbhp.co.uk.

Reservations:
Made for min. 1 week with £10 deposit p/week, plus £1 fee. Short break reservations available - ring for details.

see colour advert between pages 65/65

177 Binghams Farm Touring Caravan Park, Melplash, nr. Bridport

Small, purpose built park in rural Brit Valley location, open all year.

Binghams has a pleasant situation 2 miles from the market town of Bridport, with views seaward towards West Bay and inland across Beaminster Downs and Pilsdon Hill. The park provides an area of individual pitches with 10A electricity and over 20 hardstandings, nicely landscaped with shrubs and trees growing between the pitches, plus an open sloping field overlooking the valley with 20 electric hook-ups. The good heated toilet block, reception and games room (with table tennis) have been sympathetically converted from the original farm buildings with an upstairs lounge bar, games room, table tennis and pool table. The toilet blocks, with under floor heating for winter use and free hot water, provide well fitted, tiled, curtained showers, vanity style washbasins, hairdryers and a separate, fully equipped room for the less able with ramped access. Laundry room and chemical disposal point. Gas is available. The entrance to the park is neatly tarmaced and resident peacocks, ducks and chickens provide interest for children, together with swings and a sand pit. Telephone. A cottage has been converted into two flats to let. Winter caravan storage. Sea fishing and golf 3 miles, bicycle hire and riding 5 miles. A path has been provided to the river which links with the main footpaths for Bridport (20 minutes) or local hostelries. Limited bus service on the main road. The Brit Valley is an unspoilt area of West Dorset with an ancient heritage and coastal West Bay is only a couple of miles.

Directions: At main roundabout on A35 road, on east side of Bridport, take A3066 towards Beaminster. Watch for site entrance after approx. 2 miles on the left. O.S.GR: SY482963.

Charges 1999:
-- Per pitch incl. 2 persons and awning £8.00 - £11.00; extra adult £2.00; child (3-15 yrs) £1,00; dog £1.00; electricity (10A) £2.00.
-- Couples and families only.
-- No credit cards.
-- VAT included.

Open:
All year.

Address:
Melplash, nr. Bridport, Dorset DT6 3TT.

Tel:
(01308) 488234.
FAX: as phone.
E-mail: royphilpott@msn.com.

Reservations:
Made with £25 non-returnable deposit per week or part.

180 East Fleet Farm Touring Park, Chickerell, Weymouth

Genuine touring park, attractively situated on the coast by the Fleet.

East Fleet Farm has a marvellous situation on part level, part gently sloping meadows leading to the shores of the Fleet, with views across to the famous Chesil Bank with the sea beyond. The Fleet is a lagoon renowned for its wildlife and popular with bird watchers. The park has been developed within the confines of a 300-acre working dairy and arable farm and is maturing nicely as trees grow. The 270 pitches are a comfortable size so there is no feeling of crowding. Of these, 97 are level and marked with 10A electricity, 25 also having hardstanding. The central sanitary block is built in natural stone and provides adequate facilities with washbasins, coin-operated showers (one heated), shaver points, hairdryers, under cover washing up (H&C) and a fully equipped laundry room with a self-contained unit for disabled people off it. Extra toilets and a family bathroom are beside the bar. This is in a converted barn and has a terrace with views over the Fleet (open high season and B.Hs). It also provides bar meals and a games room with pool table. Reception plus shop with basic groceries, bread, papers and gas, etc. opens longer in high season. Public phone. Children's play area. Remember, elsewhere this is a working farm. The busy resort of Weymouth with its safe beaches and many watersports facilities is only 3 miles away (bicycle hire and boat launching possible). Riding or golf 2 miles. Bus service from the top of the lane (approx. ½ mile). Abbotsbury Swannery and Gardens are nearby.

Directions: Park is signed from B3157 Weymouth-Bridport road, approx. 3 miles west of Weymouth. The narrow, uneven approach road is by the army camp on the southern side of the B3157. O.S.GR: SY639798.

Charges 1999:
-- Per unit incl. 2 persons £4.50 - £10.00; extra adult £1.00 - £2.50; child (5-16 yrs) 25p - 50p; awning free - £1.75; extra car, large boat £2.50; dog 25p - 75p; electricity (10A) £1.75 - £2.25.
-- Senior citizen discount in June (10%).
-- VAT included.
-- Credit cards accepted.
Open:
15 March - 31 October.
Address:
Chickerell, Weymouth, Dorset DT3 4DW.
Tel:
(01305) 785768.
E-mail: camping@ easfleet.abel.co.uk
Reservations:
Write with £20 deposit.

East Fleet Farm
Touring Park
Chickerell, Weymouth Tel: (01305) 785768

- ● Electric Hook-ups
- ● Showers
- ● Bathroom
- ● H/C Water
- ● Shop

Peaceful and spacious park on the shores of the Fleet overlooking Chesil Bank and the sea, in an area of outstanding natural beauty
Telephone for brochure

- ● 'Old Barn' family bar & restaurant
- ● Games Room
- ● Children's Play Area
- ● Toilets
- ● Laundry

201 Sandyholme Holiday Park, Owermoigne, nr. Dorchester

Tranquil, family run park near pretty Dorset village.

In Thomas Hardy country, Sandyholme is a peaceful haven which provides 46 holiday homes (privately owned or to hire) and 40 numbered pitches for touring units on level, short grass fields with one corner lightly wooded. The next door field is operated by the local farmer on a 28 day licence with use of the park's facilities (extra facilities opened in high season ensure no problems). Two toilet blocks, although of older design, are bright and well maintained, with vanity style washbasins, pre-set showers (20p) and laundry facilities in both blocks and dishwashing sinks (10p). Chemical disposal . The Holme Club (free membership) is a pleasant provision, open every evening in Easter week, May B.H. and from Whitsun to mid Sept. It has a cosy bar and patio, and a good bar meal menu. There is a games room with a pool table. The shop/reception stocks all basic necessities including papers and gas. A good, fenced, safe based children's adventure play area is next to a rather special duck pond with an amazing variety of ducks from all over the world. There is a pleasant walk with seats around the pond (an electric fence keeps the foxes at bay!) Fishing is available on an adjacent farm, bicycle hire or golf 5 miles, riding 6 miles. There are walks and cycling direct from the site or in Puddletown and Wareham Forests, or along the coastal path. Lulworth Cove, Durdle Door and Weymouth, with its sandy beach, are all near at hand.

Directions: On A352 Dorchester - Wareham road going west, watch for short dual carriageway before Weymouth-Osmington roundabout. Turn north through Owermoigne village and park is on left (signed) in ¼ mile. O.S.GR: SY768863.

Charges 1999:
-- Per pitch incl. all persons £5.75 - £11.00; awning or pup tent £1.00; dog £1.00 p/n or £5 p/w; electricity £1.75.
-- Credit cards accepted.
-- VAT included.
Open:
Easter/1April - 31 Oct.
Address:
Moreton Road, Owermoigne, Dorchester, Dorset DT2 8HZ.
Tel:
(01305) 852677.
FAX: (01305) 854677.
Reservations:
Made with £15 deposit; include SAE for receipt.

Alan Rogers' Discount

Less 50p per night for min. 2 nights

East Dorset

Southern Tourist Board

East Dorset, Hampshire, Isle of Wight, South Wiltshire, Oxfordshire, Berkshire and Buckinghamshire

40 Chamberlayne Road, Eastleigh, Hampshire SO50 5JH
Tel: 023 8062 0006 Fax: 023 8062 0010
E-mail: 100651.3040@compuserve
Internet: http://www.visitbritain.com/southern-england

The Southern Tourist Board covers three distinctive areas:

The **South Coast** comprises Weymouth and Portland with its safe sandy beach and the Isle of Portland joined to the mainland by the unique Chesil beach, and Swanage with the famous Studland beach and Purbeck hills. The cosmopolitan resort of Bournemouth, with its seven miles of golden sand, and the New Forest renowned for its trees and ponies, with its famous yachting havens of Lymington and Buckler's Hard. The Isle of Wight is just a short ferry trip across the Solent and offers a wealth of activities for all ages with a mild and sunny climate. Day trips to France are possible from Portsmouth, the flagship of Maritime England and now the home of the Mary Rose.

Rural **Southern England** consists of green rolling hills and scenic wooded valleys covering North and West Wiltshire, parts of Dorset, Hampshire, Kennet and Avon Canal country and the New Forest and the Test Valley. Worthy of mention is the beautiful medieval city of Salisbury with its inspirational Cathedral and Close, and Winchester, the city of Kings.

Thames and Chilterns, dominated by the River Thames, its tributaries and the Chiltern Hills offers a mix of internationally famous cities and sporting events, royal pomp and traditional English village life. **Buckinghamshire** inspired John Betjeman and John Milton finished 'Paradise Lost' in his cottage at Chalfont St. Giles. Benjamin Disraeli, the 19th Century Prime Minister came from near High Wycombe and the scenic village of Great Missenden was home to the great children's story teller Roald Dahl. The Oxfordshire Cotswolds has picturesque villages, the regal splendour of Blenheim Palace and market towns such as Chipping Norton. **Berkshire** is within 50 miles of London and is well known for its racing connections.

202 Ulwell Cottage Caravan Park, Ulwell, Swanage

Family run holiday park with indoor pool and wide range of facilities for families.

Nestling under the Purbeck Hills in this unique corner of Dorset on the edge of Swanage, Ulwell Cottage provides for a range of needs. A good proportion of the park is taken by caravan holiday homes (140), but an attractive, undulating area accessed by tarmac roads is given over to 77 touring units, with 68 electric hookups (16A) and 18 hardstandings, 8 of which are serviced. The mixture of level and sloping pitches, interspersed with trees and shrubs, is quite pretty. The sanitary block which serves the touring section is modern and cheerful with bright yellow doors, and can be heated. It is supplemented by an older, but good, block in the holiday home section. They are well equipped, with vanity style washbasins, pre-set showers with dividers, laundry room and baby washing sinks in both blocks, dishwashing under cover and chemical disposal. The colourful entrance area is home to the Village Inn with a courtyard adjoining the heated indoor pool complex (both open all year and open to the public), well stocked shop for gas, etc. (Easter - mid Sept) and modern reception. The pool has an additional £4.50 per person weekly charge. The inn provides bar snacks and restaurant meals with a family room. Takeaway (Spr. B.H. - early Sept). Amusement arcade with video games, playing fields and play areas with a long slide and boat. Football skills sessions in high season. Bicycle hire or riding 2 miles, fishing 1 mile, golf 1 mile. The hill above the touring area, Nine Barrow Down, is a Site of Special Scientific Interest for butterflies overlooking Round Down. It is possible to walk to Corfe Castle this way. With Brownsea Island, Studland Bay, Corfe village and the Swanage Railway, Ulwell Cottage makes a marvellous centre for holidays.

Directions: From A351 Wareham - Swanage road, turn on B3351 Studland road just before Corfe Castle, follow signs to right for Swanage and drop down to Ulwell. O.S.GR: SZ019809.

Charges 1999:
-- Per unit incl. up to 6 persons £11.50 - £20.00, with electricity £13.50 - £22.00, fully serviced with hardstanding £15.00 - £23.50.
-- Less £2.00 for two persons only, less £1.00 for three persons.
-- VAT included.
-- Credit cards accepted.

Open:
All year except 8 Jan - 28 Feb.

Address:
Ulwell, Swanage, Dorset BH19 3DG.

Tel:
(01929) 422823.
FAX: (01929) 421500.

Reservations:
Made with 25% deposit; Sat.- Sat. only in high season.

see colour advert between pages 65/65

203 Wareham Forest Tourist Park, nr. Wareham

see colour advert
between pages 65/65

Well run park in forest setting with swimming pool.

A peacefully located, spacious park in an unspoilt corner of Dorset, this site becomes very busy in high season. Developed to high standards by the present owners, it provides formal pitching, with or without hardstanding, for caravans or natural pitches for tents in pine wood or open field. Drainage appears satisfactory. The setting in Wareham Forest is attractive offering space for 200 units, 102 with hardstanding, 200 with electricity and 8 luxury pitches on hardstanding with water, drainage, TV aerial, dustbin and light (available 1 March - 31 Oct. only). A cafeteria for breakfasts, etc. (open in the main season) looks out over a patio-terrace onto the free, open-air swimming pool, which can be heated (60 x 20 ft and open all day in peak season), with a surrounding, grassed sunbathing area. Small shop with off-licence and gas (limited hours) and busy games room with amusement machines next door. The two well maintained toilet blocks are spacious and of a good standard and have some washbasins in private cubicles for ladies (plus adjustable showers on payment). The block used in the winter is centrally heated. Facilities for disabled people, well equipped laundry rooms, chemical disposal and motorcaravan service point. Large children's adventure play area on sand and grass. Dogs are welcome on leads. Forest walks. Fishing 5 miles, bicycle hire or golf 3 miles, riding 8 miles. In high season a bus service to Wareham leaves the site six times daily (mornings and teatime). The park is well situated to explore the Dorset coast and Thomas Hardy country. All year caravan storage facilities. Entrance closed 11 pm. - 7 am. Resident wardens on site.

Directions: Park is north of Wareham between Wareham and Bere Regis, located off the A35 road. O.S.GR: SY899903.

Charges 2000:
-- Per pitch: standard £4.00 - £6.00, serviced £6.00 - £8.00; adult £1.80 - £3.00; child (2-14 yrs) £1.00 - £2.00; awning, extra car 50p - £1.00; dog 50p - £1.50; electricity £2.00 - £2.25.
-- Couples/families only.
-- Discount for OAPs in low season.
-- VAT included.
-- Credit cards accepted.

Open:
All year.

Address:
North Trigon, Wareham, Dorset BH20 7NZ.

Tel/Fax:
(01929) 551393.

Reservations:
Made with £25 deposit and £2 fee, balance 28 days before arrival. High season min. 7 days for electric or serviced pitch, 3 days others.

204 Manor Farm Caravan Park, Wareham

Small, rural park near the Purbecks beside a working farm.

David and Gillian Topp own and carefully run this small, simple park which is set in a hedged, level field, now semi-broken up by newly planted evergreens. It provides 50 level, well spaced pitches, some seasonal, with 43 electrical connections (16A), on neatly cut grass. The toilet block (key system) is at the top of the field and is timber clad but modern inside with all necessary facilities and kept very clean. Hot water is available but showers are metered. There is a toilet for disabled people in the men's room. Sink for washing up and one for laundry with spin dryer (all metered), chemical disposal. An original recycling point is to be found next door for rubbish. Ice pack service and gas. Sturdy children's play unit. East Stoke village has a pub, Wool is 2 miles with a pub and shops, Wareham and Swanage are near. Fishing, bicycle hire, boat launching, riding all 3 miles, golf 4 miles. Public telephone. Caravan storage. Dogs accepted at owner's discretion.

Directions: Off A352 Wareham-Wool road, turn into lane by church, over manned level crossing and park is ½ mile on right. Or from B3070 turn right signed East Stoke, then right signed Manor Farm and site is on left. O.S.GR: SY872867.

Charges 1999:
-- Per unit incl. 3 persons £9.25 - £11.50; extra person (3 yrs and over) 50p - 75p; dog £1.50; electricity (6A) £2.00.
-- No groups, singles, motorcycles or rallies.
-- No credit cards.

Open:
April - 30 September.

Address:
1 Manor Farm Cottage, East Stoke, Wareham, Dorset BH20 6AW.

Tel:
(01929) 462870.

Reservations:
Made with £20 deposit.

205 Rowlands-Wait Touring Park, Bere Regis

Pretty, rural site with good facilities and views.

Bernard and Linda Hammick have worked hard to make Rowlands-Wait into a most attractive park catering for all types of humans and units! The top of the park, edged by mature woods (full of bluebells in spring) is a haven for tents (and squirrels) with marvellous views and providing 30 places in three descending fields. The rest of the park is a little more formal, and nearer to the central toilet block, but most pitches back on to hedging or trees and they are generally level. The toilet block is purpose built and well equipped, with free hot water except for the showers (10p, 3-4 minutes). There is a laundry room, covered dishwashing area, recycling bins and chemical disposal. A shop cum reception provides milk, papers and basic essentials and a freezer for ice packs. The village, a 10 minute walk, has shops, two pubs, etc. plus a bus service for Dorchester and Poole. A play area for little ones with miniature assault course and castle is well placed near reception and there is a games room with pool table, table tennis and two video machines behind the sanitary block and crazy golf. Public phone. Bring your own bikes or bicycle hire can be arranged and there are many walks available from the park and information on wildlife. A torch is useful. Fishing 5 miles, golf 3 miles, riding 9 miles. A warm welcome awaits, particularly for those new to camping and caravanning. A reader reports the park as "very friendly and relaxed, with few rules". The park takes bookings for groups or rallies all year. No charge is made for dogs in October. A member of the Countryside Discovery group.

Directions: Park is south of Bere Regis, just off the road to Wool, well signed from A35/A31 roundabout. O.S.GR: SY842933.

Charges 1999:
-- Per unit incl. 2 persons £5.90 - £8.90; adult £1.40 - £1.90; child (under 16 yrs) 90p; awning or pup tent £1.00; electricity (10A) £2.00; dog free - 60p; extra car, boat or trailer £1.00.
-- Credit cards accepted.

Open:
16 March - 31 October, and winter by arrangement.

Address:
Rye Hill, Bere Regis, Dorset BH20 7LP.

Tel:
(01929) 472727.
FAX: as phone.
E-mail: rwtp@ btinternet.com.

Reservations:
Made with £15 deposit per week.

Alan Rogers' Discount

Less 50p per night

206 Wilksworth Farm Caravan Park, Wimborne Minster

Spacious, quiet park with heated outdoor pool, for families.

Wilksworth Farm has a lovely rural situation just outside Wimborne and around 10 miles from the beaches between Poole and Bournemouth. With its duck pond at the entrance, it is a quiet, well designed park on good quality ground with fairly level grass and with some views. It takes 65 caravans (awning ground-sheets up in daytime) and 25 tents mainly on grass but with some hardstandings. All pitches have electrical connections, 10 with water and drainage also. There are also some 77 privately owned and self contained caravan holiday homes (one for hire). The central toilet block, converted from an original farm barn, is of good quality and well maintained (heated); it should be ample for these numbers. It has free hot water in showers and washbasins, set in vanity-type flat surfaces in recessed alcoves. There are toilet facilities for disabled visitors, a shower/bath for children and a baby changing point, three covered, outside washing-up sinks and a laundry room with telephone. Amenities include a heated 40 x 20 ft. swimming pool (unsupervised, but fenced and gated, open May - Sept) with a small children's pool with paved surround, reception cum shop (basics only, limited hours, Easter - 30 Sept), gas supplies, barbecue, BMX track, golf practice net and two tennis courts, one full and one short course size. Football ground and excellent children's adventure section. Dog exercise paddock. Games room with table tennis, pool, some games machines, etc. Freezer for ice packs. A new coffee shop (unlicensed, attractively designed in keeping with the listed buildings, adjoins the games room, with a full menu and takeaway service (open weekends and B.Hs only outside the main season). Golf, fishing and riding 3 miles. Tower Park leisure and entertainment centre is 6 miles, Kingston Lacy (NT) 3 miles and Wimborne town centre (with its Minster) 1 mile. Winter caravan storage.

Directions: Park is 1 mile north of Wimborne, west off the B3078 road to Cranborne. O.S.GR: SU010019.

Charges 1999:
-- Per pitch incl. 2 adults £6.00 - £12.00; child (3-16 yrs) £1.00 July, Aug. & Spr. B.H - other times one free with each adult; dog £1.00; extra adult £2.00; boat, extra car or pup tent £1.00; electricity £2.00; full services £1.00.
-- VAT included.
-- No credit cards.

Open:
1 March - 30 October.

Address:
Cranborne Road, Wimborne, Dorset BH21 4HW.

Tel:
(01202) 885467.

Reservations:
Advised for July/Aug. and B.Hs. Made with payment in full at booking or £20 per week deposit; balance more than 28 days beforehand (min. 5 days at B.Hs).

East Dorset

207 The Inside Park Caravan & Camping Park, nr. Blandford Forum

Small, family run, rural park ideal for touring Dorset.

The Inside Park is set in the grounds of an 18th century country house which burned down in 1941. Family owned and carefully managed alongside a dairy and arable farm, it is a must for those interested in local history or arboriculture and is a haven for wildlife and birds. The reception/toilet block and games room block are respectively the coach house and stables of the old house. The 9-acre camping field, a little distant, lies in a sheltered, gently sloping dry valley containing superb tree specimens - notably cedars, with walnuts in one part - and a dog graveyard dating back to the early 1700s under a large Cedar of Lebanon. In total there are 125 spacious pitches, 90 with electricity (10A) and some in wooded glades. The six acres adjoining are the old pleasure gardens of the house where campers can walk and exercise dogs in the former garden, now mostly overgrown and providing what must be one of the largest children's campsite adventure-lands in the UK. The toilet block houses comfortably sized showers (pre-set, push button type with curtain), washbasins (some in cubicles) and toilets, all with free hot water and non-slip floors. A room for use by disabled visitors or mothers and babies has been added, plus new dishwashing sinks. A laundry room is in the same block. Chemical toilet disposal and recycling bins are provided. Spacious games room with pool tables, table tennis, etc. and a tourist information section. Safe based children's adventure play area with trampolines and organised farm tours. Shop with basics, gas and camping provisions (open limited periods out of main season). Public telephone. No vehicle access to the park is allowed after 10.30 pm. (separate late arrivals area and car park). Day kennelling facilities for dogs. Winter caravan storage. The market town of Blandford with its leisure and swimming centre (temporary membership for Inside Park guests) is 2 miles and the area is excellent for walking and cycling (test your fitness on a 5 mile mountain bike course). Fishing and riding 2 miles, golf 3 miles. Extensive walking routes are marked through the farm and woodland, with a guide showing points of interest available in the shop.

Directions: Park is about 2 miles southwest of Blandford and is signed from roundabout junction of A354 and A350 roads. If approaching from the Shaftesbury direction, do not go into Blandford but follow the bypass to the last roundabout and follow camp signs. O.S.GR: ST864045.

Charges 1999:
-- Per pitch £3.00 - £4.70; adult £2.45 - £3.00; child (5-16 yrs) free - £1.10; dog 50p - 80p; electricity £2.00; tent light free - £1.00.
-- VAT included.
-- Credit cards accepted.

Open:
Easter - 31 October.

Address:
Blandford Forum, Dorset DT11 9AD.

Tel:
(01258) 453719.
FAX: (01258) 459921.
E-mail: inspark@aol.com.

Reservations:
Essential for B.Hs and high season; made with £10 deposit (min. 4 nights 13 July - 1 Sept).

THE INSIDE PARK
BLANDFORD FORUM, DORSET

So relaxing - you won't want to leave !

- ✪ Extra Large Pitches
- ✪ All Modern Facilities - FREE Hot Water
- ✪ Ideal Family Site - Quiet & Secluded
- ✪ Electric Hookups
- ✪ Well Stocked Site Shop
- ✪ Launderette
- ✪ Caravan Storage Facility

- Imaginative Children's Play Area ✪
- Indoor Games Room ✪
- Dogs Welcome ✪
- Mountain Bike Trails ✪
- Farm Tours & Tractor Rides ✪
- Abundant Wildlife ✪
- Extensive Waymarked Country Walks ✪

BROCHURE - 01258 453719
http://members.aol.com/inspark/inspark

For a list of parks which do not accept dogs, or where certain restrictions apply - see page 236

Dogs are banned from many beaches, either all year round or in the summer months. Ask for details from local authorities or the park of your choice.

208 Merley Court Touring Park, Wimborne Minster

Award winning, family run park with excellent amenities and heated outdoor pool.

Merley Court must be one of the best examples today of a family touring park and is a credit to the Wright family. It is a well planned, attractively landscaped park, run with consistent care and attention to very high standards. The latest addition is the Leisure Garden, an historic walled garden (the Grade II listed walls date back to the 18th century) formerly part of the Merley House estate, the design and construction of which was overseen by John Nash. With flower collections, rock garden and sunken garden lovingly tended by Mrs Wright, it offers space for picnics and recreation facilities including croquet, crazy golf, petanque, badminton, volleyball and basketball or perhaps just an evening stroll. The touring area has 160 pitches for all types of unit, all with 16A electricity, on clearly marked neat lawns interspersed with a variety of shrubs, palms and plants and the odd ornamental urn. This provision includes 11 neat all-service pitches with water, waste water and satellite TV connection. Some attractive tent pitches nestle in a small wooded valley with woodland walks and a dog walk, complete with the graves of past doggie friends. The three heated toilet blocks are well designed and of good quality, with free hot water in washbasins with shelf and mirror, two with pre-set well equipped showers. There are separate facilities for disabled visitors and for babies, excellent dishwashing and laundry facilities, chemical disposal and a motorcaravan service point. A large, well appointed indoor games room with pool tables and a family room adjoin the club complex with lounge bar, where meals are available (limited hours in low and mid seasons). The complex is exceptionally well furnished and the family room opens out onto a spacious and attractive sheltered patio, which leads through to the paved, walled pool area. The pool (30 x 20 ft) with children's section is open mid May - Sept. Other amenities include an all-weather tennis court, outdoor table tennis and two good children's playgrounds. An enlarged shop in the Leisure Gardens carries gas and caravan accessories and there is a useful takeaway with café. A tourist information centre and two public phones complete the wide range of facilities, all exceptionally well maintained. The park is only 6 miles from Poole, 8 from Bournemouth. The Tower Park leisure and entertainment centre is nearby, Kingston Lacy House, Knoll Gardens and Brownsea Island are also near. Fishing, bicycle hire, riding and golf all within 5 miles. No dogs are accepted in high season. Caravan storage (all year). Conference/meeting venue available in the Orangery within the Leisure Garden. A member of the Best of British group.

Directions: Park is signed at an exit from A31/A349 roundabout on the Wimborne bypass. O.S.GR: ST008984.

Charges 2000:
-- Per standard pitch (caravan, small tent or motorcaravan - no awning) incl. 2 persons £7.00 - £12.00, all service pitch (excl. electricity) £9.50 - £14.50; extra adult £3.00; child (3-13 yrs) £2.00; awning (no tent as well as awning) £1.00; dog (outside 15/7-1/9) £1.00; extra car/boat (on car park) £1.00; electricity (16A) £2.00.
-- Min. 5 nights Easter, 7 nights Spr B.H. and high season.
-- Less 10% for senior citizens in low season (excl. B.Hs).
-- Credit cards accepted.
-- VAT included.

Open:
All year except 8 Jan - 28 Feb.

Address:
Merley,
Wimborne,
Nr. Poole,
Dorset BH21 3AA.

Tel:
(01202) 881488.
FAX: (01202) 881484.
E-mail: holidays@merley-court.co.uk.

Reservations:
Made with deposit (£35 p/w), balance due 28 days before arrival.

See colour feature for `BEST of BRITISH' between pages 96/97

209 Whitemead Caravan Park, Wool, nr. Wareham

Pleasant, small, family run park between Dorchester and Wareham.

The Church family are continuing to make various improvements to this rather pleasant little park which is within walking distance of the village of Wool. Providing 95 numbered pitches on flat grass sloping gently north and orchard-like in parts, it is very natural with open views over the Frome Valley water meadows. They are well spaced and mostly back onto hedges or fences. There are 65 electrical connections for tourers (10A) and no caravan holiday homes. The single, comfortably sized toilet block provides free hot water both in the washbasins, set in flat surfaces, and the pre-set hot showers (with adjustable flow in ladies) and a baby room which doubles as a facility for disabled visitors. Also provided are a washing machine, spin and tumble dryers and chemical disposal facilities. A small shop (limited hours) doubles as reception. Gas is available. Information room. Children's playground with sand or grass base. Public phone. A fish and chip van calls three nights weekly in high season. The Ship Inn is 300 m. The park is 4½ miles from the nearest beach at Lulworth and is handily placed for many attractions in this part of Dorset (train services and limited bus service close). Riding or golf 3 miles. Caravan storage available. Possibly some rail noise.

Directions: Turn off main A352 on eastern edge of Wool, just north of level crossing, onto East Burton road. Site is 300 m. on right. O.S.GR: SY841871.

Charges 1999:
-- Per caravan, tent or motorcaravan £4.00 - £7.75; person (over 5 yrs) 85p; awning or tent (over 15 x 15) £1.00 - £1.50; extra car, boat free - £1.75; dog 50p; electricity £1.85.
-- No credit cards.
-- VAT included.

Open:
20 March - 31 October.

Address:
East Burton Road, Wool, Dorset BH20 6HG.

Tel/Fax:
(01929) 462241.

Reservations:
Made with £15 deposit, min. 3 nights at B.Hs.

East Dorset

210 Sandford Holiday Park, Holton Heath, nr. Poole

Pleasant, well run park with many first-class amenities near popular coastal areas; holiday caravans and large touring section.

Sandford Park has a large permanent section with 248 static holiday homes and lodges. However, the touring sections can accommodate 460 units of any type, mainly on individual pitches, on level grass with mature hedging in the main area. All have 10A electrical connections. Early booking is advisable. The main toilet block in the touring area provides facilities for the disabled and a baby room. It is supplemented by the former main block and subsidiary `portacabin' style units in the touring and static areas (one a bath block). Free hot water in the washbasins, set vanity-style in flat surfaces, and in the pre-set showers (under pressure at peak times). Plenty of water points around. Dogs or pets are permitted in the touring section from 5 Sept. onwards with a dog walk provided. Sandford is a large, very busy holiday park with a wide range of entertainment. The clubhouse (free membership) is spacious with dance floor, bar and seating area, and caters for different tastes and age groups. There is also a large air conditioned ballroom for entertainment and dancing. Both are open over a long season. There is a variety of bars, restaurants (book in busy periods) and simple hot meals and takeaway elsewhere in peak season. The outdoor swimming pool (25 m. long, open May-Oct. and supervised) and a very large play pool (0-2 ft.) with a sandy beach, ideal for children, are attractively situated with a snack bar and terraced area. An impressive indoor pool is a nice addition, also a separate soft indoor play area for children (open April - Oct and Christmas, also supervised). Large supermarket and other shops, including well stocked camping accessory shop (all open peak season only). Large launderette. Ladies' hairdresser. TV lounges. On site are a children's playground, two tennis courts, mountain bike hire, table tennis, two short mat bowling greens (outdoor) and large crazy golf course. Public phones. Many activities nearby include riding stables and fishing (9 miles).

Directions: Park is just west off the A351 (Wareham - Poole) road at Holton Heath. O.S.GR: SY940913.

Charges guide:
-- Per pitch free - £5.75, acc. to season; adult £2.25; child (3-13 yrs) £1.50 - £2.50; extra car free - £1.50; awning free; electricity £2.50; `super hook-up (electricity, TV, water) £4.50; dog (1 only, after 4 Sept) £2.50; boat and trailer £1.50 - £2.00; visitor £3.95, child £1.75).
-- Club membership included.
-- Special offers and special interest weeks - details from park.
-- VAT included.
-- Credit cards accepted.

Open:
Easter - January incl.

Address:
Holton Heath, nr. Poole, Dorset BH16 6JZ.

Tel:
(01202) 631600.

Reservations:
Early booking advisable (min. 3 days) - write to park.

see colour advert between pages 65/65

211 Pear Tree Touring Park, Organford, nr. Poole

Neat, well cared for, family run park catering for families and couples only.

Pear Tree is obviously the pride and joy of its owners, Mr and Mrs Broome, and this clearly shows. Set in 7½ acres, with mature tress and views across to Wareham Forest, the 125 good sized, grassy pitches are separated into areas by high hedges and shrubs. There are 120 pitches with 10A electricity, 43 with full services (water, waste water and electricity) of which 14 have hardstanding. The main heated sanitary block is opened by key and has vanity style washbasins and controllable showers (coin operated, hot water 20p throughout), with a baby changing unit and two WCs for disabled visitors. All is kept spotlessly clean. Also here is a `state of the art' chemical disposal point. Another small block with washbasins and WCs only, is near the tent area, which is a lovely secluded spot with many mature trees. Reception and a small shop supplying milk, bread, gas and other basics is at the park entrance where the gates (with key) are closed at 9 pm. (no late arrivals area, so book in before 9 pm). Public telephone and tourist information. Motorcaravan service point. Only breathable groundsheets are permitted with awnings. Dogs are only accepted outside July/Aug. and there is a bridle path extending into Wareham Forest for exercise. A large, fenced children's play field is at the top of the park with swings, climbing frame, trampolines and ball games area. There is no restaurant but a fish and chip van calls three times weekly in high season and the Clay Pipe Inn is just 500 m. away. Also 500 m. is a coarse fishing lake (day tickets from reception) and bicycle hire. Riding 5 miles, golf 2 miles. A bus service stops nearby for Wareham (2½ miles) or Poole (8 miles). All year caravan or boat storage available.

Directions: Park is just west off A351 (Wareham - Poole) road at Holton Heath near Sandford Park. O.S.GR: SY940915.

Charges 2000:
-- Per unit incl. 2 persons £7.50 - £10.00; extra adult £3.00; child (3-14 yrs) £1.50; extra tent £2.50; awning free; dog (not July/Aug) £2.00; extra car or boat £3.00; electricity (10A) £2.20 - £2.50.
-- Security key deposit £10 (refundable).
-- VAT included.
-- Credit cards accepted.

Open:
Easter - mid October.

Address:
Organford, Poole, Dorset BH16 6LA.

Tel:
(01202) 622434.
FAX: (01202) 631985.
E-mail: enquiries@ pear tree-touringpark. freeserve.co.uk.

Reservations:
Made for min. 4 nights with £25 deposit.

212 Hoburne Park, Christchurch

Well kept holiday and touring site with many amenities; no tents.

This well kept and tidy park, with a range of good quality amenities, is conveniently situated for Bournemouth or the New Forest. There are 285 level, grass touring pitches (for caravans or motorcaravans), all with 16A electricity and some with individual water supply and hardstanding, in three separated hedged, neat grass areas. The park also caters for 305 caravan holiday homes to hire. Amenities include an outdoor pool, with paved and grass sunbathing areas, children's pool and an attractive indoor leisure pool with sauna, spa bath, solarium and steam rooms. We continue to be impressed with the number of lifeguards on duty and attendance to safety here and at other Hoburne parks. A large reception area, restaurant, snack bar, takeaway, well furnished bar with terrace, video games room and snooker room form part of the indoor complex area. A large adventure play area is near this main complex together with tennis, crazy golf and a field area with goal posts. A programme of entertainment is organised in season. A well stocked shop and launderette complete the facilities. Sanitary facilities are modern with free hot showers in blocks central to each field area, with additional facilities attached to the main building. A baby room with bath is in one block, changing units in all blocks. Free hairdryers. Chemical disposal. Many large sites have a somewhat frenzied atmosphere in the high season. This one can be busy but the atmosphere is pleasantly quiet and relaxed. No tents, trailer tents or pup tents are permitted. Dogs and pets not accepted. American motorhomes accepted in limited numbers up to 30 ft. Fishing or golf 3 miles, bicycle hire or boat slipway 2 miles, riding 6 miles. A well managed park, the flag flier of the Hoburne group.

Charges 2000:
-- Per unit, incl. electricity and awning (up to 3 x 9m.) £11.00 - £25.00.
-- Weekly rates and special weekend breaks.
-- VAT included.
-- Credit cards accepted.
Open:
March - October.
Address:
Hoburne Lane, Christchurch, Dorset BH23 4HU.
Tel:
(01425) 273379.
FAX: (01425) 270705.
E-mail: enquiries@hoburne.co.uk.
Reservations:
Made with payment in full (6 days or less) or £50 deposit; min. periods 4 nights for B.Hs, 7 nights mid July - end Aug.

Directions: Park is signed (left) from roundabout 2 miles east of Christchurch on the A337. From Lyndhurst, travel south on A35 to the junction with A337 - turn left onto A337 then left again at the first roundabout. O.S.GR: SZ169928.

HOBURNE PARK
Award Winning Holiday Park
TOURING PITCHES

Impressive family location close to Bournemouth, the New Forest and the Solent beaches. Touring pitches inclusive of electricity, hot showers, awning (if space), VAT and use of most Park facilities for up to 6 people. For FREE colour brochure or credit card bookings please contact:

HOBURNE PARK, RG1, Hoburne Lane,
Christchurch, Dorset BH23 4HU.

Telephone: 01425 273379

e-mail - enquiries@hoburne.co.uk   www.hoburne.co.uk

213 Grove Farm Meadow Holiday Park, Christchurch

Quiet traditional park with holiday vans, with small provision for touring caravans.

The grassed flood bank which separates the River Stour from this park provides an attractive walkway and the bank, kept natural, is well populated by a range of ducks and a swan family - early in the season they parade their young through the park. Caravan holiday homes (118 privately owned, 77 for hire) are regularly sited in rows. For touring units there are 44 level grass pitches all with 15A electricity, clearly numbered, backing on to fencing or hedging and accessed by tarmac roads. The sanitary block is tiled and provides vanity style washbasins, free hot showers, a bathroom for each sex (50p), a separate toilet and washbasin with ramped access for disabled visitors, and a baby room. Dishwashing sinks, together with spin dryer, iron and board and a line are provided. A games room has a pool table and video games, a play area is beside the river bank and there is a good, well stocked shop, 8-8 in high season but limited hours in early March and late Oct. The impressive modern reception has good tourist information. Fishing is available on the park and bicycle hire can be arranged. Boat launching 4 miles. Nearby is a public 9 hole golf course. Bournemouth is 10 minutes by car, Christchurch 5. Grove Farm Meadow is the parent site of Mount Pleasant (number 214) and is a more traditional, peaceful type of park.

Charges guide:
-- Per pitch incl. 2 persons, 10A electricity and awning £8.50 - £16.00; extra person over 5 yrs £1.50; extra car or boat £1.50.
-- VAT included.
-- Credit cards accepted.
Open:
1 March - 31 October.
Address:
Meadowbank Holidays, Stour Way, Christchurch, Dorset BH23 2PQ.
Tel:
(01202) 483597.
FAX: (01202) 483878.
Reservations:
Made for Sat-Sat or Sun-Sun in high season, min. 3 nights at other times; contact park for details.

Directions: From A388 Ringwood - Bournemouth take B3073 for Christchurch. Turn right at first roundabout and Stour Way is third right. O.S.GR: SZ136946.

214 Mount Pleasant Touring Park, Christchurch, nr. Bournemouth

Neat tidy park on edge of New Forest, within 3 miles of Bournemouth centre.

A surprisingly pretty, 'rural' park for its situation near Bournemouth, the pitches at Mount Pleasant are on mostly level, sandy grass with circular connecting tarmac roads, neatly fenced and interspersed with pine trees and rhododendron bushes. In total there are 175 pitches for all types of units, 87 of them marked and with 10A electricity, with a separate tenting area. Two good, purpose built, modern toilet blocks are well maintained and fully tiled, with vanity style washbasins with free hot water (some washbasins in cubicles), adjustable hot water to free, well equipped roomy showers, plus toddler room and separate, en-suite unit for disabled people. A good basic shop and information area are in reception and a mobile takeaway, open all season (closed afternoons), is very popular, especially for breakfasts! Mountain bike hire can be arranged. Fishing 2 miles, boat launching facilities 4 miles. Fenced adventure play area and direct access to the forest for dog walking, etc. A card operated security barrier is at the entrance. Bournemouth is around 10 minutes by car (depending on the traffic; Tesco hypermarket, 7 minutes. Dry ski centre within ½ mile with bars and restaurants. The nearest bus service is 2 miles. Barbecues are allowed. Due to its situation between Bournemouth airport and the A338 dual-carriageway there may be road or aircraft noise. Despite this it is a very popular, well run park.

Directions: From A338 Ringwood-Bournemouth road, take B3073 towards Hurn airport. Follow signs at mini-roundabout to Matchams Lane. O.S.GR: SZ129987.

Charges guide:
-- Per unit incl. up to 2 persons £7.50 - £14.50; small tent £5.50 - £11.00; extra person (over 4 yrs) £1.00 - £2.00; extra car, boat or trailer £1.50 - £2.00; dog £1.00 - £1.50; electricity (6A) £2.00.
-- Credit cards accepted.

Open:
1 March - 31 October.

Address:
Matchams Lane, Hurn, Christchurch, Dorset BH23 6AW.

Tel:
(01202) 475474.

Reservations:
Accepted only for weekly bookings (Sat-Sat), with £30 deposit (non-refundable).

225 Bashley Park, New Milton

Pleasant park with pools and evening entertainment; no tents.

A well run park with many holiday homes (380 including 40 for hire), Bashley Park also has a very sizeable tourist section and can take 420 touring units (tents, trailer tents and pup tents are not accepted). Spread over three flat meadows plus a woodland area complete with visiting squirrels, pitches are all individual ones with electricity, marked out but not separated. Groundsheets must be lifted daily. The four toilet blocks, one central to each area, are well constructed buildings, fully tiled with modern fittings. They have free hot water, vanity style washbasins and push-button, pre-set showers (no dividers, but shower heads are set fairly low). Set in pleasant park-like surroundings not far from beaches, Bournemouth and the New Forest, the site has a good clubhouse with excellent facilities overlooking an 18 m. circular outdoor swimming pool (heated mid-May - mid-Sept) and 18 m. paddling pool, a sensible size and fun with its geysers and beach effect. An indoor pool complex houses a water flume, sauna, spa bath and steam room. There are evening entertainments (also for children) in the club with music Spr.B.H. to mid-September; it has a ballroom, large lounges and bars, restaurant, simple hot takeaway all day, TV room. Also a video arcade and games room with two full-size snooker tables, plus pool tables in other rooms. Very well equipped children's play area, crazy golf, 9-hole, `par 3' golf course on site, bicycle hire and three tennis courts. Fishing or riding 1 mile. Shop (mid-May to end Sept). Launderette. Up to 6 American motorhomes accepted (40 ft. max). One dog is allowed per unit. A popular park with lots going on, part of the Hoburne group.

Directions: Park is on B3055 road about ¼ mile east of the crossroads with the B3058 in Bashley village. O.S.GR: SZ246969.

Charges 2000:
-- Per unit incl. all persons and electricity £10.00 - £25.00; multi service pitch £10.50 - £27.50; pet £2.00.
-- Weekend breaks available.
-- VAT included.
-- Credit cards accepted.

Open:
28 February - 31 October.

Address:
Sway Road, New Milton, Hampshire BH25 5QR.

Tel:
(01425) 612340.
FAX: (01425) 612602.
E-mail: enquiries@ hoburne.co.uk.

Reservations:
Necessary for peak season and made for any length: 1-6 nights with payment in full at booking; 7+ nights, £50 p/w. deposit, balance 3 weeks before arrival.

229 Sandy Balls Holiday Centre, Godshill, Fordingbridge

Amazing holiday park with excellent range of facilities for all types of touring unit and with holiday homes and lodges to hire.

Sandy Balls must be one of the oldest 'camp sites' in the UK, celebrating its 75th anniversary in 1995. Ernest Westlake, grandfather of the present owners and an educationalist and idealist, bought the ancient woodland overlooking the Avon Valley in 1919 to save it from the axe and today, while the majestic oaks, beeches, Scots pine and larch have matured, new facilities have been designed to be in sympathy with the setting. Sandy Balls is now an award winning park, high above the sweep of the Avon River and protected as a nature reserve. There is much to discover in the history of the park, such as how it came to get its name, the significance of the organisation founded by Ernest Westlake ('The Order of Woodcraft Chivalry') and his commitment to life-long learning. Perhaps visit Good Friday Hill and try to absorb the atmosphere and some of the thinking behind the development of Sandy Balls to what it is today, deserving of the entry which it has maintained in these guides for over 30 years.

It continues to be a very well run and modern thinking park set within 120 acres and with a wide range of leisure facilities developed around a 'village' centre. Open all year, it covers an extensive area in a series of fields which include terrain of different types: light woodland with 186 caravan and chalet holiday homes (many for rent), and some tent areas with unmarked pitches, tourist units for the most part on open meadows, and some general parts including woodland not used for camping. They include over 300 all service pitches for touring units with electrical connections (10-16A), water, drainaway and TV connection - site satellite dish, on concrete or gravel with gravel hardstanding for awnings (steel pegs can be provided if required). In winter only 50 pitches are available. There are four modern toilet blocks (three very modern, with under-floor heating) and one of `portacabin' type which remains as overflow in the tenting field (28 day). One block has a bath in each section and all have cubicled washbasins. Hot water is free and showers are of the pre-mixed type. The blocks are spacious and airy and should be adequate for peak season, with 'Northfield' having been added to provide extra, good quality facilities. Toilets for disabled visitors and baby changing facilities are provided in at least two blocks. Excellent launderette plus washing machines in all the toilet blocks. Chemical disposal and motorcaravan service point. New recycling stations - look for the green coloured sheds. The central area with the park's facilities is pleasantly laid out and designed to blend with the forest surroundings. There is a large indoor heated swimming pool (66 x 30 ft.) and a solar heated outdoor pool, with lifeguards and free at all times (in high season, sessions are timed according to demand). Other facilities include a well equipped fitness gym, jacuzzi spa bath, steam room, toning tables, sauna and solarium and dance studios. There is a modern Spar supermarket, a takeaway service and a licensed pub complete with bar, family room, with wide screen and patio area and with entertainment every evening in high season. Games room with pool and table tennis, children's adventure playgrounds and two other play areas for younger children are provided, plus a soft play area for 2-5 year olds (Mon-Sat, £2 p/hour). Bicycle hire, petanque, archery, orienteering, hot air balloon rides along the Avon valley. River fishing on permit, riding nearby. New on site in '99, Valencio's, a pizzeria with bar for eating in or takeaway. The park also owns the Fighting Cocks pub, ¼ mile away. Tourist information and a gift shop, plus telephones. The park has recently won a 'Good Lighting Award' from the British Astronomical Association for the design of its lighting which enables visitors to better appreciate the night sky; a new and unusual award for a park to win. Sandy Balls provides a range of all-round family entertainment, including a woodland leisure trail where wild animals and birds can be observed in their natural surroundings, as well as the New Forest on your doorstep, and even clay-modelling tuition for the children. Dogs are only allowed on certain fields. An ideal park for families and couples.

Directions: Park is northwest off B3078 (Fordingbridge - Cadnam) just west of Godshill village, and about 1½ miles east of Fordingbridge. O.S.GR: SU168147.

Charges 1999:
-- Serviced pitch weekends £15.50 - £18.00, mid-week £11.75 - £18.00; non-serviced pitch £12.50 - £14.75 or £10.50 - £14.75.
-- Mid and high seasons only: adult £1.50 - £2.50, young adult (12-17 yrs) £1.00 - £1.75, child (3-11 yrs) 50p - £1.00; additional car or m/cycle 50p - 75p; dog 75p - £1.25.
-- VAT included.
-- Credit cards accepted.
Open:
All year.
Address:
Sandy Balls Estate, Godshill, Fordingbridge, Hampshire SP6 2JY.
Tel:
(01425) 653042.
FAX: (01425) 653067.
E-mail: post@sandy-balls.co.uk.
Reservations:
Made with deposit and compulsory cancellation insurance - contact park for details.

see colour advert between pages 65/65

Hampshire

226 Camping International, St Leonards, nr. Ringwood

Well kept, lively, family managed touring park with small heated pool, close to New Forest and Bournemouth.

Now incorporating Redcote Holiday Park, Camping International has a neat, compact appearance and closer inspection of the facilities confirms that everything is orderly, clean, and well cared for. The flat, grassy terrain is divided into two parts. The first, which is the original Camping International, comprises 80 numbered pitches, quite close together, all with electricity and 30 with gravel area for awnings. This is the more lively part with a central bar, pool and children's adventure play area, shop, reception and tourist information. The second part, formerly Redcote, is the quieter area taking 125 units on a flat, grassy meadow with some hardstanding and does not accept dogs. A games room has five pool tables, table tennis, amusement machines and under-5s' playroom. To one side is a fully fenced ball game area. Both parts have fully equipped sanitary facilities with hot showers on meters. The block in the second part is larger and more functional with plenty of toilets including one for mother and child. Both have facilities for babies, covered dishwashing facilities (H&C), laundry rooms and chemical disposal. Motorcaravan sevice point. The `Old Trout' pub has a pleasant licensed bar, family room, TV and video room. A patio overlooks the children's adventure play area and neatly paved small pool (1 m. deep) and paddling pool. Hot food and takeaway are available at most times in high season. Public phones. Well stocked shop with camping accessories. Secure caravan storage. Fishing, golf or bicycle hire 2 miles, riding ½ mile. The park is well situated to tour the New Forest, Bournemouth, Beaulieu, etc. and is essentially a park for families. It is also very popular, particularly with visitors from the continent, so reservation is advisable for July/Aug. Possible road noise from the A31 on some pitches.

Charges 2000:
-- Per unit incl. 2 persons £8.30 - £12.50; extra person (4 yrs and over) £1.60 - £1.80; awning or extra car £1.60 - £2.00; dog £1.50 - £1.80; electricity £2.50.
-- VAT included.
-- Credit cards accepted.

Open:
1 March - 31 October.

Address:
229 Ringwood Road, St Leonards, nr. Ringwood, Hants BH24 2SD.

Tel:
(01202) 872817 or 872742.
FAX: (01202) 893986.
E-mail: campint@global.co.uk.

Reservations:
Made with £40 deposit.

Directions: Park is off main A31 road to south at second roundabout travelling west from Ringwood (3 miles). Turn off at camp signs. O.S.GR: SU106024.

231 Hollands Wood Camping and Caravanning Site, Brockenhurst

Spacious, level Forestry Commission site in the heart of the New Forest.

Hollands Wood is a large 168 acre secluded site in a natural woodland setting (mainly oak) with an abundance of wild-life, including the famous New Forest ponies. The site is arranged informally with 600 unmarked pitches but it is stipulated that there must be at least 20 feet between each unit. There are no electrical connections and possible traffic noise from the A337 which runs alongside one boundary. New for '99 was a dog free zone within the site. Two large utilitarian toilet blocks (and a third smaller, older one) have free hot showers, hot and cold water to open washbasins, free hairdryer, razor points, two laundry rooms with washing machines and dryers, water points, chemical disposal, facilities for disabled people and baby changing surfaces. These facilites are under pressure at peak times. There is no shop, but the site is only about ½ mile from Brockenhurst village with shops for supplies and gas, etc, plus trains and buses. Night security with the barrier closed 23.30 - 07.30 hrs (overnight overflow area). Public telephones. Torches essential. Motorcaravan service point. It can get very busy and we include the smaller Ashurst site as an alternative.

Charges 1999:
-- Per unit incl. up to 4 persons £7.00 - £12.30; extra person (over 5 yrs) £1.00; extra car, trailer or pup tent £3.70.
-- Weekend prices higher.
-- Less 20% all year for disabled guests and excl. 9/7-30/8 for senior citizens.
-- Credit cards accepted

Open:
25 March - 28 September.

Reservations:
Necessary for B.Hs and peak times (min. 3 nights with £30 deposit). Contact (at all times): Forest Holidays, Forestry Commission, 231 Corstorphine Road, Edinburgh EH12 7AT. Tel : (0131) 314 6505.

Directions: Site entrance is on east side of A337 Lyndhurst - Lymington road, half a mile north of Brockenhurst. O.S.GR: SU303038

230 Ashurst Caravan and Camping Site, Ashurst, nr. Lyndhurst

Attractive Forestry Commission site on the fringe of the New Forest.

A smaller site than Hollands Wood (23 acres), Ashurst is set in a mixture of oak woodland and grass and heathland which is open to the grazing animals of the Forest. Of the 280 pitches, 180 have been gravelled to provide semi-hardstanding; otherwise you pitch where you like, applying the 20 ft. rule on ground that can be uneven. There are no electricity connections on this site. Some noise must be expected from the adjacent railway line - the station is just five minutes walk away. The single central sanitary block is fairly plain, but provides everything necessary, including hairdryers, a well equipped unit for visitors with disabilities (key required) and a good laundry room. It appears to be well maintained but could be under pressure when the site is full. Within easy access of all pitches are 8 water points. There are chemical disposal and motorcaravan service points. Reception is run by the very helpful site managers. There is a late arrivals area and separate car-parking area for those arriving or returning after the gate has closed (11.30 pm). A nearby pub is accessible by footpath across an adjacent field and shops and local buses are within a five minute walk. Guided forest walks and Activity Walks for children are organised during the main season. A local garage sells gas. Public telephone. A torch is useful. No dogs are accepted.

Directions: Site is 2 miles east of Lyndhurst, set back from the A35 Southampton - Bournemouth road. O.S.GR: SU332102.

Charges 1999:
-- Per unit incl. up to 4 persons £6.20 - £11.00; extra person (over 5 yrs) £1.00; extra car, trailer or pup tent £3.50.
-- Weekend prices higher.
-- Less 20% all year for disabled guests and outside 9/7-30/8 for senior citizens.
-- Credit cards accepted

Open:
25 March - 28 September.

Reservations:
Necessary for B.Hs and peak times (min. 3 nights with £30 deposit).
Contact (at all times): Forest Holidays, Forestry Commission, 231 Corstorphine Road, Edinburgh EH12 7AT.
Tel: (0131) 314 6505.

234 Shamba Touring Park, St Leonards, nr. Ringwood

Friendly, family run park with outdoor pool on Dorset/Hampshire borders.

The Gray family have been gradually upgrading Shamba over the last few years and it is developing into a comfortable park with good sized, well drained pitches (150 in total, all with 10A electricity). Most of the amenities are good including a well stocked shop and a cosy bar offering bar snacks, takeaway service and a small family room, heated and with a pool table. At the rear is an open terrace area overlooking the heated outdoor pool, which is very popular with children and carefully fenced. Also popular with children is a large play area and a games room with video games and table football. The owners have a young family themselves and seem to be aware of their needs, even down to providing a small child's toilet and basins in the toilet blocks. The showers, in a separate heated block, are controllable with seat and divider. The rest of the provision is adequate but is a little dated; however, it is kept clean and provides free hot water, make-up area for ladies, Belfast sink for the baby, covered dishwashing sinks (H&C), plus a laundry sink, two washing machines and two dryers, and chemical disposal facilities. This is the area where improvements are planned in the not so distant future. The Grays live on site and have managed to create a relaxed, pleasant atmosphere. Bournemouth with its beaches is 8 miles, Ringwood 2½ miles and the Moors Valley Country Park 1 mile. Riding stables and a fishing lake are just 500 yds. Note: site is near the A31 so there could be some road noise.

Directions: Site is signed directly off the A31 Ringwood - Wimborne Road, 400 yds. down a small lane. Approaching from the east, after passing Little Chef, you will need to go round the next roundabout back on yourself, then immediately left down lane. O.S.GR: SU104026.

Charges guide:
-- Per pitch incl. up to 6 persons £8.00 - £12.00; extra person £1.00 - £2.00; electricity £2.00; dog free - £1.50.

Open:
1 March - 31 October

Address:
Ringwood Road, St Leonards, Ringwood, Hampshire BH24 2SB.

Tel:
(01202) 873302.

Reservations:
Made with non-returnable deposit of £25.

A 7 acre Holiday Park set in wooded surroundings some 8 miles from Bournemouth and ideally situated for the New Forest.
This family Park is secluded and caters for discerning holidaymakers

- Large, level, well drained Pitches
- Licensed Clubhouse
- Shop and Off Licence
- Take Away Food Bar / Bar Meals
- Electricity Hook-ups
- Launderette

- Games Room
- Children's Playground
- Pre-bookable Pitches
- Horse Riding, Fishing & Sailing nearby
- Plus Winter Storage

H O L I D A Y PARK For a relaxing holiday, come to Shamba Holiday Park. Telephone now for our brochure and booking form.

HEATED SWIMMING POOL Shamba Holiday Park, 230 Ringwood Road,
(01202) 873302 St. Leonards, Ringwood, Hants BH24 2SB

Hampshire

235 Red Shoot Camping Park, Linwood, nr. Ringwood

Rural retreat in the heart of the New Forest.

Set on three acres of open, slightly sloping, level grass-land, this park has panoramic views of the surrounding countryside and forest, and is very popular in high season. There are around 130 good sized pitches, 45 with electric hook-ups (16A), served by a circular gravel roadway. There is no site lighting so a torch would be useful. The sanitary facilities are fairly modern, well maintained, practical but not luxurious, including push-button hot showers, dishwashing sinks under cover, with free hot water throughout. The laundry has a washing machine and dryer, and there is a good unit for disabled visitors. A very well stocked shop provides fresh and frozen foods, camping equipment and gas, wine and beer, toys and gifts plus maps and guides. Also on site is a fenced adventure style playground on a bark safety base, mountain bike and tandem hire. The adjacent Red Shoot Inn (separate ownership) serves hot or cold meals and brews its own real ales - Forest Gold and Tom's Tipple. There are ample opportunities for walking, cycling and naturalist pursuits. Nearby Ringwood has a market on Wednesday and other local attractions include watersports at the New Forest Water Park near Ringwood, a Doll Museum in Fordingbridge, cider making in Burley and Breamore House, just north of Fordingbridge. The campsite keeps an extensive range of tourist information brochures.

Directions: From A338 about 1.75 miles north of Ringwood, turn east (signed Linwood, Moyles Court). Follow signs, over staggered cross-roads, and continue straight on for another 1.75 miles to Red Shoot Inn. O.S.GR: SU188095.

Charges 1999:
-- Per adult £3.65; child 5-14 yrs £2.10, 0-4 yrs 85p; car £1.05; m/cycle £1.00; day visitor 50p; electricity £2.00; awning £1.30; dog 65p.
-- VAT not included.
-- Min. stays at B.Hs.
-- Less 20% in low seasons (min. 3 nights).

Open:
1 March - 31 October.

Address:
Linwood, nr. Ringwood, Hampshire BH24 3QT.

Tel:
(01425) 473789 or 478940.
FAX: (01425) 471558.

Reservations:
Advised for w/ends, B.Hs and peak season (school holidays) and made with £15 deposit per week or part week.

228 Lytton Lawn Touring Park, Lymington

Modern, well equipped park with access to leisure complex, near Milford on Sea.

Lytton Lawn is the touring arm of Shorefield Country Park, a holiday home park and leisure centre. Situated 2½ miles from Shorefield, campers and caravanners staying at Lytton Lawn are entitled to free membership of the Leisure Club. The comprehensive facilities at Shorefield are of a very good standard and are free (except tennis). They comprise a very attractive indoor pool (20 m. heated), solarium, sauna, spa bath and steam room, dance studios, bicycle hire and two all weather tennis courts, open all year with fully trained attendants. Outdoor pools and crazy golf (Easter - Sept). Restaurant facilities include a bistro (Easter - 2 Nov). A range of entertainment and activity programmes, fitness classes and treatments, are all well managed and organised. Lytton Lawn provides 126 marked pitches, including 43 'premier' pitches (hardstanding, 16A electricity, pitch light, satellite TV, water and waste water outlet) in a hedged area of natural grass. This section, with its heated toilet block, is open for a longer season (March - 5 Jan). The rest of the pitches, all with electrical connections (tenters note), are in the adjoining, but separate, gently sloping field, edged with mature trees and hedges and with a further toilet block. Access roads are either tarmac or un-made gravel. Both areas have purpose built, modern toilet blocks which are fully tiled, heated and well fitted, with free hot water, vanity style washbasins and showers with dressing area. Dishwashing, washing machine and dryer, plus chemical disposal in each block. Baby changing facilities in one block. Simple shop (limited opening out of main season), with supermarket and takeaway (main season) at Shorefield. The fenced children's play area is small but there is a fairly large field with goal posts. Barbecues are allowed. Public phone. The village pub is a 10 minute walk. The New Forest, Isle of Wight, Bournemouth, Southampton and the beach at Milford on Sea are near, as are golf, riding, coarse fishing (all within 3 miles), sailing, windsurfing and boat launching facilities (1½ miles).

Directions: From M27 follow signs for Lyndhurst and Lymington on A337. Continue towards New Milton and Lytton Lawn is signed at Everton, Shorefield is signed at Downton. O.S.GR: SZ293937.

Charges 1999:
-- Per 'premier' pitch incl. all persons, electricity, water, drainage and TV connection £10.00 - £22.00; basic pitch incl. electricity £9.00 - £20.00; pup tent or awning free, together £2.50; dog (1 only) £2.50; extra car £3.50.
-- Less 40% Mon - Thurs in certain periods.
-- Min. weekly charge at busy times.
-- Credit cards accepted.
-- VAT included.

Open:
All year except 4 Jan - 28 Feb.

Address:
Shorefield Country Parks, Shorefield Road, Milford on Sea, nr. Lymington, Hampshire SO41 0LH.

Tel:
(01590) 648331.
FAX: (01590) 645610.
E-mail: holidays@shorefield.co.uk.

Reservations:
Made with deposit and cancellation insurance - contact park for details.

see colour advert between pages 65/65

82

232 Camping and Caravanning Club Site Chichester, Southbourne

Small, well kept touring park near the Hampshire/Sussex coast.

This is a neat park, just to the west of Chichester and north of Bosham harbour. Formerly an orchard, it is rectangular in shape with 60 pitches on flat, well mown lawns on either side of gravel roads. All pitches have 16A electricity, 13 with level hardstanding. Situated on the main A259 road, although the new A27 bypass takes most of the through traffic, there may be some traffic noise in some parts (not busy at night). Opposite the park are orchards through which paths lead to the seashore and the location is ideal for touring this part of the south coast or inland. The well designed, brick built sanitary block is of first class quality. Fully tiled and heated in cool weather, there is free hot water in washbasins set in flat units, showers and sinks, with facilities for people with disabilities (access by key). Chemical disposal point. Dogs are accepted on leads. No ball games or children's bicycles permitted on the park. Gas available. There are shops, restaurants and pubs within easy walking distance in the nearby village and the park is on a main bus route. Fishing or golf 5 miles, riding 6 miles. Dogs can be walked in the lane opposite the entrance. Unfortunately there is no overnight area for late arrivals; the gates are shut between 11 pm. and 7 am. with no parking outside. Chichester has a leisure centre and market day is on Wednesday. An excellent caravan shop is near.

Charges 2000:
-- Per 2 adults £7.50 - £10.60; child (6-18 yrs) £1.65; non-member pitch fee £4.30; electricity £1.60 - £2.35.
-- VAT included. .
-- Credit cards accepted.
Open:
All year.
Address:
Main Road, Southbourne, Hampshire PO10 8JH.
Tel:
(01243) 373202 (no calls after 8 pm).
Reservations:
Necessary and made with deposit (min. 2 nights); contact the wardens.

Directions: Park is on main A259 Chichester - Havant road at Southbourne, 750 yards past Chichester Caravans on the right. O.S.GR: SU774056.

245 The Orchards Holiday Caravan Park, Newbridge, nr. Yarmouth

Peaceful, spacious family park, well kept and with indoor and outdoor pools.

In a village situation in the quieter western part of the island, The Orchards is a busy and lively family holiday park combining 61 holiday caravans (in a separate area) with a neat touring area. Run personally by the proprietor, it provides a pleasant, comfortable base from which to explore, about 4 miles from the beaches and from Yarmouth. A pool complex provides a medium size, heated swimming pool and children's pool (late May - mid Sept) with a grass sunbathing area, supplemented by a supervised irregularly shaped indoor pool with spa pool (on payment, open all year), attractively glass walled with terrace and café bar for relaxing - a nice addition. About 175 marked pitches are arranged on gently sloping meadow, broken up by apple trees, mature hedges and fences. All have electricity and 41 have hardstanding, including 5 with water hook up and drain (more planned). Sanitary facilities are provided by three blocks of varying age and size which together should be an ample provision. Hot water is free for the washbasins (some with shelf, others set in flat surfaces and a few in private cabins), the controllable hot showers and for dishwashing. There are also baths on payment and toilet facilities for disabled visitors (a hardstanding pitch close by can be reserved). Free irons and hairdryers (10p coin) are thoughtfully provided, with full laundry facilities. There are facilities for chemical disposal, a motor-caravan service point, ice pack and battery charging services and gas supplies. The large reception provides useful tourist information and there is a well stocked shop and takeaway service (April - Oct, limited opening at quiet times). Dog walk area. A meetings room (up to 50 persons) is suitable for small rallies. Children's play equipment, pool, table tennis, TV and amusements rooms complete the facil-ities (there is no evening entertainment on site). Coarse fishing on site (no closed season). Bicycle hire, boat launching 4 miles, riding 1 mile. Walks from the park. Membership is available for the village social club and a small discount at Freshwater golf course (4 miles) – ask at reception. Golfing and walking holidays available. Limited caravan storage available. Part of the Caravan Club's 'managed under contract' scheme, non-members are also very welcome, the park is also a member of the Best of British group.

Charges 1999:
-- Per adult £1.25; adult £3.05 - £4.75; child £1.45 - £3.00; awning free; pup tent £1.50; electricity (16A) £2.05 - £2.75; dog 50p - £1.20; no pitch fee for hikers or cyclists; all-service pitch plus £3.10.
-- Packages incl. ferry travel available - ring park for best deal.
-- VAT included.
-- Credit cards accepted.
Open:
All year excl. 2 Jan - 12 Feb.
Address:
Newbridge, Yarmouth, I.O.W. PO41 0TS.
Tel:
(01983) 531331 or 531350.
FAX: (01983) 531666.
E-mail: info@orchards-holiday-park.co.uk.
Reservations:
Made for min. 5 days with £25 p/wk deposit.

See colour feature for 'BEST of BRITISH' between pages 96/97

Directions: Park is in Newbridge village, signed north from B3401 (Yarmouth - Newport) road. O.S.GR: SZ412878.

Isle of Wight

The island is a popular destination with a certain old world charm, combining coast and countryside activities and scenery with a mild, sunny climate and a network of footpaths and bridleways. It has a wide range of tourist attractions and sports facilities. Ferry companies offer mid-week discount packages for touring caravan owners. We found that most of the park owners are knowledgeable about deals and we suggest you contact the parks and let them arrange the most economical crossing.

244 Adgestone Camping Park, nr. Sandown

Well run touring park with swimming pool, popular with families.

Nestling at the foot of Brading Down, near the Adgestone Vineyard and with pleasant views across the valley, Adgestone provides a relaxed holiday atmosphere for families, complementing the attractions of nearby beaches and amenities at Sandown and Shanklin. About 200 marked pitches, all with electric hook-up available are divided into groups by tidy bar-rail fences, hedges and many attractive, ornamental trees. A further group of pitches can be found close to the banks of the small River Yar on the park's perimeter, where you can take a peaceful stroll or go fishing. There are no caravan holiday homes. Two, low, neat sanitary blocks offer very clean facilities with free hot water to controllable showers and washbasins with some in private cabins also providing 3 en-suite family shower rooms, 3 toddler/baby care areas and full facilities for the disabled. Fully equipped launderette, also hair care areas with hairdryers and sockets. Amenities on the park include floodlit swimming and paddling pools, heated from mid-May, but open earlier for brave swimmers, with a sheltered, grass sunbathing area, beautifully kept with colourful flower displays, as there are elsewhere on the park. Two sturdy children's adventure playgrounds (grass based) with a Tudor style playhouse for the little ones. Table tennis room, petanque court, volleyball and football pitch with goal posts. Good sized fenced and hedged dog exercise field. Barbecues allowed and are for hire from reception. Two public phones and post box. Ice pack and battery charging services and tourist information. Well stocked, licensed shop with wide range of camping and caravan accessories - in fact it is the island's main stockist. Good value takeaway (limited opening before Whit B.H). There is a small, private fishing lake and access to walks and bridleways on the Downs behind the park. One mile to bus route and pub.

Directions: Park is signed only from A3055 at Lake (a place) between Sandown and Shanklin. Leave A3055 just west of railway bridge, by Manor House pub. 1 mile to park. O.S.GR: SZ590855.

Charges guide:
-- Per adult £3.80 - £5.50; child (3-15 yrs) £1.90 - £3.25; dog £1.30; electricity £2.00; extra car £1.50; pup tent or awning free.
-- Off peak concessions for the over 50s.
-- Ferry packages available - park will help get best deal.
-- Good behaviour deposit required for young persons.
-- VAT included.
-- Credit cards accepted.

Open:
Easter - end September.

Address:
Adgestone, nr. Sandown, I.O.W. PO36 0HL.

Tel:
(01983) 403432 or 403989.
FAX: (01983) 404955.

Reservations:
Deposit £5 per night booked on standard tariff; balance payable on arrival.

Lower Adgestone Road, Nr Sandown
Isle of Wight, PO36 0HL
Tel: 01983 403432/403989

WINNERS OF AA's BEST CAMPSITE AWARD 1997/98 FOR SOUTHERN ENGLAND

Superb family run park set in beautiful countryside with lovely walks all around, but only 1½ miles to sandy beach. Excellent toilet and disabled facilities include family shower rooms and baby bathing areas. Well stocked shop with off-licence and extensive range of camping and caravan accessories. Pets welcome.

● PADDLING POOL ● SWIMMING POOL

● TAKEAWAY FOOD ● ADVENTURE PLAY AREAS

● PRIVATE RIVER AND POND FISHING

● PACKAGE HOLIDAYS INCLUSIVE OF FERRIES

● CONCESSIONS FOR COUPLES 50 AND OVER

'Rallies are most welcome'

Red Funnel Ferries

As the original cross-Solent operator, Red Funnel celebrated 135 years of running a ferry service between Southampton and Cowes with the introduction of three super new car ferries. The new ships have been fitted out to a very high standard and we were very impressed with the on-board facilities which include a shop, bar, restaurant, seating areas and sun deck. Each vessel is able to carry up to 140 cars and there are 19 sailings a day in high season. The crossing time is 55 minutes.

see colour opposite page

247 Southland Camping Park, Newchurch, nr. Sandown

Quiet, well run touring park 3 miles from popular resorts.

Southland was opened in 1981 in the grounds of a former nursery and has matured nicely with many attractive shrubs and trees. In the peaceful country setting of the Arreton valley, it is a sheltered park with 120 large, level pitches backing on to and separated by hedging. Comfortable and spacious, all have electricity (10/16A) and some water points. A modern building houses reception and the shop, with tourist information. The excellent, well maintained toilet block has recently been extended ('99). The ladies' is modern, light and airy with washbasins in spacious cubicles, low level basins for children, push-button hot showers, three basin and shower cubicles and a hairdressing area. The men's gains extra space and more facilities. Bathroom (on payment), baby room, a good unit for disabled people, and two family shower rooms also suitable for disabled people. A rustic building houses laundry and dishwashing sinks (H&C) and there are plentiful water points, chemical disposal and a motorcaravan service point. A quiet, well kept park, a fenced children's play area is in the top corner and dog walks are provided (more than one dog by prior arrangement only). Nearby Arreton and Newchurch have craft shops and in August the National Garlic Festival. Sandown and Shanklin are 3 miles, the beach at Lake, 2½ miles. A bus route stops at the top of the road, two pubs are within walking distance and there is access to walks. The park has arranged concessions at the Heights Sports Centre. Fishing ½ mile, riding 2 miles, bicycle hire or golf 3 miles. A member of the Countryside Discovery group.

Directions: Park is signed from A3055/6 Newport-Sandown road, southeast of Arreton. O.S.GR: SZ557847.

Charges 2000:
-- Per adult £3.50 - £5.20; child (3-15 yrs) £1.60 - £2.50; electricity £2.00; dog £1.10.
-- Packages incl. ferry travel available.
-- Special low season offers.
-- VAT included
-- Credit cards accepted.
Open:
Easter - end September.
Address:
Newchurch, Sandown, IOW PO36 0LZ
Tel:
(01983) 865385.
FAX: (01983) 867663.
E-mail:
info@southland.co.uk.
Reservations:
Made for any length with £30 deposit per pitch, per week (or part week).

248 Appuldurcombe Gardens Caravan and Camping Park, Wroxall

Pleasant, family park with heated outdoor pool, with some holiday caravans.

This well kept little park would be a pleasant spot for a stay on the Isle of Wight. Quietly situated in a village and once part of the grounds of Appuldurcombe House, it is a little back from the sea - Ventnor beach 2½ miles and Shanklin 3 - with distant views and good walks nearby. It has a sheltered, heated swimming pool (60 x 25 ft, Spr. BH.- end Aug) and an attractive bar and lounge, with dance floor, beside the pool, where there is limited entertainment at Spr. B.H. and school holidays. It is therefore quite a lively park. There are also 40 holiday caravans for hire in the attractive, old walled garden and two flats. The 100 marked touring pitches, 46 with electricity (10A), are on either side of gravel roads on a slightly sloping meadow. A further field with a pond is available for recreation and a little stream flows past the reception block. Two small sanitary units serve the site. The older unit, now very dated, is behind reception and to one side of the touring field. The other unit, more recently refurbished, is in the old walled garden. Washbasins are set in flat surfaces, showers are on payment in the old unit (10p), but free in the refurbished one. Dishwashing sinks and facilities for disabled visitors. Small shop (in school holidays, otherwise limited). TV room. Fishing, bicycle hire, riding, golf and boat launching within 3 miles. The park can be peaceful and quiet in early and late season, whilst being busily active in high season.

Directions: From A3020 Newport - Sandown road turn right on Shanklin road. Follow through Godshill to Whiteley Bank roundabout and turn right for Wroxall. Continue for 1 mile past Donkey Sanctuary and site is to right in village - watch for sign. The entrance to the site access lane is off a narrow road on a blind bend and the access lane itself is too narrow for two units to pass (unguarded stream on one side and corners with jutting out walls). O.S.GR: SZ548803.

Charges 1999:
-- Per adult £2.65 - £4.40; child (3-13 yrs) £1.75 - £2.00; pitch free - £1.50; dog 50p or £3.00 per week; awning free; electricity £2.00.
-- Credit cards accepted.
-- VAT included.
Open:
1 March - 31 October.
Address:
Wroxall, nr. Ventnor, I.O.W. PO38 3EP.
Tel:
(01983) 852597.
FAX: (01983) 856225.
Reservations:
Made with £10 non-refundable deposit per week booked.

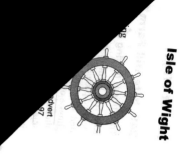

...le of island.

...of outstanding natural beauty, its ...d of Wootton Creek where you may ...below the site you might catch a ...nt – the red squirrel. Fifty unmarked ...with 19 electric hook-ups (10A), a ...e area for ball games, etc. (kite flying ...er cables). The nicely tiled modern ...ntrollable, high pressure showers, a ..., a fully equipped room for disabled ...cilities and gas supplies are available from reception. Torches wou.. .. .. Wootton Bridge village has a fish and chip shop, a launderette and a mini-market which is open long hours, and several supermarkets are only ten minutes away by car. Fishing, riding and golf, all within 3 miles. A bus stop is close (every 15 minutes to most parts of the island). The Firestone Copse, managed by the Forestry Commission, is near with walking trails and wildlife. Nearby attractions include the Steam Railway, Butterfly World, Brickfields Horse Country, Robin Hill Theme Park, and Haseley Manor - the island's oldest manor.

Charges 2000:
-- Per adult £3.00 - £3.50; child (5-15 yrs) £1.50 - £2.10; electricity £2.00.
-- VAT included.
Open:
All year.
Address:
Firestone Copse Road, Wootton Bridge, Ryde, I.O.W. PO33 4LE.
Tel:
(01983) 882543.
Reservations:
Advisable for B.Hs and peak season, made with £15 p/week deposit.

Directions: From A3054 (Newport - Ryde road), just east of Wootton Bridge, half way up hill (where site is signed) turn right into lane, site entrance is 250 yds. on right. O.S.GR: SZ550918.

250 Heathfield Farm Camping, Freshwater

Quiet family camping site, with views over the Solent.

Heathfield is a pleasant contrast to many of the other sites on the island, in that it is a 'no frills' sort of place, very popular with tenters, cyclists and small camper vans. Despite its name, it is no longer a working farm. The large, open meadow provides 60 large, level pitches, 30 with electricity (10A), and a very large open area for non-electric pitches. The main sanitary unit is housed in a modern, ingeniously customised, 'portacabin' type unit which provides WCs, washbasins (one cubicle for ladies) and showers - these are slightly different in that they have two push-button controls, one for pre-mixed hot water, the other for cold only (provided at the special request of some of the regular customers). To the side of this unit are covered laundry and dishwashing sinks. A second smaller unit has WCs and washbasins only. Further facilities include a baby room, a red telephone kiosk, recycling bins, chemical disposal and a new motorcaravan service point by the entrance. Also here is a late arrivals and parking area on grass. A play field for ball games also has two picnic tables and two barbecues provided. There is no shop as you are only eight minutes walk from the centre of Freshwater, but Gaz and an ice pack service are provided. Nearby Ivylands Holiday Park is under the same ownership and the laundry facilities there may be used by Heathfield campers. No commercial vehicles are accepted and the gate is locked 22.30-07.00. The site overlooks Colwell Bay and across the Solent towards Milford-on-Sea and Hurst Castle. It is ideal for visiting attractions on the western side of the island including Totland and Freshwater Bays, The Needles and Old Battery, Compton Down, and Mottistone Manor Garden. The Military road which runs from Freshwater Bay to St Catherine's Point gives spectacular coastal views.

Charges 1999:
-- Per adult £3.00 - £3.50; child (3-15 yrs) £1.25 - £1.75; extra car 50p; dog 50p; electricity £1.75.
-- VAT included.
-- No credit cards.
Open:
1 May - 30 September.
Address:
Ivylands Holiday Park, The Broadway, Totland Bay, I.O.W. PO39 0AN.
Tel:
(01983) 756756.
FAX: (01983) 752480.
Reservations:
Advisable for B.Hs and peak season; contact site.

Directions: From A3054 north of Totland and Colwell turn into Heathfield Road where site is signed. Site entrance is on right after a short distance. O.S.GR: SZ334878

257 Lincoln Farm Park, Standlake, nr. Witney

Family run park with indoor leisure facilities in quiet, rural position.

From its immaculately tended grounds and quality facilities, to the efficient and friendly staff, this park is a credit to its owner. Situated in a small, quiet village it is well set back and screened by mature trees, with wide gravel roads, hedged enclosures, attractive brick pathways and good lighting. All 87 numbered, level touring pitches are generously sized and have electrical connections (10/16A), 75 with gravel hardstanding and adjacent grass for awnings, and 22 fully serviced (fresh and waste water, electricity and TV). The two toilet blocks are of notable quality, from Cotswold stone exteriors and colourful hanging baskets, to tiled and pine clad interiors, with background music and enormous plant displays. Showers (sensibly sized and designed), washbasins in cubicles, WCs, hairdryers, ample shelf space and heating make them a pleasure to use. A well equipped, separate unit for disabled people is adjacent to a specially reserved pitch with direct access. Two family bathrooms (incorporating baby bath and changing facilities) complete the sanitary amenities. Everything is well maintained and exceptionally clean. Each block also contains a laundry room, dishwashing sinks under cover (more throughout the site), freezers, fridges and microwaves; the latter being welcome provision for campers. Other amenities include a small shop, with basic supplies, telephone box, information kiosk, outdoor chess/draughts, putting green and sizeable adventure play area (bark chipping and rubber base), motorcaravan service point, chemical disposal and battery charging. Although only a relatively small site its leisure facilities are quite outstanding. One indoor swimming pool is always appreciated, but two (30' x 15' and 40' x 20') plus a toddlers' pool, spa pools, saunas, steam room, sun bed and a fitness suite really offer something rather special. Charges for all of these are modest, and outside of the open sessions everything can be hired privately by the hour. Dogs are welcome (2 per pitch) with allocated walks. Fishing (lake and river) 300 yds - 5 miles, riding centre and water sports nearby, plus Oxford and the Cotswolds conveniently close. A member of the Best of British group.

Directions: Take A415 Witney - Abingdon road and turn into Standlake High Street by garage; park is 300 yds on the right. O.S.GR: SP396029.

Charges 1999:
-- Per unit incl. 2 persons £10.75 - £12.75; extra adult £2.25; child (5-14 yrs) £1.25; full awning (no groundsheets) £1.25, porch awning 75p; electricity £2.00 - £2.50; `super' pitch (excl. electricity) £6.00; extra pup tent £1.25; dog free.
-- Low season offers.
-- VAT included.
-- Credit cards accepted.

Open:
1 February - 26 Nov.

Address:
High Street, Standlake, nr. Witney, Oxon OX8 7RH.

Tel:
(01865) 300239.

Reservations:
Made with £10 non-returnable deposit.

See colour feature for 'BEST of BRITISH' between pages 96/97

260 Barnstones Caravan and Camping Park, Great Bourton

Small, tidy park, 3 miles from Banbury, open all year round.

This small, neat park provides an excellent point from which to explore the Cotswolds, Oxford and Stratford-upon-Avon. The 49 level pitches all have gravel hardstanding with a grass area for awnings (no groundsheets allowed) and 10A electricity; 20 of these are fully serviced. Shrubs, flowers and a central gravel road convey a tidy impression throughout and the low level lighting is subtle but effective. The newly upgraded toilet block is small, but it can be heated and is quite adequate for the number of people it serves. It houses vanity style washbasins, WCs and adjustable unisex showers, all with free hot water. There is chemical disposal asnd a separate dishwashing and laundry room. The small, fenced play area for children (grass and bark chipping base) is adjacent to the entrance road. A fenced dog walk and rally field is near the main road, so some traffic noise is to be expected. All arrivals are required to report to the warden's caravan at the park entrance. Gas is available but no on-site shop - the nearest village is 1 mile, a supermarket 3 miles and a pub 150 yds. Fishing, bicycle hire, golf and riding, all within 3 miles.

Directions: From M40 take exit 11 for Banbury. Turn off following signs for Chipping Norton, straight on at two small roundabouts. At third roundabout turn right on A423 signed Southam and in 2½ miles turn right signed Great Bourton, Site entrance is 100 yds on right. O.S.GR: SP455454.

Charges 2000:
-- Per unit incl. 2 persons £5.50; extra person 5-12 yrs 50p, over 12 yrs £1.00; 1-man tent £3.50; awning 50p - £1.00; electricity £1.50; fully serviced pitch incl. electricity £8.50.
-- OAPs less 50p per night.
-- No credit cards.

Open:
All year.

Address:
Great Bourton, nr. Banbury, Oxfordshire OX17 1QU.

Tel:
(01295) 750289.

Reservations:
Contact park.

Alan Rogers' Discount

Less 50p per night, per unit all year

Oxfordshire

258 Cotswold View Caravan and Camping Site, Charlbury

Well run family site with good facilities in quiet location.

On the edge of the Cotswolds and surrounded by fine views, this site offers a warm welcome. It successfully combines a working farm, touring site and self catering country cottages. Wide gravel or tarmac roads ensure easy access to all of the pitches in the 10-acre touring area. A second new toilet block, together with the original, very well maintained block, provide excellent facilities for the expanded site which now has 125 all electric pitches (10A). The newly developed area will naturally take some time to mature, but the work has been undertaken to a high standard throughout and the owner is justifiably proud of this latest development. All of the facilities are free (except baths, 50p) and washbasins in cubicles, showers with ample changing space, two family rooms, hairdryers, razor points, soft piped music, central heating and full length mirrors show careful attention to detail. Both blocks have good units for disabled people. There are baby changing facilities, a laundry room, freezers for ice packs and dishwashing sinks under cover (free hot water). Plenty of fresh and waste water points and a motorcaravan service point complete the amenities. The small reception also serves as a shop that is licensed and sells freshly baked bread, home-made cakes and eggs from their own hens. Farmhouse breakfasts (ordered the night before) are served in the farmhouse itself. The farm's animals (sheep, hens, pigs, rabbits, ducks, goats, ponies and a donkey) add great interest to one's stay. Well defined and maintained trails around the enclosures enable the animals to be safely observed, whilst additional trails and woodland plantations provide more walking opportunities, particularly for dogs who can be allowed off the lead. Children have a central, sheltered grassed area in which to play, whilst a small games room should be ready for 2000. A hard tennis court and bicycle hire are available. American motorhomes accepted. B&B is offered at the farmhouse. Fishing 1 mile, riding 10 miles, golf 7 miles. Convenient for touring the Cotswolds, there is also a good train service for day trips to London.

Charges 2000:
-- Per unit incl. 2 persons £8.00 - £11.00; extra adult £1.75; child (5-16 yrs) £1.00; electricity £2.00; dog free.
-- VAT included.
Open:
1 April - 31 October.
Address:
Enstone Road, Charlbury, Oxfordshire OX7 3JH.
Tel:
(01608) 810314.
FAX: (01608) 811891.
Reservations:
Advisable for B.H.s and peak season.

Directions: From A44 Oxford - Stratford-on-Avon road, take B4022 to Charlbury, just south of Enstone. Park is 2 miles on left. O.S.GR: SP365210.

262 Wysdom Touring Park Caravan Site, Burford

Very small garden-like site only a few minutes walk from Burford town centre.

You will have to go a long way before you find anything else remotely like this place! The land is owned by Burford School and the enterprising caretaker and his wife, caravanners themselves, suggested that they create this wonderful place to raise money for the hard pressed school (hence cheques payable to Burford School). It is really like putting your caravan or motorcaravan (no tents permitted) into their own private garden. The 19 pitches are separated from each other by hedges, all have electricity hook-ups (16A) and a picnic table and some have their own tap. The small sanitary building offers all you need including chemical disposal, although with only one shower and one toilet per sex, whilst it meets statistical requirements there may be a queue at times. When we visited, the site was a true riot of colour. The town of Burford is yards away with its famous shop lined hill full of antique shops and all those 'interesting' shops it is so much fun rooting about in. The site is immediately next to Burford Golf Club and, for those interested, you can walk from your caravan to the first tee. A great location for exploring the Cotswolds, Burford calls itself the 'Gateway to the Cotswolds'. There is a narrow turn into the site off the school drive and this site is not therefore considered suitable for large motorhomes.

Charges 1999:
-- Per unit incl. 2 persons and electricity £6.00; extra person £1.50; dog in excess of one 50p.
-- No credit cards.
Open:
All year.
Address:
The Bungalow, Burford School, Burford, Oxon OX18 4JG.
Tel:
(01993) 823207.
Reservations:
Contact park.

Directions: From roundabout on A40 at Burford, take A361 and site is a few yards on the right signed Burford School. Once in school drive watch for narrow entrance to site on right in about 100 yards. O.S.GR: SP249117.

261 Bo Peep Farm Caravan Park, Adderbury, nr. Banbury

Peaceful, friendly park in rural setting with extensive walks and good views.

Set amongst 85 acres of farmland and woodland, there is an air of spacious informality about this park and it blends perfectly with the views surrounding it. Part of the Caravan Club's `managed under contact' scheme, non-members are also very welcome. All 82 numbered, grass pitches are large, have 16A electricity and, with the exception of eight that slope gently, are quite level. Gravel roads connect the various areas, such as Poppy Field, The Paddocks and The Warren, with reasonable shelter provided by hedges and trees. Pitches are mostly set around the perimeters, leaving central areas free for a liberal sprinkling of picnic tables. The original toilet block, not modern but heated, clean and fresh has been supplemented by a larger, purpose-built unit, equally clean and heated. There are now ample showers (with seat, hooks and changing space), vanity style washbasins, WCs and hairdryers. A small shop stocks gas and basics, information centre (with maps, leaflets, etc). Other facilities include chemical disposal, a motorcaravan service point, caravan cleaning area and telephone, with undercover dishwashing sinks, laundry rooms and low level lighting. Children are welcome but there is no play area. A network of circular walks around the site, including the pleasant river walk, has wide, well-kept paths and is being continually extended and developed; even bench seats and waste bins are provided. Dogs are also welcome on these walks, even without a lead. A 15 acre field has been acquired for recreation and in the longer term, a lake is planned, plus the reclaiming of farmland to redevelop as woodland and more walks, a clear indication that owners Andrew and Margaret Hodge seek to improve a notable site even further. Fishing (apply to office). Next door is a golf course. Banbury is just 3 miles, the famous Blenheim Palace 6. Great day trips to Stratford upon Avon, Warwick and its castle and even Silverstone can be entertained from this base. Caravan storage.

Charges 2000:
-- Per adult £3.90; child (over 5 yrs) £1.20; pitch (non-member) £4.00; electricity £1.50.
-- Tent campers: per adult £4.00; child £1.20.
-- No credit cards.
Open:
26 March - 1 November.
Address:
Aynho Road, Adderbury, Banbury, Oxon OX17 3NP.
Tel:
(01295) 810605.
FAX: as phone.
E-mail: warden@ bo-peep.co.uk.
Reservations:
Advised and made with £10 deposit.

Directions: The village of Adderbury is on the A4260 Banbury - Oxford road. At traffic lights in Adderbury turn on B4100 signed Aynho; park is clearly signed, ½ mile on the right (½ mile drive). O.S.GR: SP482353.

269 Wellington Country Park, Riseley, nr. Reading

Quiet, wooded touring site within popular country park.

The Wellington Country Park is open to all on payment of an entry fee (entry for campers included in pitch fee) and many visit it for a day out. It contains a boating and fishing lake, a large adventure playground and other activities for children, nature trails, deer park, fitness course, crazy golf, narrow-gauge railway, animal farm and a dairy museum. Within the 350 acre park, the camping site is situated in a woodland area. It has 70 pitches, 18 with hardstanding and 42 with electricity hook-ups (10A). There are several individual pitches and some small groups all within woodland clearings which gives a very rustic and casual feel to this site. It is a very pleasant setting and we found it quite nostalgic, the site being of the older and more traditional style of camping found frequently some 20 years ago. Once the Country Park closes at 5.30 pm. all is very quiet. There is limited site lighting and a torch is advised. Access is through a locked gate (deposit for key) and you must make advance arrangements if you plan to arrive after 5.30 pm when the main park shop closes. However, there is a late arrivals field at the entrance, although this has no sanitation at all. It is admitted that our serious query about the standard of the sanitary facilities on site is valid and at the time of our inspection there was much talk about upgrading over the winter. We are told that this is a priority – the ladies' for 2000, the men's for 2001 – this would make a huge difference. The present facilities go back many years and do not compare favourably with standards now seen. However, this is a very special place and we recommend it for those who prefer the quiet and simple style of camping. Free hot water is plentiful, three pre-set showers in each section are adequate, there are good dishwashing sinks, an ample laundry and chemical disposal. A small shop stocks basics (no gas) with very limited hours. Public phones are at the sanitary block and near reception. Riding nearby. This site is just 30 minutes drive from Legoland and Windsor. Further site lighting is planned for 2000.

north of M3 exit 5.
O.S.GR: SU727628.

Charges guide:
-- Per unit incl. up to 2 adults and 2 children £12.50 for Fri, Sat and Sunday nights, B.Hs and high season; Mon - Thursday off-peak £7.00; extra adult £1.25; child 75p; pup tent 75p; electricity £1.75.
-- Fee includes fishing permit for ONE person.
-- VAT included.
-- Credit cards accepted.
Open:
1 March - 31 October.
Address:
Riseley, nr. Reading, Berkshire RG7 1SP.
Tel:
(0118) 9326444.
FAX: (0118) 9326445.
Reservations:
Made with £12.50 non-returnable deposit (min 2 nights July/Aug. or 3 nights at B.Hs).

Directions: Park is signed at Riseley, off A32/A33 road between Reading and Basingstoke, and from M4. It is about 4 miles south of M4 exit 11 and 7 miles

275 Highclere Farm Country Touring Park, Seer Green

Useful country park for London or Legoland.

Only 25 miles from London and 10 from Legoland and Windsor, this is a peaceful park that backs onto fields and woodland. Developed around a working chicken farm, there are also angora goats, a few large sheep and horses to provide that country feel. There are 60 level grass pitches, most with 10A electricity and 45 with gravel hardstanding, the rest being reserved for tents. The heated sanitary facilities have been converted from a chicken house and offer two large showers per sex and one unisex unit (20p) with screened cabinets that provide plenty of room for the family. Likewise are roomy toilets, washbasins with room for wash bags, etc, hairdryers (20p); all is very clean and cosy. A unit with toilet and washbasin is provided for disabled people. A laundry room has washing machine, dryer, spin dryer and iron, plus washing up and laundry sinks. Converted chicken houses also form the basis for the excellent en-suite bed and breakfast facilities. The atmosphere is friendly, but informal, with reception doubling as a small shop that can supply all sizes of fresh eggs. A fenced children's play area and a footpath are at the top of the site. Fishing 8 miles, bicycle hire 3 miles, riding or golf within 1 mile. A bus service to Uxbridge passes the site, London is 35 minutes by train, whilst Windsor Castle and Thorpe Park are also within easy reach. A member of the Countryside Discovery group.

Charges 1999:
-- Per unit £9.50 - £10.00; 1-man tent £7.00; extra pup tent £1.00; electricity £1.50 - £2.00; awning, dog or extra car free.
-- Credit cards accepted (min. £20).
-- VAT included.
Open:
All year except February.
Address:
Newbarn Lane, Seer Green, Beaconsfield, Buckinghamshire HP9 2QZ.
Tel:
(01494) 874505.
FAX: (01494) 875238.
Reservations:
Contact park.

Directions: From M40 take exit 2, then follow A40 towards London. Take first left for Seer Green, then follow site signs. O.S.GR: SU977927.

281 Camping and Caravanning Club Site, Chertsey

Splendidly located site on banks of the River Thames.

This is an old-established site (1926), a flagship of the Club, which is only a few minutes walk from the shops and amenities of Chertsey. Lovely flower displays greet you as you drive in - an indication of a well cared for site. There are 200 numbered pitches in total (for all types of unit), 95 with 10A electricity and 19 with hardstanding. They are either in open, field-like areas, beside the river creek or in little nooks and corners, which avoids the regularity of some sites. Squirrels, rabbits and ducks abound and mature trees and plants create a pretty site, with views across the water and towards Chertsey bridge, although unfortunately there is some road noise and, depending on flight paths, aircraft noise. The main toilet block is centrally situated by the recreation hall with table tennis. The other is at the entrance in the same building as reception and shop. They are well equipped with free hot water, washbasins in cabins, hairdryers and laundry and dishwashing rooms. Separate facilities are approached via a ramp for wheelchair users. There is an area for hanging clothes out, a chemical disposal point and a motorcaravan service point. A good, under cover tourist information area is next to reception, again suitable for disabled people, plus a children's play area on bark and short dog walk areas. Shop (well stocked with essentials and gas) open 8-11 am. and 4-6 pm. Public phone. The rail station for London is at Chertsey or Weybridge. Fishing is possible (£1 per day, NRA licence needed). Caravan storage..

Charges 2000:
-- Per 2 adults £7.50 - £10.60; child (6-18 yrs) £1.65; non-member pitch fee £4.30; electricity £1.60 - £2.35.
-- VAT included.
-- Credit cards accepted.
Open:
All year.
Address:
Bridge Road, Chertsey, Surrey KT16 8JX.
Tel:
(01932) 562405.
(no calls after 8 pm).
Reservations:
Necessary and made with deposit; contact the wardens.

Directions: Suggested: from M25 use junction 11. Turn left at roundabout in the direction of Shepperton and continue to second set of traffic lights. Turn right then almost immediately left watching for green Club camp sign just before Chertsey bridge; the opening is narrow. O.S.GR: TQ052667.

For lists of parks which offer facilities on site for FISHING, GOLF, HORSE RIDING, BICYCLE HIRE or BOAT LAUNCHING see pages 237 - 239

South East England Tourist Board

East Sussex, West Sussex, Surrey and Kent

The Old Brew House, Warwick Park,

Tunbridge Wells, Kent TN2 5TU

Tel: (01892) 540766 Fax: (01892) 511008

The South East England Tourist Board covers the counties of **East Sussex** and **West Sussex**, **Kent** and **Surrey** and is the most affluent and heavily populated of the tourist board areas.

Kent with its apple orchards, hop fields and vineyards is affectionately known as the 'Garden of England'. Architectural styles are especially distinctive in the Weald of Kent and Sussex, where tile-hung houses can be seen in many villages, as well as thatched houses and oasthouses - most of these have now been converted into dwellings as the production of beer from locally grown hops has almost ceased.

The scenery varies from gentle, undulating landscapes to steep escarpments on the edges of the North and South Downs and dramatic coastal cliffs, notably at Beachy Head, where the South Downs meet the sea. At the foot of the white cliffs of Dover, where the North Downs reach the coast, the Channel Tunnel heads beneath the sea on its way to France.

Its coastline has many traditional seaside resorts and busy ports, while inland there are magnificent castles - Leeds, Bodiam, Hever and Arundel - and stately homes and amazing gardens such as Sissinghurst. Brighton boasts the extraordinary Royal Pavilion, pleasure palace of the Prince Regent, where a riot of domes and minarets determines its unmistakable outline.

Canterbury has been the centre of the English Church since AD597 when St. Augustine converted King Ethelbert of Kent to Christianity and subsequently became the first archbishop. The cathedral became a centre of pilgrimage after Thomas à Becket was murdered there in 1170.

Chartwell is the home of Sir Winston Churchill and the rooms where he did so much of his writing look much as he left them (note: the National Trust enforces timed ticketing to alleviate long waits). The elegant Regency spa town of Royal Tunbridge Wells has been a fashionable market town for many years; the Pantiles was an established shopping centre in the 17th century.

London is little more than an hour away and there is easy road and rail access to northern France for day trips.

282 Camping and Caravanning Club Site Horsley, East Horsley

Pretty site with small lake and good facilities.

London and all the sights are only 40 minutes away by train but Horsley is a delightful, quiet unspoilt site with a good duck and goose population on its part lily covered lake. It provides 135 pitches, of which 60 have 10A electrical connections; 29 are all weather pitches (most with electricity). Seventeen of the pitches are around the bank of the lake, the rest further back in three hedged, grass fields with mostly level ground but with some slope in places. There is a range of mature trees and a woodland dog walk area (may be muddy). There are two purpose built, heated toilet blocks, one part of the entrance building which includes reception. Fittings and design are good, with free hot water, well equipped showers, hairdryers, some washbasins in cabins, Belfast sink and parent and child room with vanity style basin, toilet and wide surface area. There are also well designed facilities for disabled people, a chemical disposal point and new drying areas. A recreation hall with TV and table tennis (bring your own bats) is sometimes used for bingo. Children's play area. Basic provisions, gas and books are kept in reception. Shops and the station are 1 mile, pubs 1½-2 miles. Fishing is possible from May (£3 per day, NRA licence required). Golf 1½ miles, riding 2 miles. Resident wardens will make you comfortable. Guildford and the R.H.S. gardens at Wisley are close by.

Charges 2000:
-- Per 2 adults £7.50 - £10.60; child (6-18 yrs) £1.65; non-member pitch fee £4.30; electricity £1.60 - £2.35.
-- VAT included.

Open:
March - November

Address:
Ockham Road North, East Horsley, Surrey KT24 6PE.

Tel:
(01483) 283273 (no calls after 8 pm.)

Reservations:
Necessary and made with deposit; contact the wardens.

Directions: From M25 junction 10, travel 2½-3 miles towards Guildford and take first left on B2039 to Ockham and East Horsley, continuing through Ockham towards East Horsley. Site is on right - watch carefully for small club sign. O.S.GR: TQ083552.

Sussex

289 White Rose Touring Park, Wick, nr. Littlehampton

Small, well organised park close to West Sussex seaside resorts.

Situated about midway between the imposing castle at Arundel and the beaches of Littlehampton, White Rose makes an excellent base from which to enjoy the many attractions of this popular district. Watersports centres, race courses, beaches, historical and cultural interests, downland walks and the resorts of Bognor and Brighton are within easy reach. There are 140 pitches available for tourists, 88 with electricity (10/16A). The flat grassy meadow is surrounded by trees and divided into two areas. The first part has pitches on either side of concrete access roads which are individually hedged, as on the continent, with electricity hook-ups and shared water/waste water connections. The second area includes 14 super pitches (each having electricity, fresh and waste water and sewage connections, TV aerial socket and night light), full sized pitches with no electricity, plus special pitches for small tents and small motorcaravans. The central toilet block is fully tiled with free hot water in washbasins set in flat units and showers with hot water controlled by push-button taps. Two washrooms are provided for disabled people (key from reception). Chemical disposal point. Reception has a few basic supplies and gas available; a supermarket is ¼ mile away. Fishing, boat launching, bicycle hire, riding and golf within 2 miles. Special dog walking area and a central play area for children. A busy road runs along one side of the park and road noise could be disturbing in the early mornings during the week to a few pitches.

Directions: Take A284 Littlehampton road from A27 just to the east of Arundel station, pass the campsite behind the pub at this junction and park is signed along on the left. O.S.GR: TQ026041.

Charges 1999:
-- Per pitch incl. unit, car and up to 4 people: super pitch £15.00, pitch with electricity £13.00, no services £11.00; extra person £2.50; extra car £2.00.
-- Trailed boats by prior arrangement only.
-- Reductions for 1 week or 1 month outside 10 July - 31 Aug.
-- Credit cards accepted.
Open:
All year except 14 Jan - 15 March.
Address:
Mill Lane, Wick, W. Sussex BN17 7PH
Tel:
(01903) 716176.
FAX: (01903) 732671.
Reservations:
Made with deposit of 1 nights fee p/week reserved.

288 Raylands Caravan Park, Southwater, nr. Horsham

Spacious park with excellent facilities in rural environment.

A pleasant, reasonably priced park (owned by Roundstone Caravans at Southwater), deep in the heart of the Sussex countryside, Raylands is well maintained and thoughtfully landscaped. The 65 caravan holiday homes occupy an area of their own and touring units use marked, numbered pitches on gently sloping grass meadows separated into smaller areas by trees and hard access roads, with electricity (15A) available to 50 of the 65 pitches. The park manager seems to have engendered a friendly atmosphere and is willing to advise on the very numerous attractions the locality has to offer. London and Brighton are easily reached by rail from nearby Horsham and the region abounds with places of historical, cultural and sporting interests. The clubhouse (weekends only in low season) has snacks and good value full meals at weekends (to early Sept) with a special bar/dining room for non-smokers and children's games room with pool, table tennis, video games and TV. An adult's games room has pool, darts and a small library. The single toilet block (unheated) is centrally situated and is a modern building of good quality with free hot water in the basins and hot showers on payment. There are separate en-suite facilities for disabled visitors, a laundry room with washing machine, dryer, a dishwashing sink with free hot water and chemical disposal facilities. No shop on site but a supermarket and other shops are under 2 miles. Public telephone. Large dog exercise field complete with seats at the far end and another large field for children's ball games. Tennis court. Swimming pool 3 miles. Fishing, bicycle hire riding and golf, all 2 miles. Some road noise from the A24.

Directions: Leave A24 Worthing - London road for Southwater and follow signs for approx. 2 miles on narrow lanes to park. O.S.GR: TQ170265.

Charges 1999:
-- Per pitch incl. 2 persons £9.00; extra person 50p; hiker or cyclist tent, 1 person £6.00 - £9.00; electricity £1.50.
-- No credit cards.
Open:
1 March - 31 October.
Address:
Jackrells Lane, Southwater, Sussex. RH13 7DH.
Tel:
(01403) 731822.
FAX: (01403) 732828.
Reservations:
Essential for BHs, advisable for peak season, with £10 deposit.

294 Honeybridge Park, Dial Post, nr. Horsham

Touring park in the South Downs area.

Since '97 the new owners at Honeybridge have been developing this 15 acre park which now has around 100 pitches, including 40 gravel hardstandings. Some are individually hedged, although these are usually taken by longer stay units. The others are on slightly sloping grass with little to separate them, with around 62 electric hook-ups (16A). The reception building houses a small shop, and the park provides a discount voucher pack for local facilities on booking in. The sanitary unit can be heated in cool weather and provides all modern facilities including some washbasins in cubicles and push-button hot showers. In addition there is a unit for disabled persons, dishwashing and laundry sinks, plus a washing machine and dryer. A large wooden, adventure-style playground is provided for the children on an area of grass well away from the pitches, and simple family enter-tainment is organised on special occasions. This site is ideally situated for visiting the South Downs with its many attractive villages. There is a pub, restaurant and tea shop in Dial Post. Billingshurst and Horsham are both 8 miles away.

Directions: Two miles south of the junction of A24 and A272 at Dial Post, turn east by Old Barn nurseries. Follow signs to site (½ mile). O.S.GR: TQ150190.

Charges 1999:
-- Per pitch £2.50; adult £2.50 - £3.50; child £1.00; electricity £2.00.
-- VAT included.
-- Credit cards accepted.
Open:
All year.
Address:
Honeybridge Lane,
Dial Post, West Sussex
RH13 8NX.
Tel/Fax:
(01403) 710923.
Reservations:
Made with £5 per night deposit (June-Aug), other times £5 for 3 nights, £10 over 3 nights and B.H's.

295 Washington Caravan and Camping Park, Washington

Unusual site near Worthing with superb equestrian facilities.

A campsite with a bias towards tenting families, there are only 21 hardstanding pitches for caravans or motorcaravans, and a large gently sloping grassy field with enough space for 80 tents. The 23 electric hook-ups (16A) are on slot meters (50p). The sanitary facilities are housed in a heated chalet style building and are of an excellent standard, including spacious shower rooms (on payment), and indoor dishwashing and laundry facilities. There is no shop but eggs, bread, butter and milk can be obtained from the reception office. Security is good, but unobtrusive. There is some road noise from the A24. The latest development is a new equestrian centre adjacent to the campsite, including an Olympic standard floodlit arena, a small children's pony arena, stabling and paddock facilities. Excellent riding opportunities on the bridle paths of the South Downs Way. Local attractions (all with free admission, check opening times) include Highdown Chalk Gardens at Worthing, Nutbourne Vineyard near Pulborough, and Steyning Museum. Eating out options include the local pub and a nearby restaurant.

Directions: Site entrance is just east of the junction of the A24 and A283 at Washington, 6 miles north of Worthing. O.S.GR: TQ125130

Charges 1999:
-- Per caravan or motor-caravan (incl. 2 persons) £8.00; tent £1.50; person £3.00; car £1.00; m/cycle £1.00; electricity (metered) 50p.
-- VAT included.
Open:
All year.
Address:
London Road,
Washington,
West Sussex RH20 4AJ.
Tel:
(01903) 892869.
FAX: (01903) 893252.
Reservations:
Contact site for details

290 Horam Manor Touring Park, Horam, nr. Eastbourne

Secluded rural park in the heart of the Sussex countryside.

The touring park is part of, but under separate management from, Horam Manor which has a farm museum, nature trail (free access for campers) and Merrydown Winery. The 90 pitches, 52 with electricity, are on two open meadows joined by a tarmac/gravel road. The field nearer reception is undulating, the second field is flatter but slopes - levelling blocks are needed for motorcaravans. Pitches are generous size, those with electricity being numbered and marked, the rest not. Both areas are ringed with a variety of mainly tall trees. The park, back from the main Eastbourne to Tunbridge Wells road, is a haven of peace and tranquillity. The modern, well built sanitary block at the entrance to the larger field has free hot water in washbasins (set in flat surfaces), showers, laundry and washing up sinks. A family room (key access) has shower, washbasin and toilet and is suitable for disabled visitors. Washing machine. Chemical disposal. Gas available. No shop but the village is close, with supermarkets in Heathfield, 3 miles. Two inns are within walking distance and the Barn cafe at the Farm Centre serves drinks and snacks (10 am. - 5 pm). The Craft Centre has some interesting exhibits and riding stables. The nature trail has walks from ½ -1½ hours in length (written guide available). Fishing is available in 10 lakes on the estate (adults £3). Bicycle hire and golf within 1 mile. Dogs are accepted (max. 2 per unit).

Directions: Entry to the park is signed at the recreation ground at southern edge of Horam village. O.S.GR: TQ577169.

Charges 2000:
-- Per unit incl. 2 adults and 2 children (under 18 yrs) £11.85; extra adult £3.50; extra child 95p; electricity £1.85; extended awning £2.50; dogs (max 2) free.
-- No credit cards.
-- VAT included.
Open:
1 March - 31 October.
Address:
Horam, nr. Heathfield,
E. Sussex TN21 0YD.
Tel:
(01435) 813662.
E-mail: horam.manor
@virgin.net.
Reservations:
Telephone or write to park.

Sussex

293 Sheepcote Valley Caravan Club Site, Brighton

Excellent site in quiet location within boundary of popular resort.

Brighton is without doubt the South of England's most popular seaside resort and now that the Caravan Club has taken over and modernised the Sheepcote Valley Site, there is a first class base from which to enjoy the many and diverse attractions both in the town and this area of the south coast. The site occupies a quiet situation in an almost fully enclosed valley in the South Downs, a mile north of the town's interesting Marina which has a superstore and good variety of shops and restaurants. It is adjacent to extensive recreation grounds and the centre of Brighton is only two miles away with a bus service from the entry road. A wide tarmac road winds its way through the site from reception, with pitches on either side, leading to terraces with grass pitches on the lower slopes of the valley. 82 pitches have hardstanding, there are 13 with water, drainage and TV sockets and all have electricity (16A). Two grass terraces are for tents and these have hard parking near as a low fence prevents cars being taken onto the camping areas. Although there are a number of trees, many of these are young so do not provide shade as yet. Flower beds add to the attractiveness of the site. Two well built, brick, heated sanitary blocks have excellent facilities including free hot water in washbasins (all in private cabins), showers and sinks. In the main season a `portacabin' type building provides additional services near the tent places. There is a well equipped room for wheel chair users, another one for walking disabled and two baby and toddler wash rooms. Other facilities include washing machines, dryers, iron and spin dryer, a motorcaravan service point, chemical toilet disposal points and a children's play area with safety base. Gas is available. The site fully lives up to the very high standards expected from the Caravan Club and provides a first class venue both for a quiet holiday and as a base from which to explore this interesting and historic town and delightful Sussex downland countryside either by car or on foot. A wide variety of tourist attractions is displayed in reception. Non-members are welcome.

Charges 1999:
-- (Non members) Per pitch £6.00 - £7.00; person £3.25 - £4.00; child (5-16 yrs) £1.10 - £1.20; electricity £1.45 - £2.20.
-- VAT included.
-- Credit cards accepted.

Open:
All year.

Address:
East Brighton Park, Brighton, Sussex BN2 5TS.

Tel:
(01273) 626546.

Reservations:
Advised for high season with £5 deposit.

Directions: Site is in eastern part of Brighton and well signed from A259 coast road opposite the Marina through to site entrance. O.S.GR: TQ341043.

292 Bay View Caravan and Camping Park, Pevensey Bay

Friendly beach-side park for couples and families only.

The Adams family have developed Bay View with care over the last few years, a fact which is obvious as soon as you arrive and see the tidy state of everything. There are 3½ acres of mainly flat grass with gravel access roads and a low bank on three sides giving some shelter if it is windy. Careful use of fencing adds to the attractiveness, whilst also keeping the rabbits off the flowers. The 49 pitches (80 sq.m, all with 10/16A electricity and 10 with hardstanding) are neatly marked out by numbered posts, while 5 caravan holiday homes for hire are at the back of the park. There are plenty of water and waste water points. A well made, fenced children's play area on a bark surface has adventure equipment (10 years and under) and is very popular. The centrally placed sanitary facilities are housed in a very well maintained `portacabin' style building which will be heated when necessary. Hot water is free to the washbasins, dishwashing and laundry sinks and on payment (20p) for the showers. There are chemical disposal and motorcaravan services and a laundry room has a washing machine, dryer, spin dryer, iron and board, plus tourist information. Reception is combined with a well stocked shop which is good value and open long hours (the owners live next to it). Gas available. A large `overflow' field opposite the entrance with small `portacabin' style sanitary facilities is for use in the peak season. At other times this space may be used for games. Apart from all the attractions of Sussex, from this very pleasant park you may swim, fish, windsurf, sail or just enjoy the view. Bicycle hire 1 mile, golf 2 miles. Winter caravan storage available. A new marina complex is under construction nearby.

Charges 2000:
-- Per caravan, motor-caravan or trailer/family tent £4.60 - £5.15; adult £2.15 - £2.40; child (2-16 yrs) £1.50 - £1.65; awning £1.50 - £1.65; dog 60p - £1.00; electricity £2.00.
-- VAT included.
-- Couple and families only - no commercial vehicles, large vans or pick-ups.
-- No credit cards.

Open:
Easter/1 April - October.

Address:
Old Martello Road, Pevensey Bay, East Sussex BN24 6DX.

Tel:
(01323) 768688.
FAX: (01323) 769637.
E-mail: bayviewcara-vanpark@tesco.net.

Reservations:
Made with deposit (£25) - contact park.

Directions: Park is about 1 mile west of Pevensey Bay and 2 miles east of Eastbourne, off the A259 Pevensey Bay road. O.S.GR: TQ648028.

296 Whydown Farm Tourist Caravan Park, Sedlescombe, nr. Battle

Small touring park in '1066' country, ideal for couples.

This peaceful, traditional style two acre park has just 26 pitches arranged on grassy terraces, all with electric hook-ups. It is advisable to telephone to make sure space is available before travelling long distances. The tiny, but well maintained sanitary unit has coloured fittings and towel rails and includes controllable hot showers (on payment), laundry facilities with a washing machine and dryer, plus dishwashing sinks, and a suite for disabled persons. Local attractions include the very pretty village of Sedlescombe, two steam railways, an organic vineyard, Rye with its quaint cobbled streets and of course Battle itself.

Directions: From A21, 100 yards south of junction with B2244 (to Sedlescombe) turn into Crazy Lane, where site is signed. O.S.GR: TQ782170.

Charges 1999:
-- Per unit incl. 2 adults £7.50 - £8.75; extra person over 12 yrs £1.25; electricity £2.00.

Open:
March - October

Address:
Crazy Lane,
Sedlescombe, nr. Battle,
East Sussex TN33 0QT.

Tel:
(01424) 870147.

Reservations:
Contact site for details.

309 Black Horse Farm Caravan Club Site, Densole, nr. Folkestone

Well organised park near Channel Ports and Tunnel.

This neat, tidy and attractive 6 acre park, owned by the Caravan Club, is situated amidst farming country in the village of Densole on the Downs just 4 miles north of Folkestone, 8 northeast of Dover and 11 south of Canterbury. This makes it ideal for a night stop travelling to or from the continent, or a base for visiting the many attractions of this part of southeast England. Accessed directly from the A260, the tarmac entrance road leads past reception towards the top field which has gravel hardstanding pitches with a grass area for awnings (possibly some road noise), past hedging to the smaller middle area with 8 hardstandings, then to the large bottom field which has been redeveloped to give 104 large pitches, all with electricity. A late arrivals area at the entrance has 4 electrical hook-ups and places for storage. The carefully thought out and well constructed toilet blocks, one below reception and the other at the far end of the site, have washbasins set in flat surfaces (in cabins with curtains), good sized showers, a baby room and facilities for disabled visitors, laundry and washing-up facilities, all with free hot water and well heated in cool weather. Chemical disposal, motorcaravan service point and gas supplies. Opposite the site is a general store and newsagent and within 100 m, a pub and filling station. Riding 1 mile, golf or fishing 5 miles. Caravan storage.

Directions: Directly by the A260 Folkestone - Canterbury road, 2 miles north of junction with A20. Follow signs for Canterbury. O.S.GR: TR211418.

Charges 1999:
-- Per adult £2.00 - £4.00; child (5-17 yrs) £1.00 - £1.20; pitch (non-member) £6.00 - £7.00; electricity £1.45 (summer) - £2.20.
-- VAT included.
-- Credit cards accepted.

Open:
All year.

Address:
385 Canterbury Road,
Densole, Folkestone,
Kent CT18 7BG.

Tel:
(01303) 892665
(not after 8 pm.).

Reservations:
Advised at all times - write to or phone the Warden.

310 Hawthorn Farm Caravan & Camping Site, Martin Mill, nr. Dover

Large, relaxed park close to Dover, useful for continental ferries.

Hawthorn Farm, set in 27 acres, is an extensive park taking 224 touring units of any type on several large meadows which could accommodate far more, plus 157 privately owned caravan holiday homes in their own areas. Campers not requiring electricity choose their own spot, most staying near the two toilet blocks leaving the farthest fields to those liking solitude. There are 120 pitches with electricity (10/16A), 46 of which are large pitches separated by hedges, the remainder in glades either side of tarmac roadways. The sanitary blocks (now heated) are well tiled and of good quality, providing free hot water to washbasins set in flat surfaces, roomy pre-set showers with seat and screen, plus covered dishwashing and laundry sinks. There are chemical disposal and motorcaravan service facilities and a launderette. Breakfast and other snacks are served at the shop (closed 31/10) and a pub is nearby. This is a well run, relaxed park with plenty of room and mature hedging and trees making an attractive environment. A torch would be useful. Riding ½ mile, golf 3 miles, bicycle hire, fishing and boat launching 4 miles. Caravan storage available. Being only 4 miles from Dover docks, it is a very useful park for those using the ferries and is popular with continental visitors. Close to the sea at St Margaret's Bay, it is a fairly quiet situation apart from some rail noise (no trains 23.30 - 05.30). Gates close at 8 pm. - cards are available. A member of the Best of British group.

Directions: Park is north of the A258 road (Dover - Deal), with signs to park and Martin Mill where you turn off about 4 miles from Dover. O.S.GR: TR341464.

Charges 1999:
-- Per car, caravan/tent incl. 2 persons £9.00 - £11.00; extra adult £2.00 - £2.50; child (7-16 yrs) £1.50 - £2.00; hikers and bikers (2 man tent) less £2.00; dog £1.00; electricity £2.00.
-- Less 10% for 4 nights booked.
-- VAT included.

Open:
1 March - 30 November or mid-December by arrangement.

Address:
Martin Mill, Dover,
Kent CT15 5LA.

Tel:
(01304) 852658.
FAX: (01304) 853417.
E-mail: keat@
martex.co.uk.

Reservations:
Contact park for details.

Kent

306 Yew Tree Caravan Park, Petham, nr. Canterbury

Tranquil country site with swimming pool.

Yew Tree Park, a small site, is located in the heart of the Kent countryside overlooking the Chartham Downs. Just 5 miles south of Canterbury and 8 miles north of the M20, it is ideally placed either to explore the delights of the ancient city or the many attractions of eastern and coastal Kent. Its nearness to the channel ports also makes it useful for a night stop on the way to, or on return from, the continent. If catching a late evening ferry you may remain on site after 12 noon for a small payment. Apart from the peaceful environment, the main feature of the park is the swimming pool (60 x 30 ft. open June-Sept) which is surrounded by caravan holiday homes and apartments, but is available to all campers. There are 45 pitches for tourers, 20 with electricity (10A), marked on mainly level grass either side of the entrance road, the remainder unmarked on a rather attractive, sloping area which is left natural with trees and bushes creating cosy little recesses in which to pitch. The main brick-built sanitary blocks (one for each sex) are behind reception. They can be heated and each has four washbasins (warm water from a single tap), four toilets and four showers (on payment), with two more toilets on the edge of the camping area. Recently added is a toilet/shower room for families or disabled visitors. Clothes and dishwashing facilities are provided, plus a washing machine, dryer and iron and chemical disposal. Gas supplies. This neat, tidy, well cared for park which the resident proprietors, Derek and Dee Zanders, have created makes an excellent base away from the hurly-burly of life where you can enjoy the rural scenery and also have the opportunity for walking, riding, visiting local places of interest or for cross-Channel excursions. Riding 4 miles, golf 6 miles. The County cricket ground is 4 miles. Tourist information. Dogs are not accepted. Torches may be useful.

Directions: Park is on B2068 Canterbury-Folkestone road. From south, take exit 11 from the M20. From Canterbury, ignore signs to Petham and Waltham on B2068 and continue towards Folkestone. From either direction, turn into road beside the Chequers Inn, turn left into park and follow road to owners' house/reception. O.S.GR: TR138507.

Charges 1999:
-- First two adults £3.00 - £3.80 per person; extra adult £2.00 - £2.80; child 2-11 yrs 75p - £1.10, 12-16 yrs £1.00 - £1.60; caravan or trailer tent £2.00 - £3.50; motor-caravan £1.30 - £2.80; car £1.00; electricity (deposit required) £1.75 - £2.00.
-- VAT included.
-- Credit cards accepted.

Open:
March - October.

Address:
Stone Street, Petham, Kent CT4 5PL.

Tel:
(01227) 700306.
FAX: as phone.

Reservations:
Made with deposit of £5 per night.

307 Camping and Caravanning Club Site, Canterbury

Ideal site for touring northern Kent or as a stop-over for the ferry or the Tunnel.

Situated just off the A257 Sandwich road, about 1½ miles from the centre of Canterbury, this site is an ideal base for exploring Canterbury and the north Kent coast, as well as being a good stop-over to and from the Dover ferries, and the Folkestone Channel Tunnel terminal. There are 210 pitches, 85 with electric hook-ups (16A) and, except at the very height of the season, you are likely to find a pitch, although not necessarily with electricity. Most of the pitches are on well kept grass with hundreds of saplings planted, but there are also 24 pitches with hardstanding. Some pitches do slope so blocks are advised. A good sized over-night area for late arrivals can be reached even when the barriers are down. Two modern, heated toilet blocks, the main one also with a laundry room plus a room for washing dishes, an outside vegetable preparation area, chemical disposal point and recycling bins. Not far from the second block is a motorcaravan service point where chemical toilets may also be emptied. Reception stocks a small range of essential foods, milk, papers and gas, and there is an excellent tourist information room next door. Not far from reception is a children's play area with equipment on bark chippings. The site is adjacent to Bekepond nature reserve and within walking distance of Howletts Zoo. Golf adjacent, bicycle hire 2 miles. Although the busy A257 is close, there is minimal noise from the traffic. Note: power lines cross the site.

Directions: From A2 take Canterbury exit and follow signs for Sandwich - A257. After passing Howe military barracks turn right into Bekesbourne Lane opposite golf course. O.S. GR: TR173575.

Charges 2000:
-- Per 2 adults £7.50 - £10.60; child (6-18 yrs) £1.65; non-member pitch fee £4.30; electricity £1.60 - £2.35.
-- VAT included.
-- Credit cards accepted.

Open:
All year.

Address:
Bekesbourne Lane, Canterbury, Kent CT3 4AB.

Tel:
(01227) 463216
(no calls after 8 pm).

Reservations:
Necessary and made with deposit; contact the wardens.

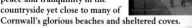

International Caravan & Camping Park

FOREST GLADE HOLIDAY PARK, CULLOMPTON, DEVON EX15 2DT

*A small country estate surrounded by forest in which deer roam.
Situated in an area of outstanding natural beauty.*
Large, flat, sheltered camping/touring pitches
Modern facilities building, luxury 2/6 berth full service
holiday homes, also self contained flat for 2 persons.

DELUXE

FREE Indoor Heated Pool

COUNTRY HOLIDAY PARK

Shop, Take Away Food, Tennis Court, Adventure Play Area, Games Room, Electric Hook-up Points. Riding Forest & Hill Walks, Gliding, Fishing & Golf are all nearby. Freedom for the children, peace for the adults. Central for touring S.W. Easy access coast and moors.
Motor caravans welcome.
Facilities for the Disabled.
Dogs welcome.
Tourers please book in advance.

FREE COLOUR BROCHURE
Tel: (01404) 841381
(Evgs to 8pm)
Fax: (01404) 841593
www.forestglade.mcmail.com

... for an
*unforgettable
holiday in
glorious Devon*

Jan and Paul Harper welcome you to their 4-pennant park with all individually-hedged pitches and top quality facilities. We are conveniently situated 1 mile from the end of M5 alongside the A38 and are an ideal centre for visits to Torquay, Dartmoor and the beaches of South Devon. Please telephone for our colour brochure illustrating the local attractions and the Park's facilities.

Kennford International Caravan Park, Exeter, Devon EX6 7YN Tel/Fax: 01392 833046

APPOINTED

Ideal for
**BOURNEMOUTH
POOLE, SANDBANKS
NEW FOREST**

AA **Campsite of the Year** *1999*
Practical Caravan **Best Family Park** *1993 and 1997*

For a free colour brochure describing our superb facilities, please write or telephone:
Merley Court Touring Park
Merley, Wimborne, Nr Poole Dorset BH21 3AA
Tel: **01202 881488**

Highlands End and
Golden Cap Holiday Parks

- *Choice of two select family parks on West Dorset Heritage coastline*
- *Indoor heated swimming pool*
- *Caravan holiday homes for hire & for sale*
- *Excellent facilities for tourers & tents*

Set in exceptionally beautiful countryside of West Dorset, both of our parks are ideally situated for a quiet stay or as a centre for touring. Quiet beaches, countryside walks with panoramic views, as well as places of interest, and welcoming country inns make West Dorset a place to come back to year after year.

Eype, Bridport, Dorset, DT6 6AR
FOR A FREE COLOUR BROCHURE
from Martin & Vanessa Cox

Tel: 01308 422139
Fax: 425672 Email: highlands@wdlh.co.uk
Website: www.wdlh.co.uk

———*West Dorset at its best*———

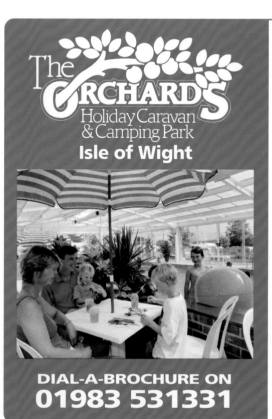

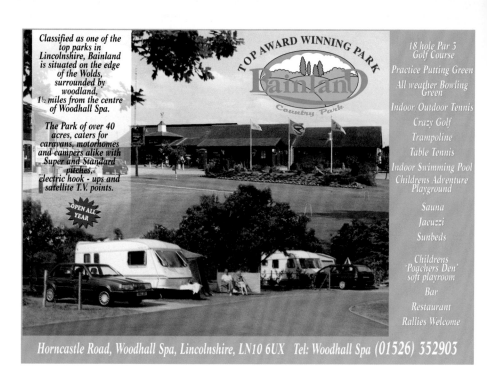

ENGLISH TOURIST BOARD
★ ★ ★ ★ ★
TOURING PARK

THE Best of British
CARAVAN & CAMPING PARKS

Ord House
Country Park

Pride of Northumbria Caravan Park of the Year 1997 / 98 / 99

An Award Winning Park situated in North Northumberland's "Secret Kingdom" about two miles from the Scottish Border.

Tourers, Motor Homes and Tents welcome. Luxury Heated Toilets and Shower Facilities. Country Pub with Bar, Lounge and Family Room. Play Area and 6 Hole Practice Golf Course. Superb Caravan and Camping Accessory Shop.

East Ord, Berwick-upon-Tweed, Northumberland, TD15 2NS
Tel: 01289 305288
Fax: 01289 330832
www.ordhouse.co.uk

PARK OF
BRANDEDLEYS

A top Award Winning family park with full facilities set superbly at the centre of this delightful holiday area.

THE Best of British

NOW OPEN ALL YEAR

- ● INDOOR POOL
- ● OUTDOOR POOL
- ● GAMES ROOM
- ● TENNIS COURT
- ● BADMINTON
- ● PLAY AREAS
- ● PUTTING COURSE
- ● RESTAURANT & BAR

Crocketford, Dumfires, DG2 8RG
Telephone: 01556 690250 Fax: 01556 690681

HOLGATES COUNTRYSIDE PARKS

The MOTOR Caravanners' CLUB

™

311 Quex Caravan Park, Birchington, nr. Margate

Peaceful site in a secluded location; no tents accepted.

This park does not accept tents and, although there are a fair number of privately owned holiday homes, they do not intrude on the touring area which is in a sheltered glade under tall trees. There are 60 touring pitches with 48 electric hook-ups (16A) and a well equipped central sanitary unit. This is in a chalet style building with all the usual facilities including free controllable hot showers, dishwashing sinks under cover at the rear, and a laundry room with sink, washing machine and dryer. When we visited there was no heating, but there are plans to remedy this. There is a well stocked shop on site, although there are many super-markets close by, and reception can provide you with a map of the local area. Local attractions include Quex House and gardens, the model village and motor museum at Ramsgate, while in the seaside resort of Margate you can walk through 1000 years of history at the Caves, or visit the Hollywood Bowl. A new member of the Best of British group.

Directions: From roundabout at junction of A28 and A299, take A28 east towards Birchington and Margate. At Birchington carry straight on at roundabout by church, then take next right, then right again, and left at mini roundabout. Site is on right in ½ mile (well signed). O.S.GR: TR320685.

Charges 1999:
-- Per unit incl. 2 adults £9.00 - £11.00; extra adult £2.00 - £2.50; child (7-16 yrs) £1.50 - £2.00; dog £1.00; electricity £2.00.
-- Less 10% for 4 nights booked (and paid for on arrival).
-- VAT included.

Open:
7 March - 7 November.

Address:
Park Road, Birchington, Kent CT7 0BL.

Tel:
(01843) 841273.

Reservations:
Contact site for details.

304 Broadhembury Holiday Park, Ashford

Small, pleasant touring park with some holiday homes, near to Folkestone and ferries.

In quiet countryside just outside Ashford, this well landscaped, sheltered park takes 65 touring units of any type, plus 25 caravan holiday homes (5 for hire). All pitches are on level, neatly cut grass backing onto hedges, 50 have electrical connections (10A), 4 are fully serviced and 8 have double hardstanding plus a grass area for an awning. The park is friendly and popular and often becomes full in the main season, with a good proportion of continental visitors, so reservation is advisable. The single small toilet block is kept very clean, can be heated in cool weather and has free hot water to washbasins (with shelf and mirror) and showers. Alongside are partially covered dishwashing sinks with hot and cold water. There is a small laundry room, chemical disposal and motorcaravan service point. Other facilities include a TV and pool room, games room with table tennis, children's playground (grass or wood-chip bases) and play field away from the touring area, public phone and a dog exercise field. Security arrangements are excellent - the gates are closed at 11 pm. in high season with coded entry. The new reception building at the park entrance also contains a well stocked shop and comprehensive tourist information. Fishing 500 m, bicycle hire or riding 2 miles and golf 1 mile. For those who would like a trip to France, the new International Railway Terminal is at Ashford (Paris in 2 hours) - take your passport. A member of the Best of British group.

Directions: From M20 junction 10 take A2070 road. After 2 miles follow sign for Kingsnorth. Turn left at the second crossroads in Kingsnorth village. O.S.GR: TR010382.

Charges 2000:
-- Per unit incl. 2 persons £11.00 - £13.00; extra adult £2.00; child (5-16 yrs) £1.50; extra car £2.00; electricity (10A) £2.00; awning or pup tent included.
-- Less 10% excl. July/Aug. for bookings of 7 nights or more.
-- VAT included.
-- Credit cards accepted.

Open:
All year.

Address:
Steeds Lane, Kingsnorth, Ashford, Kent TN26 1NQ.

Tel/Fax:
(01233) 620859.

E-mail: holidays@broad-hembury.co.uk.

Reservations:
Essential for B.Hs and peak season; made with £5 per night deposit (min. 3 nights at Easter or Spr. B.H). Balance 21 days before arrival for B.Hs, on arrival at other times.

Alan Rogers' Discount

Less 10% excl. July/Aug & B.Hs. (no other discounts)

Kent

303 Tanner Farm Touring Caravan and Camping Park, Marden

Quality park in quiet, spacious, rural setting.

Developed as part of a family working farm, Tanner Farm is recognised as a top class park. This is the heart of the Weald of Kent with orchards, hop gardens, lovely countryside and delightful small villages. The owners are much concerned with conserving the natural beauty of the environment and visitors are welcome to walk around the farm and see the Shire horses at work. The park extends over 15 acres, most of which is level and part a gentle slope. The grass meadowland has been semi-landscaped by planting saplings, etc. which units back onto (the owners don't wish to regiment pitches into rows). Places are numbered but not marked, allowing plenty of space between units which, with large open areas, gives a pleasant, comfortable atmosphere. There are 100 pitches, all with 16A electricity, 13 with hardstanding, 4 with water tap and 1 with waste water point also. The farm drive links the park with the B2079 and a group of refurbished oast houses (listed heritage buildings) with a duck pond in front, along with rare pigs and piglets, pygmy goats, lambs, etc. make a focal point. The traditional farm building on the right at the entrance houses a small shop (limited stock and opening hours in winter) and reception. Gas is supplied. The two heated sanitary units are well tiled and given a most pleasant appearance with interior flower arrangements, hanging baskets and flower beds. Hot water is free for the washbasins (private cubicles in both units), which have mirrors and shaver points, in the showers and in the dishwashing sinks. There are purpose built facilities for disabled visitors, a small launderette, chemical disposal and motorcaravan service point. A bathroom (£1 token) and baby facilities have been added in the newer block (this block is not opened Nov - Easter). Small children's play area with swings and adventure climbing frame and fishing on site (on payment). Dogs are accepted on leads with paths for exercise. There is good lighting around the park, but a torch may be useful. The friendly management advise on local attractions, shops and pubs. There are many National Trust attractions in the area (Sissinghurst, Scotney Castle, Bodiam Castle), riding and golf within 6 miles, leisure centres and sailing facilities near and good shopping facilities at Maidstone and Tunbridge Wells. Caravan storage all year. The park is a member of the Caravan Club's 'managed under contract' scheme although non-members are also very welcome. A popular park, early reservation is advised.

Directions: Park is 2½ miles south of Marden on B2079 towards Goudhurst. O.S.GR: TQ732417.

Charges 1999:
-- Per pitch £3.00; adult £2.60 - £3.90; child £1.10 - £1.20; 2-man tent plus car (all incl.) £8.00 - £8.50, plus bicycles £5.50 - £6.00; electricity £1.45 - £2.20; all service pitch +£2.00.
-- Only one car per pitch permitted.
-- VAT included.
-- Credit cards accepted.

Open:
All year.

Address:
Goudhurst Road, Marden, Kent TN12 9ND.

Tel:
(01622) 832399.
FAX: (01622) 832472.

Reservations:
Essential for high season and B.Hs, recommended for other times. Made with deposit (£5 for 1-3 nights; £10 over 3 nights and B.Hs).

TANNER FARM
TOURING CARAVAN & CAMPING
PARK
Goudhurst Road, Marden, Kent TN12 9ND
Tel: 01622 832399 Fax: 01622 832472

Attractively landscaped, peaceful Touring Park set in the centre of 150 acre idyllic Weald family farm.
Spotless facilities. Central for a wealth of attractions, including our own Shire Horses.
★ Open All Year ★ 100 Electric Touring Pitches ★ Centrally Heated Toilet Block ★ Free Showers
★ Dogs Welcome on Leads ★ Children's Play Area ★ Shop/Gas Supplies
★ Launderette ★ Hard Standings ★ Disabled Facilities
'Phone 01622 832399 for bookings and brochure

For a list of parks which are open all year - see page 234

305 Pine Lodge Touring Park, Bearsted, nr. Maidstone

Useful park near main London - Folkestone - Dover M20 motorway.

Set in the heart of Kent, near Leeds Castle and central for the historical and scenic attractions of this county, this park is on a slight slope, the rectangular field surrounded by rolling hills, farmland and trees. A gravel, one-way road circles the site with pitches set against hedges around the perimeter and around a figure of eight in the centre with picnic areas. Trees have been planted but these at present are for decoration and will take a while to grow enough to provide shade. Of the 100 pitches, 85 have electricity (10A) and several have hardstanding. Water points, fenced central refuse, motorcaravan services, chemical disposal and waste water area. Access from the A20 road is wide but there may be background traffic noise. The new, good sanitary facilities are situated at the entrance to the park and include vanity style washbasins (free hot water), metered showers (token), laundry and washing up facilities, plus a shower and toilet room for disabled visitors. Basic supplies and gas are available from reception which also has tourist information. Local shops 1 mile (Bearsted) or 3½ miles (Maidstone). Fishing 3 miles, riding 2 miles, golf 1 mile. The park is very convenient for events staged at Leeds Castle and is a useful overnight stop between London and the channel ports. A small children's play area is in a corner of the site, well away from the entrance. No dogs are admitted.

Directions: From M20 junction 8, at A20 roundabout, turn towards Bearsted and Maidstone and park is about ½ mile on the left. O.S.GR: TQ808548.

Charges 1999:
-- Per unit incl. 2 adults £9.00 - £10.00; extra adult £2.00; child (3-14 yrs) £1.00; electricity £1.50 - £2.25; awning or extra tent £1.00; hikers or cyclists please enquire. -- Credit cards accepted.

Open:
All year.

Address:
A20 Ashford Road, Hollingbourne, nr Maidstone, Kent ME17 1XH.

Tel:
(01622) 730018. FAX: (01622) 734498.

Reservations:
Contact park.

312 Gate House Wood Touring Park, Wrotham Heath

Sheltered park within easy reach of Brands Hatch.

This park, which opened for its first season in '98, has been created in a former quarry where all the pitches are on well drained grass. A spacious paved entrance with a new reception building and well stocked shop, leads on to the park itself. The 60 pitches are level and open with a few small trees, four water and fire points, two brick built barbecue units, and 40 electricity hook-ups (10A). A children's playground has swings, seesaw and a slide all set on a safety base, and the entire site is enclosed by grassy banks on three sides, with a wild flower walk around the top. The comprehensive sanitary facilities are smart, well maintained and include open washbasins and push-button hot showers, with a well equipped family room, which is also fully designed for disabled people. The laundry and dishwashing room is at one end of the modern heated building, and there is free hot water throughout. No dogs or other pets, commercial vehicles or caravans and motorcaravans greater than 25' overall are admitted. Local attractions include Brands Hatch Circuit, the International Karting Circuit at Buckmore Park, and the nearby Country Park at West Malling. Within walking distance of the park are three pubs and a Cantonese restaurant. Trains run to London Victoria from Borough Green (2½ miles).

Directions: From M26 junction 2a, take A20 eastwards towards Wrotham Heath and Maidstone. Just past junction with A25, and opposite the Royal Oak pub, turn left into Ford Lane, and park is immediately on left. O.S.GR: TQ630580.

Charges 1999:
-- Per unit incl. 2 adults £8.00 - £9.50; hiker's tent (incl. 2 adults) £6.00 - £7.00; extra adult £1.50; child (3-12 yrs) £1.00; awning £1.00; extra car £1.00; electricity £1.70 - £2.20. -- VAT included.

Open:
All year excl. first two weeks Jan.

Address:
Ford Lane, Wrotham Heath, Sevenoaks, Kent TN15 7SD.

Tel/Fax:
(01732) 843062.

Reservations:
Made with deposit (£5 for 3 days, £10 over 3 days or £10 p/week for longer stays).

For travel further afield, remember the other ALAN ROGERS' titles – the GOOD CAMPS GUIDES for FRANCE and EUROPE

★ Independent site assessors make regular monitoring visits

★ Consistently revised and updated – sites included on merit only

★ Discount vouchers for selected sites, ferries and tourist attractions

London

London Tourist Board & Convention Bureau

Glen House, Stag Place,
Victoria, London SW1E 5LT
Tel: 0171 932 2000 Fax: 0171 932 0222
Internet: www.LondonTown.com.

London is the largest city in Europe, covering some 610 square miles with a population of nearly seven million.

However, the centre is fairly compact and covers the financial district called 'The City', the entertainment and shopping area known as 'The West End' and Westminster, seat of Parliament and home of royalty.

London's wealthiest neighbourhoods, such as Knightsbridge, Kensington and Chelsea, lie to the west. East of the city is the culturally intriguing East End and the ambitious Docklands devel-

opment and, further down-river, historical Greenwich.

As we go to press, the mighty Millennium Dome is taking shape beside the Thames on the Greenwich peninsula. The Millennium Bridge is being built across the Thames near St Paul's Cathedral and the massive Millennium Wheel should soon be in place opposite the Houses of Parliament. It will be the world's largest Ferris wheel standing as high as Cairo's Great Pyramid and its glass capsules will give 1,000 riders at a time stunning 30-mile views of London.

327 Crystal Palace Caravan Club Site, Crystal Palace, London

Busy but friendly site with easy access for central London attractions.

The Caravan Club's site at Crystal Palace in south London provides easy access to the city centre and all its many attractions. A pleasant and efficiently run site, it is arranged in terraces overlooking the ruins of the old Crystal Palace, its park and the National Sports Centre. It is surprisingly quiet given its location (with the possible exception of regular police sirens and over-flying aircraft). In peak season it is even busier than Abbey Wood with many overseas visitors and advance booking is always necessary. However, as most of the pitches are on gravel hardstanding, it is particularly useful for out of season stays. There are places for 84 caravans or motorcaravans, all with electricity connections (16A). Tents are placed on the site's well mown lawns at the top of the site near reception. In summer an overflow area across the approach road (with portacabin style sanitary facilities) takes further tents or small motorcaravans. The single toilet block can be heated in cool weather and has free hot water in the washbasins (with shelf and mirror, curtained for ladies) and controllable showers, a WC and washbasin for disabled visitors and a laundry room. Washing up sinks and neat rubbish bins are outside, under cover. Chemical disposal and motorcaravan service facilities. Gas is available from reception where there is plenty of tourist information (travel cards for sale). Shops, pubs, etc. are ¼ mile away. Many buses stop outside the site, including services to central London. The Crystal Palace park is extensive and provides open spaces for strolls or picnics and plenty of activities for children. The Sports Centre has two swimming pools, tennis and squash courts and gym facilities, with national events in a variety of sports to watch at certain times. The park and the Sports Centre are due for substantial redevelopment and when this begins access will obviously be restricted. An area at the site entrance should be used for arrivals after 10.30 pm.- the pitch areas have a coded security barrier.

Charges 1999:
-- Per pitch £6.50 - £9.00; adult £3.25 - £4.00; child (5-16 yrs) £1.10 - £1.20; electricity £2.20 - £1.45.
-- Caravan Club members pay less.
-- Tent campers - apply to site.
-- VAT included.
-- Credit cards accepted.
Open:
All year.
Address:
Crystal Palace Parade, London SE19 1UF.
Tel:
(020) 8778 7155.
(08.00-20.00 hrs).
FAX: (020) 8676 0980.
Reservations:
Essential at all times and made with £5 deposit - contact site.

Directions: On A205 South Circular road travelling east, pass Dulwich College and Golf Course on right (avoid College Road - width restriction), turn right at traffic lights (Harvester pub on left). Within ¼ mile at traffic lights turn right into Sydenham Hill; in 350 yds at roundabout turn left (still Sydenham Hill). Site entrance is 1 mile opposite mini-roundabouts (take care on these). Travelling west on A205 South Circular, immediately after passing under Catford railway bridge, keep left on A212 signed Crystal Palace. After 2¾ miles site entrance is on left at top of Westwood Hill before two mini-roundabouts. O.S.GR: TQ341724.

321 Lee Valley Caravan Park, Dobbs Weir, Hoddesdon

Pleasant park north of London in Lee Valley Park.

Stretching for 23 miles along the Lee Valley and covering 10,000 acres from Ware to the east end of London, Lee Valley park is administered by the Lee Valley Regional Park Authority. Extensive development of the Park into a leisure area now means it offers a wide variety of outdoor and sporting pursuits, including riding, water sports, golf, cycle tracks and places of interest. Set between Hoddesdon, Broxbourne and Nazeing, and under the same management as Lee Valley Campsite (no. 325), this park is situated in the far north of the complex. The touring section, which consists of a large, open, well mown meadow with space for 100 units, 36 with electricity (10A), is quite separate from 100 caravan holiday homes. There is no shade in the touring area, but tall trees surrounding the site offer adequate shelter, and it has a neat, tidy and well cared for appearance. A single sanitary block (access by key) is of good quality with free hot water to washbasins, showers and sinks. Other facilities include a parent and child room, laundry, en-suite facilities for disabled people and chemical disposal. No shop on site, but a free bus service to a nearby superstore is offered three times a week, and there is a bar/restaurant just 100 yds from the entrance. Some fishing is possible from the canal towpath that runs past the site, with further opportunities nearby and a swimming pool is just 2 miles away. Bicycle hire 3 miles. Trains run from Broxbourne (about 2 miles) to London, with the journey taking about 30 minutes. Dobbs Weir industrial estate and garden centres are near, but surrounding trees screen out noise and create some privacy.

Directions: From M25 exit 25 take A10 north for 4 miles; take the Hoddesdon exit, turn left at second roundabout following signs for Dobbs Weir and park is on right within 1 mile. O.S.GR: TL383082.

Charges 1999:
-- Per adult £5.05; child (under 16 yrs) £2.05; electricity £2.25.
-- Min. charge £7.10 (but not backpackers).
-- VAT included.
-- Credit cards accepted.
-- Checking out time 5 pm.

Open:
W/end before Easter - 31 October.

Address:
Charlton Meadows, Essex Road, Dobbs Weir, Hoddesdon, Hertfordshire EN11 0AS.

Tel:
(01992) 462090.
FAX: (01992) 462090.

Reservations:
Made with £5 deposit - write to park for reservation form. (For information contact PO Box 88, Enfield, Middlesex; tel: 01992 700766).

see colour advert between pages 128/129

325 Lee Valley Campsite, Chingford, North London

Friendly and well run park, conveniently placed for visits to the London area.

This site provides an excellent base for visits to the capital, having both easy access to the M25 and excellent public transport links into the centre of London. Closely situated to Epping Forest and in the heart of the Lee Valley, there is much to enjoy in the surrounding area, from walking and cycling, to golf, fishing and riding. With capacity for 200 units of all types the site is mostly level, with several bush sheltered avenues and plenty of trees throughout. There are 20 pitches with tarmac hardstanding and 100 with electricity (10A). Three toilet blocks, one of which is heated, are of good quality and more than adequate with free hot water to washbasins and controllable showers, two excellent units for disabled visitors, a few washing up sinks and chemical disposal. There is a well equipped laundry room, motorcaravan service point and a shop. Children's playground, but no other on-site amenities, but those staying here are often out visiting London. A local bus stops by the site at fairly frequent intervals in season, with another alternative, and equally good service, every 20 minutes to Walthamstow underground station just 500 yds away. Alternatively you can park at South Woodford or Chingford stations and go by train.

Directions: From M25 take exit 26 (Waltham Abbey) from where site is signed; take A112 road towards Chingford and the site is 3 miles on right. It can also be approached on A112 from the North Circular Road. O.S.GR: TQ378970.

Charges 2000:
-- Per adult £5.40; child (under 16 yrs) £2.40; electricity £2.25.
-- Min. charge £7.80.
-- VAT included.
-- Credit cards accepted.

Open:
1 April - 28 October.

Address:
Sewardstone Road, Chingford, London E4 7RA.

Tel:
020 8529 5689.
FAX: 020 8559 4070.
E-mail: scs@leevalley park.org.uk.

Reservations:
Any length up to 14 days with £5 deposit. (For information see address above).

IMPORTANT LONDON EVENTS

January -International Boat Show, Earl's Court.

March - Ideal Home Exhibition. Earls Court.

April - London Marathon.

May- Chelsea Flower Show. Chelsea Royal Hospital.

June - Beating the Retreat. Horse Guard's Parade Trooping the Colour. Queen's official Birthday. Starts at Buckingham Palace.

June - Biggin Hill International Air Fair

Late June/early July - Wimbledon Lawn Tennis Championship

August B.H. Weekend- Notting Hill Carnival. Europe's largest outdoor festival.

October - Annual Full Tidal Closure. Lifting of the Thames Flood Barrier

November - London to Brighton Veteran Car Run

December - Olympia International Showjumping Championships, Olympia

326 Abbey Wood Caravan and Camping Site, Abbey Wood

Quietly situated Caravan Club site in S.E. London with rail links to the city centre.

This site is run by the Caravan Club and there are reductions for their members. It is one of the nearest sites to London and it becomes very full and crowded in the summer months with campers of many nationalities. Reservations are made for all units except tents and are very advisable for July/Aug. and B.Hs. Tent campers, for whom there is a special railed area, with cars parked separately, must take their chance. Stays are limited to a maximum of 14 days. Although within a built-up area, this grassy site is in a quiet and pleasant setting with many mature trees. Most parts, especially those for caravans, are sloping but many of the 360 pitches are levelled. A curving line of gravel hardstandings is available for 14 motorcaravans. The three traditional type toilet blocks, all heated in cool weather, have free hot water in the washbasins (with shelf and mirror, curtained for ladies), mostly controllable showers, washing-up sinks and laundry room. Chemical disposal and motorcaravan service facilities. There is not much on-site activity but nearly all those staying here want to visit London. There is a train service every 15 minutes from Abbey Wood station (5 mins walk) to either Charing Cross or Cannon Street. Bread, milk and cold drinks are available from the office in high season. Gas is available. A good travel and information centre (open 8.30- 11 am) can provide tickets for travel and attractions. Children's playground with sand base. Golf 4 miles. Sports centre at Crook Log, 1 mile. The Royal Observatory and the Thames Barrier are nearby. Dogs are accepted on leads. A car park at the entrance has electrical connections for late arrivals (after 10.30 pm). Security could be a problem - be aware.

Charges 1999:
-- Per pitch £6.00 - £8.50; adult £3.25 - £4.00; child (5-16 yrs) £1.10 - £1.20; electricity £2.20 - £1.45; extra car £1.00.
-- Caravan Club members pay less.
-- Tent campers - apply to site.
-- VAT included.
-- Credit cards accepted.
Open:
All year.
Address:
Federation Road, Abbey Wood, London SE2 0LS.
Tel:
010 8311 1465 (08.00-20.00 hrs).
FAX: 010 8311 7708.
Reservations:
Essential for Easter, Spring B.H. July/Aug with £5 deposit.

Directions: From east on M2/A2 or from central London: on A2 turn off at A221 junction (third exit off the A2) into Danson Road (signed Bexleyheath, Welling and Sidcup). Follow sign Bexleyheath to Crook Log (A207 junction); at traffic lights turn right and immediately left into Brampton Road. In 1½ miles at traffic lights turn left into Bostal Road (A206); in ¾ mile at traffic lights turn right into Basildon Road (B213). In 300 yds turn right into McLeod Road, in about ½ mile at roundabout turn right into Knee Hill; in 100 yds turn right (second right) into Federation Road. Site on left in 50 yds. From M25, north, west or south approach: leave at junction 2 onto A2 (signed London), then as above. Note: route is well signed with International caravan and camping signs. O.S.GR: TQ472785.

322 Ashridge Farm Touring Caravan Park, Ashwell, nr. Baldock

Farm site with excellent modern facilities.

This family run site is in a rural location on the edge of the interesting village of Ashwell. The grassy touring field has been divided into four small areas, and has room for 30 units, all with electricity (10A). There is an area (with a small plastic play frame) set aside for children, but ball games are not permitted - there is an excellent children's playground in the village. The modern heated sanitary unit is well equipped. The spacious showers have full screens and large shower trays, all washbasins are in cubicles, and the dishwashing sink is in the foyer. In addition, there are facilities for visitors with disabilities, a motorcaravan disposal point and gas is available from reception. Recycling bins are to be found in the lane or the village. The Friends of Ashwell Village Museum have thoughtfully produced a guided walk sheet for the village with some 23 sights to see. Other places of interest close by are Imperial War Museum at Duxford, Shuttleworth Air Museum, Wimpole Hall and Model Farm and The Lodge - RSPB headquarters and nature reserve near Sandy. A new barrier has been added (£5 deposit for card).

Charges 1999:
-- Per unit incl. 2 adults £5.90; extra adult £2.40; child £1.20; electricity £1.60 (summer) - £2.10 (winter).
-- VAT included.
Open:
All year.
Address:
1 Ashwell Street, Ashwell, Baldock, Hertfordshire SG7 5QF.
Tel:
(01462) 742527.
FAX as phone.
Reservations:
Recommended for B.Hs, peak season and Christmas.

Directions: Ashwell lies to the north of Baldock between A1 and A505, and is best approached from A505 turning at Odsey. Site access is via Ashwell Street, a lane turning off Station Road on eastern edge of village. O.S.GR: TL275398.

East of England Tourist Board

Essex, Suffolk, Norfolk, Cambridgeshire, Lincolnshire Hertfordshire and Bedfordshire

Toppesfield Hall, Hadleigh, Suffolk IP7 5DM
Tel: (01473) 822922 FAX (01473) 823063
E-mail: info@e-anglia-tourist-board.org.uk
Internet: http://www.e-anglia-tourist-board.org.uk/eatb/

Covering the seven counties of **Cambridgeshire, Essex, Hertfordshire, Bedfordshire, Norfolk, Suffolk** and **Lincolnshire**. The region as a whole is characterised by a bracing windswept climate, prairie-like fields of wheat, sugar-beet and rape and no significant industrial centres. The legacy of the medieval wool trade when the region was the best-off and most populated in England is evident in the rich array of parish churches, often faced in flint and sometimes thatched, and the handsome market towns.

Norfolk is best experienced in the quiet resorts, bird reserves, dunes and sand marshes of the north coast. The Broads have a charm of their own. Norwich is a city on a human scale, and well worth a visit

The Fens of **Cambridgeshire** are absolutely flat, criss-crossed by drainage canals installed by Dutch engineers in the 17th century and the peat rich soil makes this one of England's most fertile agricultural areas. Ely cathedral is not to be missed nor the college courts and 'backs' at Cambridge where the

punt (a flat-bottomed boat propelled by a long pole) is the traditional form of transport.

Suffolk's undulating country has been immortalised by John Constable. Lavenham is one of the best preserved villages with timbered halls, and houses covered in ornamental plaster work. Suffolk's charming coast is part reed-fringed, part heath-topped, with small time soothing resorts. Aldeburgh and the 'Maltings' hold one of the most prestigious festivals of Music and Arts, founded by the famous British composer, Benjamin Britten.

The Roman town of Colchester is the principle reason for visiting **Essex**, perhaps the least attractive of the counties.

Hatfield House in **Hertfordshire** is one of England's finest stately homes and more grand country houses can be found in **Bedfordshire**.

Lincolnshire is green and rolling in the wolds to the north and flat in its bulb-growing fenland to the south. The city of Lincoln has one of the country's most impressive cathedrals.

---

330 The Grange Country Park, East Bergholt, nr. Colchester

Pleasant well tended all year park with heated pool and high season entertainment.

This neat 11 acre site, set in the heart of Constable country, offers 120 pitches, many with electricity connections (16A). All are on flat grass with mature trees and there are well lit, tarmac roads throughout the site. There are now 41 fully serviced 'executive' pitches (operated by credit card), a separate area for tents and 52 privately owned caravan holiday homes; seven of which are for hire. In addition to a communal barbecue point many pitches are now provided with their own facilities (equipment can be hired from reception). Three modern, heated sanitary blocks with good, clean facilities have free hot water; also an en suite unit for disabled people and two laundry rooms. A range of amenities includes a 60 x 30 ft. outdoor, heated swimming pool plus children's paddling pool (open Whitsun - 7 Sept, lifeguard in high season), with snacks available, and a sauna and solarium. There is also a free house bar and restaurant, entertainment in high season, games and TV room and a small children's play area on grass and matting. Well stocked shop (April - Sept, limited hours out of peak season). Single groups and motorbikes are not accepted; and no one night bookings are taken in high season. Dogs are accepted (max. 2, no dangerous breeds) and a dog walk and nature trail are offered. Limited facilities available during winter (Nov. - March). A member of the Best of British group.

Directions: Park is between Ipswich (8 miles) and Colchester (10 miles). Follow signs for East Bergholt from the A12 (4 miles). O.S.GR: TL097352.

Charges guide:
-- Per pitch incl. 2 adults £8.00 - £12.00; premier pitch incl. 2 adults, electricity and awning £14.00 - £20.00; extra adult £1.50 - £2.50; child £1.00 - £2.00; pup tent £1.00 - £2.00; electricity £2.25 - £2.50; dogs (max. 2) £0.50 - £1.00.
-- VAT included.

Open:
All year except 4 Jan. - 1 Feb.

Address:
East Bergholt, Colchester, Essex CO7 6UX.

Tel:
(01206) 298567/298912. FAX: (01206) 298770.

Reservations:
Made with £10 deposit and £2 fee.

Suffolk

332 Lakeside Leisure Park, Saxmundham

Large modern holiday park with own fishing lakes and swimming pool.

Set in 46 acres with two fishing lakes, this site has a total of nearly 500 pitches. Although 151 pitches are occupied by privately owned caravan holiday homes, they are in separate areas from the touring park and are fairly unobtrusive. The 275 touring pitches, 168 with electricity (10/16A), are arranged on large grassy fields, sloping in places, with some new plantings separating the rows, and there is a separate area for tents. Two substantial, brick built sanitary units are well tiled and with modern fittings providing washbasins in cubicles and good quality hot showers on payment. The top block is closed in early Sept. A laundry has washing machines, dryers and ironing facilities, dishwashing sinks are under cover at the end of each building, and there is a spacious, well equipped unit for disabled persons. The good value restaurant seats 50 and a large bar has space for around 400-500 (both open weekends only after Sept). A variety of entertainment is provided in the main season. A takeaway van operates at peak times. Games room. The heated outdoor swimming pool (60 x 25 ft) and children's paddling pool are open May - end Sept. Fishing permits are available in advance from reception. Barrier gate (£10 deposit). The seaside villages of Southwold and Aldeburgh are within easy reach, also for birdwatchers, Minsmere Nature Reserve. Nearby attractions include Bruisyard Vineyard with its Winery and Herb Centre, aand steam rollers and traction engines at Longshop Museum in Leiston. The East Anglia Transport Museum at Carlton Colville near Lowestoft or the Stoneham Barns shopping and leisure complex are within easy driving distance.

Charges 2000:
-- Per unit incl. 2 adults £5.00; American motorhome £12.00; extra adult or child £2.00; extra car £1.50; awning or pup tent £1.75; electricity £2.00 (American motor home £4.00); dog £1.50.
-- No credit cards.
-- VAT included.

Open:
Easter - 8 October.

Address:
Saxmundham,
Suffolk IP17 2QP.

Tel:
(01728) 603344.
FAX: as phone.

Reservations:
Advised for B.Hs and peak season and made with £15 deposit.

Directions: From A12 by Saxmundham, turn west on B1119 Framlingham road for about 1½ miles. On a double bend take minor road to the right signed Kelsale. Site is signed on left. O.S.GR: TM370645.

331 Low House Touring Caravan Centre, Foxhall, nr. Ipswich

Small tranquil touring park, open all year; tents accepted subject to space.

Set in 3½ acres, this beautiful garden site has 30 pitches, all with electricity (most 16A, some 10A) and an abundance of trees, shrubs and flowers. In two sections, you drive through one field (the rally field) to reach the garden area - we understand from the owner that there are 90 different varieties of trees on site and an ornamental tree walk can be followed around the edge of the park. Pitches back onto trees offering plenty of shade and the opportunity to observe a range of wildlife, the rally field having a more open aspect. Tents are accepted only if space is available. Reception and the office are in the cottage and there is a small, modern, heated sanitary block which is spotlessly clean with hot showers (50p). There are no dishwashing sinks. Chemical disposal. No on-site provision facilities but a supermarket is 2 miles away (towards Ipswich), frozen goods can be stored and Calor gas is available. A good bus service to Ipswich stops just outside the site. A small children's adventure play area is on grass, with the added attraction of a pets corner, with rabbits and ornamental fowl. Public phone. A torch would be useful. The enthusiastic and helpful owner, John Booth, has made arrangements for site residents to join the Civil Service club which is just 5 minutes walk with a bar, good value meals and a sports centre. There is also a pub in Bucklesham village (1½ miles) and other good pubs nearby. Golf 2 miles. The centre lies between Felixstowe (8 miles) and Ipswich (5 miles) and would be a useful stopover for the Felixstowe port or Harwich.

Charges 1999:
-- Per unit incl. 2 adults and children £6.50; adult (over 16 yrs) £2.00; awning no charge (but please lift groundsheets); extra car 50p; electricity (16A) £1.50.
-- No commercial vehicles.
-- No credit cards or Eurocheques.

Open:
All year.

Address:
Bucklesham Road,
Foxhall, nr. Ipswich,
Suffolk IP10 0AU.

Tel:
(01473) 659437.
FAX: (01473) 659880.

Reservations:
Advance booking advised
- phone any time.

Alan Rogers' Discount

Less 10%

Directions: Turn off A14 (was A45) Ipswich ring road (south) via slip road onto A1156 (signed Ipswich East). Follow road over the bridge which crosses over the A45 and almost immediately turn right (no sign). After ½ mile turn right again (signed Bucklesham) and site is on left after ¼ mile. O.S.GR: TM225423.

351 Liffens Holiday Park, Burgh Castle, nr. Great Yarmouth

Long established family holiday site with outdoor pool.

This popular family holiday park is in a semi-rural location, but within easy reach of Great Yarmouth. On site there is an area with 109 privately owned caravan holiday homes, plus 35 site owned units for rent. A separate grassy open area provides around 150 touring pitches, some slightly sloping, with only 100 having electrical hook-ups (16A), plus 2 fully serviced pitches. Two sanitary units of differing ages provide clean but fairly standard facilities with pre-set hot showers, open style washbasins, a unit for disabled persons, a baby room, and dishwashing sinks. There is, however, free hot water throughout. The laundry, in a separate older unit, has washing machines, dryers, spinners and irons. Chemical disposal and motorcaravan service points. Gas is available. Other facilities include a large restaurant/bar which has club style entertainment in season, and a takeaway service (noon-7pm). This overlooks a heated outdoor swimming pool (60 x 30 ft) which opens from May. Campers can also use the indoor pool and other facilities at Liffens Welcome Holiday Centre nearby. The excellent children's playground and a fenced hard surfaced multi-court for ball games are far enough from the pitches to preserve peace and quiet. The site also operates a post office/shop which is adjacent to the site, and a regular bus service runs from here to Great Yarmouth. Golf 2 miles, fishing ¼ mile. A Roman fortress borders the site.

Directions: From junction of the A12 and A143 at roundabout south of Great Yarmouth take Burgh Road westwards, straight over at next roundabout, then second left into Butt Lane. Site is on right. Avoid width restricted road closer to Great Yarmouth. O.S.GR: TM490050.

Charges 1999:
-- Per unit incl. 4 persons £7.00 - £12.50; extra person free - £1.00; fully serviced pitch plus £3.00; awning or boat free - £1.00; extra pup tent £5.00; electricity £2.00; dog (one only) £1.00 - £1.50.
-- Special offer breaks available.
-- Credit cards accepted.
-- VAT included.

Open:
2 April - 30 October.

Address:
Burgh Castle,
Great Yarmouth,
Norfolk NR31 9QB.

Tel:
(01493) 780357.
FAX: (01493) 782383.

Reservations:
Advisable for B.Hs,
weekends and electric hook-ups, with £20 p/week deposit.

see colour advert
between pages 128/129

349 The Grange Touring Park, Ormesby St Margaret

Very appealing and well appointed, family touring site, near Great Yarmouth.

The overall appearance of this site is that of a garden, with many hanging baskets, flower beds, bluebells and daffodils under the trees in spring, and all carefully tended by the resident wardens. Of the 70 level grassy pitches, 62 have electricity (5A) and all are arranged around tarmac access roads. The modern stylish sanitary building is exceptionally well appointed, beautifully tiled and spotlessly clean, housing all the usual facilities including a baby changing room in the ladies' and with free hot water throughout. The laundry room has a washing machine, dryer and a mangle (very popular we were told), and washing lines are provided at the rear of the building. Other facilities include children's swings, a mobile shop calls daily in high season and gas is available from reception. Next to the campsite is The Grange itself - a free house offering a wide range of meals, beers and real ale, plus children's play equipment. The site owner also has a holiday campsite at Hemsby (4 miles) with its own wide sandy beach, which guests at The Grange are welcome to use. Fishing 4 miles, golf 3 miles. Local attractions include Caister Castle and Motor Museum, Norfolk Rare Breed Centre, Yarmouth greyhound stadium and ten pin bowling.

Directions: Site is north of Great Yarmouth and east of Ormesby St Margaret, just south of the roundabout where the B1159 joins the A149. O.S.GR: TG515140.

Charges 1999:
-- Per unit incl. 4 persons £6.00 - £11.00; extra adult £2.00; awning £2.00; electricity £1.50; extra car or boat £2.00; first dog free, extra dog by arrangement £2.00.
-- Credit cards accepted.
-- VAT included.

Open:
20 March - 26 September.

Address:
Yarmouth Road,
Ormesby St Margaret,
Great Yarmouth,
Norfolk NR29 3QG.

Tel:
(01493) 730306.
FAX: (01493) 730188.

Reservations:
Advisable for B.Hs (min. 3 nights), school holidays and peak season and made with deposit (£10 for under 7 days or £20 per week).

Norfolk

339 The Dower House Touring Park, Thetford Forest

Peaceful park in a woodland setting.

The Dower House is situated in 20 acres of Britain's largest woodland forest on the Suffolk and Norfolk borders, it provides quiet woodland walks (you may be asked to `donate' a walk) and cycle ways, with an abundance of wildlife. It is also an ideal centre from which to explore Breckland. The present owners acquired the park some years ago and have worked hard to upgrade the facilities. There is provision for 60 tents and 100 vans on unmarked, fairly level, open grass with some mature oaks, in four field areas surrounded by the forest, with the Dower House in the centre. Electrical hook-ups (10-16A) are available on three fields with wheel hardstandings on one. Six new pitches for visitors with mobility problems are linked by path to the main facilities. A smallish swimming pool (only 1.1 m. deep, late May - early Sept), with a paddling pool alongside, is attractively situated in front of the house. The Dower House, as well as being the home of the owners, houses a pleasant, enlarged bar which provides the history of the house and also serves bar food (weekends only in low season), TV and quiet rooms, and a takeaway (no games machines). A patio area is used for special feature weekends (eg. Morris dancing, Star Gazers and Swinging 60s). A separate licensed shop doubles as reception and opens daily in the season, on request at other times. There are two toilet blocks – a small, refurbished one near the entrance, and a larger one with free hot water in the row of washbasins with mirrors, shaver points and a baby room. The showers (5 for each sex and 20p for 4 mins with meter outside door) are in a separate building which also houses a unit for disabled people. Dishwashing room, including a lower sink for children or the disabled. Laundry room with washing machine and dryer. Chemical disposal. Gas supplies. Public phone. Information room. A torch would be useful. Fishing nearby (1½ miles). Very large, open air market at Snetterton motor racing circuit (2-3 miles) on Sundays.

Charges 1999:
-- Per unit incl. 2 persons £6.95 - £9.15; extra adult 50p - £1.50; extra child (4-17 yrs) 40p - 85p; hikers or cyclists (2 persons) incl. tent £4.85 - £6.50; electricity £2.00 - £2.25; visitor £1.00 - £2.00 per car; dog or awning free.
-- VAT included.
-- Credit cards accepted.

Open:
20 March - 1 October.

Address:
Thetford Forest,
East Harling,
Norfolk NR16 2SE.

Tel:
(01953) 717314.
FAX: (01953) 717843.

Reservations:
Accepted by phone; deposit of £10 required for electricity.

Directions: From A11 (Thetford-Norwich) road follow signs to East Harling and park is signed. Turn right at the church and right at T junction; park is on right. From A1066 Thetford-Garboldisham road follow signs for East Harling and park is on left after passing Forestry Commission site. Follow unmade road for approx. 1 mile driving slowly past the Gamekeepers cottage. O.S.GR: TL969853.

348 Little Lakeland Caravan Park, Wortwell, nr. Harleston

Traditional, mature little site with own fishing lake.

This peaceful hideaway is tucked behind the houses and gardens that border the village main street. There are 57 pitches with a number of caravan holiday homes and long stay units, but there should always be around 25 places for tourers. The pitches are mostly individual with mature hedges and trees separating them. A newly constructed, heated sanitary unit is well tiled and has washbasins in vanity style units (all in cubicles for ladies, one for men), and modern spacious, controllable showers. Hot water is free throughout. The laundry has a washing machine, dryer, spin dryer and ironing facilities and a well equipped room for disabled visitors also has facilities for baby changing. A further unit (also heated) by reception provides a shower, WC and basin per sex and is used mostly in the colder months. There is a small children's play area, and a library of paperback books in the summer-house. Reception stocks gas and some basic essentials. Recycling bins. Fishing in the lake is free for campers, max. 4 rods per unit. Riding 6 miles, golf 4 miles. The village has a post office and general store, a pub and garage. Places to visit nearby include The Cider Place at Ilketshall St Lawrence, the Otter Trust at Earsham, and there are numerous local way-marked walks around Wortwell and nearby Harleston, which also has a market every Wednesday. A member of the Countryside Discovery group.

Charges 2000:
-- Per unit incl. 2 adults £7.60 - £9.50; extra adult £2.00; child (4-16 yrs.) £1.00; electricity (10A max) £1.60; extra vehicle £1.00.
-- VAT included.
-- No credit cards.

Open:
15 March - 31 October.

Address:
Wortwell, Harleston,
Norfolk IP20 0EL.

Tel:
(01986) 788646.
FAX: as phone.

Reservations:
Advisable for B.Hs and peak season; made with £20 deposit or full fee if less.

Directions: Approaching from Diss, leave A143 at roundabout signed Wortwell. Continue to village, pass `The Bell' public house then a garage on the right, after which turn right at first bungalow (Little Lakeland Lodge) watching carefully for signs. Site is down lane, 250 yards on right. O.S.GR: TM270850.

338 Clippesby Holidays, Clippesby, nr. Acle

Beautiful, self-contained, friendly, family park in the middle of the Broads.

A `gem' of a park, in the grounds of a private estate where one can wander at will, Clippesby offers the choice of pitching in shady secluded woodland or on more open parkland with mature colourful trees and shrubs on gently sloping lawns. All 100 pitches are well spaced and numbered (70 with 10A electricity). Hardstanding is available in the parking area. Three timbered toilet blocks are well placed, with heating, free hot water in washbasins (some cabins), 10 showers in total including 2 in the Pinewoods block which are large enough to take a family or a wheelchair. Showers are free but hot water for dishwashing is 20p - the park is not on mains services. The real pleasures of Clippesby are the beautiful environment, the friendly welcome from the family who live in the Hall and the thoughtful facilities planned with a degree of originality not often found on British sites. You come on them unexpectedly; a sunken grass tennis court, small heated swimming pool with mellow flagstone patio behind the Hall, the timber adventure playground, putting and recreation greens and the mature garden area around the single storey Hall. The Muskett Arms (evenings only in low season), with attractive and comfortable family bar and a sheltered courtyard outside, provides evening meals, music nights, barbecue evenings and other family entertainment, again individual in design. Honey Bun's, by reception, comprises a shop to meet basic needs, a coffee bar for home-made breakfast, lunches, teas and takeaways, a gift and local craft shop, children's video shows and equipment hire including board games. All fascinating and open from end-May, 9 am.-5 pm. in the main season. Facilities also include a unit for disabled visitors, chemical disposal, washing machine and dryer, gas supplies and bicycle hire, but remember your torch and wellington boots - the environment is very natural and is deliberately kept that way. Dogs have a dog walk (max. 1 per pitch). Reservations are advised for peak periods and visitors return year after year. There are 23 cottages around the park for hire, all in keeping with the environment (all year). Sunday evening services are held in the beautiful Saxon church on the estate. Children can roam at will, and in safety, and parents can unwind in this comfortable park, never mind all the attractions of the Broads and Great Yarmouth on your doorstep and only the peacocks to disturb you! Riding 3 miles, golf 5 miles, fishing 2 miles.

Directions: Park is signed off B1152 about a mile north of the junction with A1064, 2 miles south of the junction with A419. O.S. GR: TG423145.

Charges 1999:
-- Per unit incl. 2 adults £8.50 - £15.00 (hiker's tent £13.50); unit 20 ft. or over plus £2.00 in high season; extra adult or visitor £1.00 - £1.95; child or student (over 3 yrs) 50p - 75p; awning £1.00 - £1.95; extra car £1.00 - £2.50 (free on car park); pup tent or boat trailer 45p - 95p; dog £1.00 - £1.95; electricity £2.00 (20 m. lead required).
-- VAT included.
-- Credit cards accepted.

Open:
Easter w/end, then 1 May - last w/end in September.

Address:
Clippesby Hall,
Clippesby,
Norfolk NR29 3BL.

Tel:
(01493) 367800.
FAX: (01493) 367809.
E-mail: holidays@ clippesby.ndirect.co.uk.

Reservations:
Made with deposit (£20 per week or part week).

Alan Rogers' Discount

Less 50p per night

343 Kelling Heath Holiday Park, Weybourne, nr. Sheringham

Spacious, heathland park with a range of amenities overlooking north Norfolk coast.

Kelling Heath is a holiday park situated in a 250-acre estate in a designated area of outstanding natural beauty and the 384 caravan holiday homes (36 to let, the rest privately owned) and the 300 touring pitches blend easily into the part-wooded, part-open heathland. A wide range of on-site facilities, including a club complex, swimming pool (May-end Aug) and nature trail, provide activities for all ages. The touring area is quiet and peaceful, away from the facilities, on fairly level grass amid pine trees and open heathland with gorse and heather. It has 246 marked pitches with electrical hook-ups (13A) and a further 54 unmarked. Purpose built toilet blocks of brick and local stone, including a new, heated block serve the site. They provide free pre-set hot showers, washbasins (a few in private cabins), an excellent supply of toilets, provision for disabled people, chemical disposal, baby bath and in season, a nappy disposal service. There are washing machines (3), tumble dryers (2) and irons from reception (with £20 deposit). The central reception area between the statics and the tourers has been attractively paved and pedestrianised with village stores, bar and band-stand. `The Forge', the complex comprising an entertainment bar, adults only bar, family room and pool area, provides a comprehensive range of entertainment and amusements all season. An adventure playground with assault course is near and the nature trail starts and ends here. Other facilities include two hard tennis courts, a small outdoor, heated fun pool (main season only), sports field, play areas (some rather hidden from the pitches) and a small lake for free fishing (permit holders only). Well stocked supermarket and takeaway. Gas is available. Torch useful. A range of information is available on places to visit and the North Norfolk Steam Railway has a halt within walking distance, giving access to Cromer.

Directions: Park is signed on A148 the Holt - Cromer road between High Kelling and Bodham. On A149 Sheringham road turn right at the church in Weybourne. O.S.GR: TG117418.

Charges guide:
-- Per unit £7.95 - £13.25; pitch with electricity £9.95 - £15.25; extra person (under 16 yrs) free- £1.95; awning, extra car or pup tent free - £2.00; dog (max. 2) £1.50.
-- Min. 7 day stay in high season.
-- No single sex groups.
-- Credit cards accepted.
-- VAT included.

Open:
19 March - 31 October, (full facilities: Easter, Mayday w/ends and 20/5-9/9).

Address:
Weybourne, Sheringham, Norfolk NR25 7HW.

Tel:
(01263) 708181.
Reservations:
(01263) 588181.

Reservations:
Necessary for July/Aug. on a weekly basis with £15 deposit.

Alan Rogers' Discount

Less 10%
excl. Juy/Aug

350 Woodhill Park, East Runton, nr. Cromer

Seaside site with good views and traditional atmosphere.

Situated on the cliff top, on a large gently sloping open grassy field, are 113 marked touring pitches, all with electricity (16A), many of which have wonderful views over the surrounding countryside. A small number of holiday homes which are located nearer to the cliff edge unfortunately have the best sea views, although perhaps at times a little bracing! The three sanitary units (the newest of which is part of the reception building) provide a more than adequate supply of WCs and washbasins, but could be a little short of showers at peak times. There is, however, free hot water throughout, a laundry with washing machines and dryer (iron available from reception), a fully equipped unit for disabled persons and chemical disposal facilities. A very well stocked mini-market had a good range of beers, wines and magazines, alongside the usual groceries, toys and sweets, plus gas exchange. There is a good adventure playground for the children, plenty of space for ball games and new crazy golf. A 9 hole golf course is adjacent to the site. Bicycle hire nearby. Although the site is fenced there is access to the cliff top path, a possible hazard for small children. Nearby attractions include `Karttrax' at Cromer (go-karting), boat trips to see the seals off Blakeney Point, the Shire Horse Centre at West Runton, the North Norfolk Steam Railway, and at Sheringham you can find `The Splash' fun pool complex with wave machine.

Directions: Site is beside the A149 coast road between East and West Runton. O.S.GR: TG190420.

Charges guide:
-- Per unit £6.25 - £7.00; small pitch (non-electric) £4.35 - £5.20; adult £1.17 - £1.45; child 60p - 80p; electricity £1.25; multi-service pitch plus £2.20 - 2.70; dog 80p.
-- VAT included.

Open:
20 March - 31 October.

Address:
Cromer Road, East Runton, Cromer, Norfolk NR27 9PX.

Tel:
(01263) 512242.
FAX: (01263) 515326.

Reservations:
Accepted for min. 3 nights with £15 p/week non returnable booking fee.

PRETTY NORTH NORFOLK
SET BETWEEN CROMER & SHERINGHAM
Award winning Woodhill is one of Norfolk's finest parks. Set in countryside overlooking the sea, you will find **peace & tranquillity**. Developed to the highest standards our peaceful park specialises in touring & camping, with **multi-service & super size hook-up pitches**, superb toilet & cleansing facilities.

We also **luxury caravan holiday homes**, which overlook the sea, boasting **central heating, satellite T.V., barbecue** and many other extras.

WE THINK YOU'LL FIND, AS MANY DO - THAT YOU WILL RETURN.
Send for brochure to Mrs E. Woods
WOODHILL PARK, CROMER ROAD,
EAST RUNTON, CROMER, NORFOLK NR27 9PX.
Tel: 01263 512242 www.woodhill-park.com

ROSE AWARD

EXCELLENT

NORTH NORFOLK
DISTRICT COUNCIL
A W A R D O F
E X C E L L E N C E
W I N N E R

346 The Garden Caravan Site, Barmer Hall, Syderstone

Imaginative touring site in an enclosed, south facing, walled garden, near Kings Lynn.

This newly developed site has 30 spacious marked pitches, all on gently sloping grass in the most attractive setting behind the Hall itself. There are 30 electrical connections (16A), each with a TV hook-up as reception is variable, possibly due to the high wall and woodland surrounding the site. However, this does mean that the site is peaceful and a little sun-trap, a haven from the busy world outside. Attractive mature trees, shrubs and climbers provide shade at various times of the day. Reception is housed in a small kiosk (not always manned, so pitch yourself and pay later). There is no shop, but gas, ices, soft drinks and free range fresh eggs are usually available. The sanitary facilities are in a new building (heated when necessary) providing the usual facilities with extremely spacious hot showers, free hot water throughout, dishwashing sinks under cover at one end of the building and chemical disposal. The site is not far from Sandringham, and there are plenty of peaceful lanes to explore on a bicycle or take a woodland walk from the little door in the wall at the rear of the site. Maybe visit Norfolk Lavender, Langham Glass or the Thursford Collection of steam engines, organs and Wurlitzer fame. The North Norfolk coast and beaches, numerous golf courses and bird sanctuaries are all within easy reach. Bicycle hire 4 miles, riding 6 miles, golf 10 miles.

Directions: Approx. 4 miles west of Fakenham turn off A148, taking B1454 northwards and turning to Barmer Hall after a further 4 miles, where site is signed - the road is marked `unsuitable for motor vehicles' but ignore this and follow past and behind the Hall and farm buildings. O.S.GR: TF810330.

Charges 1999:
-- Per adult £3.50 - £4.00; child £1.00; electricity £2.00; TV aerial hook-up 50p.
-- VAT included.
-- No credit cards.

Open:
1 March - 1 November.

Address:
Barmer Hall, Syderstone, Kings Lynn, Norfolk.

Tel:
(01485) 578220 (house) or 578178 (site).
FAX: (01485) 578178.

Reservations:
Advised for B.Hs and peak season; contact site for details.

Alan Rogers' Discount

Less 10% per adult in June

340 The Old Brick Kilns Caravan & Camping Park, Little Barney

Tranquil, rural site on split levels with good quality facilities, near Fakenham.

This family run park, owned by Alan and Pam Greenhalgh, has been developed on the site of an old brick kiln resulting in land on varying levels. It provides areas of pitches (eg. the Dell, the Orchard) which have been well drained and grassed over. Banks around the park and trees provide shelter, home for a variety of wildlife with a wide range of trees and shrubs. There are new garden areas, including a butterfly garden, and a central conservation pond is the main feature. There are 60 pitches, all with electricity (10/16A) and semi hardstanding. Drinking water is supplied by a 285 ft. bore and excellent, roofed service areas provide water and waste disposal. Toilet facilities are very good with under floor heating, washbasins in curtained cubicles, free hot water, hand and hair dryers. There are facilities for babies and disabled people (unisex), a laundry room and dishwashing (H&C), chemical disposal. A small toilet block at the furthest end and motorcaravan services complete the provision. Amenities include a large, comfortable bar area and à la carte restaurant, open selected evenings and weekends. Patio area outside with barbecue. TV room, an information centre, table tennis, bicycle hire, giant chess and mini library. The reception area also provides a shop and gas is available. The children's play area is fenced, with bark surface. Telephone. Dogs are accepted on leads with a dog walk provided. Winter caravan storage available. B&B is also available. Gas barbecues for hire. Fishing on site, riding 6 miles, golf 5 or 8 miles. A friendly, helpful atmosphere prevails and as the park is 8 miles from the coast, it is ideally situated to explore North Norfolk. A member of the Best of British group.

Directions: From Fakenham take A148 Cromer road. After 6 miles, fork right on B1354 Aylsham road and in 300 yds, turn right, signed Barney, and then first left on a narrow country lane with passing places, for ¾ mile. O.S.GR: TG004332.

Charges 2000:
-- Per pitch £5.00 - £7.50; adult £2.00; child 4-15 yrs £1.00 - £1.50, 0-3 yrs 50p - 75p; awning free; extra pup tent £1.00 - £1.50; extra car on pitch £1.50 - £2.50; dog (max. 2) free; visitor £1.00; electricity £2.00.
-- VAT included.
-- Credit cards accepted.

Open:
1 March - 31 October.

Address:
Little Barney Lane, Barney, Fakenham, Norfolk NR21 0NL.

Tel:
(01328) 878305. FAX: (01328) 878948. E-mail: enquire@old-brick-kilns.co.uk.

Reservations:
Advised and made with £15 deposit (non-refundable).

344 Gatton Waters Lakeside Touring Site, Hillington

Peaceful park set round fishing lakes, for adults only, near Sandringham.

Developed by James and Carolyn Donaldson around two fishing lakes (formerly stone quarries), Gatton Waters has a pleasant open aspect. The reception/bar, housed in an old Norfolk barn, provides a nice welcome and serves real ale (closed Tuesdays). Evening meals and Sunday lunches are served (weekends only out of main season and not October) and a welcome addition is a non-smoking lounge. The 60 caravan and 30 tent pitches are set further away, around the lakes and quite a number are occupied by seasonal caravans. However, there is room for those seeking either to fish (day tickets available) or for a quiet base to visit Sandringham (2½ miles) or the north Norfolk Coast (8 miles). Everything is kept as natural as possible. We heard skylarks and watched leverets when we visited and there are many types of ducks, etc. on the lakes. A new toilet block can be heated and provides free hot water, vanity style washbasins, push-button showers and a washing up sink. Chemical disposal and motorcaravan services. Ask at reception about laundry. Extra facilities are available in two `portacabin' units and at reception. B&B is also offered. Dogs are welcome on leads. Caravan storage available. Riding or golf 8 miles. The owners made the decision to go `adult only' in '98 in keeping with the natural relaxed atmosphere of the site.

Directions: From Kings Lynn follow A148 Cromer road. Site is signed after sign to West Newton but before sign to Sandringham and village of Hillington (all to the left). O.S.GR: TF705255.

Charges 1999:
-- Per unit incl. 2 persons: caravan or trailer tent £4.00 - £8.00; tent incl. 2 persons £4.00 - £7.00; extra person £1.00; electricity £1.75 - £2.00.
-- VAT included.
-- No credit cards.

Open:
April - 5 October.

Address:
Hillington, nr. Sandringham, Kings Lynn, Norfolk PE31 6BJ.

Tel:
(01485) 600643.

Reservations:
Advisable during peak periods and made for min. 3 days at B.Hs. for electricity with £10 deposit.

342 Two Mills Touring Park, North Walsham

Small, sheltered and secluded park but for adults only.

Two Mills is a quiet site situated in the bowl of a former quarry and is therefore a real sun trap, both secluded and sheltered. The park is neatly maintained with natural areas, varied trees, wild flowers and birds. It is a good centre to explore the North Norfolk coast, the Broads or for visiting Norwich and a footpath from the park joins the Weavers Way. Including five 'panorama' pitches (with patio area, water and waste water drainage), there are 60 level, marked, grassy pitches, 50 for touring units, all at least 11 m. wide and with electricity (10/16A), 7 with hardstanding. The central, very well maintained and heated toilet block has free hot water in the curtained showers and washbasins (some in cabins), en-suite facilities for disabled people, laundry and dishwashing rooms and chemical disposal. Small shop with comprehensive tourist information and community room with TV and tea and coffee facilities. The town is 20 minute walk. Dogs accepted by arrangement only (several breeds not welcome) with kennels and dog walk provided. No plastic groundsheets. Public phone. Ice service. Hotel/pub across the road. Fishing, golf or riding 5 miles, bicycle hire 1½ and the coast is 5 miles. Adults only accepted.

Directions: Approach from southeast on A149 and watch for caravan sign approx. 1½ miles before North Walsham (also signed White Horse Common). The road runs parallel to the A149; site is on right after 1¼ miles. O.S.GR: TG292287.

Charges 2000:
-- Per unit incl. 2 adults £7.50 - £10.50; panorama pitch £87.50 - £112.00 per week; extra person £2.50; awning £1.00 - £1.50; dog 50p; electricity £2.00.
-- B.H's (min. stay 3 nights) £28.50 - £34.50.
– Special offers available.
-- Credit cards accepted.

Open:
All year excl. 4/1-28/2.

Address:
Scarborough Hill, North Walsham, Norfolk NR28 9NA.

Tel/Fax:
(01692) 405829.

Reservations:
Made with £10 deposit; balance on arrival.

345 Little Haven Caravan & Camping Park, Erpingham, nr. Norwich

Secluded and pretty, touring site for adults only.

Within easy reach of the coast and the Broads, this is an attractive and peaceful little site with excellent facilities. The 24 grassy pitches, all with electricity (16A), are arranged around the outside of a gravel access road, with a central lawn and decorative pergola, neat little garden and seating area. The well maintained sanitary unit is heated and provides modern facilities including spacious hot showers and two covered dishwashing and laundry sinks at one end of the building. Hot water is free throughout. There is no shop, gas is available at Alby Service Station, and there are two pubs which serve food and traditional ales within walking distance. An ideal base for cycling, walking, horse riding, or just relaxing, the Weavers Way footpath is within half a mile of the site, whilst a riding stables and craft centre are at nearby Alby. Also close by is magnificent Blickling Hall with its superb state rooms, gardens and park, or a short drive takes you to the historic market town of Aylsham. Note: this site is unsuitable for American motorhomes. Only adults and accompanied children over 14 years are accepted.

Directions: From A140 Cromer - Norwich road, going south towards Aylsham and 3 miles south of Roughton, past Horseshoes pub and Alby crafts, take first right signed Erpingham 2 miles. Site is 175 yards on right. O.S.GR: TG190320.

Charges 1999:
-- Per unit incl. 2 adults £7.00 - £8.00; extra adult £2.00; extra car £1.00; full awning £1.00; porch awning or extra small tent 50p; electricity £1.50 (May - Aug) - £2.00.
– Special offers available.
-- VAT included.

Open:
1 March - 31 October.

Address:
The Street, Erpingham, Norwich, Norfolk NR11 7QD.

Tel/Fax:
(01263) 768959.

Reservations:
Advised in peak season; with £10 deposit.

347 Breckland Meadows Touring Park, Swaffham

Small touring park within walking distance of historic market town.

This is a pleasant little park which would make a good base to explore the local area. The 45 pitches are on fairly level, neat grass, all with electricity (16A). There may be some road noise at times but newly planted trees should reduce this as they mature. Adjacent to the site is the Swaefas Way, a seven mile circular walk which links to the more well known Peddars Way. The toilet block has been completely refurbished and is neat, clean and heated when necessary. It provides all the usual facilities, a separate toilet and washbasin unit for disabled visitors, outside covered washing up facilities and chemical disposal. Gas is available. Fishing 5 miles, riding 4 miles, golf 2 miles. Local attractions include Cockley Cley Medieval Iceni Village and Saxon Church, Castle Acre Priory, Oxburgh Hall and the Thursford Collection of steam engines, mechanical organs and Wurlitzer fame. Swaffham (½ mile) is a historic market town with a popular Saturday market.

Directions: Park is just west of Swaffham on the old A47, approx. ½ mile from the town centre. O.S.GR: TF820080.

Charges 2000:
-- Per unit incl. 2 adults £5.00 - £8.00; extra adult £1.00; child (5-15) 50p; electricity £2.00.
-- Credit cards accepted.

Open:
1 March - early Nov.

Address:
Lynn Road, Swaffham.

Tel:
(01760) 721246.
FAX: (01760) 725994.
E-mail: breckland-meadows@tesco.net.

Reservations:
Essential for B.Hs and advised for peak season; with deposit (£5-£10).

Cambridgeshire

355 Old Manor Caravan Park, Grafham Water, Grafham

Clean, peaceful and friendly park, situated near large reservoir.

Set in six acres of level grounds there is a history to this site. The old white cottage (now the reception) was once occupied by Oliver Cromwell, and the grounds formed part of his garden. Even today the horse pond and part of the moat still remain. A gravel road serves the 80 numbered and generously sized grass pitches (65 with 10A electrical connections). Privacy and shade is provided by varied and plentiful trees and hedges throughout. The park is well drained, neat and carefully maintained, with ample service points for water and refuse. The single, tiled, heated toilet block is thoughtfully planned and exceptionally clean. Hot water is controllable, whilst all showers and washbasins are in generously sized cubicles. Dishwashing and laundry rooms, similarly tiled and equally clean, are further complemented by free deep freezers for ice blocks and food storage. Facilities for disabled visitors are provided with a ramp. Basic provisions are kept in reception, with the nearest shops being at West Perry or Buckden (5 and 3 miles respectively). Leisure facilities comprise a small playground, with bark chipping base and a large, solar-heated, outdoor pool (unsupervised). Sailing, fishing, cycle hire, nature trails and bird watching can be found at nearby Grafham Water. Cambridge, The Imperial War Museum at Duxford, Woburn Abbey, the Shuttleworth Collection at Old Warden are nearby too. Public phone and post box. Dogs are welcome on leads, but must be exercised off-site.

Directions: Leave the A1 at Buckden roundabout and follow B661 towards Grafham Water for approx. ½ mile. O.S.GR: TL160680.

Charges 1999:
-- Per unit incl. 2 adults £9.00 - £11.00; extra person £2.50 - £3.00; child free - £1.50; extra car or boat £1.50; electricity £1.70.
-- VAT included.
-- No credit cards.

Open:
February - November.

Address:
Church Lane, Grafham Water, Grafham, Cambridgeshire PE18 0BB.

Tel:
(01480) 810264.

Reservations:
Made with £10 non-returnable deposit (min 3 nights at B.Hs).

358 Ferry Meadows Caravan Club Site, Peterborough

Family holiday site in extensive country park.

Only 3 miles from Peterborough and closer still to the East of England Showground, Ferry Meadows occupies 30 acres of the much larger Nene Country Park. The meadows, lakes and woodlands provide ample opportunities to sample the numerous facilities on offer, more of which later. Open all year, the site provides 254 pitches in total, 160 grass pitches on one side of the park and 94 gravel hardstandings on the newer side, just across the road. Privacy, shade and character are assured by the abundance of trees, bushes and shrubs that are part of the park as a whole. All pitches have electricity (16A) and tents are accepted on the grassed section of the site. Two modern, heated toilet blocks are of the usual good Club standard, with free, controllable showers, curtained washbasins, hand and hair dryers and en-suite facilities for disabled visitors. Each section has dishwashing sinks under cover, as well as a laundry room with sinks, a washing machine, dryer and ironing. There are chemical disposal facilities, numerous points for waste and drinking water, plus a motorcaravan service point and a barrier system to prevent unauthorised access. Families with children may prefer the grass section, from where they can keep a watchful eye on the well-equipped children's play area. The site office stocks basic provisions (nearest shops 1½ miles) and there is an entire room devoted to tourist information and ideas on where to go. Returning to the Country Park, it covers over 500 acres within which are miles of walks and cycle ways, horse routes, lakes for coarse fishing, sailing and windsurfing, a wetland nature reserve, archery field, two golf courses and a miniature railway. Well laid out for the disabled visitor, free wheelchair hire is available. Also passing within nostalgic earshot and yielding the occasional aroma of bygone eras is the Nene Valley Steam Railway, complete with Thomas the Tank Engine. Peterborough also offers ice and roller skating, whilst other attractions include Spalding Flower Festival and Burghley Park.

Directions: From A1 south, don't turn onto A1139, but turn left at next junction (signed Showground, Chesterton, Alwalton). At T-junction turn left on A605, continue straight at three roundabouts, following signs for Nene Park to site in Ham Lane. O.S.GR: TL151975.

Charges guide:
-- Per adult £2.00 - £4.00; child £1.10 - £1.20; non-member pitch fee £6.00 - £7.00; electricity £1.45 - £2.20.
-- Credit cards accepted

Open:
All year.

Address:
Ham Lane, Peterborough PE2 5UU.

Tel:
(01733) 233526.

Reservations:
Essential for B.Hs, July/Aug and all w/ends.

356 Highfield Farm Camping Park, Comberton, nr. Cambridge

Quality, peaceful and very well kept, family run park.

Situated five miles from Cambridge, this eight acre park is a delightfully quiet touring location. Family run, the welcome is warm and the facilities of superior quality. Divided into five enclosures by hedges and conifers, there are also shady glades for those who wish to retreat even further. One enclosure is usually reserved for those without children. Offering 60 numbered pitches for caravans or motorcaravans, and 60 for tents, personal space is further enhanced by the fact that the centre of all enclosures is left free. All pitches have 10A electricity, 50 have gravel hardstanding, and most are level. Three, heated toilet blocks provide a more than adequate coverage. The original block offers controllable showers on payment, free hot water to washbasins and an additional set of unisex showers. The other two blocks (fully tiled) provide a combination of showers on payment (10p), free hot water to washbasins, some open plan, others in cubicles, and ample toilets; all of which are outstandingly clean and well maintained. There is no dedicated provision for disabled people, but one block has extra wide doors and easy access. Laundry facilities comprise two washing machines, tumble dryers, spin dryer, iron and board, plus sinks and baby bath. Hot water is free to ten covered dishwashing sinks spaced throughout the site. Chemical disposal facilities and motorcaravan service point. Basic provisions and gas are available from reception and there are nearby shops and pubs. Two play areas, swings and tree house, plus further space for football and bicycle hire. Fishing 3½ miles, riding 3 miles, golf 2 miles. A small kiosk offers tourist information about the area. Public phone and post box. Extensive dog walk. Gates closed midnight - 7.30 am. A member of the Best of British group.

Directions: Park is 5 miles southwest of Cambridge town centre near eastern edge of Comberton village. From M11 take exit 12, the A603 towards Sandy and right after ½ mile on B1046 to Comberton. From A428 turn south at Hardwick roundabout to Comberton. O.S.GR: TL391571.

Charges 2000:
-- Per caravan/large tent incl. 2 persons £7.50 - £9.00; motorcaravan or small tent £7.25 - £8.50; m/cyclist and tent £6.25 - £7.25; hiker/cyclist and tent £6.25 - £7.00; extra adult £1.50 - £2.00; child (5-16 yrs) £1.00 - £1.50; awning or pup tent £1.00; porch awning 50p; electricity £1.85.
-- No credit cards.
-- VAT included.

Open:
21 March - 31 October.

Address:
Long Road, Comberton, Cambridge CB3 7DG.

Tel:
(01223) 262308.

FAX: as phone.

Reservations:
Made for any length with £10 deposit and 50p fee.

Alan Rogers' Discount

Less 10% for senior citizens, 3 nights or more in low season

See colour feature for 'BEST of BRITISH' between pages 96/97

357 Park Lane Touring Caravan & Camping Park, Godmanchester

Neat, well organised and attractive town park, near Huntingdon.

Personally run by owners, Alan and Kay Mills, and just 10 minutes walk from the town of Huntingdon, Park Lane provides 50 marked pitches on a neat, level and well drained grass field, 45 of which have electricity (10A). Sheltered by the bank of the A14 Huntingdon – Cambridge dual-carriageway there can be some noise but, we are told, after one night you do not notice it. A circular, gravel road, an orchard area for tents below the bank, some mixed trees and a smaller beech hedge area for those seeking seclusion, create a pleasant ambience, enhanced by the neat gravel entrance (gates closed 11.30 p.m.), with an attractive water feature manned by an army of watchful gnomes. Reception is in a static caravan, where tourist information and gas are available. The toilet block, to one edge of the park, is a little dated, but very well maintained nonetheless. Hot water is free to the open plan washbasins, but on payment in the showers. Also accommodated within the block are a baby bath, sink for clothes washing, washing machine, iron, board and hairdryers. Dishwashing sinks adjoin the block, under cover. There are toilets for disabled visitors, chemical disposal, a central waste disposal area and four water points at the end of the block. No bicycles or ball games are permitted. Dog walk. Public phone. Winter caravan storage. The Black Bull is virtually at the bottom of the drive for food or drink, a shop is 200 yds. Fishing 300 yds. The river and boats are nearby with St. Ives and St. Neots both being attractive places to sail along to. Also reasonably near are Grafham Water, for sailing and fishing, not to mention Cambridge, Ely and Duxford. A useful and pleasant park to know.

Directions: From A14 (was A604) northbound, take Huntingdon exit and pick up signs for Godmanchester. O.S. GR: TL245709.

Charges 1999:
--Per caravan, tent or motorcaravan £3.50: adult £2.50; child (3-15 yrs) £1.00; awning £1.25; electricity (10A) £2.00.
-- No credit cards.

Open:
Mid March - end Oct.

Address:
Godmanchester, Huntingdon, Cambridgeshire PE18 8AF.

Tel:
(01480) 453740.

FAX: as phone.

E-mail:
parklane@touringpark39.freeserve.co.uk.

Reservations:
Advisable for B.Hs; contact park.

113

Lincolnshire

366 Walesby Woodlands Caravan Park, nr. Market Rasen

Family owned, small, pleasant touring park near to the Wolds.

This park is surrounded by mature Forestry Commission woodland and is therefore very peaceful and sheltered. About 1½ miles distant is the small town of Market Rasen, but further afield and within easy driving distance, are Lincoln, the Wolds and the coast. There are 64 well spaced pitches, 61 with 10A electricity, marked out on a single, mainly flat, grassy field sectioned by double rows of trees and divided by a central gravel track. The one toilet block, operated by key, has fully tiled surfaces and toilet facilities for disabled people. Hot water is free to pre-set showers (curtain screen, seat, hook but no shelf), vanity style washbasins with ample mirrors, hooks etc. and outside, covered, dishwashing sinks. Chemical disposal facilities. The same block also houses a laundry room and a small shop with an information section (all season). Battery charging and gas are available. A children's play area is on grass to one end of the site (no kite flying - overhead wires). Fishing 3 miles, riding 2 miles, golf 1½ miles. Winter caravan storage. The Viking Way passes through Walesby and there are many other shorter walks in the forest and surrounding area.

Charges 2000:
-- Per unit incl. 2 persons £7.50; extra person £1.25; child (2-12 yrs) £1.00; awning or child's pup tent £1.25; electricity £1.50.
-- Credit cards accepted.
Open:
1 March - 31 October.
Address:
Walesby, Market Rasen, Lincolnshire LN8 3UN.
Tel:
(01673) 843285.
Reservations:
Any length, with deposit.

Directions: Park is northeast of, and signed from, the main approach roads to Market Rasen. O.S.GR: TF117907.

369 Bainland Country Park, Woodhall Spa, nr. Lincoln

Quality family park with many amenities including indoor pool.

Bainland, under its enthusiastic manager, has developed into a first class park, comparing favourably with European sites. There are now 150 spacious, level pitches in hedged bays, linked by circular roadways, forming circles and islands. Of these, 51 are `super' pitches with hardstanding for car and caravan, honey-combed for awning, individual water, drainage and chemical disposal, electricity and TV aerial hook-ups. The remainder of the pitches are either on gravel hardstandings or level grass, all with 16A electricity. There are 10 caravan holiday homes and 25 bungalows to hire. Two excellent toilet blocks can be heated and are well equipped for all basic necessities (except, perhaps, for showers in peak times), and in addition provide a baby care centre, unisex shower room for families, hair care room, family bathroom, fully equipped unit for disabled people, laundry room, chemical disposal, enclosed dishwashing and separate hand washing sinks. The park is also well equipped with bins, water points and motor-caravan service points. The efficient, friendly reception (8 am.- 10 pm.) is housed in a pleasant Swiss-style building adjacent to the shop (groceries, souvenirs and licensed, open March - Oct). Also here is the heated indoor pool and jacuzzi, etc. (under 16s must be accompanied by an adult). This is overlooked by the bistro (all year) and spacious bar area, which also overlooks the golf course and outdoor bowls area. A super children's adventure play area has been created in a large hollow with a sand base in addition to a trampoline, crazy golf, croquet, TV and games room and soft play area. For adults there is an 18 hole, par 3 golf course, a tennis club with a year round floodlit tennis dome with 3-4 courts including badminton (the dome comes off in summer). The bar and bistro are open to the public; the great range of leisure activities, including the pool, are individually booked and paid for at reception. Barbecues, jazz, country and western, and even medieval evenings are organised! Bicycle hire on site. Fishing 3 miles, riding 6 miles. Bainland is 1½ miles from Woodhall Spa, with its old fashioned charm and Dambusters associations, yet deep in the heart of the Lincolnshire Wolds, surrounded by mature trees and with direct access to woods for walking dogs. Winter caravan storage. An impressive park of a high standard, offering much yet still able to provide peace and quiet. A member of the Best of British group.

Charges 1999:
-- Per unit incl. electricity and awning £9.00 - £14.00; serviced pitch £11.00 - £17.00; pup tent free - £3.00.
-- Firework display (min. 2 nights, 5/6 Nov) £24.00; serviced pitch £29.00.
-- Discounts for senior citizens.
-- VAT included.
-- Credit cards accepted
Open:
All year (in winter, super pitches only).
Address:
Horncastle Road, Woodhall Spa, Lincs LN10 6UX.
Tel:
(01526) 352903.
FAX: (01526) 353730.
E-mail: bookings@bainland.com.
Reservations:
Recommended and made for any length. Deposit at B.Hs. only (one night's fee).

See colour feature for `BEST of BRITISH' between pages 96/97

Directions: Entrance to park is off B1191 Horncastle road just outside Woodhall Spa by derestriction sign. O.S.GR: TF214637.

367 Lakeside Park, North Somercotes, nr. Louth

Large family park near coast with comprehensive entertainment (no tents).

With a splendid water feature at the entrance, good tarmac access roads and well tended grounds throughout, first impressions are most rewarding. Set in 47 acres of pine forest, this park is continually seeking to improve and develop the service it offers. The majority is occupied by 300 privately owned holiday homes, all proudly maintained, with the touring section in a separate 15 acre field, but furthest from the leisure areas and activities. Although rather open, a programme of long term landscaping has commenced, intended to impart more character to this area. The number of grass based touring pitches, all level and with 16A electricity has been reduced to 150, whilst hardstanding `super' pitches have been increased to 50. The original heated sanitary facilities, washbasins, showers and toilets, are augmented by another newer block so provision should be adequate (although showers are rather slow to drain and cleaning can be variable). Indoor dishwashing facilities and a launderette are nearby, with another launderette near the shop. Chemical disposal and motorcaravan service facilities. Two play areas in the touring section, plus an amusement arcade and games room near the leisure area. The outdoor pool remains popular (from July), although the heated indoor 'Tropicana' complex, with jacuzzi and sauna, is an outstanding facility and well worth the small charge. Both pools are well maintained and supervised at all times. An impressive, new development, with family, cabaret room and stylish bar is the Waterfront Club, providing a varied entertainment programme all season. Bar meals and Sunday lunches available, with takeaway also (daily 12-2 and 6-11 except Sunday), plus a well stocked, licensed shop (from April). Visitors have free use of the large, 7 acre fishing lake. A new all-weather tennis court has been added and a nine hole golf course will be completed for 2000. Riding 4 miles. Staff are friendly and helpful, with security barrier (£10 deposit) and night patrols. Gas available. Caravan storage. The nearest beach, at Mablethorpe, is 15 minutes by car, and Grimsby, Alford and Louth are also accessible. No tents are accepted.

Directions: Park is on A1031, 7 miles north of Mablethorpe towards Cleethorpes. O.S.GR: TF430960.

Charges 1999:
-- Per unit incl. up to 5 persons, awning and electricity £7.00 - £17.00; `super' pitch plus £3.00; extra person £5.00; dog £1.00; extra car £2.00.
-- Club membership £1 per party/extra persons per night.
-- Min. stays at B.Hs.
-- VAT included.
-- Credit cards accepted.

Open:
March - end November.

Address:
North Somercotes, nr. Louth, Lincolnshire LN11 7RB.

Tel:
(01507) 358315 or 358428.
FAX: (01507) 358135.
E-mail: lakeside@ donamott.com.

Reservations:
Advised for B.Hs and main summer season with deposit (£5 per night booked, min. 3 nights for electricity at B.Hs).

373 Skegness Sands Touring Site, Skegness

Modern, well appointed, touring site, adjacent to promenade and beach.

This very well organised touring site is actually part of a much larger caravan holiday home park, but it has its own entrance and, indeed, its own, more intimate character. There are 85 pitches, all level and with electricity (16A). Most are grass although there are now 21 gravel hardstandings, 4 of which are fully serviced. Site lighting is good throughout, there are regular security patrols and the vehicle entry gates are locked 11 pm - 6 am. The good quality, heated sanitary unit is fully tiled with washbasins in curtained cubicles and good adjustable hot showers, plus three family bathrooms comprising WC, washbasin and shower. A well equipped room for disabled people also doubles as a baby room. Two dishwashing sinks are outside under cover, a laundry room has two washing machines and dryers and there are chemical disposal facilities. Hot water is free throughout. Tourist information is available in reception and gas – there is no shop on site but a small store is immediately opposite the site entrance. Other amenities include a hairdressing salon and an indoor heated swimming pool (open end May - 30 Sept; adult £1, child 50p) which is located in the 'static' area of the site. A small children's playground (for under 5's) is on a grassy area towards the promenade. The gate to the promenade is kept locked at all times, campers getting a key. Pubs, fast food outlets and a supermarket are all within easy walking distance. Local attractions include Funcoast World, Fantasy Island, Hardys Animal Farm, a seal sanctuary, stock car racing, ten pin bowling and golf. The site is a member of the Caravan Club's 'managed under contract' scheme, members and non-members are all made very welcome.

Directions: Site is north of Skegness. Turn from the A52 opposite the 'Garden City' public house into Winthorpe Avenue and the site entrance is on the left at far end of road. O.S.GR: TF570640.

Charges 1999:
-- Per adult £2.60 - £4.00; child (5-16 yrs) £1.10 - £1.20; non-member pitch fee £6.00 - £7.00; electricity £1.50 (summer) - £2.25 (winter); fully serviced pitch plus £3.00.
-- Credit cards accepted.

Open:
All year.

Address:
Winthorpe Avenue, Skegness, Lincolnshire PE25 1QZ.

Tel:
(01754) 761484.

Reservations:
Advised for B.Hs, school holidays and peak season; contact site.

Lincolnshire

365 Cherry Tree Site, Sutton-on-Sea, nr. Mablethorpe

Small, well kept, good value park.

Cherry Tree is a good example of a small touring park, carefully developed by caring and enthusiastic owners. The grass is neatly trimmed and well drained, and is divided by evergreen hedging to site your unit against. Some are well grown, the rest newly planted, and connected by a one-way circular gravel road allowing for 60 good sized pitches all with 10A electricity. The brick built toilet block can be heated and is immaculately kept, providing vanity style washbasins and controllable hot showers (20p). A nice new en-suite unit for those with disabilities is a good addition. A combined dishwashing and laundry room complete with washing machine, spin dryer and tumble dryer, and outside, two water points, a chemical disposal point and a waste disposal area provide for all practical needs. There is also a neat reception, public telephone and a well fenced children's play area again on neat grass. Gas is available. Buses stop outside hourly, and a shop and pub are within 10 minutes walk. It is also possible to walk to the sea via the road. Tennis and bowls nearby, fishing 1½ miles, golf 1 mile, riding 4 miles. Mablethorpe beach is known for its sand yacht racing and Skegness, with all its popular attractions is just down the road. Dogs are welcome on leads if exercised off the park and, for campers, a very warm welcome awaits from George and Carol Boulton.

Directions: Park is 1½ miles south of Sutton-on-Sea on the A52 coast road to Skegness, with the entrance leading off a lay-by on the left. O.S.GR: TF518828.

Charges 1999:
-- Per unit incl. 2 persons £5.00 - £7.00; extra person 50p - 75p; electricity £1.75.
-- Min. stay 3 nights at B.Hs.
-- No credit cards.

Open:
March - 31 October

Address:
Huttoft Road,
Sutton-on-Sea,
Lincolnshire LN12 2RU.

Tel:
(01507) 441626.
FAX: as phone.

Reservations:
Made with £10 deposit (non-returnable).

371 Manby Caravan Park, Manby, nr. Louth

Campsite with its own affordable Health and Fitness centre adjacent.

Although there is nothing remarkable about the campsite here, it's what goes with it that makes it that bit special. The site occupies a large, level and open grassy field with a sanitary unit in the centre. This provides all the usual facilities including a well equipped room for disabled persons. There are 125 pitches, but the site rarely has more than 50 units, and there are 48 electric hook-ups (16A). However, within a few yards you can enter a different world where, for a few pounds sterling, you can loose many more pounds in weight. Guests are assessed and given an individual fitness programme. The Centre has an indoor swimming pool with splash area and spa, a steam room and a sauna, with showers and changing rooms, also a vertical `all round' sun-bed cubicle. The aerobics room has a specially sprung floor, whilst the fitness suite is equipped with the latest cardio vascular machines, a fully supervised weights section for the totally dedicated, plus toning tables. The reception desk can provide full details. In addition there is a small coffee bar/bistro with takeaway facility, a hairdressing salon, and a small shop with the filling station.

Directions: Site is on B1200 about 4 miles east of Louth, entrance is beside Rix Garage, adjacent to the Manby Arms public house. O.S.GR: TF392874.

Charges 2000:
-- Per unit incl. 2 adults and 2 children £8.50; electricity £1.95; pup tent or awning £1.00; dog 50p.
-- VAT included.
-- Credit cards accepted.

Open:
Easter - 7 November.

Address:
Manby Middlegate,
Manby, Louth,
Lincolnshire LN11 8SX.

Tel:
(01507) 328232.
FAX: as phone.

Reservations:
Not usually necessary except at B.Hs (made with one night pitch fee).

For lists of parks which offer facilities on site for
FISHING, GOLF, HORSE RIDING, BICYCLE HIRE
or BOAT LAUNCHING see pages 237 - 239

375 Foreman's Bridge Caravan Park, Sutton St James, nr. Spalding

Peaceful, comfortable, Fenland touring site.

Not only is Foreman's Bridge an extremely pleasant little park, but it also provides a good base from which to explore the Fens, including Spalding, famous for its annual flower festival. Fishing and cycling are also to be recommended, indeed bicycle hire and fishing licences are both available from the site. Arranged around a large, level and grassy meadow there are 40 pitches, 32 of which have electricity (10A) and 7 have gravel hardstanding. Fruit trees, flower beds, hanging baskets and planted troughs punctuate the site with bursts of vibrant colour. The modern sanitary unit provides spacious individual shower rooms with seats and washbasins (showers on payment), and the thoughtful provision of soap, tissues, hand towels and pot pourri. Dishwashing sinks are in their own room, the laundry room has a washing machine, dryer and ironing facilities and the site recycles glass, aluminium and paper. There are chemical disposal and motorcaravan service points. Basic provisions and gas are available on site, but the nearest shop is just two miles away. Seven site owned mobile homes are for rent, as well as two comfortable and well equipped cottages. The adjacent Fenland 'drain' is suitable for fishing, but could be a hazard for young children. Riding 8 miles, golf 5 miles. Winter caravan storage. This site is unsuitable for American or large motorhomes. Site barrier (£5 deposit for card).

Directions: From A17 Spalding - Kings Lynn road turn south on B1390 at Long Sutton towards Sutton St James for approx. 2 miles. Site entrance is on the left immediately after the bridge. O.S.GR: TF410198.

Charges 1999:
--Per unit incl. 2 adults and 2 children £5.50; small 1 person tent £4.50; extra adult £2.00; child £1.00; awning £1.00; dog 50p; electricity £1.50.
-- VAT included.

Open:
1 March - 30 November.

Address:
Sutton St James, Spalding, Lincolnshire PE21 0HU.

Tel:
(01945) 440346.

Reservations:
Advisable for Flower Festival, B.Hs (min. 3 nights), and peak season; made with £10 deposit.

Alan Rogers' Discount

Less 10% for 2 or more nights

370 Pilgrims Way Caravan and Camping Park, Fishtoft, nr. Boston

Excellent touring site, with cosy facilities, close to historic Boston.

Located in a rural setting this delightful, family run site is two miles from Boston and its famous church tower. There are 20 individual pitches of which 5 have hardstanding, whilst all have access to electricity (10A). Housed in a good quality conversion at one end of what was once a workshop, the sanitary facilities have been thoughtfully planned and are exceptionally clean and well maintained. Entry is by keypad and all of the usual facilities are provided, including well fitted, pre-set hot showers with seats and changing space, open washbasins in vanity units, dishwashing and laundry sinks, chemical disposal, plus an excellent fully equipped unit for disabled persons. Hot water is free throughout. Laundry with washing machine and dryer. Although there is no shop, gas is available on site and a mini-market, baker and fuel station are within 1 mile, a supermarket just 2 miles. Groundsheets, kite flying and ball games are not allowed and the site is not really suitable for American motorhomes. Local attractions include the 'Boston stump', the Pilgrim Fathers Memorial and Maud Foster Windmill, all in and around the town. Further afield is Heckington village and its unique eight sailed windmill (6 miles) and the Aviation Heritage Centre (12 miles). Boston market days are on Wednesdays and Saturdays and the town also has a fine marina, two sports and leisure centres (one with swimming pools) and there is a ten-pin bowling alley and a tennis centre. Golf, fishing, bicycle hire and riding within 2 miles.

Directions: From A52, 1 mile east of junction with A16, turn south by the 'Ball House' public house, continuing past the Boston Bowl towards Fishtoft, where the site is on your left. O.DS.GR: TF360420.

Charges 2000:
-- Per unit incl. 2 persons £7.50; electricity £2.00; extra person or car £1.00.
-- VAT included.
-- No credit cards.

Open:
Easter - 30 September.

Address:
Church Green Road, Fishtoft, Boston, Lincolnshire PE21 0QY.

Tel:
(01205) 366646.
FAX: as phone.

Reservations:
Advised for B.Hs and peak season; contact park.

Derbyshire

Heart of England Tourist Board

Derbyshire, Nottinghamshire, Staffordshire, Leicestershire, Northamptonshire, West Midlands, Warwickshire, Gloucestershire, Worcestershire, Shropshire and Herefordshire

Larkhill Road, Worcester WR5 2EZ
Tel: (01905) 763436 Fax: (01905) 763450
or Premier House, 15 Wheeler Gate, Nottingham NG1 2NA
Tel: (0115) 988 1778 Fax: (0115) 958 9671
E-mail: marketatheart_tourist_board.org.uk
Internet: www.visitbritain.com/heart-of-england

This central area of England, bordering Wales on the west and with Birmingham, at its heart covers:

Derbyshire – The Peak District is ideal for leisure and activity holidays, with spectacular crags, dales and moorland. There are ample opportunities for walking, cycling or the more daring challenges of rock climbing, gliding or hang-gliding.

Staffordshire – Stunning countryside and moorlands, combine with Britain's number one theme park, Alton Towers. Stoke on Trent, the birthplace of British ceramics, is where Josiah Wedgwood, Sir Henry Doulton and Josiah Spode worked their magic transforming base clay to objects of beauty. Visitor centres and factory shops tell their story.

Nottinghamshire – Nottingham Castle above the city presides over a modern vibrant city and nearby Sherwood Forest is still alive with tales of Robin Hood and his merry men.

Leicestershire – Home to the pork pie of Melton Mowbury fame and Stilton cheese.

Rutland – England's smallest county, just 20 miles across. Rutland Water is a Mecca for watersports.

Northamptonshire – known as the county of 'spires and squires', Kings and Queens of England

used to hunt in Rockingham Forest but today its royal connection is centred on Althorp the resting place of Diana, Princess of Wales. It is also home to Silverstone, Britain's Formula 1 Grand Prix circuit.

Warwickshire – Shakespeare Country, birthplace of the world's greatest playwright and home of the Earls of Warwick. Warwick castle must be the finest mediaeval castle in England.

Birmingham – one of the UK's most important cities and a leading international centre.

Worcestershire – Ranks as one of England's most attractive counties. Home to Malvern Water, Worcestershire Sauce and the Morgan sports car.

Shropshire & Herefordshire – Where England meets Wales and a mix of heritage and history brought to life in Ellis Peters' Brother Cadfeal series, the medieval whodunits based on Shrewsbury. Herefordshire is the home of cider and timber framed buildings are a feature.

Gloucestershire – From the Cotswold hills and villages, the Forest of Dean, the Wye valley to Regency Cheltenham with its world standard festivals of literature, jazz and famous for its horse racing not to mention the art of chasing a Double Gloucestershire cheese down a hill!

380 Highfields Camping and Caravan Park, nr. Ashbourne

Quiet, spacious park in Peak District National Park.

The Redfern family run Highfields, which is set on high, flat ground in the Peak District National Park with marvellous views. It takes 50 touring units and 50 seasonal vans in open, hedged fields accessed by tarmac roads, with an area for tents, another for vans with concrete slabs for jockey wheels and an area for adults only. There are 8 hardstandings and 89 electrical connections (5A), with 55 privately owned caravan holiday homes in separate fields. The main toilet block is kept locked (deposit for key) and is well maintained. Hot water is free to the washbasins, but metered to laundry and dishwashing sinks, and to the showers. A baby bath and chemical disposal are provided. A smaller block is in the far static field and further facilities are by the new clubroom. All blocks are heated when necessary. There is a shop for basics and gas, a children's playground, bicycle hire and a dog exercise field. A room, complete with in-built barbecue, table and chairs, is available for hire. Public phone. An indoor, heated swimming pool is open all season (restricted times if the park is not very full), with a small charge (80p per session). Although not supervised at all times, the pool is monitored from reception by closed circuit TV. Pub and restaurant close. Fishing 3 miles, golf 5 miles, riding 2 miles, boat launching 5 miles. People frequently venture off the site to enjoy the Peak District - Dovedale and Ilam are only a mile or two's distance by footpath and the Tissington Trail with access to the High Peak Trail passes by the park. American motorhomes are accepted. Winter caravan storage.

Charges 2000:
-- Per unit incl. 2 persons £10.00; extra adult £1.50; child (under 16 yrs) 50p; electricity (5A) £2.00.
-- Credit cards accepted.
-- VAT included.
Open:
1 March - 31 October.
Address:
Fenny Bentley,
nr Ashbourne,
Derbyshire DE6 1LE.
Tel:
(01335) 350228.
FAX: (01335) 350253.
Reservations:
Made with payment of one night's fee; min. stay at B.Hs - 3 nights.

Directions: Park is west off A515 (Buxton - Ashbourne) just north of Fenny Bentley (sharp turn to site approaching from Ashbourne). O.S.GR: SK170510.

385 Rivendale Caravan and Leisure Park, Alsop-en-le-Dale

Brand new park in course of development in the Peak National Park

When we visited this new park at the invitation of the owners we were immediately struck by the size of the project they had taken on. The reception and shop building you first see on arrival has been carefully renovated and there is now a small cafe within this building and an excellent bar should be open for 2000 (limited opening in low seasons). Moving into the park proper which is situated in an old quarry, we were impressed by the continued effort which has been incurred since our last visit. There are 80 pitches completed, all with hardstanding and 16A electrical hook up. Set out in small groups with names such as 'Little Delving' or 'Crickhollow', each pitch is separated from its neighbour and some have a grass area. The sanitary facilities are first rate with under-floor, computer controlled central heating, excellent free showers, washbasins (with cubicles for ladies), an excellent shower room for disabled visitors and chemical disposal. The touring park will eventually take up about 11 acres of the total land space of 37 and a newly levelled field will take caravans and tents in the 2000 season with a limited number of electricity points. The park is situated almost on The Tissington Trail offering superb walks and off road cycling and, with the Peak National Park on hand and wonderful towns such Ashbourne, Bakewell and even Buxton nearby, there is lots to do and see here. Riding 3 miles, fishing 5 miles, bicycle hire 2½ miles. The important thing to remember about this park is that it is new and needs to mature which will, of course, take time. It is a credit to the owners who deserve congratulations for providing such an excellent park.

Directions: Park is by A515 Buxton - Ashbourne road at Alsop-en-le-Dale, about 7 miles north of Ashbourne. O.S.GR: SK161566.

Charges 1999:
-- Per pitch incl. 2 adults £5.80 - £7.80; pitch with water connection plus £2.70; extra adult £1.00; child (4-15 yrs) 50p; awning £1.50; extra car £1.00; dog 50p; electricity £2.20.
-- Credit cards accepted.
-- VAT included.

Open:
All year excl. February.

Address:
Buxton Road, Alsop-en-le-Dale, Ashbourne, Derbyshire DE6 1QU.

Tel:
(01332) 843000.
FAX: (01332) 842311.

E-mail:
alsopdale@aol.com.

Reservations:
Made with £10 deposit; contact park.

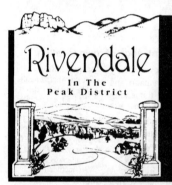

A peaceful 37 acre park with a superb, south-facing, sheltered pitching area in a natural sun-trap. Ideal for cycling and rambling in the surrounding Peak District with lots to see and do close by - from sailing at Carsington Water - to a day out at Chatsworth and Alton Towers.

Rivendale
In The
Peak District

Tel: 01332 843000 or 01335 310311
Fax: 01332 842311

Convenient for Chatsworth, Alton Towers, Dovedale, Hartington, Bakewell, Ashbourne.

383 The Firs Farm, Nether Heage, Ambergate, nr. Belper

Neat and tidy park with views over the Derwent Valley.

We were impressed with the facilities and helpful attitude of the owners at Firs Farm. The views across and along the wooded Derwent Valley are marvellous and the owners have thoughtfully provided a picnic terrace with tables. Pitches further back have pleasant flowers and shrubs to compensate for the lack of a front line position for the view. There are 60 large, level pitches for touring units, all with 10A electricity and about 50% with gravel hardstanding. The attractive toilet block to one side of the park, with a veranda and set in its own garden featuring flowering cherries, is heated, double glazed and curtained! Spotlessly clean, it provides modern fittings including washbasins in cubicles and controllable showers with stools. Under the veranda are washing up sinks, tourist information and a seat - very pleasant. A sauna is also provided (£5 charge). Chemical disposal point. No laundry facilities, but a launderette is at Belper (1½ miles) with shops, etc. A pub is a half mile walk, with other restaurants within driving distance. Fishing 1 mile, riding 1½ miles, golf 5 miles, bicycle hire 7 miles. Caravan storage available.

Directions: From A6 road, ¼ mile north of Belper, turn right into Broadholme Lane and follow signs.O.S.GR: SK354504.

Charges 2000:
-- Per unit incl. 2 persons £8.00; extra person £2.00; awning or pup tent £1.50; electricity (10A) £1.75.
-- No credit cards.

Open:
All year.

Address:
Crich Lane, Nether Heage, Ambergate, Belper, Derbyshire DE56 2JH.

Tel:
(01773) 852913.

Reservations:
Essential for B.Hs and peak season; contact park.

Derbyshire

382 Darwin Forest Country Park, Darley Moor, Two Dales

Well maintained park for caravans and motorhomes in the heart of the Derbyshire Dales, with indoor pool.

Between Matlock and Bakewell, this park, as its name implies, is set amongst 44 acres of mixed woodland close to the Peak District National Park. A large proportion of the park is given over to pine lodges for holiday letting but it also provides 50 touring pitches. All with hardstanding and electric hook-up (10A), they are clearly defined with hedging or open fencing in level grass bays amongst the pines - the unspoilt woodland is home to a variety of birds and wildlife. The modern toilet block is tiled and well equipped (including music) providing free hot showers, washbasins in cabins, free hairdryers, a full unit for disabled people, laundry room and covered washing up area. The pleasant Forester's Inn provides meals and a new beer garden. A small shop has basics and Calor gas (all year). Amenities include a children's adventure play area on bark, separate games room with pool tables, new tennis court and short-tennis and minigolf. The heated, indoor swimming pool (40 x 20 ft.) has a railed off children's section, spectator area and terrace, with good changing and shower facilities (see charges below). Fishing 2 miles, bicycle hire 8 miles, riding 2 miles, golf 4 miles. This is a useful park from which to explore the picturesque towns and villages of the Peak District - 4 miles from Chatsworth House, 40 mins. from Alton Towers. The Peak District Steam Railway currently operates a 2 mile section from Darley Dale to Matlock Riverside.

Directions: Park is best approached via the A632 Chesterfield - Matlock road. North of Matlock take the B5057 signed Darley Dale and park is on the right before descending into the village of Two Dales. O.S.GR: SK287633.

Charges 1999:
-- Per unit incl. all persons: Fri. and Sat. nights £12.00, other nights £10.00 - £12.00, acc. to season; awning £2.00; electricity £2.00 - £2.50.
-- Pool charges: adult £1.00 - £2.50, child (4-14 yrs) 50p - £1.50.
-- VAT included.
-- Credit cards accepted.

Open:
All year excl. 1/1-28/2.

Address:
Darley Moor, Two Dales, Matlock, Derbyshire DE4 5LN.

Tel:
(01629) 732428.
FAX: (01629) 735015.
E-mail: darwin@pinelog.co.uk.

Reservations:
Advised and made with deposit; contact park.

384 Lime Tree Park, Buxton

Select park with high quality modern facilities in convenient, edge of town location.

This park is a very good base for touring the Peak District. A new sanitary building serves the caravan and motorcaravan area, complete with patio and pergola frontage, together with the refitted original unit which serves the tenting area, provide ample facilities for all. Both units are heated, attractively tiled and have top quality fittings including brass taps. They provide WCs, washbasins, both open and in cubicles, controllable showers with dividers, shelf and seats, a baby room with the very latest design of baby bath, and a family room with facilities for disabled people. Dishwashing sinks are outside under cover and there are chemical disposal points, motorcaravan service area and good site lighting. A washing machine and dryer are provided in the laundry room, hot water is free throughout. The 99 touring pitches, of which 64 have access to electricity (10A), are on the two upper terraces which have the best views but are slightly more exposed until the new plantings mature. Below are areas set aside for late arrivals and the caravan holiday homes (26 privately owned and 10 for rent). Also on site is a small shop with gas and basics, public telephone and a small children's playground with rubber safety base. A new games/TV room alongside reception is now completed. The nearest pub serving food is just around the corner and Buxton town centre is a comfortable stroll away. Fishing, bicycle hire, riding and golf, all within 5 miles. Alton Towers is 22 miles..

Directions: From Buxton take A515 (Ashbourne) road south, turning sharp left into Dukes Drive after the hospital on the outskirts of the town, under the railway viaduct, and site is on right. O.S.GR: SK069725

Charges 2000:
-- Per unit incl. 2 adults £8.00 - £10.00; extra adult £1.50; extra child (5-15 yrs) 75p; hiker, cyclist or m/cyclist £3.50 - £4.00; awning £1.50; dog 50p; extra car £1.00; electricity £2.00.
-- Credit cards accepted.
-- VAT included.

Open:
1 March - 31 October

Address:
Dukes Drive, Buxton, Derbyshire SK17 9RP.

Tel:
(01298) 22988.

Reservations:
Made with £10 deposit; write to or phone park for details.

For a list of parks which are open all year - see page 234

394 Smeaton's Lakes Touring Caravan Park, South Muskham

New touring site, popular with fishermen, near Newark-on-Trent.
This site is really here for fishermen, with tarmac access roads and a modern
building housing reception and the sanitary facilities, it is set in 82 acres with
three fishing lakes. Reception keeps gas, soft drinks, dairy produce, sweets,
crisps, etc. and newspapers can be ordered. The sanitary facilities (with keypad
access) are heated, with open style washbasins, pre-set hot showers, free hot water
throughout and a good unit for disabled people, but no laundry room. There are
42 pitches on grass, 7 hardstandings, 32 electrical connections (16A), and a
separate rally field for 100 units. The fishing lakes include coarse, carp and pike
lakes and river fishing, with concessions. This site is probably the best choice for
visiting events at nearby Newark Showground, or Newark town (1 mile) with its
castle, the Millgate Folk Museum, and the Air Museum. Newark has a Flea
market (Mon and Thurs), a general market (Wed, Fri and Sat), and a car boot sale
(Sun). A bus stop is at the end of the entry lane and buses run into Newark every
hour until 10 pm. It is also central for visiting Southwell Cathedral, Lincoln with
its castle and cathedral and Nottingham with its Lace Hall, Castle or Caves.

Directions: Site lies on A6065 west of the town, south of junction of A616
towards Ollerton (well signed). O.S.GR: SK792558.

Charges 1999:
-- Per unit incl. 2 adults
£7.50 - £8.50; extra adult
£1.00 - £1.50; children
(over 5 yrs) 75p - £1.00;
electricity £2.00 - £2.50.
-- VAT included.
-- No credit cards.
Open:
All year.
Address:
Great North Road,
South Muskham,
Newark-on-Trent,
Nottinghamshire
NG23 6ED
Tel:
(01636) 605088 or
673250.
Reservations:
Contact site.

395 Orchard Park Touring Caravan and Camping Park, Tuxford

Rural family run site, created in old fruit orchard.
This well established site is in a quiet location and has 65 pitches. There are also
23 hardstandings, most of which were occupied by longer stay or seasonal units
at the time of our visit. All pitches have access to electricity (10A). Reception is
at the owners' house and includes a small shop with basic essentials and gas, more
services (some open to 10 pm) are in the village (½ mile). The specially designed
sanitary unit (with loudspeakers and piped music) has the usual facilities
including spacious pre-mixed hot showers, a well equipped room for disabled
persons and free hot water throughout. The laundry has washing machines, dryer
and sinks and there are two dishwashing sinks outside. At the far end of the park
is a children's play area with swings, slide etc. and a nature walk with wild
flowers, birds and butterflies. Local attractions include the Tuxford Windmill,
Sundown Adventureland theme park, Laxton Medieval village and Victorian
Times, with working horse drawn carriage driving centre, at nearby Kirton.

Directions: From the A1 turn onto A6075 towards Lincoln, continue through
village to the eastern outskirts, turning right towards High Marnham. Site is on
right ½ mile after railway bridge (well signed in village). O.S.GR: SK750710.

Charges 1999:
-- Per unit incl. 2 adults
£7.00 - £7.50; extra adult
£1.00; child (4-15 yrs)
50p; awning or pup tent
£1.00; electricity £1.50.
-- Credit cards accepted.
-- VAT included.
Open
March - October
Address:
Marnham Road, Tuxford,
Nottinghamshire
NG22 0PY.
Tel:
(01777) 870228.
Reservations:
Advised for B.Hs (min. 3
nights) and peak season
with £10 deposit.

392 Riverside Caravan Park, Worksop

Town centre touring site adjacent to county cricket ground.
An excellent, attractive and surprisingly peaceful site, Riverside is within easy
walking distance of the town centre pedestrian precinct and shops. The
Chesterfield Canal runs close to the northern side of the site offering delightful
towpath walks or fishing and, for those who cannot resist the thwack of leather on
willow, this site is ideal. Of the 60 marked level pitches, 50 are on gravel hardstanding, some separated by trees and low rails, and all have electricity (10A).
There is excellent site lighting. The modern sanitary unit near reception can be
heated and has all the usual facilities, although showers are on payment (20p). No
laundry, but a launderette is close in the town. Activities locally include squash,
flat or crown green bowling, bicycle hire and campers are also very welcome at
the Cricket Ground clubhouse. Worksop provides well for golfers with three
courses. One of the town's most interesting buildings, the medieval Priory Gatehouse, is open free of charge, market days are Wednesday, Friday and Saturday.
This is also a good base for exploring Creswell Craggs, Clumber Park, the
Dukeries Cycle Trail, and Rufford Mill Craft Centre and Country Park.

Directions: Easiest approach is from roundabout west of the town (A57) - third
roundabout from the A1, junction of A57/A60. Turn into Newcastle Avenue, then
left into Stubbing Lane, right into Central Avenue, left into Cricket Ground,
follow through to camping site (well signed). O.S.GR: SK580790.

Charges 2000:
-- Per adult £3.50 - £3.75;
child (5-16 yrs) £1.30;
electricity £1.60 - £2.00.
-- No credit cards.
-- VAT included.
Open:
All year.
Address:
Central Avenue,
Worksop,
Nottinghamshire
S80 1ER.
Tel:
(01909) 474118.
Reservations:
Advised for B.Hs, peak
season and weekends,
with £5 deposit.

Staffordshire

396 Silvertrees Caravan Park, Rugeley

Small, peaceful park in light woodland for caravans and motorhomes only.

Silvertrees, as its name suggests, is in a beautifully wooded setting with many silver birches on the edge of Cannock Chase. In the evenings the deer roam down the little valley in which the site is situated and there is evidence of much more animal and bird life. The park is actually designated a Site of Special Scientific Interest (SSSI) and comprises three paddock areas with 50 mobile homes (most privately owned, 10 to hire), plus 50 touring pitches on gently sloping grass. Double paving stones for the main wheels mark each pitch – chocks would be useful. All the pitches have 16A electrical connections. The small, heated toilet block provides vanity style washbasins (H&C), 2 showers each for men and women (20p) with shared changing area, laundry and dishwashing sink (20p) and a washing machine. It could be under pressure at B.Hs. Chemical disposal facilities. A small, unheated fun pool (3 ft deep and open April - Sept) is to be found in the valley bottom – it is a real sun trap. Amenities include a good tennis court, adventure play area, ball field and a comfortable games room with table tennis, video games, TV and an unusual ceiling. The park is set in 20 acres of woodland so there is plenty to do on site, never mind the natural heathland of the Chase. Helpful wardens and the owners live on site. There is a little library in reception and much useful tourist information in the games room. Gas supplies. Most dogs are accepted (not certain breeds). Barbecues must be raised off the ground. Fishing 1 mile, riding 6 miles, golf 3 miles. Supermarket 2 miles. Bus service outside park. A pub with food is within walking distance. Alton Towers is nearby. A member of the Countryside Discovery group.

Directions: Park is 2 miles from Rugeley just off the Penkridge - Rugeley road. It is signed from Rugeley off the A51. O.S.GR: SK014173.

Charges 1999:
-- Per pitch incl. 2 persons and electricity £7.00 - £9.00; extra person £1.00; awning £2.00.
-- Credit cards accepted.
-- VAT included.
Open:
April - October.
Address:
Stafford Brook Road, Penkridge Bank, Rugeley, Staffordshire WS15 2TX.
Tel:
(01889) 582185.
FAX: as phone.
Reservations:
Essential at B.Hs. (when min. 3 nights); contact park for details.

397 Glencote Caravan Park, Cheddleton, nr. Leek

Pleasant, family run park, 3 miles south of market town, at entrance to Churnet Valley.

A 6 acre park, Glencote has 60 numbered pitches set on flat grass, 50 of which have patio style hardstandings, with a tarmac, curved central access road. All pitches have electrical connections (10A) and a dedicated water supply. There are six caravan holiday homes for hire, plus two privately owned. Attractive flowerbeds and trees make a very pleasant environment. The good, modern toilet block is centrally situated and can be heated. Facilities include free, controllable showers, vanity style washbasins (one private cabin for ladies), hair dryer, razor points and mirrors, a small laundry room, two dishwashing sinks under cover (free hot water) and chemical disposal. Gas is available. An attractive, sunken children's play area, on grass and bark with an abundance of shrubs and flowers, sits alongside the small (fenced) coarse fishing pool. In the village of Cheddleton, ½ mile away, is a small supermarket and a post office. There is also a variety of inns within easy walking distance – the Boat Inn beside the canal is very good value. Attractions nearby include a renovated Flint Mill powered by two giant water wheels and Cheddleton railway centre. The Churnet Valley, an Area of Outstanding Natural Beauty is good for walking, the Staffordshire Way is also near. For the more energetic, canoeing and hang gliding opportunities are close. Riding 10 miles, bicycle hire 5 miles, golf 4 miles. Alton Towers is 10 miles (you may leave your unit on site after 3 pm. for an additional £2 charge).

Directions: Park is signed off A520 Leek - Stone road, 3½ miles south of Leek on northern edge of Cheddleton Village. O.S.GR: SJ982524.

Charges 1999:
-- Per unit incl. 2 persons £8.50; child (under 16 yrs) £1.50; extra adult £2.00; electricity £1.80.
-- For each 7 nights booked, one night free (except electricity).
-- Min. stay of 3 nights at B.Hs.
-- Credit cards accepted.
-- VAT included.
Open:
Easter - end October.
Address:
Station Road, Cheddleton, nr. Leek, Staffs ST13 7EE.
Tel:
(01538) 360745.
FAX: (01538) 361788.
Reservations:
Made with deposit of £18 (2 nights) or £25 (over 2 nights).

410 Cotswold Hoburne, South Cerney, Cirencester

Good touring park with holiday caravans and a variety of watersports amenities close.

Since the park is adjacent to the Cotswold Water Park, those staying will have easy access to the varied watersports there which include sailboarding and water ski-ing. On the park itself there is a lake with pedaloes and canoes for hire. Its wide range of other amenities include an outdoor (44 x 22 ft) heated swimming pool (open Whitsun - early September) and an impressive, large indoor leisure complex including pool with flume, spa bath, sauna, steam room (all free) and sun bed. There are 300 well marked touring pitches for any type of unit, all with hardstanding (only fairly level) and grass surround for awning or tent. Of good size but with nothing between them, all have electrical connections (some need long leads). Also 150 holiday units, mainly for letting. Six toilet blocks are all quite small but are clean and well maintained. Hot water is free in the washbasins and pre-set showers. Baby changing facilities. Basic facilities for visitors with disabilities are to be found in the clubhouse, but are locked at night. The site has heavy weekend trade. The large clubhouse has a big general lounge with giant TV screen, entertainment at times, food service (or food bar in lounge), big games room and a lounge bar which overlooks the outdoor pool and lake with a patio. Supermarket. Launderette. Activities include a football field, tennis courts, a good quality adventure playground with bark base and crazy golf. Fishing lake (permits from reception). No dogs or pets are accepted. Part of the Hoburne group.

Directions: Three miles from Cirencester on A419, turn right towards Cotswold Water Park at new roundabout on bypass onto B4696. Take second right and follow signs. O.S.GR: SU055957.

Charges 2000:
-- Touring pitch incl. electricity £9.00 - £23.00; pup tent £3.00.
-- Weekly rates and weekend breaks available.
-- VAT included.
-- Credit cards accepted.

Open:
March - 31 October.

Address:
Broadway Lane, South Cerney, Cirencester Glos. GL7 5UQ.

Tel:
(01285) 860216.
FAX: (01285) 862106.
E-mail: enquiries@hoburne.co.uk.

Reservations:
Bookings of 1-6 nights payable in full at time of reservation; caravans with £50 deposit for 1 week. Min. 4 nights booking at B.Hs.

COTSWOLD HOBURNE

Award Winning Holiday Park

HOLIDAY CARAVANS • LODGES • TOURING PITCHES

Superb family holiday Park with extensive facilities, set in 70 acres of the Cotswold Water Park. Large range of accommodation positioned around two fish - stocked lakes. Indoor leisure complex includes fun pool. For FREE colour brochure or credit card bookings please contact:

COTSWOLD HOBURNE, RG1, Broadway Lane, South Cerney, Cirencester, Gloucestershire GL7 5UQ.

Telephone: 01285 860216

e-mail - enquiries@hoburne.co.uk   www.hoburne.co.uk

ROSE AWARD

412 Briarfields Caravan and Camping, Cheltenham

Park close to M5 for night stop or for visiting the Cotswolds and local towns.

Newly planted saplings (in addition to the mature trees already here) and 3,000 rosewall bushes will mature to enhance the overall appearance and security of this developing park. Just a mile from the M5, a short entrance drive leads from the B4063 to the 75 flat, grassy pitches, 6 now with hardstanding. Set around the tarmac access road and in the central area, all have electrical connections (16A) and are well lit. The heated sanitary building (with coded locks) has washbasins in cabins, curtained showers with shared undressing area and excellent facilities for disabled visitors, plus a large laundry and dishwashing room. Just across the road, in the owner's holiday home park, is a well stocked, licensed mini market. A pub, a short walk away, offers meals and a children's garden. Cheltenham Racecourse is 4 miles and there is a golf course open to all just a few minutes up the road. Some road noise is to be expected.

Directions: From M5 exit 11 take A40 towards Cheltenham. In ½ mile turn left on B4063 Gloucester road and park entrance is shortly on the left at motel. Via Cheltenham take signs for M5 and look for B4063 as above. O.S.GR: SO922220.

Charges guide:
-- Per unit £6.50; hardstanding £1.00; electricity £1.90.
-- Credit cards accepted.

Open:
All year.

Address:
Gloucester Road, Cheltenham, Gloucestershire GL51 0SX.

Tel:
(01242) 235324. Mobile: 0836-274440.
FAX: as phone.

Reservations:
Advised at times of race meetings - contact park.

Gloucestershire / Warwickshire

411 Tewkesbury Caravan Club Site, Tewkesbury

Attractive site in a beautiful part of the country.

There are two important reasons why the Caravan Club site at Tewkesbury is so popular: firstly, it is within five minutes walk of the town centre and is overlooked by the Norman Abbey, the focal point of the town and secondly, it is a good base for exploring the eastern end of the Cotswolds as well as some of the country's most delightful towns. Gloucester, Cheltenham, Stow-on-the-Wold, Bourton-on-the-Water, Chipping Norton and Broadway are just a few that immediately spring to mind. The Malvern hills are also within driving distance. The site, which accepts non-members and campers with tents, covers nine acres and has 170 pitches reached by tarmac roads. All are on grass, but some slope so blocks are essential, and all have electric hook-ups (16A). There are three toilet blocks, although the one in the reception building has no showers. One block has facilities for disabled visitors and two have laundry rooms. All the blocks are built and maintained to the Club's usual high standards and can be heated. Chemical disposal and motorcaravan service facilities are provided. The entrance to the site is locked at night but there is a late arrivals area just outside it. The reception sells basic supplies and gas, and food shops, restaurants, pubs, etc. are all within easy walking distance. Adjoining reception is a tourist information room and a dog walk is provided in the adjacent field. Fishing 400 yds, riding 5 miles, golf 1 mile. Although one of the largest sites operated by the Caravan Club, Tewkesbury's popularity is such that booking is essential at B.H.s and during the period June to August. A further factor contributing to its popularity must be the friendly and helpful wardens.

Directions: From all directions follow signs for town centre and head for the Abbey which is easily distinguished. Turn by the Abbey into Gander Lane, follow down passing two car parks to site at end of the lane. O.S.GR: SO894324.

Charges 1999:
-- Non-member pitch fee £5.00; adult £3.25 - £4.00; child (5-17 yrs) £1.10 - £1.20; awning free; electricity £2.20 - £1.45.
-- Credit cards accepted.
Open:
End March - early November.
Address:
Gander Lane,
Tewkesbury,
Gloucestershire
GL20 5PG.
Tel:
(01684) 294035
(8 am. - 8 pm).
Reservations:
Accepted and are essential all B.Hs. and June-Aug.

407 Somers Wood Caravan and Camping Park, Meriden

Useful park in light pine woods near the N.E.C. for adults only, open all year.

Log buildings which blend comfortably into their surroundings have been used for reception, the owners' home at the entrance and for the sanitary facilities at this park. An oval, gravel road provides access to the 48 large pitches, 42 of which have 10A electricity connections. In winter, drainage can be a problem, although there are 30 pitches with hardstanding. Pines, silver birch, foxgloves and natural grass providing pleasant surroundings with glimpses of the fishing lake, which adjoins the site, along with an 18 hole golf course and driving range. The centrally situated sanitary facilities are satisfactory and can be heated, providing free, hot showers and vanity style washbasins with plenty of mirrors. Two dishwashing sinks with hot water are on the veranda area to one side of the block (no laundry sinks). Refuse areas, water taps and a simple chemical disposal point (short hose) complete the facilities. Pigmy goats neatly fenced in with their own log hut and hens and ducks provide entertainment. There is a supply of tourist information in reception which also has a public phone. This is a very useful park for those visiting the NEC, but it can get heavy usage at times. Dogs are accepted. Only gas barbecues are permitted. Local shops and a restaurant are less than 1 mile and visitors are also welcome to use the bar and restaurant at the golf club. Children are not accepted.

Directions: From M42 junction 6 (NEC) take A45 towards Coventry. Almost immediately, on left-hand side, take A452 signed Leamington. Turn right at roundabout on A452 then turn left into Hampton Lane at the next roundabout, signed Stonesbridge Golf Centre and site is signed with golf and fishing centres on the left. O.S.GR: SP228819.

Charges 1999:
-- Per pitch incl. 2 persons £9.00; 1-man tent £6.00; extra adult £1.00; awning or extra car £1.00; electricity £2.50 (Apr-Sept) - £3.00 (Oct-March).
-- No credit cards.
-- VAT included.
Open:
All year.
Address:
Somers Road,
Meriden, N.
Warwickshire
CV7 7PL.
Tel:
(01676) 522978.
Reservations:
Recommended for B.Hs and certain NEC exhibitions; made with deposit of £3 per night booked.

Alan Rogers' Discount

 Less mid-week for the over 50s

124

390 Bosworth Water Trust, Market Bosworth

Water Sports Centre with touring site adjacent.

Essentially designed for the water sports enthusiast, the camping area at Bosworth has 80 pitches on mostly level grass with electricity (5A) available to 31. The good quality, heated sanitary facilities in the main building are designed more for the watersports users, with communal showers and changing area, however the adjacent small `portacabin' style unit does have conventional separate shower cubicles. This unit may be replaced in the future, as the current facilities could be slightly over-stretched during peak times. Reception serves a good range of snacks, soft drinks, ices, etc. Gas is availabe and chemical disposal facilities. This RYA recognised centre offers a range of watersports - dinghy and board sailing, canoeing, rowing and fishing (swimming is not advised in the lake). Tuition is available for all watersports activities, lifejackets and wet suits can be hired, and there is a `Kids' Club' every Saturday (call site for brochure). On arrival you will need £2 to operate the Centre's entrance barrier. Riding 1 mile, golf ½ mile. Local attractions include Snibston Discovery Park, Twycross Zoo, Mallory Park motor racing circuit, steam trains and the battlefields.

Directions: Site is off B585 about 1 mile west of Market Bosworth. O.S.GR: SK370020.

Charges 2000:
-- Per unit incl. all persons £8.00; pup tent £2.00; awning £1.00; extra car £1.00; electricity £2.00.
-- Fishing and lake fees: 50% discount.
-- VAT included.
-- No credit cards.
Open:
All year.
Address:
Market Bosworth, Nuneaton, Warwickshire CV13 6PD.
Tel/Fax:
(01455) 291876.
Reservations:
Advised at B.Hs, school holidays and peak season.

404 Camping and Caravanning Club Site Clent Hills, Romsley

Surprisingly pretty and tranquil site close to Birmingham and motorways.

This site, conveniently close to Birmingham and only a couple of miles or so off the M5/M42 intersection, is a real surprise in terms of being quiet and peaceful and very pretty with good views. Its only disadvantage is that it is on sloping ground, but the present, very helpful wardens are happy to assist in pitching anyone who has a problem in getting level (mainly motorcaravanners); in fact, there are some level pitches and these are all earmarked for motorcaravans. The 130 pitches are all of a good size, 47 with electrical connections (10A). The central sanitary block can be heated and provides the latest facilities, including hot showers, washbasins in cabins, hairdryers, baby room and a toilet and shower for disabled people. It was spotless when seen in high season. Chemical disposal point. A new reception building with excellent tourist information, gas, arrivals area and larger car parking area are at the entrance. A small children's play area has a bark safety surface. Generally this is a well run and attractive site, very usefully situated. Fishing 3 miles, riding 1 mile.

Directions: From M5 junction 4 take A491, branch right to Romsley on B4551 and watch for site signs in Romsley village by shops. Site is on left. O.S.GR: SO955795.

Charges 2000:
-- Per 2 adults £7.30 - £10.40; child (6-18 yrs) £1.60; non-member pitch fee £4.20; electricity £1.55 - £2.30.
-- VAT included.
-- Credit cards accepted.
Open:
March - November.
Address:
Fieldhouse Lane, Romsley, Halesowen, B62 0NH.
Tel:
(01562) 710015 (no calls after 8 pm).
Reservations:
Necessary and made with deposit; contact the wardens.

419 Kingsgreen Caravan Park, Berrow, nr. Malvern

Friendly, comfortable, farm site, with good facilities and views of the Malvern hills.

In an attractive rural location, this site is ideal for adults who like the quiet life, so there are no amusements for children. The surrounding countryside is ideal for walking or cycling, and the small, fenced fishing lake on the site is well stocked (£3 per day). There are 45 level, grassy pitches all with electricity (16A), plus an additional area for tents. Some old orchard trees provide a little shade in parts. The modern facilities (key on deposit) provide good hot showers with changing area, curtain and seat (token from reception, 25p), WCs, washbasins in open worktops, plus a separate unit for disabled people (WC and washbasin). Dishwashing sinks are under cover at the rear of the building and there is a chemical disposal point, but no laundry facilities. Gas and barbecue fuels are available and a milkman calls daily with milk, eggs, bread, soft drinks, etc. The nearest pub is 2 miles. The site is 7 miles from the market town of Ledbury with its half timbered buildings and within easy driving distance of Malvern, the Three Counties showground, Cotswolds, Forest of Dean or Tewkesbury with its 12th century Abbey. Bicycle hire 2 miles, riding 3 miles, golf 5 miles.

Directions: From M50 junction 2, take A417 towards Gloucester, then first left, where site is signed, also signed the Malverns, back over the motorway. Site is 2 miles from the M50. O.S.GR: SO767338.

Charges 1999:
-- Per unit incl. 2 adults £6.00; tent incl. 2 adults £5.00 - £6.00, acc. to size; extra person over 2 yrs £1.00; dog 50p; awning £1.00; electricity £1.50.
-- Credit cards accepted.
-- VAT not included.
Open:
1 March - 31 October.
Address:
Kingsgreen, Berrow, Malvern, Worcestershire WR13 6AQ.
Tel/Fax:
(01531) 650272.
Reservations:
Essential for peak season and B.Hs. - contact site.

Worcestershire

420 The Boyce Caravan Park, Stanford Bishop, nr. Worcester

Very peaceful site on rolling downland, with distant views of the Malvern Hills.

Within its 17 acres The Boyce has 20 touring pitches and 140 permanent holiday homes. The relatively new landscaping and screening is maturing. Electrical connections (10A) are available on a limited number of pitches. The modern sanitary unit, built in '89 to serve the touring section and can be heated, providing WCs, washbasins in worktops, controllable hot showers with curtain and seat (10p for 4 mins), and a hairdrying area. A utility room houses dishwashing and laundry sinks, washing machine, dryer, iron, and a freezer for campers' use. There is a chemical disposal point and gas is available. A fenced and gated playground for smaller children, and plenty of open space for ball games are provided. The adjacent disused railway line is now the dog walk (no dangerous breeds). Coarse fishing is available across a meadow, and the area is rich in wildlife. Nearby Shortwood Farm has Jacob sheep, cider making, sheep shearing and a farm trail, and at the Pig Pen you can handle the piglets (wellingtons recommended). Reception has good tourist information including maps of local walks. The local pub is 500 m. and serves meals including breakfast. Riding 5 miles and several golf courses in the area. Bromyard with its shops and restaurants is 4 miles, and the cathedral cities of Hereford and Worcester are within easy driving distance.

Directions: From A44 (Worcester - Leominster), turn on B4220 1 mile east of Bromyard. After 2 miles, turn opposite 'Herefordshire House' inn (signed Linley Green), site is 500 m. and signed. O.S.GR: SO698527.

Charges 1999:
-- Per unit incl. 4 adults £7.50; extra person over 5 yrs £1.00; extra car £1.00; 1-man tent £4.00; awning/pup tent £1.50; electricity £1.50.
-- No tent pitches at B.H. weekends.
-- VAT included.
-- No credit cards.
Open:
1 March - 31 October.
Address:
Stanford Bishop,
Bringsty,
nr. Worcester
WR6 5UB.
Tel:
(01885) 483439
(evenings).
Reservations:
Contact site for details.

421 Lickhill Manor Caravan Park, Stourport-on-Severn

Well managed touring or holiday site in attractive parkland setting on outskirts of town.

This park is within easy walking distance (15 minutes) of the town centre via a footpath along the River Severn which lies a short distance below the site. There are opportunities for fishing and boating. The touring field has 90 marked, level, grassy pitches accessed via gravel roadways, all with electricity (10/16A). The 124 holiday homes, well screened from the touring area amongst tree lined avenues, are not visually intrusive, and there is a separate rally field. There is an extended children's playground and the site has recently created wildlife ponds and planted over 1,000 native trees and shrubs. A second sanitary building was added in '98 to serve the touring pitches. This heated building provides sparkling modern facilities including a comprehensively equipped suite for disabled guests which also double as a family washroom with facilities for baby changing. There are roomy showers with good seats and plenty of hooks and a good number of washbasins and WCs. Chemical disposal and motorcaravan service points are provided. This, together with the older unit at the other end of the park, now provides a good supply of all facilities. Gas is available on site. With its new sanitary block, roads and landscaping and friendly welcoming staff, this park promises to mature into one of the best in the area. Stourport is a lively bustling town with some splendid public parks, amusements and sports facilities. Riding 1 mile, bicycle hire 3 miles. Six golf courses within 5 miles. A small parade of shops and the nearest pub are 10 minutes walk. Kidderminster, the Forestry Commission Visitor Centre at Bewdley, the Severn Valley Railway and West Midland Safari Park are a short drive from the site.

Directions: From centre of Stourport take B4195 northwest towards Bewdley. After 1 mile turn left at crossroads (traffic lights), into Lickhill Road North where site is signed. O.S.GR: SO790730.

Charges 1999:
-- Per caravan or motor-caravan £6.00 - £9.25; small tent £6.00; large tent £8.25; awning £1.50; extra car, trailer or boat £1.00; electricity £2.00.
-- Weekly rates available.
-- VAT included.
-- Credit cards accepted.
Open:
All year.
Address:
Stourport-on-Severn,
Worcestershire
DY13 8RL.
Tel:
(01299) 871041.
FAX: (01299) 827527.
Reservations:
Recommended for B.Hs. and peak season; contact park.

Alan Rogers' Discount

 Less 10%

418 Ranch Caravan Park, Honeybourne, nr. Evesham

Popular touring park in 50 acres for caravans only, close to the Cotswolds.

The Vale of Evesham is noted for being a sheltered area growing fruit and other produce from early spring through to late autumn. Ranch lies not far from both Evesham and Broadway in quiet country surroundings, and is also only half an hour's drive from Stratford-on-Avon. A free swimming pool (55 x 30 ft.) with slide is open and heated June - Sept. The park takes 120 touring units - caravans, motorcaravans or trailer tents but not other tents - on flat, partly undulating, hedged meadows with well mown grass and a spacious feel. Pitches are not marked but the staff site units. There are around 100 electrical connections (10A) and 8 fully serviced pitches (electricity, TV, water and sewer connections). There are 169 caravan holiday homes in their own section (4 to rent). Two very well appointed, modern sanitary blocks, with free hot water to washbasins and hot showers on payment, make a good provision. Self-service shop (reduced hours mid and low seasons). Gas available. The comfortable clubhouse (weekends only in early and late season) offers a wide range of value for money meals and entertainment is arranged at B.H. weekends and Saturdays in school holidays. A small games room has TV (incl. Sky), video machines and pool table. Children's playground. Laundry room. Fishing 2 miles, bicycle hire 4 miles, and riding stables close. American motorhomes not accepted. Caravan storage.

Directions: From A44 Broadway take B4632 for approx. 2 miles and follow signs for Honeybourne down unclassified road (Ryknild Street, Roman road). Park is through village on left by station. O.S.GR: SP112444.

Charges 1999:
-- Per unit incl. 2 adults £7.00 - £12.00; extra person (over 5) free - £1.50; awning free - £1.50; electricity £2.50; full services £2.25; dog free - £1.50.
-- One free night for every 7 booked.
-- VAT included.
-- Credit cards accepted.

Open:
1 March - 30 November.

Address:
Honeybourne,
nr. Evesham,
Worcs. WR11 5QG.

Tel:
(01386) 830744.
FAX: (01386) 833503.

Reservations:
Made with £5 per night deposit and essential for B.Hs. (when min. 3 days) and peak weeks.

CARAVAN PARK — RANCH — **HOLIDAY CENTRE**

- ESTABLISHED FAMILY-RUN PARK
- LOCATED IN THE VALE OF EVESHAM
- TOURERS WELCOME
- ELECTRIC AND MULTISERVICE HOOK-UPS AVAILABLE
- LICENSED CLUB SERVING MEALS
- HEATED OUTDOOR SWIMMING POOL
- SHOP
- LAUNDRY

HONEYBOURNE, EVESHAM, WORCS. WR11 5QG
Tel: EVESHAM (01386) 830744

432 Broadmeadow Caravan and Camping Park, Ross-on-Wye

Modern, spacious site, convenient for town with open views and own fishing lake.

The approach to this site is unusual, but persevere and you will find one of the best laid out, immaculately maintained sites with the very highest quality facilities. A recently constructed level site, it offers 150 large pitches on open grass, and is especially good for tents. It has excellent illumination and two superb modern sanitary buildings with free hot water throughout. Each includes push-button showers with dividers and seats, washbasins, hairdryers, baby changing rooms, family bathrooms each with WC, basin and bath, and a comprehensive unit for disabled visitors with alarm and handrails. A dishwashing room with separate vegetable sinks, laundry with sinks, washing machine, dryer, iron (tokens from reception) plus chemical disposal, are also provided at each building. A keypad entry system is used on all external doors. Each set of four pitches has a service post with water, drain, electricity points (16A) and site lighting, and is within view of the clock-tower on one of the sanitary buildings. Small fenced playground. Well fenced fishing lake (coarse fishing £5 per day). The town centre is within easy walking distance and the supermarket is 200 m. Although the A40 relief road is at the eastern end of the site, traffic noise should not be too intrusive (but tenters be aware). Bicycle hire in town, riding 8 miles, golf 3 miles. This is a good base for touring Herefordshire, the Wye Valley or the Forest of Dean.

Directions: From A40 relief road turn into Ross at roundabout, take first right into industrial estate, then right in ½ mile, before Safeway supermarket, where site is signed. O.S.GR: SO610240.

Charges 1999:
-- Per pitch £5.50 - £6.50; adult £2.25; child (6-14 yrs) £1.75; awning or pup tent £1.75; extra car £1.50; hiker/cyclist and tent £5.00 - £6.00; dog £1.00; electricity £2.25.
-- VAT included.
-- Credit cards accepted.

Open:
Easter/1 April - 31 Oct.

Address:
Broadmeadow,
Ross-on-Wye,
Herefordshire HR9 7BH.

Tel:
(01989) 768076.
FAX (01989) 566030.

Reservations:
Made with £10 deposit; contact park.

430 Poston Mill Park, Peterchurch, Golden Valley

Pleasant, neat park in farmland, a mile from Peterchurch in heart of the Golden Valley.

Poston Mill Park offers 92 touring pitches set on level grass with some very pleasant pitches near the River Dore with mature trees around the perimeter. All pitches have electricity, water and TV connections (leads to hire), and 10 have waste water and sewage outlets. Also 30 seasonal pitches and 72 caravan holiday homes (2 to rent). There is one central sanitary block with a smaller block near the holiday home area, of reasonably modern construction. There are controllable showers (free), mainly semi-open washbasins, a unit for disabled people (toilet and basin), baby room and chemical disposal. Motorcaravan service point, small, well equipped laundry room with fridge and a freezer for ice packs. Within the park's 33 acres activities include a pleasant, large children's play area on grass with pitch and putt, tennis, petanque, croquet, bicycle hire, golf driving range, a football pitch and a games room with snooker and darts. An attractive walk along one side of the park, edging the River Dore (fishing available), follows the line of the old Golden Valley railway with a footpath from the site over the fields. Next to the park is the Poston Mill restaurant for lunches, evening meals and takeaway. The restaurant has a TV room and sells bread and milk. Gas supplies. Peterchurch village is only 1 mile. Bicycle hire. Riding 3 miles. American motorhomes are welcome. Winter caravan storage. A member of the Best of British group.

Charges 1999:
-- Per unit incl. 2 adults £7.50 - £10.00; 1 man tent £4.75 - £5.75; extra person £1.00; child (3-10 yrs) 50p; awning £1.50; electricity £1.75; TV hook-up 50p - £1.50.
-- Credit cards accepted.

Open:
All year.

Address:
Peterchurch, Golden Valley, Herefordshire HR2 0SF.

Tel:
(01981) 550225.
FAX: (01981) 550885.
E-mail: enquiries@poston-mill.co.uk.

Reservations:
Made with £10 deposit, imn. 3 nights for B.Hs.

Directions: Park is 1 mile SE of Peterchurch on B4348 road. O.S.GR: SO356371.

431 Luck's All Caravan and Camping Park, Mordiford, Hereford

Spacious site beside the River Wye, with good countryside views, canoeing and fishing.

Set in around 9½ acres on the bank of the river Wye, Luck's All has 80 large, well spaced and level touring pitches, of which 41 have electricity (10/16A). A small, unfenced playground and a large grassy area for children's games are provided. The river is open to the site but lifebelts and safety messages are in evidence. Canoes can be hired and fishing permits are obtainable from the local tackle shop. The site shop has basics and gas, plus home-made cakes (mini-market 1½ miles). The main sanitary facilities are housed in a new building which provides WCs, open washbasins, showers (20p) with curtains and seats, and a separate unit for disabled visitors with ramp, WC, basin, shower and hand-dryer. Dishwashing sinks and chemical disposal. A smaller, older unit near the entrance provides extra facilities for peak periods, also a laundry room with sink, washing machine, dryer and ironing. Worthy of a visit are the Cider Museum and King Offa Distillery in Hereford and Belmont Abbey. Golf 5 miles, bicycle hire 9 miles. Winter caravan storage. A member of the Countryside Discovery group.

Charges 1999:
-- Per unit incl. 2 adults £7.00 - £7.50; extra person over 5 yrs £1.00; dog 75p; awning £1.00 - £1.25; electricity £2.00.
-- Credit cards accepted.
-- VAT included.

Open:
Easter/1 April - 31 Oct.

Address:
Luck's All, Mordiford, Hereford HR1 4LP.

Tel:
(01432) 870213.

Reservations:
Essential for B.Hs. and peak season and made with £15 deposit.

Directions: Between Mordiford and Fownhope, 5 miles southeast of Hereford on B4224, the site is well signed. O.S.GR: SO571355.

Alan Rogers' Discount
Less £1 per night

442 Severn Gorge Caravan Park, Tweedale, nr. Telford

Mature park in woodland setting, ideal for visiting Ironbridge Museums.

With 16 acres, this touring park has 110 pitches including a few seasonal tourers, 16 hardstanding pitches and 60 electric hook ups (10/16A). The sanitary buildings can be heated and provide comprehensive facilities with free showers, facilities for disabled visitors and a baby room, plus a dishwashing conservatory leading to an ample laundry. Chemical disposal and motorcaravan service points. A small, limited shop opens daily and gas is available. Amenities include bicycle hire, a small play area and a large field with three hole pitch and putt. A small lake (unfenced) is stocked for fishing. Dogs are welcome but with a maximum of two per pitch. No kite flying because of nearby overhead cables. There could be some road noise from the A442 which runs down one boundary. A pub is just 10 minutes away serving meals. The main local attraction has to be the Ironbridge Museums, featuring the Blists Mill Victorian Town. Hawkstone Park, with its walks and follies, is popular and the Cosford Aerospace Museum is essential for those interested in aviation. Golf 1 mile, riding 3 miles. Winter caravan storage.

Charges 1999:
-- Per unit £3.50 - £4.50; adult £2.25 - £2.75; child (5-15 yrs) £1.00; awning £1.00; hardstanding £1.00; extra vehicle £1.50; dog (max 2) 60p; electricity £2.00.
-- VAT included.
-- Credit cards accepted.

Open:
All year.

Address:
Bridgnorth Road, Tweedale, Telford, Shropshire TF7 4JB.

Tel/Fax:
(01952) 684789.

Reservations:
Contact park for details.

Directions: From M54 junction 4 follow signs (A442) onto the A442 signed Kidderminster. Take slip road signed Bridgnorth to next roundabout, turn right and pick up park signs. O.S.GR: SJ704052.

Perfectly Placed for London, the Millennium City

When you visit the Millennium City stay in Lee Valley Regional Park.

There are 5 camping and caravan sites to choose from in Lee Valley Regional Park all within easy reach of The Dome and London's West End on public transport. What's more, all sites have modern facilities, offer value for money and are located in pleasant surroundings with their own local leisure attractions.

Lee Valley Leisure Centre Campsite, Picketts Lock, Edmonton, North London

Only 34 mins from the West End. The site also boasts a large leisure centre, 18 hole golf course and 12 screen UCI cinema.
Tel: 020 8803 6900
Fax: 020 8884 4975

Lee Valley Cycle Circuit Campsite, Leyton, East London

Set in 40 acres of open parkland, this site is only 4 miles from the Tower of London. Stay here and you'll reach London's major attractions in less than 30 minutes.
Tel: 020 8534 6085
Fax: 020 8536 0959

Lee Valley Caravan Park, Dobbs Weir, Hoddesdon, Herts

Enjoy the peace and tranquillity of this riverside site with good fishing, walking and boating nearby. Get to the West End by train and tube in under an hour.
Tel/Fax: 01992 462090

Lee Valley Campsite, Chingford, London

Situated on the edge of Epping Forest and close to the historic town of Waltham Abbey, this site is easily accessible from the M25 and just 42 minutes from the West End by public transport.
Tel: 020 8529 5689
Fax: 020 8559 4070

Roydon Mill Leisure Park

Ideal for families, Roydon Mill offers a 40 acre water-sports lake with man-made beach and pool. Licensed club with regular entertainment. Trains from adjacent station give fast, easy access to London and Cambridge.
Tel: 01279 792777
Fax: 01279 792695

For more information, call our Information Centre on 01992 702200 or find us on the web at:
www.leevalleypark.org.uk

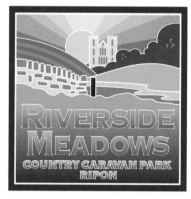

438 Fernwood Caravan Park, Lyneal, nr. Ellesmere

Quiet, pretty park in semi-woodland near Welsh border, for caravans and motorhomes.

Fernwood is set in a lovely area known as the Shropshire Lake District – the mere at Ellesmere is the largest of nine meres – and the picturesque Shropshire Union Canal is only a few minutes walk. The park itself, with its floral landscaping, the setting and attention to detail, all of a very high standard, with planted and natural vegetation blending harmoniously, is a real oasis of calm and rural tranquillity. In addition to 165 caravan holiday homes, used normally only by their owners, the park takes 60 caravans, motorcaravans or trailer tents, but no other tents in several well cut, grassy enclosures (plus 25 seasonal long stay). Some are in light woodland, others in more open, but still relatively sheltered situations. All 60 pitches have electricity (10A). Siting is carried out by the management and there is always generous spacing, even when the site is full. The excellent, refurbished sanitary block for tourers can be heated and has free hot water to washbasins (with good shelves) and pre-set hot showers, a unit for disabled people, but no dishwashing sinks. There are water points, chemical disposal and motorcaravan service points. A well tiled laundry room is near the shop, and adjacent are ladies and men's WCs. Other facilities include the small shop, which doubles as reception (from 1 April, sometimes limited hours). There is a coarse fishing lake, 40 acres of woodland for walking and a grass children's play area. Public phone.

Charges 1999:
-- Per unit incl. electricity £9.50 - £13.50; awning free - £1.50; extra car free - £1.00.
-- One night free for each 7 booked in advance.
-- VAT included.
-- No credit cards.

Open:
1 March - 30 November.

Address:
Lyneal, nr. Ellesmere, Shropshire SY12 0QF.

Tel:
(01948) 710221.
FAX: (01948) 710324.

Reservations:
Necessary for peak season and B.Hs (min. 3 nights) with deposit of £5 per night.

Directions: Park is just northeast of Lyneal village, signed southwest off the B5063 Ellesmere - Wem road, about 1½ miles from junction of the B5063 with the A495. O.S.GR: SJ453338.

- ESTABLISHED FAMILY-RUN PARK
- PEACEFUL WOODLAND SETTING
- TOURERS WELCOME
- ALL PITCHES HAVE ELECTRICAL HOOK-UPS
- PICTURESQUE LAKE
- CHILDRENS PLAY AREA
- SHOP
- LAUNDRY

LYNEAL NR. ELLESMERE SHROPSHIRE SY12 0QF TEL: (01948) 710221

439 Westbrook Park, Little Hereford, nr. Ludlow

Peaceful orchard park beside the River Teme on a working farm.

Bordering the River Teme, 45 pitches are neatly spaced on level grass underneath the apple trees. A new timber cabin for reception is planned for the '99 season. Accessed by a tarmac or gravel roadway, electricity (6A) and TV hook-up are available to all, with hardstanding, water and waste water drainage for some. A timber-clad sanitary block offers roomy, curtained showers (20p for 5 minutes), curtained washbasins (H&C), and plenty of mirrors. With a laundry room with washing machine and dryer plus sinks for laundry and for washing up (hot water 10p), it is a well maintained provision. Note that bicycles are no longer permitted at this park. There are riverside walks, also a nearby pub, and fishing is available (£2.50 per day). Children's play equipment includes an old tractor and amazing tree stumps, but the favourites are Gert and Daisy the Shetland ponies - note they must not be fed the cider apples as they can become very ill. Children can help at apple harvest (autumn half term) and possibly at lambing – yes, it is a working farm. The local market towns of Tenbury Wells, Leominster and Ludlow are only few miles away. Caravan `storage and use' available.

Charges guide:
-- Per unit incl. 2 adults £6.50 - £7.75; one man tent £4.75 - £5.75; extra person (over 3 yrs) 50p; awning or adjoining pup tent £1.50; dog 50p; electricity £1.75; TV hook-up £1.00 (own lead 50p).
-- Min. B.H. 3 nights.

Open:
All year.

Address:
Little Hereford, Ludlow, Shropshire SY8 4AU.

Tel:
(01584) 711280.
FAX: (01584) 711460.

Reservations:
Recommended for B.Hs; made with £10 deposit.

Directions: From A49 (Ludlow - Leominster) turn east at Woofferton on A456 signed Tenbury Wells, Kidderminster. After 2 miles turn right just before river bridge and Temeside Inn. Park is down lane on the left. O.S.GR: SO547679.

Shropshire

440 Stanmore Hall Touring Park, Bridgnorth

Good quality park overlooking lake in the Severn Valley.

Situated in the former grounds of Stanmore Hall, this site's huge lily pond, fine mature trees and beautifully manicured lawns give a mark of quality. Open views take precedence over maximising the number of units per square metre, with the result that all pitches are generously sized. In addition, caravans can be orientated in any direction the owner wishes, thus breaking the feeling of regimentation. There are 101 'standard' pitches, 95 grass and 6 hardstanding, all level with 16A hook-ups and TV connections. Of these, 31 grass pitches are reserved for adult only use (21 years). A further 30 hardstanding 'super-pitches' offer TV satellite reception as well. Access and internal roads are all tarmac surfaced; site lighting is adequate and reassuring. Reception is located within the shop which is licensed and well stocked (open all year) - there are even caravan accessories and repair items. The adjacent conservatory and patio overlook the lake, home for everything from humbler ducks to the resident peacocks who strut proudly around their domain. Access to the heated sanitary block is by key. Washbasins in cubicles, ample hot water, hairdryers, and a room for disabled people (which includes baby equipment), demonstrate thoughtful design. Its laundry facilities comprise two sinks, a washing machine, tumble dryer and spin dryer. Chemical disposal and motorcaravan service points. Limited, bark based children's play area. Overall the facilities are excellent and the cleanliness outstanding. But there's something else, too; this is a peaceful site with personality. Little wonder it needs advance booking and people keep returning to enjoy its atmosphere. Open all year round, there are even groups who spend Christmas and New Year at Stanmore Hall. The Severn Valley is full of interest – Bridgnorth nearby, the Clee Hills, Ironbridge Gorge Museum, and Midland Motor Museum on the doorstep are just a few suggestions. Fishing and bicycle hire at Bridgnorth (1½ miles), golf 2 miles. Dogs are welcome, but with a limit of two per unit. A member of the Caravan Club's managed under contract scheme, non-members are also very welcome.

Charges 1999:
-- Per pitch £3.80 - £4.20; adult £3.30 - £4.20; child £1.45 - £1.60; awning 60p; dog 75p; extra car or trailer £1.20; electricity £2.00 - £2.75; full services £2.50 - £3.00.
-- Credit cards accepted.
Open:
All year.
Address:
Stourbridge Road, Bridgnorth, Shropshire WV15 6DT.
Tel:
(01746) 761761.
Reservations:
Advisable and made with £10 deposit.

Directions: Site is 1½ miles from Bridgnorth on the A458 (signed Stourbridge). Signs for the Motor Museum are especially helpful. O.S.GR: SO742923.

441 Beaconsfield Farm Touring Caravan Park, Shrewsbury

Purpose designed park just north of historic market town; adults only in peak season.

A neat stone entrance way and a tarmac driveway of half a mile through open fields lead to this park, with security barrier in operation. Neatly laid out in a rural situation, with a well stocked trout fishing lake and a small coarse pool forming the main feature, the ground has been levelled and grassed to provide 60 well spaced pitches. With 16A electricity available to all, 12 to one side on a slightly higher terrace are 'de-luxe' pitches with full services on hardstanding, plus a further 10 with hardstanding. The park is well lit with a circular tarmac road and two brick refuse, water and chemical disposal areas. A large timber chalet with tiled Canadian maple roof provides reception and heated sanitary facilities. An indoor heated pool is open all year with two daily open sessions (adults £2.50, children £1) and by private hire at other times (£3 and £1, min. £10 per hour). Adjacent to reception and the pool is the coffee shop, open during reception hours. Toilet facilities (with £2 key deposit) are of excellent quality, as is everything featured on the park. They have curtained, roomy, pre-set showers, vanity style washbasins (H&C), mirrors, free hairdryers, washing up room, also with washing machine, dryer, 2 free irons and boards. Motorcaravan service point. There is no children's play area, but a central grass area is available for ball games. Only two dogs per unit are accepted. Last arrivals 7 pm. (8 pm. Fridays). Golf 3 miles. Limousins and pedigree Suffolk sheep graze in neighbouring fields and a `park and ride' operates nearby for those interested in Shrewsbury and its medieval past, bought to life by the Brother Cadfael novels. This is a top class park, maturing by the year. This is now an adults only touring park (25 yrs) in the summer months. A member of the Best of British group and the Countryside Discovery group..

Charges guide:
-- Per grass pitch incl. unit and 2 persons £8.00 - £10.00; de-luxe pitch £10.00 - £12.00; extra adult £3.00; child (3-14 yrs) £2.00; awning or child's tent £1.50; extra car or boat £1.00; dog (max. 2) 75p; electricity £2.00.
-- No credit cards.
Open:
All year.
Address:
Battlefield, Shrewsbury, Shropshire SY4 4AA.
Tel:
(01939) 210370 or 210399.
FAX: (01939) 210349.
Reservations:
Recommended for B.Hs and July/Aug. and made with £20 deposit.

Directions: Site is north of Shrewsbury and off the A49 Whitchurch road just before the village of Hadnall. Turn opposite the New Inn at brown camping sign towards Astley and park entrance is 400 m. on right. O.S.GR: SJ523196.

See colour feature for `BEST of BRITISH' between pages 96/97

Yorkshire

Yorkshire Tourist Board
North, South, East and West Yorkshire

312 Tadcaster Road, York YO2 2HF
Tel: (01904) 707961 Fax: (01904) 701414
E-mail: ytb@yorkshire-tourist-board.org.uk

Yorkshire, vast and beautiful, the land of the White Rose was once a kingdom in its own right. and its people are proud of its heritage; their welcome warm if their character is a little blunt.

Today more than 1,000 square miles of Yorkshire are protected as National Parks, Areas of Outstanding Natural Beauty and Heritage Coast and visitors are encouraged to park the car and 'go green'. Guided walks, way-marked paths and bridleways all explore deepest Yorkshire. The latest long distance challenge is the 240 km. Trans-Pennine Trail from Liverpool to Hull - part of a new Euro 'superpath'!

North Yorkshire offers the Yorkshire Dales and the North York Moors, with ruined abbeys and castles on both fringes of which magnificent Fountains Abbey, now a World Heritage site is the best known also Castle Howard of 'Brideshead Revisited' fame.

The gentle spa town of Harrogate with its antique shops, tea-rooms and colourful gardens is now an important conference centre.

Harewood House, six miles to the south is one of the finest mansions in England.

Ancient streets, buildings and museums make York one of England's most fascinating cities. Explore the Shambles or walk the medieval walls for much of their 2¼ mile length. The Jorvik Viking Centre is a popular experience involving travelling back in time through the history of York to a Viking Age, brought to life with the aid of sound effects and smells.

West and **South Yorkshire** are largely industrial, the charm of their cities - Leeds, Bradford and Sheffield depends mainly on their Victorian industrial legacy. Today Bradford's top attraction is the National Museum of Photography, Film and Television, free and very popular with children. Haworth is however on the literary trail as the home of the Bronte sisters.

One must not forget the coast line, the traditional resorts of Scarborough, Bridlington, Filey and timeless fishing harbours such as Whitby and Robin Hood's Bay.

However perhaps our knowledge of Yorkshire today is coloured by the TV series such as 'The Last of the Summer Wine', 'All Creatures Great and Small', 'Heartbeat' and 'Emmerdale'.

---

450 Waudby's Caravan and Camping Park, South Cave, nr. Hull

Small, tidy park with excellent toilet facilities.

Waudby's is very well placed for visiting the Yorkshire Wolds, or for over-nighting to or from P&O North Sea ferries (2 miles). The fact that it is beside the road and its location by the Waudby's caravan centre should not deter you from giving this little site a visit. There are only 20 pitches, with grass banks and hedges or small fencing, and all have electrical connections (10/16A). Units over 20 ft (6 m) in length cannot be accepted because of space restrictions. The tiled toilet block can be heated and is well maintained. It provides large, free, controllable showers and washbasins in cubicles. All are available to wheelchair users and are kept very clean and tidy. Chemical disposal and motorcaravan service points. Gas available. The small town of South Cave is within walking distance, with a shop, restaurant and bars and the charming, historic town of Beverley, with its beautiful Minster is only 12 miles. A bus to Hull passes the gate. Fishing ½ mile, golf 1 mile. There is a resident warden and the owners are also always around. Waudby's is a site well worth considering.

Directions: Park is south of A63 motorway at exit for village of South Cave; clearly signed. O.S.GR: SE914316.

Charges 1999:
-- Per unit incl. 2 persons £4.50; extra person (over 5 yrs) 50p; full awning £1.20; electricity £1.75.
-- Credit cards accepted.

Open:
1 April - 6 January.

Address:
Brough Road, South Cave, East Yorkshire HU15 2DB.

Tel:
(01430) 422523.
FAX: (01430) 424777.
E-mail:
site@waudbys.co.uk.

Reservations:
Advised for B.H.s and w/ends with £1 deposit per night booked.

Yorkshire

451 Thorpe Hall Caravan and Camping Site, Rudston, Bridlington

Pleasant touring park, west of Bridlington.

This small park in the grounds of Thorpe Hall, just outside the village of Rudston and 4½ miles from the sea at Bridlington is enthusiastically managed by Jayne Chatterton. It is set on flat grass, largely enclosed by the old kitchen garden wall. The 90 pitches are numbered and well spaced with a free area in the centre and with 78 electrical hook-ups (16A) and TV connections. A separate area takes tents and there are no caravan holiday homes. There is always a chance of finding space, though it is best to book for B.H.s and peak weeks. The solid, central toilet block can be heated and has free hot water in the washbasins, with shelf and mirror, and in the pre-set showers with turn-on tap. Ladies have three washbasins in private cabins and a bath. There are hair washing and drying facilities, a well equipped unit with bath for disabled visitors, launderette, covered dishwashing sinks and chemical disposal. Small shop with gas, essentials and local produce with adjacent patio. Public phone. Games room with two pool tables and table tennis, tourist information area and satellite TV room. Five acre games field and children's play area on grass and sand. Dog walk. Information sheets on a range of local walks are available and Thorpe Hall Gardens are open to park visitors between 1-4 pm. There is a footpath to the village with a shop, post office, garage, a pub serving bar meals and a new restaurant, plus a twice weekly bus service to Bridlington. The site's own coarse fishing lake is now open nearby. Bicycle hire, golf and boat launching at Bridlington (4½ miles), riding 2 miles. A member of the Countryside Discovery group.

Charges 1999:
-- Per unit incl. all persons £5.65 - £10.35; tent field £4.65 - £9.35; extra car £1.00; electricity (16A) £2.00.
-- Less 10% on booked stays of 7 days or over.
-- No credit cards.
-- VAT included.

Open:
1 March - 31 October.

Address:
Rudston, Driffield, East Yorkshire YO25 4JE.

Tel:
(01262) 420393.
FAX: (01262) 420588.
E-mail: caravansite @thorpehall.co.uk.

Reservations:
Made with advance payment (min. 4 nights at Spr. B.H).

Directions: Site is by the B1253 road, 4½ miles from Bridlington, on east side of Rudston . O.S.GR: TA105676.

473 Far Grange Park, Skipsea, nr. Driffield

Large family site with something for everyone.

Far Grange is a very well maintained holiday park which will especially appeal to families. A comprehensive leisure centre is located at the park entrance, well away from the touring pitches. The indoor pool, fitness suite, sauna and solarium (with charges) are excellent facilities with lifeguards who are happy to give assistance to swimmers with disabilities if needed. This area also includes bars with shows, cabaret acts and dancing (adults only). A family room provides games and shows for children and discos for teenagers. These rooms are very tastefully decorated and furnished, making a pleasant, relaxing environment. There are also facilities for pool, snooker, darts and a TV room (all requiring children to be accompanied by parents). Bar meals are served in the evenings and Sunday lunches also. Outside is an attractive patio area. The park grounds are extensive with plenty of room for team games, tennis, a fitness trail for young and old, an excellent adventure playground with a skateboard ramp, and a play area for younger children (both with rubber safety bases). Adjacent (but not owned by the park) is golf, pitch and putt and bowls and, across the road from the entrance, is the park's own country park with fishing and wildfowl lake, visitor centre and a dipping pond for youngsters. It is an idyllic place to get away for a walk and a picnic. In the central reception area is a well stocked supermarket (with gas), takeaway, amusement arcade and a well appointed laundry. The tiled toilet blocks are heated in low season and provide showers, some washbasins in cabins, baths and mother and baby rooms, also a bathroom for wheelchair users. These facilities are clean and well maintained. The 130 touring pitches all have electrical hook-ups (10A) and include 66 `super' pitches (these available for long weekends all winter). The cliffs here are high and in summer a steel stairway is put in place to give access to the long beach. This is a large, popular site with many caravan holiday homes and seasonal tourers, but with lots of space and plenty to do whatever the weather.

Charges 1999:
-- Per unit incl. 2 persons £11.00 - £14.00, 3 persons £11.00 - £15.00, 4 persons £11.00 - £16.00; `super' pitch £16.00 - £19.00; extra person (3 yrs and over), dog, car or small tent all £1.00.
-- Min. charge for Easter £55.
-- Less 10% for booked stays over 7 days excl. March and Oct.
-- VAT included.

Open:
1 March - 31 October.

Address:
Skipsea, Driffield, East Yorkshire YO25 8SY.

Tel:
(01262) 468293 or 468248.
FAX: (01262) 468648.

Reservations:
Made with £20 per week deposit (min. 7 days B.Hs and high season).

Directions: From A165 (Bridlington - Beverley) take B1242 Skipsea road. Park is on seaward side of this, 1½ miles south of Skipsea. O.S.GR: TA186530.

452 Flower of May Holiday Park, Lebberston, Scarborough

Large, family owned park with indoor pools.

Flower of May is a large park for both touring caravans and caravan holiday homes situated on the cliff tops, 4½ miles from Scarborough and 2½ miles from Filey. There is a cliff walk to the beach but it is only suitable for the reasonably active - there is an easier walk down from a car park one mile away. The entrance to the park is very colourful and the reception office is light and airy. Leisure facilities are grouped around reception. The indoor pool has areas for both adults and children, a water flume and jacuzzi. In the same building are two squash courts, 10 pin bowling, table tennis and amusement machines. The leisure centre is also open to the public (concessionary rates for campers) but during the high season it is only available to local regulars and the caravanners and campers on the park. There is also a pay and play golf course (£5 a round). The park is licensed for 300 touring units and 184 caravan holiday homes (45 to hire, the remainder privately owned). The touring pitches are pretty level, arranged in wide avenues mainly on grass and divided by shrubs. There are 210 with electricity (5A), including 50 `star' pitches with water and drainage also. The three toilet blocks have all been refurbished in a light and colourful style, fully tiled with washbasins in both cabins and vanity style. Roomy showers are pre-set with free hot water, plus baby rooms, facilities for disabled visitors and chemical disposal. A well stocked and licensed shop (close end Sept) is near the leisure centre, as is the laundry room. Amenities include two modern bar lounges (also to end Sept), one for families and one for adults only, with discos in season, a games room with TV, large adventure playground with safety base, and a café plus takeaway fish and chips. The Plough Inn near the park entrance offers a good bar meal. There is a dog exercise area, but numbers and breeds are limited (one per pitch) and not allowed at all at B.Hs and the six week summer holiday. Fishing, boat slipway or riding 2 miles, bicycle hire 4 miles. Flower of May also owns Riverside Meadows at Ripon (no. 476).

Charges 1999:
-- Per unit incl. up to 4 persons £7.00 - £11.50; awning £2.00; extra person (over 3 yrs) £2.00; extra car (on car park only) £2.00; dog (see above) £1.00; electricity £2.00; `star' pitch £4.00 extra.
-- 10% discount on pitch fee for weekly bookings.
-- No credit cards.
-- VAT included.

Open:
Easter - 31 October.

Address:
Lebberston Cliff, Scarborough, N. Yorkshire YO11 3NU.

Tel:
(01723) 584311.

Reservations:
Made with £20 deposit per week and £1 booking fee (Sat.-Sat. only for Spr. B.H. and 13/7-31/8).

see colour advert between pages 128/129

Directions: Park is signed from roundabout at junction of A165 and B1261 from where it is 600 yds. O.S.GR: TA088836.

453 Northcliffe Holiday Park, High Hawsker, nr. Whitby

Very high quality, family park with splendid sea views.

Within the North Yorkshire Moors National Park, Northcliffe caters for 170 caravan holiday homes as well as tourers, but they are entirely separate. The park is modern, well planned and attractive, the very friendly owners keeping everything neat and tidy - the toilet facilities are especially good. Totally refurbished and extended in '99, the block is heated in early and late seasons and uses a coded number pad entry system. Fully tiled, there are free hot showers, some washbasins in cabins, good facilities for babies and new facilities for disabled visitors. There is also a dishwashing room, a well equipped laundry and chemical disposal. When we visited everything was spotless. A well stocked shop (with gas) incorporates an attractive tea-room with a good range of reasonably priced food to eat in or takeaway (8-8 in high season, mornings and evenings in low season). Two play areas have good quality fittings with safety bases, and are both fenced. There is lots of grass for team games and an indoor room with pool table and amusement machines. The 30 touring pitches are a good size, all with electrical hook-up, and 16 of them fully serviced. These 16 have 16A electricity, the rest have 10A. Many trees and flowering bushes have been planted to provide wind breaks. The park is situated on the Heritage Coast and one can walk the Cleveland Way into Whitby or to Robin Hood's Bay. Available at reception are leaflets on walks and countryside notes (60p and produced by the park). Fishing 4 miles, riding 2 miles, golf 4 or 6 miles. Whitby and Scarborough with their sandy beaches are within easy reach as are the moors. York is about an hour away. Dogs are not accepted. A new member of the Best of British group.

Charges 1999:
-- Per unit incl. up to 6 persons in 1 family £6.00 - £10.50; pitch incl. electricity £8.00 - £12.50; `super' pitch £8.50 - £14.00; backpacker (no car) £3.00 - £4.00 per person; extra person, pup tent £1.00 - £2.00.
-- Less 10% if 7 nights booked.
-- Credit cards accepted (surcharge).
-- VAT included.

Open:
14 March - 31 October.

Address:
High Hawsker, nr. Whitby, N. Yorks YO22 4LL.

Tel:
(01947) 880477.
FAX: (01947) 880972.
E-mail: enquiries@north-cliffe.com.

Reservations:
Made with deposit and fee, min. 2-6 nights acc. to pitch type and season; contact park for details.

Directions: Three miles south of Whitby on the A171 (Scarborough) road turn left onto the B1447 signed High Hawsker and Robin Hood's Bay. Go through Hawsker village and continue on Robin Hood's Bay road. At top of hill turn left onto private road - go on ½ mile towards sea. O.S.GR: NZ936080.

Yorkshire

454 St Helens in the Park, Wykeham, nr. Scarborough

Spacious, high quality touring park with views.

Situated 6 miles from Scarborough, St Helens has been carefully planned and, set within 30 acres of parkland, the 250 level pitches have a spacious feel. There are 52 pitches with hardstanding but these are used by seasonal lets in summer (available to tourers in winter). Electrical hook-ups (10A) are available on 240 pitches, also in the late arrivals area. The whole park is maintained to a high standard and all the buildings are in local stone. The toilet blocks are well equipped, with free hot water and washbasins, both vanity style and in cabins, pre-set showers and baby baths. Everything is clean and well maintained and all four blocks have dishwashing sinks under cover. A good laundry room is next to the well stocked shop (open Mar-Oct). Small games room with pool table and amusement machines and a takeaway cabin provides simple meals on certain evenings each week during busy periods. The adventure playground, set on bark, is part of a three acre area set aside for children with goal posts and a mountain bike track. There is a telephone chalet with a large selection of tourist information. The Downe Arms (a short walk) is known for its good food and it occasionally has family discos in high season. Nearby Wykeham Lakes offer fishing (trout and coarse), scuba diving, windsurfing and sailing (in your own boat). Dogs are accepted, with a dog walk and a field to run in. Buses pass the gate.

Directions: Park access road leads off the A170 (Pickering - Scarborough) road in Wykeham village 2 miles west of junction with B1262. O.S.GR: SE963835.

Charges guide:
-- Per unit incl. 2 persons £7.00 - £9.00; extra person (over 5 yrs) £1.00; awning £1.70; porch awning £1.20; pup tent £6.00; dog free; electricity £2.00.
-- Special winter rates.
-- VAT included.
-- Credit cards accepted.

Open:
All year,
(reduced facilities Nov-Feb).

Address:
Wykeham, Scarborough, N. Yorks YO13 9QD.

Tel/Fax:
(01723) 862771.

Reservations:
Made with £10 deposit (min. 4 nights for Spr. and Aug. B.Hs).

455 Cayton Village Caravan Park, Cayton, nr. Scarborough

Quiet, spacious touring park close to the attractions of Scarborough.

Cayton Village Caravan Park can only be described as a gem. Just three miles from the hustle and bustle of Scarborough, it is a peaceful, attractive haven. Originally just a flat field with caravans around the perimeter, four years of hard work, a lot of time and even more expense has produced a park which is very pleasing to the eye and of which the owner, Carol, can be justly proud. The entrance is a mass of flowers and the late arrivals area has electrical hook-ups, very handy because the gates are locked at night and anyone leaving early is also expected to use it so as not to disturb others. Reception and the shop are side by side, both open 8.30 am. to 8 pm. Reception has quantities of tourist information, and the shop has a very comprehensive range which includes gas and caravan spares. There are four toilet blocks, including one new in '97. Three (with coded locks) are heated, with very high quality tiling and fittings. Hot water is free, there are hand dryers, soap and hair dryers, and washbasins are in vanity units. Some showers are pre-set, others controllable and there are also two family shower rooms, a family bathroom, baby changing facilities and chemical disposal. The older block is 'portacabin' style with no showers. It is really not needed, but the regulars around it like to use the facilities. The 200 pitches, of which 160 are for touring units, are numbered and everyone is taken to their pitch – a nice personal touch. There are 7 'super' pitches. Dogs are accepted on leads and a superb dog walk is provided (an enormous well mown field, floodlit at night). A short walk across a field takes you to Cayton Village which has a popular pub providing excellent meals, a shop/post office and a church. A regular bus service passes the gate to Scarborough or Filey. The North York Moors are a short distance away, as is the Forestry Commission's Dalby Forest Drive with its scenic drive, mountain bike trails and way-marked walks. The steam railway at Pickering is a big attraction. Fishing and bicycle hire ½ mile, riding 4 miles, golf 3 miles.

Directions: From A64 Malton - Scarborough road turn right at roundabout (with supermarket and pub) signed Filey and Cayton. Follow signs for Cayton, in Cayton Village take second left after the Blacksmiths Arms down Mill Lane (at brown caravan site sign) and park is 200 yds. From roundabout to park is 2¼ miles. From A165 turn inland at Cayton Bay traffic lights and park is ½ mile on right. O.S.GR: TA057837.

Charges 2000:
-- Per unit incl. 4 persons £6.00 - £10.00; extra adult £1.50; child £1.00; awning £2.00; dog £1.00; electricity £2.00.
-- No credit cards.
-- VAT included.

Open:
Easter - 1 October.

Address:
D23 Mill Lane,
Cayton Bay,
Scarborough,
North Yorkshire
YO11 3NN.

Tel:
(01723) 583171 (winter (01904) 624630).

Reservations:
Are advised and made for min. 3 nights (4 at B.Hs) with £20 deposit.

456 Golden Square Caravan and Camping Park, Oswaldkirk

Popular, high quality, family owned touring park.

Mr and Mrs Armstrong are local farmers who have worked hard to turn an old quarry into a very attractive, well drained caravan park. A number of levelled bays have superb views over the Vale of Pickering. The 130 pitches are not separated but they have markers and mainly back onto grass banks. In very dry weather the ground can be hard (steel pegs needed). There are 130 pitches with electricity (10A), 24 have drainage and 6 are 'deluxe' pitches (with waste water, sewage, electricity, water and TV aerial connection). The two heated toilet blocks are of excellent quality, with washbasins in vanity units (some in cabins) with free hot water. Showers are pre-set and metered, the heated bathroom (50p) also houses baby changing facilities. Both ladies and men have full facilities for disabled visitors. Dishwashing sinks are under cover and the laundry houses washers, dryers, a spin dryer and iron and board. All these amenities are made attractive by the care Mrs Armstrong takes in providing plants and flower arrangements. Chemical disposal and motorcaravan service point. This year sees a new tourist information room, which also houses a microwave and an extra iron and board. The licensed shop is very well stocked, selling fresh bread and cakes, dairy produce, vegetables, groceries, newspapers, gas and gifts. Two excellent play areas allow tiny tots to be kept separate from older children. Games field and a barn with table tennis and pool table. Bicycle hire on site. Visitors may have membership of Ampleforth College sports centre, with its indoor pool, tennis and gym, etc. Riding 2 miles, golf 3 miles, fishing 5 miles. The area abounds with footpaths and three well known long distance footpaths are near. Dog owners have two or three enormous fields for exercising, alongside the park. Nearby Helmsley and Ampleforth have shops and pubs with food. All year caravan storage.

Charges 1999:
-- Per unit incl. 2 persons and all children up to 10 yrs £6.00 - £9.25; extra person (10 yrs or over) £1.00; full awning £1.40; porch awning £1.00; extra car £1.00; electricity £2.00; hikers/bikers £3.00 - £3.50 per person; 'deluxe' pitch £15.00 - £20.00, all incl.
-- VAT included.

Open:
1 March - 31 October.

Address:
Oswaldkirk,
York YO62 5YQ.

Tel:
(01439) 788269.
FAX: (01439) 788236.

Reservations:
Essential for B.Hs and made with £10 deposit (£20 for B.Hs).

Directions: Park is on Helmsley - Ampleforth road on the 'caravan route' avoiding the banned Sutton Bank on A170 Thirsk road. Turn off B1257 to west at sign by Golden Square Farm, 1 mile south of junction with A170. O.S.GR: SE605797.

CARAVAN &

CAMPING PARK

OSWALDKIRK YORK
Tel: 01439 788269
Fax: 01439 788236

**Regional 'Loo of the Year' winner
6 times between 1988-1997
North Yorks Moors National Park**

Helmsley 2 miles, Ampleforth 1 mile. Secluded site surrounded by open countryside and woodland with magnificent views. Luxury heated toilet block and bathroom. Electric hook-ups. Shop. Launderette. Covered washing up sinks. Indoor and outdoor play areas. Indoor sports centre nearby. Dogs welcome with dog walks available.

Deluxe all service pitches.
Storage compound. Seasonal pitches.

457 Wombleton Caravan and Camping Park, Kirkbymoorside

Neat and tidy, well manicured park in popular area.

Since 1990 the Proctors have worked very hard to produce an attractive family park. There are 88 touring pitches set amongst flowering trees, which in spring look a picture. The site is level and open with a circular tarmac road, sheltered from the surrounding farmland by tall trees. Electricity (5/10A) is available for all the pitches (a long lead may be needed). The centrally situated toilet block is exceptionally well maintained. Metered showers have saloon type doors, the washbasins (some in cabins) have hot water. In the same building are washing up sinks and a laundry with washing machine, dryer and iron and outside is a chemical disposal point. Children are well catered for with a good fenced play area (parents are requested to supervise their children). Basic provisions are kept in reception and gas. The village pub is 1mile, Helmsley and Kirkbymoorside are about 4 miles. The sea, the moors and York are all an easy drive away. An indoor swimming pool is at Pickering and an outdoor pool at Helmsley. Riding or bicycle hire 4 miles, golf 3 miles. Seasonal pitches and caravan storage available.

Charges 1999:
-- Per unit incl. 2 persons £6.00 - £7.00; extra person £1.00; awning £1,50; electricity £2.00; extra car £1.00.
-- No credit cards.

Open:
1 March - 31 October.

Address:
Wombleton,
Kirkbymoorside,
N. Yorks YO62 7RY.

Tel:
(01751) 431684.

Reservations:
Made with £10 deposit.

Directions: From Helmsley take A170 (Scarborough). After 4 miles turn right to Wombleton, through village and then left to park in ¼ mile. O.S.GR: SE670835.

458 Foxholme Touring Caravan and Camping Park, Harome

Well shaded touring park for caravans and a few tents, near Helmsley.

Foxholme is an unusual park with only 60 pitches for caravans and a small field for a few tents. Nearly all the pitches are individual ones in clearings in the quite dense coniferous plantation. The trees give a lot of shade and quite a lot of privacy (manoeuvring may be difficult on some pitches). All pitches have electricity (6A, a few need long leads) and 20 places have hardstanding. Some picnic tables are provided. The toilet block is of good quality, built in local stone, with all washbasins in private cubicles and free hot showers.Also part of this building is a laundry room with washing machine and sinks and a washing up room (H&C). Two further small blocks provide WCs only in other parts of the park, there are two chemical disposal points and a motorcaravan service point. The site is managed by a warden and his wife with reception usually open 9 am. - 9 pm. with an hour for lunch. Very basic provisions are kept. Public phone. The park is set in quiet countryside and would be a good base for touring, being within striking distance of the moors, the coast and York. There are no on site activities but the indoor pool at the Pheasant Hotel in Harome may be used by campers (£2 per session). The nearest shops are at Helmsley and Kirkbymoorside, both about 4 miles away, where there is also bicycle hire. Riding and golf also 4 miles. Caravan storage available. A torch would be useful.

Charges 2000:
-- Per unit £7.00 - £7.50; awning £1.50; extra car 60p; electricity £2.00.
-- No credit cards.
-- VAT included.

Open:
Mid March - 31 October.

Address:
Harome, Helmsley, North Yorkshire YO62 5JG.

Tel:
(01439) 770416, 771241 or 771696.
FAX: (01439) 771744.

Reservations:
Made for any dates with £10 deposit.

Directions: Turn south off the A170 between adjoining villages of Beadlam (to west) and Nawton (to east) at sign to Ryedale School, then 1 mile to park on left (passing another park on right). From east ignore first camp sign at turning before Nawton. From west turn right ¼ mile east of Helmsley, signed Harome, turn left at church, go through village and follow camp signs. O.S.GR: SE661831.

FOXHOLME TOURING CARAVAN PARK

HAROME, HELMSLEY, NORTH YORKSHIRE YO62 5JG
Telephone: (01439) 771241, 770416 or 771696   Fax: (01439) 771744

AA 3 PENNANT - CARAVAN CLUB APPROVED - CAMPING CLUB APPROVED

A quiet, rural site for touring vans, motor caravans and some tents. All pitches in well sheltered clearings in the 6 acres of 38 year old woodland. All weather roads; Some hardstandings; Luxury toilet block graded excellent by the A.A. Washbasins in cubicles; H&C showers; Laundry room; Small shop; Gas exchange; Mains electric hook-ups available.

BEAUTIFUL COUNTRYSIDE, CLOSE TO THE NORTH YORK MOORS NATIONAL PARK
Please send stamp for brochure to G.C. Binks

---

460 Vale of Pickering Caravan Park, Allerston, nr. Pickering

Well designed, neat and tidy, family owned park.

Vale of Pickering is a level park edged by grassy banks and, although over the 12 or so years that the site has been developing these have been partly hidden by foliage, trees and attractive flower beds, they do give shelter from the wind. The owners, who are local farmers, have put a lot of thought into planning the site. There are 130 pitches, 75 of which are for touring units, all with electrical connections (10A). The well maintained, tiled toilet block has washbasins (some in cabins), coin-operated showers with curtains, hooks, shelves and mirrors, and also a bath. A separate toilet and washbasin are provided for visitors with disabilities. Chemical disposal facilities, motorcaravan service point, launderette, dishwashing sinks (2p for hot water) and a microwave oven. A well stocked, licensed shop also stocks a few caravan accessories (open according to demand in low season). Tourist information is provided in a separate wooden chalet. A fish and chip van calls twice weekly in main season and a local pub is at Yedingham, 1½ miles. Fishing 1 mile, bicycle hire and riding 3 miles, golf 5 miles. There is a good play area with safety bases and a playing field for football, etc. Dogs are accepted with a dog walk provided.

Charges guide:
-- Per unit incl. 2 adults and 2 children (under 12 yrs) £6.00 - £9.00; extra adult or child £1.00; awning £1.50; electricity £2.00; large tent plus £1.50; hardstanding 50p; 2 dogs free, extra £1.00.
-- No credit cards.

Open:
14 March - 31 October.

Address:
Carr House Farm, Allerston, N. Yorks, YO18 7PQ.

Tel:
(01723) 859280/850060.

Reservations:
Made with £10 deposit (min. 3 nights at B.Hs with £20 deposit).

Directions: Park is 1 mile off the main A170 (Scarborough - Helmsley) road at the village of Allerston. O.S.GR: SE879808.

474 Jasmine Park, Snainton, nr. Scarborough

Quiet, well manicured park in the Vale of Pickering.

This is an area of North Yorkshire that is very popular so although we have other parks nearby, we feel there is room for another. Jasmine is a very attractive, well manicured park with a colourful floral entrance. Set in the Vale of Pickering, the park is level, well drained and protected by a coniferous hedge. All pitches are on grass, with electricity (10A) for all caravans and some tents. The sanitary block is kept very clean and provides adjustable showers (on payment) and a large room for families or disabled visitors containing a bath, shower, WC and washbasin (access by key). A laundry room has dishwashing sinks, washing machine, dryer and iron (hot water metered). Chemical disposal. There is no playground but a field is provided for games. Dogs are welcome (no dog walk). Tourist information is in a log cabin and the owners are happy to advise. A licensed shop sells essentials and gas. The market town of Pickering and seaside Scarborough are both 8 miles. Many local attractions are within easy reach, including Castle Howard, Dalby Forest, Sledmere House, Nunington Hall, Goathland (the setting for ITV's 'Heartbeat') and the North York Moors Railway. Closer are facilities for riding, fishing, bowls and golf, also quiet lanes for cycling. With 11 privately owned log cabins, some seasonal tourers and a caravan holiday home for hire, this is a quiet park for a restful holiday. A member of the Countryside Discovery group.

Charges 1999:
-- Per unit incl. 2 persons £6.00 - £9.50; extra adult £1.00; child (6-13 yrs) 75p; awning or tent over 150 sq.ft. £1.50; extra car £1.00; electricity £2.00.
-- Min. stay at Easter 4 nights, other B.Hs 3 nights.
Open:
1 March - 31 December.
Address:
Cross Lane, Snainton, Scarborough, N. Yorks YO13 9BE.
Tel:
(01723) 859240, FAX: as phone.
Reservations:
Made with £10 deposit and S.A.E.

Directions: Snainton is on the A170 (Pickering-Scarborough). Park is signed at eastern end of the village. Follow to park on left in 1 mile. O.S.GR: SE928813.

463 Ripley Caravan Park, Ripley

Spacious, family run touring park with heated indoor pool.

Peter and Valerie House are the resident owners of Ripley Park, an 18 acre grass park accommodating 130 units. On fairly level grass, undulating in parts, with 130 electrical connections (10A) and 10 hardstandings, some pitches are marked, others carefully spaced (allowing the grass to recover) and all connected by a circular gravel road. Recent developments include electric hook-ups, water points and refuse areas, and 2,000 trees have been planted. The park has a fairly open field like aspect, with growing trees and a small pond (lake) with ducks provides an attractive feature. The central, attractively designed toilet block provides push-button hot showers, washbasins in curtained cubicles, baby bath and a separate unit for disabled people with a shower. It can be heated and has been extended to provide extra, smart facilities. Small laundry, washing up sinks under cover, chemical disposal and motorcaravan service point. The leisure block beside the entrance with the reception and shop (with gas), offers a games room with TV, playroom and a heated indoor pool (50p per person) and sauna. Adventure play equipment and football area. Dogs welcome but max. two per unit unless by prior arrangement. Winter caravan storage. The park is at the gateway to the Yorkshire Dales National Park and almost midway between the spa town of Harrogate and historic Knaresborough. The village of Ripley, dominated by its castle, is within walking distance. Fishing, riding or golf 3 miles. Bus service 150 yds.

Charges 1999:
-- Per unit incl. 2 adults £6.75 - £8.00; extra adult £2.00; child (5-18 yrs) £1.00; awning £1.50; porch awning, child's pup tent or extra car £1.00; electricity £1.95.
-- VAT included.
Open:
Easter - 31 October.
Address:
Ripley, Harrogate, Yorks HG3 3AU.
Tel/Fax:
(01423) 770050.
Reservations:
Made with £10 deposit, min. 3 nights at B.Hs.

Alan Rogers' Discount

Less 10% in low season, for min. 7 days

Directions: About 4 miles north of Harrogate, site access is 150 yds. down the B6165 Knaresborough road from A61 roundabout junction. O.S.GR: SE291601.

Ripley Caravan Park
where the country and enjoyment comes naturally...

This luxury touring caravan park in the beautiful North Yorkshire countryside is within easy reach of Ripley Castle, village and only ten minutes north of Harrogate.
First class facilities include new extended shower facilities, amenities for the disabled; there is a shop, laundry, games rooms, telephone, children's playground and play area, electric hook-up points and indoor heated swimming pool.
For further information: -
Peter & Valerie House, Ripley Caravan Park
Ripley, Harrogate, HG3 3AU
Tel: (01423) 770050 *Dogs permitted*

BRONZE

Yorkshire

465 Fangfoss Old Station Caravan Park, Fangfoss, nr. York

Small, rural, family run park at the foot of the Yorkshire Wolds.

The Station House and platform give this site character, its rural situation amongst rolling farmland gives it peace and quietness and its owners, a friendly welcome and clean and comfortable facilities. The grassed over track and sidings provide hardstanding and, with the adjacent fairly level grass field, give a total of 45 marked pitches, 18 with hardstanding and 36 with 10A electricity. All units are sited. A modern, centrally situated toilet block provides free adjustable hot showers, vanity style washbasins (two in cubicles for ladies). A separate wooden utility block 'The Wendy House' provides covered washing up sinks and a laundry sink with free hot water and a food preparation bar (useful for tenters). No washing machine but a laundry service is offered. Chemical disposal. Reception carries food essentials with an off-licence facility, gas and tourist information. Some play equipment on grass, public telephone, central refuse area and 6 water points. York is 10 miles (with 'park and ride' facilities), Hull 28 miles and the Yorkshire Wolds 5 miles. There are nearby market towns and a variety of pubs and restaurants within a 6 mile radius. Fangfoss is 1 mile, Pocklington 4, with sports facilities, etc. Fishing, bicycle hire, riding and golf within 4 miles. This is an area to encourage walkers and cyclists. Winter caravan storage.

Directions: Park is clearly signed on A166 from Stamford Bridge. Using A1079 York - Hull road, follow signs at Wilberfoss Village for 1½ miles (in a northerly direction). O.S.GR: SE748527.

Charges 2000:
-- Per unit incl. up to 4 persons £7.70 - £8.70; trailer tent £8.70 - £9.70; 2-man tent £6.00; awning £1.80; porch awning 90p; extra person £1.00; extra car £1.50; electricity £2.00.
-- Credit cards accepted.
Open:
1 March - 31 October.
Address:
Fangfoss, York YO41 5QB.
Tel:
(01759) 380491.
Reservations:
Made with £15 deposit, or full payment in advance for electric pitch at B.Hs.

461 Moorside Caravan Park, Strensall, nr. York

Adults only park with a neat and tidy appearance.

Strensall is only a few miles from York, one of England's most attractive cities and Moorside will provide a peaceful haven after a day's sightseeing. It will impress you with its pretty fishing lake, masses of flowers and the quietness (except for the odd passing daytime train). There are 57 marked pitches on neat well trimmed grass, most with electricity (5/10A) and 18 with paved hardstanding. The purpose built toilet block can be heated and houses immaculately kept facilities with very spacious showers and washbasins in cubicles for ladies. One WC is suitable for use by visitors with disabilities. Fully equipped laundry room, also housing a public phone, washing up area and chemical disposal. Reception has books to borrow and tourist information. The whole park is very well maintained and is a very pleasant environment. The small lake is well stocked (coarse fishing charge). The pitches bordering the lake are the most popular. Dogs are accepted (poop scoops provided) and there is a good dog walk off site. York golf course is almost opposite the site entrance and Strensall village with shops and places to eat is less than a mile away. Caravan storage available.

Directions: From A1237 York outer ring road, follow Flaxton road. Park entrance is on left past signs to Strensall village and Golf Club. O.S.GR: SE647614.

Charges 1999:
-- Per unit £6.00 - £9.00; awning £1.00; hardstanding 50p; electricity £1.50.
-- No credit cards.
Open:
1 March - end October.
Address:
Flaxton Road, Strensall, York Y032 5XF.
Tel:
(01904) 491208 or 491865.
Reservations:
Contact park.

464 Goose Wood Caravan Park, Sutton-on-the-Forest, York

Family owned park in natural woodland setting 6 miles from York, for caravans and motorcaravans only.

Goose Wood provides a quiet, relaxed atmosphere from which to explore York itself or the surrounding Yorkshire Dales, Wolds or Moors. The park has a well kept air and rural atmosphere, with 75 well spaced and marked pitches on level grass, all with electricity (16A) and 75 with paved hardstanding and patio pitch. No tents or trailer tents are accepted. The excellent toilet block, modern and well maintained, provides good facilities including free showers (four minute push-button which also operates the light and is located outside cubicle), a bathroom (£1) and hairdryers. A separate unit provides four extra toilets and washbasins, and coin-operated washing up sinks. Chemical disposal, a motorcaravan service point, laundry room, small shop with gas supplies and a public phone complete the practical facilities supporting the needs of the discerning visitor. For children, there is a `super plus' adventure playground in the trees at one side of the site and, for adults, a small coarse fishing lake and attractive, natural woodland for walking, plus a large scale chess set. Dogs are welcome on a lead (max. two per pitch), to be exercised in nearby woodland. The park is popular with families in high season when it can be busy at weekends. A 'park and ride' scheme for York operates from nearby all year, six days a week or there is a local bus every two hours, six days a week. The park is 1¼ miles from Sutton village and only 7 miles from `Water World' a new water leisure centre with pool, slides, wave machines, etc. Riding or golf 1 mile. A member of the Best of British group.

Directions: Park is 6 miles north of York; from the A1237 York outer ring-road take the B1363 for Sutton-on-the-Forest and Stillington, taking the first right after the Haxby and Wigginton junction and follow camp signs. O.S.GR: SE595636.

Charges 2000:
-- Per unit incl. 1 or 2 persons and car £8.50 - £10.50; extra person £1.00; awning (no groundsheet), extra pup tent (1 only) or extra car £1.00; electricity (16A) £2.50; hardstanding free.
-- No credit cards.
-- VAT included.

Open:
2 weeks before Easter - 31 October.

Address:
Sutton-on-the-Forest, York YO61 1ET,

Tel:
(01347) 810829.

Reservations:
Made with £20 deposit (min. 3 nights at B.Hs).

See colour feature for `BEST of BRITISH' between pages 96/97

462 Rawcliffe Manor Caravan Park, Rawcliffe, York

Very good quality, neat touring park close to the city of York.

Don't be put off by the road down to Rawcliffe Manor – admittedly it is not a very nice ride, past an industrial estate and new houses, but you will be rewarded. The park itself comes as a very pleasant surprise. The 120 touring pitches are on flat, very well manicured grass with some tarmac and concrete hardstandings. Originally in the middle of the countryside, the park is now surrounded by houses and a shopping centre. However, the hedges have grown so there is no feeling of being overshadowed. Over the years much money has gone into updating and redesigning the facilities. There are hedged bays, flower beds and all the pitches are fully serviced, giving 10A electricity, satellite TV, water and drainage connections. American motorhomes can be catered for, mainly in the quieter periods (contact park for details). Being a city site, Rawcliffe naturally gets very busy. There are two modern toilet blocks (opened by security codes and heated in winter). Tastefully tiled, they have free hot water in fully controllable showers and washbasins (some in cabins, others vanity style, baby baths, hair dryers and excellent facilities for disabled visitors. Both blocks have laundry rooms with washing machines, dryers, spin dryers and irons. Chemical disposal and motorcaravan service point. Gas is available. The clubhouse at the entrance has a large bar and lounge, with bar meals, takeaway service and a separate restaurant. All this can be used by the general public (weekends only Oct-April). Entertainment is organised frequently in the bar in high season. A games room for both adults and children with pool tables, etc. opens out onto a well equipped children's play area (bark safety base) where barbecues are held in high season. Foreign visitors make full use of a boules pitch. This is not really a suitable site for dogs being surrounded by houses as it is, but they are accepted and there is a small dog walk provided. A very short walk takes you to an 'out of town' shopping centre, with a 12 screen cinema and 10 pin bowling, also a park and ride bus into York. Also near is the local park with tennis courts, and a cycle route is adjacent. Golf 1 mile, riding 3 miles.

Directions: Park is ½ mile off A19 York - Thirsk road at A1237 junction (York side) with the new northern bypass. O.S.GR: SE583552.

Charges 1999:
-- Per unit incl. 2 persons £8.00 - £11.50; small camper van less £1.00; small tent (no car) incl. 2 persons £7.00 - £8.00, 1 person £4.50 - £5.50; extra adult £1.60; child 5-11 yrs £1.20, 12-16 yrs £1.40; awning (grass friendly) £1.20; extra car £2.00; electricity £2.00 (plus 80p Dec-Feb); satellite TV £1.00 - £1.20; m/cycle £1.50; dog £1.00.
-- Less 10% in low season for senior citizens.
-- VAT included.
-- Credit cards accepted.

Open:
All year.

Address:
Manor Lane, Shipton Road, York YO30 5TZ.

Tel:
(01904) 624422.
FAX: (01904) 640845.

Reservations:
Made for min. 3 nights with £25 deposit; contact park for details.

471 Rudding Holiday Park, Follifoot, Harrogate

Touring park set in quiet, mature parkland, with swimming pool and golf course.

The extensive part wooded, part open grounds of Rudding Park are very attractive, peaceful and well laid out. All 141 pitches have electricity (10-16A). One camping area is sloping but terraces provide level pitches and further pitches are in the very sheltered old walled garden. There are 17 'super pitches' (full services including satellite TV connections). A separate area contains 52 owner occupied caravan holiday homes and pine chalets. Some of the touring pitches are let on a seasonal basis. The two toilet blocks are tiled and of a good standard, centrally heated and well maintained. We found them to be very clean, although they may be under pressure when the park is full. All hot water is free, there are some washbasins in cabins, pre-set showers (button beside the door), soap and hand dryers, a baby room and bathroom and ladies have free hairdryers. A laundry room at each block contains washing machines, dryers, sinks and irons and boards and disabled people have well appointed facilities. Chemical disposal and motor-caravan service point. A heated outdoor swimming and paddling pool with sunbathing areas is open from Spr. B.H.– early Sept. and is supervised at all times (charged). The large, well stocked, self-service shop is open all season (sometimes limited hours). Gas supplies. On the outer edge of the park is an 18 hole golf course and driving range, together with the 'Inn in the Park', a bar and restaurant which is open twice daily during B.Hs and school holidays, otherwise only at weekends. Children have an adventure playground on bark chippings, football pitch, games room and minigolf. Bicycle hire on site. Dogs are provided with a dog walk. Caravan storage. Buses pass the gate hourly on their way to Harrogate and Knaresborough. Fishing 2 miles, riding 1 mile. Tennis, markets, pubs and restaurants are all within a few miles, and the majestic City of York is less than an hour away. This is an attractive park with something for all the family.

Directions: Park is 3 miles south of Harrogate clearly signed between the A658 and A661 roads. O.S.GR: SE333528.

Charges 1999:
-- Per pitch £9.00 - £12.50; awning £1.00 - £2.00; electricity £2.50; `super' pitch incl. awning and electricity £16.00 - £21.00; 2-man tent £6.50 - £8.00; extra car £1.00; dog (on lead) free.
-- Special offers - contact park.
-- VAT included.
-- Credit cards accepted
Open:
15 March - 3 November.
Address:
Follifoot, Harrogate, North Yorkshire HG3 1JH.
Tel:
(01423) 870439.
FAX: (01423) 870859.
Reservations:
Made with full advance payment (essential for B.H. w/ends).

Alan Rogers' Discount

Less £1 p/night with card

470 Nostell Priory Holiday Park, Nostell, nr. Wakefield

Attractive, quiet woodland park.

A tranquil, secluded park within the estate of Nostell Priory, this site provides 60 touring pitches, all with electrical connections (5A), in a grassy, flat and sheltered area edged with mature trees. There is a hardstanding area suitable for motorcar-avans, plus 80 caravan holiday homes in a separate area (5 for hire). Amenities are designed to blend into the environment in rustic wood, including the sanitary block which, although older in style, is very clean and well maintained. Accessed by key, it has roomy showers (20p), vanity style washbasins and a separate room for dishwashing (free hot water) and laundry with two washing machines and a dryer (opening times on the door). Chemical disposal and motorcaravan service facilities are provided. There is a children's play area (no ball games on the site). Milk and papers can be ordered at reception, the nearest shops are 2 miles. Nostell Priory with its collection of Chippendale furniture and attractive gardens is well worth a visit. The Dales, York and the Peak District are all an easy drive away. A fishing lake is within the grounds, with golf and watersports locally (details in reception). Golf 5 miles, boat launching 8 miles. The park is very well cared for and the natural environment is encouraged so there is an abundance of birds and wildlife. Dogs are accepted (max. 2). A rally field is adjacent to the site. Buses pass the end of the drive (½ mile long).

Directions: Park entrance is off A638 Wakefield - Doncaster road, 5 miles southeast of Wakefield. Follow drive for ½ mile keeping the rose nursery on your left. O.S.GR: SE394181.

Charges 1999:
-- Per unit incl. 2 persons £7.50 - £8.50; extra person (over 7 yrs) 50p; extra vehicle or porch awning £1.00; awning £1.25; dog (max. 2) £1.00.
-- Less 10% for 7 night bookings.
-- Less 10% for senior citizens.
-- No single sex groups or units over 21'6" length.
-- VAT included.
Open:
1 April - 30 September.
Address:
Nostell, Wakefield, W. Yorks WF4 1QD.
Tel:
(01924) 863938.
FAX: (01924) 862226.
Reservations:
Advised and made with £5 deposit and 50p fee (min. 2 nights).

TOURING CARAVANS and Family Camping

Award winning holiday park - your gateway to the Yorkshire Dales

RUDDING
holiday PARK

ROSE
AWARD

- Heated swimming pool & children's paddling pool
- Licensed bar serving meals ● Free showers
- Children's playground ● Games room and bicycle hire ● Laundrette ● Park lighting
- Electrical hook-up points ● 18 hole pay & play golf course plus floodlit driving range

SUPERSITES: These individual pitches have a hard standing for touring caravans, 16 amp electricity, water, direct drainage, TV and satellite hook-up and a picnic table. *Please send for free illustrated brochure:*

Rudding Holiday Park, Follifoot, Harrogate HG3 1JH. Tel: 01423 870439 Fax: 01423 870859

---

469 Constable Burton Hall Caravan Park, nr. Leyburn

Tranquil park in beautiful Wensleydale for caravans and motorcaravans only.

This is a park where the emphasis is on peace and quiet, the wardens working to provide a relaxing environment. In the grounds of the Hall, it has a spacious, park-like feel to it. On part level, part sloping, well trimmed grass, the 120 pitches are of a good size and all have electricity(10A). The two sanitary blocks, built of local stone and blending in with the local surroundings, have been refurbished recently, are well tiled and kept immaculately clean, and can be heated. Washbasins are in vanity style units and the showers are controllable and free. The former deer barn has been adapted for use as a laundry room, tourist information room and extra washrooms with basins for both men and women. The park is ideally placed for visiting the Northern Dales. The gardens of the Hall are open to the public, with a collection of maples and terraced gardens developed by Mrs Vida Burton. There is no shop but nearby Leyburn will provide for needs. Opposite the entrance is the Wyvill Arms for bar meals. Public telephone. Gas supplies. Chemical disposal. Fishing, riding or golf within 4 miles. Gates closed 10 pm - 8 am.

Directions: Park is by the A684 between Bedale and Leyburn, ½ mile from the village of Constable Burton on the Leyburn side. O.S.GR: SE152907.

Charges 2000:
-- Per unit incl. 2 persons £7.50 - £10.00; extra adult £2.00; child 75p; awning £1.80; extra car 50p; electricity £2.00.
-- No credit cards.
-- VAT included.

Open:
Late March - 31 October.

Address:
Constable Burton Hall, nr. Leyburn, N. Yorks DL8 5LJ.

Tel:
(01677) 450428.
FAX: (01677) 450622.

Reservations:
Made with deposit (£20 for B.Hs. £5 other times).

---

475 Howgill Lodge Caravan and Camping Park, Barden, nr. Skipton

Small, traditional, family site, set in the heart of the Dales.

Arranged on a sloping hillside, the terraced pitches at Howgill Lodge have fantastic views. It is a small park catering for the needs of walkers, tourers and the people who like to just relax. The whole area is a haven for both experienced walkers or the casual rambler, without having to move your car. All the pitches at the upper part of the park are on hardstanding and have electricity connections, the lower ones are mainly on grass (30 in total). Picnic tables and chairs are provided. The sanitary facilities, which can be heated, are at the entrance, close to reception, with dishwashing sinks outside, under cover. Showers are large and adjustable (on payment). The laundry room is fully equipped with washing machine, dryer and iron and four unisex showers are also here. Outdoor washing lines are provided. A small block housing WCs, with another one planned, are lower down the site for tent campers. Reception also houses the small shop selling most of the basics including fresh foods. A dog walk is provided; there is no children's play area. Fishing licences are available from reception. Part of the farmhouse has been tastefully converted into a licensed restaurant, open six days a week (noon - 6 pm) in season, weekends only in winter. B&B is offered and there are 4 caravan holiday homes for rent. Skipton, a market town, is only 8 miles and the well known Bolton Abbey, with its beautiful riverside walks is 3 miles. Pretty villages abound in the area, all with attractive inns and nearby Embsay has the Dales Railway with steam trains. This very pleasant park, with clean facilities, has a very relaxing feel to it. A member of the Countryside Discovery group.

Directions: Turn off A59 (Skipton - Harrogate) at roundabout on B6100 Bolton Abbey, Burnsall road. Three miles past Bolton Abbey at Barden Towers, bear right signed Appletreewick and Pateley Bridge. This road is fairly narrow for 1¼ miles with passing places. Park signed on right at phone box. O.S.GR: SE055582.

Charges 1999:
-- Per unit incl. 2 persons £9.50, incl. family £11.50; tent or motor-caravan £9.00 or £10.50; awning or extra car £2.00; hiker £3.30.
-- VAT included.

Open:
1 April - 31 October.

Address:
Barden, Skipton, N. Yorks BD23 6DJ.

Tel:
(01756) 720655.

Reservations:
Made with £10 deposit.

467 Wood Nook Caravan Park, Threshfield, Skipton

Small, family run, rural park in the heart of Wharfedale, popular for walking holidays.

The access road to Wood Nook is narrow for a short distance, but you will find it is well worth this slight inconvenience. Set in the Yorkshire Dales National Park, the site includes six acres of woodland with quite rare flora and wildlife. Reception is in the farmhouse and, if you are lucky, the peacocks will come out to greet you. The small shop is also at the farm (from Easter, gas and basics only). Farm buildings have been converted to provide modern, neat sanitary facilities which can be heated, are well maintained and kept very clean (opened by key). Washbasins are in cubicles for ladies, there are hairdryers and the showers (in another building) are roomy, tiled and coin operated. The laundry has a washing machine, dryer, spin dryer and iron, with clothes lines available. Dishwashing sinks are outside but under cover. Chemical disposal and motorcaravan service points. A wooden chalet provides tourist information. The gently sloping fields have gravel roads and provide 25 pitches with gravel hardstanding. All have electricity (10A, long leads may be required) and there are water and chemical disposal points. There is also room for 24 tents and the park also has 10 caravan holiday homes to let. A small, attractive children's play area with good quality equipment is on top of a small hill, between the touring fields and farmhouse buildings. The Thompson family are very friendly, trying always to have time for a chat, although Wood Nook is still a working farm producing beef cattle. Dogs are accepted with a good area provided for walking. American motorhomes are taken by prior arrangement. The Old Hall Inn at Threshfield offers bar food and there is a leisure centre with swimming pool nearby. Fishing or bicycle hire 2 miles, riding 3 miles, golf 9 miles. The park itself adjoins the fells, with direct access from the top of the site. A visit to the nearby village of Grassington is a must, with its cobbled main street and quaint gift shops. All in all, this is a peaceful park from which to explore the Yorkshire Dales.

Charges 2000:
-- Per adult £2.00; child 3-15 yrs 75p, 16-17 yrs as part of a family unit £1.25; pitch incl. car £4.00; awning £1.00; hiker/cyclist £3.00; electricity £1.80.
-- Credit cards accepted.

Open:
1 March - 31 October.

Address:
Skirethorns, Threshfield, Skipton, N. Yorks, BD23 5NU.

Tel:
(01756) 752412.

FAX: as phone. E-mail: enquiries@wood-nook.demon.co.uk.

Reservations:
Necessary for high season and B.H.s with £10 deposit.

Directions: From Skipton take B6265 to Threshfield, then B6160. After 50 yds turn left into Skirethorns Lane and follow signs for 600 yds, up narrow lane then 300 yds. O.S.GR: SD974641.

468 Street Head Caravan Park, Newbiggin, nr. Leyburn

Small, rural park with marvellous views.

Street Head is a no frills, simple site situated next door to the local hostelry. There are 50 privately owned caravan holiday homes arranged over two areas, while a separate, fairly level, hedged field with a circular gravel road provides 25 pitches for touring units. Each has hardstanding and 10A electricity. A further separate sloping field is for tents. At the entrance housed in traditional, stone buildings are reception and the sanitary facilities. These provide metered hot showers (20p), free hot water to washbasins, but metered for washing up sinks, washing machine and dryer, plus chemical disposal. Public telephone. Basic essentials and gas are available in reception (only open for two hours morning and afternoon in the main season, less in low season). However, Thoralby village (¼ mile) has a post office/general store and West Burton (1½ miles) is very pretty with a pub and shops. Bar snacks are served next door at the Street Head Inn. Aysgarth Falls are only 1½ miles and there are local markets at Hawes and Leyburn. Bicycle hire ½ mile, fishing 4 miles. Caravan storage available.

Charges 1999:
-- Per unit £9.00; hikers' tent £8.00; awning £2.00; electricity £2.00.
-- No credit cards.

Open:
1 March - end October.

Address:
Newbiggin,
Bishopdale, Leyburn,
North Yorkshire
DL8 3TE.

Tel:
(01969) 663472 or 663571.

Reservations:
Advised at B.Hs; contact site.

Directions: From A684 travelling west take the B6160 to Kettlewell just after Swinithwaite. Continue to Newbiggin past turning to West Burton (park is on right beside road). O.S.GR: SD998862.

472 Knight Stainforth Hall Caravan and Camping Park, nr. Settle

Traditional campsite in the Ribble Valley with outstanding scenery.

This park is located in the heart of the Yorkshire Dales and the whole area is a paradise for hill-walking, fishing and pot-holing. The camping area is on slightly sloping grass, sheltered by mature woodland in a very attractive setting. There are 100 touring pitches, 50 with electricity (10A) and 10 with hardstanding. A separate area houses 60 privately owned caravan holiday homes. Buildings near the farmhouse provide reception, a games/TV room and a shop (with basics). The sanitary facilities are in converted stone barns. One houses pre-mixed hot showers plus a room with dishwashing sinks, the other building providing WCs and washbasins, including three curtained cubicles for ladies, plus a laundry room (with washing machine and dryers) and chemical disposal. The facilities are practical rather than luxurious, but there is heating and a good supply of free hot water throughout. Refurbishment is planned. A gate leads from the bottom of the camping field giving access to the river bank where the Ribble bubbles over small waterfalls and rocks and whirls around deep pools where, we are told, campers do swim in warm weather. This is not fenced and children should be supervised, although it is a super location for a family picnic. Fishing permits and licenses are available from reception and one can fish for trout (or salmon when available). A partially fenced children's playground is on site. Settle is only 2 miles away, as is Giggleswick and its well known school. Train buffs will want to travel on the Settle-Carlisle railway with the famous Ribblehead Viaduct. The magic of the Dales National Park is on the doorstep and just off the A65 to the west of Settle at Felzor is the Dales Falconry and Conservation Centre. Bicycle hire on site, riding or golf 3 miles. Security barrier at entrance (£10 deposit).

Charges 1999:
-- Per unit incl. 2 adults £8.30; extra adult £2.00; extra child £1.00; backpacker £3.75; extra vehicle £1.00; electricity £1.70.
-- Weekly rate: 7 nights for the price of 6.
-- Deposit for amenity block key £2.
-- VAT included.
-- Credit cards accepted.

Open:
1 March - 31 October.

Address:
Little Stainforth, Settle, North Yorkshire
BD24 0DP.

Tel:
(01729) 822200.
FAX: (01729) 823387.
E-mail: knight-camp@aol.com.

Reservations:
Write or phone for details.

Directions: From Settle town centre, drive west towards Giggleswick. Ignore turning marked Stainforth and Horton, and after 200 yards turn right into Stackhouse Lane (signed Knight Stainforth). After 2 miles turn right at cross-roads. O.S.GR: SD815671.

Yorkshire

466 Woodhouse Farm Caravan & Camping Park, Winksley, nr. Ripon

Secluded family park on former working farm.

This unsophisticated park is only 6 miles from Ripon and about 4 miles from the World Heritage site of Fountains Abbey. It is a very rural park with a spacious feel and various pitching areas tucked away in woodland areas or around the edges of hedged fields with the centres left clear for children. There are hard roads and most of the 160 pitches have 10A electricity, 50 also with hardstanding. The farm buildings at the entrance house a reception and shop plus some of the sanitary facilities. These are supplemented by a separate block nearer the pitches which includes unisex showers (20p) that are roomy with shelf, curtain, etc. and open direct to the outside. Clean and functional, there is free hot water to vanity style washbasins (some in cabins) and for covered dishwashing sinks. A well equipped laundry is in the main building. Chemical disposal and motorcaravan services. There are 56 acres in total, 17½ devoted to the site and 20 acres of woodland for walks, etc. with a good area where dogs can run free. The 2½ acre fishing lake (day tickets from reception) is a big attraction and provides a pleasant area for picnics or walks. Children have a games room, table tennis, pool table and TV, with an additional pool table and TV tucked away for adults. Play equipment with rubber bases is placed at strategic points around the park. Riding 3 miles, golf 6 miles. The Yorkshire Dales of Nidderdale, Wharfedale, Wensleydale and Swaledale are all within easy reach and there are numerous villages around with attractive country inns supplying both food and drinks. The small historic city of Ripon has a beautiful cathedral. Woodhouse Farm is a quiet, secluded location from which many excursions can be made. As in most parts of the Dales, the peace is occasionally disturbed by passing jet aircraft, but happily not very often. Caravan storage available.

Charges 2000:
-- Per caravan and car or motorcaravan incl. 2 persons £7.50; tent £7.00; cyclist or hiker with tent £4.00; extra person (over 5 yrs) 75p; awning, pup tent £2.00; extra car £1.00 (on visitors car park); electricity £2.00.
-- Plus £1 on hook-up pitches at B.Hs.
-- Credit cards accepted.
-- VAT included.
Open:
1 March - 31 October.
Address:
Winksley, nr. Ripon, North Yorkshire HG4 3PG.
Tel:
(01765) 658309.
FAX: (01765) 658882.
E-mail: woodhouse-farm@btinternet.com.
Reservations:
Contact park.

Directions: From Ripon take Fountains Abbey - Pateley Bridge road (B6265). After approx. 3½ miles turn right to Grantley and then follow campsite signs for further 1-2 miles. O.S.GR: SE241715.

476 Riverside Meadows Country Caravan Park, Ripon

Busy park only a short walk from Ripon.

Riverside Meadows has a new name and new owners who have lots of experience in the caravan park world. All the facilities are being upgraded and brought up to their demanding standards. This is a rural park, although the approach to it belies that fact. The short approach from the main road passes a row of houses and a factory, but once they are passed, the park opens up before you and you are once again back in the countryside. There are plenty of caravan holiday homes but they are, on the whole, quite separate from the touring units. The pitches, practically all with electrical hook-ups, are mainly on gently sloping grass with just a few hardstandings. A meadow separates the park from the River Ure, a favourite place for strolling and fishing (licenses available) The tiled toilet block is new, with large, pre-set hot showers and washbasins set in vanity units. A baby room, dishwashing room, a fully fitted shower room for disabled visitors and a chemical disposal point are provided. There are also laundry facilities. Planned for the 2000 season are a new shop, reception, swimming pool and sauna, bar with snacks and a games room. A good dog walk is provided (max. 2 dogs per unit) which can be extended to a two mile round walk. There is a golf course within a mile and the delightful market town (city) of Ripon with its ancient cathedral is only 15 minutes walk. Close to Ripon is the Lightwater Valley theme park, and a little further are Fountains Abbey, Harrogate, Knaresborough, the Yorkshire Dales and Thirsk with its market and the new James Herriot centre. There is lots to see and do on and off the park for both families and couples.

Charges 1999:
-- Per unit incl. 4 persons £6.50 - £12.00; extra person £2.00; awning or extra car £2.00; dog (max. 2) £1.00; electricity £2.00.
-- No credit cards.
Open:
Early March - 31 Oct.
Address:
Ure Bank Top, Ripon, North Yorkshire HG4 1JD.
Tel:
(01765) 602964.
Reservations:
Made for min. 3 nights with £20 per week deposit.

see colour advert between pages 128/129

Directions: At the most northern roundabout on the Ripon bypass (A61), turn onto the A6108 signed Ripon, Masham and Leyburn. Go straight on at mini-roundabout and ark is signed. O.S.GR: SE317727.

North West Tourist Board

Cheshire, Lancashire, Merseyside, Greater Manchester
and the High Peaks of Derbyshire

Swan House, Swan Meadow Road,
Wigan Pier, Wigan WN3 5BB
Tel: (01942) 821222 Fax: (01942) 820002

The North West Tourist Board includes the counties of Cheshire, Greater Manchester, Lancashire and Merseyside, and the High Peak District of Derbyshire.

The north of England expresses itself in a scale and sternness not found in the south of the country, with some magnificent scenery. However, the area suffers from the legacy of the cotton industry and the effects of the Industrial Revolution.

Merseyside with Manchester and Liverpool was at the heart of the cotton business, expanded rapidly and then experienced economic decline. Now **Greater Manchester** is England's second largest urban area, boasting a very vibrant night life and, with Liverpool, brings together one of the most innovative music and arts scenes in Britain. Liverpool's once thriving docks are now clustered with museums and each pub, restaurant and corner claim a Beatles connection.

Cheshire has distinctive timber framed houses best seen in Chester, which is also a Roman city well worth visiting. Again much of the region was, and is still, industrial; cotton mills can be visited at Style.

The most well known resorts are **Lancashire's** Blackpool and Morecambe, still with a fairly strong working class flavour developed from the past. Brash and cheerful Blackpool with its three piers and dominated by the Tower, still attracts many visitors who go, not only to visit the Pleasure Beach with its 140 rides, but to see the famous 'illuminations' in September and October. Morecambe is more family orientated

The **Peak District** National Park wedged between industrial giants like Manchester, Sheffield, Nottingham and Stoke on Trent, serves as a playground to 17 million urban neighbours and receives over 26 million visitors a year.

---

528 Abbey Farm Caravan Park, Ormskirk

Quiet, well equipped, family park beside Abbey ruins with views over open farmland.

This is an ideal base for a longer stay with plenty of interest in the local area, including Ormskirk parish church, unusual for having both a tower and a spire. Market days are on Thursday and Saturday. The park is divided into small paddocks, one of which is for 44 privately owned seasonal units, one for tents, the others for touring units, plus a rally field for special events. The 60 touring pitches, all with electricity (10 or 16A), are on neatly mown level grass, separated by small shrubs and colourful flower borders. Some mature trees provide shade in parts. Children have a field to themselves, with a small adventure playground and space for ball games. A farm walk and a fishing lake have been created. A little well stocked shop shares space with reception, with butcher and baker calling twice weekly. The main, heated sanitary building is modern and spotless, provides WCs, washbasins, controllable hot showers with curtain and seat, hand-dryer and hairdryer, plus a dual-purpose family bathroom, which includes facilities for disabled people (£5 deposit for key, small charge for the non-disabled). A second smaller unit has WCs and washbasins, but no showers. Hot water is free. Dishwashing sinks are under cover at both units and a laundry room has washing machine, dryer, spinner, ironing board and airing cupboard (£5 key deposit). There is a small free lending library, with a good stock of tourist information. The site organises two events annually - a barbecue in early June and a Bonfire Night in November. Wigan Pier, the British Commercial Vehicle Museum, Aintree for the Grand National, the annual Beatles Festival or Southport Flower Show and Martin Mere Nature reserve are some of the attractions within easy reach. A member of the Countryside Discovery group.

Directions: From M6 junction 27 take A5209 (Parbold) road. After 5 miles turn left (just before garage) on B5240, and then first right into Hobcross Lane, following signs to site. O.S.GR: SD433099.

Charges 2000:
-- Per unit incl. 2 adults standard pitch £7.75 - £10.75, serviced pitch £10.75 - £12.00; extra adult £1.75; child (5-15 yrs) £1.00; small tent £5.00 - £6.50; hiker's tent incl. 1 adult £3.50 - £4.50; porch awning 50p, standard awning £1.00 - £1.50; extra car/trailer 50p; electricity £1.50 - £2.00.
-- Less 10% for 7 nights booked on or before arrival.
-- VAT included.
-- Credit cards accepted.

Open:
All year.

Address:
Dark Lane, Ormskirk, Lancashire L40 5TX.

Tel/Fax:
(01695) 572686.

Reservations:
Essential for high season or B.Hs. Min charge 3 nights for B.Hs. + £10 deposit.

Lancashire

529 Royal Umpire Caravan Park, Croston, nr Preston

Good, spacious park near coast and M6 motorway for overnight stops or longer stays.

Royal Umpire is owned by a well known major caravan dealer and has been improved and developed to a high standard. The entrance to the park is neat and tidy with the reception block, security barrier and an unusual sunken garden area. Comprising 58 acres with 200 pitches, most with 10A electricity, the top rows have neat hardstanding with TV and water connections and back onto high hedging and are connected by tarmac roads. The lower rows are a little less neat, with gravel roads and growing hedges or banks. There are 4 'super' pitches and around 50 pitches are available for longer stays. The two tiled toilet blocks, one beside reception, are excellent with well equipped showers, free hot water, and are kept spotlessly clean. There are fully equipped laundry and dishwashing sinks and special facilities for disabled visitors which are shared with baby facilities (entrance with key, £2 deposit). Chemical disposal and motorcaravan services. Among the general facilities are a licensed shop, large indoor recreation area with table tennis, pool and various games, a super adventure playground on bark, a field area for ball games and a leisure area consisting of an outdoor shuffle board, boules, chess and draughts overlooking the sunken garden. Outside information area. First aid room. Dog walk. Fishing on site, riding 2 miles. There is a separate field for rallies. A good choice of pubs serving bar or restaurant meals nearby. It is a tidy, well run site with a good welcome from the managers, Norman and Christine Roberts. Gates closed 11 pm. - 7 am. (outside parking provided). The first park to be awarded BS5750, this is reflected in the good management of the park. A member of the Best of British group.

Directions: From north use M6 exit 28 joining A49 going south (parallel to M6) for 2 miles. Then right across M6 on A581 to Croston (approx. 4 miles). From the south use M6 exit 27 onto A5209 but immediately right on B5250 and follow towards Eccleston, joining A581 at Newtown (approx. 5 miles). Site is clearly signed with wide entrance east of Croston. O.S.GR: SD505189.

Charges guide:
-- Per standard pitch incl. 2 persons, electricity and awning £7.70 - £12.35, `Royal' pitch £10.70 - £15.35, `Super Royal' £11.80 - £16.50; backpacker/cyclist £2.95; extra adult £2.35; extra child (5-16 yrs) £1.60; extra car, boat £1.10.
-- Less 10% for 7 nights pre-booked.
-- Mid-week stays less.
-- VAT included.
-- Credit cards accepted.

Open:
All year.

Address:
Southport Road,
Croston, nr. Preston,
Lancs PR5 7JB.

Tel:
(01772) 600257.
FAX: (01772) 600662.

Reservations:
Made with £5 per night deposit and £1 fee.

See colour feature for
`BEST of BRITISH'
between pages 96/97

530 Kneps Farm Holiday Park, Thornton Cleveleys, nr. Blackpool

Well established park with top class modern facilities, adjacent to Wyre Country Park.

This well managed park is still operated by the family who opened it in 1967, and it makes an excellent base from which to explore the area. A card operated barrier system flanks the reception building which also houses the well stocked shop. The small, fenced children's playground is nearby. The 70 marked and numbered touring pitches are generally on hardstandings with electricity (10A) available to most, and all are accessed from tarmac roads. There are also some grassy pitches and a separate area with 80 caravan holiday homes (78 privately owned, 2 for rent). The excellent, large, heated sanitary building has a main hall accessed from either end and is decorated with artificial plants. It is warm and inviting and has free hot water throughout. Along one side are ten individual family bathrooms, each providing a WC, basin and bath/shower. To the other side are separate toilet facilities with electric hand-wash units for men and women, a very well equipped room for disabled visitors, notice boards and a haircare/shaving centre. The building has external access to dishwashing sinks, baby/first aid room, laundry room with washing machines, dryers, spinner and ironing facility, and a chemical disposal point. A path leads through a gate at the back of the site into the Wyre Country Park. Just down the lane is a public slip-way and the Wyreside Ecology Centre. A list and map are provided of local services and amenities, including pubs, restaurants, takeaway, etc. Other local attractions include Marsh Mill Village with a restored windmill, the Freeport Shopping and Leisure village at nearby Fleetwood (discount shopping), and several bird-watching sites around the estuary and country park. Fishing ¼ mile, riding ½ mile, golf 2 miles.

Directions: From M55 junction 3, take A585 towards Fleetwood. Turn right at traffic lights by Shell station (for Thornton-Cleveleys), straight across next traffic lights, then right at the next roundabout by River Wyre Hotel. After one mile (past school) turn right into Stanah Road, continue into River Road and site entrance is ahead of you. O.S.GR: SD350430.

Charges 1999:
-- Per unit incl. 2 adults and 2 children £10.50 - £14.00; adult couple £8.50 - £11.00; single adult £6.50 - £8.00; extra adult £2.00 - £3.00; extra child £1.00 - £1.50; extra vehicle £1.00 - £2.00; electricity £1.75 - £2.20.
-- Special Senior Citizen rates.
-- Refundable deposit for barrier card and amenity unit key £10.
-- VAT included.
-- Credit cards accepted.

Open:
1 March - 15 November.

Address:
River Road, Thornton-Cleveleys, Lancashire FY5 5LR.

Tel:
(01253) 823632.
FAX (01253) 863967.

Reservations:
Essential for B.Hs. and peak season and illumina-tions, and made with £10 deposit.

531 Pipers Height Caravan and Camping Park, Peel, nr. Blackpool

Family site in open country with modern facilities, clubroom, bar and restaurant.

Only 4 miles south of Blackpool, this smaller, modestly priced site is a useful alternative to the larger holiday sites nearer to town, and is also convenient for visiting Lytham St Anne's with its attractive gardens. There are 140 pitches with electricity (10A) on concrete hardstandings and a further grassy area for tents which also has a small adventure type playground in one corner. Unlike many sites in this area, there are only 20 holiday homes at Pipers Height. Due to its rather flat and exposed location it can be windy at times, even with two grassy dividing banks topped with small trees and shrubs, and there are no dividing hedges between the pitches. The modern sanitary unit can be heated and provides WCs, washbasins in vanity units, hot showers with curtain and seat, with a separate unit for disabled visitors and a chemical disposal point. Hot water is free throughout. Refundable deposit is payable for the amenity building key and barrier card £4. There are dishwashing sinks and a laundry with washing machine and dryer. The main building houses the reception which controls the entry barrier, a small shop with gas and basic supplies (open mid-peak season), and a games room with pool table and TV. The large club room/lounge with bar and restaurant is open evenings in peak season and weekends at other times, providing disco or cabaret entertainment during peak season. Hourly bus service to Blackpool. Riding 1 mile, golf 3 miles. No commercial vehicles are accepted.

Directions: From M6 junction 32 take M55 towards Blackpool. Leave at junction 4, taking first left off roundabout, then right at traffic lights into Peel Road, where site is signed. O.S.GR: SD355327.

Charges 2000:
-- Per unit incl. up to 4 adults £11.00; extra adult £2.00; child (3-12 yrs) £1.00; extra car £2.00; awning £1.50; electricity £1.50.
-- Special half price rates for low season.
-- VAT included.
-- No credit cards.
Open:
1 March - 30 November.
Address:
Peel Road,
Peel, Blackpool,
Lancashire FY4 5JT.
Tel:
(01253) 763767.
Reservations:
Essential for B.Hs, peak season and the illuminations (Sept/Oct) and made with £10 deposit.

532 Bridge House Marina and Caravan Park, Nateby, Garstang

Small, friendly park on bank of Lancaster Canal, close to M6; for caravans, motorcaravans and trailer tents only.

A useful little park making a good stopover close to the M6 and A6, Bridge House is also only 12 miles from Morecambe and 15 from Blackpool. Adjacent to the Marina (with joint reception/shop) and the Lancaster Canal, the park has 50 pitches on flat grass, all marked but with nothing between them; giving a pleasant open feel about the place. Caravans, motorcaravans and trailer tents are taken, but not other tents, with 32 hardstandings and 37 16A electrical connections (note: no groundsheets). It can become full, especially at B.Hs. The heated, tiled toilet block has washbasins set in flat surfaces, well spaced out with free hot showers, hairdryer, dishwashing room (free hot water) and laundry room with washing machine and dryer, plus hot water (10p). Shop with provisions, gas and boat accessories. Public phone. Some children's play equipment and large grass play area. No other on-site amenities but pub with meals and shops quite close. Boat slipway on site, fishing nearby, golf 1½miles. Dogs are permitted (on leads) with a pleasant exercise area on the old railway line behind the site. Caravan storage.

Directions: Garstang is on the A6 between exits 32 and 33 of the M6. Follow A6 Garstang bypass and turn off west by The Flag pub. After 20 yds turn right into Nateby crossing lane. O.S.GR: SD483458.

Charges 1999:
-- Per unit £6.50; awning 80p; porch awning 50p; electricity £1.50.
-- VAT included.
-- Credit cards accepted.
Open:
All year except 5 Jan - 28 Feb.
Address:
Nateby, Garstang, nr. Preston, Lancs PR3 0JJ.
Tel:
(01995) 603207.
FAX: (01995) 601612.
Reservations:
Made for any length without deposit.

Nateby, Garstang, Nr. Preston, Lancashire, PR3 0JJ

This small, quiet and pleasant touring site overlooking the Bowland Hills is family owned and operated, ideally situated for Blackpool, Morecambe and the Lake District.

The Park caters for fifty tourers and is adjacent to our Boating Marina alongside the Lancaster Canal. We are ideally situated for the holidaymaker wishing to spend a holiday in the country or a night halt for people travelling north or south.

★ Electric hook-up
★ Shop, Laundry room
★ Children's play area

★ Dogs welcome on lead
★ Fishing permits available
★ Pony trekking by arrangement

Lancashire

534 Old Hall Caravan Park, Capernwray, Carnforth

Newly developed, secluded, small touring park in woodland clearing (no tents).

A half mile woodland driveway (tarmac) leads you from the lane to this delightful park with its 38 touring pitches, nestling in a sheltered clearing with bluebells in the woods and a small stream nearby. It is a site for those who like peace and quiet, walking, cycling or bird-watching, with 80 acres of woodland to wander around and all manner of wildlife to observe. Although this site also has a holiday home park of 140 units adjacent, it is so well screened you would hardly know it was there. All the touring pitches are on gravel hardstanding with electricity (10A) and TV hook-ups; no tents are taken. The excellent, modern sanitary building can be heated, provides free hot water throughout and has a keypad entry system. It provides WCs, vanity style washbasins with soap dispensers and hand-dryers, controllable hot showers with curtain and seat, and free hairdryers. There are covered dishwashing sinks outside, a laundry room with washing machine, dryer and iron, and a dual purpose family room with facilities for disabled visitors, plus a chemical disposal point. Other facilities on site include a good selection of tourist information, public telephone, a fenced children's playground and a small football field for ball games. No shop but gas is available and there is a daily delivery of milk, eggs and papers. Shops, pubs and restaurants are in Carnforth (3 miles). The site is ideally located for touring the Trough of Bowland, Lake District and Yorkshire Dales, with Morecambe, Lancaster, Kirkstone Pass, plus numerous castles, gardens and other tourist attractions all within an easy hour's drive. Caravan storage.

Charges 2000:
-- Per unit all inclusive £10.00 - £12.00; awning £1.00 - £2.00; electricity £2.00.
-- No credit cards.
-- VAT included.

Open:
1 March - 31 October.

Address:
Capernwray, Carnforth, Lancashire LA6 1AD.

Tel:
(01524) 733276.
FAX (01524) 734488.
E-mail: oldhall@ charis.co.uk.

Reservations:
Advised all year because of limited touring pitch availability; contact park.

Directions: From M6 junction 35 take link road signed Over Kellet, turning left on B6254. At Over Kellet village green turn left (signed Capernwray), and follow road for 1½ miles. Old Hall is signed on the right; continue up a half mile drive to site. O.S.GR: SD530720.

535 Holgates Caravan Park, Silverdale, nr. Carnforth

Attractive site in craggy, part-wooded, hillside location, with views over Morecambe Bay.

This is a high quality park in an outstanding location. It takes 70 touring units, with 339 privately owned caravan holiday homes and 11 to rent located in woodland away from the tourist pitches. There are just 5 grassy pitches for tents and the remaining 65 large touring pitches, all with electricity (16A), free TV connection, individual drainage and water points are on gravel hardstandings. Two modern, heated, sanitary buildings are built from local stone and have top quality fittings, providing push-button hot showers and private cubicles with WC and washbasin. Dishwashing sinks and chemical disposal points are at each unit. There is excellent separate provision for disabled visitors at one unit, with a reserved pitch and parking bay adjacent. Hot water is free throughout. The main complex with reception and entrance barrier, was redeveloped for the '99 season. It provides a well stocked supermarket, boutique, launderette, games room with pool table and video games, lounge bar, restaurant with good value meals and a terrace with views over the bay, plus a new heated indoor swimming pool (17 x 17 m) with a spa pool, steam room and sauna (all free to campers, no unaccompanied under 10s). There are good changing rooms, a baby room and lockers and a lifeguard on duty. Children have a choice of two adventure playgrounds and plenty of space for ball games. Also on site is a small but challenging golf course (75p per person). Facilities may be limited mid-week in January and early February. Opportunities for riding, cycling, walking and fishing all within 7 miles. Morecambe or Lancaster are just 12 miles and Kendal is 15 miles. Gas available. Note: Admission restrictions include no unaccompanied under 18's or single sex groups, no dangerous breeds of dog or commercial vehicles. Minimum stays apply for all B.H. weekends (contact park for details).

Charges 1999:
-- Per unit incl. 2 adults and 2 children £9.00 - £17.75; extra adult £4.00; extra child (5-17 yrs) £2.00; awning/pup tent £2.00; electricity (16A) £2.50.
-- VAT included.
-- Credit cards accepted.

Open:
All year except 7 Nov. - 21 Dec. incl.

Address:
Middlebarrow Plain, Cove Road, Silverdale, Carnforth, Lancashire LA5 0SH.

Tel:
(01524) 701508.
FAX: (01524) 701580.

Reservations:
Essential for B.Hs and peak season; made with £10 deposit for 1 or 2 nights, £20 for longer.

Directions: From traffic lights in centre of Carnforth take road to Silverdale under low bridge (12' 9"). After 1 mile turn left signed Silverdale and after 2½ miles over a level crossing carry on and then turn right at T junction. Follow the Holgates signs from here watching for left fork followed by right fork (narrow roads). O.S.GR: SD460755.

148

Cumbria Tourist Board

Ashleigh, Holly Road, Windermere LA23 2AQ
Tel: (015394) 44444 Fax: (015394) 44041
E-mail: mail@cumbria-tourist-board.co.uk
Internet: www.golakes.co.uk

Cumbria, perhaps better known as the Lake District, is unique in its richness and variety of landscape, climate, culture and history. At its centre is the Lake District National Park with a core of rugged fells, gleaming lakes and peaceful valleys providing the ideal country for sailing, walking, climbing and cycling.

The 16 lakes all have their own unique charm and character, from Ullswater with its sailing boats, to Windermere with its powerboats and water-skiers. Walks range from gentle strolls by lakes or through ancient woodlands to long distance routes or the climb to the summit of Scafell Pike, at 3,210 ft. England's highest mountain.

To the West of Cumbria are the quietest lakes and valleys, a long coastline of beaches and high cliffs and the historic ports of Whitehaven and Maryport with developments for visitors.

East of the Lake District is the Eden Valley, a lush area of rich farmland, meandering rivers and quiet, winding lanes linking pretty villages.

To the North lies Hadrian's Wall and the border with Scotland where a dramatic and often violent history is etched into the face of Carlisle and the borderlands around about.

Evidence of Cumbria's rich heritage can be found in the historic houses, castles, museums and the splendid gardens of the county. It's literary legacy ranges from William Wordsworth , Samuel Taylor Coleridge, John Ruskin to the popular children's writer's namely Beatrix Potter and Arthur Ransom of Swallows and Amazons Fame. Not to mention Alfred Wainwright creator of the wonderful hand drawn Wainwright guides to the Lakeland fells and many other books about Cumbria.

New Millennium Developments

Theatre by the Lake, Keswick, opened 19 Aug 99. The biggest new attraction in Cumbria and the only professional performing theatre in the county

Rheged – Upland Kingdom Discovery Centre, opens Easter 2000. The centre-piece will be a large format film taking visitors on a journey from the Dark Ages and King Arthur to the present day.

The Rum Story, due to open Easter 2000. This new attraction will tell the story of Whitehaven's role as the UK's main rum Import centre in the 1800.

552 Skelwith Fold Caravan Park, Ambleside

Spacious, family owned park for caravans, motorcaravans and trailer tents only in southern Lake District.

Skelwith Fold was developed in the extensive grounds of a country estate taking advantage of the wealth of mature trees and shrubs. The 300 privately owned caravan holiday homes and 150 touring pitches are absorbed into this unspoilt natural environment, sharing it with red squirrels and other wildlife in several discrete areas branching off the central, mile long main driveway. Touring pitches are on gravel hardstanding and metal pegs will be necessary for awnings. Electric hook-ups (10A) and basic amenities are available in all areas. Eight toilet blocks, well situated to serve all areas, provide free hot showers and all usual facilities including laundry, drying and ironing rooms. There is a well stocked, licensed self-service shop, together with a store for gas, battery charging and caravan spares and accessories. Public telephones. Whilst there is an adventure play area, most youngsters and indeed their parents will find endless pleasure exploring over 90 acres of wild woodland and, if early risers, it is possible to see deer, foxes, etc. taking their breakfast in the almost hidden tarn deep in the woods. It is a fascinating site at any time of the year, but beautiful in the spring with wild daffodils, bluebells and later rhododendrons and azaleas. Family recreational area with picnic tables and goal posts. Reservation is essential for July, August and B.Hs. It is 1½ miles to Ambleside village and pubs within walking distance.

Charges guide:
-- Per caravan or trailer tent £10.00; motor-caravan £9.50 (both + £1.00 in August); awning £2.50; extra car or boat £4.00; electricity £1.50 (or £1.75 before 1 May, after 30 Sept).
-- Discounts for weekly or monthly stays.
-- Credit cards accepted.
-- VAT included.

Open:
1 March - 15 November.

Address:
Ambleside, Cumbria LA22 0HX.

Tel:
(015394) 32277.
FAX: (015394) 34344.

Reservations:
Essential for July/Aug and B.Hs. and made for min. 3 days with £10 deposit.

Directions: From Ambleside take the A593 in the direction of Coniston. Pass through Clappergate and on the far outskirts watch for the B5286 to Hawkshead on the left. Park is clearly signed approx. 1 mile down this road on the right. O.S.GR: NY358028.

Cumbria

553 Walls Caravan and Camping Park, Ravenglass

Small, neat, well equipped park in west Cumbria.

Set in 5 acres of existing woodland amongst a variety of mature trees, Walls was once part of the large Pennington Estate. It has space for 25 touring units on hardstanding pitches with a grass verge for awnings (plus 25 seasonal units). A circular gravel road provides access and all pitches have electrical hook-ups (10A). A small grass area at the top and back of the park provides an attractive spot for 10 tents overlooking fields. An attractively designed central courtyard complex includes the owner's home, reception with tourist information, `shop' (only a few basic necessities, plus gas) and a good modern toilet block with all the usual amenities and H&C water throughout. This is very well kept and has a comfortable feeling often missing in British campsite toilet blocks. There is also a laundry room, with baby bath, washing machine, tumble and spin dryers, iron and board and a separate room with dishwashing facilities and further tourist information. Chemical disposal facilities and motorcaravan service point. All is excellently maintained by Keith and Stephanie Bridges, who have used the site since it was first developed and now own it and provide a very warm welcome. Dogs are permitted but must be exercised off the park and 'poop-scoops' used. Fishing and bicycle hire 3 miles, boat launching 1½ miles, golf 6 miles. Winter caravan storage. It is a useful site for all sorts of walking - estuary, river or fell - or to explore the Cumbria coast with its Roman connections, the western Lake District or to enjoy the Ravenglass and Eskdale Miniature Railway. The small village of Ravenglass, a single, cottage lined street, is within walking distance and does provide a pub and holds a Charter Fair in June to coincide with the Three Peaks Race.

Directions: Park is just off A595 (between Egremont and Millom) on road into village of Ravenglass. O.S.GR: SD096965.

Charges 2000:
-- Per caravan, frame or trailer tent incl. 2 adults £8.50, motorcaravan £8.00; medium tent (2 persons) £7.50; small tent (1 person) £3.50; extra person £1.00; child under 16 yrs free; awning, extra car or dog 50p; electricity £1.50.
-- No credit cards.

Open:
1 March - 15 November.

Address:
Ravenglass, Cumbria CA18 1SR.

Tel:
(01229) 717250.

Reservations:
Contact park.

561 Waterfoot Caravan Park, Pooley Bridge

Quiet family park for caravans and motorcaravans only.

Waterfoot is set in 22 acres of partially wooded land, developed in the fifties from a private estate. The 126 private caravan holiday homes are quite separate from the 57 touring pitches. Lake Ullswater is only about 400 yds away and a half mile stroll through bluebell woods brings you to the village of Pooley Bridge. Here are a post office/general store, hotels and restaurants. Waterfoot's touring pitches are arranged very informally in a large clearing. Most are level, there are some hardstandings and all have 10A electricity. The heated toilet block is close by and contains some vanity style washbasins with others in large cubicles which also contain free adjustable showers. These are activated by a button on the wall outside the cubicle and give 5 minutes showering time. A hairdressing area has mirrors, shelves and free hair dryers. The dishwashing room is large, light and airy with free hot water and the laundry has a washing machine, dryer and spin dryer, plus a free iron. In a separate building is chemical disposal (with flush). Close to the pitches is a large fenced field with play equipment to suit all ages and goal posts for football. A small shop sells basics, gas and newspapers. The bar (with strictly enforced, separate family room) opens weekend evenings in low season and every evening in high season. This is in a large, imposing mansion which has been in the past a family home then a golf hotel. Dogs are accepted with a small dog walk provided and there are public footpaths straight from the park. Fishing close, boat slipway or riding 1½ miles, golf 5 miles. The regular lake steamer service calls at Pooley Bridge, the Ullswater yacht club is only 10 minutes drive and the market town of Penrith is 5 miles. The historic house and gardens of Dalemain are a short walk.

Directions: From M6 junction 40, take A66 signed Keswick. After 0.5 miles at roundabout take A592 signed Ullswater and site is on right after 4 miles. O.S.GR: NY460245.

Charges 1999:
-- Per unit £11.50, with electricity £13.00.
-- VAT included.
-- No credit cards.

Open:
1 March - 31 October.

Address:
Pooley Bridge, Penrith, Cumbria CA11 0JF.

Tel:
(017684) 86302. FAX (017684) 86728.

Reservations:
Essential for B.Hs and summer holidays; contact the Warden.

555 Limefitt Park, Windermere

Well managed and popular Lake District park.

Limefitt Park is owned and run by the Whiteley family who also own Fallbarrow Park and is centrally situated for the southern lakes. It has fine views and walks, with the beck running alongside. With various active pursuits nearby and some evening entertainment, it is very well managed and is for families or couples (no organised groups of young people). The 145 pitches for touring caravans are good and flat, with hardstanding, electricity (10A) and water, with cars parked at an angle on further hardstanding in front. The remainder of the park is on flat or slightly sloping grass with some terracing and shade provided by trees with numbered pitches for tents or more caravans or motorcaravans. The ground by the beck has been developed for 45 log cabins (for private sale) and there are 20 caravan holiday homes (9 for hire), plus another field for 20 long stay caravans. The sanitary facilities consist of one large, central block for the tenting area and a smaller block for the caravan area, accessed by combination locks. Both are of excellent quality, amongst the best we have seen and are well maintained and fully tiled with free hot water and modern fittings including oval washbasins, with mixer taps, flat surfaces, mirrors and side lighting. There are toddlers' rooms with half-size bath and changing facilities, covered washing-up sinks and chemical disposal. Well stocked supermarket and licensed bar lounge with real ales, bar meals and weekly entertainment, both open all season, and takeaway. This should give good coverage all season. Campers' kitchen (metered), gas supplies, launderette and motorcaravan service point. Sporting activities include walking and fishing, and local facilities, including bicycle hire, can be booked from the park. Riding 3 miles, golf 5 miles. Games room with many machines. Play field and adventure playground on grass by the river and small beach area with picnic tables. American motorhomes, dogs or boats are not accepted. No single persons, no groups and no rallies are accepted; to quote, "in order to preserve Limefitt's unique atmosphere and provide restful nights ... we accept families and couples only." The park is popular for a long season, reservation is advisable.

Directions: Limefitt Park lies 2½ miles north up the A592 from its junction with the A591 north of Windermere. O.S.GR: NY416030.

Charges 2000:
-- Per unit incl. 2 persons, electricity and TV hook-up £9.50 - £13.00; tent £9.00 - £12.50; extra adult £2.00 - £2.50; child (2-14 yrs) £1.00 - £1.25; awning, pup tent, trailer or 2nd car £2.00 - £2.50.
-- Max. charge 1 family per pitch £11.50 - £15.50 (excl. supplements).
-- Prices are higher for stays not booked in advance.
-- VAT included.
-- Credit cards accepted.

Open:
31 March - 30 October.

Address:
Windermere, Cumbria LA23 1PA.

Tel:
(015394) 32300 ext. 49. FAX: (015394) 32848.

Reservations:
Made with full payment at time of booking; cancellation insurance available.

see colour advert between pages 128/129

556 Sykeside Camping Park, Patterdale, nr. Penrith

Touring park in attractive Lake District location for tents and a few motorcaravans.

This small, family owned site, set in the northern lakes area and surrounded by fells, is ideal for active holidays with walking or climbing on high hills, and the small lake of Brotherswater ¼ mile away. It would also be useful for a touring holiday and is a little away from the busiest areas. It takes 100 tents which could include a few motorcaravans, but no caravans, on flat grass in the valley floor. Pitches are not marked and campers arrange themselves. Reservations are advisable for peak times. There are 16 electrical connections (5/10A). The stone-built building, an original barn, near the entrance, 200 m. from the field, houses all the facilities, including the washing and toilet block which has washbasins with free hot water (one private cubicle in ladies' and make-up section) and hot showers (20p); a little basic but updating is planned. Chemical disposal, small launderette and dishwashing room. The self-service shop doubles as reception, with camping equipment, gas and an ice-pack service. Public telephone. A cosy, licensed bar and restaurant serves breakfast (8.15-10 am) and evening meals (6-9 pm, bar open 5-11 pm). Bunkhouse accommodation is provided for 30 persons in various groupings. As well as fell and hill walking, fishing is available nearby. Bicycle hire 3 miles, riding 8 miles, golf 10 miles. The family also own the Brotherswater Inn, 200 m. from the site overlooking the fells which is open all day including meals and has rooms to let.

Directions: On west side of A592 road about 2 miles south of Patterdale, which lies at the southwestern end of Ullswater. O.S.GR: NY396005.

Charges 2000:
-- Per adult £2.00 - £2.50; child (4-14 yrs) £1.30 - £1.50; car or m/cycle £2.00 - £2.50; motor-caravan, tent or awning £2.00 - £2.50; dog £1.00; electricity £1.50.
-- Min. charge for motor-caravan £5 per night.
-- VAT included.
-- Credit cards accepted.

Open:
All year.

Address:
Brotherswater, Patterdale, Penrith, Cumbria CA11 0NZ.

Tel:
(017684) 82239. FAX: (017684) 82558.

Reservations:
Made with £10 per pitch deposit with balance on arrival. Easter or Spr. B.H. - min. 3 and 4 days respectively.

see colour advert between pages 128/129

Cumbria

554 Fallbarrow Park, Bowness, Windermere

Quality park with Lake Windermere frontage, for caravans and motorcaravans only.

Fallbarrow Park is most attractively situated alongside Lake Windermere with a lake frontage of about 600 m; one can stroll among the lawns and gardens near the lake. Founded in the mid-fifties by the Whiteley family, Fallbarrow is still owned and managed by them. Over the years improvements have been made, and each year finds new projects – at present, 'green' issues, for example, recycling, biodegradable products, nest boxes, etc. The major part of the park is occupied by seasonal holiday homes – about 70 for letting and 180 private ones. There are also 72 level touring pitches in two areas. The 'Glade" area amongst tall trees has pitches all with hardstanding and electric hook-up (10/16A), the `Lake' area (not actually by the lake, but some pitches have lake views) with 38 fenced or hedged, fully serviced pitches including TV aerial connections. The park is very popular and reservations are essential for June - Sept. and B.Hs. American motorhomes are accepted by prior arrangement. There is a motorcaravan service point and the site is well lit. Two excellent toilet blocks serve the touring sections (access by combination locks). With top quality fittings and heating when required, they provide vanity style washbasins, free controllable showers, make up and haircare areas and a baby room. There are dishwashing sinks and a very well equipped laundry which also houses a freezer. The Boathouse pub has a spacious and comfortable lounge with bar meals and snacks, and an attractive outdoor terrace. TV lounge with occasional entertainment and a large games room with pool table and games machines. The supermarket is very well stocked. Gas supplies. Public phones. Dogs are accepted (only one per booking) with an exercise area provided. Reception is smart and comfortable, with lots of tourist information. The site has a boat park with winter storage and two launching ramps and three jetties can cater for craft up to 18 ft in length. Fishing on site. Bicycle hire 1 mile, riding 2 miles, golf 3 miles. The centre of Bowness is only a short walk and facilities for pony trekking and numerous visitor attractions are close.

Directions: Park is beside the A592 road just north of Bowness town centre. O.S.GR: SD401971.

Charges 2000:
-- Per unit inclusive: Glade pitch £11.35 - £15.95, Lake pitch £13.25 - £18.65; awning £2.95 - £4.00; boat (max 18 ft.) £10.00; car-top dinghy £5.00; sailboard or canoe £2.00; second car £2.50.
-- VAT included.
-- Credit cards accepted.
Open:
10 March - 4 November.
Address:
Rayrigg Road, Windermere, Cumbria LA23 3DL.
Tel:
(015394) 44422, ext. 49. FAX: (015394) 88736.
Reservations:
Made for 3 nights min. (7 at Spring B.H.). Payment in full at time of booking.

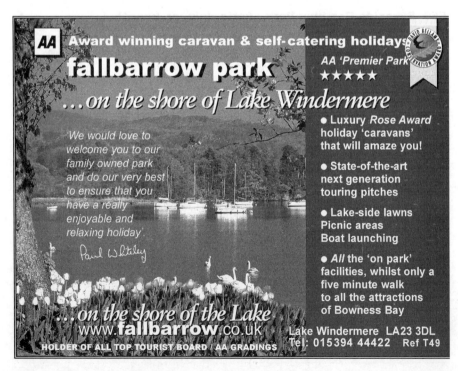

562 Cove Camping Park, Watermillock, nr. Penrith

Quiet, peaceful park with views over Lake Ullswater.

Cove Camping is a delightful small site, some of the 50 pitches having great views over Lake Ullswater. The grass is well trimmed, there are speed ramps and the site is well lit. The tiled toilet blocks are immaculate and heated in low seasons, providing adjustable showers, some washbasins in cabins and, for ladies, a hairdressing area. Dividing the ladies' and men's facilities is a foyer containing a freezer, coffee machine and tourist information. The laundry has a washing machine, dryer and an iron, there are washing up sinks in a separate area and chemical disposal. Gas supplies. At the top of the park are 15 level pitches with electric hook-ups and one hardstanding. The rest of the site is quite sloping. Rubbish and recycling bins are hidden behind larch lap fencing. Small, grass based play area. Fishing 1½ miles, riding 3 miles, golf 6 mile, bicycle hire 7 miles (will deliver). Dogs are welcome with two fields for exercise. A shop is near. The park is well situated for walking. The road up from the A592 is narrow, but a self imposed one way system is generally adhered to and the warden will advise on a different way to leave the site.

Directions: From A66 Penrith - Keswick road, take A592 south, signed Ullswater. Turn right at Brackenrigg Inn (site signed) and follow road uphill to park on left (this road is narrow). O.S.GR: NY431236.

Charges 2000:
-- Per person (over 3 yrs) £1.80 - £1.90; caravan, motorcaravan or tent £3.60 - £3.80; pup tent or awning £1.80 - £1.90; car, boat or m/cycle £1.80 - £1.90; dog 50p.
-- No credit cards.

Open:
Easter - 31 October.

Address:
Ullswater, Watermillock, nr. Penrith, Cumbria CA11 0LS.

Tel:
(017684) 86549.

Reservations:
Made with deposit (caravans or motorcaravans £10, tents £5); contact park.

551 The Larches Caravan Park, Mealsgate, nr. Carlisle

Peaceful, quality, family run park with excellent sanitary facilities, for adults only.

Mealsgate and The Larches lie on the Carlisle – Cockermouth road, a little removed from the hectic centre of the Lakes, yet with easy access to it (and good views towards it) and to other attractions situated near – the Western Borders, Northumberland, etc. The park takes 73 touring units of any type with 100 privately owned holiday leisure homes. Touring pitches are in different grassy areas with tall, mature trees, shrubs and accompanying wildlife. Some are sloping and irregular, others on marked hardstandings, with electricity (10A), water and waste water connections. The sanitary blocks are a feature of the site, particularly one of outstanding quality consisting of en-suite facilities for both sexes. The block also includes a purpose designed unit for disabled people of either sex and can be heated. The second block is also excellent, fully tiled with the ladies' wash-basins in cubicles and men's set in flat surfaces, and controllable hot showers. Chemical disposal facilities. A well stocked shop, includes gas, camping accessories and off-licence, with events in the district displayed in the window. Amenities include table tennis, TV room in a summer-house, camping kitchen with metered power to cooker, microwave and breakfast bar, laundry room and a telephone. A small indoor, heated swimming pool has been added (small charge). Caravan storage. Everyone is loaned comprehensive tourist information. Fishing 8 miles, bicycle hire 7 miles, riding 10 miles, golf 3½ miles. There are bus routes to Carlisle and Keswick, walks from the park and good restaurants nearby. The Elliotts provide a warm welcome at this peaceful, well organised park, which is an ideal haven for couples - only adult visitors are accepted.

Directions: Park entrance is south off A595 (Carlisle - Cockermouth) road just southwest of Mealsgate. O.S.GR: NY206415.

Charges 1999:
-- Per unit incl. 2 adults £7.00 - £9.00; backpacker £4.00 - £5.00; extra person, awning or car £1.00; electricity £2.00.
-- Discounts for senior citizens and bookings over 7 nights.
-- VAT included.
-- No credit cards.

Open:
1 March - 31 October.

Address:
Mealsgate, nr. Carlisle, Cumbria CA5 1LQ.

Tel:
(016973) 71379.
FAX: (016973) 71782.

Reservations:
Made with £1 per night deposit, balance on arrival.

THE LARCHES
Caravan Park

Mealsgate, Cumbria Tel: (016973) 71379

Adults Only

The Larches, where a warm and friendly welcome awaits you on this family-run Park, offering not only the tranquillity of a quiet rural setting but also the kind of facilities which offer a relaxed and refreshing holiday. The toilet block houses suites of beautifully tiled rooms, each complete with shower, toilet, hairdrier, shower point and vanity unit. A unisex unit for disabled persons is also available with plenty of space for a wheelchair and a helper if necessary. The well stocked shop supplies everything from food to camping accessories. Small indoor heated swimming pool (small charge). The park provides an ideal touring base. **ADAC**

Cumbria

557 Wild Rose Park, Appleby-in-Westmorland

Well organised, neat park in the Eden Valley with excellent facilities and holiday homes.

The entrance to Wild Rose is very inviting with its well mown grass, trim borders and colourful flower displays. The first impression is of well maintained facilities and the feeling that nothing but the best will do. This is reflected throughout the park and each year the owners find something new to provide or something to upgrade. There are three touring areas, two with their own warden to ensure that everything is always spick and span. The top areas have been upgraded to provide neat, level, fully serviced pitches. Separated by newly planted hedges (plus a small fence until the hedge grows), many have views. The lower touring area on a slightly sloping field caters for both tents and caravans. Next to this are six individual 'super' pitches which are fenced or hedged with full services, some including patio, barbecue, picnic table, grass area and satellite TV connections. Owner occupied caravan holiday homes occupy their own areas and do not intrude. The final touring field is for 60 tents, gently sloping with an oval roadway linked to the large field or ball game area with its special viewpoint.

The three toilet blocks (two heated) are of excellent quality, well maintained and kept spotlessly clean. Nothing is forgotten – washbasins are mainly in private cubicles, showers are free and there are hair washing basins, hairdryers, baby baths and bottle warmers, soap and hand dryers, plus full facilities for disabled visitors, a fully equipped laundry with washing lines and drying rooms, and chemical disposal. The kidney shaped outdoor swimming pool has a landscaped sunbathing area on grass and flagstones, with sunbeds, tables and chairs. Heated mid-May - mid-Sept and open 10 am.- 10 pm, this is a popular, free attraction. The shop is exceptionally well stocked (Easter - Nov) and the licensed restaurant (with takeaway) has a conservatory/coffee lounge. Sunday lunches are very popular. Amenities for children include a well kept, fenced play area with safety bases, an indoor playroom for under fives, a games room with table tennis and video games for older children and two TV rooms, one with a cinema style screen. Bicycle hire, BMX track, half court tennis and a field for ball games on site. Dogs are accepted (excluding dangerous breeds) with a small dog walk. New 'state of the art' entrance barrier and intercom (pass from reception with deposit). Wild Rose has a fully deserved, excellent reputation, which the owners strive to maintain and improve. Nothing is overlooked from recycling bins, electric dust carts to keep the noise down, 'sac-o-matic' special bags in the dog walk and cycle racks placed around the park. Motorcaravan service point. Gas available. Caravan storage. In a peaceful rural situation, the Yorkshire Dales and the Lake District are within easy reach and there are many public footpaths in the area. Fishing, golf or riding within 4 miles. A member of the Best of British group.

Directions: Park is signed south off B6260 road 1½ miles southwest of Appleby. Follow signs to park, in the direction of Ormside. O.S.GR: NY697165.

Charges 1999:
-- Per unit incl. 2 persons: standard pitch £7.50 - £12.40; super pitch £12.50 - £25.00; walker or cyclist £3.00; extra person (over 4 yrs) £1.50; awning, extra car, toilet or pup tent £1.80; electricity summer £2.00, winter £2.50; dog 50p.
-- 10% discount for 7 nights or more.
-- Special winter or long-stay rates.
-- VAT included.
-- Credit cards accepted.

Open:
All year.

Address:
Ormside,
Appleby-in-Westmorland,
Cumbria CA16 6EJ.

Tel:
(017683) 51077.
FAX: (017683) 52551.
E-mail: mail@wildrose.co.uk.

Reservations:
Essential for B.Hs and July/Aug; made with deposit of £5 per night + £2 fee, remainder on arrival. Min. 3 nights at B.Hs.

560 Pennine View Caravan and Camping Park, Kirkby Stephen

Small, strictly touring site, suitable for night halts.

Pennine View was opened in 1990 and is built on reclaimed land from a former railway goods yard. This 'strictly touring' park has a very attractive rockery at the entrance and the whole site is very neat, tidy and well maintained. All very level, numbered pitches with gravel hardstanding are arranged around the perimeter, with grass pitches in the centre. The pitches are of a good size, some being especially large, and are all are supplied with electric hook-ups (16A). One end of the park adjoins the River Eden with steps leading down from the site to huge projecting stone slabs on the river bank (good for sunbathing). There are trout but a licence is needed for fishing. The modern toilet block is built of local stone and is accessed by a digital keypad (as is the phone box). There are individual wash cubicles and spacious free showers. Hair dryers (20p) but also sockets for the visitors' own equipment. A deep sink is provided to bath the baby in, and both ladies and men have a large unit for disabled visitors with a toilet, washbasin, shower, grab handles and shaver points. Well equipped laundry room with washing machine, dryer, spin dryer and iron and washing up sinks with free hot water, outside but under cover. There is no shop but gas is sold in reception and the hotel nearby offers bar meals and takeaway pizzas. Kirkby Stephen is 1 mile and, although only a small town, its shops should fill most needs. Dogs are accepted (to be exercised off site). Large American motorhomes are not accepted.

Charges 2000:
-- Per adult £3.60 - £3.80; child (4-15 yrs) £1.40; pitch £1.00 - £2.00; extra car £1.00; electricity £1.50 - £2.00; cyclist or backpacker £3.60 - £4.00 per person.
-- VAT included.

Open:
1 March - 31 October.

Address:
Station Road, Kirkby Stephen, Cumbria CA17 4SZ.

Tel:
(017683) 71717.

Reservations:
Made with £5 deposit; min. 3 days Easter and B.Hs..

Directions: Park is on the A685, under a mile south of Kirkby Stephen. Turn left at small site sign opposite the Croglin Castle hotel. Site is 50 yds on right. O.S. GR: NY772075.

559 Westmorland Caravan Site, Tebay, nr. Penrith

Ideal stopover on the M6, for caravans and motorcaravans only.

This caravan park is the ideal stopover for anyone heading either north or south, near the M6 motorway, but far enough away for the traffic noise not to be too disturbing. The 41 level touring pitches, most with electrical hook-up (10/16A), are on gravel and divided into bays of about six or seven units. These are backed by grassy banks alive with rabbits and birds - a long list in the office describes the large variety of birds to be seen on the site and the manager, Mrs Scales, is only too pleased to discuss them with you. The heated toilet block is kept very clean. Showers are pre-set and coin operated (10p), all other hot water is free, there are sinks for clothes and dishwashing, a laundry with washing machine, spin dryer, dryer and iron and two chemical disposal points. The site has no shop (although reception sells gas) but there are shops and restaurants five minutes walk away at the motorway service area. The site is well lit and there is a late arrivals area. Dogs are accepted with a good walk around the perimeter of the site.

Charges 1999:
-- Per unit £8.00 - £9.00; awning £1.00 - £1.50; electricity £1.00.
-- OAPs less £1.00.
-- Special rates for 3 or 7 days.
-- 10% discount on hotel and café meals.
-- VAT included.
-- No credit cards.

Address:
Orton, Penrith, Cumbria CA10 3SB.

Tel/Fax:
(015396) 24511.

Reservations:
Advised for B.Hs and July/Aug; contact park.

Directions: Northbound, just north of junction 38, exit M6 at Tebay Services (site signed). Southbound, stay on M6 to junction 38 then return north on M6 to Tebay Services. O.S.GR: NY607060.

For a list of parks which are open all year - see page 234

Northumberland

Northumbria Tourist Board

Northumberland, Durham, Tyne and Wear and Cleveland
Aykley Heads, Durham DH1 5UX
Tel: (0191) 375 3000 Fax: (0191) 386 0899
E-mail: enquiries@ntb.org.uk   Internet: http://www.ntb.org.uk

Northumbria covers the counties of **Northumberland, Durham, Tyne and Wear** and the **Tees Valley** area. Even before the Victorians invented tourism travellers were drawn to this vast empty area between England's industrial belt and the rugged wilderness of Scotland, bisected by the Pennine Mountains and the start of the Pennine Way.

The Pennine Way was the country's first official long-distance path and still the longest (268 miles), stretching from the Peak National Park to the border. Northumberland borders Scotland and is an ancient rugged area dotted with forts from its passionate past when the Scottish raiding parties ventured south.

The 400 square mile Northumberland National Park stretches south from the now peaceful Cheviot Hills near the border, through the Simonside Hills, to the crags of Whin Sill, where it engulfs part of Hadrian's Wall. When the Romans ruled, this line marked the northern limit of their Empire. The surviving sections of this 73 mile long fortification must be the most impressive legacy of Roman rule. The best part, popular for walking, is along the crest of Whin Sill crags around Housesteads fort, the most complete fort on the wall.

The coastline is not to be forgotten, deserted white sandy beaches, majestic castles, including Bamburgh and islands. Lindisfarne known for its links with St Cuthbert and early Christianity and the Farnes, remembered locally through the daring of Grace Darling, now a bird sanctuary.

The City of **Newcastle**, home of the 'Geordies', perhaps looks a little worn and grimy by day but comes to life at night when a good time is had by all in the pubs and clubs.

The small city of **Durham** has a more historical feel, dominated by England's greatest Norman Cathedral. Surrounded on three side by the river Wear, with cobbled medieval streets and restricted car access it is a popular with tourists.For hundreds of years Durham was a quasi-regal state called a 'palatinate' with its own currency, arms and courts with the governors and prince bishops living in the castle, divided from the cathedral by Palace Green. Today it is all part of the university, the third oldest after Oxford and Cambridge in England.

The North East was a coal-producing and ship-building area and proud of its heritage but the decline in these industries has had its affect on the area from Middlesbrough to Tyne and Wear.

---

576 Percy Wood Caravan Park, Swarland, nr. Morpeth

Well equipped, quality woodland site, open 11 months of the year.

Percy Wood provides excellent, modern facilities whilst still maintaining the feel of camping in woodland. A lot of thought and effort has gone into developing a park which blends with its natural surroundings. There are 60 level touring pitches, all with electricity (10A), 20 with hardstanding and full services. A grass tent field with 5A electricity has a more open aspect with views. The central sanitary block is of wooden construction (heated) and in consequence blends in naturally with the woodland surroundings. It is very well equipped with controllable showers, open, vanity style washbasins, free hot water throughout, dish-washing under cover, a laundry room, baby room and chemical disposal and motorcaravan service facilities. Reception provides basics including gas and local tourist information, the village store and post office is just ½ mile away and local pubs and a restaurant are within a mile. Children's play area, outdoor table tennis and games room with two pool tables and video games. Six caravan holiday homes for hire (plus 60 privately owned). Dogs are accepted on leads (but not certain breeds). On the boundary of the park is an 18 hole golf course, with a bar and restaurant, and membership can be arranged. Fishing 1½ miles. An excellent area for rambling, walking and for nature lovers generally, the park is only 4 miles from Throughton Wood and on the bus route for Alnwick and Rothbury. Druridge Bay Country Park is near (lake visitor centre, good for watersports).

Directions: Park is about 2 miles west of the A1 (only signed northbound), 3 miles from the A697. It is 12 miles north of Morpeth and 7 miles south of Alnwick. O.S.GR: NU160042.

Charges 1999:
-- Per unit incl. 2 persons and 10A electricity £8.50 - £10.00; fully serviced pitch in July/Aug plus £1.50; camping field incl. 2 persons and 5A electricity £8.00; extra person (over 5 yrs) £1.00; dog 50p; extra car £1.00.
-- Credit cards accepted.
Open:
All year except February.
Address:
Swarland, Morpeth, Northumberland NE65 9JW.
Tel:
(01670) 787649.
FAX: (01670) 787034.
Reservations:
Made with 10% deposit, min. £10 (non-refundable).

577 Dunstan Hill Camping and Caravanning Club Site, nr. Alnwick

Peaceful site within a mile of one of Northumberland's golden beaches.

Northumberland is not very well blessed with good campsites, so Dunstan Hill makes a welcome addition to this guide. Situated in a quiet lane between Embleton and Craster this is a rural site with a tree belt to shelter it from the north wind and access to the beach by a level footpath through the fields, across the golf course and past the ruins of Dunstanburgh Castle. This is 1-1½ miles by car. With gravel access roads, the site has 150 level, well spaced pitches, 78 with 16A electricity. Two heated sanitary blocks have some washbasins in cubicles, free controllable showers, hairdryers and a washroom for children with deep sinks. The fully equipped suite for disabled visitors is in one block, the laundry in the other. Chemical disposal. All is very clean and well maintained. Reception is located in a new building and is manned by very helpful wardens. It also contains the small shop which has gas, basic provisions and ices. Bread and milk can be ordered and the paper man visits. A large area for outside parking and late arrivals is at the entrance. A tourist information room and a small childrens play area are provided. Torches would be useful. This is a wonderful area to visit, with its unspoilt beaches and the whole area is steeped in history with Holy Island, the Farne Islands, Bamburgh, Dunstanburgh, Walkworth and Alnwick castles. Buses pass the site entrance. Fishing 1½ miles, riding 8 miles.

Charges 2000:
-- Per 2 adults £7.50 - £10.60; child (6-18 yrs) £1.65; non-member pitch fee £4.30; electricity £1.60 - £2.35.
-- VAT included.
-- Credit cards accepted.
Open:
March - November.
Address:
Dunstan Hill, Dunstan, Alnwick, Northumberland NE66 3TQ.
Tel:
(01665) 576310, (no calls after 8 pm).
Reservations:
Necessary and made with deposit; contact the wardens.

Directions: From A1 just north of Alnwick take B1340 or B6347 (further north) for Embleton. Site signed in Embleton. Avoid signs to Dunstanburgh Castle, take those for Craster. Site is (south) on left in ½ mile. O.S.GR: NU236214.

575 Waren Caravan and Camping Park, Bamburgh

Spacious family park with good sea views, with touring area.

Northumberland has very few quality parks in proportion to its size but Waren Park provides a friendly, family atmosphere, with marvellous views. It has been developed from 100 acres of undulating private heath and woodland and provides a static park (caravans for hire), a 4 acre, self contained touring area and a separate tenting area, enclosed by shelter banks and with its own on-site warden. There are 170 clearly marked pitches on level grass, 84 with electrical connections (10A). The toilet block is a rather basic provision but functional and supplemented in peak season with a second block in the static area. It provides free hot water in washbasins (with shelves and mirrors), showers and baby changing equipment. A laundry room has washing, drying and ironing facilities and washing up sinks with free hot water. The facilities are due to be updated and at present could do with a little 'TLC'. Amenities include a licensed well stocked shop, games room, pool table and well equipped children's play park. The reception/shop area has been rebuilt to include a coffee shop (licensed) with bar snacks available and an attractive terrace overlooking the outdoor heated splash pools (small hexagonal pool and deeper 9 x 6 m. pool, open June - Sept). Playing field. Weekly barbecues. Dog walks. Video transmission available. As well as the spacious grounds to wander in, there is much to see nearby from historic castles, the Farne Islands to the Cheviot Hills. Golf, birdwatching and riding all nearby. Holiday homes to let.

Charges guide:
-- Per unit incl. 2 persons £7.75 - £11.50; extra person (over 5 yrs) £1.00; boat or awning £1.50; dog £1.00; electricity £2.00.
-- Less 10% for bookings of 7 days or over.
-- Credit cards accepted.
-- VAT included.
Open:
Easter/1 April - end Oct.
Address:
Waren Mill, Bamburgh, Northumberland NE70 7EE.
Tel:
(01668) 214366.
FAX: (01668) 214224.
Reservations:
Early reservation advised for high season (50 pitches for reservation). Deposit of one night's charge plus £1 fee.

Directions: Follow B1342 from A1 to Waren Mill towards Bamburgh. After Budle Bay turn right and follow signs. O.S.GR: NU154342.

Northumberland

578 Brown Rigg Caravan & Camping Park, Bellingham, nr. Hexham

Interesting, newly developed park in the heart of Northumberland.

Bellingham is tucked away amidst heather clad moors in the North Tyne valley, just below the Scottish Borders on the edge of the Northumberland National Park, 'full of history, myth and legend', to quote from the Bellingham town guide. John Mowatt went to school here and has returned with his wife and family to establish Brown Rigg in part of the grounds of his old school. The park has been open for few years now and provides 70 pitches, 26 with electricity (10/16A), for all types of unit on a level grass field between the moor and the road. Reception with shop, the games room and the sanitary facilities have all been converted from the former wooden school dormitory buildings with a central courtyard area and are rather distinctive. Ladies' facilities are finished in pine and provide washbasins in cubicles, controllable showers on payment (10p), free hairdryer and a baby bath can be provided. The men's have been tiled. In total, it is a good provision, cleverly adapted and well maintained and is operated on a key system. There is a washing machine and dryer, free iron and board, laundry and dish washing sinks with free hot water, chemical disposal and motorcaravan service point. Reception provides tourist information and basic food supplies, gas and battery charging. Games room with pool and table tennis, TV room. Public phone. Children's play area. A tea shop and craft centre are planned. Bellingham is ½ mile away and a new 18 hole golf course has been opened recently. Fishing or golf within 1 mile, bicycle hire 7 miles, boat launching 7 miles, riding 10 miles. The Pennine Way passes the entrance and Kielder Water is 9 miles to the west, as is Hadrian's Wall to the south.

Directions: Park is on the B6320, south of Bellingham. O.S.GR: NY835826.

Charges 1999:
--Per unit incl. 2 adults £7.00 - £8.50; small frame tent £6.50 - £7.50; 2-man tent £6.00 - £7.50; 1-man tent £3.50 - £4.50; child's pup tent £2.00; extra adult £1.50; child (6-14 yrs) £1.00; awning £1.00; one dog free, others 50p; electricity £1.50 - £2.00.
-- Book for 7 nights, stay 1 free.
-- No credit cards.

Open:
Easter - 31 October.

Address:
Bellingham, nr. Hexham, Northumberland NE48 2JY.

Tel:
(01434) 220175.
FAX: as phone.

Reservations:
Made with £10 deposit for bookings.

580 Ord House Country Park, East Ord, nr. Berwick-upon-Tweed

Large holiday home park with well equipped touring area.

Ord House, an 18th century mansion house, has been converted to provide a bar, lounge bar and family room with meals available in each. Outside office hours, reception is also here. The 40 acre park caters for about 200 privately owned holiday homes, but there are also 75 touring pitches and an area for 9 tents. In seven small, tidy sections, from a secluded, walled orchard to open areas near the sanitary block or the playground, the pitches are of reasonable size with varying degree of slope. All have electricity (10A), some have water and drainage too. The modern, heated sanitary building has good facilities with free hot water to showers, open washbasins, two excellent large family bathrooms (with two showers, a bath, WC and washbasin) and upgraded facilities for disabled visitors. Dishwashing, laundry, chemical disposal facilities are all well provided for, plus a motorcaravan service point. Other amenities include a very popular golf practise area, bicycle hire, crazy golf, table tennis and draughts as part of the children's play area which has swings, etc. on a bark base. Although the majority of the park is taken by holiday homes, this does allow other facilities, such as the bars, to remain open for a long season (not Tuesdays in April, May, June and Sept or Tues/Wed. in March, Nov and Dec). Public phones. Tourist information available in reception. Gas supplies. Fishing 1½ miles, riding 8 miles, golf 2 miles. A post office stores is just 50 m. from the entrance (open daily 6 am.- 6 pm, incl. Sun. in high season). No transit vans or commercial vehicles accepted, dogs are accepted by prior arrangement (max. two, not certain breeds). A member of the Best of British group.

Directions: From the A1 Berwick bypass take East Ord exit and follow signs. O.S.GR: NT982515.

Charges 1999:
-- Per unit incl. up to 4 people £7.50 - £12.25; extra adult £2.00; child 6-15 yrs £1.00, 0-5 yrs free; awning £2.00; electricity £2.00; water and drainage £2.00; dog free - £1.00; extra car, boat and trailer by prior arrangement.
-- Credit cards accepted.

Open:
All year
excl. 10 Jan - 8 March.

Address:
Ord House, East Ord, Berwick-upon-Tweed, Northumberland TD15 2NS.

Tel:
(01289) 305288.
FAX: (01289) 330832.
E-mail: enquiries@ordhouse.co.uk.

Reservations:
Advisable at all times, essential in high seasons (min. 3 nights at B.Hs) - contact park for details.

See colour feature for `BEST of BRITISH' between pages 96/97

571 Doe Park Touring Caravan Park, Cotherstone, Barnard Castle

Peaceful site in the old mould with character, ideal for couples (caravans and motorhomes only).

This is Hannah Hauxwell country and the Dales, less frequented than other upland areas, provide wonderful walking country; indeed part of the Pennine Way runs near the site. The farm and park are close to where the River Balder joins the Tees at Cotherstone and the ancient oak wood beside the river is an SSSI (Site of Special Scientific Interest) for its insects and flowers, but is also a haven for bird-watchers. Reception is in the farmhouse, formerly Leadgard Hall, a mellow three storey, Grade II listed building with a history of its own. Mr and Mrs Lamb make you very welcome and personally take you to your pitch. The farm is a traditional Dales livestock farm, non-intensive where the animals fatten naturally and visitors are welcome. The camping fields with a lovely open aspect are of natural grass, neatly kept and the 70 pitches are spacious (all with 10A electricity, 20 with hardstanding). The newer ones have open fields in front, ideal for children. Two toilet areas, one part of the farmhouse, the other built in natural stone, provide en-suite toilets and washbasins and metered showers with curtain and stool. Dishwashing and a small laundry in the farmhouse. New chemical disposal. A new heated toilet block has been added in '99 with further WCs and washbasins and a large unisex unit for visitors with disabilities. Eggs and milk can be ordered with gas and battery charging available. A regular bus service passes the farm from Barnard Castle to Middleton and there is a local leisure centre with a swimming pool (4 miles). The village of Cotherstone is ½ mile with post office and a restaurant with bar meals, a pleasant walk by road or river bank. River fishing on site, reservoirs 3 miles, bicycle hire or golf 4 miles, riding 2 miles. Dogs and pets are accepted by arrangement only.

Charges 2000:
-- Per car and caravan incl. 2 persons £6.50 - £7.00; motorcaravan £6.00 - £6.50; extra person (over 7 yrs) 80p - £1.00; electricity £1.80.
Open:
1 March - 31 October.
Address:
Cotherstone,
Barnard Castle,
Co. Durham DL12 9UQ.
Tel:
(01833) 650302.
FAX: as phone.
Reservations:
Made with £10 deposit (send SAE); min. 3 days at B.Hs.

Directions: Follow B6277 from Barnard Castle in direction of Middleton in Teesdale. The farm is signed on the left just after Cotherstone village (there is no need to go into Barnard Castle). O.S.GR: NZ005204.

572 Camping and Caravanning Club Site Barnard Castle

Family site taking all types of unit including tents, also accepting non-members.

For those readers with tents who wish to visit this area, we have added this new Club site as unfortunately nearby Doe Park does not take tents. The Camping and Caravanning Club site at Barnard Castle was only opened in '96. Originally level farm fields, one side of the site is bordered by mature trees and 11,000 young trees and bushes have been planted so eventually it will become an even more attractive location. Most of the 90 pitches are on grass, with 56 electrical hook-ups (16 A) plus 12 hardstanding pitches which have a gravel base with room for both car and caravan and space for an awning on grass. Both the toilet block and reception (another large spacious room) are built of local stone and, true to the club's reputation, there is always a warm welcome on arrival. The centrally positioned toilet facilities are of good quality and kept spotlessly clean, the whole building having a feeling of spaciousness. Washbasins are in cubicles and the free, controllable showers are roomy. A large laundry has a washing machine, dryer, iron and sink with outside lines provided. Chemical disposal, dishwashing sinks, a baby room and a large, fully equipped unisex unit for visitors with disabilities are also here. Gas supplies available. Central children's play area with rubber safety base. Barnard Castle, an old town with its market cross still standing, is well worth a visit. The Bowes museum in the town is a French style chateau housing one of Britain's finest art collections. Raby Castle, near Staindrop, is a very impressive mediaeval castle, formerly the seat of the powerful Neville family. Durham has a castle and cathedral (both World Heritage Sites). High Force, England's highest waterfall is about 12 miles away, and the forest of Hamsterly about 16 miles. A riding centre is next to the site and a public footpath leads from the site to Barnard Castle, with a network of public footpaths in the area. Dogs are accepted with a dog walk provided. Fishing 4 miles, golf 2½ miles.

Charges 2000:
-- Per 2 adults £7.50 - £10.60; child (6-18 yrs) £1.65; non-member pitch fee £4.30; backpacker £4.80 - £6.10; electricity £1.60 - £2.35.
-- VAT included.
-- Credit cards accepted.
Open:
March - November.
Address:
Dockenflatts Lane,
Lartington,
Barnard Castle,
Co. Durham DL12 9DG.
Tel:
(01833) 630228,
(no calls after 8 pm).
Reservations:
Necessary and made with deposit; contact the wardens.

Directions: Follow B6277 from Barnard Castle (towards Middleton in Teesdale) for 1 mile to Lartington. Turn left at club sign into narrow lane with passing places to site entrance on left (no need to go into Barnard Castle). O.S.GR: NZ025168.

WALES

Wales Tourist Board

Brunel House, 2 Fitzalan Road, Cardiff CF2 1UY
Tel: (01222) 475226 www.visitwales.com

Wales, with its history of cross-border struggle with England, has a distinctive culture and few parts of the world can contain as much varied scenery in such a restricted area. No passport is needed to enter Wales but once you have crossed the border you know you are in another country. Its seemingly impenetrable ancient Celtic language manifests itself not only in unpronounceable place names but in signs such as 'Croeso i Cymru' (Welcome to Wales). Everyone speaks English, but many locals use Welsh as their first language. Devolution is now a fact and the Welsh parliament sits in Cardiff. Perhaps the Welsh identity is expressed in its

number of Nonconformist chapels, its male voice choirs, its national sport of rugby and its eisteddfodau, emotive celebrations of Welsh artistic endeavour. The hills contribute to a wet climate, but the frequent rains create a lush green landscape, with rivers, foaming waterfalls and an abundance of lakes, some of which are man-made sources of water for thirsty towns, as well as being scenic attractions or centres for watersports.

We have divided this Welsh section into three parts: South, Mid and North Wales with a short introduction to each and contact addresses.

South Wales

Tourism information for South and West Wales may also be obtained from:

Tourism South and West Wales, Charter Court, Enterprise Park, Swansea SA7 9DB
Tel: (01792) 781212 Fax: 01792 781300
or Old Bridge, Haverfordwest SA61 2EZ Tel: (01437) 766388 Fax: (01437) 766008

The highest proportion of Wales' 2.8 million inhabitants live in the south, between the country's small capital Cardiff and Swansea and in the working-class settlements of 'The Valleys' across a massive coal field. It is here that some of the now defunct mines have been turned into tourist attractions.

To the east and the border, the wooded Wye Valley is a tight concentration of fine scenery and historic monuments. To the West, the remote Pembrokeshire Coast National Park, which winds its way round inlets and coves, cliffs and beaches around the coastline is marked by a long distance footpath.

592 The Bridge Caravan Park and Camping Site, Dingestow

Quiet, family run park in village 4 miles from Monmouth.

The Bridge Caravan Park was established in 1979, being a working farm until a few years ago. Still in the hands of the Holmes family, it provides a peaceful haven bordered by the River Trothy and woodland on one side and by the farm buildings and church on the other. Over half the park is taken up by seasonal long stay pitches. The touring area is to one side, edged by the river at a lower level. Neat, level grass accessed by a circular tarmac roadway provides 33 pitches for caravans and motorcaravans with electricity (10A) and 16 hardstandings. A further 20 places for tents are available, all with electricity (5A), and there are three holiday homes for hire. A pleasant, friendly atmosphere prevails. The purpose built, central toilet block is well maintained and now has a separate shower section, with metered showers in excellent cubicles with dry area, seat and hooks. A bathroom for disabled visitors has also been added here, but this does not have a shower. There is hot water to washbasins in cubicles and hairdryers. A fully equipped laundry and dishwashing room has free hot water. Gas is available on site. Nearby is a village shop and Post Office and there is a children's play area in the village also. A local pub offers good food a short walk away. River fishing is possible. Bicycle hire 6 miles, boat slipway 4 miles, golf 3 miles.

Charges 2000:
-- Per unit incl. 2 adults £8.00; extra adult £1.50; child (5-14 yrs) £1.00; awning £1.00; electricity 10A £2.00, 5A £1.50.
-- No credit cards.

Open:
Easter - 30 October.

Address:
Dingestow, Monmouth, Gwent NP5 4DY.

Tel:
(01600) 740241.

Reservations:
Contact park.

Directions: Park is signed off A40 road by junction with A449 (about 4½ miles from junction). O.S.GR: SO458099.

160

France for beginners

NOT VENTURED ACROSS THE CHANNEL YET? FANCY THE CAMARADERIE AND FUN OF TRAVELLING IN AN ESCORTED GROUP?

At the Alan Rogers Travel Service we know that for many the first trip abroad can be a big step. That's why we invite you to join us on a fabulous escorted trip to a delightful hidden part of Northern France, less than an hour from Calais. We've put together an exciting 7 night programme, staying at the lovely Camping Château de Gandspette situated in the heart of the Audomarais National Park, twinned with the Norfolk Broads.

The Programme

Meeting at an Alan Rogers selected site in Kent for drinks, we'll take a morning Dover-Calais ferry next day, arriving at Château de Gandspette in time for lunch. There'll be plenty of time during the week to explore this fascinating area: delightful countryside, mediaeval cobbled towns like Arras and Cambrai, First World War battlefields, and of course St Omer with its pretty square, restaurants and colourful market. There's so much to see and your experienced escorts, both seasoned caravanners, will always be on hand for advice.

What's included

- 7 nights pitch fees
- Welcome drinks
- Return Dover-Calais crossing
- Farewell dinner
- Comprehensive Travel Pack
- Insurance for two people with car + caravan/motorhome

ALL THIS FOR JUST

£499

9th -16th June
2 people with car + caravan/motorhome

Numbers are strictly limited - So call now for details or book today

01892 61 51 41

quoting AR4S

THE ALAN ROGERS'
travel service

In association with

FOUR SEASONS TOURING

8 Garden Street, Tunbridge Wells. TN1 2XB email: travelservice@alanrogers.com website: www.alanrogers.com

Channel express.

Brittany · Jersey · Guernsey

If you're travelling to Brittany or the Channel Islands for your holiday next year, the first thing you need is your copy of the Condor 2000 Car Ferries Brochure.

With services, up to 3 times daily from Weymouth or Poole you can be in St. Malo in as little as 5 hours, Guernsey 2 hours or Jersey from 3¹/₄ hours.

INFORMATION & RESERVATIONS: 01305 761551

CONDOR Ferries

UK · JERSEY · GUERNSEY · ST. M

SANDOWN AIRPORT

AVIATION MUSEUM

Come and see the Island's unique Air Museum

with aircraft and exhibits from both World Wars, together with classic jets and displays relating to the Battle of Britain, the Blitz and the Home Front – something for everyone interested in the history of aviation

★ SOUVENIR & GIFT SHOP ★ COFFEE SHOP

OPENING TIMES
SUMMER: MAY-SEPT 10am-6pm
WINTER: OCT-APRIL 10am-4pm
(Except 23, 24, 25, 26 December)

★ FREE PARKING

Embassy Way, Sandown Airfield, Sandown.
Tel/Fax: 01983-404448

ELECTROLUX –
FOR THE LIFE OF LEISURE

With the life we lead today leisure is of increasing importance, so is the need to have cool fresh food and drinks to hand wherever you are.

Electrolux have the most comprehensive range of portable refrigerators and coolers in the industry. They have a product for every conceivable use and application.

The mobilLife range of portable refrigerators is ideal for use either at home or away. There are models suitable for use on outings with the kids, or just in the garden for barbecues.

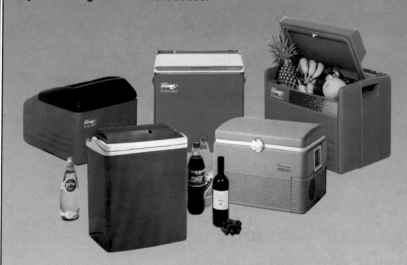

HOLIDAY

Stocking up for the holiday? Taking the children or grandchildren with you? Where to store the left-over Christmas turkey?

Electrolux has the answer. Their top of the range mobilLifes are portable top-opening absorption refrigerators. There is a choice of models and they are all three-way just like the model fitted in a caravan. You can run from gas or 230v while stationary, or plug into the cigar lighter 12v socket whilst on the move. They are ideal when you are camping, or useful as an additional refrigerator at home. Whatever the occasion Electrolux can help solve the problem.

Sitting in your car in long summer traffic jams in the sweltering heat, wouldn't it be great to just reach into the back of your car and take out a long cool drink?

Electrolux mobilLife thermoelectric coolers work on the Peltier system from a 12v supply, so you can plug them directly into the cigarette lighter of the car, and have cool drinks to hand at any time. No more do you need to search for a roadside café, or queue in busy motorway service stations. Refreshment is to hand at any time of day or night. With the aid of an adaptor, you can run your mobilLife cooler on the 24v system on a truck or boat. A 230v adaptor means you can use it at home as well. Some of the products even allow you to reverse the plug and use your mobilLife as a food warmer, ideal for an outing on colder days, or for keeping the takeaway warm.

Reasonably priced, these coolers are also ideal for day trips and excursions. Whatever the application Electrolux has a portable product to suit.

WIDEN YOUR HORIZONS WITH CALOR GAS

Holidaymakers throughout the UK benefit from using Calor gas

Established in 1935, Calor Gas pioneered the development of liquefied petroleum gas (LPG) as a clean, efficient and convenient source of fuel for heating, cooking and lighting for caravanners and campers. Calor gas is a reliable, flexible fuel which has now been in use in caravanning and camping for over 60 years.

Calor Gas has developed strong links with the tourism and leisure sector and its support to the caravan industry is demonstrated through its close association with national organisations including the British Holiday and Home Parks Association, the National Caravan Council and the national Tourist Boards. A good example of Calor's support is the annual Calor Gas Caravan Park Awards scheme. The scheme encourages parks to improve facilities and services, providing caravanners and campers with all the ingredients for a first class holiday.

Calor also continues to work closely with major appliance manufacturers to develop new products and has recently launched its Calor Choice range of top quality, competitively priced

Calor-powered patio heaters enhance alfresco evenings

appliances. The range includes barbecues and patio heaters, designed to enable caravanners and campers to further enjoy their holidays with relaxed evenings of alfresco dining and drinking.

Appliances from the Calor Choice range are available from Calor's nationwide network of over 10,000 dealers and stockists, which supply gas and related products to all parts of the UK mainland and many of the surrounding islands. For details of your nearest Calor stockist, or for further information on the use of LPG in caravanning and camping please call Calor Gas free on *0800 626626*.

CALOR Gas

606 Tredegar House Caravan Club Site, Newport

Immaculate new site, ideally situated for breaking the journey or longer stays.

This newly developed Caravan Club site accommodates 82 caravans, all with 16A electricity hook-up and 40 with gravel hardstanding. A further grass area is allocated for 30 tents, with use limited to families and couples - no single sex groups are accepted. The sanitary block is of an excellent standard with a digital lock system. It provides showers and washbasins in cubicles, all with hooks, mirrors and seats, a bathroom for visitors with disabilities and a baby and toddler bathroom complete with small bath, toilet, washbasin and changing unit. The usual dishwashing, laundry and chemical disposal facilities are also here. Entry to and exit from the park are controlled by a barrier (card required). Calor gas can be purchased from the warden but no other facilities are considered necessary as a large supermarket is just three minutes away. The site itself is situated within the gardens and park of Tredegar House, a 17th century house and country park which is open to the public to discover what life was like 'above' and 'below' stairs. Newport is some 3 miles away and is a good shopping centre and Cardiff with its castle, shops and much more is only 9 miles. On site there is a well stocked tourist information centre for places of interest, places to eat, etc. Caravan Club policy is to charge non-members an extra £5 per night - or invite them to join, of course - so for those who choose not to join the Club and particularly for overseas visitors, site fees can be high if you are a larger group. Those affected by this policy may wish to consider staying at Cwmcarn Forest Drive Campsite (no. 593) where the charges could well be half that of this most excellent club site and is 15 minutes away.

Charges 1999:
-- Per pitch £6.00; adult £2.60 - £3.90; child (5-16 yrs) £1.10 - £1.20; electricity £1.45 (26/3-4/10) - £2.20.
-- Credit cards accepted.
-- VAT included.
Open: All year.
Address: Newport, Gwent NP1 9YW.
Tel: (01633) 815600.
FAX: (01633) 816372.
E-mail: cc92@gofornet.co.uk
Reservations: Advised for peak season - contact the warden.

Directions: From M4 take exit 28 or from A48 junction with the M4 follow brown signs for Tredegar House. The caravan park is indicated to the left at the house entrance. O.S.GR: ST299855.

593 Cwmcarn Forest Drive Campsite, Cwmcarn, nr. Newport

Small, council owned park in a beautiful setting.

Set in a narrow, sheltered valley with magnificent wooded slopes (it's hard to believe it was once the site of the Cwmcarn Colliery), this park is not only central for the many attractions of this part of Wales, but there is now also much of the natural environment to enjoy including a small fishing lake. The seven mile forest drive (open daily in season) shares its Visitor Centre with the camp reception and has much to offer - bird watching, badger seeking, the Twmbarlwm ancient hill fort to visit with its magnificent views across the Severn to Somerset, Devon and Gloucestershire. Guided walks are available. The site has a slightly wild feel, but is stunningly located and has 40 well spaced, flat pitches (30 with 15A electric hook-ups, 3 with concrete hardstanding and with tarmac for the car) spread over three small fields between the Visitor Centre and the small lake (fishing permits available). There is one well equipped, heated toilet block (£5 deposit for key) including toilet facilities for the disabled, chemical disposal facilities, laundry with washing machine, dryer, iron and board, and a kitchen with two washing up sinks, small cooker and fridge (hot water free). Telephone. The Visitor Centre has a coffee shop open 1-5.30 pm. at weekends from Easter. A variety of shops, a leisure centre, pubs and takeaway food are available in the village ¾ mile away. Riding 2 miles, golf 6 miles. Pets are welcome under control. Wardens are on hand daily and the Visitor Centre and reception are manned 9 am - 5 pm. - arrive before then. Rallies can be accommodated.

Charges 1999:
-- Per unit £6.60 - £7.70; large tent £5.70 - £6.70; small ridge tent £4.20 - £5.30; electricity £2.00.
-- Credit cards accepted.
-- VAT included.
Open: January - December.
Address: The Warden, Cwmcarn Forest Drive Campsite, Cwmcarn, Crosskeys, nr. Newport NP1 7FA.
Tel: (01495) 272001.
Reservations: No stated policy. 14 day max. stay.

Directions: Cwmcarn Forest Drive is well signed from junction 28 on M4. From the Midlands and the `Heads of the Valleys' road (A465), take A467 south to Cwmcarn. O.S.GR: ST230935.

South Wales

594 Pembrey Country Park Caravan Club Site, Pembrey, Llanelli

Comfortable, quiet site with access to Pembrey Country Park and beach.

A sheltered peaceful park, this Caravan Club site provides 115 level grassy pitches, accessed by a semi-circular tarmac, one-way road and pleasantly interspersed with clumps of bushes and trees. All but 4 of the pitches have electric hook-ups (16A) and tents are taken providing there is room (steel tent or awning pegs may be needed). The heated sanitary block, well situated for all the pitches, is of the usual good Club standard with curtained washbasins, well equipped, controllable, free hot showers, hand and hair dryers and en-suite facilities for the handicapped (with key). A laundry room has two sinks (H&C) and a washing machine, dryer and ironing board, three dishwashing sinks are under cover, chemical disposal facilities, a motorcaravan service point, four neat service points for drinking water and waste water, plus two large rubbish bins. A small children's play area, giant draughts set and boules pitch are alongside a tarmac area near the reception, which also sells gas, toilet chemicals, bottled water, sweets and barbecue charcoal, and has a small library. However the real plus for this site is its proximity to the Country Park – access to this is free on foot direct from the site, or the Club has organised a special weekly car pass for £6.50. The Park covers 520 acres of grass and woodland, with 7 miles of soft sandy beaches, about a mile of which has a `Blue Flag' rating (dogs are limited to a special area). There are some 64 miles of walks and cycle ways, picnic and conservation areas, a wealth of birds and butterflies, pitch and putt, narrow gauge railway, a dry ski slope (excellent value) and toboggan run, plus an orienteering course, nature trails, and equestrian centre – all part of a really wonderful provision which is both quiet and safe for families. A small drawback could be some noise during the day from aircraft or from occasional meetings at the nearby Pembrey motor racing circuit (on the other hand, enthusiasts can watch the racing from the bicycle trail!) Plenty of family orientated pubs nearby serve good value meals and the Gower Peninsula is only 20 miles away.

Directions: Leave M4 at junction 48 onto A4138. After 4 miles turn right onto A484 at roundabout signed Carmarthen. Continue for 7 miles to Pembrey. The Country Park is signed off the A484 in Pembrey village; site entrance is on right 100 yds before park gates. O.S.GR: SN415005.

Charges 1999:
-- Per pitch (non-member) £6.00 - £7.00; adult £2.60 - £4.00; child (5-16 yrs) £1.10 - £1.20; electricity £1.45 - £2.20.
-- Credit cards accepted.

Open:
All year except 5 Jan. - 26 March.

Address:
Pembrey, Llanelli, Carmarthenshire SA16 0EJ.

Tel:
(01554) 834369, (not after 8 pm).

Reservations:
Essential for July/Aug. and B.Hs; contact the Warden.

607 Camping and Caravan Club Site Rhandirmwyn, nr. Llandovery

Countryside site in a very scenic location

This is a popular site with those who like a peaceful life with no on-site entertainment, just fresh air and beautiful countryside. The site is only a short drive from the magnificent Llyn Brianne reservoir and close to the Dinas RSPB nature reserve, where a two mile trail runs through oak and alder woodland alongside the River Tywi and the wildlife includes many species of birds including red kites. The site is in a sheltered valley with 90 pitches on level grass, 48 electric hook-ups (16A), and six hardstandings. The single heated sanitary block is kept very clean and tidy, with controllable hot showers, washbasins (some in cubicles), WCs, dishwashing sinks and a laundry with a washing machine, dryer, and ironing centre. The chemical disposal point is in a small building near the site entrance, and there is a drive-over motorcaravan service point. The village is within walking distance although there is a fairly steep hill to negotiate (but the return is much easier), and you can take a short cut through the woodland grove dedicated to John Lloyd, a former Chairman of the Club. The village has a Post Office and general store, and the Royal Oak Inn serves good value meals.

Directions: From centre of Llandovery take A485 towards Builth Wells, after a short distance turn left, signed Rhandirmwyn, continue for approx. 7 miles along country lanes. O.S.GR: SN779435

Charges 2000:
-- Per adult £3.75 - £5.30; child £1.60; non member pitch fee £4.20; electricity £1.60 - £2.35.

Open:
March - November.

Address:
Rhandirmwyn, Llandovery, Carmarthenshire SA20 0NT.

Tel:
(01550) 760257 (not after 8 pm).

Reservations:
Advised for high season and made with deposit; contact the wardens.

596 Abermarlais Caravan Park, Llangadog, nr. Llandeilo

Sheltered park close to main holiday route, in natural setting.

Apart from the attractions of south or mid Wales for a stay, this family run park could also double as a useful transit stop for those en-route to Pembrokeshire. Up to 88 touring units are accommodated in one flattish, tapering 5-acre grass field edged by mature trees and a stream. Pitches are numbered, and generously spaced around the perimeter or on either side of a central, hedged spine at the wider end, with 42 electrical hook-ups (10A) and some hardstanding. Backpackers have a small, separate area. The park is set in a sheltered valley with a range of wildlife and 9 acres of woodland walks. There is also an old walled garden, with some pitches and lawns for softball games, which screens the park, both audibly and visibly, from the A40 road. However, the most sought after pitches are beside the stream, loved by children and a haven for wildlife. The one small toilet block is older in style, but it can be heated and is clean and adequate with free hot water to washbasins (shelf and mirror) and controllable showers. There are two external, covered washing-up sinks (free hot water), chemical disposal, but no laundry facilities - nearest about 5 miles away. Motorcaravan service point. A small shop doubles as reception and gas supplies are available. Play area with tennis and volleyball nets and play equipment. No other major on-site amenities and a torch would be useful. Little Chef restaurant near and pubs, etc. at Llangadog. Fishing 2 miles, riding 5 miles. Winter caravan storage.

Directions: Park is on the A40, between the junctions with the A4069 and A482, between Llandovery and Llandeilo. O.S.GR: SN685295.

Charges 2000:
-- Per pitch £4.50; adult £1.50; child (over 5 yrs) £1.00; awning 60p; electricity £1.75.
-- No credit cards.

Open:
14 March - 14 November.

Address:
Llangadog, nr. Llandeilo, Carmarthenshire SA19 9NG.

Tel:
(01550) 777868 or 777797.

Reservations:
Any length, with £5 deposit.

595 Afon Lodge Caravan Park, St. Clears, nr. Carmarthen

Small park in a peaceful, rural setting, personally run by new owners.

Formerly known as Parciau Bach Caravan Park, there are some narrow lanes to be negotiated to get here, but it is well worth it to enjoy the quality and peaceful setting. The 26 privately owned caravan holiday homes (and 5 site-owned for letting) are hidden in the wooded slopes at the back of the park - a haven for wild flowers and squirrels. The open field for tents is sloping, but now has individual terraced places with dividing shrub hedges (10 pitches) and a lower level, part terraced for 25 caravan pitches, all with electrical hook-ups (16A), 9 with hardstanding, water and TV connections. All are on neatly cut grass with views across the valley. A wooded stream area unfortunately does not belong to the park but further up on the park is a small wildlife pond. The owner's pine chalet home, sited on the slope between the touring field and the wooded area houses reception, a tourist information room and two small toilet units for both sexes with separate showers, toilets and washbasins with hairdryer for each. The other toilet block, open in high season only, is in the wooded area reached by a steepish, hard-core path and steps through the trees, lit at night. Free hot water is provided and the showers have the necessary seat, hook and curtain - however, it has to be admitted that this needs updating now. There is also a laundry room, two dishwashing sinks, one beside reception, one near the tent area, and chemical disposal. Adventure play unit and new pets corner. Shop at reception (Easter - end Oct). Bar snacks and evening meals are available at the Parciau Bach Inn (separate ownership) situated above the site. Telephone. A haven of tranquility, even when we visited in peak season, if you tire of the rural atmosphere, Tenby is only 18 miles, with the 7 mile long Pendine sands 6 miles away or to the north, the Preseli mountains. Riding ½ mile, fishing 2 miles, golf 5 miles. Birdwatching opportunities abound. A member of the Countryside Discovery group.

Directions: From St Clears traffic lights, take road to Llanboidy forking right after 100 yds. Follow this road for almost 2 miles and turn right. After less than a mile turn right at small crossroads and park is on left. O.S.GR: SN298184.

Charges 2000:
-- Per unit £6.50 - £9.00; 2 person tent £5.00 - £7.50; awning £1.00; electricity £1.80; TV connection 50p.
-- No credit cards.

Open:
All year except 9 Jan. - 1 March.

Address:
Parciau Bach, St. Clears, Carmarthenshire SA33 4LG.

Tel:
(01994) 230647.

Reservations:
May be advisable for B.Hs; contact park for details.

South Wales

597 Noble Court Holiday Caravan and Camping Park, Narberth

Family owned park with good facilities, centrally situated for southwest Wales.

The neat entrance sets the standard for Noble Court which is part caravan holiday homes (60) and part touring. Arranged over four hedged fields, each one at a slightly lower level, with an additional tenting field, the last has lovely views over the rural Welsh countryside. All 92 touring pitches have electricity, 25 on grass terraces with waste water connection, fresh water supply and 16A electricity, and the others mainly on gravel based hardstanding. An area is available for rallies. Gas supplies are available. Well equipped sanitary facilities in two similar, well equipped blocks feature pine doors. They provide vanity style washbasins and reasonably sized showers with a movable shelf, and all hot water is free. There is a laundry, covered dishwashing sinks and chemical disposal. Facilities for disabled people with ramped access are in the lower block (access by key). Children have an adventure play area on bark and there is good access to a further 20 acres of rural land for walking. There is an excellent bar/restaurant, TV room and games room, plus an outdoor heated pool (35 x 20 ft) with a beach effect and children's splash pool, nicely paved (open Spr. B.H. - early Sept). A new ½ acre coarse fishing lake is excellent with free use for campers. Noble Court is centrally situated for all Pembrokeshire has to offer and is easily accessed from the A40. Bicycle hire 5 miles, riding 4 miles, golf 3 miles, boat launching 8 miles. The market town of Narberth is ½ mile.

Directions: Going west on A40 ignore roundabout with sign to Narberth (on A478) and continue to next junction signed Narberth (B4313) with camping sign. Site is ½ mile on the left and you come on it quite suddenly. O.S.GR: SN111158.

Charges 2000:
-- Per pitch incl. up to 4 persons with electricity £8.00 - £15.00; extra person £1.25; child (under 12 yrs) £1.00.
-- Tent pitch £8.00 all year.
-- 2 night specials.
-- Credit cards accepted.
-- VAT included.
Open:
1 March - 30 November.
Address:
Redstone Road, Narberth, Pembrokeshire SA67 7ES.
Tel:
(01834) 861191.
FAX: (01834) 861484.
Reservations:
Recommended for electricity; contact park for details.

598 Moreton Farm Leisure Park, Saundersfoot

Well run park with modern facilities, 4 miles from Tenby.

Moreton Farm has been developed in a secluded valley, a 10-20 minute walk from Saundersfoot. It provides 20 caravan and 40 tent pitches on two sloping, neatly cut grass fields, with 12 pine holiday lodges and 4 cottages for letting, occupying another field. The site is approached under a railway bridge (height 10'9", width across the top 6'6", but with alternative access over the railway line for larger vehicles). There are a few trains during the day, none at night. The toilet block (heated) is light and airy, providing excellent facilities with pre-set hot showers (metered), vanity style washbasins (H&C) with soap and hand dryers, a ramp to a unit for disabled visitors with toilet and washbasin, baby bath, under cover dishwashing sinks and laundry facilities with a fenced, outside clothes drying area provided. A small shop, part of reception, provides basics and gas. Telephone. Children's playground on bark and grass. An attractive lake at the bottom of the valley is home to ducks, geese and chickens (fishing is no longer available)- pride of place must go to 'Missy and her girls'! Fishing or riding 1 mile, bicycle hire 2 miles, golf 4 miles. Pembroke and Carew castles and a variety of visitor attractions are close. This is a quiet family site. No dogs or pets are accepted.

Directions: From A477 Carmarthen - Pembroke road take A478 for Tenby at Kilgelly. Park is signed on left after 1½ miles. Watch carefully for sign and park is ½ mile up poorly made-up road and under bridge. O.S.GR: SN122047.

Charges 1999:
-- Per caravan £8.00 - £9.50; trailer tent or motorcaravan £7.00 - £8.50; tent £5.00 - £6.00; awning £1.50; electricity £2.00.
-- VAT included.
-- No credit cards.
Open:
1 March - 31 October.
Address:
Moreton, Saundersfoot, Pembrokeshire SA69 9EA.
Tel:
(01834) 812016.
FAX: (01834) 811890.
E-mail: moretonfarm @btconnect.com.
Reservations:
Made with deposit (£20 p/wk caravans, £15 p/wk tents), balance 28 days before arrival.

599 Freshwater East Caravan Club Site, nr. Pembroke

Park with excellent facilities, a few minutes from the beach.

This Caravan Club site in the Pembrokeshire Coast National Park is open to non-members (for all units). At the bottom of a hill, it has 126 mainly level, grassy pitches bounded by trees and with electrical hook-ups available. The heated toilet block is modern and in pristine condition with free, controllable showers, washbasins in cubicles, free hairdryers or sockets for your own. There are facilities for disabled visitors, a fully equipped laundry room, chemical disposal and a waste point for motorcaravans. Small play area. Gas supplies. Public phone. Shop ½ mile. The beach and the Pembroke Coastal Path are about a 5 minute walk. This is an excellent area for walking with magnificent cliff views and birdwatching. Fishing within 5 miles. You will find St. David's, the smallest cathedral city, well worth a visit. Note: booster aerial connections are available for a small extra charge including the loan of a connecting cable. Dogs are accepted.

Directions: From the east on A477, fork left 1¼ miles past Milton onto A4075 Pembroke road. After 2 miles in Pembroke (after railway bridge) turn sharp left at roundabout on A4139 Tenby road. In 1¾ miles in Lamphey turn right onto B4584 signed Freshwater East. In 1¾ miles turn right signed Stackpole and Trewent and after 400 yds at foot of hill, right into lane at Club sign. Note: do not tow to beach area. O.S.GR: SS015979.

Charges 1999:
-- Per pitch £6.00 - £7.00; adult £2.00 - £4.00; child (5-16 yrs) £1.10 - £1.20; extra car and trailer (in excess of 2 units) £1.00; electricity £1.45 - £2.20.
-- Credit cards accepted.
Open:
26 March - 1 November.
Address:
Freshwater East, Lamphey, Pembroke SA71 5NL.
Tel:
(01646) 672341, not after 8 pm.
Reservations:
Write to or phone the Warden at site.

600 Gwaun Vale Holiday Touring Park, Llanychaer, Fishguard

Small park with marvellous views, very convenient for Fishguard and the ferries.

In a superb rural setting, with cows in the field behind and wonderful views across the countryside towards the sea, Gwaun Vale provides 28 pitches. On mainly level grass, with one terrace above another, connected by an oval, gravel and tarmac roadway, 5 pitches have hardstanding and 19 have electricity connections (10A). There are plenty of water points and several picnic tables. A useful little shop doubles as reception with a well presented display of tourist information and variety of books on local walks to buy or borrow. One can also borrow a barbecue, iron and board, a boules set, baby bath or videos! The sanitary block, beside reception and to one side of the site, although of older style, is neat, clean and heated with plenty of mirrors, hooks and shelves. It has well equipped hot showers (20p, but for a long time) and washbasins including one in the ladies' with a WC. A cheerful laundry room with laundry sink, washing machine and dryer and two dishwashing sinks, is also well provided with tourist information. Chemical disposal facilities are outside. A children's play area is in a small sloping fenced field with adventure type equipment and a field for dogs next door complete with a useful seat - to watch dog and child! A family pub serving bar meals is within easy walking distance. Fishing, bicycle hire and riding 2 miles. Golf 7 miles. Day trips to Ireland are possible, as well as windsurfing, boating and fishing trips, and the Pembroke coastal footpath is nearby. A `must' to see is Wales' answer to the Bayeux Tapestry, a 100 ft. long tapestry on view in Fishguard (the French invaded Britain in 1797 and the tapestry, embroidered by 70 local women, gives a carefully researched account of this invasion and its defeat - full of life and humour).

Charges 1999:
-- Per unit incl. 1 or 2 persons £6.00 - £7.00, 3 or 4 persons £7.00 - £8.00, 5+ persons £8.00 - £9.00; electricity (10A) £1.50; awning, dog, extra car no charge.
-- No credit cards.
Open:
1 March - 31 October.
Address:
Llanychaer, Fishguard, Pembrokeshire SA65 9TA.
Tel:
(01348) 874698.
Reservations:
Advised for high season and B.Hs. and made with £10 deposit and 50p fee.

Directions: Park is on the right, 1½ miles from Fishguard; follow brown camping signs from centre. O.S.GR: SM977356.

South Wales

601 Cenarth Falls Holiday Park, Cenarth, Newcastle Emlyn

Excellent provision for tourers near the renowned Cenarth Falls.

The Davies family have developed an attractively landscaped, part wooded holiday home park with 80 privately owned units and 7 for hire. However, a neat well cared for, sheltered grassy area at the top of the park provides 30 touring pitches, 17 with sunken grid hardstanding and all with electricity (10A). Accessed via a semi-circular tarmac road, they enjoy views across the Teifi valley. An excellent, heated sanitary block complements this provision. Accessed by key, it uses a 'P.I.R.' system which controls heating, lighting, water and air-freshener on entry - very efficient. Tiled with non-slip floors, both men and ladies have an en-suite family room (doubling as provision for disabled visitors), an additional well equipped shower and also one washbasin in a roomy cabin. A laundry room has two washing machines and two dryers, for the use of the whole park. There are no laundry sinks, but two dishwashing sinks are under cover, neatly equipped with bowl and rack. There is easy ramped access, even to the chemical disposal unit. A 'state of the art', electrically operated motorcaravan service point using the van's own pump system is most impressive. A welcoming reception area doubles as a shop for essential groceries, papers, gas, etc. while the 'Fisherman's Cove', a friendly little private bar (automatic membership for all guests, weekends only in Oct, closed Nov), serves good value, home cooked meals, together with some entertainment, especially at weekends. Children's play area and games room with pool table and video game machine. A kidney shaped heated swimming pool with landscaped surrounds and sun-beds is very pleasant (open 1 May - mid Sept). Fishing ¼ mile, bicycle hire 8 miles, riding 7 miles, golf 10 miles. A footpath leads to the village and the famous Cenarth Falls (with leaping salmon). The National Coracle Centre is worth a visit. A member of the Best of British group.

Directions: Follow A484 Cardigan - Newcastle Emlyn road and park is signed before Cenarth village. O.S.GR: SN265421.

Charges 2000:
-- Per unit incl. 1 car and up to 4 people £8.00 - £15.00; extra person £2.00; awning £2.00; extra pup tent (space permitting) £2.50; dog £1.00; electricity (10A) £2.00.
-- Credit cards accepted.
-- VAT included.
Open:
1 March - mid November.
Address:
Cenarth,
Newcastle Emlyn,
Ceredigion
SA38 9JS.
Tel:
(01239) 710345.
FAX: as phone.
Reservations:
Made with 33% deposit; contact park.

See colour feature for `BEST of BRITISH` between pages 96/97

608 Llwyngwair Manor Holiday Park, Newport, nr. Fishguard

Riverside hotel and caravan park on the Pembrokeshire coast.

A feeling of grandeur strikes you when you turn into the drive at Llwyngwair Manor. As you turn the corner and come over a small hill, there are neatly sited and cared for caravan holiday homes and soon the ivy-clad manor house comes into view. The Manor is run as an hotel, but this is also where you check in for the touring park which you will see signed to the left of the open area in front of the house (take it steady here – there are a lot of fairly serious speed humps). The touring park is behind the manor and is laid out in two areas, the first with electricity available on the right hand side. The far area is for those who book in advance and all pitches have electricity. These are only 5A because of the limited supply coming to the whole holiday park, so those with state of the art electric water and space heating will need to watch out. The new sanitary block is mid-way and equi-distant from both camping areas. It is of a good modern standard, with spacious showers with a good dry area but, rather disappointingly, no soap tray and only one small hook. Washbasins are in cubicles in the shower area and there are separate rooms with toilets which also have washbasins. A bathroom for disabled visitors has excellent facilities, a family bathroom (key from the hotel) and chemical disposal facilities. The River Nevem runs through the park, right down one side of the touring area so those with small children need to take care. On the other hand, fishermen should be overjoyed as it is claimed that salmon and sea trout swim up and down and you have ½ mile over which you are invited to fish. The hotel provides food and drink (bar 11 am. - midnight, food noon - 1.30 and 6 - 9.30 pm. but shorter hours on Sunday). All children must be out of the bar by 9 pm. A tennis court, boules, snooker room and a TV lounge may be used by touring visitors. Apart from wonderful St Davids, the Dyfed Shire Horse Farm and the Oakwood Coaster Country Park are both very popular with visitors and a day trip to Ireland can be taken by ferry from nearby Fishguard. There are lovely walks, beaches and the beautiful small town of Newport nearby.

Directions: Park entrance is off the A487, 1 mile east of Newport. O.S.GR: SN072391.

Charges 1999:
-- Per unit £9.00; awning £1.00; electricity £2.00.
-- Weekly rates available.
-- Credit cards accepted.
Open:
April - end September.
Address:
Newport,
Pembrokeshire
SA42 0LX.
Tel:
(01239) 820498.
Reservations:
Advised in high season and B.Hs; contact park.

603 Brynich Caravan Park, Brecon

Well kept, family run park with picturesque setting and views towards Brecon Beacons.

Brynich has been gradually developed over the years by Colin and Maureen Jones to a very high standard. Originally farmland near the Brecon bypass, there are now three hedged camping fields, neatly mown and level with tarmac roads and a mixture of hardwood trees and shrubs maturing nicely, providing for 130 touring units of all types with 106 electricity points (10/16A). Two modern toilet blocks, which can be heated, have free hot water throughout, well equipped showers, washbasins in cubicles, washing up sinks, a laundry room and chemical disposal points. Two fully equipped units for visitors with disabilities are in one block, one providing left handed toilet facilities, the other right handed (key system) and a baby unit including bath. In total it is an excellent provision. A nice addition in a sloping field leading down to a stream is an extensive dog walk on one side of the Brynich Brook and an adventure play area, reached by stepping stones, on the opposite side. The stream is shallow and an added attraction along with the play equipment. Seats have also been provided. For smaller children there is some play equipment near reception and there is a large field for ball games. Reception and a well stocked shop (with gas) are in a building at the entrance. Motorcaravan service point. Within the Brecon Beacons National Park, this is a good area for hill walking and climbing. There are also two golf courses and possibilities for watersports. A local pub serving 'pub grub' is within walking distance. Fishing or bicycle hire 1½ miles, riding 2 miles, golf 3 miles. Access to the towpath of the Brecon and Monmouthshire Canal is only 200 yds from the park. Market days in Brecon on Tuesday and Friday. A member of the Best of British group.

Directions: Park entrance is off A470 (Builth Wells) road, 250 yds. from junction with the A40 (Abergavenny) road, 1 mile east of Brecon. O.S.GR: SO069278.

Charges 2000:
-- Per unit incl. 2 persons £8.50 - £9.50, 1 person £6.50 - £7.50; extra adult £2.25 - £2.75; child (4-16 yrs) £1.25 - £1.50; backpacker £4.00 - £4.50; awning £1.50 - £1.75; electricity £2.00 - £2.25; dog 50p.
-- Credit cards accepted.

Open:
29 March - 31 October.

Address:
Brecon, Powys LD3 7SH.

Tel:
(01874) 623325.
FAX: as phone.
E-mail: brynich@aol.com.

Reservations:
Advisable for hook-ups at B.Hs. and made with £10 deposit.

See colour feature for 'BEST of BRITISH' between pages 96/97

604 Pencelli Castle Caravan and Camping, Pencelli, nr. Brecon

Small park with character, charm and atmosphere in beautiful setting of the Usk Valley.

Pencelli Castle has been developed to a high standard by Gerwyn and Liz Rees. It is unusual to find a site which blends a high standard of facilities with relaxed, rural informality. Majestic trees border the main area and an adjacent rally or tent field, beyond which is the Brecon-Monmouth canal where gaily painted narrow boats (hired from the next village) and canoes slip silently past. Substantial development over the winter of 1999/2000 will mean that from Easter you will find the park in three sections, the first around a circular access road with 14 fully serviced pitches on hardstandings on the outside and a further 6 grass fully serviced pitches within the circle (all with 16A electricity). Two further fields to the right have 20 electric pitches (10A) and plenty of space for a 40 pitches without electricity for tents. A new block will provide showers, washbasins in cabins, dishwashing facilities and a laundry, together with two bathrooms for those with disabilities. The whole building will be heated as from Easter the park will be open all year round. The present, first rate facilities housed in small outhouses will be used at peak times only, although the old laundry room is to be converted into a drying room principally for hikers' use. The historic house, dating back to 1593, occupies the site of Pencelli castle (c. 1080 AD). Arched barns house old machinery including two rare Fordson tractors. There is an excellent, fenced children's play area. Reception is the farmhouse kitchen where, along with a warm welcome, there is plenty of local information. The Taff trail is nearby for mountain bikers, hill walkers reach the tops of the Brecon Beacons from here and there is an easy towpath ramble to Tal y Bont where its pubs and post office, with tea room, offer a village welcome. Bicycle hire, boat launching 150 yds, riding 2 miles, fishing 3 miles, golf 5 miles. No site shop (but gas is available). American RVs accepted. Regrettably no dogs - this is sheep country, but wait until you see the red deer.

Directions: From A40 Brecon bypass take B4558 south at sign for Llanfrynach to Pencelli village (2-3 miles); site is on the left. O.S.GR: SO096248.

Charges 1999:
-- Per unit incl. 2 persons £8.50; extra adult £2.00; child (5-13 yrs) £1.50; awning £1.50; electricity £2.00.
-- Tents: adult £4.00; child (5-13 yrs) £2.00, under 5 free.
-- No credit cards.

Open:
All year from Easter 2000.

Address:
Pencelli, Brecon, Powys LD3 7LX.

Tel:
(01874) 665451.
FAX: (01874) 665452.
E-mail: pencelli.castle@virgin.net.

Reservations:
Advised for peak season and B.Hs; contact site for details.

Mid Wales

628 Aeron Coast Caravan Park, Aberaeron

Family park with wide range of recreational facilities, on west coast of Wales.

Although Aeron Coast has many caravan holiday homes (150 privately owned), it provides for touring units in two fields separated from the beach and sea by a high bank (although the best beach is on the south side of this traditional fishing village). Pitches are on level grass with units well spaced in lines. There are two toilet blocks, one of older design but now updated, the other completed for '99 with excellent facilities, including large, free family showers and facilities for disabled people and babies. Chemical disposal and basic motorcaravan service point. The main attraction is the excellent recreational provision, both in and out of doors which includes a heated kidney shaped pool (June - Sept) plus toddlers' pool (unsupervised) and paved, walled area for sunbathing, tennis court and small half-court for youngsters, football and a sand pit. The indoor leisure area provides an under-5s' room with slide, teenagers' only room with juke box, table tennis, pool and games machines, a large entertainment room and TV room. In high season these are looked after by students who arrange activities such as tennis tournaments, rounders, treasure hunts, teenage discos or free films if the weather is poor. A club house and bar complete the amenities (from Easter) with family room, bar meals and takeaway. Reception keeps a range of tourist information and there is a shop at the petrol station at the entrance. Telephone. Only one dog per unit is accepted. Fishing and boat launching ½ mile, bicycle hire 6 miles, riding or golf 5 miles. A steam railway, craft centre, woollen mills and potteries are near.

Charges 2000:
-- Per unit incl. 2 persons £7.00 - £10.00; extra person over 12 yrs £1.00, 2-12 yrs 50p; electricity £1.50.
-- No credit cards.

Open:
1 March - 31 October.

Address:
North Road, Aberaeron, Ceredigion SA46 0JF.

Tel:
(01545) 570349.

Reservations:
Made with £10 deposit.

Alan Rogers' Discount

 Less 50p per unit per night, excl. Bank & school holidays

Directions: Park is on northern outskirts of Aberaeron village with entrance on the right beside an Texaco petrol station - not too easily seen. O.S.GR: SN461633.

629 Glan-y-Mor Leisure Park, Clarach Bay, Aberystwyth

Busy, sea front, holiday-style park with many holiday homes and touring sections.

Glan-y-Mor has an enviable situation on this part of the Cambrian coast, on an attractive bay beside the beach, yet within easy reach of Aberystwyth. On a wet day you may not wish to go far with the comprehensive leisure centre on site - it is open eight months of the year with reduced entry for campers. The balance of pitches is very much in favour of caravan holiday homes (3:1) which dominate the open park and bay, but there are 60 touring pitches, 45 with electricity (10A). They are rather pressed together in two sections on the lower part of the park. In high season, tents or motorcaravans can opt for space and fine views (but beware of winds) on a ridge of higher ground. An excellent, heated toilet block on the lower touring area has dishwashing, free hot water and laundry room, a toilet for disabled people and chemical disposal. Motorcaravan service point. A 'porta-cabin' type block (high season) is on the ridge ground. Further facilities for disabled people are at the leisure centre (RADAR key). This well equipped centre offers a heated pool, jacuzzi, solarium, sauna, steam room and gym. The complex also includes reception, amusement room, 10-pin bowling, bar, buffet bar and dance room (free entertainment nightly, Easter and May-Oct). Elsewhere are a supermarket, play area and a sports field. Licensed restaurant and takeaway (from Easter). Ice pack service and gas. Winter caravan storage. No dogs are accepted in high seasons. This is an ideal site for those wanting 'all the bells and whistles'!

Charges 2000:
-- Per unit incl. 2 persons £6.00 - £12.00; child free; extra person over 18 yrs £2.00; awning £3.00; electricity £2.00; dog £2.00.
-- Top camping area max. £10 plus £2 electricity.
-- Club membership (not Leisure complex) incl.
-- VAT included.
-- Credit cards accepted.

Open:
1 March - 31 October.

Address:
Clarach Bay, Aberystwyth, Ceredigion SY23 3DT.

Tel:
(01970) 828900.
FAX: (01970) 828890.

Reservations:
Any length, with £20 deposit; balance 28 days before arrival.

Directions: Clarach is signed west from the A487 (Aberystwyth - Machynlleth) in village of Bow Street. Follow signs over crossroads to beach and park. Access for caravans from Aberystwyth on B4572 is difficult. O.S.GR: SN580850.

630 Ocean View Caravan Park, Clarach Bay, Aberystwyth

Small, quiet holiday home park, with good provision for tourers and no entertainment.

The two, gently sloping, neatly cut grass fields for tourers at Ocean View have good views over Clarach Bay. Offering 24 numbered touring pitches, some of which have electrical hook-ups (5 or 10A), they are for all types of unit. There are some level pitches at the top, mainly for motorcaravans. There are also 50 privately owned caravan holiday homes, plus 3 for hire, also 4 cottages. A neat clean sanitary block provides free hot showers and laundry facilities, as well as washbasins, mirrors, hooks, shaver points, hand-dryers, soap, dishwashing sinks and chemical disposal. The usual water and waste water points and refuse bins are also provided. A football field, complete with goal posts, a dog walking area, picnic tables, public telephone and a small reception area (with gas supplies) complete the on-site facilities. Everything else, including bars and shops, is only 200 m. away beside the safe sand and pebble beach. This is sheltered by steep shale cliffs, along the top of which there are many walks enjoying magnificent views in the direction of both Borth and Aberystwyth. Golf 2 miles, riding 5 miles.

Charges 2000:
-- Per unit incl. 2 persons £6.50 - £9.00; extra person 2-12 yrs 50p, over 12 yrs £1.00; awning free - £1.00; dog £1.00; electricity £1.50 - £2.00.
-- One night stay + £1.00.
-- Credit cards accepted.
-- VAT included.
Open:
April - October.
Address:
Clarach Bay,
Aberystwyth,
Ceredigion SY23 3DT.
Tel:
(01970) 828425/623361.
FAX: (01970) 820215.
E-mail: alan@ grover10.freeserve.co.uk.
Reservations:
Made with £20 deposit.

Directions: Clarach is signed west from A487 (Aberystwyth - Machynlleth) in village of Bow Street. Follow signs over crossroads to beach and park. Access for caravans from Aberystwyth on A4572 is difficult. O.S.GR: SN592842.

Alan Rogers' Discount

Less £1 per 2 night stay, excl. Bank & school holidays

632 Fforest Fields Caravan and Camping Park, nr. Builth Wells

Secluded 'different' park set on family hill farm in the heart of Radnorshire.

This truly rural park has glorious views of the surrounding hills and a distinctly family atmosphere. This is simple country camping and caravanning at its best, without man-made distractions or intrusions - a place to unwind and watch the stars. The facilities include 50 large pitches on level grass, with 16A electrical connections, on a spacious and peaceful, carefully landscaped field by a stream. The sanitary facilities are acceptable, if not especially luxurious, with free hot showers (with seat, curtain and hook), open washbasins with mirrors, razor points, baby bath, dishwashing and laundry facilities including washing machines and a dryer, chemical disposal and heating in cool weather. Milk, eggs and orange juice are sold in reception and gas, otherwise there are few other on-site facilities, but the village of Hundred House, one mile away, has a pub, village stores and post office. George and Kate, the enthusiastic owners, have opened up much of the farm for moderate or ample woodland and moorland trails which can be enjoyed with much wildlife to see. Indeed wildlife is actively encouraged with nesting boxes for owls, song-birds and bats, by leaving field margins un-mown to encourage small mammals and by yearly tree planting. Dog 'Scampers'. A torch is useful. Fishing 3 miles, bicycle hire or golf 5 miles, riding 10 miles. George and Kate also run a para-gliding school where beginners are welcome.

Charges 2000:
-- Per caravan or trailer tent £7.50; motorcaravan or family tent £6.50; small tent £3.00 - £6.50; awning or child's tent £1.00; electricity £1.50.
-- No credit cards.
Open:
Easter/1 April - 31 Oct.
Address:
Hundred House, Builth Wells, Powys LD1 5RT.
Tel:
(01982) 570406.
FAX: (01982) 570444.
E-mail: paramania@ btinternet.
Reservations:
Contact park.

Directions: Park is signed off A481 between Hundred House and Builth Wells. O.S.GR: SO098535.

This delightful campsite is spacious, level and really peaceful. It nestles in a woodland bowl straddling a mountain stream in which children love to play. It has very clean modern toilets and free showers. There are no statics and no clubhouse. 16 amp electrics, laundry and plenty of space. Lovely walks direct from site and dogs are welcome. Reservations are free and no deposit required. Family run. Phone for brochure which will be sent by return. You'll wonder why you haven't been before!

01982 570406
www.fforestfields.co.uk

FFOREST FIELDS

'Simple country camping at its best'
Alan Rogers

- No statics
- No Clubhouse
- No Traffic Noise
- No Booking Deposit
- No Extras
- Excellent free facilities
- Family run
- 'A gem of a site'

★★★

RAC

AA

ENVIRONMENTAL AWARD
GOLD

631 Disserth Caravan Park, Disserth, nr. Llandrindod Wells

Small, family owned riverside park with some caravan holiday homes.

In a secluded situation between the ancient church of Disserth and the Ithon river and sheltered by a wooded cliff formed by river action, yet with handy access to many attractions in mid-Wales, Disserth provides a good base for families with an outdoor disposition. Up to 40 caravans, motorcaravans and tents are taken on one meadow adjacent to the river made attractive with shrubs and trees, a beautiful setting. The pitches are marked and spacing is generous with electrical hook-ups (10A) for all places. The pride of the park is the homely restaurant/coffee shop with an upstairs bar serving real ales (open at weekends and at peak times). Small, yet nicely converted from an old barn, this provides a restful evening haven after a day out. Reasonably priced meals are served in the evenings (7.30 - 9.30 pm). The toilet block provides free hot showers (3M, 3F) and, for ladies, a hair drying cubicle and three washbasins in cubicles. Laundry room, separate dishwashing sinks with hot water and chemical disposal facilities. These facilities are perhaps a little rustic for some but are adequate. There are colour coded bins for recycling certain rubbish. Small shop, information kiosk, public telephone, private fishing and access to the river with a pebbled beach. Bicycle hire 3 miles, riding 6 miles, golf 3 miles. Torches advised. Winter caravan storage. Two holiday homes to let, 17 others privately owned. A member of the Countryside Discovery group.

Directions: Follow signs for Disserth and Park, either west off A483 at Howey, or east from B4358 around eastern edge of Newbridge-on-Wye. O.S.GR: SO035585.

Charges 2000:
-- Per unit, incl. 2 adults £6.75 - £7.95; extra adult £1.95; child (3-15 yrs) £1.00; full awning 85p, porch 50p; electricity £1.95; single hiker and tent £4.95.
-- Credit cards accepted.
-- VAT included.

Open:
1 March - 31 October.

Address:
Disserth, Howey, Llandrindod Wells, Powys LD1 6NL.

Tel:
(01597) 860277.
FAX: as phone.
E-mail: graham@ disserth.freeserve.co.uk.

Reservations:
Made with £5 deposit (non-returnable).

Graham and Audrey Houghton invite you to

DISSERTH CARAVAN PARK

DISSERTH, HOWEY, LLANDRINDOD WELLS LD1 6NL

Telephone: 01597-860277

DELIGHTFUL
IDYLLIC
SMALL
SELECT
ENCHANTING
RELAXING
TRANQUIL
HIDDEN

MEMBER

IT ALL ADDS UP TO "DISSERTH"
A SECRET PLACE WORTH FINDING

Riverside camping, touring and holiday caravans. Peace and quiet with private fishing

'A COUNTRYSIDE DISCOVERY PARK'

PARC TEITHIO
★★★★
TOURING PARK

---

633 Daisy Bank Touring Caravan Park, Churchstoke

Pretty, tranquil 'adults only' park in Camlad Valley with wide views, ideal for walkers.

Attractively landscaped with 'old English' flower beds and many different trees and shrubs, this small park has been carefully developed by its owners, Brian and Joan Totterdell. The Welsh hills to the north and the Shropshire hills to the south overlook the two fields of 20 pitches each. The field nearer to the road (perhaps a little noise) is slightly sloping but there are hardstandings, while the second field is more level. All pitches have 10A electricity and most have water and waste water drainage. TV hook up leads can be borrowed. The heated toilet block, cheerful with stencils, plants and music, provides roomy showers (25p/5 mins), vanity style washbasins with free hot water. Covered washing up sinks (H&C) are at rear of block, but there are no laundry facilities (launderette at Churchstoke, 2 miles). There is a carefully screened refuse point with chemical disposal. Other amenities include brick built barbecues, a dog walk plus a small area for dogs to run free (dog grooming possible), and a new putting green (free loan of clubs and balls). With many walks in the area, including Offa's Dyke, a series of leaflets is available centred on Bishop's Castle 3 miles away. Tourist information is provided and a public phone. Supermarket 2 miles and many eating places near. Bicycle hire, riding or fishing 3 miles. Mr Totterdell will site your van for you and there is a late arrivals area with hook-up. A security bar at the entrance has to be lifted for motorcaravans. Gas supplies. Winter caravan storage. Although technically in Wales, the park is 500 yds from the Shropshire border, an area rich in history.

Directions: Site is by A489 road 2 miles east of Churchstoke in the direction of Craven Arms. O.S.GR: SO303929.

Charges 1999:
-- Per unit incl. 2 adults £6.50; extra person £1.50; awning £1.00; porch awning 50p; dog 50p; electricity £1.50 - £1.75; TV aerial hook-up free.
-- Adult only park.
-- No credit cards.

Open:
February - end Nov.

Address:
Churchstoke, Montgomeryshire, SY15 6EB.

Tel:
(01588) 620471.

Reservations:
Contact park.

636 Pen-y-Garth Caravan and Camping Park, Bala

Tranquil park set in a high valley; an ideal touring base.

A beautifully landscaped and located touring park, Pen-y-Garth has 63 pitches (35 with 10A electrical hook-ups) and two rally fields. Adjacent to the touring area are 54 caravan holiday homes, mainly privately owned (5 for hire). The newly renovated main sanitary block offers clean and well maintained facilities with free controllable showers. In addition to this block, there are two further men's and ladies' toilets and showers on payment (10p or 20p). Also provided are facilities for dishwashing (one with a free freezer), a laundry and a small games room for children. At reception there is a well stocked shop with gas, tourist information and Sara's, a lovely small, bistro-style licensed restaurant which is open most weekends for evening bar meals (but you should enquire about opening times when booking). There is a wonderful 6 acre recreation field opposite (but owned by the park) to burn off excess energy prior to that bistro supper. Watersports are plentiful in this area with the National White Water Centre 5 miles away and Lake Bala and Lake Vyrnwy close. Portmeirion, Snowdonia, Bodnant Gardens and many of those little railways are easy day trips from this park. Fishing, bicycle hire, riding and golf, all within 3 miles. Dogs are accepted by prior arrangement.

Directions: Take B4391 from Bala and in 1 mile turn right uphill at sign. Park is 600 yds on right before road narrows. O.S.GR: SH940349.

Charges 1999:
-- Per unit incl. 2 persons £6.95 - £8.50; extra person (over 5 yrs) £1.60; awning £1.60; electricity £1.70.
-- Less 25% for one person with small tent.
-- VAT included.
-- Credit cards accepted.
Open:
1 March - 31 October.
Address:
Bala,
Gwynedd LL23 7ES.
Tel:
(01678) 520485 (mobile: 0780 8198717).
FAX: (01678) 520401.
Reservations:
Made with 25% deposit (min. 3 nights at B.Hs).

637 Hendre Mynach Touring Caravan and Camping Park, Llanaber

True family park between mountains and beach, near Barmouth.

A neat and tidy park, colourful flowers and top rate facilities make an instant impression on arrival down the steep entrance to this park (help is available to get out if you are worried). There are two toilet blocks, one modern and one traditional, but both offering excellent facilities including spacious showers (20p) and washbasins in cubicles in the new block. Extra showers are provided in mobile units which are used in peak times and, although this is a large park, the facilities should cope well even when it is full. The 220 pitches are in various areas, with substantial tent areas identified. Twenty gravel hardstandings are available and around the park there are 120 electricity hook-ups (10A) and ample water points. An on-site shop is well stocked and incorporates a snack bar and takeaway (open 8.30 am. - 9 pm. in peak times, less at quieter times). The quaint old seaside and fishing town of Barmouth is just ¾ mile – a 15-20 minute walk along the prom. The local pub offers a courtesy bus service from the park (7.30 pm. - 11 pm.) and serves bar snacks, etc. The beach is only 100 yards but a railway line runs between the park and the beach. This can be crossed at any of three points by pedestrian operated gates - this could be a worry for those with young children.

Directions: Park is off the A496 road north of Barmouth in village of Llanaber with entrance down a steep drive. O.S.GR: SH608168.

Charges 1999:
-- Per unit incl. 2 persons £8.00 - £13.00; electricity (10A) £2.00; extra adult £2.00; child (2-15 yrs) £1.00; first dog free, extra dog 50p.
-- Credit cards accepted.
Open:
1 March - 30 November.
Address:
Llanaber, Barmouth,
Gwynedd LL42 1YR.
Tel:
(01341) 280262.
FAX: (01341) 280586.
E-mail: mynach@ btinternet.com.
Reservations:
Made with £20 deposit and £1.50 booking fee.

635 Barcdy Caravan and Camping Park, Talsarnau, nr. Harlech

Rurally situated park with good facilities and marvellous views.

Barcdy is partly in a sheltered vale, partly on a plateau top and partly in open fields edged by woods, with fells to the rear and views across the Lleyn peninsula in one direction and towards Snowdon range in another. The park provides for all tastes with 108 level or sloping grass pitches, including 38 for tourers and 40 for tents, with or without 10A electricity (44 points), plus 30 caravan holiday homes (3 for hire). There are two toilet blocks, the one at the top of the valley opened in high season only. Facilities include large, comfortable showers which open direct to the outside except for one in each section. Hot water is metered to the showers (25p) and dishwashing sinks (10p). Excellent chemical disposal point. A shop opens 8.30-11 am and 4-7 pm (Spr. B.H, then mid July-end Aug) for essentials and gas. The farm includes 28 acres of fields and natural oak woods (a haven for children) and further up the hills are the two Tecwyn lakes for fishing or just to relax by and enjoy the views. Riding 4 miles, golf 4 or 6 miles. Harlech beach and castle are 4 miles, the village of Portmeirion is nearby and Snowdonia is on your doorstep. No dogs accepted. A member of the Countryside Discovery group.

Directions: Park is just off the A496 between villages of Llandecwyn and Talsarnau, 4 miles north of Harlech. O.S.GR: SH622371.

Charges 1999:
-- Per unit incl. 2 persons £7.50 - £9.50; extra adult £3.00; child (up to 16 yrs) £1.50; awning free - £1.00; electricity (10A) £1.95.
-- Credit cards accepted.
Open:
Easter - 31 October.
Address:
Talsarnau, nr. Harlech,
Gwynedd LL47 6YG.
Tel:
(01766) 770736.
Reservations:
Contact park.

Mid Wales

Tourism information for Mid Wales may also be obtained from:
Mid Wales Tourism Ltd. The Station, Machynlleth SY20 8TG
Tel: 01654 702653 Fax: 01654 703235 E-mail: info@brilliantbreaks.demon.co.uk

The hinterland of Mid Wales is upland country, covered in traditional sheep hill farms where market towns come to life once a week for livestock markets. The high grassy plateaux of the Brecon Beacon National Park define its southern limits, north of which lie Wales' spa towns. Llandridnod Wells is the only one to have remained active where you can drink a glass of its famous water at the Victoria pump room. To the West, stunning drovers' routes weave across the lonesome Cambrian Mountains. The coastline of Cardigan Bay is not as scenic as that of Pembrokeshire nor as interesting as that of the north coast.

North Wales

658 Camping and Caravanning Club Site Llanystumdwy, Criccieth

Small, well maintained park with good facilities, overlooking mountains and sea.

One of the oldest Camping and Caravanning Club sites, Llanystumdwy is on sloping grass, but the wardens are very helpful and know their site and can advise on the most suitable pitch and even have a supply of chocks. There are 60 pitches in total (20 ft. spacing), 45 with 10A electricity, spaced over two hedged fields with mainly caravans in the top field, motorcaravans and tents lower down. A purpose built toilet block to one side provides excellent, full facilities for the disabled including access ramp. Tiled and nicely finished with green fittings, it has free hot water (you can set your own temperature in the showers), one washbasin each in a cubicle for male and female and extra large sinks. Facilities for babies, hairdryers and laundry (taps with fitting for disabled people). Chemical disposal point, enclosed with bolt, and neat, fenced refuse points located about the park. Gas is available. A small dog walk is provided but main exercising should be off the park. Public telephone. A little library with a supply of tourist information is next to the small reception. A shop and pub are in the village and a bus leaves each hour from outside the site to Pwllheli or Porthmadog. This is a good base from which to explore the Lleyn peninsula or Snowdonia National Park. Portmeirion with its Italianate village is near. Riding or fishing ½ mile, golf 2½ miles.

Charges 2000:
-- Per 2 adults £7.50 - £10.60; child (6-18 yrs) £1.60; non-member pitch fee £4.30; electricity £1.60 - £2.35.
-- VAT included.
-- Credit cards accepted.
Open:
March - November.
Address:
C&C Club Site, Tyddyn Sianel, Llanystumdwy, Criccieth, Gwynedd LL52 0LS.
Tel:
(01766) 522855.
(no calls after 8 pm).
Reservations:
Necessary and made with deposit - contact the wardens.

Directions: Follow A497 from Criccieth west and take the second right to Llanystumdwy. Site is on the right. O.S.GR: SH469384.

659 Beddgelert Caravan and Camping Site, Beddgelert

Well equipped Forestry Commission site in the heart of Snowdonia.

Set in a marvellous, natural, wooded environment on the slopes of Snowdon with abundant fauna and flora, tumbling streams and always something to watch from the cheeky squirrels to the smallest bird in Britain, this site is well equipped and well managed. Two fully equipped sanitary blocks clad in natural wood provide large, free hot showers (with good dry areas), washbasins and washing up sinks (both with H&C). There is laundry equipment in one block. A small unit provides extra washbasins and toilets in peak season and there is a toilet and washbasin for the disabled. The site provides 280 pitches – tents in a semi-wooded field area and caravans with numbered hardstandings amongst the trees with 10A electricity. Tents may pitch where they like in their areas leaving 6 m. between units. Metal tent pegs may be best (available from the shop). There are plenty of water points, central refuse areas and two chemical disposal points are provided together with a motorcaravan emptying point. Reception is central, as is a well provisioned shop. Free maps of the forest walks are provided in reception and orienteering and fishing possible. A bus service stops at the top of the entrance lane (two hourly for Caernarfon and Porthmadog). A pub is within walking distance (¾ mile) and other eating places nearby. Bicycle hire within 500 m. in forest. There is a well equipped children's adventure playground, but we wonder if it is used considering what nature has provided – water, trees, rocks, etc!

Charges 1999:
-- Per adult £3.40 - £4.30; child (5-14 yrs) £1.50 - £2.10; extra car, trailer or pup tent £2.50; electricity £2.10 - £2.30.
-- Weekend prices higher.
-- Credit cards accepted.
Open:
All year.
Address:
Beddgelert Campsite, Beddgelert, Gwynedd LL55 4UU.
Tel:
(01766) 890288.
Reservations:
Necessary for B.Hs and peak times (min. 3 nights with £30 deposit). Contact (at all times): Forest Holidays, Forestry Commission, 231 Corstorphine Road, Edinburgh EH12 7AT. Tel: (0131) 314 6505.

Directions: Site is clearly signed to the left 1 mile north of Beddgelert on A4085 Caernarfon road. O.S.GR: SH578490.

North Wales

Tourism information for North Wales may also be obtained from:
North Wales Tourism Ltd. 77 Conway Road, Colwyn Bay LL29 7LN
Tel: 01492 531731 Fax: 01492 530059 E-mail: croes@nwt.co.uk www.nwt.co.uk

North Wales is very much the most nationalist part of the country but, having said that, it is well worth visiting. Not only is peppered with impressive medieval castles such as Conway, Caernarfon and Harlech, but it also contains the country's most magnificent scenery in the mountains of the Snowdonia National Park and several small privately or voluntarily operated railway lines such as Ffestiniog, Bala or Llanberis not to mention the unusual Italianate village of Portmeirion.

660 Bryn Gloch Caravan and Camping Park, Betws Garmon

Well run and family owned touring park in the impressive Snowdonia area.

Bryn Gloch is a neat, well kept and quiet country park taking some 160 units on five flat, wide meadows, with 12 caravan holiday homes. There are tarmac roads and free areas are allowed in the middle for play. With 150 electrical connections (10A) available, there are 8 all weather pitches, 6 'super' pitches and 8 serviced pitches (shared). The sanitary arrangements have been extensively upgraded and the two original blocks are now of very commendable standard. A further, purpose built shower and toilet block has been added. The far field has been equipped with a 'portacabin' style unit containing all facilities, for use in peak season. There is free hot water in the washbasins (some private cabins) and in the pre-set showers and indoor washing-up sinks. An excellent building houses a family bathroom (£1 for hot water), baby changing room and complete facilities for disabled visitors (coded access). Chemical disposal point. Fishing is possible on the river bordering the park with a barbecue and picnic area, adventure play area and field for ball games. There is a shop (1/3-30/10), well equipped laundry and separate drying room, TV and games rooms with pool tables, amusement machines and tourist information are located in one complex by the reception; this building also houses an extra shower and toilet per sex. Other amenities include minigolf, a public phone and a car wash and motorcaravan service point. Riding 2½ miles, bicycle hire or golf 5 miles, as is Caernarfon with its famous castle. Bungalow and bunk type self catering accommodation is for rent.

Directions: Park is just beyond Waunfawr, 4½ miles southeast of Caernarfon on A4085 towards Beddgelert. Watch for signs and park entrance is opposite St Garmon church. O.S.GR: SH538578.

Charges 1999:
-- Per unit incl. 2 persons £8.50 (caravans over 18 ft. plus £1); extra adult £2.00; child (3-16 yrs) £1.50; awning or pup tent £1.50; dog 50p; electricity £2.30; 'super' pitch incl. electricity, etc. plus £5.30; serviced pitch plus £4.30.
-- VAT included.
-- Credit cards accepted.
Open:
All year, limited facilities 1 Nov - 1 March.
Address:
Betws Garmon, nr. Caernarfon, Gwynedd LL54 7YY.
Tel/Fax:
(01286) 650216.
E-mail: eurig@ easynet.co.uk.
Reservations:
Necessary for B.Hs. (min. 3 nights) with payment in full; other times with deposit of 1st night's fee.

661 Cadnant Valley Caravan Park, Caernarfon

Pretty town park 10 minutes walk from Caernarfon centre.

This is an older style, town centre park where the fairly steep road past reception leads you to a hidden, tree lined valley area with a little stream, complete with two bridges, which once fed the moat of the historic Caernarfon Castle. The shower and toilet blocks (with free hot water), whilst somewhat dated, are satisfactory and to one side of the site, which has 69 marked, level pitches (35 with 16A electricity and 5 hardstandings). You can choose a secluded area across the stream, a more open, central grass area or a terraced pitch, depending on your unit. Cadnant's natural environment has been enhanced with plants, shrubs and stepping stone paths; even the play area blends in and provides solid, rustic equipment on safety matting. Fully equipped laundry room, under cover dishwashing (with H&C) and chemical disposal. Reception keeps gas and tourist information. A small supermarket is 30 yds but the main shops and restaurants are only a 5-6 minute walk and Caernarfon's leisure centre with pool is 400 yds. Fishing 1 mile, riding and golf 2 miles, bicycle hire ½ mile. Easily accessible by public transport are Bangor, Llanberis/Snowdon and Porthmadog. It is nice to find such a site within town centre walking distance, never mind the added attractions of this historic area of Wales. The park is, however, within the town and in an urban area so there may be odd extra noise. Dogs are welcome on a lead, small dog area provided.

Directions: Park is on A4086 Llanberis road. From town centre watch carefully for park entrance after second roundabout, opposite a school and just before the fire station. O.S.GR: SH488628.

Charges 2000:
-- Per unit incl. 2 persons £7.00 - £9.00, 1 person £5.50 - £7.00; 2-man tent and car £6.00 - £8.00; backpacker (no car) £4.00; extra adult £1.50; child (4-16 yrs) £1.00; dog or extra car 50p; electricity £2.00.
-- No credit cards.
Open:
14 March - 31 October.
Address:
Llanberis Road, Caernarfon, Gwynedd LL55 2DF.
Tel:
(01286) 673196.
Reservations:
Advised for high season and made with £10 deposit.

North Wales

664 Home Farm Caravan Park, Marianglas, Anglesey

Good quality site with excellent facilities for children.

A tarmac drive through an open field leads to this neatly laid out park, with caravan holiday homes to one side. Nestling below what was once a Celtic hill fort, later decimated as a quarry, it is edged with mature trees and farmland. There is a circular, tarmac access road for the 61 well spaced and numbered pitches, which include 9 fully serviced with electricity, water and waste water and a further 13 with electricity and water, All of these have hardstanding with 16A electricity; other pitches all have 10A supply. On neatly cut grass, some areas are slightly sloping, and there is a separate area for tents. Two purpose built toilet blocks, one part of the reception building, are of the same design, fully tiled and can be heated. They provide excellent roomy showers with curtains, vanity style washbasins (H&C), free hairdryer, soap and hand dryer, en-suite provision for people with disabilities (with key) and an excellent small bathroom for children with baby bath and curtain for privacy, a laundry room and good washing up facilities. Neat refuse, water and waste points, chemical disposal, motorcaravan point, and a public telephone complete the facilities. Reception provides basic essentials, gas and some caravan accessories, alongside tourist information. The 'piece de resistance' of this park must be the children's indoor play area, large super adventure play equipment, complete with tunnels, bridges on safe rubber matting, not to mention an outside fenced play area. TV and a pool table complete the provision, although there are fields available for sports, football, etc. and walking. Fishing or golf 2 miles, riding 8 miles. Various beaches, sandy or rocky, are within a mile. A member of the Best of British group.

Charges 1999:
-- Per unit incl. 2 persons £7.50 - £9.00, large or trailer tent £7.50 - £10.50; extra person (over 5 yrs), car or boat £1.50; awning or extra pup tent £1.50; electricity £2.00; fully serviced pitch plus £2.00.
-- Credit cards accepted.

Open:
April - October.

Address:
Marianglas,
Isle of Anglesey
LL73 8PH.

Tel:
(01248) 410614.
FAX: (01248) 410900.

Reservations:
Essential for peak season (min. 3 days at B.Hs) and made with £15 deposit.

Directions: From the Britannia Bridge take second exit left signed Benllech and Amlwch on the A5025. Two miles after Benllech keep left at roundabout and park entrance is approx. 300 yards on left beyond the church. O.S.GR: SH498850.

669 Bron-Y-Wendon Touring Caravan Park, Llanddulas, Colwyn Bay

Mature, 'non-seaside' type of park beside the sea.

Bron Y Wendon is right by the sea between Abergele and Colwyn Bay on the beautiful North Wales coast road. However, this is a quiet park which, by its own admission, is not really geared up for the family unit - there is no children's playground here, although there is a games room with table tennis and a separate TV room. On the day we visited there was wall-to-wall blue sky, a slight breeze and a fantastic blue sea - quite something. The site is manicured to the highest standards. Two sanitary blocks provide excellent facilities, the top block, which can be heated, having men's and women's shower rooms separate from the toilets and washbasins. There are also good facilities for disabled visitors. Chemical disposal facilities and a laundry with washing machines and dryers are also provided. The park caters for a large number of seasonal caravans on pitches with gravel bases which are all kept very tidy. There are a further 65 touring pitches, all grass based and all with electrical hook ups (16A). All pitches have coastal views and the sea and beach are just a short walk away. A mobile shop visits the park daily and gas is available on site. Very close by is the village of Llanddulas which has shops and several good pubs. Colwyn Bay, Conwy, Anglesey, Llandudno, Snowdonia and Chester are all within easy reach of the park, so there is lots to do. Having said how peaceful and quiet everything is (particularly for a seaside park in this area), there could be a little road noise from the adjacent A55 and during our visit a small train passed on the tracks between the park and the sea (just a few yards) and at night with little else going on it could be just noticeable.

Charges 1999:
-- Per pitch £5.00 - £7.00; person £1.50; child (2-12 yrs) £1.00; awning £2.00; electricity (16A) £2.00.
-- VAT included.
-- Credit cards accepted.

Open:
21 March - 30 October.

Address:
Wern Road, Llanddulas,
Colwyn Bay LL22 8HG.

Tel:
(01492) 512903.
FAX: as phone.

Reservations:
Made with £5 deposit;
contact park.

Alan Rogers' Discount

Less 50p per unit, per night

Directions: From A55 Chester - Conwy road at Llanddulas junction (A547). Turn right opposite Shell garage and park is approx. ¼ mile, signed on coast side of the road. O.S.GR: SH897785.

665 Hunter's Hamlet Touring Caravan Park, nr. Abergele

Small, family owned, quality park with beautiful rural views.

The design, layout and facilities of this purpose built site are of a very high standard and the Hunter family are justifiably proud of the park, which is licensed for all units except tents (trailer tents allowed). On a gently sloping hillside providing panoramic views, one area provides 15 well spaced pitches with hardstanding and 10A electricity hook-ups, with access from a circular, hard-core road. A new area has been developed next to this of a similar design but with 8 pitches fully serviced by new tourer `superpitches' (water, waste water, sewerage, TV and electricity connections). Shrubs and bushes at various stages of growth enhance both areas. An excellent purpose built, heated sanitary block has fully tiled facilities including showers en-suite with toilets for both sexes, vanity style washbasins and hairdryers. There is the nice provision of sinks for laundry and dishwashing (H&C), washing machine and dryer, iron and board, freezer and fridge. A family bathroom (metered) has been added, there are separate toilet and shower facilities for visitors with disabilities, plus chemical disposal and refuse points. A natural play area incorporating rustic adventure equipment set amongst mature beech trees with a small bubbling stream (supervised by the ducks) is a children's paradise. Table tennis and pool in a barn also. Milk and papers can be ordered and the Hunters will do their best to meet your needs, even to survival rations! Public telephone. Only two dogs per unit allowed (not certain breeds in July/Aug. and B.Hs). Self catering flat available. All year caravan storage. Fishing (2 miles). The park is well situated to tour Snowdonia and Anglesey and is within easy reach of Llandudno and Rhyl.

Charges 1999:
-- Per unit incl. 2 adults and 2 children: basic pitch £8.00 - £10.00, `super' pitch (fully incl.) £15.00 - £18.00; extra person £2.00; awning £2.00; extra car £2.00; electricity (10A) £2.00.
-- Less £5 on weekly bookings.
-- Aug. B.H, plus £1.00.
-- Credit cards accepted.

Open:
21 March - 31 October.

Address:
Sirior Goch Farm,
Betws-yn-Rhos,
Abergele,
LL22 8PL.

Tel:
(01745) 832237.
FAX: as phone.

Reservations:
Made with £2 per night deposit (min. £10). B.H. bookings min. 4 nights.

Directions: From Abergele take the A548 south for 2¾ miles; turn onto the B5381 in the direction of Betws-yn-Rhos and park is on left after ½ mile. To date there are no local authority caravan signs so watch carefully for the farm after turning - it can be identified by a artistically painted sign with the house and farm name: `Sirior Goch Farm' and Hunter's Hamlet. O.S.GR: SH929736.

670 Ty Ucha Caravan Park, Llangollen

Quiet, family owned park in the Vale of Llangollen, for caravans and motorhomes only.

Only a mile from Llangollen, world famous for the Eisteddfod, Ty Ucha has a rather dramatic setting, nestling under its own mountain and with views across the valley to craggy Dinas Bran castle. It is a neat, ordered park, carefully managed by the owners, providing 40 pitches (30 with 10A electrical hook-up) well spaced round a large, grassy field with an open centre for a play area and a small paddock area. One side slopes gently and is bounded by a stream and wood. A path leads from here for various mountain walks, depending on your energy and ability. The single toilet block, although of `portacabin' style, is clean and well maintained and can be heated. It provides two metered showers for each sex (a little cramped), small washbasins with free hot water, shelf and mirror, toilets and chemical disposal. A dishwashing sink with cold water is outside. There are no laundry facilities but there is a launderette in Llangollen. Gas is available. Games room with table tennis. Because of overhead cables, kite flying is forbidden; no bike riding either. The paddock area provides for those who prefer to be without the company of children or dogs. Public telephone. Late arrivals area. There is an hotel ½ mile away where reasonably priced meals are available. Fishing 1 mile, golf ½ mile. Eisteddfod is an international festival of music and dance held for six days starting on the first Tuesday of the first full week in July every year - a very busy time for the area.

Charges 2000:
-- Per caravan incl. 2 persons £7.00, motor-caravan £6.00; extra person £1.00; awning (environmental ground-sheets) £1.00; electricity £2.00.
-- Reductions for OAPs for weekly stays.
-- No credit cards.

Open:
Easter - October.

Address:
Maesmawr Road,
Llangollen,
Denbighshire LL20 7PP.

Tel:
(01978) 860677.

Reservations:
Necessary for B.Hs. and Eisteddfod and made with £10 deposit; 3 days min. at B.H.s.

Directions: Park is signed off A5 road, 1 mile east of Llangollen (250 yds). O.S.GR: SJ228411.

Alan Rogers' Discount

Less 50p per unit, per night

North Wales

667 The Plassey Touring and Leisure Park, Eyton, nr. Wrexham

Spacious, rural 250-acre park in the Dee Valley, offering many activities.

The Plassey is not just a touring park but is also a leisure and craft centre with a friendly, busy atmosphere and pleasant environment. The Edwardian farm buildings have recently been tastefully converted to provide a restaurant, coffee shop, health, beauty and hair studio, small garden centre and 16 different craft and retail units, open all year to the public. Other amenities include a 9 hole golf course, fishing pools and countryside footpaths. Unusually there is also a small brewery on site, producing its own unique Plassey Bitter! The park itself is spacious with pitches around the outer edges of a series of fields forming circles. There are 120 pitches with electrical connections (16A) and 15 hardstandings, plus two fields of seasonal caravans which will put pressure on the facilities. The original toilet facilities beside the entrance and under the clubhouse have been refurbished to a good standard. These are to be supplemented for the 2000 season by a new heated shower and toilet block in the top field area (to replace a 'porta-cabin' style unit). Showers are free and there are dishwashing sinks, a laundry room, chemical disposal and motorcaravan services. The Tree Tops clubhouse, serving Plassey Bitter, overlooks the park and has a children's room (open March - Oct). A good adventure playground beside a small wood has equipment for smaller children on bark chippings (note: bicycles, skateboards or footballs are not allowed on the site). Badminton courts including an indoor one can be booked and there is an indoor, heated swimming pool with sun-bed and sauna (May - Sept, limited hours mid-week). Shop (all season) and gas. Winter caravan storage. Riding or bicycle hire 5 miles. There is much to do and to look at in a rural setting at the Plassey but it is probably best enjoyed mid-week and avoiding the busy Bank Holidays. Certainly for peace and quiet. you should try and pitch away from reception, the clubhouse and arcade games.

Directions: Follow brown and cream signs (for The Plassey) from the A483 Chester - Oswestry bypass onto the B5426 and park is 2½ miles. Also signed from the A528 Marchwiel - Overton road. O.S.GR: SJ349452.

Charges 2000:
-- Per unit incl. 2 adults, 2 children, electricity and club membership £10.00 - £12.00; extra person, dog or extra car £1.00; awning £2.00.
-- Includes club membership, coarse fishing, badminton and table tennis (own racquets and bats required).
-- B.H. supplement £1 per night.
-- Discount for weekly booking.
-- VAT included.
-- Credit cards accepted.

Open:
5 March - 7 November.

Address:
Eyton,
Wrexham LL13 0SP.

Tel:
(01978) 780277.
FAX: (01978) 780019.

Reservations:
Necessary for weekends, B.Hs and July/Aug. and made with £20 deposit.

Alan Rogers' Discount

Less 50p per unit, per night

668 James' Caravan Park, Ruabon, nr. Wrexham

All year site, easily accessible and with good facilities.

Open all year, this park has a heated toilet block and attractive, park-like surroundings with mature trees and neat, short grass. However, edged by two main roads it is subject to some road noise. The old farm buildings and owner's collection of original farm machinery, carefully restored and maintained, add interest to the park. The heated toilet block offers roomy showers (20p) with a useful rail to help those of advancing age with feet washing, curtain and shelf, vanity style washbasins with good mirrors and a hairdryer for ladies (20p). En-suite facilities for visitors with disabilities have a special 'clos o mat' toilet! The park has over 40 pitches, some level and some on a slope, with informal siting giving either a view or shade. Electricity (6A) is available all over, although a long lead may be useful. Tourist information, free freezer for ice packs and a telephone are in the foyer of the toilet block. Chemical disposal and motorcaravan service point. Gas available. The village is a 10 minute walk with a Spar shop, fish and chips, a launderette and four pubs. Golf 3 miles. This is a useful park with easy access from the A483 Wrexham - Oswestry road (road noise).

Directions: Park is at junction of A483/A539 Llangollen road and is accessible from the west-bound A539. O.S.GR: SJ302434.

Charges 1999:
-- Per unit incl. 2 persons £7.00; extra person £1.00; awning £1.00; extra car £1.00; dog 50p; electricity £2.00.
-- No credit cards.

Open:
All year.

Address:
Ruabon,
Wrexham LL14 6DW.

Tel:
(01978) 820148.
FAX: as phone.
E-Mail: ray@
carastay.demon.co.uk.

Reservations:
Contact park for details.

Tourist Information:
A list of quarterly events is available free from the Wales Tourist Board, PO Box 1 Cardiff CF1 2XN.

SCOTLAND

Scottish Tourist Board

23 Ravelston Terrace, Edinburgh EH4 3EU
Tel: (0131) 332 2433 Fax: (0131) 315 2906
Internet: http://www.holiday.scotland.net

We have used the following Regional Tourist Areas to list our parks:

1. Scottish Lowlands   2. Heart of Scotland   3. Grampian   4. Highlands and Islands

Scotland provides superb opportunities to enjoy wild and grand scenery. It also offers towns and cities with a rich cultural life and over the centuries has had a disproportionately large impact on the world with many of its philosophers, scientists and inventors being responsible for the ideas on which we base our understanding of the world.

The area we identify as the **Scottish Lowlands** or Southern Scotland, covers Dumfries and Galloway, the Scottish Borders, Edinburgh and Lothians, Greater Glasgow and the Clyde valley.

In Dumfries and Galloway lonely hills roll down to pastures and dark woods which in turn give way to rich farmlands and a sunny south facing coast and a mild climate allows for some magnificent gardens to visit. The Borders is an area of tranquil villages, bustling textile towns and a wild coastline running north from Berwick-upon-Tweed. There are magnificent historic houses, great Border abbeys, working woollen mills and craft workshops. Sir

Walter Scott, the famous Scottish writer, lived at Abbotsford near Melrose and is buried at Dryburgh Abbey, one of the four abbeys which once were influential in Borders life. The Lothians, bordered by the sea waters of the Firth of Forth to the unspoiled Pentland Hills, has a beautiful coastline and rich countryside. Edinburgh with its castle which is open all year is dealt with elsewhere as is Glasgow. Paisley is known for the Paisley shawl and Lanark for the enlightened industrialist Robert Owen whose Utopian ideas on workers welfare in his textile mills which became world famous.

Heart of Scotland covering Loch Lomand, Stirling and the Trossachs, Perthshire, Angus, Dundee and the Kingdom of Fife. Here the Lowlands meet the mountains of the north and west and in old days all routes led to Stirling. Because of its strategic position whoever held Stirling Castle controlled the Scottish nation.

Continued on page 177

Continued on page 177

692 Cressfield Caravan Park, Ecclefechan, nr. Lockerbie

Purpose designed, well run, modern park just north of the border, open all year.

Cressfield is close to main routes (A74M/M6) and is an ideal transit park, although the Solway Firth or Dumfries and Galloway tourist features are nearby. It has been developed in pleasant undulating countryside, next to the village of Ecclefechan, to a very high standard and is personally managed by the owner. The park provides 153 pitches of which 37 are for touring units, the remainder being taken up by holiday homes and seasonal vans. The park is pleasantly landscaped (trees are growing well) and the level pitches, mostly with hardstanding, are connected by tarmac or gravel roads and provided with 16A electric hook-ups. A good rally field is also fully equipped with electrical hook-ups. The modern, heated toilet block is cenral, operated on a key system and provides excellent facilities including free, well equipped showers, washbasins in cubicles, hair-dryers (metered) and a bath is a welcome addition in the ladies' (20p). A toilet and washbasin are provided for disabled visitors, plus shower seats, in both the male and female sections. Excellent laundry room, washing up area under cover, bin store, chemical disposal and motorcaravan service point. Large dog exercise field and dog waste bins. Other amenities include a well equipped, fenced children's play area, 9 hole putting green and a sports field with goal posts (not in wet weather or Nov-March), tennis and badminton nets and netball posts. Giant chess and draughts, plus boules. There is no shop but it is only ¼ mile from the village and adjacent to the park is an hotel for a drink or a meal. Gas available on site. For the more active there are seven golf courses nearby, opportunities for coarse or game fishing, cycling, walking, birdwatching and historical Solway to explore. Boat launching 8 miles. Some road noise is possible.

Charges 1999:
-- Per unit incl. 2 adults £6.50 - £8.00; awning, extra car or small tent £1.00; extra adult £2.00; child (under 16 yrs) £1.00; car and small tent £6.50 - £7.00; walkers or cyclists with 2-man tent £5.00; electricity £2.00 - £2.50.
-- B.H.s - £2 extra per night, per unit.
-- No credit cards.
-- VAT included.

Open:
All year.

Address:
Ecclefechan,
nr. Lockerbie,
Dumfries and Galloway
DG11 3DR.

Tel:
(01576) 300702.
FAX: (01576) 300702.

Reservations:
Phone bookings accepted.

Alan Rogers' Discount

Less 50p per unit, per night

Directions: Approaching from north or south on A74(M) (10 miles north of Gretna, 5 miles south of Lockerbie) take exit 19 for Ecclefechan and follow B7076 for ½ mile to south side of village; park is signed. O.S.GR: NY196744.

Lowlands

Continued from previous page
The Trossachs with their heather-clad hills are the home of Rob Roy the Scottish folk hero . The Kingdom of Fife boasts two ancient 'capitals'. Dunfermline, the seat of early Celtic kings and the final resting place of Robert the Bruce and St Andrews, the ecclesiastical capital, now a university town and the 'Home of Golf'.

Grampian includes the Grampian Highlands, Aberdeen and the North East Coast and is probably beat known for Royal Deeside where Prince Albert built Balmoral Castle as a summer home for Queen

Victoria and the Malt Whisky Trail. This is a signposted route featuring seven whisky distilleries, each with excellent interpretation facilities for visitors.

The **Highlands and Islands** one of the last wildernesses in Europe, from the soaring beauty of Glencoe to the to the idyllic charm of the Isles, and from the crashing waves of the northern coastline to the silence of the windswept moors. Home to the Loch Ness Monster and the famous Fort William to Mallaig railway, one of the greatest railway journeys in the world.

691 Hoddom Castle Caravan Park, Lockerbie

Attractive site in well landscaped, spacious park.

The oldest part of Hoddom Castle is a 16th century Borders Pele Tower, or fortified keep. This was extended to form a residence for a Lancashire cotton magnate, became a youth hostel and was then taken over by the army during WW2. Since then parts have been demolished but the original border keep still survives, unfortunately in a semi-derelict state. The site's bar and restaurant have been developed in the courtyard area from the coach houses and the main ladies' toilet block was the stables. The park is well laid out on mainly sloping ground with many mature and beautiful trees, originally part of an arboretum. The drive to the site is ¾ mile long with a one way system. Many of the 120 numbered pitches have good views of the castle and have gravel hardstandings with grass for awnings, most with electrical connections (10A). In front of the castle are flat fields for tents and caravans not needing electricity. The main toilet block can be heated and is very well appointed with washbasins in cubicles and free hot showers. A new unit for disabled visitors provides a shower, WC, hairdryer, etc. The other two blocks are tiled and are kept very clean, with washbasins and WCs. Each block has dishwashing sinks and there is a well equipped laundry room at the castle. Behind the castle a building houses a chemical disposal point (with washbasin and soap) and near this, a motorcaravan service point. Reception is combined with the licensed shop (gas available). Amenities include the comfortable bar lounge with family room and TV, the restaurant and takeaway (restricted opening outside high seasons) and a games room with pool tables, table tennis and video games. Large, grass play area, crazy golf, bicycle hire and mountain bike trail. The park's 9 hole golf course is in an attractive setting alongside the Annan river, where fishing is possible for salmon and trout (tickets available). Coarse fishing is also possible elsewhere on the estate. Guided walks are organised in high season. Tennis near. Caravan storage. This is a peaceful place from which to explore historic southwest Scotland.

Directions: Leave A74M at junction 19 (Ecclefechan) and follow signs to park. Leave A75 at Annan juncion (west end of Annan by-pass) and follow signs. O.S.GR: NY155725.

Charges 2000:
-- Per unit incl. up to 4 persons £6.00 - £11.50; small tent incl. 1 or 2 persons £5.00 - £8.50; extra person £2.00; awning £2.00; electricity (10A) £2.00.
-- VAT included.
-- Credit cards accepted.

Open:
1 April - 25 October.

Address:
Hoddom, Lockerbie, Dumfriesshire DG11 1AS.

Tel:
(01576) 300251.
FAX: (01576) 300757.

Reservations:
Necessary for July/Aug and B.Hs. Any length with deductible £5 deposit.

CC Approved

  Approved
CCGBI Approved

A.A. Best Scottish Campsite 1996/97

HODDOM CASTLE

10 minutes from A74 (M) and A75. Ideal stopping place or base for travelling North, South or to Ireland; exploring SW Scotland, the Borders or the Lake District. Mains toilets, showers, electric hook-ups, launderette, shop, play area, bar.
FISHING (on our own waters) Salmon, sea tout and brown trout on River Annan. Coarse fishing at Kellhead Quarry.
GOLF 9 hole course at Hoddom Castle, 18 hole course at Powfoot. WALKING Woodland walks, nature trails, guided walks.
Adjacent to Caravan Park.

Enquiries to: Warden, Hoddom Castle, Lockerbie, Dumfriesshire. Tel: 01576 300251

693 Park of Brandedleys, Crocketford, nr. Dumfries

Good quality, friendly park providing a range of facilities including swimming pools.

Brandedleys is a first class park providing pitches for some 80 caravans and a limited number of tents, plus 27 self-contained holiday homes (12 of which, with two cottages and three chalets, are let) in three or four flat and variably sloping fields with tarred access roads. It has excellent installations and amenities. Caravan pitches are on lawns or terraced hardstandings, many with a pleasant outlook across a loch. There are 80 electrical connections (10A), 21 pitches with water and drainage also, plus some 'premier' pitches with TV connection and picnic bench. The main heated toilet block has been extensively modernised with clean, well appointed cubicled showers with toilet and washbasin (just one for men), in addition to the normally provided showers, washbasins and toilets, full length mirror, hand and hairdryers and a bathroom for disabled visitors. Also a laundry room, baby and hair care room, covered dishwashing sinks and chemical disposal. There is a second block of equal size and standard in the lower field with laundry and dishwashing facilities also. It is excellently equipped and maintained. A small, heated outdoor swimming pool is open when the weather is suitable and the heated indoor pool adjacent to the bar/restaurant is open all season with changing room (both pools free) and a sauna. Shop with good stocks. Bar and licensed restaurant with full menu at reasonable prices, and open for lunch and dinner, with patio area overlooking Auchenreoch Loch. Takeaway food to order (6.15-9.30 pm). All-weather tennis courts, outdoor badminton court and draught board. Games room with TV. Table tennis, pool table and 'air hockey' table. Football pitch. Putting course and golf driving net. Small playground with grass base and adventure play area for older children by the pool. Dog exercise area. Public phone. Fishing (½ mile), golf, riding and pony trekking all nearby. Walks on open moors or forest and beautiful sandy beaches 12 miles away. A popular, quality park and a member of the Best of British group.

Charges 1999:
-- Per unit incl. 2 persons £9.00 - £15.00; extra adult £2.00; child (5-17 yrs) £1.50; awning £2.00; extra small tent £3.00; extra car £1.00; electricity £2.00; individual water/drainage £2.00; premier pitch £5.00; dog £1.00.
-- Less 5-10% for weekly bookings acc. to season.
-- VAT included.
-- Credit cards accepted.
Open:
All year.
Address:
Crocketford, Dumfries, Dumfries and Galloway DG2 8RG.
Tel:
(01556) 690250.
FAX: (01556) 690681.
Reservations:
Recommended for peak dates and made for min. 2 days, £20 deposit per pitch.

Directions: Park is 9 miles from Dumfries on south side of the A75 Dumfries - Stranraer road, just west of the village of Crocketford. O.S.GR: NX830725.

See colour feature for 'BEST of BRITISH' between pages 96/97

694 Caldons Caravan and Camping Site, Galloway Forest Park

Truly peaceful Forestry Commission site ideal for exploring vast Forest Park.

The drawbacks first - Scotland is known for its midges and they love the combination of water and trees here (mid June - end Aug), so follow the site manager's advice on where to pitch (away from the trees) and use repellents. Secondly, the sanitary facilities, with the notable exception of the expensively refurbished ladies' toilets, are adequate rather than luxurious but are well maintained and clean with free hot water to showers and washbasins. Facilities for disabled visitors are good. The benefits are a wonderfully quiet and relaxing streamside site, close to the loch with mountain views, and a perfect base for exploring this enormous 240 square mile Forest Park. The site has 160 large pitches, 50 with 10A electricity and 15 with hardstanding. They are in several different areas offering shady, flat pitches or an open, sloping area. Situated in the beautiful Glen Trool, the Loch Trool Trail oak and pinewoods are a naturalist's delight. The trail starts at the site and takes walkers on a 5 mile circuit of the Loch with spectacular loch views and passing Bruce's Stone, commemorating his first victory over the English in 1307 (this can also be reached by car). There are many other walks and drives into the moorland and rugged hills. At the site, children can play on varied play equipment (on bark) or splash around in the Caldon Burn. Neither boating nor fishing is permitted in Loch Trool, but permits (from £6.50 for adults, £1.50 for children) for fishing elsewhere in the park are cheap for Scotland. In spring and early summer goats roam the site with their kids. Picnic benches, games rooms with table tennis and pool, and a rest room with drinks machine are provided. There is a shop for basic supplies, plus a launderette and dishwashing facilities. Access to the site makes it unsuitable for very large units. Dogs are accepted. Caravan storage. The village of Glentrool is 4 miles, with a pub at Bargrennan, 5 miles.

Charges 1999:
-- Per unit incl. up to 4 persons £6.00 - £7.50; extra person (over 5 yrs) £1.00; extra car, trailer or pup tent £2.50; electricity £2.10.
-- VAT included.
Open:
25 March - 28 September.
Address:
Glentrool, Newton Stewart, Wigtownshire DG8 6SU.
Tel:
(01671) 840218, or out of season (0131) 314 6505.
Reservations:
Necessary for B.Hs and peak times; made for min. 3 nights with £30 deposit. Contact site when open or Forest Holidays, Forestry Commission, 231 Corstorphine Road, Edinburgh EH12 7AT. Tel: (0131) 314 6505.

Directions: From A714 Newton Stewart - Girvan road turn east at Bargrennan and right just past Glentrool, following signs on single track forest road with passing places. O.S.GR: NX400790.

Lowlands

695 Brighouse Bay Holiday Park, Borgue, Kirkcudbright

Seaside park with exceptional all weather facilities.

Hidden away within 1,200 exclusive acres, on a quiet, unspoilt peninsula, this spacious family park is only some 200 yards through bluebell woods from a lovely sheltered bay. It has 120 self-contained holiday caravans of which about 30 are let, the rest privately owned. Over 90% of the 120 touring caravan pitches have electricity (16A), some with hardstanding and some with water, drainage and TV aerial. The three tenting areas are on fairly flat, undulating ground and some pitches have electricity. The well maintained main toilet block is large with ample washbasins with shelf and free hot showers. It also has 10 unisex cabins with shower, basin and WC, and 12 with washbasin and WC, a launderette and covered dishwashing sinks. A second, excellent block next to the tenting areas has en-suite shower rooms (one for disabled people) and bathroom, separate washing cubicles, free hot showers, baby room, laundry sinks and covered dishwashing sinks. One section is heated in winter. Chemical disposal, motorcaravan service point and gas supplies. On site leisure facilities include a golf and leisure club with 16.5 m. pool, water features, jacuzzi, steam room, fitness room, sun-bed, games room (all on payment) and clubhouse bar and bistro. The 18 hole, par 72 golf course extends onto the headland with superb views over the Irish Sea to the Isle of Man and Cumbria. Like the park, these facilities are open all year. The BHS approved pony trekking centre (Easter - Sept) on the farm offers treks for complete beginners, slow hacks for the nervous or inexperienced or gallops on the beach for the more experienced. Other amenities include mountain bike hire, quad bikes, boating pond, 10 pin bowling, playgrounds including a new 'high-tech' play area, putting, coarse fishing ponds plus sea angling and an all-tide slipway for boating enthusiasts. Cottages, 10 pine lodges, chalets and centrally heated caravans may be rented all year. Licensed supermarket and takeaway meals. Advance booking is advised. Caravan storage. A well run park of high standard and a member of the Best of British group.

Directions: From Kirkcudbright turn south off A755 onto B727 (to Borgue); after 4 miles Brighouse Bay is signed to south. From west take B727 to Borgue and beyond, turning south as above. Or follow Brighouse Bay signs off A75 just east of Gatehouse of Fleet. O.S.GR: NX630455.

Charges 1999:
-- Per unit incl. 2 persons £9.00 - £12.25; extra adult £2.00 - £2.20; child (4-15) £1.25 - £1.50; full awning £1.80 - £2.00; porch awning, extra car or small pup tent £1.00; electricity £2.70 - £2.25; electricity and TV hook-up £3.00 - £2.85; fully serviced pitch £4.20 - £3.95; trailed craft £3.00 - £3.20, other craft £1.50 - £1.60; dog £1.00.
-- Winter rate: from £12.00 incl. all pitch fees.
-- Up to 10% reduction for weekly bookings.
-- Credit cards accepted.
-- VAT included.

Open:
All year.

Address:
Brighouse Bay, Borgue, Kirkcudbright, Dumfries and Galloway DG6 4TS.

Tel:
(01557) 870267.
FAX: (01557) 870319.
E-mail: arogers@brighouse-bay.co.uk

Reservations:
Made with £17 deposit plus £3 booking fee for each pitch booked.

See colour feature for 'BEST of BRITISH' between pages 96/97

702 Aird Donald Caravan Park, Stranraer

Tidy site suitable for night halt or longer.

Aird Donald makes a good stopping off place when travelling to and from the Irish ferries, but it is also useful for seeing the sights around Stranraer. The park comprises 12 acres surrounded by conifers, flowering trees and shrubs and the 300 yard drive is lit and lined with well trimmed conifers. There are grass areas for caravans or tents and hardstandings with electricity hook-up (these very handy for hardy winter tourers). A small play area caters for young children, but the local leisure centre is a walk away and caters for everything from swimming, table tennis, gym, etc, and a theatre which hosts everything from country and western to opera. It also has bar facilities. The site has two toilet blocks; the old original one is very basic with free showers and this is open all the time. The other is new, modern and heated. Kept very clean with excellent, tiled facilities, this one is kept locked with a key deposit of £5 - we recommend you use this facility. It has two types of shower, an electric one which is metered (20p) and two others which are free (strange, because they are all excellent). Washbasins are in vanity units, ladies having one in a cubicle. Both sexes have hair dryers. A unit for visitors with disabilities has a washbasin and WC. Dishwashing sinks and a small laundry with sinks, dryer, twin-tub washing machine, an old fashioned mangle and clothes lines are provided. Chemical disposal and motorcaravan service facilities. The area has three world famous gardens to visit, numerous golf courses, fishing, riding and watersports.

Directions: Enter Stranraer on A75 road. Watch for narrow site entrance on left entering town, opposite school. O.S.GR: NX075605.

Charges 2000:
-- Per unit incl. 2 adults, 1 child and electricity £10.40.
-- No credit cards.

Open:
All year.

Address:
London Road, Stranraer, Wigtownshire, DG9 8RN.

Tel:
(01776) 702025.
E-mail: aird@mimman.u-net.com.

Reservations:
Contact park.

701 Camping and Caravanning Club Site Culzean Castle, Maybole

Quiet family Club site near Ayr, with fantastic views, also taking non members.

Culzean Castle (pronounced Kullayne), with its grounds and 17 miles of footpaths, is next door to the Camping and Caravanning Club site and visitors are given a pass to walk in the grounds (when open) as many times as they wish. The 18th century, cliff top castle is built on the site of a former ancient castle and its armoury exhibition is superb. Besides the woodland walks, adventure playground, deer park and aviary, there are three miles of rocky shore, small sandy beaches and stunning views of the Firth of Clyde. A full programme of events is staged at the castle over the season, including special children's weeks, sheep-dog trials, bands, battle re-enactments, ranger walks and craft fairs. The campsite has 90 pitches, some level others slightly sloping, and 60 have electrical hook-ups (10A). A few level pitches are suitable for motorcaravans and 20 pitches have hard-standing. American style motorhomes (less than 27 ft. only) are advised to make prior arrangements, as large pitches are limited. A small shop with very basic provisions opens for short periods morning and evening. The very clean toilet blocks can be heated and provide washbasins (in cubicles and vanity style), free showers of a satisfactory size, dishwashing sinks with hot water, chemical disposal and a well equipped laundry with clothes lines. A unit for disabled visitors has a WC, washbasin and shower - an excellent facility. Should you have your fill of the castle and its grounds, Maybole with shops, etc. is only 4 miles and the area has a wealth of places to visit. A new information hut was added in '99. Dogs are accepted and there are miles of walks. Buses pass the gate. Golf or bicycle hire 4 miles, riding 2 miles, fishing 8 miles.

Charges 2000:
-- Per 2 adults £7.50 - £10.60; child (6-18 yrs) £1.60; non-member pitch fee £4.30; electricity £1.60 - £2.35.
-- VAT included.
-- Credit cards accepted.
Open:
March - November.
Address:
Maybole, Strathclyde KA19 8JK.
Tel:
(01655) 760627, (no calls after 8 pm).
Reservations:
Advised for high season and made with deposit; contact the wardens.

Directions: From Maybole follow signs for Culzean Castle and Country Park, turning in the town on B7023 which runs into the A719. Country Park entrance is clearly signed on right after 3¾ miles; entrance to caravan park is on the right in Country Park drive. O.S.GR: NS247103.

703 Gibson Park Caravan Club Site, Melrose

Beautiful small park on town edge.

This is an ideal transit park, being so close to the A68, but also a perfect base for exploring this Southern Scotland area or indeed a trip to Edinburgh, as this is only 35 miles away taking your car or one of the regular buses which run from the park entrance. Situated on the edge of the little town of Melrose, a five minute walk, shops, pubs and restaurants are all in easy reach. This small, three acre park has only 60 touring pitches plus, unusually, an extra 12 tent pitches (summer only) next to the adjacent rugby pitch. All touring pitches have electricity (16A) and TV connections (otherwise it is a bad signal here), 51 have hardstanding and 10 are serviced with water and drainage. Excellent drinking water and waste water points are around the park, which has a one way system on tarmac roads. Sanitary facil-ities are in a new building and are first rate with spacious showers, washbasins in cabins, centrally heated and all fitted out with purpose made faced boarding which gives a very pleasing finish.There are facilities for laundry and a separate room with shower and WC for disabled visitors. Motorcaravan service point. Gas available. This is Sir Walter Scott country - visit Abbotsford House, his romantic mansion on the banks of the River Tweed. Melrose's Abbey ruins are believed to be the final resting place of Robert The Bruce and the starting place of St Cuthbert's Way. A new cross-border 62 mile trail leads to Northumberland's Lindisfarne.

Charges 1999:
-- Per pitch £6.00 - £7.00; adult £3.90 - £4.00; child (5-16 yrs) £1.20; extra car, boat or trailer (in excess of 2 units) £1.00; electricity £1.45 (26/3-4/10) - £2.20; TV hook-up 55p (bring own cable); serviced pitch £1.00.
-- Tent pitches £6.90 - £12.50.
-- Credit cards accepted.
-- VAT included.
Open:
All year.
Address:
High Street, Melrose TD6 9RY.
Tel:
(01896) 822969.
Reservations:
Made with £5 per night deposit - contact park.

Directions: Turn left off A68 Jedburgh - Lauder road at roundabout about 2½ miles past Newton St Boswell on A6091 Galashiels road. In about 3¼ miles at roundabout turn right on B6374 to Melrose. Site on right at filling station opposite Melrose Rugby Club, just before entering town centre. O.S.GR: NT545340.

Lowlands

696 Crossburn Caravan Park, Peebles

Peaceful, friendly small park, suitable as a night stop.

Half a mile north of the town centre, Crossburn is on the south side of the A703 road. The entrance has a fairly steep slope down to reception and the shop which sells basic food items (the town is so close) and a large selection of camping accessories. Passing the caravans for sale and the holiday homes you might think that this is not the site for you, but persevere as the touring area is very pleasant, with attractive trees and bushes. Of the 50 pitches, 46 have electricity (16A), 20 have hardstanding, 8 are fully serviced. There is also a sheltered area for tents. There are two sanitary blocks, the smaller one (which can be heated) with fairly basic facilities, the other more modern with washbasins in cubicles, hairdryers and spacious, controllable free showers. A campers' kitchen (key at reception) gives free use of a hot plate, kettle and fridge. Adjacent is a large games room with table tennis and games machines. The field behind the resident donkey has a 9-hole putting green. A good play area is on bark and there is a dog walk along the side of the burn. Mountain bike hire. If you decide to stay longer, the area has many places to visit and things to do and Edinburgh is only 40 minutes drive. Perhaps the night halt may turn into a longer visit.

Charges 2000:
-- Per unit from £8.00;
awning £2.00; hiker or cyclist plus tent £5.00;
electricity £2.00.
-- Credit cards accepted.
Open:
Easter/1 April - end Oct.
Address:
Edinburgh Road,
Peebles EH45 8ED.
Tel:
(01721) 720501.
FAX: as phone.
E-mail: enquiries@cross-burncaravans.co.uk.
Reservations:
Advised for July/Aug.
and made with £14 deposit including £2 fee.

Directions: Park is by the A703, ½ mile north of Peebles. O.S.GR: NT248417.

697 The Monks' Muir, Haddington, nr. Edinburgh

Small, relaxed, 'individual' park, open all year and handy for visiting Edinburgh.

The Monks' Muir is just back from the A1 road (the layout makes traffic noise minimal), a few minutes from Haddington and about 20 minutes by rail or an hour by bus from Edinburgh from just outside the site. It therefore provides a base from which to explore the city, to enjoy the golden beaches of East Lothian, discover the border country or just play golf! A continental style café cum delicatessen shop provides the atmosphere which sets the style of the park. The stock in the shop is wide ranging with an excellent choice of coffee. This park has extensive development plans which will take some years to complete. As a result, with the steadily increasing number of static units, the touring area will initially decrease and become even further away from the toilet blocks. Eventually a new area is to be developed for touring. There are no marked pitches for about 40 units which are taken on mostly fairly level grass beyond a line of holiday homes. Finding a place either side of the central gravel road amongst the odd tree contributes to the friendly and relaxed atmosphere. There are 35 electrical connections (12A) on an elongated strip of land between the fields, finishing with a natural play area for children. The main toilet block, a fair walk now from the touring pitches, provides toilets, showers and washbasins with free hot water plus hand and hair dryers. Outside washing-up sinks have free hot water and a fully equipped laundry room also provides tourist information. A second smaller block nearer the touring units ensures an adequate provision. One block is closed in low season. Chemical disposal and motorcaravan services. Public phone. A boules pitch and bicycle hire are on the park, fishing and golf within 2 miles. Douglas and Deirdre Macfarlane have planted thousands of trees and shrubs and the park has its own garden centre. Caravan holiday homes for hire (8). Caravan storage.

Charges 1999:
-- Per unit £7.50 - £8.30, large motorhome £10.80 - £12.00, 2 man tent and car £5.60 - £6.20;
m/cyclist and tent £4.50 - £5.00, cyclist or walker and tent £2.00 - £3.00;
person (14 yrs or over) £1.85 - £1.95; child (0-13 yrs) free; full awning or pup tent (May - Aug) £3.00; electricity £1.80 - £2.20.
-- Less 10-20% for 7 day or more stays outside July/Aug.
-- VAT included.
-- Credit cards accepted.
Open:
All year.
Address:
Haddington, East Lothian EH41 3SB.
Tel:
(01620) 860340.
FAX: (01620) 861770.
E-mail: monksmuir@aol.com.
Reservations:
Made with £7 deposit and £3 booking fee.

Directions: Park is on the north side of the A1, halfway between East Linton and Haddington. O.S.GR: NT 559762 .

698 Drum Mohr Caravan Park, Musselburgh, nr. Edinburgh

Family owned, attractively laid out touring park on east side of Edinburgh.

Although adjacent to built-up areas, this is a secluded, well kept modern park, convenient for Edinburgh and the Lothian and Borders regions. Carefully landscaped, there are many attractive plants, flowers and hedging. There are 120 pitches, 40 with hardstanding, for touring units of any type, well spaced out on gently sloping grass in groups of 12 or more, marked with white posts. There is electricity on 110 and 7 are fully serviced with water and waste water connections also. Free space is left for play and recreation. The two toilet blocks are clean, attractive, of ample size and can be heated. They have washbasins set in flat surfaces with free hot water in these and four external washing-up sinks, but hot water is on payment for the showers (outside the cubicle) and laundry sinks. Laundry facilities are in each block, chemical disposal and motorcaravan service point. There is a well stocked, licensed shop (gas, bread and papers to order) and a children's playground on sand, but no other on-site activities. However, the town amenities are quite close, as is a golf course. Musselburgh centre is 1½ miles, Edinburgh 7, with a frequent bus service to the latter. A well run park, managed personally by the owner, Mr Melville. A member of the Best of British group.

Directions: From Edinburgh follow A1 signs for Berwick on Tweed for 6-7 miles. Turn off for Wallyford and follow camp and Mining Museum signs. From south follow A1 taking junction after Tranent village (A199 Musselburgh) and follow signs. O.S.GR: NT371732.

Charges 1999:
-- Per unit incl. 2 persons £8.00 - £10.00; extra person (over 3 yrs) £1.00; extra pup tent or awning £1.00; electricity £2.00; fully serviced pitch incl. electricity + £6.00; extra car £1.00.
-- VAT included.
-- Credit cards accepted.
Open:
1 March - 31 October.
Address:
Levenhall, Musselburgh, East Lothian EH21 8JS.
Tel:
0131 665 6867.
FAX: 0131 653 6859.
Reservations:
Made for any length with deposit of one night's charge plus £1 fee.

699 Mortonhall Caravan Park, Edinburgh

Attractive, large touring park in the mature grounds of Mortonhall mansion.

The Mortonhall park makes a good base to see the historic city of Edinburgh and buses to the City leave from the park entrance every ten minutes (parking in Edinburgh is not easy). Although only 4 miles from the city centre, Mortonhall is in quiet mature parkland, easy to find with access off the ring road. The park can accommodate 250 units mostly on numbered pitches on a slight slope with nothing to separate them but marked by jockey wheel points. There are over 170 places with electricity (10A), 16 with hardstanding, water and drainage, and many places for tents. Holiday caravans to let. The park is very popular but only part is reserved and early arrival may find space. Two modern toilet blocks have free hot water in individual washbasins, showers and outside, uncovered dishwashing sinks. A third excellent, new facility at the top of the park has eight unisex units incorporating shower, washbasin and WC, with covered dishwashing sinks. The courtyard area provides further standard facilities and 'portacabin' type units are added for the high season to serve the large number of tents. There are facilities for disabled visitors, water points, chemical disposal units and laundry room with washing machines and dryer. Self-service shop. An attractive courtyard houses a bar and restaurant, open to all, with good value meals in pleasant surroundings. Games room. TV room. Table tennis, children's play area on sand. Late arrivals area with hook-ups. Torches useful. Golf courses and driving range very near.

Directions: Park is well signed south of the city, 5 minutes from A720 city by-pass. Take Mortonhall exit from the Straiton junction and follow camping signs. Entrance road is alongside Klondyke Garden Centre. O.S.GR: NT262686.

Charges 1999:
-- Per unit incl. 2 persons £8.25 - £12.75; extra person (5 yrs and over) £1.00; serviced pitch + £4.00; electricity £3.00; awning £2.50 - £5.00; porch awning £2.50; dog £1.00.
-- Credit cards accepted.
-- VAT included.
Open:
14 March - 31 October.
Address:
38 Mortonhall Gate, Frogston Road East, Edinburgh, East Lothian EH16 6TJ.
Tel:
0131 664 1533.
FAX: 0131 664 5387.
E-mail@
mhallcp@aol.com.
Reservations:
Made with 1 night's charge plus £1.50 fee.

Lowlands

EDINBURGH

The capital, a World Heritage Centre and now the home of the Scottish Parliament, is one of the most beautiful cities in the world dominated by its castle. At the very heart is the Royal Mile where you can stroll through the centuries from Parliament Square, the magnificent 15th century St Giles' Cathedral and down to the Palace of Holyroodhouse, the Queens's official Edinburgh residence. Further north of the city is the historic Port of Leith, with its restaurants, bistros and pubs and now home to HM Yacht Britannia and the future focus of Conran's Cruise Ship Terminal which promises to be architecturally spectacular. The most exciting developments yet include Sir Michael Hopkin's 'Dynamic Earth' exhibition – a huge tented structure at the foot of Arthur's Seat which describes the evolution of the planet, and the new Museum of Scotland where you can absorb the essence of Scottish architecture and material culture from beam engines to Bonnie Prince Charlie.

704 Slatebarns Caravan Park, Roslin, nr. Edinburgh

Small, select park for city and country.

Slatebarns is a small, well groomed park, perfectly located for that trip to Edinburgh. It has only 30 pitches, all with electricity hook-ups (10A), some with hardstanding and some on grass (steel awning pegs useful). This recently developed park has a small purpose built toilet block with well equipped showers, washbasins in cubicles for ladies and an excellent separate provision for those with disabilities. Plentiful water points, waste water points, a very practical motorcaravan service point and chemical disposal complete the facilities. The small reception office within this block doubles as tourist information. A public telephone is on hand and a good launderette with washing machine, dryer and spin dryer is impressive. Gas is available. Buses run from the village (five minutes' walk) regularly into Edinburgh (30 minute journey, 6 miles), although they are less frequent in the evening. In the village there are shops, pubs and hotels for all that you may need. Slatebarns is a small park with little on site for children or teenagers. Managed under contract for the Caravan Club, non-members are also very welcome. An ideal base to get away from the bustle after a full day in Edinburgh, or equally attractive as a touring base or country hideaway.

Charges 1999:
-- Per pitch £1.00; adult £3.25 - £3.75; child £1.10; electricity £1.50 - £2.00 (Oct).

Open:
Easter - 31 October.

Address:
Slatebarns, Roslin, Mid Lothian EH25 9PU.

Tel:
0131 440 2192 (up to 8 pm).

Reservations:
Contact park for details.

Directions: From Straiton junction on A720 (Edinburgh bypass) go south on A701 signed Bilston, Penicuik. At roundabout in Bilston turn left on B7006 signed Roslin. After 1 mile continue over crossroads signed Rosslyn Chapel. Site entrance is immediately past Chapel. O.S.GR: NT275632.

700 Strathclyde Country Park Caravan Site, Bothwell, Motherwell

Good touring site near Glasgow in Country Park with many amenities.

The 1,200 acre Country Park is a large green area less than 15 miles from the centre of Glasgow and is suitable for both overnight or period stays (max. 14 days). The very well kept park, open to all, has a large water sports centre offering sailing, water skiing, windsurfing, canoeing, rowing (all with craft for hire), a water bus, a selection of family `fun boats' and bicycle hire, plus Scotland's own theme park only ½ mile from the site. Also provided within the park are coarse fishing, nature trails, children's adventure play area, sandy beaches and an 18 hole golf course. The site has 100 numbered pitches for caravans, all with electrical connections (10A). Arranged in semi-circular groups on flat grass they are served by made-up access roads and the site is well lit. There is also a camping field which holds 150 or more for special events. Four solidly built modern toilet blocks make a good provision, with free hot water to close together washbasins (shelf and mirror) and showers. Enclosed sinks for dishwashing or food preparation and launderette (irons from reception). Block 4 has facilities for visitors with disabilities. Motorcaravan service point and chemical disposal facilities. Gas is available and bread, milk and basics are kept in reception (shop 1 mile). Within the park are bar and restaurant facilities (100 yds). Children's play equipment on bark. Public phone. 24 hour security. American motorhomes accepted up to 22 ft. The site is close to the motorway so there may be some traffic noise.

Charges 1999:
-- Per caravan pitch incl. 2 persons £8.00; awning £1.90; tent pitch £6.90; small ridge tent £3.60; extra adult £4.00; child 75p; electricity £2.20. -- No credit cards.

Open:
Easter - late October.

Address:
Information and enquiries: Strathclyde Country Park, 366 Hamilton Road, Motherwell ML1 3ED.

Tel:
(01698) 266155. FAX: (01698) 252925. E-mail: strathclydepark@ northlan.gov.uk.

Reservations:
Made for any period with deposit of one night's fee.

Directions: Take exit 5 from M74 and follow sign for Strathclyde Country Park. Turn first left for site. O.S.GR: NS720584.

724 Tullichewan Holiday Park, Balloch

Good touring park south of Loch Lomond, open all year.

Almost, but not quite, on the banks of Loch Lomond (10 minutes or ¼ mile), this family owned, landscaped and well planned park is suitable for both transit or longer stays. It takes 120 touring units, including 30 tents, all on well spaced, numbered pitches. On flat or gently sloping grass, most have hardstandings, 106 have electrical connections (10A) and 8 have water and waste water too. The single heated toilet block has been totally refitted over the past two winters and is kept in an excellent state. It is large with plenty of WCs and basins, hot showers (some with WC), new baths, a shower room for disabled visitors and two baby baths. Water and refuse points are around the site, and there are covered dish-washing sinks, a launderette, chemical disposal and motorcaravan service points. A well stocked shop is combined with reception. Amenities include a games room with TV, table tennis, pool table and a children's playground on grass and bark. A leisure suite provides a sauna, sun-bed and spa-bath on payment. Bicycle hire on site, fishing and boat launching ¼ mile, riding 4 miles, golf 5 miles. There are watersports activities and boat trips on Loch Lomond and rail and road connec-tions to Glasgow. Dog walks (`owners must be kept on leads at all times'). Pine lodges and caravan holiday homes for letting. Public phone. Restaurants and bar meals in Balloch (5 mins). American motorhomes accepted with prior notice. Caravan storage. This is a well run park with very helpful wardens and reception staff. A member of the Best of British group.

Directions: Turn off A82 road 17 miles northwest of Glasgow on A811 Stirling road. Site is in Balloch at southern end of Loch Lomond and is well signed. O.S.GR: NS389816.

See colour feature for `BEST of BRITISH' between pages 96/97

Charges 1999:
-- Per unit incl. up to 2 persons £10.00 - £12.00 (all persons in winter £8.00); extra adult £1.50; child (3-12 yrs) £1.00; awning £1.50 - £2.00; extra small tent £2.00 - £2.50; electricity £2.00, £2.50 in winter; serviced pitch with electricity £4.00 - £4.50; hikers (2, no car) £6.50 - £9.00.
-- VAT included.
-- Credit cards accepted.

Open:
All year except Nov; (reduced facilities Dec-March).

Address:
Balloch, Loch Lomond G83 8QP.

Tel:
(01389) 759475.
FAX: (01389) 755563.
E-mail: tullichewan@ holiday-parks.co.uk.

Reservations:
Any length with first night's charge and £2 fee.

725 Glen Dochart Caravan Park, Luib, Crianlarich

Small, neat park in beautiful Highland Glen setting.

The mountains and river which flows through the Glen to Loch Tay provide a dramatic setting for this park which is located on the site of the former Luib railway station on part of the line which used to connect east and west Scotland. It is a quiet site, just off the A85 Perth - Oban road, and is ideal for hill walking or fishing holidays, with a watersports centre close by. It is personally supervised by the Donaldson family who provide a warm welcome. There are 48 holiday homes at one end of the site, with space for 45 touring units on either gravel or grass pitches with 38 electrical hook ups (10A). A new toilet block was opened in '98. This provides excellent toilet cubicles, complete with handbasins, for both men and women, plus the usual facilities. Regretably there is a shortage of hooks, shelves and soap-dishes which makes use more difficult and the mop and bucket provided are essential because, at the time of our visit, the whole of the shower cubicle floor flooded on showering. A shower room for families or disabled visitors will be ready this year and the laundry and dishwashing room is good. It has to be acknowledged that this new building is a great improvement and consid-erably better than many. A combined reception and licensed shop are in the former station house, the former platform providing some of the hardstandings. Dogs are accepted, with walks along the old railway track and a large wood to run free in. Fishing permits for the River Dochart are available in reception. A hotel within walking distance provides meals and bar snacks. The Falls of Dochart at the delightful village of Killin, 7 miles away are well worth a visit

Directions: Park is mid-way between Killin and Crianlarich on the A85 road. O.S.GR: NN467278.

Charges 1999:
-- Per unit incl. 2 persons £8.50 - £9.50; extra adult £1.00; child 50p; extra car, boat or awning 50p; electricity £1.50.
-- Credit cards accepted.
-- VAT included.

Open:
Mid March - end Oct.

Address:
Luib, Crianlarich, Perthshire FK20 8QT.

Tel:
(01567) 820637.
FAX: as phone.

Reservations:
Advisable for July/Aug, and made with £7.50 deposit per pitch.

GLASGOW

One of the most magnificent 19th century cities in Europe and now known as Scotland's style capital with its art deco brasseries, stylish shops and cultural centres boasting more than 30 art galleries and museums. Worth visiting is the new elegant Gallery of Modern Art in Queen Street and Charles Rennie Mackintosh's finest building - The Glasgow School of Art. Also interesting along the banks of the River Clyde is the restored Carlton Terrace and Glasgow's newest landmark, the Clyde Auditorium, popularly known The 'Armadillo', due to its distinctive shape.

723 Trossachs Holiday Park, Aberfoyle

Well run, friendly family park, ideal for exploring the Trossachs and Loch Lomond.

Nestling on the side of a hill 3 miles south of Aberfoyle, this is an excellent base for touring this famously beautiful area. Lochs Lomond, Ard, Venachar and others are within easy reach, as are the Queen Elizabeth Forest Park and, of course, the Trossachs. The park specialises in sales and hire of top class mountain bikes. A very neat and tidy park, there are 45 well laid out and marked pitches arranged on terraces with hardstanding. All have electricity and TV connections and most have water and drainage also. There are trees between the terraces and lovely views across the valley. A modern wooden building houses the sanitary facilities which offer a satisfactory supply of toilets, showers and washbasins, the ladies' area being rather larger, with two private cabins. The building also contains a laundry room and a large games room with TV and lots of seating. There are several items of play equipment on gravel. The park purchased the adjoining oak and bluebell woods in '97. A 'passport' scheme arranged with a local leisure centre (10 miles) provides facilities for swimming, sauna, solarium, badminton, tennis, windsurfing, etc. Nearby are opportunities for golfing, boat launching and fishing (3 miles). A well stocked shop (all season) and the bike shop are either side of reception, where you will receive a warm welcome from Joe and Hazel Norman. Luxury caravans (12) for hire in separate section. A new member of the Best of British group.

Directions: Park is 3 miles south of Aberfoyle on the A81 road, well signed. O.S.GR: NS544976.

Charges 1999:
-- Per unit incl. 2 persons £8.50 - £10.50; extra adult £2.00; child (2-14 yrs) £1.25; awning £1.50 - £2.00; small pup tent £3.00; electricity and TV connection, hardstanding pitch £2.00; all services £3.00.
-- VAT included.
-- Credit cards accepted.
Open:
1 March - 31 October.
Address:
Aberfoyle,
Stirling FK8 3SA.
Tel:
(01877) 382614 (24 hrs).
FAX: (01877) 382732.
E-mail: trossachsholiday park@ compuserve.com.
Reservations:
Advised; min. 3 days with £15 deposit.

726 Ardgartan Caravan and Camping Site, Arrochar, nr. Tarbet

Forestry Commission site on banks of Loch Long with mountains all around.

Ardgartan, a rugged site in the Argyll Forest Park, is splendidly situated with lovely views of Loch Long and with lots of sightseeing and activity opportunities. At the northern end of the Cowal Peninsula, it is on a promontory on the shores of Loch Long, there is good sea fishing and facilities for launching small boats. The 160 touring pitches are in sections which are well divided by grass giving an uncrowded air. Most with hardstanding and marked by numbered posts, they are accessed from hard surface roads and 46 have electrical hook-ups. There are additional grass areas for tents. The main sanitary block is opposite the reception and shop with two small others (one for each sex) close by for the busiest periods. It is a basic, but clean provision with facilities for disabled visitors and a launderette. These facilities may be quite stretched when the park is busy. Play equipment is provided (with bark surfaces) and barbecues are allowed. Arrochar village (2 miles) has fuel, general stores and a restaurant. Walking and climbing, as well as sea and river fishing (permits obtainable locally), are all available nearby. The site gate is locked 10.30 pm. - 7.30 am.

Directions: From A82 (Glasgow-Crianlarich) take A83 at Tarbet signed Arrochar and Cambletown. Site is 2 miles past Arrochar, the entrance on a bend. O.S.GR: NN275030.

Charges 1999:
-- Per adult £2.90 - £4.10; child (5-14 yrs) £1.20 - £1.80; electricity £2.10.
-- Credit cards accepted.
Open:
25 March - 25 October.
Address:
Ardgartan, Arrochar, Dunbartonshire
G83 7AR.
Tel:
(01301) 702293.
Reservations:
Necessary peak times (min. 3 nights with £30 deposit); contact site.
Brochure requests: Forest Holidays, Forestry Commission, 231 Corstorphine Road, Edinburgh EH12 7AT.
Tel: (0131) 314 6505.

727 Auchterarder Caravan Park, Nether Coul, Auchterarder

Small, family run park in sheltered position.

This is a charming small park, purpose designed and landscaped by the owners Stuart and Susie Robertson. It is conveniently situated for exploring central Scotland and the Highlands with many leisure activities close at hand, particularly golf, and within walking distance of the village (1 mile). The 21 original pitches, all with electricity (6A) and hardstanding, 12 with drainage also, are well spaced around the edge of the elongated, level grass park. Marked pitches with grass frontage back on to raised banks which are planted with trees. More pitches have been developed to one side of the park, along with a fishing pond (exclusively for campers) and woodland walk. A tarmac hold-over area at the entrance for late arrivals (with electricity) ensures no one is disturbed. A modern pine chalet, blending with the environment, is also at the entrance housing reception, a small shop with basic items (milk delivered daily), small library and excellent sanitary facilities with a key system and piped music. These include roomy toilets, controllable hot showers with dressing area, seat, shelf, hooks and vanity style washbasins with large mirrors. A toilet for disabled people is provided in both the male and female units. Laundry room with sink and washing machine - an iron can be provided as well. Under cover washing up with free hot water. Chemical disposal. Two secluded chalets (self catering) for hire and B&B. Public phones. Bicycle hire 1½ miles. With plenty of outdoor pursuits including fishing and golf locally, the historic cities of Perth and Stirling are less than half an hour's drive away. Caravan storage. There is easy access from the nearby A9 road which does create some background road noise, although it is peaceful at night.

Charges 1999:
-- Per unit incl. up to 4 persons £8.00; tent and vehicle from £6.00; extra person (over 5 yrs) £1.00; awning £1.00; porch awning 50p; electricity and drainage £1.50 - £2.50.
-- VAT included.

Open:
All year.

Address:
Nether Coul,
Auchterarder,
Perthshire PH3 1ET.

Tel:
(01764) 663119.
FAX: as phone.

Reservations:
Advisable July/Aug. and made with deposit of one night's charge and booking fee (£1). Bookings held until 5 pm. on day reserved.

Directions: Park is between the A9 and A824 roads east of Auchterarder village, only ½ mile from the main road. It is reached by turning on to the B8062 (Dunning) road from the A824. O.S.GR: NN964138.

728 Nether Craig Caravan Park, by Alyth, Blairgowrie

Very attractive, family run touring park in truly peaceful Glenisla.

Richard and June Nicoll farmed in Glenisla before developing Nether Craig which is attractively designed and beautifully landscaped, with views across the Strathmore valley to the long range of the Sidlaw hills. The 40 large pitches are accessed from a circular, gravel road; 26 have hardstanding (for awnings too) and 10A electrical connections. The majority are level and there are 9 large tent pitches on flat grass. The central, modern, purpose built toilet block can be heated and provides free pre-set hot showers with dressing area, seat, shelf and hooks, vanity style washbasins and free hairdryers for both male and female. A complete unit for disabled visitors (entry by key) also includes a hairdryer. Chemical disposal. Separate sinks for dishwashing and clothes are provided in the laundry room with metered hot water, washing machine, dryer and iron, with a rotary clothes line outside near the dog walk. It is a good provision which is very well maintained. There is a personal welcome for all visitors at the attractive wooden chalet beside the entrance (with a slope for wheelchairs) which doubles as reception and shop providing the necessary essentials, gas and tourist information. Children have swings and other play equipment, plus a small football field opposite the entrance. A one mile circular woodland walk from the park has picnic benches and a leaflet guide is provided. Otherwise you can just enjoy the peace of the Angus Glens by hill walking, birdwatching, fishing or pony trekking. Three golf courses are within 4 miles. Alyth with its Arthurian connections is only 4 miles away and Glamis Castle, the childhood home of the Queen Mother, is nearby, as is the beautiful Glenshee and Braemar with its castle. Caravan storage.

Charges 1999:
-- Per unit incl. 2 persons £9.00 - £11.00; extra person £1.00; electricity £1.70.
-- VAT included.
-- No credit cards.

Open:
15 March - 31 October.

Address:
By Alyth, Blairgowrie, Perthshire PH11 8HN.

Tel:
(01575) 560204.
FAX: (01575) 560315.
E-mail: nethercraig@lineone.net.

Reservations:
Advisable for main season - contact park.

Directions: From A926 Blairgowrie - Kirriemuir road, at roundabout south of Alyth join B954 signed Glenisla. Follow caravan signs for 4 miles and turn right onto unclassified road signed Nether Craig. Park is on left after ½ mile. O.S.GR: NO265528.

Heart of Scotland

729 Craigtoun Meadows Holiday Park, St Andrews

Attractively laid out park with individual pitches; holiday homes to let.

Though outnumbered by caravan holiday homes, the touring section on this park is an important subsidiary. The facilities offered are both well designed and comprehensive with 70 units taken on gently sloping land. Caravans go on individual hardstandings with grass alongside for awnings on most pitches. All caravan pitches are equipped with electricity (16A), water and drainage and have been redesigned to increase size (130 sq.m.). There are 24 larger `patio' pitches with summer house, barbecue patio, picnic table and chairs, partially screened. Tents are taken on a grassy meadow at one end, also with electricity available. Only `breathable' type groundsheets to be used in awnings. The 157 caravan holiday homes stand round the outer parts of the site; 32 are owned and let by the park. An excellent, de-luxe, centrally heated sanitary building serves the touring area. All washbasins are in cabins and each toilet has its own basin. Showers are unisex, as are two bathrooms, there are hand and hair dryers, facilities for disabled people and babies, a dishwashing room and chemical disposal. All is free in this first-rate provision. Amenities on the park include a shop and an attractive little licensed restaurant (both restricted hours in low seasons) which also provides a takeaway. Launderette. Games room and mini-gym. Well equipped children's playground and play field and 8 acres of woodland. Barbecue area. Public phone (card). All weather tennis court. Small information room. Dogs are accepted (good dog walk). A well run park, 2 miles from St Andrews with its golf courses and sandy beaches. Buses pass the entrance. Craigtoun park with boating pond and miniature railway, etc. is within walking distance.

Charges 2000:
-- Per unit incl. 2 persons and electricity £14.00 - £20.00, 3-6 persons £15.00 - £21.00;
backpacker's tent (max. 2 persons) £12.00.
-- Credit cards accepted.
-- VAT included.

Open:
1 March - 31 October.

Address:
Mount Melville,
St. Andrews,
Fife KY16 8PQ.

Tel:
(01334) 475959.
FAX: (01334) 476424.
E-mail: craigtoun@aol.com.

Reservations:
Advised for main season; any length with full payment at time of booking.

Directions: From M90 junction 8 take A91 to St. Andrews. Just after sign for Guardbridge (to left, A919), turn right at site sign and sign for `Strathkinness, 1¾ miles'. Go through village, over crossroads at end of village, left at next crossroads, then ¾ mile to park. O.S.GR: NO482151.

730 Blair Castle Caravan Park, Blair Atholl

Well kept park in attractive, spacious setting with some holiday homes.

This attractive park is set in the grounds of Blair Castle, the traditional home of the Dukes of Atholl. The castle is open to the public, its 32 fully furnished rooms showing a picture of Scottish life from the 16th century to the present day. The caravan park has a wonderful feeling of spaciousness with a large central area left free for children's play or for general use. There is space for 283 touring units with 191 electricity connections (10A), 144 hardstandings and 42 fully serviced pitches with water and waste water facilities also. A motorcaravan service point is provided and American motorhomes are accepted (max. 30 ft or 5 tons). Caravan holiday homes, 85 privately owned and 28 for hire, are in separate areas. The original sanitary building has been updated in parts but is only open at peak times. The four newer blocks can be heated and are of excellent quality with very high standards of cleanliness. They have large, free hot shower cubicles, some also incorporating WC and washbasin, and further cubicles with WC and washbasin. Three blocks have facilities for disabled visitors, one with WC and washbasin, the others with a bath also. There are baby changing mats, chemical disposal points and dishwashing sinks. A good launderette has washing machines, dryers, spin dryer and irons plus a separate drying room and outside lines. Gas is available. The large self-service, licensed shop (all season) is well stocked and a coffee shop sells home made cakes, snacks and takeaway (June, July and Aug). Near reception is a games room with pool, table tennis and table football, plus a TV room. Mountain bike hire, riding, golf and fishing within 1 mile and the castle grounds provide many walking trails. The village is within walking distance with hotels, shops, a water mill craft centre and folk museum. A quality park, quiet at night and well managed. Member of the Best of British group.

Charges 2000:
-- Per unit with all persons £8.50 - £10.50;
extra person £1.00; child (5-12 yrs) 50p; awning or pup tent £1.50 - £2.00;
dog 50p; electricity £1.50 - £2.00.
-- VAT included.
-- Credit cards accepted.

Open:
1 April - 30 October.

Address:
Blair Atholl, Pitlochry, Perthshire PH18 5SR.

Tel:
(01796) 481263.
FAX: (01796) 481587.

Reservations:
Made with any length deposit of 1 night's charge + £2 booking fee except 15/7-15/8 when min. 3 nights and payment in full.

Directions: From A9 just north of Pitlochry take B8079 into Blair Atholl. Park in grounds of Blair Castle, well signed. O.S.GR: NN868659.

See colour feature for
`BEST of BRITISH'
between pages 96/97

188

731 Twenty Shilling Wood Caravan Park, Comrie, nr. Crieff

Secluded family park, taking caravans and motorcaravans only.

Everyone gets a warm welcome from the Lowe family when they arrive at Twenty Shilling. Set amongst 10.5 acres of wooded hillside, this unusual park has a few touring pitches plus a number of owner occupied caravan holiday homes. However, because of terracing and landscaping not many of them are visible and flowering trees and shrubs help to hide them. The lowest level is the entrance which has a late arrivals area and visitor car park. The drive then rises to reception (there is no shop but rolls, milk and papers can be ordered here). Alongside is a games room with pool table and table tennis (both free). There is masses of tourist information in the lounge area which has comfortable seating and a well stocked library and where responsible parents can keep an eye on the children whilst they use the games equipment. The fenced adventure playground is on bark and for all ages. An automatic barrier has been installed (£10 deposit for card). The 20 pitches are all level, on gravel with grass bays between them. All have electric hook-ups (10A) and, because of the poor TV reception, also have a free TV aerial hook up with lead provided. You will be escorted to your pitch and sited. The toilet blocks are of an older design but are kept very clean and bright, and have been refurbished to give some washbasins in cubicles and tiled shower cubicles with plenty of space to change. Showers are spacious, controllable and on payment. The dishwashing area leads into the laundry with washing machine, dryer, iron and clothes lines. Up to two dogs per pitch are accepted with a dog walk provided. Buses pass the gate. Comrie is 1 mile where most things can be purchased. There are many walks in the area from strenuous Munros to a gentle stroll to the Devil's Cauldron waterfall. Glen Turret, Scotland's oldest distillery is at Crieff, 7 miles away, Auchingarrich Wildlife centre is 2½ miles, there are watersports at Loch Earn, 11 miles and riding and golf at Comrie. A member of the Countryside Discovery group.

Charges 2000:
-- Per unit incl. 2 adults £8.00 - £11.00; extra person (over 5 yrs) £1.00; awning (rock pegs required) £1.00; electricity and TV hook-up £2.00.
-- Credit cards accepted.
Open:
23 March - 23 October.
Address:
Comrie,
Perthshire PH6 2JY.
Tel:
(01764) 670411.
FAX: as phone.
E-mail: alowe20@
aol.com.
Reservations:
Advised for B.Hs and July/Aug; made with £10 deposit.

Directions: Park is on north side of A85 Crieff - Lochearmead road, about ¾ mile west of B827 junction, ½ mile west of Comrie. O.S.GR: NN762222.

732 Witches Craig Caravan Park, Blairlogie, nr. Stirling

Neat and tidy park, nestling under the Ochil Hills.

Witches Craig is a friendly park and the Stephen family take great pride in the fact that so many satisfied families return year after year. They take each visitor to their pitch to make sure that they are happy with it. All the 60 pitches have electrical hook-ups (10A) and 14 have hardstanding, 7 of which are enormous taking American style motorhomes easily. The whole site is reasonably level. The toilet and shower block is modern, can be heated and was very clean when we visited. There are vanity style washbasins and a cubicle with washbasin and WC for ladies. Showers are on payment, adjustable with a dividing curtain. Soap, hand and hairdryers are provided for men and women, plus a baby bath and mat. The unit for dusabled campers is excellent. Laundry with washing machine, dryer and spin dryer and washing up sinks. Tourist information is kept in reception, and bread, milk, drinks and papers are available daily (supermarket 2½ miles). A large play area is fenced and surrounded by flowering shrubs with equipment on grass or rubber, also a field for games. The park covers 5 acres and there is a pleasant welcoming feel with everything well maintained and the grass well manicured. Seven owner occupied park homes are well kept and surrounded by shrubs. Dogs are accepted with a good walk up into the hills from the back of the site. The area has a wealth of historic attractions, starting with the Wallace Monument which almost overlooks the park. Its 220 ft. tower dominates the surrounding area and the climb up its 246 steps gives spectacular views. Stirling is known as the 'Gateway to the Highlands' and its magnificent castle is world renowned. Within 10 miles there are castles, museums, cathedrals and parks. A leaflet of local walks is usually available in reception. Riding or bicycle hire 2 miles, fishing 3 miles, golf 1 mile. Buses stop at the park entrance. Being by the A91, there is some day-time road noise. Trees have been planted to try to minimise this but the further back onto the park you go, the less the traffic is heard.

Charges 1999:
-- Per unit incl. 2 adults £9.20 - £10.20; extra adult £1.30; child (2-13 yrs) 80p; extra car £1.30; awning (no groundsheets) or extra small tent £1.80; electricity £1.80; walker with tent £3.95 - £4.95 per person.
-- VAT included.
-- No credit cards.
Open:
1 April - 31 October.
Address
Blairlogie,
Stirling FK9 5PX.
Tel:
(01786) 474947.
Reservations:
Made without deposit; contact park.

Directions: Park is on A91, 2 miles northeast of Stirling. O.S.GR: NS822968.

Grampian

755 Huntly Castle Caravan Park, Huntly

New, family park with indoor Activity Centre.

Huntly Caravan Park was opened in '95 and its hard-working owners, Hugh and Debbie Ballantyne, are justly proud of their neat, well landscaped 15 acre site which is managed under contract for the Caravan Club (but non-members are also welcome). The 90 level, grass touring pitches are separated and numbered with everyone shown to their pitch. Arranged in three bays with banks of heathers and flowering shrubs separating them, 66 pitches have electric hook-ups (16A) and 15 are fully serviced with water and waste water also. Two areas have central play areas and all have easy access to a toilet block, as has the camping area. Campers are provided with a covered cooking shelter (with work tops) should the weather turn inclement. The three heated toilet blocks are well designed and maintained, with washbasins both in cubicles and vanity style and large, free showers with lots of changing space. Each block also has a family shower room (even larger), dishwashing sinks with free hot water, chemical disposal facilities and a superb room for disabled visitors. Also one well equipped laundry room. The park also has 39 privately owned caravan holiday homes, plus 3 to hire. The Activity Centre near the entrance contains two indoor safe play areas (one for up to 2 yrs old, the other up to 9 yrs). In addition there are snooker and pool tables, table tennis, badminton and short tennis. There is a charge for these facilities which are also open to the public, with tea, coffee and ices sold (open weekends and all local school holidays). Dogs are accepted with many good walks from the park. No shop on site but milk and papers may be ordered and the town of Huntly is only 10 minutes walk, with its shops and pubs. The castle is well worth a visit. The area abounds with things to do, from forest trails to walk or cycle, a falconry centre, malt whisky distilleries and an all year Nordic ski track. Fishing, golf or bicycle hire within ½ mile, riding 5 miles. A member of the Best of British group.

Charges guide;
-- Per standard pitch incl. 2 persons £8.75; electricity £2.00; awning £1.50; porch awning 75p; extra adult £2.00; child (5-16 yrs) £1.00; fully serviced pitch plus £1.50; tent incl. 2 persons £7.50 - £8.75.
-- VAT included.
-- Credit cards accepted.
Open:
24 March - 29 October.
Address:
Huntly,
Aberdeenshire
AB54 4UJ.
Tel:
(01466) 794999.
Reservations:
Contact park.

Directions: Site is well signed from the A96 Keith - Aberdeen road. O.S.GR: NJ526402.

753 Aden Country Park Caravan Park, Mintlaw, nr. Peterhead

Landscaped park in large country park with many attractions.

Aden Country Park is owned by the local authority and is open to the public offering several attractions for visitors including an Agricultural Heritage Centre, Wildlife Centre, Nature Trail, restaurant and craft shops, as well as open and woodland areas, with a lake, for walking and recreation. The caravan and camping site is on one side of the park. Beautifully landscaped and well laid out with trees, bushes and hedges, it is kept very neat and tidy. It provides 48 numbered pitches for touring units, with varying degrees of slope (some level) and all with electrical hook-ups (16A), plus an area for tents. There are also 12 caravan holiday homes in a row on the left as you enter. A modern, fully tiled sanitary block, with good facilities for disabled visitors, was very clean when we visited. It can be heated and provides free, pre-set hot showers, with dressing area, plenty of toilets and vanity type washbasins, with hairdryer for ladies, a baby bath and chemical disposal. Dishwashing and laundry facilities are together, with washing machines, tumble and spin dryers and an iron, all metered. Large dog walking area. Facilities for children include two games areas and various items of play equipment (with safety surfaces). There is a small shop (sweets and ice-creams) in the reception area, the restaurant in the Heritage Centre is available for meals and Mintlaw is ½ mile for shopping. Fishing 1 mile, riding 2 miles, golf 3 miles. The park is in a most attractive area and one could spend plenty of time enjoying all it has to offer.

Charges 1999:
-- Per caravan or motor-caravan £8.65; tent £7.50; small tent or awning £3.50; electricity £1.75.
-- Reductions for OAPs out of season.
-- Credit cards accepted.
Open:
Easter - 25 October.
Address:
Old Deer, Mintlaw,
Aberdeenshire.
Tel:
(01771) 623460.
Reservations:
Advisable for weekends; write to park for details.

Directions: Approaching Mintlaw from the west on A950 road, park is shortly after sign for Mintlaw station. From the east, go to the western outskirts of the village and entrance is on left - `Aden Country Park and Farm Heritage Centre'. O.S.GR: NJ985484.

754 Aberlour Gardens Caravan and Camping Park, Aberlour

Pleasant park within the large walled garden of the Aberlour Estate.

Mr and Mrs Moss, the new owners, have made improvements to this sheltered, five acre, family run park on Speyside which provides a very natural setting amidst spruce and Scots pine. Of the 61 level pitches, 26 are for holiday homes (1 for rent) and 6 for seasonal units, leaving the remainder for touring units. All have electrical connections (10A) and 4 are 'all-weather' pitches. The toilet block can be heated and has vanity style washbasins (with shelves, mirrors, soap and towels), four large unisex showers on payment and facilities for visitors with disabilities. Laundry facilities, chemical disposal and motorcaravan service point. A small licensed shop stocks basics and has an information area. Children's play area. Public telephone. Dogs are welcome if kept under control. Caravan storage available. This is an ideal area for walking, birdwatching, fishing (salmon, 1 or 5 miles), pony trekking or for following the only Malt Whisky Trail in the world. Golf 4 miles, riding ½ mile, swimming or bicycle hire 1 mile, bowls 2 miles.

Directions: Turn off A95 between Aberlour and Craigellachie onto unclassified road and site is signed in 500 yds. Vehicles over 10' 6" high should use A941 Dufftown Road (site is signed). O.S.GR: NJ282432.

Charges 1999:
-- Per caravan, motorcaravan or trailer tent incl. 2 persons £6.50 - £9.00; tent £6.50 - £8.00; extra person £2.00; child (5-16) £1.00; electricity £1.50 - £1.75.
-- No credit cards.

Open:
1 April - 31 October.

Address:
Aberlour-on-Spey, Banffshire AB38 9LD.

Tel/Fax:
(01340) 871586.

E-mail: abergard@compuserve.com.

Reservations:
Advised for July/Aug; with deposit (1 night fee).

766 Spindrift Caravan and Camping Park, Little Kildrummie, Nairn

Attractive, quiet, small family run park near popular resort.

Mr and Mrs Guillot have put a lot of thought into the landscaping of their park, making it into an absolute gem. It is situated in an elevated position overlooking the distant Monadlaith mountains and a short walk from the River Nairn. The popular seaside resort of Nairn with its shops, restaurants, beach and harbour is some 2 miles away and it is said to take 30 minutes to walk via the riverside path. The park is surrounded by trees and is arranged on three terraces (roads down to the lower pitches have been re-laid and give easy access). The lowest level is used primarily for tents. With 40 pitches altogether, there are 28 electrical connections (16A), all on the highest terrace, although if you have a long cable, reached from the second level too. Two modern sanitary blocks are both well equipped with free controllable hot showers, vanity style washbasins, free hair dryers and chemical disposal. The large laundry room has dishwashing and laundry sinks with free hot water, a washing machine, dryer and iron. A thoughtful addition is a table and chairs for use in inclement weather. The front porch of the owners house is used as reception (gas available), providing tourist information and a phone (left open at all times). There is no shop but Nairn is near. A bus passes the lane end (400 yds). Dogs are accepted with the river footpath easily accessible. Salmon fishing permits at the park. Bicycle hire, riding, golf and boat launching within 2 miles.

Directions: From A96 just west of Nairn take B9090 south towards Cawdor. Pass through residential area out into the country for about 1½ miles and follow Little Kildrummie sign to right. O.S.GR: NH863537.

Charges 2000:
-- Per unit incl. 2 adults and 2 children £5.50 - £8.50; small tent (2 adults) £5.50 - £7.50; extra adult free - £1.00; child free - 50p; awning free - £1.00; electricity (15A) £1.50.
-- No credit cards.

Open:
1 April - 31 October.

Address:
Little Kildrummie, Nairn, Highlands IV12 5QU.

Tel:
(01667) 453992.

Reservations:
Advisable for July/Aug. with £5 deposit.

769 Torvean Caravan Park, Inverness

Small, neat, select touring park for caravans only.

Torvean is situated on the outskirts of Inverness beside the Caledonian Canal and within easy reach of the town's amenities which include an ice rink, theatre and leisure sports centre. Excursions to the coast and Highlands, including Loch Ness, are possible in several directions. The pitches on level grass are well spaced and clearly marked with a tarmac access road and street lighting giving a very neat appearance. There are 50 touring pitches, 45 with electricity (10A) and 10 caravan holiday homes for hire. Torvean offers a children's play area on bark, a well equipped launderette and public phone. The two toilet blocks are of good quality with free hot water in basins, set in flat surface with shelves and mirrors - ladies have two cubicles with washbasin and toilet and a hair wash cubicle. Controllable hot showers on payment, hand and hair dryers, a suite for disabled people with toilet and shower and chemical disposal. Dog walking area. Reservations are necessary for July/Aug. Golf adjacent. Bicycle hire or fishing 3 miles.

Directions: Park is off the main A82 road on the southwest outskirts of the town by the Tomnahurich Canal Bridge. O.S.GR: NH638438.

Charges guide:
-- Per unit incl. 2 adults £9.00 - £9.50; electricity £2.00; extra adult £1.50; child (under 16) 75p; awning £3.00; small dog £1.00 (one only).
-- No credit cards.

Open:
Easter - end-October.

Address:
Glenurquhart Road, Inverness IV3 6JL.

Tel:
(01463) 220582.
FAX: (01463) 233051.

Reservations:
Made deposit and £1 fee.

Highlands and Islands

767 Grantown-on-Spey Caravan Park, Grantown-on-Spey

Family run touring park with good sanitary facilities.

Sandra McKelvie and her son John Fleming own and personally run this park, continually upgrading an already excellent provision. Quietly and peacefully situated on the edge of the little town with views of the mountains in the distance, it consists of well tended grassy lawns, terraced or slightly sloping with made-up access roads and, where the rabbits allow, colourful flower beds. Recent landscaping included the planting of many trees which are growing well. For tourers, there are 100 caravan pitches, plus 50 which may be occupied by seasonal vans (many on hardstandings) and room for perhaps 50 tents. There are 80 electrical connections (10A) and 12 large pitches with water and drainage. You are escorted to your pitch and given any help necessary. Caravan holiday homes are mostly separated to either end. Sanitary facilities in two clean, modern blocks, are of good quality and beautifully maintained, with a small night unit at the opposite end. Facilities include free hot water in individual washbasins and controllable showers, covered dishwashing sinks behind each block, a laundry room with washing machines, spin dryers and irons and chemical disposal. Motorcaravan service point. Games room with table tennis and pool table. Football pitch. Two public phones. Dog exercise area with hill top view! Gates closed 10.30 pm. - 7.30 am. Gas is available, but no shop - the town is close. Grantown is a pleasant touring base for the Cairngorms and for the Malt Whisky Trail. Fishing, golf and mountain bike hire within 1 mile, riding 3 miles. Winter caravan storage. A peaceful park with a warden on site at all times.

Charges 1999:
-- Per pitch incl. 2 persons £7.00 - £9.50; 2 man tent and vehicle £6.00 - £7.00; hiker's 2 man tent £5.00 - £6.00; awning or extra pup tent £1.50; extra person £1.00; electricity £2.00.
-- VAT included.
-- Credit cards accepted.

Open:
31 March - 31 October.

Address:
Seafield Avenue, Grantown on Spey, Moray PH26 3JQ.

Tel:
(01479) 872474. FAX: (01479) 873696. E-mail: findahome@ prodigy.net.

Reservations:
Made with £5 deposit.

Directions: Park is signed from the town centre. O.S.GR: NJ028283.

768 Glenmore Caravan and Camping Site, Glenmore, Aviemore

Forestry Commission site well situated for watersports and exploring the Cairngorms.

The Glenmore Forest site lies close to the sandy shore of Loch Morlich amidst conifer woods and surrounded on three sides by the impressive Cairngorm mountains. It is conveniently situated for a range of activities, including skiing (extensive lift system), orienteering, hill and mountain walking (way-marked walks), fishing (trout and pike) and non-motorized watersports on the Loch. The site itself is attractively laid out in a fairly informal style in several adjoining areas connected by narrow part gravel, part tarmac roadways with access to the lochside. One of these areas, the Pinewood Area, is very popular and has 32 hardstandings (some distance from the toilet block). Of the 220 marked pitches on fairly level grass, 137 have electricity (10A). There are two very basic toilet blocks with heating and free hot water to the washbasins, but only one shower/laundry block which is some distance from the majority of the pitches and reached by an underpass. Opened by electronic key pad (you are given a number), it is a large heated block with free hot showers, providing basic facilities. There is a separate unit for visitors with disabilities. The site has a range of amenities, also open to the general public, which include a well stocked shop, a café serving a variety of meals and snacks, Forestry Commission visitor centre and souvenir shop (better than average quality souvenirs). The Aviemore centre providing a wide range of indoor and outdoor recreations is only 7 miles and there are several golf courses within a range of 15 miles, as well as fishing and boat trips. No night time supervision.

Charges 1999:
-- Per unit incl. up to 4 persons £7.70 - £9.00; `select' pitch +3.20; electricity £2.10; extra car, trailer or child's tent £2.50.
-- Weekend prices higher.
-- Credit cards accepted.

Open:
All year excl. 1/11-15/12.

Address:
Glenmore, Aviemore, Inverness-shire PH22 1QU.

Tel:
(01479) 861271, or out of season (0131) 314 6505.

Reservations:
Necessary for B.Hs and peak times; made for min. 3 nights with £30 deposit. Contact site when open, otherwise Forest Holidays, Forestry Commission, 231 Corstorphine Road, Edinburgh EH12 7AT. Tel: (0131) 314 6505.

Directions: Immediately south of Aviemore on B9152 (not A9 bypass) take B970 then follow sign for Cairngorm and Loch Morlich. Site entrance is on right past the loch. O.S.GR: NH975097.

20 00
SELECTED AND INSPECTED

ALAN ROGERS'
GOOD CAMPS GUIDE

DISCOUNT CARD A

CAMPSITE DISCOUNT VOUCHER

VALID 01 JAN - 31 DEC 2000

This voucher entitles the holder to the discounts shown against the relevant campsite report in this guide. This portion of the voucher should be retained by the holder, but made available for inspection at the campsite(s) concerned when booking in and/or departure.

VOUCHER NUMBER

02619

B00/

Save Money!

20 00
SELECTED AND INSPECTED

ALAN ROGERS'
GOOD CAMPS GUIDE

DISCOUNT CARD B

TRAVEL & BREAKDOWN INSURANCE DISCOUNT VOUCHER

VALID 01 JAN - 31 DEC 2000

This voucher entitles the holder to a discount of 10% on Travel & Breakdown Insurance arrangements made via this Guide. Please call 01308 897809 or write to Deneway Guides & Travel Ltd., Chesil Lodge, West Bexington, Dorchester, DT2 9DG - for a proposal form which will need to be completed and sent to Deneway Guides & Travel along with payment for the relevant premium, and this voucher at least one week before you intend to travel.

VOUCHER NUMBER

02619

B00/

Save Money!

20 00
SELECTED AND INSPECTED

ALAN ROGERS'
GOOD CAMPS GUIDE

DISCOUNT CARD C

IRISH FERRIES DISCOUNT VOUCHER

VALID 09 JAN - 15 DEC 2000

(WITH THE EXCEPTIONS DETAILED OPPOSITE)

This voucher entitles the holder to the following 50% reductions with Irish Ferries on all their routes between Britain and Ireland between 09 Jan - 15 Dec 2000 except during the period indicated below:

Reductions: For caravans and trailer tents - a discount of 50% off the published brochure tariff for towed caravan or trailer tents when making a standard return fare booking for a car, caravan or trailer tent and up to five adults, excluding the months of July & August. For motorcaravans any prevailing overheight supplement will be waived.

How to book: For telephone bookings, telephone 08705 171717, quoting this voucher number and the brochure/fare code No C016 at the time of booking. The voucher itself must be sent to Irish Ferries when confirming/paying for your booking.

VOUCHER NUMBER

02619

B00/

Save Money!

ALAN ROGERS GOOD CAMPS GUIDES 2000 DISCOUNT VOUCHER

Valid as shown on opposite side

NAME:

ADDRESS:

SIGNATURE:

Save Mon

ALAN ROGERS GOOD CAMPS GUIDES 2000 DISCOUNT VOUCHER

Valid as shown on opposite side

NAME:

ADDRESS:

SIGNATURE:

Save Mon

ALAN ROGERS GOOD CAMPS GUIDES 2000 DISCOUNT VOUCHER

Valid as shown on opposite side

NAME:

ADDRESS:

SIGNATURE:

Save Mon

ALAN ROGERS'
GOOD CAMPS GUIDE

DISCOUNT CARD D

AVIATION MUSEUM DISCOUNT VOUCHER

VALID 01 JAN - 31 DEC 2000

This voucher entitles the holder to a 20% discount on entry fees to The Island Aeroplane Company's Aviation Museum. This voucher should be retained by the holder but made available for inspection at the Museum on arrival.

VOUCHER NUMBER

02663
B00/

Save Money!

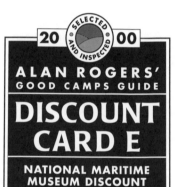

ALAN ROGERS'
GOOD CAMPS GUIDE

DISCOUNT CARD E

NATIONAL MARITIME MUSEUM DISCOUNT VOUCHER

VALID 01 JAN - 31 DEC 2000

VOUCHER NUMBER

02663
B00/

Alan Rogers Good Camps Guides/ National Maritime Museum Promotion ref ALA/B00
This voucher entitles the holder to a discount of 20% off the normal price of admission for adults and children, but cannot be used in conjunction with any other special offer, family or season tickets

Save Money!

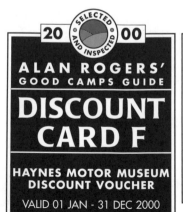

ALAN ROGERS'
GOOD CAMPS GUIDE

DISCOUNT CARD F

HAYNES MOTOR MUSEUM DISCOUNT VOUCHER

VALID 01 JAN - 31 DEC 2000

THE UK'S MOST EXTENSIVE COLLECTION OF MOTOR VEHICLES FROM AROUND THE WORLD

HAYNES
MOTOR
MUSEUM

Save 50p per person off the full admission price, up to a maximum of six people.

UP TO **£3** **VOUCHER**

This offer applies until 31 December 2000 and is not valid in conjunction with any other voucher scheme, discounts or family tickets. Haynes Motor Museum, Sparkford, Nr Yeovil, Somerset BA22 7LH Tel: 01963 440804

ALAN ROGERS GOOD CAMPS GUIDES 2000 DISCOUNT VOUCHER

Valid as shown on opposite side

NAME:

ADDRESS:

SIGNATURE:

Save Mon ▲ 🚐

CARD E NATIONAL MARITIME MUSEUM DISCOUNT VOUCHER

Valid 01 Jan - 31 Dec 2000 (Not to be used in conjunction with any other offer)

NAME:

ADDRESS:

SIGNATURE:

Save Mon ▲ 🚐

ALAN ROGERS GOOD CAMPS GUIDES 2000 DISCOUNT VOUCHER

Valid as shown on opposite side

NAME:

ADDRESS:

SIGNATURE:

Haynes
THE BOOK ®

Save Mon ▲ 🚐

773 Scourie Caravan and Camping Park, Scourie, nr. Handa Island

Family park with own restaurant, close to ferries for Handa Island Bird Sanctuary.

Mr Mackenzie has carefully nurtured this park over many years, developing a number of firm terraces with 60 pitches which gives it an attractive layout - there is nothing regimented here. Perched on the edge of the bay in an elevated position, practically everyone has a view of the sea. A short walk along the shore footpath leads to a small sandy beach. The park has tarmac and gravel access roads, with well drained grass pitches and some hard-core hardstandings with 10A electric hook-ups. A few are on an area which is unfenced from the rocks (young children would need to be supervised here). Reception, alongside the modern toilet block, contains a wealth of tourist information and maps. The toilet facilities can be heated and have free hot water to vanity style washbasins and controllable free showers (no divider or seat). A laundry room provides washing machines, dryers, spin dryer and iron, plus sinks for clothes and dishwashing, there is a very good unit for visitors with disabilities, chemical disposal and a motorcaravan service point. The 'Anchorage' restaurant at the entrance to the park (used as reception at quiet times) is large and well appointed with meals at reasonable prices cooked to order (1/5-15/9). Mr Mackenzie claims that this is the only caravan park in the world from where, depending on the season, you can see palm trees, Highland cattle and Great Northern divers from your pitch. Red throated divers have also been seen. Trips to Handa Island (a special protection area for seabird colonies) are available from here and Tarbet. There are boat launching facilities and the clear water makes this area ideal for diving. Fishing permits (brown trout) can be arranged. The village has a well stocked shop with post office, gas is available from the local petrol station and mobile banks visit regularly.

Charges 1999:
-- Per unit incl. 2 adults £8.00, 1 adult £7.00; extra adult £1.00; child (3-16 yrs) 50p; hiker and tent £5.00; extra tent, vehicle or awning £1.00; electricity £2.00.
-- No credit cards.

Open:
1 April - 30 September, but phone first to check.

Address:
Harbour Road, Scourie, Sutherland IV27 4TG.

Tel:
(01971) 502060.

Reservations:
Not made.

Directions: Park is by Scourie village on A894 road in northwest Sutherland. O.S.GR: NC153446.

772 Woodend Camping and Caravan Park, Achnairn, Lairg

Delightful, peaceful and welcoming park overlooking Loch Shin.

Mrs Cathie Ross runs this small, simple and friendly park single-handedly and provides a wonderfully warm Scottish welcome to visitors. On a hill with open, panoramic views across the Loch to the hills beyond and all around, the large camping field is undulating and gently sloping with plenty of reasonably flat areas for 55 tourers. Most of the 22 electrical hook-ups (16A) are in a line near the top of the field, close to the large, fenced children's play area which has several items of equipment on grass. The modernised sanitary facilities are kept very clean and are quite satisfactory, with hot water for showers, chemical disposal, dishwashing on small payment, with books and magazines to borrow in the dishwashing room. A laundry with two machines and a dryer is just behind and a kitchen and eating room for tent campers are provided. Reception and a shop are at the house, where Sunday papers can be ordered, strawberries are on sale in season and daily milk and bread may be ordered. Fishing licences for the Loch (your catch will be frozen for you) are available. Besides fishing, there are opportunities for hill walking, mountain bikes can be hired in Lairg (5 miles) and there are several scenic golf courses within 20-30 miles. The famous Falls of Shin with a Visitor Centre is an ideal place to see the salmon leap (about 10 miles). Caravan holiday homes (5) to rent.

Charges guide:
-- Per unit (all) £5.50; electricity £1.00.
-- No credit cards.

Open:
1 April - 30 September.

Address:
Achnairn, Lairg, Sutherland IV27 4DN.

Tel:
(01549) 402248.
FAX: as phone.

Reservations:
Not considered necessary.

Directions: Achnairn is near the southern end of Loch Shin. Turn off the A838 single track road at signs for Woodend. From the A9 coming north take the A836 at Bonar Bridge, 11 miles northwest of Tain. O.S.GR: NC558127.

Highlands and Islands

770 Pitgrudy Caravan Park, Dornoch

Quiet park with marvellous views, in the heart of the Highlands.

Pitgrudy is in a rural situation with superb views over the Dornoch Firth and the surrounding Ross-shire hills. There are 40 touring pitches, mostly on slightly sloping grass and with electrical connections (10A). A few have hardstanding and six are fully serviced. Located at the top of the park are 35 caravan holiday homes, 25 privately owned and 10 to hire. The whole park is on immaculately tended grass with tarmac roads. Sanitary facilities are provided in a modern, superior 'portacabin' style unit. Very clean and well equipped, the showers are controllable and free. A laundry has a washing machine, dryer and iron and there are separate dishwashing sinks. Chemical disposal. Gas is available but there is no shop - Dornoch, a pleasant little town, is less than a mile away with shops, restaurants, plus the cathedral. A safe sandy beach is 1 mile and the area is good for walking and golf (there are 7 courses within 15 miles of the park). Fishing 1 miles, bicycle hire or boat launching 3 miles, riding 5 miles. A member of the Best of British group. Bookings and enquiries to: GNR Sutherland, Caravan Sales, Edderton, Tain, Ross-shire IV19 1JY.

Directions: At the war memorial in Dornoch, turn north (park signed) on B9168. Park is ½ mile on the right (45 miles north of Inverness). O.S.GR: NH795911.

Charges guide:
-- Per unit incl. 2 persons £7.50 - £9.00; tent and car £7.00 - £8.50; extra adult £1.00; child (under 16 yrs) 50p; awning £1.50; dog (max. 2) free; electricity £2.00.
-- No credit cards.
Open:
25 April - 30 September.
Address:
Poles Road, Dornoch, Highland IV25 3HY.
Tel:
(01862) 821253 (9-5.30).
FAX: (01862) 821382.
Reservations:
Made with deposit (1st night's rent) and £1 fee (see address above).

771 Ardmair Point Caravan Park, Ardmair Point, nr. Ullapool

Spectacularly situated park on bay at Loch Kanaird.

Just 3 miles north of Ullapool and overlooking the little Loch Kanaird, just round the corner from Loch Broom, this park has splendid views all round. The 68 touring pitches are arranged mainly on grass around the edge of the bay in front of the shingle beach. Electrical hook-ups (10A) are available and some gravel hardstandings are on the other side of the access road, just past the well equipped second sanitary block. This block, with wonderful views from the large windows in the launderette and dishwashing rooms, provides good facilities including free hot showers and washbasins set in flat surfaces, plus large en-suite rooms for disabled people. Tents pitches, together with cheaper pitches for some tourers are in a large field behind the other sanitary facilities (also good). Other amenities include a motorcaravan service point, reception and a shop, housed in the same building and a children's play park. The park provides rowing and motorboats for hire and arranges fishing trips. Golf or bicycle hire 3 miles. Seals are regularly seen in the bay and the whole area is full of interest, including visits to Inverewe Gardens and the Isle Martin bird and seal colonies.

Directions: Park is off the A835 road, 3 miles north of Ullapool. O.S.GR: NH109983.

Charges 1999:
-- Per unit incl. 2 persons £8.00 - £10.00; awning £2.00; extra adult £2.00 - £3.00; child (over 5 yrs) £1.00 - £1.50; extra tent £1.50 - £2.50; electricity (10A) £2.00.
-- Credit cards accepted.
-- VAT included.
Open:
1 May - late September, depending on the weather, if in doubt phone.
Address:
Ardmair Point, Ullapool, Ross-shire IV26 2TN.
Tel:
(01854) 612054.
FAX: (01854) 612757.
E-mail: p.fraser@ btinternet.com.
Reservations:
Recommended for July/Aug. (min. 2 nights).

774 Loch Greshornish Camping Site, Edinbane, Isle of Skye

Simple, spacious site overlooking the Loch in northwest Skye.

This is a simple site with basic facilities in a beautiful, peaceful setting with views over the loch to the low hills to the northwest of Skye. There are 30 level grass pitches for motorcaravans and caravans, 18 with 10A electric hook-ups. There are also places for up to 100 tents (but numbers never reach that level). The sanitary facilities are satisfactory, old but light and airy, very well painted and spotlessly clean when we visited. They provide free hot water to showers (a little cramped) and washbasins, plus a dishwashing sink for each sex. Hair dryer on payment. The only acknowledgement of any clothes washing needs was a tumble dryer in a little cabin outside. There is no shop and Portree, the nearest town, is 15 miles. The local village has a hotel for drinks and meals.

Directions: Site is 15 miles west of Portree on the A850 Dunvegan road by Edinbane. O.S.GR: NG343524.

Charges guide:
-- Per unit incl. 2 persons £7.00; extra person over 5 yrs £1.00; electricity £1.50.
Open:
Easter - 12 October.
Address:
Arnisort, Edinbane, Isle of Skye IV51 9PS.
Tel:
(01470) 582230.
Reservations:
Advised for high season - contact site.

775 Staffin Caravan and Camping Site, Staffin, Isle of Skye

Simple hillside site with wonderful views in northeast Skye.

The camping site is on the side of a hill just outside Staffin, where the broad sweep of the bay is dotted with working crofts running down to the sea. A marked walk from the site leads to the seashore and slipway (good for walking dogs but too far to be taking a boat). With 50 pitches, the site is quite sloping but there are 18 reasonably level pitches with hardstanding for caravans and motorcaravans, all with electrical hook-ups (16A) The sanitary block is tiled with large, controllable, free showers and vanity style washbasins. Washing up sinks are unfortunately not under cover and have only cold water. There is also an older block but this is only open at very busy times. Chemical disposal facilities are also out in the open. A large hardstanding area has a motorcaravan service point and gas is for sale. Staffin village is 400 yds and has a large shop (open six days a week), a restaurant, launderette (useful as the site has no laundry), plus a public phone. Skye has many activities to offer and for the truly dedicated walker the Cuillins are the big attraction but the hills above Staffin look demanding! Cottage for rent. Fishing or boat launching 1 mile, bicycle hire 5 miles, riding 9 miles.

Directions: Site is 15 miles north of Portree on A855 (2 miles of single track at the start), just before Staffin on the right and up a slope. O.S.GR: NG496668.

Charges 1999:
-- Per unit (all) incl. 2 persons £7.00; extra adult £3.00; child 5-12 yrs £1.00, 13-18 yrs £1.50; electricity £1.50.
-- No credit cards.

Open:
1 April - 30 September (maybe into October if weather fine).

Address:
Staffin,
Isle of Skye IV51 9JS.

Tel:
(01470) 562213.

Reservations:
Maybe necessary for peak periods (made with £10 deposit), but will always try to fit you in.

776 Reraig Caravan Site, Balmacara, Kyle of Lochalsh

Small, quiet park with views over to Skye; only small tents accepted.

This is a small, level park close to Loch Alsh and with a wooded hillside behind (criss-crossed with woodland walks). Mainly grass, it is sheltered from the prevailing winds by the hill and provides just 45 numbered pitches, 36 with electrical connections (10A) and some hardstandings. Large tents and trailer tents are not accepted at all. Small tents are permitted at the discretion of the owner, so it would be advisable to telephone first if this affects you. Awnings are not permitted during July and August. The ground can be stony so there could be a problem with tent pegs. The single sanitary block has had some refurbishment and was very clean when we visited. Washbasins are in vanity units with pine surrounds and very decorative mirrors (children have their own low basins), controllable hot showers are on payment, as are hair dryers, and a room at the end of the block provides sinks for clothes and dishwashing (free hot water). Use of a spin dryer is free. Chemical disposal. Adjacent to the park is the Balmacara Hotel (with bar), shop (selling gas), sub-post office, off licence and petrol station. Riding 1 or 3½ miles. An attractive little park with well cut grass, Reraig makes a good base from which to explore the Isle of Skye and the pretty village of Plockton with its palm trees (remember Hamish Macbeth on TV?) Reservations are not necessary but it is advisable to arrive before mid-afternoon in July and August.

Directions: Take A87 towards Kyle of Lochalsh. Park is signed very soon after sign for Balmacara, on the right just before hotel and petrol station. O.S.GR: NG815272.

Charges 2000:
-- Per unit incl. 2 persons £7.50; extra person £1.20 (tbc); electricity £1.50; awning (May, June, Sept only) £1.30.
-- Credit cards accepted.

Open:
1 May - 30 September.

Address:
Balmacara, Kyle of Lochalsh, Ross-shire IV40 8DH.

Tel:
(01599) 566215.

Reservations:
Not necessary so not accepted by phone; if considered essential, by letter enclosing cheque/PO for first night's fee (non-returnable).

For lists of parks which offer facilities on site for FISHING, GOLF, HORSE RIDING, BICYCLE HIRE or BOAT LAUNCHING see pages 237 - 239

Highlands and Islands

778 Faichem Park, Faichem, Invergarry

Small unsophisticated site near Loch Ness with wonderful views.

Faichem Park is situated on a hillside in a beautiful setting with glorious views over Ben Tee (2,955 ft). The road up to the site has been tarmaced so it is now accessible to all except American motorhomes. For the children there is the attraction of helping to feed the animals - sheep and lambs, chickens, many types of ducks and strange marvellous looking types of pheasants (Mr Wilson's hobby), the pony and the white `runner' ducks which march like soldiers around the park and farm. There are 30 pitches with plenty of space, including 14 with electrical connections and 10 with level concrete hardstanding. A log type cabin houses the sanitary facilities which are older in style but very clean and well painted (key, £1 deposit). Hot water to the showers is metered but is free to the washbasins (with soap). Hair and hand dryers, plus dishwashing sinks are provided. The chemical disposal unit is of a very high standard. Gas is available and free range eggs are sold at the farm but there is no shop (closest 2 miles towards Fort William). The village is ½ mile with a hotel. Dogs are accepted (but care is needed with the livestock) and there is an excellent area above the site for walks. TV reception is good. There are numerous places to fish in the area, golf in Fort Augustus and Fort William, pony trekking, a pleasure cruiser on Loch Ness (you might see Nessie) and the Great Glen water park (2 miles). Bicycle hire or boat slipway 2 miles, golf 7 miles. Pine lodges and a cottage to let.

Charges 2000:
-- Per unit incl. 2 persons £6.50 - £7.00; extra adult 50p; extra child 25p; electricity £1.50 - £2.00.
-- No credit cards.

Open:
15 March - 15 October.

Address:
Ardgarry Farm,
Faichem, Invergarry,
Inverness-shire

Tel:
(01809) 501226.
FAX: (01809) 501307.

Reservations:
Advisable in main season and made with small deposit.

Directions: From A82 at Invergarry take A87 (towardsKyle of Lochalsh) and continue for 1 mile. Turn right at Faichem sign and bear left up hill, farmhouse and reception is first entrance on the right, the site is second. O.S.GR: NH285023.

779 Invercoe Caravan and Camping Park, Invercoe, Glencoe

Family owned park in magnificent historical setting.

On the edge of Loch Leven, surrounded by mountains and forest, Iain and Lynn Brown are continually developing this attractively located park. It provides places for 55 caravans and 60 tents on level grass with gravel access roads and 4 hardstandings. You choose your own numbered pitch, those at the loch side being very popular, although the 36 with electricity (10A) are to the back of the park. Five caravan holiday homes and three chalets are for hire. Adjoining the shop (May - end Sept) near the entrance is the nicely refurbished toilet block which can be heated and has free hot showers and vanity style washbasins (shower/wash room locked 10 pm. - 7 am). Dishwashing under cover, excellent laundry facilities with a drying room, and chemical disposal facilities are provided. Public phone. Play area with swings. The village with pub and restaurant is within walking distance. There is much to do for the active with hill walking, climbing, boating, pony riding and sea loch or fresh water fishing in this area of outstanding natural beauty, with the Visitor's Centre at Glencoe just a couple of miles away.

Charges 1999:
-- Per unit incl. 2 persons £10.00; extra adult £1.00; child (over 2 yrs) 50p; awning £1.50; boat on trailer £1.00; electricity (10A) £1.50; tent incl. 2 persons, no car £8.00.
-- Senior citizens less £1.00 excl. July/Aug.
-- No credit cards.
-- VAT included.

Open:
Easter/1 April - end Oct.

Address:
Invercoe, Glencoe,
Argyll PA39 4HP.

Tel/Fax:
(01855) 811210.
E-mail: invercoe@
sol.co.uk.

Reservations:
Advised for electricity for peak season; made with £17 deposit and £3 fee.

Directions: Follow A82 Crianlarich - Fort William road to Glencoe village and turn onto the B863; park is ½ mile along, well signed. O.S.GR: NN098594.

780 Resipole Farm Caravan and Camping Park, Acharacle

Beautifully situated park on the loch shores, with good facilities.

This quiet, open park is marvellously set on the banks of Loch Sunart, 8 miles from Strontian, in the Ardnamurchan peninsula, with views across the water and is regularly visited by wild deer. It offers a good base for exploring this scenic area or, more locally, for fishing, boating (from the site's slipway) and walking in the unspoilt countryside. There are 60 touring pitches, 24 with hardstanding of which 4 have all services and 20 have electrical hook-ups (10A). Tents are sited by the hedges. Some caravans and cabins to rent. The central, modern sanitary block can be heated and provides free, pre-set showers, washbasins in rows, shaver points and hair dryers. All was very clean when seen, good dishwashing facilities are in separate rooms and there is excellent provision for disabled visitors. Chemical disposal, laundry facilities and a public phone. Adjoining the farmhouse is a bar and restaurant with good value, home made food in the evenings (vegetarians also). The park has its own 9 hole golf course. Riding 5 miles. Caravan storage. Resipole Farm is well located for day trips to Mull via the Lochaline ferry.

Directions: From A82 Fort William road, take Corran ferry 5 miles north of Ballachulish, 8 miles south of Fort William. On leaving ferry, turn south on A861. Park is on north bank of Loch Sunart, 8 miles west of Strontian. The road is single track for 8 miles approaching Resipole, but it is worth it. O.S.GR: NM676740.

Charges guide:
-- Per unit, incl. 2 persons £8.50 - £9.50; extra adult £1.50; child up to 5 yrs 50p, 6-12 yrs £1.00, 13 yrs upwards £1.50; electricity £1.50.
-- VAT included.
-- Credit cards accepted.
Open:
1 April - 31 October.
Address:
Loch Sunart, Acharacle, Argyll PH36 4HX.
Tel:
(01967) 431235.
FAX: (01967) 431777.
E-mail: info@ resipole.co.uk.
Reservations:
Advised for hook-ups,any period with 1 night's fee.

781 Camping and Caravanning Club Site Oban, Barcaldine

Small friendly site in a sheltered location north of Oban.

This Camping and Caravanning Club site at Barcaldine 12 miles north of Oban, is small and intimate taking 86 units. Arranged in the walled garden of Barcaldine House, the walls give it some protection from the wind and make it quite a sun trap. There are 16 level pitches with hardstanding and 45 electrical hook-ups (10/15A). Being a small site, it has a friendly feel to it, due no doubt to the welcome new arrivals receive. Through the garden gate, one is immediately in the Barcaldine forest with its miles of forest tracks. The central, heated toilet block is kept very clean with free hot showers, hair dryers and plenty of washbasins and WCs. The laundry is next to the small shop for basic provisions and gas. A motorcaravan service point is provided and an excellent unit for disabled visitors. The play area is small but has a safety base. Unusually for a club site there is a bar. A very comfortable area, only open until 10.30 pm. (no children after 8.30 pm), bar meals are served 6-8 pm. most evenings The loch across the road is handy for sea fishing. Sea Life Centre 2 miles and a not too frequent bus passes the gate.

Directions: Park entrance is off the A828 road on south side of Loch Creran, 6 miles north of Connel Bridge. O.S.GR: NM966420.

Charges 2000:
-- Per 2 adults £6.30 - £9.60; child (6-18 yrs) £1.55; non-member pitch fee £4.30; electricity £1.60 - £2.35.
-- VAT included.
-- Credit cards accepted.
Open:
March - November.
Address:
Barcaldine by Connel, Argyll PA37 1SG.
Tel:
(01631) 720348 (no calls after 8 pm).
Reservations:
Needed for high season and made with deposit; contact the wardens.

782 Oban Divers Caravan Park, Oban

Scenic, peaceful and friendly park close to Oban.

Set most attractively in valley, yet close to Oban, this park has been thoughtfully developed as an extension to the garden of the owner's family home and diving business. A small stream runs through the park, with several types of young eucalyptus and bamboo growing and fuchsias at the entrance. There are only 45 pitches with 12 hardstandings, 34 electrical connections and plenty of space. Tents are placed mainly on a higher back terrace. Sanitary facilities are in two chalets, the smaller one near the tent pitches. The main chalet provides comfortable facilities with two of the three ladies' washbasins in cabins and dishwashing, laundry (with a popular mangle!), drying and chemical disposal rooms. Small shop at reception with gas, divers' shop with hot drinks machine, a covered barbecue and a motorcaravan service point. An open fronted room is provided for tenters. Children's play items on gravel. Definitely no dogs. The park is unsuitable for largest units. Bunk houses for groups to rent. Fishing 1 mile, bicycle hire 2 miles, riding or golf 3 miles. A member of the Countryside Discovery group.

Directions: From north follow A85 one way system through town to traffic island then take ferry terminal exit (Albany St). By Job Centre turn left and then follow signs to Camping Glenshellach. From south to traffic island, then as above. Site is 2 miles from Oban on single track road (passing places). O.S.GR: NM841277.

Charges 2000:
-- Per unit £7.00; person 50p; electricity (10A) £1.50; awning or extra car £1.00.
-- Less £1.00 for senior citizens excl. B.Hs and July/Aug.
-- No credit cards.
Open:
Mid March - end Oct.
Address:
Glenshellach Road, Oban, Argyll PA34 4QJ.
Tel/Fax:
(01631) 562755.
E-mail: obandivers@ tesco.net.
Reservations:
Made with £10 deposit.

783 Glen Nevis Caravan and Camping Park, Fort William

Spacious touring park in wonderful situation by Ben Nevis range.

Just outside Fort William in a most attractive and quiet situation with views of Ben Nevis, this park is used by those on active pursuits as well as sightseeing tourists. It comprises 7 quite spacious fields, divided between caravans and tents (steel pegs required). It is licensed for 250 touring caravans but with no special tent limits. The large touring pitches, many with hardstanding, are marked with wooden fence dividers, 174 with electricity (13A) and a further 100 with water and drainage also. If reception is closed (possible in low season) you site yourself. There are regular security patrols at night in busy periods. Holiday caravans and cottages may be hired at the adjacent, site owned holiday park. Four modern toilet blocks make a good provision with plentiful WCs, washbasins and hot showers on payment (20p), with extra showers in two blocks; free hairdryers and units for disabled visitors. An excellent new block has some washbasins in cubicles, showers, a second laundry room and further facilities for the disabled. Washing-up sinks and ample water points. Motorcaravan service point. Amenities include a shop (Easter - mid Oct), barbecue area and snack bar (May - mid-Sept). The park's own modern restaurant and bar with good value bar meals is a short stroll from the park, open to all. Public phones. Children's play area on bark. Riding, golf and fishing near. A well managed park with bustling, but pleasing ambience, watched over by Ben Nevis. Around 1,000 acres of the Glen Nevis estate are open to campers to see the wildlife and explore this lovely area.

Directions: Turn off A82 to east at roundabout just north of Fort William following camp sign. O.S.GR: NN124723.

Charges guide:
-- Per caravan £5.50 - £8.00; motorcaravan or tent £5.20 - £7.70; small tent £4.70 - £7.00; backpackers: 1 person £3.10 - £4.60, 2 £3.80 - £5.60; person £1.00 - £1.40; awning 80p - £1.20; fully serviced pitch extra £1.30 - £1.90.
-- VAT included.
-- Credit cards accepted.
Open:
15 March - 31 October.
Address:
Glen Nevis, Fort William, Inverness-shire PH33 6SX.
Tel:
(01397) 702191.
FAX: (01397) 703904.
E-mail: holidays@ glen-nevis.demon.co.uk
Reservations:
Advised for July/Aug; contact park.

Glen Nevis Caravan & Camping Park

Glen Nevis
Fort William PH33 6SX
Tel: 01397 702191

EXCELLENT

This award-winning environmental park - **Calor 1998 Best Park in Scotland -
David Bellamy Gold Conservation Award** - situated at the foot of Ben Nevis, Britain's
highest mountain, offers modern, clean and well-equipped facilities including Motor caravan service point. Many pitches are fully serviced with electricity, water and drainage
Showers, scullery, laundry. licensed shop, gas and play areas are all on park
with our own spacious restaurant and lounge only a few minutes walk.
Holiday Caravans, Cottages, Lodges on adjacent park. Colour brochures available.

---

784 North Ledaig Caravan Park, Connel, by Oban

Friendly park with splendid views, for caravans, motorvans and trailer tents only.

This park has magnificent views over the Sound of Mull. A member of the Caravan Club's managed under contract scheme, non-members are also welcome. There are 260 pitches, 230 with electricity (10A) and 228 with hardstanding. Some 140 are for non-members (caravans, motorhomes or trailer tents only). The main sanitary block is central - you may have a bit of a walk depending on your pitch but a new block is planned within the next couple of years. The current facilities are excellent and include full facilities for disabled visitors and for mothers and babies, both with access by key. There are free hot showers, washbasins in private cabins for ladies, (with one for men), a well equipped laundry with irons for hire, and dishwashing. Chemical disposal points and motorcaravan service area. Further, well renovated sanitary facilities are behind reception, which also provides a well stocked, licensed shop. A dog walk is provided. A play area and a mountain bike track are planned and across the road, a 30 acre nature reserve is taking shape with ponds and walks (strictly no dogs) to attract wildlife. Being well organised and run, this is a quiet park which makes a good base for exploring the area, visiting the islands from Oban, or relaxing on the shores of the loch. Fishing and sailing are possible from the site (slipway for small boats), hill walking or riding are close by. Buses pass the gate 5 or 6 times a day. Caravan storage.

Directions: Park is about 1 mile north of Connel Bridge, on the A828 Oban - Fort William road, 7 miles from Oban. O.S.GR: NM913456.

Charges 1999:
-- Non members: Per pitch £2.00 - £3.00; adult £2.60 - £4.00; child (5-17 yrs) £1.10 - £1.20; electricity £1.45 - £2.20; extra car, trailer or m/cycle £1.00.
-- VAT included.
-- No credit cards.
Open:
27 March - 31 October.
Address:
Connel, by Oban, Argyll PA37 1RT.
Tel:
(01631) 710291.
FAX: as phone.
Reservations:
Any length, with £10 deposit incl. £1 non-returnable fee.

785 Linnhe Caravan and Chalet Park, Corpach, nr. Fort William

Quiet, well run park in a fine setting for caravans, motorcaravans and small tents only.

This park has a very peaceful situation overlooking Loch Eil, beautifully landscaped and with wonderful views. There are individual pitches with hardstanding for 65 touring units (12 seasonal) on terraces leading down to the water's edge. They include 32 special ones with electrical connection (16A), water and drainaway, plus 30 with electricity only (10A). A separate area on the lochside takes 15 small tents (no reservation). There are also 64 caravan holiday homes and 12 centrally heated pine chalets for hire. The toilet facilities are of an excellent standard and can be heated in the cooler months, providing free hot showers and baths (£1), a dishwashing room, chemical disposal. There is a first class laundry, toddlers' play room and separate outdoor clothing drying room (charged per night). Two well equipped children's play areas are on safe standing, there is a barbecue area, public phones, gas and a self-service, licensed shop (Whit-end Sept). Fishing is free on Loch Eil and you are welcome to fish from the park's private beach or bring your own boat and use the slipway and dinghy park. Large motorhomes are accepted but it is best to book first. About 5 miles from Fort William on `The Road to the Isles', the park is conveniently placed for touring the Western Highlands. Easily accessible are Ben Nevis and the Nevis range (cable car to 2,000 ft.), geological, Jacobite and Commando museums, distillery visits, seal island trips, the Mallaig steam railway and the Caledonian Canal. Bicycle hire 2½ miles, riding or golf 5 miles. Up to two dogs per pitch are accepted. Caravan storage available. A member of the Best of British group.

Charges 2000:
-- Per unit incl. 2 persons, with electricity £11.00 - £13.00, special pitch £11.50 - £14.00; small tent pitch £8.00 - £10.00; awning, extra tent or car £1.50; extra person £1.00; dog (max. 2) 50p.
-- VAT included.
-- Credit cards accepted.

Open:
All year excl. 1/11-19/12.

Address:
Corpach, Fort William, Inverness-shire PH33 7NL.

Tel:
(01397) 772376.
FAX: (01397) 772007.
E-mail: holidays@linnhe.demon.co.uk.

Reservations:
Made with £25 deposit for min. 3 nights.

Directions: Park entrance is off A830 Fort William - Mallaig road, 1 mile west of Corpach. O.S.GR: NN072772.

786 Glendaruel Caravan Park, Glendaruel, Kyles of Bute

Peaceful family park set in former wooded gardens surrounded by the Cowal hills.

Glendaruel is set in South Argyll in the area of Scotland bounded by the Kyles of Bute and Loch Fyne, yet is less than 2 hours by road from Glasgow and serviced by ferries from Gourock and the Isle of Bute, with a new summer service between Tarbert and Portavadie opening up the Mull of Kintyre. The park itself is set in the wooded gardens of the former Glendaruel House in a secluded glen surrounded by the Cowal hills. It makes an ideal centre for touring this beautiful area of Scotland. The park takes 35 units on numbered hardstandings with electrical connections (10A), plus 10 tents, on flat oval meadows bordered by over 50 different varieties of mature trees with more tent pitches planned. There are also 28 privately owned holiday homes, plus 2 for hire, in a separate area. The toilet block is ageing but is kept very neat and tidy, can be heated and has a good supply of toilets, washbasins and showers (2M, 2F), hair and hand dryers and a washing machine and dryer. A covered area has picnic tables for campers' use in bad weather and dishwashing sinks (H&C). Chemical disposal. Gas available. The stables of the original house have been converted to provide an attractive little shop selling basics, local produce, venison, salmon, wines (some Scottish!) and some tourist gifts (hours may be limited in low season) and a games room with pool table, table tennis and amusement machines. New for '99 was a children's play centre for under 12s. Bicycle hire (adults only). Fishing on site (sea fishing and boat slipway 5 miles). Adventure centre and sailing school close. Golf 12 miles. Dogs are accepted by prior arrangement. Glendaruel is a park for families with young children or for older couples to relax and to enjoy the beautiful views across the Sound of Bute from Tighnabruaich or the botanical gardens which flourish in the climate. The owners, Quin and Anne Craig, provide a warm welcome and will advise on what to do - they are justifiably proud of their park and its beautiful environment. A member of the Best of British group.

Charges 1999:
-- Per unit incl. 2 persons £8.00 - £10.00; tent per person, no car £3.50 - £4.00; extra adult £1.50 - £2.00; child (4-15 yrs) 75p - £1.00; awning, extra tent, extra car, trailer or boat £1.50; electricity (10A) £2.00.
-- Special weekly rates and senior citizen discount outside July/Aug.
-- VAT included.
-- Credit cards accepted.

Open:
1 April - 29 October.

Address:
Glendaruel, Argyll PA22 3AB.

Tel:
(01369) 820267.
FAX: (01359) 820367.

Reservations:
Any length, with £10 deposit and £2 fee.

Alan Rogers' Discount

Local discount vouchers

Directions: Entrance is off A886 road 13 miles south of Strachur. Alternatively there are two ferry services from Gourock to Dunoon, then on B836 which joins the A886 about 4 miles south of the park - this route not recommended for touring caravans. Note: the park has discount arrangements ·with Western Ferries so contact the park before making arrangements (allow 7 days for postage of tickets). O.S.GR: NS001865.

NORTHERN IRELAND

Northern Ireland Tourist Board
59 North Street, Belfast BT1 1NB
Tel: (01232) 246609 Fax: (01232) 312424
Internet: http://www.ni-tourism.com

IRISH REPUBLIC

Irish Tourist Board
150 New Bond Street, London W1Y 0AQ
Tel: (0171) 518 0800 Fax: (0171) 493 9065
Internet: http://www./ireland.travel.ie
Travel enquiries: (0171) 493 3201

`You're welcome' is not said lightly to the visitor who sets foot in Ireland, it is said with sincerity. On this `Emerald Isle' you will find friendly and hospitable people, spectacular scenery and a selection of good campsites, in both north and south of the country, to suit your particular needs. Whether you choose to be sited by a lough shore, at the foothills of a mountain range or close by golden sands and mysterious rock formations, the scenery is stunning and the pace of life slow. With the help of information and maps available from both Tourist Offices you discover for yourself, not only the beauty spots, but also many historic and interesting routes to follow. In such areas we have endeavoured to locate well run sites that range from family parks where children can find day long amusement, to the more simple site offering total relaxation, all of good quality.

A British visitor to the Republic of Ireland does not require a passport (and one may take the dog!). British currency is accepted in most outlets although we quote charges in Irish punts (IR£), currently valued at slightly below the UK£. Travel insurance is advisable when travelling in the south (see our special discount rates for Heritage Insurance).

To telephone the Irish Republic from the UK, replace the first `0' given in the number with the country code: 00 353. For example: (094) 88100 becomes 00 353 94 88100.

The following ferry services are expected to operate between the UK mainland ad Ireland in 2000:

Irish Ferries
(see advert opposite page xxx)
(01233) 211211 for brochures, etc.
or (0990) 171717 for bookings/enquiries
Holyhead - Dublin (3¼ hours), Fastcraft 109 mins
Pembroke - Rosslare (3¾ hours)

P&O European Ferries
(01581) 200276   Cairnryan - Larne:
Ferry (2¼ hours, 2 sailings daily each way)
Jet Liner (1 hour, 5 sailings daily each way)

Sea Cat Scotland
(0990) 523523
Stranraer - Belfast (1½ hours, 4 daily each way)
Heysham - Belfast (4 hours, 2 daily)
Troon - Belfast (2½ hours, 2 daily)

Swansea Cork Ferries
(01792) 456116
Swansea - Cork (10 hrs, mid-March - early Nov)

Stena Line
(see advert between pages xxxxx)
(0990) 707070 Frequent sailings:
Fishguard - Rosslare: Ferry (3½ hours, 2 sailings daily each way), Lynx (99 mins)
Holyhead - Dun Laoghaire: Ferry (3½ hrs), Sea Linx (110 mins) or HSS (99 mins)
Stranraer - Belfast: Ferry (3¼ hrs), HSS (105 mins)

Norse Irish Ferries
(01232) 779090
Liverpool - Belfast (8½ hrs, overnight daily, day service up to 3 weekly)

Outdoor Freedom Holidays.....The Green Option for the New Millennium

Ireland, one of Europe's best-kept secrets, is the Caravan and Camping destination for the discerning traveller. You take control of your holiday from start to finish, go as you please, and do as little or as much as you like. It's all on offer in Ireland, rugged coastlines, inland waterways, lakes and rivers, Celtic monuments, churches and castles, rolling hills and lush green valleys. Plus, of course, Ireland's legendary hostelries and the friendliest people you're ever likely to meet. Pick up a copy of the 2000 Caravan and Camping Annual at your local tourist office today - it's a breath of fresh air.
Alternatively contact ICC direct at: Fax: 00 353 98 28237

e-mail: info@camping-ireland.ie
Website: http//www.camping-ireland.ie
PO Box ICC, Box 4443, Dublin 2, Ireland

831 Carnfunnock Country Park Caravan Site, Drain's Bay, Larne

Modern site in magnificent parkland setting overlooking the sea.

In exceptional scenic surroundings, 3½ miles north of the market town of Larne on the famed Antrim Coast Road this is a caravanner's delight. The 28 level `super' pitches have hardstanding, water, electricity (15A), drainage and individual pitch lighting, with ample space for an awning and car parking. The site has a neat appearance with a tarmac road following through to the rear where a number of pitches are placed in a circular position. There is additional road lighting, refuse area and allocated space for tents. A small, modern building beside the entrance gates houses sanitary facilities (entry by key). There are two shower units, washbasins, shaver points, WCs, facilities for disabled people, dishwashing sinks and a chemical disposal point. Motorcaravan service point. Run by the Borough Council and supervised by a manager, the Country Park is immaculately kept. The Visitor Centre includes a gift shop and information about local attractions, and the restaurant/coffee shop is pleasant and looks towards the sea. Spending time around the parkland, you will find a walled time garden with historic sundials, a maze, forest walk, children's adventure playground, putting green, 9 hole golf course, wildlife garden and miniature railway. Fishing and boat launching 400 m.

Charges 1999:
-- Per caravan or motor-caravan £13.00, 5 nights £59.00, 7 nights £80.00 (electricity included); tent £7.00.
-- No credit cards or Eurocheques.
Open:
Easter - 30 September.
Address:
Coast Road, Drain's Bay, Larne, Co. Antrim BT40 2QG.
Tel:
028 2827 0541 or 028 2826 0088.
Reservations:
Advisable for peak periods and B.Hs.

Directions: From ferry terminal in Larne, follow signs for Coast Road and Carnfunnock Country Park. Well signed 3½ miles on A2 coast road.

Caravan & Camping in Carnfunnock Country Park

Excellent caravan and camping facilities amidst the magnificent scenery of the Antrim Coast. Carnfunnock offers something for everyone - a modern reception building and coffee shop, a unique walled time garden, a maze, a par 3 nine hole golf course, children's activity centre, and a play area, attractive woodland walks and open spaces. For action packed family fun or simply a relaxing break, Carnfunnock has it all!

For further information please contact:-

LARNE
Tourist Information
C E N T R E

Tourist Information Centre
Narrow Gauge Road, Larne
County Antrim. BT40 1XB
℃ **(01574) 260088**

832 Curran Court Caravan Park, Larne

Well kept site convenient for ferry terminal, an ideal night stop.

Formerly run by the local borough council, the park is now managed by the Curran Court Hotel (opposite the park). Attractive garden areas add to the charm of this small, neat site which is very conveniently situated for the ferry terminal and only a few minutes walk from the sea. The 29 pitches, all with hardstanding and electricity connections, give adequate space off the tarmac road and there is a separate tent area of 1½ acres. The sanitary block is clean and adequate without being luxurious, with free controllable hot showers (2 for men, 1 for ladies) and there is a laundry room with dishwashing facilities. Plans are in hand for a new block, plus another 31 pitches. Children's play area with good equipment and safety surfaces. Bowls and putting are available on site and many other amenities are very close including a shop (100 yds), the hotel for food and drink, tennis and a leisure centre with swimming pool (300 yds). Fishing, bicycle hire and boat launching 500 yds. Larne market is on Wednesdays. You may consider using this site as a short term base for discovering the area as well as an ideal overnight stop. The warden can usually find room for tourists so reservations are not normally necessary.

Charges 2000:
-- Per caravan or motor-caravan £9.00; tent £6.00; electricity £1.50.
-- Credit cards accepted.
Open:
Easter - 30 September.
Address:
Curran Road, Larne, Co. Antrim.
Tel:
028 2827 3797.
FAX: 028 2826 0096.
Reservations:
Not normally considered necessary.

Directions: Immediately after leaving the ferry terminal, turn right and follow camp signs. Site is just ¼ mile on the left.

Antrim

834 Drumaheglis Marina and Caravan Park, Ballymoney

Well kept site on the banks of the River Bann, convenient for the Causeway coast.

A caravan park which continually maintains a high standard, Drumaheglis is popular throughout the season. Situated on the banks of the lower Bann, approximately 4 miles from the town of Ballymoney, it appeals to watersports enthusiasts or makes an ideal base for exploring this scenic corner of Northern Ireland. The marina offers superb facilities for boat launching, water-skiing, cruising, canoeing or fishing, whilst getting out and about can take you to the Giant's Causeway, seaside resorts such as Portrush or Portstewart, the sands of Whitepark Bay, the Glens of Antrim or the picturesque villages of the Antrim coast road. For tourers only, this site instantly appeals, for it is well laid out with trees, shrubs, flower beds and tarmac roads. Electricity (5A) and water points are available on 52 pitches, of which 47 have hardstanding. The toilet blocks are modern and were spotlessly clean when we visited. They house showers which are free, individual wash cubicles, toilets and facilities for disabled visitors, plus four new family shower rooms. There are razor points, hand dryers, dishwashing sinks, washing machine and dryer and chemical disposal point. A children's play area, barbecue and picnic areas are added facilities. Ballymoney is a popular shopping town and the Riada Centre is a leading leisure establishment with a health suite which incorporates a high-tech fitness studio, sports hall, etc. Bicycle hire and golf 4 miles, riding ½ mile. There is much to see and do within this Borough and of interest is the Heritage Centre in Charlotte Street.

Charges guide:
-- Per unit incl. electricity £11.00, per 7 days £66.00; unserviced £10.00, per 7 days £60.00.
-- No credit cards.

Open:
Easter - 1 October.

Address:
36 Glenstall Road, Ballymoney, Co. Antrim BT53 7QN.

Tel:
028 2766 6466. Ballymoney Borough Council: Tel: 028 2766 2280; FAX: 028 2766 7659.

Reservations:
Essential for peak periods and weekends.

Directions: From the A26/B62 Portrush - Ballymoney roundabout continue for about 1 mile on A26 towards Coleraine. Site clearly signed - follow International camping signs.

835 Bush Caravan Park, Bushmills

Family run park, an ideal base for touring the North Antrim Coast.

This is a small, select park only minutes away from two renowned attractions, the Giant's Causeway and the Old Bushmills Distillery. This fact alone makes Bush a popular location, but its fast growing reputation for friendliness and top class facilities makes it equally appealing. Conveniently sited just off the main Ballymoney - Portrush Road (B62) it is approached by a short drive. The site itself is partly surrounded by mature trees and hedging, but views across the countryside can still be appreciated. Although there is no appointed reception area, the owners live on the farm or a part-time warden is usually to hand. There are 22 well laid out and spacious pitches, all with hardstanding and electricity hook-up (16A), also a grass area to accommodate tents. The sanitary block which is to the right of the entrance is opened by key. It is modern, clean and equipped to a high standard. Walls and floors are fully tiled and facilities include controllable showers (by token) with curtain divider, seat and hooks. There are open style washbasins, hairdryer, mirrors, etc. Excellent provision is made for people with disabilities. Additional facilities include a laundry and dishwashing room with two sinks, washing machine and dryers, plus a separate chemical disposal unit. A children's play area on grass is in a central position. Unique features on site are murals depicting the famed scenery, sights and legends of the Causeway Coast. A further novelty is the Bushmills barrels used to house rubbish containers. The enthusiastic owners organise tours to the Distillery and coastal trips - a musical evening cannot be ruled out.

Charges guide:
Per unit incl. all persons £9.00; frame tent £8.00; small tent £5.00; awning £1.00; electricity £1.00.

Open:
Easter - 31 October.

Address:
95 Priestland Road, Bushmills, Co. Antrim BT57 8UJ.

Tel:
028 2073 1678 or 028 7035 4240. FAX: 028 7035 1998.

Reservations:
Advised for high season or weekends.

Directions: From Ballymoney A26/B62 roundabout proceed north on B62 direction Portrush for 6½ miles. Turn right onto B17. Site is 350 yds on the left.

Tourist Information:

Bushmills has the oldest licensed whiskey distillery in the world. It first received its license in 1608, though distilling has taken place here since at least the 13th century. To earn your free dram, you have to tour the distillery. You may just get a shot of all three types – the malt, Black Bush and regular Bushmills!

860 Bellemont Caravan Park, Coleraine

Well kept park close to Coleraine and Portstewart.

This brand new park makes an immediately favourable impression with its white concrete roads, its perfect grass areas and well laid out appearance. The gently sloping ground rises at the far right of the park to give views over Portstewart and towards the sea. To the left of the entrance and security gate are five new privately owned caravan holiday homes. Tents are pitched to the right and there are 30 touring pitches, all with hardstanding, electric hook up and water. These are spacious and well distributed around this open, parkland style setting. In a central position stands a gleaming white building, with flower tubs decorating the forecourt, which houses reception and heated sanitary facilities. These include washbasins, mirrors, electric points, soap and hand-dryer. Showers (token operated) are a good size and well equipped with seat, hooks, soap dish and changing space. For people with disabilities a separate unit comprises a shower, WC, washbasin, hand-dryer and seat. There is a laundry room with two washing machines, two dryers and iron (token operated), plus a dishwashing sink and drainer to the outside. Also outside is a chemical disposal unit with flush and hose. A play area for children with swings and slide on a bark surface is placed to the right of the park. Bellemont makes a good base for visiting the university town of Coleraine, the resorts and beaches of Portstewart and Portrush, or famous sights such as Dunluce Castle, Carrick-a-Rede rope bridge, the Giant's Causeway, plus the harbours which follow the North Antrim coastline. No dogs are accepted.

Charges 2000:
Per unit incl. all persons £10.00; electricity £12.00; awning £1.50.
-- No credit cards.
Open: Easter - 30 September.
Address: 10 Islandtasserty Road, Coleraine, Co. Londonderry BT52 2PN.
Tel: 028 7082 3872.
Reservations: Contact site.

Directions: From Lodge Road roundabout on eastern outskirts of Coleraine follow A29 north to fourth roundabout. Continue towards Portrush and site is clearly signed on left after ¼ mile.

859 Tullans Farm Caravan Park, Coleraine

Well run family park in rural setting convenient for the Causeway Coast.

This excellent park, opened in 1995, is set to become one of the most popular in the area. Its peaceful and quiet surroundings suggest that it is in the heart of the country, yet the University town of Coleraine is only 1 mile away, the seaside resorts of Portrush and Portstewart are within 5 miles and a shopping centre a 2 minute drive. Tucked in from the busy roads that lead to the coast, Tullans Farm is already earning a reputation for its spotlessly clean toilet block and its well cared for appearance. In a central position in the park, fronted by a large parking space, stands a long white building housing the sanitary facilities, reception, TV lounge and barn which is used for indoor recreation. The toilet and shower rooms, which include a family shower room, are spacious, modern and have facilities for the handicapped. There are washbasins set in marble top units, mirrors, soap dispensers, hand and hair dryers, even flower arrangements. Next to the toilet area is the laundry and washing up room with sinks, washing machine, dryers and a fridge for campers to use. Around the park roadways are gravel and 20 of the 32 pitches have hardstanding, all have electric hook-ups (10A). Trees and shrubs have been planted and will eventually give a more mature look. Chemical disposal, water points, rubbish bins and receptacles for cans and plastic bottles are provided. An outdoor children's play area is another attraction. In season the owners organise barbecues, barn dances and line dancing (funds in aid of charity).

Charges 1999:
-- Per unit incl. all persons and electricity £10.00; awning £1.00; family tent £7.00; 2 man tent £5.00.
Open: March - 31 October.
Address: 46 Newmills Road, Coleraine, Co. Londonderry BT52 2JB.
Tel: 028 7034 2309.
Reservations: Advisable at peak times - contact park.

Directions: From the Lodge Road roundabout (south end of Coleraine) turn east onto the A29 Portrush ring road and proceed for 1 mile. Turn right at sign for park and Windy Hall and park is clearly signed on left.

Tourist Information:

The scientific explanation for the Giant's Causeway, a promontory of 40,000 closely packed multi-sided basalt columns, is that it was formed after a volcanic eruption about 55 million years ago but myth has it that the giant Finn MacCool built it as a road to cross to Scotland – a similar but smaller causeway is visible on the island of Staffa. It is interesting that something that looks so geometrically exact can be natural. Sometimes it fails to live up to expectations – it is dwarfed by the surrounding towering cliffs.

Tyrone / Down

856 Gortin Glen Caravan and Camping Park, Gortin, nr. Omagh

Well run friendly site in beautiful Forest Park surroundings.

Pronounced 'Gorchin', this excellent, truly peaceful site is deep in Gortin Glen with splendid views of the surrounding hills and forest. The very large Gortin Glen forest embraces the 405 ha. forest park which has a 5 mile scenic road offering breathtaking views, picnic areas, nature trails, wildlife enclosures and an indoor exhibit, all open to the public. Within the park is a camping area with 24 individually numbered pitches, all with hardstanding and electricity (13A). All pitches are spacious with room for an awning. In addition there are separate areas for tents and attractive self catering cottages. The sanitary block has four controllable hot showers (10p for 8 minutes) and good facilities for people with disabilities, which mothers may also use for children. There is a laundry room with two washing machines and two dryers, also a dishwashing area with free hot water. Leisure facilities include a TV/games room with table tennis and full sized snooker table, plus a children's play area with safety base and provision for ball games. A barbecue area is located behind the main block. Reception is well stocked with tourist information on local attractions which include the Ulster History Park, Ulster American Folk Park and Sperrin Heritage Centre. Shops are in Gortin village (3 miles).

Charges guide:
-- Per caravans £7.50 (£45 per week); tent £3.50 - £7.50, acc. to size (£21 - £45 per week); electricity £1.50; awning 50p.
-- Youth groups of 10 or more £1.50 per person, per night.
Open:
All year.
Address:
1 Lisnaharney Road, Lislap, Omagh, Co. Tyrone BT79 7UG.
Tel:
028 8164 8108.
FAX: as phone.
Reservations:
Made with £15 fee for B.H. weekends.

Directions: From Omagh take B48 road signed Gortin. Proceed north for approx. seven miles and turn left immediately after Ulster History Park into site.

842 Tollymore Forest Caravan Park, Newcastle

Well run site in forest setting at foot of Mourne mountains.

This park, for tourers only, is located within the parkland of Tollymore Forest. It is discretely situated away from the public footpaths and is noted for its scenic surroundings. The forest park, which is approached by way of an ornate gateway and majestic avenue of Himalayan cedars, covers an area of almost 500 hectares. It is backed by the Mourne mountains and situated two miles from the beaches and resort of Newcastle. The site is attractively laid out with hardstanding pitches, 72 of which have electricity (6A). Toilet blocks, timbered in keeping with the setting, are clean, modern and tastefully decorated. They have free hot showers with benches and hooks, wash cubicles, facilities for disabled people, dishwashing and laundry area. Night lighting is adequate. Other amenities are a confectionery shop and tea room within close proximity. A small grocery shop is located a few yards from the exit gate of the park and gas is also available here. The Head Ranger at Tollymore is helpful and ensures that the caravan site is efficiently run and quiet, even when full. Exploring the forest park is part of the pleasure of staying here. Of note are the stone follies, bridges and entrance gates. The Shimna and Spinkwee rivers flow through the park adding a refreshing touch and tree lovers appreciate the arboretum with its many rare species.

Charges 1999:
-- Per unit incl. car and occupants £6.50 - £10.00, acc. to season; electricity £1.50.
Open:
All year.
Address:
Tollymore Forest Park (Administration), 176 Tullybrannigan Road, Newcastle, Co. Down BT33 0PW.
Tel:
028 4372 2428.
Reservations:
Advisable in high season and for B.Hs. and made with £10 deposit.

Directions: Approach Newcastle on the A24. Before entering the town, at roundabout, turn right on to A50 signed Castlewellan and follow signs for Tollymore Forest Park.

For travel further afield, remember the other ALAN ROGERS' titles –
the GOOD CAMPS GUIDES for FRANCE and EUROPE

★ Independent site assessors make regular monitoring visits

★ Consistently revised and updated – sites included on merit only

★ Discount vouchers for selected sites, ferries and tourist attractions

850 LoanEden Caravan Park, Muckross Bay, Kesh

Friendly, family owned park by the shores of Lower Lough Erne.

All caravanners who enter this exceptional park are immediately made welcome and receive the attention of the owners, Noelle and Austyn Loane. First impressions are of an overall neat and tidy appearance, with caravan holiday homes occupying the centre and left side of the park, whilst to the right stand the touring pitches. Flower beds, trees and shrubs are well maintained and an ornamental well and illuminated barbecue give added effect. What makes LoanEden special is that tourers' needs are thoughtfully catered for and not secondary to the static owners. The 24 touring and 12 long-stay pitches are level with hardstanding and water, electricity and drainage connections and a rubbish bin; also a dividing grass area on which to erect an awning. Night lighting is good. Cleanliness is utmost and the immaculate, ultra modern toilet block is tiled, housing WCs, facilities for disabled people, showers, washbasins, washing machines, dryers and dishwashing and laundry sinks. Nothing has been forgotten - there are soap dispensers, hand dryers, paper towels, hooks and points for hairdryers and razors. Motorcaravan service point. There is a vending machine for confectionery and soft drinks plus a hot food takeaway. Children have two play areas and a games room, with plans for a third play area. The `LoanEden Ramblers' club for 4-11 year olds provides activities each day (£1.50 per child). Young and old can enjoy pony and horse riding tuition under the supervision of the owners' daughter Victoria, an A.I. instructor, and son Andrew who is an international rider. Fishing and bicycle hire on site, golf 5 miles. Caravan storage . An additional 30 touring pitches, a second shower and toilet block including a campers' kitchen, go-kart track and other facilities are planned. The owners organise barbecues and barn dances in aid of charity.

Charges 2000:
-- Per caravan or motorcaravan incl. awning and electricity £12.00; tent £8.00; electricity £1.00.
Open:
All year.
Address:
Muckross Bay, Kesh, Co. Fermanagh BT93 1TX.
Tel:
028 6863 1603.
FAX: 028 6863 2300.
Reservations:
Advisable for high season and B.Hs.

Directions: From Enniskillen take A32 Omagh road for 3½ miles and branch left on B82 Kesh road. Continue for 11 miles to village of Kesh. Cross over bridge at north end of village and turn immediately left to park in ½ mile on right.

Loan Eden Caravan Park
Muckross Bay
Co. Fermanagh
N. Ireland

Tel: (013656) 31603/31129
Fax: (013656) 32300

OPEN ALL YEAR - 5✓

★ Award winning caravan park - Calor Green ★
★ Fully serviced pitches ★ Tent area ★
★ Immaculate sanitary facilities ★ Children's play areas ★
★ Quality mobile homes for sale/hire ★
★ Horse riding tuition A.I. instructor ★
★ Special on site feature - barbecue in July ★
★ Extended facilities - new toilet block, 3rd play area,
  new reception area, campers kitchen ★
★ Boat hire facilities ★ man made beach ★ Marina 5 mins walk
★ Scenic walks ★ Pony trekking ★
★ Village of Kesh - Lough Erne Hotel - Chef of the Year award ★

851 Blaney Caravan Park, Blaney

Quiet, family run park, beautifully maintained.

A park with a neat and tidy appearance and one that boasts quality rather than quantity, the 17 touring pitches, all with hardstanding and electricity, are well spaced around the perimeter and in the centre of the site. The tarmac roads are wide, with flower beds and shrubs adding detail and colour. A tent area is tucked into the bottom left hand corner and to the rear, at a higher level, are a small number of caravan holiday homes which blend unobtrusively. A modern toilet block houses showers (50p) with hot water, facilities for the disabled, and a laundry with washing machine, dryer and ironing board. Waste and chemical disposal, a dog walk and night lighting. There is a small supermarket, post office and petrol station at the entrance. For children there is a spacious, safe play area, but the farm animals may be more appealing. Boules. Central barbecue area, or barbecues are permitted, with care, on the pitches. Blaney makes a good base for hill climbing, fishing, watersports or for seeking out local beauty spots such as nearby Lough Navar Forest which commands extensive views over Lough Erne.

Charges 1999:
-- Per unit £10.00 (high season); electricity £1.00; awning free (with ventilated ground sheet); tent (2 person) £6.00.
Open:
All year.
Address:
Blaney, Co. Fermanagh BT93 7ER.
Tel:
028 6864 1634.
Reservations:
Contact park.

Directions: From Enniskillen take the A46 road towards Belleek. The park is on the right after approx. 8 miles.

Fermanagh

852 Share Holiday Village, Smith's Strand, Lisnaskea

Caravan park in a village environment, offering a package deal.

Immediately you drive into this 30 acre park in its quiet and beautiful location on the shores of Upper Lough Erne, you want to get involved in the host of attractions on offer. The 5 acre touring park is a separate part of this complex, which offers all the benefits and self contained aspects of caravanning, plus the opportunity to enjoy all the sports facilities of the village. The 15 pitches have hardstanding, electricity and space for awnings. The sanitary blocks, which can be heated and are kept very clean, have washbasins, showers, washing up and laundry facilities, including a drying room with tumble dryers, and a chemical disposal point. An important factor here is that Share is committed to the provision of facilities and opportunities for both the able bodied and the disabled. Caravanners can take temporary Leisure Suite membership for the duration of their stay (£2.50 per day, child under 5 free, and best booked and paid for in advance to ensure availability). If wanting to participate in the outdoor activities, an Activity Pass can be purchased covering sailing, canoeing, windsurfing, banana-ski, archery, mountain bikes, or you may prefer a Viking long-ship cruise. A 2½ hour session costs £5 per person and includes all equipment and instruction. Fishing, bicycle hire and boat launching all on site. This centre is an approved British Canoe Union and Royal Yachting Association teaching school and has a 30 berth marina. A multi-purpose Arts Area has been added which provides a comprehensive range of art facilities.

Charges 2000:
-- Per caravan or tent £10.00; 2 man tent £7.00.
-- Touring caravan and campsite packages available.
-- Credit cards accepted.
Open: Easter - 31 October.
Address: Smith's Strand, Lisnaskea, Co. Fermanagh BT92 0EQ
Tel: 028 6772 2122.
FAX: 028 6772 1893.
E-mail: share@dnet.co.uk.
Reservations: Advisable in peak season and for B.H.s and with deposit (weekend or midweek £20, 7 days £50; activity passes 50% of total cost per person).

Directions: From Lisnaskea village, take B127 sign to Derrylin and Smith's Strand and proceed for 3 miles. Site is clearly signed on the right.

REPUBLIC OF IRELAND
Donegal

864 Knockalla Caravan and Camping Park, Portsalon

Family run park set amidst the breathtaking scenery of Donegal.

What adds to the popularity of this site is its location, nestling between the slopes of the Knockalla Mountains and Ballymastocker Bay. The fact that the beach here has been named `the second most beautiful beach in the world' is not surprising. On entering this park, approached by an unclassified but short roadway, its elevated situation commands an immediate panoramic view of the famed Bay, Lough Swilly, Inishowen Peninsula and Dunree Head. The site is partly terraced giving an attractive, orderly layout with reception, shop and restaurant in a central position and the touring area sited to the left of reception. All 50 pitches have electrical hook-ups and hardstanding, offering a choice of solely tarmac or with adjoining grass allowing for awnings. Tents are pitched on a lower level facing reception and to the far left of the tourers. Caravan holiday homes are placed around the right hand perimeter and to the rear of the park. The main sanitary block, a white, rough cast building, is situated in the touring section. Tastefully refurbished, it is kept clean and fresh and can be heated. There are washbasins, hand dryer, hair dryer, shaver points and showers (50p token) with hooks, soap dish, curtain divider and mat. Dishwashing area and campers' kitchen with hot water. A laundry service is operated by staff. Chemical disposal and motorcaravan serice points. Gas is available. Children's play area and TV/games room. The park has a shop and café (both open July/Aug) and specialities are home made scones, apple cakes, jams, etc. plus a takeaway or table service. Full Irish breakfasts are served. Golf 3 miles, fishing, riding and bicycle hire within 10 miles.

Charges 2000:
-- Per motorcaravan, caravan or family tent IR£11.00; awning IR£1.50; tent for 1 or 2 persons IR£8.00; extra person IR£3.00; electricity (5A) IR£1.50.
-- No credit cards.
Open: 27 March - 17 September.
Address: Portsalon, Co. Donegal.
Tel: 074 59108 or 074 53213.
Reservations: Advisable for July/Aug and B.H. w/ends; contact park.

Directions: From Letterkenny take R245 to Rathmelton. Continue on R245 to Milford. Turn right on R246 to Kerrykeel. In village turn left towards Portsalon and at second crossroads turn right onto Portsalon/Knockalla coast road. Turn right to park at sign.

869 Greenlands Caravan and Camping Park, Rosses Point

Park with excellent facilities in the sand hills adjoining a championship golf course.

This is a well run park at Rosses Point, just off the N15 road and 8 km. from Sligo town. It is thoughtfully laid out with small tents placed to the front of reception and the hardstanding touring pitches separated from the trailer tent pitches which occupy the rear. The ground is undulating which adds interest to the overall appearance. Your view depends on where you are pitched - look towards Coney Island and the Blackrock lighthouse which guards the bay, take in the sight of Benbulben Mountain or appreciate the seascape and the water lapping the resort's two bathing beaches. The sanitary and laundry facilities are modern and kept exceptionally clean, with tiled walls and floors, WCs, washbasins, hot showers (50p token), razor and hairdryer points, mirrors and hand-dryers. Also dish-washing and laundry sinks, washing machine, dryer and iron. Electric hook-ups are available for touring units. Chemical disposal and motorcaravan service point. Night security. An information point and a TV room are located beside reception. There is a sand pit for children and a ground chess and draughts sets. A mini-market, restaurant and evening entertainment can be found in the village. Fishing and boat launching 100 m, golf 50 m, bicycle hire 8 km, riding 14 km. This is an excellent base from which to explore the `Yeats Country' and discover the beauty spots immortalised in his poems, such places as Lissadell, Dooney Rock, the Isle of Innisfree and the poet's burial place at Drumcliffe.

Charges 1999:
-- Per unit IR£8.50 plus 50p per person (family rate IR£8.50 - 12.00);
hiker/cyclist incl. tent IR£5.00; electricity (6A) IR£1.50.
-- Weekly rates available.
-- Credit cards accepted.
Open:
Easter - mid-September.
Address:
Rosses Point, Co. Sligo.
Tel:
071 77113.
Reservations:
Contact park.

Directions: From Sligo city travel approx. 800 m. north on N15 road, turn left onto R291 signed Rosses Point. Continue for 6.5 km. and park is on right after village.

870 Gateway Caravan and Camping Park, Ballinode, Sligo

Family run park, convenient for the beauty spots immortalised by the poet W. B. Yeats.

This is the northwest's newest park and straight away it warrants the highest accolade for its excellent design and standards set. Its situation 1.2 km. from Sligo centre means this cultural city is easily accessible, yet Gateway's off-the-road location, screened by mature trees and fencing, offers a quiet relaxing environment. After the park entrance, past the family bungalow and to the left is parking space and the reception and services block which is fronted by columns and an overhanging roof. Flower baskets add decoration and soft background music drifts through the air. Incorporated in this building are three separate rooms - one for TV, snooker and board games, the second for satellite TV and the third for selected video viewing. A passage divides the elongated building which also houses showers, WCs, washbasins with shaver points, hand-dryers and baby changing units in both the male and female areas. Showers, room for disabled visitors (with WC and shower) are entered from the outside of this block which can be heated. In an adjacent building is a dishwashing area, laundry room, fully equipped campers' kitchen plus a large indoor games room and a toddlers room with playhouses and fixed toys. An outdoor children's play area faces reception. There are 30 fully serviced touring pitches with hardstanding and satellite TV connection, 10 grass pitches with electrical hook-up for tents and 10 caravan holiday homes for hire. Touring pitches stand to the right and centre of the park, holiday homes to the left and rear, with tents pitched at the top left. Evening relax-ation could mean a 3 km. drive to romantic Half Moon Bay, or a drink in the fasci-nating surroundings of Farrells Brewery, which faces the caravan park.

Charges 1999:
-- Per unit incl. 2 persons IR£8.50; adult or child in July/Aug 50p; family rate IR£8.50 - 12.50;
m/cyclist incl. tent IR£8.50; hiker or cyclist incl. tent IR£5.00;
electricity (10A) IR£1.50.
Open:
All year.
Address:
Ballinode, Sligo, Co. Sligo.
Tel:
071 45618.
FAX: as phone.
Reservations:
Contact site.

Directions: Site is 1.2 km. northeast of Sligo city, off the N16 Enniskillen - Belfast road. Approaching from the north on the N15, turn left at second traffic lights into Ash Lane, continue for 1.1 km. and turn left at traffic lights onto the N16 Sligo - Enniskillen road. Site entrance is on left in 50 m.

Mayo

874 Cong Caravan and Camping Park, Cong, nr. Connemara

Family run touring park and hostel in a famous and scenic location.

It would be difficult to find a more idyllic and famous spot for a Caravan Park than Cong. Situated close to the shores of Lough Corrib, Cong's scenic beauty was immortalised in the film 'The Quiet Man'. This immaculately kept park, is 1.6 km. from the village of Cong, near the grounds of the magnificent and renowned Ashford Castle. The owner's house which incorporates reception, shop and the hostel, stands to the fore of the site. The 40 grass pitches, 36 with electricity, are placed at a higher level to the rear, with the tent area below and to the side - the policy on this site is for campers to 'choose a pitch' rather than have one allocated. Sanitary facilities and the holiday hostel accommodation are entered from the courtyard area. These are tastefully decorated, kept spotlessly clean and heated when necessary. Apart from the high standard of hygiene evident throughout, the toilet facilities for the campsite include hot showers with curtains, electric points, mirrors, hairdryers, washbasins, soap and hand towels. Also provided are a dish-washing area, launderette service, chemical disposal, central bin depot, barbecue, games room and extensive children's play area. Catering is also a feature. Full Irish or continental breakfast, dinner or packed lunch may be ordered, or home baked bread and scones purchased in the shop. When not spending time around the village of Cong with its picturesque river setting and Monastic relics, there is much to keep the active camper happy. Watersports, cycling, walking, climbing, caving and scenic drives can all be pursued. Riding or golf within 2 km, fishing and boat slipway 500 m. Bicycle hire on site. Not least of the 'on site' attractions at this park is a mini cinema showing 'The Quiet Man' film nightly all season.

Charges 2000:
-- Per pitch IR6.00; adult IR£1.50; child IR£1.00; awning IR£1.50; electricity (16A) IR£1.50; hiker/cyclist incl. tent and 1 person IR£6.50.
-- Credit cards accepted
Open:
All year.
Address:
Lisloughrey, Lake Road, Cong, Connemara, Co. Mayo.
Tel:
092 46089.
FAX: 092 46448.
E-mail: quiet.man.cong @iol.ie.
Reservations:
Contact park.

Directions: Leave N84 road at Ballinrobe to join R334/345 signed Cong. Turn left at end of the R345 (opposite entrance to Ashford Castle), take next road on right (approx. 300 m) and the park is on right (200 m).

875 Belleek Caravan and Camping Park, Ballina

Family owned park in a quiet woodland setting, only minutes from Ballina, a famed salmon fishing centre.

This is a park with excellent pitches and toilet block and a family committed to ensuring that it is immaculate at all times. From the entrance gate the park is approached by a road which passes reception and leads to well spaced out pitches where an overall neat appearance abounds. There are 58 pitches, 32 with hard-standing, 35 with electric hook-ups, and you have a free choice of pitch. Water points and rubbish bins are distributed around. The spotlessly clean toilet block is tastefully decorated with tiled floors, cream coloured, rough cast walls, pine ceilings and pot plants to complement the modern washbasins, showers (50p token), WCs and baby sink. There are also razor points, hand dryers, facilities for disabled people, washing up/laundry sink, two washing machines and two dryers, and chemical disposal. Housed in a separate building is a TV and games room with table tennis and football game. A campers' kitchen and emergency accom-modation with beds are also located in this building. There is a sink, free hot water, fridge, cooker, bench table and open fire. The reception area includes a shop (June-Sept) and tea room serving delicious, home baked scones and fruit cake. If required, a cooked or light breakfast, omelettes, sandwiches or salads can be ordered. There is a new children's play area, a ball area, basketball and tennis courts, plus a covered barbecue area. Sports facilities within a short distance of the park include pitch and putt, golf, swimming pool, tennis and riding. Fishing 1 km, bicycle hire 3 km, riding 6 km, golf 8 km. Other local attractions are the Blue Flag beach at Ross, Ceide Fields (Neolithic farm), Down Patrick Head, Mayo North Heritage Centre or a Seaweed bath at Kilcullen's Bath House, Enniscrone. Mobile homes for hire.

Charges 2000:
-- Per unit IR£6.00 - 7.00; adult or child IR£1.00; m/cyclist and tent IR£3.50 - 4.50; hiker or cyclist and tent IR£3.00 - 4.00; awning free - IR£1.00; extra car IR1.00; electricity (10A) IR£1.50.
-- No credit cards.
Open:
15 March - 8 October.
Address:
Ballina, Co. Mayo.
Tel:
096 71533.
E-mail: lenahan@ indigo.ie.
Reservations:
Contact park.

Alan Rogers' Discount

Less 10% for min. 3 nights

Directions: Take R314 Ballina - Killala road. Park signed on right after 1¾ miles.

876 Keel Sandybanks Caravan and Camping Park, Achill Island

Busy park with direct access to a Blue Flag beach on Achill Island.

This is a park offering a taste of island life and the opportunity to relax in dramatic, scenic surroundings. Achill, Ireland's largest island, is 15 miles long and 12 miles wide and is connected to the mainland by a bridge. The site is situated beside Keel village and approached by the R319 from the swivel bridge at Achill Sound. Although there are static holiday caravans on this site, the 42 pitches for caravans and 42 for tents are kept separate. Some with hardstanding are located at the perimeter fence overlooking the beach. Although sand based, the ground is firm and level. Roads are tarmac and there is direct access to the beach which is supervised by lifeguards. Two modern toilet blocks serve the site, one at the entrance gate beside reception and the other in a central position. Facilities include WCs (one for disabled visitors), washbasins, hot showers (50p token), heating, adequate razor points, mirrors, shelves, hooks, hair and hand dryers, dishwashing and laundry sinks and chemical disposal facilities. A barrier on site is closed 01.00 - 08.00. For children there is a play area with safety base and a TV room. Watersports enthusiasts can enjoy surfing, canoeing and board sailing on Keel Strand and Lough. Fishing trips can be arranged. Bicycle hire or golf 200 m; riding 10 km. In the village there is a food shop, takeaway, restaurants and music at night in the pubs. Occasionally a traditional music evening is organised on the site. Whilst a treat in store is the natural beauty on Achill, worth seeing are Kildownet Castle, the Slievemore deserted village and the Seal Caves.

Directions: From Achill Sound follow the R319 for 10 miles. Site is on the left before Keel village.

Charges 2000:
-- Per caravan or motor-caravan IR£6.00 - 8.50; tent IR£5.00 - 6.50; electricity (13A) IR£1.00.
-- No credit cards.
Open:
27 May - 9 September.
Address:
Keel, Achill Island, Co. Mayo.
Tel:
094 32054 or 098 43211.
Reservations:
Contact site.

877 Parkland Caravan and Camping Park, Westport

Popular park, enjoying the attractions of Westport House Country Estate.

Located in the grounds of an elegant country estate, this park offers the choice of a 'pitch only' booking, or a 'special deal' (min. stay 3 nights) which includes free admission to Westport House and children's animal and bird park, plus other activities, such as boating and fishing on the lake and river, pitch and putt, 'slippery dip', ball pond and 'supabounce', hillside train rides and new flume ride. Stay one week or more and all the above are free, plus tennis, a par-3 golf course and 20% discount on bar food in the Horse and Wagon bar on the site. From Westport Quay, you enter the grounds of the estate by way of a tree lined road that crosses the river and leads to the site. In an attractive, sheltered area of the parkland, set in the trees are 155 pitches, 65 with hardstanding. There are 76 electric hook-ups, night lighting around the site and the gate is closed 11.30 pm.- 9 am. If late, vehicles must be parked in the car park. Toilet facilities, some at various points on the site, plus a `super-loo' located in the farmyard buildings. Hot showers are free and there are facilities for disabled people. Also included are dishwashing and laundry sinks, chemical disposal, washing machines and dryers plus free ironing facilities. A well stocked shop is incorporated in the farmyard reception area and the bar offers food and musical entertainment. Within 5 km. of the estate are an 18 hole golf course and deep sea angling on Clew Bay. Westport is an attractive town with splendid Georgian houses and traditional shop fronts. There are many good restaurants and pubs. No dogs are accepted.

Directions: Take R335 Westport - Louisburgh road and follow signs for Westport Quay, then turn right into Westport House Country Estate.

Charges 2000:
-- Per unit excl. free facilities (see above), pitch only IR£16.00 - 24.50 (weekly IR£112 - 165); hiker or cyclist IR£12.00 - 13.00; electricity incl..
-- Specials (min. 3 nights) incl. free facilities from IR£129; weekly IR£275.
-- No credit cards.
Open:
20 May - 10 September.
Address:
Westport, Co. Mayo.
Tel:
098 27766.
FAX: 098 25206.
E-mail: camping@westporthouse.ie.
Reservations:
Contact park.

Mayo

878 Knock Caravan and Camping Park, Knock

Clean, friendly park with many local attractions including religious shrine.

This park is immediately south of the world famous shrine, which receives many visitors. Comfortable and clean, the square shaped campsite is kept very neat with tarmac roads and surrounded by clipped trees. The original pitches are of a decent size accommodating 38 caravans or motorcaravans, 20 tents and 14 holiday caravans (for hire). All pitches have hardstandings (5 doubles) and there are 52 electrical connections (13A), with an adequate number of water points. There is also an overflow field. The modern, heated sanitary block, with good facilities for disabled visitors and a nice sized rest room attached, has 4 controllable hot showers (on payment) and adequate washing and toilet facilities. A laundry and dishwashing room is also part of this building. Chemical disposal and motorcaravan service points, and gas supplies are provided. A children's playground is in the centre of the site. The park reports the addition of 36 new pitches and another sanitary block. Because of the religious connections of the area, the site is very busy in August and indeed there are unlikely to be any vacancies at all for 14 -16 August. Besides visiting the shrine and Knock Folk Museum, local activities include fishing (3 miles), golf and riding (both 7 miles). This is also a good centre for exploring scenic Co. Mayo.

Charges 2000:
-- Per unit IR£8.50 - 9.00; hiker or cyclist and tent IR£5.50 - 6.50; electricity (13A) IR£1.50.
-- No credit cards.

Open:
1 March - 31 October.

Address:
Claremorris Road, Knock, Co. Mayo.

Tel:
094 88100 or 88223.
FAX: 094 88295.
E-mail: info@knock-shrine.ie.

Reservations:
Taken for any length, no deposit, but see editorial for August.

Directions: Take the N17 to the Knock site which is just south of the village. Camp site is well signed.

879 Carra Caravan and Camping Park, Belcarra, Castlebar

Small, unpretentious park in a pretty village setting.

This is an ideal location for those seeking a real Irish village experience on a 'value for money' park. Family run, it is located in Belcarra, a regular winner of the 'Tidiest Mayo Village' award. Nestling at the foot of a wooded drumlin, it is surrounded by rolling hills and quiet roads which offer an away from it all feeling, yet Castlebar the county's largest town is only an 8 km. drive. On the pleasant 1.5 acre park, the 20 unmarked touring pitches, 14 with electric hook-up (13A), are on flat ground enclosed by ranch fencing and shaded in parts by trees. The basic sanitary block has adequate, well equipped showers (40p), etc. and there is a combined kitchen, dishwashing, laundry area with fridge/freezer, sink, table, chairs, washing machine and dryer. A comfortable lounge with TV, books and magazines is located at reception. An additional novel idea at Carra are eight horse-drawn caravans for hire. Also of interest are the talks that the owner Sean and daughter Deirdre give on the area. There are recommended walks and maps provided. In the village are shops, a post office and 'Flukies' cosy bar which serves Irish breakfast for IR£3.50 and where Irish stew is a speciality. There is also a leisure centre, tennis courts, a free fishing area and a special walkway to the river. Golf 8 km.

Charges 2000:
-- Per unit incl. all persons IR£5.00; electricity IR£1.00.
-- No credit cards.

Open:
10 June - 23 September (bookings accepted by arrangement outside this period).

Address:
Belcarra, Castlebar, Co. Mayo.

Tel:
094 32054.
FAX: 094 32351.

Reservations:
Contact park.

Directions: From Castlebar take N60 Claremorris road for 8.5 km. southeast and turn right at sign for Belcarra. Continue for 4.5 km. to village and site on left at end of village.

To telephone the Irish Republic from the UK, replace the first `0' given in the number with the country code: 00 353.

eg. (094) 88100 becomes 00 353 94 88100.

882 Hodson Bay Caravan and Camping Park, Kiltoom, Athlone

Peaceful, scenic park on shores of Lough Ree, in central Ireland.

This picturesque park is in a tranquil, wooded setting on the shores of Lough Ree on the River Shannon. Part of a 100 acre working farm, the site offers 19 pitches, with electricity for caravans and motorcaravans and 15 for tents, on flat grass. The central sanitary block, with good facilities for the disabled, was very clean when we visited and offers hot showers on payment 8-12 in the morning and 4-9 in the evening, plus sufficient washing and toilet facilities. A dishwashing room at the rear of the block has 2 sinks and hot water (10p). The spin and tumble dryers provided are available for use after you take your laundry to reception where it is put through an industrial machine for you. The reception block also provides a lounge area, campers' kitchen, a children's play room, TV, pool, table tennis and board games. The park has no shop but there is a mini-market at the top of the road. An hotel serving bar snacks and a carvery is close. You may fish, swim, go boating or just walk along the parks own path by the lough shore. Barbecues are permitted on site and by the lough. Horse riding and golf are available nearby. No dogs are accepted.

Directions: Leave N6 at the Roscommon/Sligo junction to join the N61. Travel 4 km. and turn right onto minor road. Site is clearly signed. Continue to park at the end of this road (2.4 km).

Charges 1999:
-- Per adult or child IR£1.00; caravan or family tent IR£6.00; car £IR1.00; motorcaravan IR£7.00; small tent (1 or 2 man) IR£5.50; hiker/ cyclist and tent IR£5.50; awning IR£2.00; extra car or tent IR£1.00; electricity IR£2.00; hardstanding IR£1.00.
Open:
9 May - 1 September.
Address:
Kiltoom, Athlone, Co. Roscommon.
Tel:
0902 92448.
Reservations:
Made for high season with IR£5 deposit.

896 Lough Ree East Caravan and Camping Park, Ballykeeran

Touring park alongside a river, screened by trees and reaching the water's edge.

Drive into the small village of Ballykeeran and this park is discretely located behind the main street. The top half of the site is in a woodland situation and after the reception and sanitary block, Lough Ree comes into view and the remaining pitches run down to the shoreline. There are 40 pitches, 20 with hardstanding and 35 with electricity. The toilet block, with partly tiled walls, is clean without being luxurious. It houses WCs, washbasins, razor and hairdryer points, mirrors and hot showers (50p). Chemical disposal. Dishwashing sinks are outside and a new laundry room has been added. A wooden chalet with accommodation and kitchen is available for the use of campers and fishermen. A restaurant and singing pub are close. With fishing right on the doorstep there are boats for hire and the site has its own private mooring buoys, plus a dinghy slip and harbour. Golf or riding 4 km.

Directions: From Athlone take the N55 in the direction of Longford for 4.8 km. Park is in the village of Ballykeeran, clearly signed.

Charges 1999:
-- Per adult IR£2.50; child (under 14) IR£1.00; caravan and car IR£4.00; motorcaravan IR£3.00; family tent IR£2.00; hiker/cyclist and tent IR£3.00; awning IR£2.00; electricity IR£1.00.
-- No credit cards.
Open:
1 April - 2 October.
Address:
Ballykeeran, Athlone, Co. Westmeath.
Tel:
0902 78561 or 0902 74414.
FAX: 0902 77017.
E-mail: athlonecamping @tinet.ie.
Reservations:
Contact park for details.

For lists of parks which offer facilities on site for FISHING, GOLF, HORSE RIDING, BICYCLE HIRE or BOAT LAUNCHING see pages 237 - 239

211

Louth / Offaly

889 Táin Holiday Village, Omeath

Fun packed holiday village, scenically set on Carlingford Lough.

This holiday complex is one of the most extensive in Ireland and is exactly what a family seeking non-stop entertainment might want. The touring park is within the 10-acre village, overlooking Carlingford Lough with views towards the Mourne mountains, whilst nestling at the foot of the Cooley mountains. The area for tourers is situated to the far right of the main buildings, entrance through a security gate is by key (deposit required). There are 87 pitches with hardstanding and electrical hook-ups, plus 10 pitches for tents. Young trees are planted and will eventually add more detail to this well laid out, but open site. The sanitary block is kept clean and can be heated. It houses WCs, hot showers, washbasins in cubicles with mirrors, etc. and facilities for disabled visitors. Dishwashing and laundry sinks with hot water, washing machines and iron, chemical disposal and motorcaravan service facilities are provided. Included in the site fees is the use of the 40,000 sq.ft. of indoor leisure facilities. These include a heated swimming pool (4-9 pm. daily) with slides, flumes and rafts, an indoor play area with free fall, ball pool, climbing room and nets, also a sports hall, gym and games room, a jacuzzi, steam room and sun beds, plus new for 2000 an indoor water play pool. Not least at Táin is a hands-on Science Interactive Centre. The licensed restaurant offers varied menus and there is a new lounge and bar (all limited opening outside July/Aug). Outdoor activities include two adventure playgrounds, tennis courts and watersports, not forgetting the pleasant grounds with neat flower beds. Fishing, bicycle hire or riding 2 km, golf 5 km. Caravan holiday homes to rent.

Directions: From Newry take B79/R173 road signed Omeath. Site is 1.6 km. south of Omeath village, on the left.

Charges 2000:
-- Per unit incl. 2 persons on fully serviced gravel pitch IR£19.00 - 21.00; tent on grass area IR£17.00 - 19.00; extra person IR£4.00 - 5.00.
-- Min. 2 nights in high season; for 1 night only prices are higher.
-- Credit cards accepted.
Open:
5 March - 31 October.
Address:
Carlingford Lough, Omeath, Co. Louth.
Tel:
042 9375385.
FAX: 042 9375417.
E-mail: tain@tinet.ie.
Reservations:
Made with deposit (caravan IR£15, tent IR£10).

906 Green Gables Caravan and Camping Park, Geashill, Tullamore

Peaceful relaxing environment in the heart of Ireland's Bogland.

The owners of Green Gables have created a natural meadow-like effect, a theme in keeping with the wide open bogland countryside which enhances this county. Opened in '96, the park has matured nicely and offers top class facilities and, most importantly, a friendly reception - in fact, here you experience Irish hospitality at its best. From the park entrance the drive leads to a parking area, clearly defined by a roundabout and a huge Ice Age stone from Boora Bog, known as 'Mona'. Reception, the Gables tea rooms and a patio area lie to the right, approached by a gateway and gravel path. The spotlessly clean sanitary block, a freshly painted, modern building, stands adjacent to reception. Its exterior is complemented with flower beds, shrubs and climbing plants which give a well cared for appearance. Facilities in the heated block include wash areas, attractive oval mirrors, hand towels, vanity unit, baby changing space and showers with hooks and seats. There are excellent facilities for disabled people, also a laundry area, washing up sink and chemical disposal. Motorcaravan sevice point and gas supplies available. Apart from 8 hardstanding pitches towards the rear of the park, the remainder are on grass. Electric hook-ups (10A) are provided on 14 and tents are catered for. The ground is gently sloping and the perimeter is surrounded by hedging. The village of Geashill is within 50 m. with old houses, stone walls, shops and three pubs. The proprietor at Hamilton's welcomes Green Gables campers in his pub where Irish culture abounds. Getting out of the village can mean taking a train from Portarlington station to Dublin city. If preferring the countryside there are cycle tours, the Grand Canal walking routes or a Bog Train tour through the historic bogland, one of Offaly's many attractions. Riding 5 km, fishing, bicycle hire or golf 10 km.

Directions: From Tullamore take R420 east for 12 km. to village of Geashill. Site is on right at end of village.

Charges 2000:
-- Per unit IR£8.00; small tent IR£6.00; adult IR£1.00; child 50p; hiker or cyclist and tent IR£5.00; electricity (10A) IR£1.50.
Open:
Easter - 31 October
Address:
Geashill, Tullamore, Co. Offaly.
Tel:
0506 43760.
FAX: as phone.
E-mail: ggcp@iol.ie.
Reservations:
Contact park.

910 Camac Valley Tourist Caravan and Camping Park, Dublin

Touring park with top class facilities convenient for ferry ports and Dublin city.

Opened in '96, this campsite is not only well placed for Dublin, but also offers a welcome stopover if travelling to the more southern counties from the north of the country, or vice versa. Despite its close proximity to the city, being located in the 300 acre Corkagh Park gives it a 'heart of the country' atmosphere. The site entrance and sign are distinctive and can be spotted in adequate time when approaching on the busy N7. Beyond the entrance gate and forecourt stands an attractive timber fronted building. Its design includes various roof levels and spacious interior layout, with large windows offering a view of the site. Housed here is reception, information, reading, TV and locker rooms plus heated sanitary facilities which include WCs, good sized showers (50p token) and central floor units with washbasins and mirrors. There are also shaver points, hand dryers, facilities for disabled people, baby changing room, laundry, washing up and chemical disposal. A second well designed and fitted sanitary block is operational, also a children's playground with wooden play frames and safety base. A shop and coffee bar open in June, July and August. There are 163 pitches, 48 for tents placed to the fore and the hardstandings for caravans laid out in bays and avenues with electrical connections, drainage and water points. Young trees separate pitches and roads are tarmac. There is an automatic gate and 24 hour security. Caravan storage. Dogs are not accepted in July/Aug. Fishing 8 km, bicycle hire 1.5 km, riding 9 km, golf 6 km. After a day of sightseeing in Dublin, which can be reached by bus from the site, Camac Valley offers a evening of relaxation with woodland and river walks in the park or a number of first class restaurants and pubs nearby.

Charges 2000:
-- Per unit incl. 2 persons IR£10.00 - 11.00, incl. up to 4 children IR£11.00 - 13.00; extra person IR£1.00; child (under 7 yrs) 50p; motorcyclist, cyclist or hiker with tent IR£3.00 - 4.00 per person; awning IR£1.00; extra small tent IR£3.00; electricity (10A) IR£1.00.
-- Credit cards accepted.

Open:
All year

Address:
Naas Road, Clondalkin, Dublin 22.

Tel:
01 464 0644.
FAX: 01 464 0643.
E-mail: camac morriscastle@tinet.ie.

Reservations:
Advance bookings necessary. (max. stay operates at certain times).

Directions: From north follow signs for West Link and M50 motorway. Exit M50 at junction 9 onto N7 Cork road. Site is on right of dual carriageway (beside Green Isle Hotel) after 2 km. and is clearly signed. At City West business park, cross over bridge and return on dual-carriageway following camp signs - site is on left after 800 m.

913 Roundwood Caravan and Camping Park, Roundwood

Excellent park in the heart of the Wicklow mountains and convenient for ferries.

This park is neatly laid out with several rows of trees dividing different areas and giving some shade and an attractive appearance. There are 37 pitches, all with electricity (5A) and 16 with hardstanding, for caravans and motorcaravans and 42 for tents, arranged off tarmac access roads (additional pitches used for holiday homes have now been given over to touring areas). There are several water point, dustbins and sink areas handily placed around the park. The sanitary block was spotless when we visited, with adequate washing and toilet facilities and spacious showers. The block also houses two dishwashing sinks with free hot water and good laundry facilities (ask for assistance at reception as machines are not self use). Chemical disposal and motorcaravan service point. Bicycle hire is available and there is a children's adventure playground, a TV room, a campers' kitchen and dining room. In the village of Roundwood you can find shops, pubs, restaurants and takeaway food and there is a Sunday market. There are excellent walks in the immediate area, around the Varty Lakes and a daily bus service to Dublin City. Close by are the Wicklow and Sally Gap, Glendalough, Powerscourt Gardens, plus many other places of natural beauty. Fishing or golf 1 km. You should enjoy this excellent park, which is set in an area of mountains, lakes, rivers and forests.

Charges 2000:
-- Per unit IR£7.00 - 8.00; adult IR£1.50; child (under 14 yrs) £1.00; electricity IR£1.50.
-- No credit cards.

Open:
31 March - 1 October.

Address:
Roundwood, Co. Wicklow.

Tel:
01 2818163.
FAX: as phone.
E-mail: dicksonn @indigo.ie.

Reservations:
Accepted without deposit and are advisable for July/Aug.

Directions: Turn off the Dublin - Wexford N11 road at Kilmacanogue in the direction of Glendalough and then 15 km. to Roundwood.

Tourist Information:

Dublin the capital of Ireland since the late 17th century is stylish and energetic with a charm of its own, The old Ireland is still present in its castles, cathedrals and fine pubs but Dublin has seen a blending of cultures that has allowed for an amazing intellectual and literary life. From Swift and Burke to Joyce and Beckett, Dublin has produced so many great writers that nearly every street contains a literary landmark. Pubs shelter Dublin's public life and a world-renowned music scene for the Irish maintain a strong public life centred around music, sports, a laid-back attitude, and, of course, drinking.

Wicklow

914 Valley Stopover and Caravan Park, Kilmacanogue

Small, family run park located in quiet, idyllic setting and convenient for Dublin ferries.

This neat and attractive ¾ acre park situated in the picturesque Rocky Valley could be used either as a transit site or for a longer stay. It has instant appeal for those who prefer the more basic `CL' type site. There are 15 grassy pitches, 11 with electric hook-ups, 3 hardstandings, 2 water points, night lighting and a security gate. Toilet facilities, which were spotlessly clean when we visited, are housed in one unit and consist of 2 WCs with washbasins, mirrors, etc. and a shower (50p). There is a dishwashing/laundry sink, a spin dryer, chemical disposal point, a campers' kitchen and hot water is constantly available. A cooked full Irish breakfast is available for IR£3.50 in the family guest house. Dairy products are available and bread can be ordered. Fishing 10 miles, bicycle hire 4 miles (can be delivered), riding 2 miles, golf 4 miles. Staying put here you are only minutes from Enniskerry which lies in the glen of the Glencullen river. Here you can enjoy a delight of forest walks, or visit Powerscourt, one of the loveliest gardens in Ireland. If wanting to be at the sea, travel 6 km. to Bray and you are in one of the oldest seaside resorts in the country. Small caravan to hire.

Directions: Turn off Dublin-Wexford N11 road at Kilmacanogue - follow signs for Glendalough. Continue for 1.6 km and take right fork signed `Waterfall'. Park is first opening on the left in approx. 200 m.

Charges 1999:
-- Per caravan or tent with car IR£7.00; motor-caravan IR£6.00; tent with bike IR£3.00; electricity £IR1.00; awning IR£1.00.
-- No credit cards.

Open:
Easter - 31 October.

Address:
Valleyview,
Killough, Kilmacanogue,
Co. Wicklow.

Tel:
01 282 9565.

Reservations:
Advised for July/Aug; contact park.

915 River Valley Caravan and Camping Park, Redcross Village

Friendly, family run park in small village in the heart of Co. Wicklow.

In the small country village of Redcross, which abounds with character and atmosphere, is where you will find this well run park. Although only 58 km. from Dublin, being based here you are in the heart of the countryside with beauty spots such as the Vale of Avoca, Glendalough and Powerscourt within driving distance, plus the safe beach of Brittas Bay 6 km. away. Although there are 80 caravan holiday homes on this park, the 100 touring pitches are together in a separate area. There are 80 with electrical connections (6A) and, with a choice of hardstanding or grass, you select your pitch. A luxurious new, heated sanitary block has a modern, well designed appearance which makes it a special feature at River Valley. Facilities for disabled visitors are excellent, hot water is available for dishwashing and there is a laundry area, chemical disposal and motorcaravan service points. Within this 12 acre site children can find day long amusement, whether it be Fort Apache, the adventure playground, the new 'tiny-tots' playground, or at the natural mountain stream where it is safe to paddle. They may, however, prefer to get to know the farm animals and birds in the pets corner. Other amenities include TV, games room, a tennis court, par-3 golf course and bowling green, plus a new sports complex with badminton courts and indoor football and basketball. An attractive wine and coffee bar with a conservatory is an inviting asset, or an alternative may be the cosy atmosphere of the restaurant where many home made, traditional dishes are on the menu (both 9 am-6 pm, 1/6-31/8). Gas is available. An excellent late arrivals area has electric hook-ups, water and night lighting. Rally area and caravan storage. No dogs are accepted in July/Aug. Fishing 4 miles, bicycle hire and boat launching 9 miles.

Directions: From Dublin follow N11 Wexford road. Turn right in Rathnew and then left (under railway bridge) onto the Wexlow-Arklow road. Continue for 11 km. and turn right at Doyle's Pub. Park is in Redcross Village, under 5 km.

Charges 2000:
-- Per caravan, motor-caravan or tent incl. 2 adults IR£10.00 - 11.00, small tent IR£9.00 - 10.00; extra adult IR£3.00; child (under 15 yrs) IR£1.00; m/cyclist, cyclist or hiker and tent incl. tent IR£5.00 - 6.00; electricity IR£1.00.
-- No credit cards.

Open:
12 March - 23 September.

Address:
Redcross Village,
Co. Wicklow.

Tel:
0404 41647.
FAX: 0404 41677.

Reservations:
Made with IR£10 deposit.

916 Moat Farm Caravan and Camping Park, Donard

Heart of the country experience within easy driving distance of Dublin or Rosslare.

Camping at its most idyllic is what can be enjoyed at this campsite. Here a true feel of the countryside abounds for it is part of a working farm environment and offers incredible vistas across a scenic landscape. Driving into the village of Donard in West Wicklow you little suspect that alongside the main street lies this tranquil 5 acre site. The entrance is approached by way of a short roadway where the ruins of a Medieval church sit high overlooking the forecourt and reception. Facing down the site is the sanitary block which is kept clean and includes WCs, large showers, sink units with marble effect tops, mirrors, soap dispensers and electric points. There are facilities for visitors with disabilities, a well equipped laundry room with sink, washing machine, dryer and ironing board. Next to this is a TV room with easy chairs and a long window giving a panoramic view over the site and beyond. Chemical disposal facilities are at the end of this building and a campers' kitchen with sinks, fridge and freezer with ice pack facilities is beside the farmyard buildings. Three large barbecues and a patio area are provided. There are 40 pitches for caravans and tents. The pitches with hardstanding to the right, some sheltered by tall trees, occupy both sides of a broad avenue. These are spacious and incorporate awning and car space, and all have electricity and drainage points. Tents are pitched on the grass area to the centre and left. This site makes a good base for touring or going on foot, for this is a walker's paradise with a 30 minute circular walkway around the perimeter of the site. Riding on site. There is fishing (3 km), mountain climbing or sites of archaeological interest nearby. Bicycle hire 15 km, golf 13 km. Caravan storage available.

Directions: From south on N81 turn off 14 km. north of Baltinglass at old Tollhouse pub. Site is clearly signed.

Charges 1999:
-- Per caravan, motor-caravan or family tent IR£8.00; adult IR£1.00; child 50p; tent (1 or 2 persons) IR£6.00; m/cyclist incl. tent IR£4.00; hiker or cyclist incl. tent IR£3.50; awning free; electricity (10A) IR£1.50.
-- No credit cards.

Open:
All year.

Address:
Donard, Co.Wicklow.

Tel:
045 404727.
FAX: as phone.

Reservations:
Contact site.

908 Forest Farm Caravan and Camping Park, Athy

Farm site with good quality facilities, off Dublin - Kilkenny road.

This new site makes an excellent stopover if travelling from Dublin to the southeast counties. It is signed on the N78 and approached by a 500 m. avenue of tall pines. Part of a working farm, the campsite spreads to the right of the modern farmhouse, which also provides B&B. The owners have cleverly utilised their land to create a site which offers 64 unmarked touring pitches on level ground. Of these, 32 are for caravans, all with electricity and 10 with hardstanding and 32 places are available for tents. The red brick sanitary block, which is heated and has double glazing, occupies a central position on site. It offers quality amenities including a comfortable lounge/games room (a TV will be supplied on request). The shower and WC areas have freshly painted yellow walls and pine doors, plus top of the range fittings. Facilities include a spacious shower unit for disabled visitors and a family room with shower and WC. There is also a laundry room, with washing machine, drier and spin drier, and dish washing sinks which are in the camper's kitchen. This is furnished with a fridge/ freezer, cooker, table and chairs. Chemical disposal facilities are in a dedicated space separate from the main building. There is a basketball net, sand pit and picnic tables, also night lighting. Full Irish breakfasts are served at the farmhouse and farm tours available on request.

Directions: Site is 4.8 km. northeast of Athy town off the main N78 Athy - Kilcullen road.

Charges 1999:
-- Per unit incl. 2 adults IR£9.00 - 10.00; child 50p; 1 or 2 person tent IR£3.00 - 4.00 p/person; m/cyclist, hiker or cyclist incl. tent IR£3.00 - 4.00 p/person; electricity (16A) IR£1.50.

Open:
All year.

Address:
Dublin Road, Athy, Co. Kildare.

Tel:
0507 31231 or 33070.
FAX: 0507 31231.
E-mail: forestfarm@ tinet.ie.

Reservations:
Contact site.

Laois / Kilkenny

920 Kirwans Caravan and Camping Park, Portlaoise

Friendly, peaceful park, ideal for exploring inland, rural Ireland.

One receives a warm welcome at this small `homely' park, located on the edge of Portlaoise and surrounded by trees. The pitches are around the edges of a flat, firm grassy meadow and you site yourself sensibly, choosing morning or afternoon sun. Flowers and shrubs have been planted and secluded seating areas provided. The site offers 16 pitches with electricity (13A) for caravans or motorcaravans and another 14 for tents. There are a couple of static vans and mobile homes for hire. Water facilities are adequate with a long hose available. The sanitary block, near the entrance, is very clean and is adequate, without being luxurious. It offers hot showers on payment and additional facilities are being added. There are dish-washing facilities and a laundry with washing machine, spin and tumble dryers – the laundry may not be used on Sundays. A TV and video room is provided and a rest room where one can make tea and coffee, plus a kitchen for groups, a children's playground, barbecue and picnic area are on site. Shops, supermarkets, etc. are close in Portlaoise, where there is a market on Thursdays. Laois is a beautiful inland county of Ireland, with picturesque small towns and many historical connections well worth exploring.

Directions: Approaching Portlaoise from the N7 Kildare - Limerick road, join the M7 bypass and branch off onto R445 signed Portlaoise centre. Continue to round-about in centre and follow signs for Limerick and Montrath. Site is on right approx. 1 mile from roundabout; watch carefully for campsite sign immediately by entrance.

Charges 1999:
-- Per unit, incl. 2 persons IR£8.00 - 15.00; m/cycle and tent incl. 1 or 2 persons IR£5.00 per person; backpacker or cyclist IR£3.00 per person; child IR£1.00; extra adult, tent, electricity, dog, awning or boat all IR£1.00 - 1.50.
Open:
1 April - 15 October.
Address:
N7 Limerick Road, Portlaoise, Co. Laois.
Tel:
0502 21688.
Reservations:
Made for any length, with deposit.

923 Nore Valley Park, Annamult, Bennettsbridge

Small working farm site, set in picturesque and peaceful surroundings.

This lovely site is set on a grassy hillock overlooking the valley and the river Nore, with a woodland setting behind. Situated on a working farm, it offers 60 pitches, 30 for caravans and motorhomes with electrical hook-up and some with hardstanding. The owners pride themselves on their home baking and farm produce and during high season cooked breakfasts are available in the small café (June-Aug). The reception area at the site entrance is in an attractive courtyard and basic items such as milk, bread, camping gaz are available. A modern sanitary block houses facilities which are kept spotlessly clean and can be heated. These include free hot showers, WCs, washbasins and two units suitable for disabled visitors. There are dishwashing sinks with hot water, a laundry room with washing machine and dryer, chemical disposal and motorcaravan services. The original sanitary block in the courtyard is for use mainly in the low season. A comfortable lounge is to be found next to the reception area, plus a games room with pool table. Crazy golf is a feature. Bicycle hire. Other facilities within the courtyard include a sand pit, pedal go-karts, tractor rides and a straw loft playing area for wet weather. At the front of the park is a children's play area on gently sloping grass and fenced. This is an ideal park for families, offering children and adults alike the opportunity to feed the animals (goats, lambs, ducks, chickens, and donkey). The park is 11 km. from Kilkenny, renowned for its castle, history and crafts, and 3 km. from the village of Bennettsbridge, where there are shops and eating places. There is plenty of scope nearby for outdoor pursuits such as canoeing, pony trekking or golf (10 km), walking and fishing (4 km). Caravan storage available. Four mobile homes for hire. Note: the animal park, tractor rides, go-karts and the café are closed on Sundays.

Directions: From Kilkenny take R700 to Bennettsbridge. Just before the bridge turn right at sign for Stoneyford and after approx. 3 km. site is signed Nore Valley Park.

Charges 2000:
-- Per person £1.00; caravan IR£8.50; trailer or chalet tent IR£8.00; motorcaravan IR£7.50; family tent IR£8.00, 2 person tent IR£5.50; awning or extra small tent IR£2.00; electricity (6A) IR£1.50.
-- Credit cards accepted.
Open:
1 March - 31 October.
Address:
Annamult, Bennettsbridge, Co. Kilkenny.
Tel:
056 27229.
FAX: 056 27748.
E-mail: norevalleypark @tinet.ie.
Reservations:
Contact park.

924 Tree Grove Caravan and Camping Park, Kilkenny

Orderly, neat and welcoming touring park within walking distance of Kilkenny.

The entrance gate to this small family run site, now into its third season, is easily spotted off the R700 road. It makes an ideal location for spending time in medieval Kilkenny, known for its elegance and famed for its beer and cats. Tree Grove has instant appeal because its young owners are friendly and have insisted on a logical layout to suit both the terrain and campers needs. It is a terraced site with the lower terrace to the right of the wide sweeping driveway laid out with 11 hardstanding pitches for caravans. All 30 pitches have electrical hook-ups (10A) and plenty of water points are to be found. On a higher level, to the left is a grass area for hikers and cyclists with further caravan and tent pitches sited near the elevated sanitary block. If needed more grass pitches face reception, which is temporarily housed in a mobile unit. Whilst there are mature trees at the entrance and around the site perimeter, many young shrubs have been planted and flower troughs effectively placed. House plants add decoration inside the toilet block giving a cared for look to this modern building. Showers are free and a family room with shower, WC and washbasin can be used by disabled people. WCs and washbasins with mirrors, shaver and hairdryer points, are in separate spacious areas. Ladies' have a vanity unit with large mirror. An open, covered kitchen for campers with fridge, work-top, sink and electric kettle adjoins a comfortable games/TV room with pool table, easy chairs and magazine rack. Next to this is a laundry room with sink, washing machine, dryer and iron. Chemical disposal. On the patio there are bench seats with tables and umbrellas. Tents to rent on site. There is much to see and do around the ancient city of Kilkenny (1.5 km) with its cobbled streets and castle. Fishing, bicycle hire and riding within 2 km. Golf 3 or 15 km. County Touring Routes are worth following.

Charges 2000:
-- Per caravan, motor-caravan or family tent incl. 2 persons IR£8.50; extra person IR£1.00; 1 man tent IR£5.00; 2 man tent IR£6.50; 4 man tent IR£7.00; car IR£1.00; awning IR£1.00; electricity (10A) IR£1.50.
-- No credit cards.
Open:
1 March - 15 November.
Address:
Danville House, Kilkenny, Co. Kilkenny.
Tel:
056 70302.
FAX: 056 21512.
E-mail: treecc@iol.ie.
Reservations:
Contact site.

Directions: Travelling north on the N10 Waterford/Kilkenny Road turn right at roundabout on ring road. Continue to 2nd roundabout and turn right onto R700. Site is 150 m. on right.

930 Morriscastle Strand Caravan and Camping Park, Kilmuckridge

Family run park with direct access to sandy beach and convenient for Rosslare Port.

Whether you use this park as a stopover, or choose it as a longer stay destination, you will find it to be in a quiet relaxing location. Situated minutes from the pretty village of Kilmuckridge it offers well maintained and clean facilities. There are 145 privately owned caravan holiday homes on site but these are unobtrusive and kept separate by high hedging. The entrance to the touring park is to the right of reception by way of a tarmac drive. This leads to the secluded, gently sloping, grass pitches which enjoy an open aspect. They overlook marshland which attracts wild geese and ducks, whilst the sea brings in crabs, eels and fish. To the right of the site lie the sand-hills and pathways to the beach which is supervised by lifeguards in high season. The 100 pitches are numbered and marked by concrete slabs, each has an electrical hook-up (6A) and drainage point. There is good night lighting and two sanitary blocks house all the toilet facilities. These include spacious WCs, washbasins, mirrors, shaver points, etc. Also unisex showers (on payment) with dividing wall, bench seat, hooks and soap dish. There is provision for disabled people, a baby bath, campers' kitchen, dishwashing area, launderette, chemical disposal and outside cold showers. Other on site facilities include a shop, snacks and takeaway in high season, also a games room, two tennis courts, football field and children's play area. Kilmuckridge is approximately 3 km. with an assortment of shops, pubs offering nightly entertainment and top class restaurants, such as The Rafters, a picturesque spot which helps characterise this charming village. Golf 5 km. Dogs are accepted only in certain areas (not with tents).

Charges 2000:
-- Per unit incl. 2 persons IR£10.00 - 11.00, incl. up to 4 children IR£11.00 - 13.00; extra person IR£3.00; child (under 7 yrs) IR£1.00; motorcyclist, cyclist or hiker with tent IR£3.00 - 4.00 per person; awning IR£1.00; extra small tent IR£3.00; electricity (5A) IR£1.00.
-- Credit cards accepted.
Open:
1 May - 25 September.
Address:
Kilmuckridge, Co. Wexford.
Tel:
053 30124 or 053 30212 (off season 01 453 5355). FAX: 053 30365 (off season 01 454 5916).
E-mail: camacmorris castle@tinet.ie.
Reservations:
Made with IR£10 deposit; contact site by phone or letter (use off season numbers Oct - April).

Directions: Site is 25 km. east of Enniscorthy. Travelling south on N11 Dublin-Wexford road branch onto R741 at Gorey. Continue for 19 km. to Ballyedmund. Turn left at petrol station and follow signs for Kilmuckridge and site.

217

Waterford

933 Casey's Caravan Park, Clonea, Dungarvan

Family run site with direct access to the beach.

Set on 20 acres of flat grass, edged by mature trees, this park offers 284 pitches which include 154 touring pitches, 118 with electrical hook-ups and 30 with hardstanding. The remainder are occupied by caravan holiday homes. The central sanitary block, operated on a key system, has good facilities kept spotlessly clean, a top priority for the owner. There are showers on payment (50p), free hot water to open style basins and washing up sinks (10p). Also housed in this block is a small laundry with machine and dryer. A further luxurious and modern block has been added with an excellent campers' kitchen, laundry room and toilet for disabled visitors. Chemical disposal. There is direct access from the park to a sandy, blue flag beach with a resident lifeguard during July/Aug. Facilities on the site include a large children's adventure play area with bark surface in its own field (not supervised by camp staff). Near the site entrance is a games room with pool table, table tennis and amusements, crazy golf and TV lounge. Gas is available. A highly recommended leisure centre is adjacent should the weather be inclement. There is no shop, but two village stores are near the beach. The park is 5½ km. from Dungarvan, a popular town for deep sea angling, from which charter boats can be hired and three 18 hole golf courses are within easy distance. Recommended drives include the scenic Vee, the Comeragh Drive and the coast road to Tramore. Dogs allowed on a lead. Full time security staff in high season.

Charges 1999:
-- Per unit IR£10.50 - 11.00; hiker or cyclist IR£4.00; electricity IR£1.00.
-- No credit cards.
Open:
28 April - 10 September.
Address:
Clonea, Dungarvan, Co. Waterford.
Tel:
058 41919.
Reservations:
Are made, but not between 9 July - 15 Aug; contact park.

Directions: From Dungarvan centre follow R675 east for 3.5 km. Look for signs on the right to Clonea Bay and site. Site is approx. 1.5 km.

 ## Casey's Caravan & Camping Park
Clonea, Dungarvan, Co Waterford Tel: 058 41919

Top class facilities	Two ablution blocks with laundry & kitchen
Playground	Games room and TV room
Electric sites for tents & tourers (5A)	EU Blue Flag beach
Dungarvan town 3½ miles	Two nearby shops with takeaway
Choice of scenic views to visit	Deep sea and river angling
18 hole golf course in easy reach	Adjacent hotel with 19 metre pool and leisure centre with bowling alley

---

934 Newtown Cove Camping and Caravan Park, Tramore

Small, well run, friendly park, 5 minutes walk from the beautiful Newtown Cove.

This park offers views of the famous and historic Metal Man and is situated 2.5 km. from Tramore beach and 11 km. from Waterford. Neatly set out on gently sloping grass with an abundance of shrubs and bushes, there are 40 pitches. All have electrical connections (10A), some hardstanding also, with access by well lit tarmac roads. There are around 50 privately owned caravan holiday homes. A modern building at the entrance houses reception, a small shop (1/6-31/8), TV room, games room and further sanitary facilities. The village of Tramore, with a wide range of shops and eating houses, is close. The main sanitary block is situated at the bottom end of the site and, although not very modern, offers good facilities which include a bathroom. Showers are on payment (50p for a token from reception). The block also provides a campers' kitchen with cooking facilities (20p), lounge and a washing up room and small laundry, with free hot water. A small children's play area set on sand is conveniently positioned in the centre of the park. A golf course is 800 m. and the choice of many delightful cliff walks in the immediate vicinity. Bicycle hire 1.5 km, fishing 400 m, riding 3 km. Dogs are allowed if kept on a lead. No bookings are taken and the park does not accept single sex groups.

Charges 1999:
-- Per unit incl. 2 persons IR£9.00 - 10.00; extra adult IR£1.50; child free - IR£1.00; hiker, cyclist or motorcyclist IR£3.50 - 4.50 per person; electricity IR£1.50.
-- No credit cards.
Open:
Easter - 26 September.
Address:
Tramore, Co. Waterford
Tel:
051 381979.
FAX: 051 381121.
Reservations:
Not necessary but for information contact park.

Directions: From Tramore on R675 coast road to Dungarvan. Turn left 2 km. from town centre, following signs.

939 Carrick-on-Suir Caravan and Camping Park, Carrick-on-Suir

Small, family run, town site in quiet and tranquil setting.

This memorable little site is not only conveniently situated off the main N24 between Waterford and Clonmel, but its owner, Frank O'Dwyer, is an excellent ambassador for his county. On his site campers are guaranteed the finest example of 'Cead Mile Failte' it is possible to encounter - personal attention and advice on where to go and what to see in the area is all part of the service. The entrance to the park is immediately past the O'Dwyers' shop, through a gate which is closed at 11 pm. The gravel drive leads past tall hedges and well kept shrubs to the right and several caravan holiday homes (for hire) to the left. The touring park lies to the rear with scenic views to the wooded hills. At present there are 30 level pitches, 23 with electricity (10A) and several with hardstanding, but this number is to be extended. There are 7 water points, chemical disposal, a motorcaravan service point and good night lighting. What makes this little site distinctive is its excellent, well designed sanitary block which has a sparkling clean freshness. The building itself is white, as are all inside fittings and the floor tiles, which are white with a black design. Facilities include WCs, showers, washbasins with mirrors, electric points, hand dryers and plenty of hot water each morning. Laundry room with washing machine and a dishwashing area also. Camper's kitchen with TV. Basic groceries and a selection of wines available from the family shop. Gas is available. Fishing 1 km, riding 6 km, golf 3 km. Carrick town centre is a five minute walk away where there are shops, pubs, restaurants, banks, sports facilities and all services, plus a castle which is open to the public. Within a short drive is the 'magic road', the Mahon Falls, a slate quarry or a romantic river walk.

Charges 1999:
-- Per unit incl. 2 adults IR£9.00 - 10.00; tent IR£6.00 - 7.00; extra adult IR£1.00 - 1.50; child IR£1.00; electricity 6A IR£1.00. 10A 1.50; hiker/cyclist incl. tent IR£3.00 - 3.50; extra car IR£1.00.
-- No credit cards.
Open:
All year except 20 Dec - 5 Jan.
Address:
Ballyrichard, Kilkenny Road, Carrick-on-Suir, Co. Tipperary.
Tel:
051 640461.
E-mail: coscamping@tinet.ie.
Reservations:
Contact site.

Directions: Approaching town on N24 road, follow signs for R690 in the direction of Kilkenny. Site is north of town, clearly signed at junction with R697.

941 The Apple Camping and Caravan Park, Cahir

Fruit farm and campsite combination offering an idyllic country holiday venue.

In one of the most delightful situations imaginable, this small farm site for tourers only is located off the N24, midway between Clonmel and Cahir. Entrance is by way of a 300 m. drive which follows straight through the heart of the farm. Apple trees guard the route, as do various non-fruit tree species, which are named and of interest to guests, who are free to spend time walking the paths around the farm. When we visited, strawberries were being gathered - the best we had tasted all season. Reception is housed with the other site facilities in a large farmyard barn. Although a rather unusual arrangement, it is very effective. Showers, WCs, washbasins with mirrors, electric points, etc. are in functional units occupying two corners of the large floor space. Kept very clean, quite modern in design and with heating, there are simple extra touches such as green curtains and green coloured concrete floor which blend with the fittings to give an attractive well maintained appearance. Facilities for disabled visitors have been added. Also in the barn are dishwashing sinks with hot water, bench seating and a fridge/freezer for the use of campers. Chemical disposal and motorcaravan service point. The 32 pitches are in a secluded situation behind the barns and are mostly grass with a few hardstandings. There are electricity connections up to 24, but some may require long cables. Amenities include a tennis court, a basketball/football pitch and children's play area. No dogs are accepted. Public phone. Fishing, golf, bicycle hire and riding within 6 km. The towns of Cahir and Clonmel are of historic interest and the countryside around boasts rivers, mountains, Celtic culture and scenic drives.

Charges 2000:
-- Per person IR£3.25 - 3.75; child (0-12 yrs) IR£1.75; electricity (13A) IR£1.00 (no charge per unit).
-- No credit cards.
Open:
1 May - 30 September.
Address:
Moorstown, Cahir, Co. Tipperary.
Tel:
052 41459.
FAX: 052 42774.
Reservations:
Contact site.

Alan Rogers' Discount

Free bottle of apple juice or fruit in season

Directions: Park is 300 m. off main N24, 9.6 km. northwest of Clonmel, 6.4 km. southeast of Cahir.

Tipperary / Limerick

938 Parsons Green Caravan and Camping Park, Clogheen

Small, family run park with excellent on-site facilities.

In a tranquil and scenic location, this open style site commands panoramic views toward the Vee Gap and Knockmealdown Mountains. Surrounded by low ranch fencing, it offers 20 pitches for caravans and motorcaravans with hardstanding and 14 on grass, all with electrical connections (6A), plus 20 pitches for tents. The sanitary facilities, to the top right of the site close to reception, are kept clean and include WCs, washbasins with mirrors and electric points, free hot showers and good facilities for disabled people (shower and toilet), plus a laundry area with washing machines, dryer and sinks, three dishwashing sinks and chemical disposal. A coffee shop is on site, ice cream, confectionery and gifts are sold and there is a takeaway. The village is within 500 m. (footpath and lighting) with shops, pubs, bank, post office, etc. The wide range of amenities on site includes a garden area, river walks, picnic area, an extensive farm museum, a pet field with selection of domestic and rare animals and birds, children's playground, minigolf, pony and trap rides, boating on the small lake and trout fishing river. TV/games room, campers' kitchen and function room. If not sitting back enjoying the scenic surroundings or participating in the many activities, there is much to see and do in this area. The manager of Parson's Green, would be more than pleased to pinpoint places of interest. Riding and golf 8 miles. Caravan holiday homes (3) and chalets (2) for hire.

Charges 1999:
-- Per caravan, family tent or motorcaravan IR£4.00; small tent IR£3.00; adult IR£2.00; child IR£1.00; awning IR£1.00; electricity IR£1.00.
-- No credit cards.
Open:
All year.
Address:
Clogheen, Co. Tipperary.
Tel:
052 65290.
FAX: 052 65504.
E-mail: pjkn@tinet.ie.
Reservations:
Contact site.

Directions: Site is in the village of Clogheen, 200 m. off the R665, 24 km. west of Clonmel, 19 km. east of Mitchelstown.

945 Curraghchase Caravan and Camping Park, Kilcornan

Beautiful, tranquil park set in Curraghchase Forest.

This 39 acre park is set in 600 acres of beech forest (known as the Coillte Forest park), 21 km. from Limerick City. Touring pitches have hardstanding with drainage and electric hook-ups, plus a separate grassy area allocated for 40 tents. One large amenities building houses a well stocked shop, TV lounge, a games room with table tennis and seating for an excellent campers' kitchen. Also within this building are the sanitary facilities which are basic. Hot water is free and showers are separated by a partition, sharing a large base with single drain and a communal dressing area with hooks and benches. Washing up sinks are available in the campers' kitchen and a small laundry with washing machines, dryers and iron. Chemical disposal. Behind the main block is a small `sun trap' picnic area. Children's play area with a bark safety base. Card telephone on site. Barbecues are allowed. There are many lovely forest walks, a nature trail and a number of rare orchids can be found. Within the forest are the ruins of Curragh (or Currah) Chase House, which was once the home of the poet Aubrey de Vere. Fishing, riding, golf and Adare village, with its interesting historical buildings and shopping facilities, are within 10 km.

Charges 2000:
-- Per caravan or family tent IR£10.00; tent incl. 1 or 2 persons IR£5.00; electricity IR£1.00.
-- No credit cards.
Open:
1 May - 11 September.
Address:
Coillte Forest Park, Kilcornan, Co. Limerick.
Tel:
061 396349 (or 061 337322 off season).
FAX: 061 338271.
E-mail: okeeffe_e@ ecoillte.ie.
Reservations:
Advisable in high season - contact site.

Directions: From Limerick city take N69 Foynes road; park entrance is at Kilcornan. Park also signed from Adare on the N20.

Tourist Information:
The West - even Dubliners will tell you that the west is the 'most Irish' part of Ireland. The West was hardest hit by the potato famine - entire villages emigrated or died. Today, every western county has less than half of its 1841 population.

901 Shannon Cottage Caravan and Camping Park, O'Brien's Bridge

Small, family run touring park offering tranquillity in a lovely location.

In a garden style setting amid trees and shrubs this is an attractive campsite on the banks of the Lower Shannon. After crossing the bridge in the village of O'Brien's Bridge, the park is within 100 m. It makes an ideal overnight halt or a convenient base for touring the mid-west. The Hyland family are dedicated to ensuring that visitors' needs are catered for. Visible from their elegant farmhouse are the 21 touring pitches, some with hardstanding and most with 5A electrical hook-up. The sanitary facilities, housed in outbuildings alongside the touring area, were spotlessly clean when we visited and can be heated. They have modern units, tiled walls and floors, pine-wood ceiling and doors and provide free hot showers, razor and hairdryer points, mirrors and hand dryers, laundry and dishwashing areas, and chemical disposal. Night lighting is provided. Important in inclement weather is the campers' indoor accommodation which includes a kitchen, dining hall and reception room. If required German and French are spoken. There is much to do when staying here. You can choose from riverside walks through the bird sanctuary, enjoy cycling, visit the traditional pubs, coarse or game angling, sailing or boating (boat hire locally). Riding 5 km, golf 10 km.

Charges 2000:
-- Per unit incl. 2 adults and 2 children IR£10.00 - 13.00; large family tent IR£12.00 - 16.00.
Open:
All year.
Address:
O'Brien's Bridge, Co. Clare.
Tel:
061 377118.
FAX: 061 377966.
E-mail: dave.hyland@ camping-ireland.ie.
Reservations:
Contact park.

Directions: From N7 (west, Dublin - Limerick) turn off at Birdhill on R466. From N7 (east, Limerick - Dublin) turn off at Daly's Cross on R525. Then follow signs to O'Brien's Bridge, cross the bridge and park is 100 m. east of the Old Bridge. From the R463 turn off at sign for O'Brien's Bridge, cross the New Bridge and park is 100 m. east of the Old Bridge.

948 Blarney Caravan and Camping Park, Blarney

Friendly, family run park easily reached from the ports of Cork and Rosslare.

There is a heart of the country feel about this 'on the farm' site, yet the city of Cork is only an 8 km. drive. What makes it so appealing is its secluded location and neatly laid out, open appearance. The terrain on the 3 acre park is elevated and gently sloping, commanding views towards Blarney Castle and the surrounding mountainous countryside. The 40 pitches, 30 of which have hardstanding and 10A electrical connections, are with caravans sited to the centre and left and tents pitched to the right. There are gravel roads, well tended young shrubs and a screen of mature trees and hedging marks the park's perimeter. Sanitary facilities are housed in converted farm buildings with the reception area and small shop abutting near the entrance. The toilet area is kept clean, showers are of a good size, free and have hooks, seat and soap rack, and there are now facilities for disabled visitors. The laundry room has stainless steel sinks, washing machine, dryer and ironing facilities and a washing up area is in the large campers' kitchen, which also has plenty of tables and seating. Other facilities include a shop (1/6-31/8), night lighting, chemical disposal, motorcaravan service point, TV lounge, phone room and an 18 hole golf and pitch and putt course. Caravan storage available. In the Blarney area, apart from the castle, house and gardens, there are shops, restaurants, pubs with traditional music and an abundance of outdoor pursuits such as walking, riding and fishing. A newly opened public bar and restaurant at 100 m. serves food all day.

Charges 1999:
-- Per caravan, family tent or motorcaravan IR£5.00 - 6.00; car and small tent IR£4.00 - 5.00; adult IR£1.50 - 2.00; child 50p - IR£1.00; hiker/cyclist and tent IR£3.00 - 3.50; motorcy-clist IR£3.50 - 4.00 per person; electricity (10A) IR£1.50; awning free - IR£1.00.
-- 7 nights for price of 6, if pre-paid.
-- Credit cards accepted.
Open:
All year.
Address:
Stoneview, Blarney, Co. Cork.
Tel:
021 385167.
FAX: as phone.
Reservations:
Contact park.

Directions: Site is 8 km. northwest of Cork, just off the N20. Take N20 from Cork for approx. 6 km. and then left on R617 to Blarney. Site clearly signed at Esso station in village, in approx. 2 km.

Cork

949 Sonas Caravan and Camping Park, Ballymacoda, nr. Youghal

Pleasant family run park in an unspoilt rural area.

What sells Sonas is its delightful situation, overlooking Youghal Bay with direct access to the beach and a birdwatchers' paradise. In this peaceful and quiet location, 4 km. from Ballymacoda village, it is easy to sit back and relax at this family run site. Pleasantly laid out, the 20 touring pitches are mostly to the right, with 12 pitches for caravans and motorcaravans, all with electric hook-ups (10A) and 10 with hardstanding. It is also possible to choose a more isolated spot around the perimeter where at least 20 tents can be pitched. Immediately in view is the main amenity block with 70 privately owned caravan holiday homes placed beyond. This building, which has a fresh and clean appearance, houses all the facilities which include reception and small shop (1/6-1/9) selling basic groceries, confectionery and with tourist information. There is a TV room, campers' kitchen, laundry and dishwashing area (washing machine, tumble and spin dryers, sinks) and the sanitary facilities. These are opened by key and include showers (£1), WCs, washbasins, with electric points, mirrors, etc. and were clean when we visited. To the rear of the block is a unit for disabled people. Chemical disposal. Also on site are a tennis court, volleyball and football pitch and a new adventure playground. Fishing 1 km, boat launching 2 km, golf 15 km. If not keeping fit, birdwatching, fishing or enjoying the beach, which is a mixture of shingle and sand but safe for swimming, take time to visit the area's many attractions which include the Cobh Heritage Centre and the historic walled port of Youghal.

Directions: From Youghal turn left off the N25 to Ballymacoda. Park is 4 km. on left after village and is signed.

Charges 2000:
-- Per unit incl. 2 adults IR£10.00 - 11.00; small tent IR£8.00; extra adult IR£1.50; child (4-14 yrs) IR£1.00; awning or extra car IR1.00; electricity IR£1.00; hardstanding IR£1.00.
-- No credit cards.

Open:
1 May - 30 September.

Address:
Ballymacoda, Co. Cork.

Tel:
024 98132.

Reservations:
Contact site.

950 The Meadow Camping Park, Glandore

Small, mature garden park on Ireland's garden route; for tents and motorcaravans only.

The stretch of coast from Cork to Skibbereen reminds British visitors of Devon before the era of mass tourism. This is rich dairy country, the green of the meadows matching the emerald colours of the travel posters. Thanks to the warm and wet Gulf Stream climate, it is also a county of gardens - and keen gardeners. The Meadows is best described not as a site, but as a one acre garden surrounded - appropriately - by lush meadows. It lies 1.5 km. east of the fishing village of Glandore. A further 5 km. west is the regional centre, Skibbereen, beyond which the landscape moves from unspoilt Devon to unspoilt Cornwall. The owners, who live on the park, have cunningly arranged accommodation for 19 pitches among the flower beds and shrubberies of their extended garden. Space is rather tight and towed caravans are therefore not encouraged. There are 6 hardstandings for motorcaravans with 5A electric hook-ups. Facilities are limited but are well designed and immaculately maintained. Among the homely features are a sitting room and a well equipped kitchen, and breakfast is available on request. Chemical disposal, washing machine and dryer. American motorhomes are accepted with an additional charge according to length. No dogs are accepted. Fishing or riding 2 km, fishing, swimming, boat launching and sailing at Glandore (2 km).

Directions: Park is 1.5 km. east of Glandore, off N71 road, on R597 mid-way between Leap and Rosscarbery (coast road).

Charges 2000:
-- Per motorcaravan incl. 2 persons IR£8.00 - 9.00; family tent incl. all persons IR£9.00 - 10.00; small tent and car £8.00; extra person IR£2.00; child (under 12) 50p; hiker or cyclist incl. tent IR£3.50 per person; electricity (5A) IR£1.00.
-- No credit cards.

Open:
15 March - 30 September.

Address:
Glandore, Co. Cork.

Tel:
028 33280.

Reservations:
Please phone site for details.

Alan Rogers' Discount

Less £1 per night

For a list of parks which are open all year - see page 234

952 Barleycove Holiday Park, Crookhaven

Family owned park on the scenically renowned Mizen Peninsula.

This long established park enjoys an idyllic situation tucked between the golden sands of Barleycove and Crookhaven Harbour. It is within an 8 km. drive of Mizen Head, Ireland's most south-westerly point, and approached along a route of unspoilt rugged countryside, offering the ideal 'away from it all' environment. It is a well cared for park with an overall neat and tidy appearance. Mobile homes, some for hire, are sited around the perimeter and within a field to the right. The 85 touring pitches all have electricity hook-ups. Some are on grass in bays of 12, divided by timber fencing and a number are unfenced, on hardstanding with drainage and rubbish disposal. Tents have a dedicated grass area. The three sanitary blocks are kept clean and well maintained. There are free hot showers, open style wash areas with light and electric points, plus a vanity unit and long mirror in the ladies. Other site facilities include a laundry, with washing machines, dryer and spin dryer, washing-up sinks, chemical disposal and motorcaravan service point. Reception, with bureau de change and tourist information, is at the park entrance. Alongside is a games room with table tennis, pool tables and games machines. Adjacent is a cafe/takeaway with outside seating, also a well stocked mini market. Ice packs are available at reception. There is a tennis court (admission free) also pitch and putt (50p adult, 20p child). Activities for children are organised in the high season. A security gate and night watchman patrol operate. Apart from discovering the natural beauty of this peninsula, of interest is Mizen Head Signal Station visitor centre, reached by a suspension bridge. Alternatively, the local friendly pubs and quality seafood restaurant at Heron's Cove offer a memorable evening out.

Charges 1999:
-- Per family unit IR£9.00 - 12.00; 2 person unit IR£8.00 - 9.50; awning (high season only) IR£2.00; m/cyclist with tent IR£2.50 - 4.00; hiker or cyclist with tent IR£2.50 - 3.50; electricity free - IR£1.00.
Open:
Easter week, then 1 May - 19 September.
Address:
Crookhaven, Co. Cork.
Tel:
(028) 35302 (low season (021) 346466).
FAX: (021) 307230.
Reservations:
Contact park

Directions: Site is 35 km. southwest of Bantry. From the N71 Bantry/Cork road join the R591 (3.2 km. south of Bantry) and follow signs for Crookhaven via Durrus, Toormore and Goleen. Site on right before Crookhaven village.

951 Eagle Point Caravan & Camping Park, Ballylickey, Bantry Bay

Spacious, well run park on a spectacular peninsula jutting into Bantry Bay.

Midway between the towns of Bantry and Glengarriff, the peninsula of Eagle Point juts into the bay. The first impression is of a country park rather than a campsite. As far as the eye can see this 20 acre, landscaped, part-terraced park, with its vast manicured grass areas separated by mature trees, shrubs and hedges, runs parallel with the shoreline. Suitable for all ages, this is a park devoted to tourers, with campers pitched mostly towards the shore. It provides 125 pitches (60 caravans, 65 tents) thus avoiding overcrowding during peak periods. There are three toilet blocks with free hot showers, all maintained and designed well above expected standards. Other facilities include electric hook-ups, bin area, laundry and dishwashing facilities, chemical disposal and motorcaravan service points, a children's play area, tennis courts, a football field to the far right, well away from the pitches, plus a supermarket at the park entrance. A wet weather timbered building towards the water's edge houses a TV room - the brightly decorated interior is guaranteed to brighten the dullest of days. Eagle Point makes an excellent base for watersports enthusiasts - swimming is safe and there is a slipway for small craft. Fishing on site. Bicycle hire 6 km, riding 10 km, golf 2 km. No dogs are accepted.

Charges 2000:
-- Per unit IR£10.50 - 13.50; extra adult IR£4.00; m/cyclist, hiker or cyclist IR£5.00 per person; extra car IR£2.00; electricity (6A) IR£1.00.
-- Credit cards accepted.
Open:
28 April - 30 September.
Address:
Ballylickey, Bantry, West Cork.
Tel:
027 50630.
Reservations:
Bookings not essential.

Directions: On coast side of the N71, 6 km. north of Bantry, 11 km. east of Glengariff. Park entrance is opposite Burmah petrol station.

To telephone the Irish Republic from the UK, replace the first `0' given in the number with the country code: 00 353.
eg. (094) 88100 becomes 00 353 94 88100.

Kerry

955 Anchor Caravan Park, Castlegregory

Secluded, mature park two minutes from a beautiful sandy beach.

Of County Kerry's three long, finger like peninsulas which jut into the sea, Dingle is the most northerly. Tralee is the main town and Anchor is 20 km. west of this famed town and under 4 km. south of Castlegregory on Tralee Bay. This five acre, family run park is in a secluded situation enclosed by shrubs and trees, with a gateway leading to the beach which is safe for bathing, boating and shore fishing. There are 30 pitches, all with electric hook-ups and some also with drainage and water points. There is night lighting around the site and, although there are holiday homes for hire, these are well apart from the touring pitches. The sanitary facilities (entry by key), are kept clean (often three or four times daily in busy periods). Included are showers, two private cabins, toilet with handrail, dishwashing and laundry facilities, chemical disposal, clothes lines and central rubbish depot. Motorcaravan service point. Children enjoy two play areas which have sand pits and swings with rubber safety matting. There is also a games/TV room. Fishing 2 km, riding or bicycle hire3 km, golf 4 km. In this area of great beauty, miles of sand abounds and taking in the panorama of mountain scenery from the top of the Conor Pass is a unique experience.

Charges 2000:
-- Per unit incl. all persons IR£9.00 - 10.00; tent incl. 1 or 2 persons IR£7.00 - 8.00; m/cyclist, hiker or cyclist incl. tent IR£7.00; electric IR£1.00; awning IR£1.00.
-- No credit cards.
Open:
Easter - 30 September.
Address:
Castlegregory, Co. Kerry.
Tel:
066 7139157.
FAX: as phone.
Reservations:
Contact site.

Directions: From Tralee follow the Dingle coast road for 19 km. Park is signed before Castlegregory.

956 Wave Crest Caravan and Camping Park, Caherdaniel

Dramatically located hillside park running down to Kenmare Bay on Ring of Kerry coast.

It would be difficult to imagine a more dramatic location than Wave Crest's. Huge boulders and rocky outcrops tumble from the park entrance on the N70 down to the seashore which forms the most southern promontory on the Ring of Kerry. There are spectacular southward views from the park across Kenmare Bay to the Beara peninsula. Sheltering on grass patches in small coves that nestle between the rocks and shrubbery, are 45 hardstanding pitches offering seclusion. Electricity connections are available (13A). Two toilet blocks house the sanitary facilities and include hot showers (50p), toilet for disabled people and dishwashing sinks. There is also a laundry service, chemical disposal, central rubbish point, shop (open May - Sept) and children's play area. A unique feature is the TV room, an old stone farm building with thatched roof. Its comfortable interior includes a stone fireplace heated by a converted cast iron marker buoy. Beside the park is a small beach or there is Derrynane Hotel with its swimming pool and tennis court. Fishing and boat launching from the site, riding 1 km, bicycle hire or golf 10 km. Caherdaniel is known for its cheerful little pubs and distinguished restaurant. The Derrynane National Park Nature Reserve is only a few km. away, as is Derrynane Cove and Bay. This park would suit older people looking for a quiet, relaxed atmosphere.

Charges 1999:
-- Per unit IR££7.50; small tent £7.00; adult IR£1.00; child 50p; hiker or cyclist incl. tent IR£3.25 per person; m/cyclist incl. tent £3.50; extra car IR£1.50; electricity (13A) IR£1.00.
-- Credit cards accepted.
Open:
15 March - 12 October. (off season by arrangement).
Address:
Caherdaniel, Ring of Kerry, Co. Kerry.
Tel:
066 9475188 or 9475483. FAX: 066 9475188.
Reservations:
Write for details.

Directions: On the N70 (Ring of Kerry), 1½ km. east of Caherdaniel.

Tourist Information:

Ring of Kerry – the Southwest's most celebrated peninsula is a well-established visitor attraction where travellers can soak up the great sea spray, grand views and pervasive quiet. The term 'Ring of Kerry' is often used to describe the entire Iveragh Peninsula, but it more correctly refers not to a region but to a set of roads: N71 from Kenmare to Killarney, R562 from Killarney to Killorglin, and the long loop of the N70 west and back to Kenmare.

For the best introduction to Ireland...

..make Irish Ferries our first connection

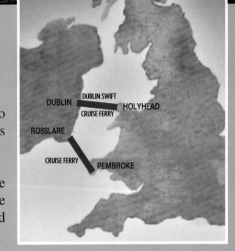

When it comes to taking you or your car to Ireland, choose to travel with the experts Irish Ferries.

With the most modern fleet of ships on the Irish Sea, great value fares and inclusive package holidays we have the island covered.

IRISH FERRIES

Ask Irish Ferries first

Call us now on 08705 17 17 17

and quote A368, or see your travel agent.

Bookings: www.irishferries.ie

No.1 to Ireland

More crossings. More craft. More choice.
(All the more reason to sail with us)

No other ferry company offers as many routes or choice of craft to Ireland than Stena Line. Take the jet-propelled Stena HSS from Holyhead to Dun Laoghaire or Stranraer to Belfast, or the speedy Stena Lynx from Fishguard to Rosslare and you'll be in Ireland in half the time of a conventional ferry. Alternatively cruise across in style on our luxurious Superferries.

Whichever route you choose, you'll find that Stena Line offers competitive rates, comfortable crossings and superior levels of service. So go with the company that leads the way. Stena Line.

For further information and to book call
08705 70 70 70
or see your travel agent

www.stenaline.com   *The world's leading ferry company*

motorhome
I R E L A N D

Motorhome Ireland offers you the freedom to tour Ireland in your own quality motorhome.

Rent in confidence from Ireland's only Motorhome centre.

MOTORHOME IRELAND LTD 8 Station Road, Saintfield, N Ireland BT24 7DU **TEL** (44) 01238 519519
FAX (44) 01238 519509 **E-MAIL** rental@motorhome-irl.co.uk **INTERNET** www.motorhome-irl.co.uk

957 Creveen Lodge Caravan and Camping Park, Healy Pass

Immaculately run, small hill farm park, overlooking Kenmare Bay.

The address of this park is rather confusing, but Healy Pass is the well known scenic summit of the road (R574) crossing the Beara Peninsula, which lies between Kenmare Bay to the north and Bantry Bay to the south. Several kilometres inland from the north coast road (R571), the R574 starts to climb steeply southward towards the Healy Pass. Here, on the mountain foothills, is Creveen Lodge, a working hill farm with a quiet, homely atmosphere. Although not so famed as the Iveragh Peninsula, around which runs the Ring of Kerry, the northern Beara is a scenically striking area of County Kerry. Creveen Lodge, which commands views across Kenmare Bay, is divided among three gently sloping fields separated by trees. Reception is to be found in the farmhouse which also offers guests a comfortable sitting room. A small separate block, which is well appointed and immaculately maintained, has toilets and showers, plus a communal room with a fridge, freezer, TV, ironing board, fireplace, tables and chairs. Full Irish breakfast is served on request. This park is carefully tended with neat rubbish bins and rustic picnic tables informally placed, plus a children's play area with slides and swings. To allow easy access, the steep farm track is divided into a simple one-way system. There are 20 pitches in total, 16 for tents and 4 for caravans with an area of hardstanding for motorcaravans. Electrical connections are available. This is walking and climbing countryside or, of interest close by, is Derreen Gardens. Fishing 2 km, bicycle hire 9 km, boat launching 9 km. Also available in the area are water sports, riding, `Seafari' cruises, shops and a restaurant.

Directions: Park is on the Healy Pass road (R574) 1.5 km. southeast of Lauragh.

Charges 2000:
-- Per unit IR£6.00; person IR£1.00; hiker or cyclist incl. tent IR£3.50 per person; electricity £1.00.
-- No credit cards.

Open:
Easter - 31 October.

Address:
Healy Pass, Lauragh, Co. Kerry.

Tel:
064 83131.
E-mail: creveen@ freeocean.net.

Reservations:
Write to site with an S.A.E.

958 Waterville Caravan & Camping Park, Waterville, Ring of Kerry

Family run park in scenic location overlooking Ballinskelligs Bay.

Drive into Waterville and immediately feel welcome - the Horgan family place emphasis on being hospitable and attentive to their guests. It is an 'away from it all' environment, picturesque and quiet. The 60 touring pitches, many with hardstanding, are located in three areas. Some are convenient for reception, whilst others are pitched to the middle and rear. There is also a sheltered corner allocated to campers, with 21 caravan holiday homes (15 for hire), unobtrusively placed around the perimeter and centre, giving the park a spacious, neatly laid out appearance. Sitting high above the bay, the view in all directions is magnificent and the well tended grounds with plants, shrubs and cordyline trees gives a tropical appearance, especially on a fine sunny day. Three sanitary blocks are all well maintained and kept clean, the newest tastefully decorated with white tiles, relieved with rows of decorative black. There are hot showers (50p token), facilities for disabled people, washing up and laundry areas, quiet room, chemical disposal facilities and a motorcaravan service point. Other facilities include a campers' kitchen, shop (with gas), takeaway (both 1/6-31/8) and TV room. As well as an outdoor children's play area and above ground swimming pool (June-Aug), there is a play room in an old horse drawn caravan and a timber house with toys and 'upstairs, downstairs'. Waterville is on the Ring of Kerry, convenient for all the scenic grandeur and attractions for which the area is famed. Fishing, golf and bicycle hire within 3 km. Waterville is also on the 'Kerry Way' walking route.

Directions: Travelling south on the N70, park is 1 km. north of Waterville, 270 m. off the main road.

Charges 2000:
-- Per unit IR£8.00 - 8.50; adult IR£1.00; child 50p; hiker or cyclist incl. tent IR£3.75 - 4.00; m/cyclist incl. tent IR£4.25 - 4.50; electricity (6A) IR£1.00; awning IR£1.50; hardstanding or extra car IR£1.00.
-- Credit cards accepted.

Open:
Easter - 16 September.

Address:
Waterville, Ring of Kerry, Co. Kerry.

Tel:
066 74191.
FAX: 066 74538.
E-mail: waterville caravans@tinet.ie.

Reservations:
Made with fee IR£5 plus IR£15 deposit.

Alan Rogers' Discount

 Less 10%

Kerry

959 Fossa Caravan and Camping Park, Killarney

Mature, well equipped park in scenic location, 5½ km. from Killarney.

A 10 minute drive from the town centre brings you to this well laid out park which is recognisable by its forecourt on which stands a distinctive building housing a roof top restaurant, reception area, shop and petrol pumps. The park is divided in two - the touring area lies to the right, tucked behind the main building, and to the left is an open grass area mainly for campers. Touring pitches, with electricity and drainage, have hardstanding and are angled between shrubs and trees in a tranquil, well cared for garden setting. To the rear at a higher level and discreetly placed are 50 caravan holiday homes (25 for hire). These are unobtrusive and sheltered by the thick foliage of the wooded slopes which climb high behind the park. The toilet facilities are modern and kept spotlessly clean. A second amenities block is placed to the far left of the grass area beside the tennis courts. Other facilities, apart from a shop (April - Sept), takeaway and restaurant (5/6-26/8), include a TV lounge, campers' kitchen, laundry room, washing up area, children's play area, picnic area, games room, bicycle hire, night lighting and security patrol. Fishing or golf 2 km, riding 3 km. Not only is Fossa convenient for Killarney, it is also en-route for the famed 'Ring of Kerry', and makes an ideal base for walkers and golfers.

Directions: Park is to the right on the R562/N72, 5½ km. west of Killarney on the road to Killorglin.

Charges 2000:
-- Per unit IR£3.00 - 3.50; adult IR£3.00; child (under 14 yrs) IR£1.00; electricity IR£1.50; m/cycle and tent p/person IR£4.25 - 4.50; hiker/ cyclist p/person IR£3.50 - 4.00; awning IR£1.50.
-- Credit cards accepted.

Open:
1 April - 30 September.

Address:
Fossa, Killarney, Co. Kerry.

Tel:
064 31497.
FAX: 064 34459.
E-mail: fossaholidays @tinet.ie.

Reservations:
Advised in high season; made for min. 3 nights with IR£10 deposit.

Alan Rogers' Discount

Less £1 per night in low season

FOSSA CARAVAN & CAMPING PARK

★ Ample hardstanding & electric hook-up ★ Separate tent area
★ Modern toilets ★ Shaving points ★ Hairdryers ★ Hot showers ★ Facilities for the disabled
★ Full laundry facilities ★ Campers kitchen ★ Free wash-up facilities
★ On site shop open 7 days Easter to Sept. ★ Restaurant (June-Aug) ★ Take away (July/Aug)
★ Children's playground ★ Tennis court ★ Games room ★ TV room ★ Bicycles for hire
★ Mobile homes for hire ★ Hostel accommodation

FOR FREE COLOUR BROCHURE WRITE TO:
Brosnan Family, Fossa Caravan & Camping Park, Fossa, Killarney, Co. Kerry, Ireland
Telephone: (064) 31497   Fax: (064) 34459

---

960 Glenross Caravan and Camping Park, Glenbeigh, Ring of Kerry

Immaculate small park on the edge of Glenbeigh Village.

Being situated on the spectacular Ring of Kerry and the Kerry Way gives this park an immediate advantage, and scenic grandeur around every bend of the road is guaranteed as Glenbeigh is approached. Quietly located before entering the village, its situation commands a fine view of Rossbeigh Strand, which is within walking distance. On arrival, a good impression is instantly created with the park well screened from the road and with new stone entrance and gates. Beyond the entrance stands a well maintained modern sanitary block which includes showers, and facilities for laundry and dishwashing. On site facilities include a games room, bicycle hire, public phone, a shelter for campers, a sun lounge and barbecue patio. There are 34 touring pitches including hardstanding pitches with electricity and, although there are six caravan holiday homes, the park is attractively laid out. Motorcaravan service point and chemical disposal. There is no catering on site but the Glenbeigh Hotel is popular and village shops are near. Watersports and tennis are near, riding and fishing 200 m. and golf 500 m. Not least is the Kerry Bog Village where you can go back in time in this reconstructed pre-famine village.

Directions: Park is on the N70 Killorglin - Glenbeigh road, on the right just before entering the village.

Charges 2000:
-- Per unit IR£3.00 - 3.50; adult IR£4.00; child (under 14) £1.00; awning IR£1.00 - 1.50; electricity (10A) IR£1.70 - 1.50; m/cyclist and tent IR£4.50 - 4.75; hiker and tent IR£4.00 - 4.50.
-- No credit cards.

Open:
5 May - 9 September.

Address:
Glenbeigh, Ring of Kerry.

Tel:
066 9768451 (May-Aug) or 064 31590 other times.
FAX: 064 37474.
E-mail: fwbcamping@ tinet.ie.

Reservations:
Write to site for details.

Alan Rogers' Discount

Less 50p per night in May, June & Sept

961 Mannix Point Camping and Caravan Park, Cahirciveen

Quiet and peaceful, beautifully located seashore park.

It is no exaggeration to describe Mannix Point as a nature lovers' paradise. It is situated in one of the most spectacular parts of the Ring of Kerry, overlooking the Portmagee Channel towards Valentia Island. Whilst the park is flat and open, it commands splendid views in all directions, it is right on marshland which teems with wildlife (2 acre nature reserve) and it has immediate access to the beach and seashore. The owner has planted around 500 plants with plans for around 1,000 more trees and shrubs. There are 42 pitches, 15 for tourers and 27 for tents, with electricity (6A) available. A charming old fisherman's cottage has been converted to provide reception. A cosy sitting room with turf fire, and 'emergency' dormitory for campers, is a feature of this site. Toilet facilities, now upgraded and immaculate, have well designed showers and free hot water. There is a modern campers' kitchen, laundry facilities, chemical disposal and motorcaravan service facilities. There is no television, but compensation comes in the form of a knowledgeable, hospitable owner who is a Bord Fáilte registered local tour guide. This park retains a wonderful air of Irish charm aided by occasional impromptu musical evenings. Watersports, bird watching, walking and photography can all be pursued here, but note that dogs are not allowed on site in June, July and August. Bicycle hire 800 m. riding 3 km, golf 14 km. Local cruises to Skelligs Rock with free transport to and from the port for walkers and cyclists. This is also an ideal resting place for people walking the Kerry Way.

Directions: Park is 250 m. off the N70 Ring of Kerry road, 800 m. southwest of Cahirciveen (or Cahersiveen) on the road towards Waterville.

Charges 1999:
-- Per adult IR£3.25 - 3.40; child IR£1.50 - 2.00; caravan or motorcaravan IR£1.00 - 2.00; tent no charge; electricity IR£1.00; hiker/cyclist, incl. tent IR£3.25 - 3.40; m/cyclist IR£3.50 - 3.90.
-- Book 7 nights, pay 6.
-- Reductions for groups if pre-paid.
Open:
15 March - 15 October, the rest of the year also, if you write first.
Address:
Cahirciveen, Co. Kerry.
Tel:
066 9472806.
FAX: as phone.
Reservations:
Made with deposit of one night's fee.

962 Fleming's White Bridge Caravan Park, Ballycasheen, Killarney

Family run, 9 acre, woodland park on eastern outskirts of Killarney.

Once past the county border, the main road from Cork to Killarney (N22) runs down the valley of the Flesk river. On the final approach to Killarney off the N22 Cork road, the river veers away from the road to enter the Lower Lake. On this prime rural position, between the road and the river, and within comfortable walking distance of the town, is Fleming's White Bridge. The ground is flat, landscaped and generously adorned with flowers, shrubs and trees. There are now 92 pitches (46 caravans and 46 tents) which extend beyond a wooden bridge to an area surrounded by mature trees and where a new toilet block, one of three, is sited. Facilities include a shop (1/6-1/9), two TV rooms, a games room, campers' shelter for wet weather, and two laundries. Hot water is free, there are also dishwashing sinks and chemical disposal facilities. This is obviously a park of which the owners are very proud. The family personally supervise the reception and grounds, maintaining high standards of hygiene, cleanliness and tidiness. There are six new luxury holiday mobile homes for hire, fishing (advice and permits provided), canoeing (own canoes), bicycle hire and woodland walks. Riding 3 km, golf 4 km. The park's convenient location, so close to Ireland's premier tourism centre does however mean that advance booking is advisable during peak summer months.

Directions: From Cork and Mallow: at N72/N22 junction continue towards Killarney and take first turn left (signed Ballycasheen Road). Proceed for 300 m. to archway entrance on left. From Limerick: follow N22 Cork road. After passing Super Valu and Killarney Heights Hotel take first right (signed Ballycasheen Road) and continue as above. From Kenmare: On N71, pass Gleneagles Hotel and Flesk Bridge. Turn right before Shell filling station into Woodlawn Road and Ballycasheen Road for continue 2 km. to archway.

Charges 2000:
-- Per unit IR£3.00 - 3.50; small tent/car or motorcaravan IR£2.50 - 3.00; adult IR£3.50; child (under 14 yrs) IR£1.00; awning IR£1.00 - 1.50; electricity (10A) IR£2.00 - 3.00; m/cyclist and tent IR£4.25 - 4.75; hiker or cyclist and tent IR£4.50 - 5.00.
-- Credit cards accepted.
Open:
17 March - 31 October.
Address:
White Bridge, Ballycasheen Road, Killarney, Co. Kerry.
Tel:
064 31590.
FAX: 064 37474.
E-mail: fwbcamping @tinet.ie.
Reservations:
Write to park with IR£5 non-refundable reservation fee, especially for peak periods.

Alan Rogers' Discount

 Less 50p per night

Kerry

963 White Villa Farm Caravan and Camping Park, Killarney

Small, welcoming park in scenic surroundings for tourers and campers only.

This is a very pleasing touring park on the N22 Killarney-Cork road. It is set in a 100 acre family operated dairy farm which stretches as far as the River Flesk, yet is only minutes away from Killarney town. Trees and shrubs surround the park but dominant is a magnificent view of the MacGillicuddy's Reeks. There are 25 pitches for caravans and tents, 15 with hardstanding and a grass area for awnings, electricity (10A), water points, rubbish disposal and night lighting. The toilet block, a sandstone coloured building to the rear of the park, is kept spotlessly clean. It houses showers (50p), a good toilet/shower room for disabled visitors, laundry area and dishwashing sinks. There is chemical disposal, a motorcaravan service area and clothes lines, plus a campers' kitchen with TV. In a central position is a children's play area, areas for basketball and a novelty is old school desks placed around the site, plus an antique green telephone box. Bicycle hire on site. Walking through the oak wood, fishing on the Flesk or visiting White Villa's Vintage Farm Museum are on site attractions. Leave the park and the scenic splendours, the allure of Killarney town and the National Park are 10 minutes away. Riding, golf and boat launching 5 km.

Directions: Travel 3 km. east from Killarney town on N22 Cork road. Park entrance is 500 m. east of N22/N72 junction. From Kenmare take R569 via Kilgarvan to the N22, then as above.

Charges 2000:
-- Per unit IR£2.00 - 3.00; adult IR£2.75; child under 14 yrs 75p, 14-18 yrs £1.25; m/cyclist incl. tent IR£3.50 - 4.00; hiker or cyclist incl. tent IR£3.25 - 3.50; electricity IR£1.00; awning IR£1.00 (July/Aug); extra tent IR£1.00 - 1.25.
-- No credit cards.

Open:
1 April - 16 October.

Address:
Cork Road (N22), Killarney, Co. Kerry.

Tel:
064 32456.

Reservations:
Made with £10 deposit in Irish or UK currency.

Alan Rogers' Discount

 Less 5% OR stay 6 nights, 7th free

964 The Flesk Muckross Caravan and Camping Park, Killarney

Seven acre park at gateway to National Park and Lakes, near Killarney town.

This family run park has undergone extensive development and offers high quality standards. Housed in one of Europe's most modern toilet blocks are well designed, heated shower and toilet areas, decorated in co-ordinating colours. Every detail has been added, including a vanity area with mirror and hair dryer and a baby bath/changing room. Pitches are well spaced and have electricity (10A), water, and drainage connections; 21 also have hardstanding with a grass area for awnings. Other on site facilities include petrol pumps, supermarket (all year), delicatessen and café (March - Oct) with extra seating on the sun terrace. There is also a laundry room, campers' kitchen with dishwashing sinks, a comfortable games room and chemical disposal point, plus night lighting and night time security checks. The grounds have been well cultivated with further shrubs, plants and an attractive barbecue and patio area. This is situated to the left of the sanitary block and is paved and sunk beneath the level roadway. Surrounded by a garden border, it has tables and chairs, making a pleasant communal meeting place which commands excellent views of Killarny's mountains. Fishing 300 m, boat launching 2 km. Winter caravan storage.

Directions: From Killarney town centre follow the N71 and signs for Killarney National Park. Site is 1½ km on the left beside the Gleneagle Hotel.

Charges 2000:
-- Per unit IR£3.00 - 3.50; adult IR£3.75; child (under 14) IR£1.00; small tent incl. 1 or 2 persons IR£2.50 - 3.00; hike or cyclist incl. tent IR£4.50 - 4.75; awning IR£1.50; electricity IR£1.75.
-- Credit cards accepted.

Open:
12 March - 31 October.

Address:
Muckross Road, Killarney, Co. Kerry.

Tel:
064 31704. FAX: 064 34681. E-mail: killarneylakes @tinet.ie.

Reservations:
Advised in peak periods.

965 Woodlands Park Touring Caravan and Camping Park, Tralee

Family run park in quiet setting minutes from Tralee centre.

Tralee is not only the Capital of County Kerry and gateway to the Dingle Peninsula, it is also Ireland's fastest growing visitor destination, with Woodlands its newest touring caravan park. Although only a ten minute walk from the town centre, this park is located on a 16 acre elevated site approached by a short roadway and bridge which straddles the River Lee. Once on site the town seems far removed for a countryside environment takes over. Hedging, trees, grazing fields and the distant Slieve Mish Mountain create the setting. The owners of Woodlands have ensured their park is designed and equipped to a high standard. A distinctive feature is its impressive yellow coloured building which houses an ''on top' family dwelling and ground floor services. This offers a spacious reception and information area, a café/snack bar, shop, games room, TV and adult room. The heated sanitary facilities, which are fully tiled with non slip flooring, include sizeable showers (50p token), washbasins and provision for disabled guests. There is a campers' kitchen, dishwashing sinks, a laundry room with washing machines and dryer, also a chemical disposal unit. Fifty pitches with hardstanding, electricity, water and drainage plus night light lie to the left and centre behind the main building, and a grass area for 40 tents is situated to the right. Young shrubs, cordyline trees and flower beds have been planted around the park and a security barrier is in operation. For children there is a fenced adventure park, or alternatively, the nearby Aqua Dome offers half price admission after 6 pm. Interesting is the award winning 'Kerry the Kingdom' museum with its incredible time car trip through the Middle Ages. Not least are the blue flag beaches on the Dingle Peninsula. Evening entertainment in Tralee means a selection of singing pubs, restaurants and the National Folk Theatre.

Directions: Site is 1 km. southwest of Tralee town centre. From N21/N69/N86 junction south of Tralee follow camp signs for 2.4 km. to park, 200 m. off the N86 Tralee - Dingle road.

Charges 1999:
-- Per unit incl. 2 adults IR£9.00 - 9.50; child (under 14 yrs) 75p; awning IR£1.50; tent incl. 1 or 2 persons IR£2.50 - 3.00; m/cyclist with tent IR£4.00 - 4.25; hiker or cyclist with tent IR£3.50 - 4.00; electricity (10A) IR1.20.

Open:
15 March - 31 October.

Address:
Dingle Road, Tralee, Co. Kerry.

Tel:
(066) 7121235.
FAX: (066) 7181199

Reservations:
Advisable for high season.

Woodlands Park

Touring Caravan & Camping Park
GRADE ★★★★

Recommended by AA, ADAC. ACSI, EUROPA, KOSMOS, ICCC, Caravan Club, ALAN ROGERS and our visitors.

Designed by campers, this family run park is located on a 16 acre parkland setting just a 10 minute walk from the centre of Tralee town, connected by bridge to the Aqua Dome (Ireland's biggest indoor waterworld). The facilities building has Euro style washrooms and shower blocks, Campers Kitchen, Laundry, Games Room, Café, TV Room and Reception. The 11 x 17 m. bays have hardstands and 10 amp electric with water and drains.

Half price admission to the Aqua Dome after 6 pm.

How to find us: From N21, N22 turn left after McDonalds and follow signs. From N69 follow signs for Dingle until Tralee marina, then turn left and straight past Aqua Dome for 200 m.

For travel further afield, remember the other ALAN ROGERS' titles –
the GOOD CAMPS GUIDES for FRANCE and EUROPE

★ Independent site assessors make regular monitoring visits

★ Consistently revised and updated – sites included on merit only

★ Discount vouchers for selected sites, ferries and tourist attractions

Jersey

Jersey Tourism

Liberation Square, St. Helier,

Jersey JE1 1BB

Tel: (01534) 500700 Fax: (01534) 500899

Guernsey and Herm

States of Guernsey Tourist Board

PO Box 13, White Rock

Guernsey

Tel: (01481) 723552

Sark

Sark Tourism Office

Sark (via Guernsey), Channel Islands.

Tel: (01481) 832345.

A visit to the Channel Islands offers a holiday in part of the British Isles, but in an area which has a definitely continental flavour. Of course, you don't need a passport or to change your money, although the proximity of the islands to the French coast might tempt one to take a day trip. All the islands have beautiful beaches and coves, pretty scenery and fascinating histories. Jersey is probably more commercially orientated, with more entertainment provided, while Guernsey will suit those who prefer a quieter, more peaceful holiday. For total relaxation, one of the smaller islands, such as Sark or Herm, where no cars are allowed, might appeal. Shopping in all the islands has the advantage of no mainland VAT - particularly useful for buying cameras, watches, jewellery and clothes.

Camping holidays on the islands are limited to TENTS only - caravans and motorcaravans are not permitted due to the narrow and sometimes crowded nature of the roads. Trailer tents (with canvas roof and walls) are permitted but on Jersey advance reservations must be made. Contact the Island Tourism authorities for more detailed information. Some of the parks we feature offer tents and camping equipment for hire, which may prove a popular option for some, and cars are also easily rented on the main islands.

Since all the parks cater solely for tents, rather than caravans or motorcaravans, this means that there tend to be very limited waste water emptying points and almost no chemical disposal facilities.

We are advised that on both Jersey and Guernsey, that political pressure is being placed for a change of policy in order to develop tourism. Guernsey is trying for caravans on the basis that, once they are on site, then only the car will run around the island, while Jersey is pushing for motorcaravans under a certain length. Both developments are likely to be some time off!

Travel between mainland Britain and the Channel Islands is not cheap, particularly if you take your car. However the Condor wave-piercing catamaran service has made travelling to the Channel Islands a very easy and much quicker proposition than ever before. We used this service, which now carries cars, and were most impressed, in respect of the speed (From Poole, Guernsey is only some 2½ hours travelling time, Jersey 1 hour longer), the comfort and the onboard service. These craft are surprisingly spacious with room to walk around (and even to go outside), a bar and snack bar and duty-free shopping facilities. Condor offer a range of fares, including a Family Saver deal. Condor may be contacted at:

Condor Ferries

Weymouth Quay, Weymouth,

Dorset DT4 8DX

Travel information and reservations:

Tel: (01305) 761551

Jersey Tourism - Events 2000

Jersey Jazz Festival, 6-9 April; European Open Karate Championships, 5-8 May; Jersey International Food Festival, 13-21 May; Jersey Festival Rose Show, 1-2 July; Jersey Garden Festival, 10-15 July; Battle of Flowers, 10 Aug; Battle of Flowers Moonlight Parade, 11 August; Foire de Jerri Country Show, 7-9 Sept; International Air Display, 14 Sept (prov).

971 Rozel Camping Park, St. Martin

Rurally situated park in quieter northeast of island, close to picturesque harbour.

This family owned park is within walking distance of the famous Jersey Zoo and the pretty harbour and fishing village of Rozel where the north coast cliff path commences. The surrounding countryside is quieter than many areas of the island. A car is probably necessary to reach the main island beaches, although a bus service does run to St Helier from close by. The park itself is quietly situated at the top of a valley (the French coast can be seen on a clear day) and is surrounded by trees providing shelter. There are two main camping areas providing 100 pitches of which some 20 are used for fully equipped tents for hire. Some pitches, mainly for smaller tents are arranged on terraced areas. The remainder are on a higher, flat field where pitches are arranged in bays with hedges growing to separate them into groups. Free parking is permitted by the tents and some electrical connections are available. Two heated sanitary buildings offer first rate facilities including excellent, free controllable showers with divider and good dry area, plentiful washbasins with mirror, shelf and shaver point and a bathroom for disabled people with a shower, toilet and washbasin in the lower block with an access ramp. A family shower room can be found in the upper block; hand dryers and a small heater for cooler weather. Dishwashing facilities are under cover, hot water is free throughout and there is a laundry and make up room. For entertainment there is a good play field with play equipment, an attractive, sheltered swimming pool (June-Sept) with children's pool and grass and terraced sunbathing areas, crazy golf, games room, reading room and TV and bicycle hire. A torch would be useful. Public telephone. Breakfast, evening meals and possibly takeaway are offered in high season (closed Mondays) and there is a shop. Fishing 1 mile, riding 3 miles, golf 4 miles. In addition to package deals for tent hire and travel, the site offers a good range of camping equipment for hire on a daily basis. Boats are only accepted on site by prior arrangement. No dogs are accepted.

Charges 2000:
-- Per person £4.40 - £6.60; child (3-11 yrs) half price; electricity £1.50.
-- Tent hire and travel packages.
-- Credit cards accepted.
Open:
19 April - 16 September.
Address:
Rozel, St. Martin, Jersey, Channel Islands JE3 6AX.
Tel:
(01534) 856797.
FAX: (01534) 856127.
Reservations:
Made for any length with £20 deposit; balance due 14 days before arrival.

Directions: On leaving the harbour by Route du Port Elizabeth, take A1 east through the tunnel and the A17. At the fourth set of traffic lights turn left on A6. Keep in the middle lane. Continue to Five Oaks and on to St Martin's church. Turn right, then immediately left at the `Royal' onto the B38 to Rozel and the park is on the right.

972 Beuvelande Camp Site, St Martin

Family run park with outstanding sanitary facilities.

What a pleasant surprise we had when we called here – the new sanitary building gives campers facilities normally associated with top class hotels. Tiled top to bottom and spotlessly clean, there are free, controllable showers, washbasins in vanity units with mirrors and electricity points, plus two fully equipped bathrooms for people with disabilities and a baby room. A licensed restaurant with covered terrace area is also situated in this building, open morning and evening at all times, but perhaps a few less hours at quiet times – 'if we are open we are open'. There are 150 pitches, 60 with fully equipped tents for hire, but with plenty of space for those with their own tents. Some electric hook ups are available and cars may be parked next to your tent. An outdoor heated pool (41 x 17 ft) has a sun terrace and simple play equipment is provided for children. Plenty of dishwashing facilities and a laundry can now be found in the original sanitary building, and a games room and TV room are provided. The well stocked shop is open 8 am. - 7 pm. during peak times and stocks gas. Ice pack and battery charging services are provided for a small charge. Car hire can be arranged and bicycle hire is possible from the site. Fishing, golf or riding within 3 km. This family run park prides itself on quality, cleanliness and hospitality.

Charges 2000:
-- Per adult £5.00 - £7.00; child 8-14 yrs £3.50, 2-8 yrs £2.50; dog £2.00.
-- Credit cards accepted.
Open:
1 May - 15 September.
Address:
St Martin, Jersey, Channel Islands JE3 6EZ.
Tel:
(01534) 853575, 852223 or 851156.
FAX: (01534) 857788.
Reservations:
Made with £30 deposit; contact park for details.

Directions: On leaving the harbour by Route du Port Elizabeth, take A1 east through the tunnel and the A17. At the fourth set of traffic lights turn left on A6. Continue to Five Oaks and on to St Martin's RC church, then right into La Longue Rue, right again Rue de L'Orme then left to site.

Guernsey

977 Vaugrat Camping, St Sampson's

Neat, well tended site, close to beach, in northwest of island.

Vaugrat is centred around attractive and interesting old granite farm buildings dating back to the 15th century, with a gravel courtyard and colourful flower beds. Owned by the Laine family, Vaugrat provides 150 pitches on flat grassy meadows, which are mostly surrounded by trees, banks and hedges to provide shelter. Tents are arranged around the edges of the fields, giving open space in the centre, and while pitches are not marked, there is sufficient room and cars may be parked next to tents. Only couples and families are accepted and the site is well run and welcoming. The site offers 25 fully equipped tents for hire. Housed in the old farmhouse, now a listed building, are the reception area, plus in the main season a shop (with ice pack hire) and upstairs Coffee Barn, with views to the sea, where breakfast is served. There is also a small games room with TV in the cider room complete with the ancient presses. The sanitary facilities are in two buildings, one of which is in the courtyard, with hot showers on payment, washbasins and hairdryers (on payment). There is a room here for disabled visitors with shower, basin and toilet (although there is a 6 inch step into the building). A laundry room here has a washing machine, dryer and iron. The other block is near the camping fields and provides toilets and washbasins in a row, set in a flat surface, plus one private cabin for ladies. Dishwashing facilities are housed in a room in this block with free hot water, with further sinks under cover outside. Chemical disposal. All these facilities are well kept and clean. A bus service is within easy reach and car or bicycle hire are arranged. Fishing, riding and golf within 1½ miles. Hotel and bar nearby. No dogs are accepted. A torch may be useful.

Charges 2000:
-- Per adult £5.25; child (under 14 yrs) £4.20; car or boat £1.05.
-- Families and couples only.
-- Fully equipped tents to hire.
-- Credit cards accepted.
Open:
1 May - 15 September.
Address:
St Sampson's, Guernsey, Channel Islands GY2 4TA.
Tel:
(01481) 57468.
FAX: (01481) 51841.
E-mail: adgould@globalnet.co.uk.
Reservations:
Made for independent campers for any length, with £10 deposit and balance on arrival. Hire details from site.

Directions: On leaving St Peter Port, turn right onto coast road for 1½ miles. At filter turn left into Vale Road. Straight over at two sets of lights then first left turn by church. Follow to crossroads (garage opposite) turn right. Carry on past Peninsula Hotel, then second left, signed for site. Site on left after high stone wall (400 yds) with concealed entrance.

978 Fauxquets Valley Farm Campsite, Castel

Attractive, rural site with good facilities in quiet, sheltered valley.

Situated in the rural centre of the island, Fauxquets is in a pretty valley, hidden down narrow lanes away from busy roads and is run by the Guille family. A car would be useful here to reach the beaches, St Peter Port and other attractions, although there is a bus service each day (20 mins walk). Once a dairy farm, there are still a few animals and hens for children to visit but the valley side has now been developed into an attractive camp site, with the old farm buildings as its centre. Plenty of trees, bushes and flowers have been planted to separate pitches and to provide shelter around the various fields which are well terraced. The 86 touring pitches are of a good size, most marked, numbered and with electricity. There are also 15 smaller places for backpackers. The site has 23 fully equipped trailer tents for hire. Sanitary facilities are good with modern, free, controllable hot showers, some washbasins set in flat surfaces, with others in private cabins and with a shower and baby bath for children. Hairdryers and irons are free. Dishwashing facilities are under cover, with free hot water and a tap to take away hot water. Laundry room with washing machine, dryer and free iron. In converted buildings around the farmhouse is a small shop with ice-pack hire and gas. The Haybarn licensed restaurant and bar provides (in high season, and for limited hours) breakfasts and evening meals. TV room, table tennis room, small children's play area and play field, nature walk, plus bicycle hire. Heated swimming pool (20 x 45 ft.) with a paddling pool and a shallow end. Fishing and boat launching 3 miles, riding and golf 2 miles. There is room to sit around the pool, including a large grassy terrace with sun-beds provided. A torch would be useful.

Charges 2000:
-- Per adult £4.40 - £5.10; child (at school) half price.
-- Fully equipped tents with fridge for hire.
-- Credit cards accepted.
Open:
Easter - 15 September.
Address:
Castel, Guernsey, Channel Islands.
Tel:
(01481) 255460.
FAX: (01481) 251797.
E-mail: fauxquets@campingguernsey.freeserve.co.uk.
Reservations:
Made for independent campers for any length, with £30 deposit. Tent hire details from site.

Directions: From St Peter Port harbour follow sign for Catel - St Andrew's. At top of hill, turn left at `filter in turn' into Queens Road, then right at another `filter in turn'. Follow road straight through traffic lights and down hill past Princess Elizabeth Hospital, through pedestrian lights and straight on at another set of lights at top of hill. Continue for ¾ mile, then turn right opposite at sign for German Underground Hospital. Fourth left is pedestrian entrance, cars 400 yds further on into gravel entrance.

983 Seagull Campsite, Herm Island

Small site on beautiful, peaceful island with no cars.

This tiny site, and indeed the island of Herm, will appeal to those who are looking for complete tranquillity and calm. Reached by boat (20 mins and approx. £6 return fare) from Guernsey, the 500 acre island allows only tractors on its narrow roads and paths (no bicycles either). One is free to stroll around the many paths, through farmland, heath and around the coast, where there are beautiful beaches. The campsite is a 20 minute uphill walk from the harbour, but your luggage will be transported for you by tractor. It consists of several terraced areas offering a total of 80 pitches, and 30 fully equipped tents for hire on flat grass areas. There are no electricity hook-ups. There is just a small, modern, but open, toilet block on site with WCs, hot showers (£1 payment - there is a shortage of water on Herm) and washbasins, plus shaver points, with a freezer for ice-packs. One may bring one's own tent and equipment or hire a tent and equipment (but not bedding, crockery and lighting) from the site. The harbour village is about ten minutes walk down the hill, where there is a small shop for provisions, gas, a post office, pub, restaurants and café. No dogs or pets are allowed. Fishing on the island. Herm is definitely not for those who like entertainment and plenty of facilities, but for total relaxation, with the absence of any bustle and noise it takes some beating!

Directions: Reached by boat from St Peter Port - report to Administration Office on arrival. Do not take your car as it is unlikely you will be able to park long term in St Peter Port.

Charges 1999:
-- Fixed site charge (irrespective of length of stay) incl. transportation of luggage £5.00.
-- Per adult £4.30; child (under 14 yrs) £2.15+.
-- Equipped tents for hire.
-- Credit cards accepted.

Open:
14 May - first w/end in September.

Address:
Herm Island,
Channel Islands
GY1 3HR.

Tel:
(01481) 722377.

Reservations:
Made for any length with £20 deposit. Details of hire tents from above address.

987 Pomme de Chien Campsite, Sark

Tiny, family oriented site in superb 'away from it all' setting.

The `island where time stands still' is an apt description of Sark, one of the smallest inhabited Channel Islands, some 45 minutes from Guernsey by boat. There is no airport, no cars or motorcycles and (apart from a tractor-drawn 'train' up Harbour Hill) the only transport is by bicycle or horse-drawn carriage. However everything you are likely to need for a tranquil holiday is provided with several small shops, pubs, hotels, restaurants, a Tourist Office and even two banks! Situated five minutes from the shops and ten from the beach, the Pomme de Chien campsite on Sark is tiny in terms of the number of pitches, totalling only 20, of which 8 are occupied by large, fully equipped frame tents (of excellent quality) available for rent. The remainder are for campers with their own tents (no caravans, motorcaravans or trailer tents of course). The pitches themselves are large, on fairly level ground, but none have electricity hook-ups. Planned for the '99 season is a new sanitary block with free hot showers, washbasins, dishwashing sinks under cover, hairdryers and public phone. This will enhance the warm welcome of the owners Chris and Jill Rang and the famous charm of Sark. Although you cannot take your car to the island, transport by the Condor service via Guernsey means you can get there in a little over three hours either with your own small tent or of course you could hire one of the site's own fully equipped ones (equipment includes everything you're likely to need except bedding and a torch). Baggage can be transferred from the Harbour right to the site by tractor trailer, at a cost of 60p per item. Fishing (10 mins. walk, bicycle hire (5 mins). Dogs are not accepted.

Directions: At the top of Harbour Hill turn left, first right, and follow the lane to the site entrance.

Charges 1999:
-- Per adult £4.50; child £2.50.
-- Hire tents from £160 per week.
-- No credit cards.

Open:
All year - independent campers June - Sept. for hire tents.

Address:
Sark, Channel Islands.

Tel:
(01481) 832316.

Reservations:
Write to site.

OPEN ALL YEAR

The following parks are understood to accept caravanners and campers all year round, although the list also includes some parks open for at least 10 months. It is always wise to phone the park to check as, for example, facilities available may be reduced.

England

West Country
002 Cardinney	*excl. Dec & Jan.*
006 River Valley	*excl. Jan & Feb*
010 Leverton Place	
037 Budemeadows	
044 Dolbeare	
080 Higher Longford	
081 Riverside	
089 Grange Court	*excl. 15/1-15/2*
091 Ross Park	*excl. Jan*
092 Finlake	
099 Kennford Int.	
135 Quantock Orchard	
140 Isle of Avalon	
141 Broadway House	*excl. Jan & Feb*
142 Southfork	
144 Baltic Wharf	
145 Bath Caravan Park	
148 Home Farm	
150 Long Hazel Int.	*excl. Jan & Feb*
151 Chew Valley	
167 Alderbury	
177 Binghams Farm	
181 Newlands	

South
202 Ulwell Cottage	*excl. 8/1-28/2*
203 Wareham Forest	
208 Merley Court	*excl. 8/1-28/2*
210 Sandford Park	*excl. 1/2-Easter*
228 Lytton Lawn	*excl. 6/1-28/2*
229 Sandy Balls	
232 Chichester	
245 The Orchards	*excl 2/1-12/2*
249 Kite Hill Farm	
260 Barnstones	
262 Wysdom	
275 Highclere Farm	*excl. Feb*
281 Chertsey	
289 White Rose	*excl. 14/1-15/3*
293 Sheepcote Valley	
294 Honeybridg	
295 Washington	
303 Tanner Farm	
304 Broadhembury	
305 Pine Lodge	
307 Canterbury	
309 Black Horse Farm	
312 Gate House Wood	*excl. 1-14 Jan*

London
322 Ashridge Farm	
326 Abbey Wood	
327 Crystal Palace	

East Anglia
330 The Grange	*excl. 3-31 Jan*
331 Low House	
342 Two Mills	*excl. 4/1-28/2*
358 Ferry Meadows	
369 Bainland	
373 Skegness Sands	

Heart of England
382 Darwin Forest	*excl. Jan & Feb.*
383 Firs Farm	
385 Rivendale	*excl. Feb*
390 Bosworth	
392 Riverside	
394 Smeaton's Lakes	
407 Somers Wood	
412 Briarfields	
421 Lickhill Manor	
430 Poston Mill	
439 Westbrook Park	
440 Stanmore Hall	
441 Beaconsfield Farm	
442 Severn Gorge	

Yorkshire
454 St Helens in the Park	
462 Rawcliffe Manor	
474 Jasmine Park	excl. Jan & Feb.

North West
528 Abbey Farm	
529 Royal Umpire	
532 Bridge House	*excl. 5/1-28/2*
535 Holgates	*excl. 7/11-20/12*

Cumbria
556 Sykeside	
557 Wild Rose	

Northumbria
576 Percy Wood	*excl. Feb*
580 Ord House	*excl. 10/1-8/3*

OPEN ALL YEAR

Wales

593 Cwmcarn Forest		633 Daisy Bank	*excl. Dec & Jan.*
595 Afon Lodge	*excl. 9/1-1/3*	659 Beddgelert	
604 Pencelli Castle		660 Bryn Gloch	
606 Tredegar House		668 James'	

Scotland

692 Cressfield	703 Gibson Park	
693 Brandedleys	724 Tullichewan	*excl. Nov*
695 Brighouse Bay	727 Auchterarder	
697 The Monk's Muir	768 Glenmore	excl. Nov
702 Aird Donald	785 Linnhe	

Northern Ireland

842 Tollymore Forest	851 Blaney
850 LoanEden	856 Gortin Glen

Republic of Ireland

870 Gateway	916 Moat Farm	
874 Cong	938 Parsons Green	
901 Shannon Cottage	939 Carrick-on-Suir	
908 Forest Farm	948 Blarney	
910 Camac Valley	961 Mannix Point	*but write first*

Channel Islands

987 Pomme de Chien

ADULTS ONLY

The following parks have made the decision not to accept children. For full details contact the parks.

001 Chacewater Park
151 Chew Valley Caravan Park
168 Plough Lane Caravan Site
344 Gatton Waters Lakeside Touring Site
342 Two Mills Touring Park
345 Little Haven Caravan and Camping Park
407 Somers Wood Caravan & Camping Park
461 Moorside Caravan Park
551 The Larches Caravan Park
633 Daisy Bank Touring Caravan Park

The following parks do not accept children at certain times or in certain areas of their site:

441 Beaconsfield Farm Touring Caravan Park (25 yrs) - high season only
380 Highfields Camping and Caravan Park - in one area only
440 Stanmore Hall Touring Park (21 yrs) - 31 grass pitches only

NATURIST PARKS

We feature just one naturist site in this guide: 024 Southleigh Manor Naturist Club

235

NO DOGS !

For the benefit of those who want to take their dogs with them and for those who do not like dogs on the parks they visit, we list here the parks which have indicated to us that they do not accept dogs. If you are planning to take your dog we do, however, advise that you phone the park first to check - there may be limits on numbers, breeds, etc. or times of the year when they are excluded.

NEVER: these parks do not accept dogs at any time.

020	Newquay Holiday Park	598	Moreton Farm
025	Pentewan Sands	604	Pencelli Castle
073	Twitchen Park	635	Barcdy
087	Beverley Holidays	782	Oban Divers
089	Grange Court	860	Bellemont
138	Blue Anchor	877	Parkland
149	Greenacres	882	Hodson Bay
212	Hoburne Park	941	The Apple
230	Ashurst	950	The Meadow
305	Pine Lodge	951	Eagle Point
306	Yew Tree	971	Rozel Camping Park
312	Gate House Wood	977	Vaugrat Camping
410	Cotswold Hoburne	983	Seagull Campsite
453	Northcliffe	987	Pomme de Chien
555	Limefitt Park		

SOMETIMES: these parks do not accept dogs at certain times of the year.

085	Galmpton	*off peak only; max. 2 per pitch*	452	Flower of May	*not in peak six weeks*
086	Ramslade	*not peak six weeks*	601	Cenarth Falls	*not in high season*
208	Merley Court	*not in high season*	629	Glan-y-Mor	*not in high seasons*
210	Sandford Park	*after 5 Sept only, and max. 1 per pitch*	910	Camac Valley	*not in July/August*
			915	River Valley	*not in July/August*
211	Pear Tree	*not in July/August*	961	Mannix Point	*not in June/July/August*

MAYBE: accepted at any time but with certain restrictions.

003	Ayr	*1 only (medium size)*	396	Silvertrees	*not certain breeds*
015	Sea View	*limited numbers/breeds*	420	The Boyce	*not certain breeds*
021	Hendra	*some areas only*	440	Stanmore Hall	*max. 2 per pitch*
022	Trevornick	*one area only*	441	Beaconsfield	*max. 2 per pitch*
029	Carlyon Bay	*some areas only*	442	Severn Gorge	*max. 2 per pitch*
038	Wooda Farm	*not certain breeds*	452	Flower of May	*only 1, not certain*
072	Easewell Farm	*max. 1 in high season*			*breeds (see above also)*
090	Widdicombe	*not certain breeds*	463	Ripley	*over 2 contact park*
093	Ashburton	*not certain breeds*	464	Goose Wood	*max. 2 per pitch*
095	River Dart	*max. 2 per pitch*	470	Nostell Priory	*max. 2 per pitch*
102	Oakdown	*not certain breeds*	476	Riverside Meadows	*max. 2 per pitch*
141	Broadway	*not certain breeds*	535	Holgates	*not certain breeds*
181	Newlands	*max. 2 per pitch*	554	Fallbarrow	*only 1 per booking*
204	Manor Farm	*at owner's discretion*	557	Wild Rose	*not certain breeds*
225	Bashley Park	*max. 1 per pitch*	571	Doe Park	*prior arrangement only*
226	International	*certain areas only*	576	Percy Wood	*not certain breeds*
228	Lytton Lawn	*max. 1 per pitch*	580	Ord House	*by prior arrangement,*
229	Sandy Balls	*certain areas only*			*not certain breeds*
231	Hollands Wood	*certain areas only*	636	Pen-y-Garth	*prior arrangement only*
247	Southland	*prior arrangement*	665	Hunter's Hamlet	*max. 2 per pitch; not*
257	Lincoln Farm	*max 2 per pitch*			*some breeds in high seasons*
290	Horam Manor	*max. 2 per pitch*	670	Ty Ucha	*not in certain areas*
330	The Grange	*max. 2; not some breeds*	731	Twenty Shilling	*max. 2 per pitch*
338	Clippesby	*max. 1 per pitch*	769	Torvean	*1 small dog only*
340	Old Brick Kilns	*max. 2 per pitch*	770	Pitgrudy	*max. 2 per pitch*
342	Two Mills	*prior arrangement only*	785	Linnhe	*max. 2 per pitch*
343	Kelling Heath	*max. 2 per pitch*	786	Glendaruel	*prior arrangement only*
351	Liffens	*max. 1 per pitch*	930	Morriscastle	*not in certain areas*

FISHING

We are pleased to include details of parks which provide facilities for fishing on the site. Many other parks, particularly in Scotland and Ireland, are in popular fishing areas and have facilities within easy reach. Where we have been given details, we have included this information in the individual site reports. It is always best to contact individual parks to check that they provide for your individual requirements.

ENGLAND

South West
006	River Valley Caravan Park
017	Trevella Caravan & Camping Park
022	Trevornick Holiday Park
025	Pentewan Sands Holiday Park
038	Wooda Farm Caravan & Camping Park
075	Minnows Camping & Caravan Park
077	Clifford Bridge Park
079	Harford Bridge Park
081	Riverside Caravan Park
092	Finlake Holiday Park
095	The River Dart Country Park
097	Cofton Country Holiday Park
137	Burrowhayes Farm
138	Blue Anchor Park
139	The Old Oaks Touring Park
142	Southfork Caravan Park
145	Bath Caravan Park
146	Lakeside Touring Caravan Park
148	Home Farm Holiday Park
174	Golden Cap Holiday Park
176	Wood Farm Caravan Park
178	Freshwater Beach Caravan Park

South
206	Wilksworth Farm Caravan Park
213	Grove Farm Meadow Holiday Park
229	Sandy Balls Holiday Centre
244	Adgestone Camping Park
245	The Orchards Holiday Caravan Park
261	Bo Peep Caravan Park
269	Wellington Country Park
281	Chertsey C&C Club Site
282	Horsley C&C Club Site
290	Horam Manor Touring Park
292	Bay View Caravan Park
303	Tanner Farm Caravan Park

East Anglia
321	Lee Valley Caravan Park
332	Lakeside Leisure Park
340	The Old Brick Kilns
343	Kelling Heath Holiday Park
344	Gatton Waters Touring Site
348	Little Lakeland Caravan Park
367	Lakeside Park
375	Foreman's Bridge Caravan Park

Heart of England
390	Bosworth Water Trust
392	Riverside Caravan Park
394	Smeaton's Lakes Touring Park
397	Glencote Caravan Park
410	Cotswold Hoburne Caravan Park
419	Kingsgreen Caravan Park
420	The Boyce Caravan Park
421	Lickhill Manor Caravan Park
430	Poston Mill Caravan Park
431	Luck's All Caravan Park
432	Broadmeadow Caravan Park

438	Fernwood Caravan Park
439	Westbrook Park
441	Beaconsfield Farm Caravan Park

Yorkshire
451	Thorpe Hall
461	Moorside Caravan Park
464	Goose Wood Caravan Park
466	Woodhouse Farm Caravan Park
470	Nostell Priory Holiday Park
472	Knight Stainforth Hall
473	Far Grange Park

North West and Cumbria
529	Royal Umpire Caravan Park
554	Fallbarrow Park
555	Limefitt Park
560	Pennine View Caravan Park

Northumbria
571	Doe Park Touring Caravan Park

WALES
592	The Bridge Caravan Park
593	Cwmcarn Forest Drive Campsite
597	Noble Court Holiday Park
631	Disserth Caravan Park
659	Forestry Commission - Beddgelert
660	Bryn Gloch Caravan Park
667	The Plassey Touring Park

SCOTLAND
691	Hoddom Castle Caravan Park
694	Forestry Commission - Caldons
695	Brighouse Bay Holiday Park
700	Strathclyde Country Park
726	Ardgartan Campsite
727	Auchterarder Caravan Park
766	Spindrift Caravan Park
771	Ardmair Point Caravan Park
772	Woodend Caravan Park
780	Resipole Farm Caravan Park
784	North Ledaig Caravan Park
785	Linnhe Caravan Park
786	Glendaruel Caravan Park

NORTHERN IRELAND
831	Carnfunnock Country Park
834	Drumaheglis Caravan Park
850	LoanEden Caravan Park
852	Share Holiday Village

IRISH REPUBLIC
877	Parkland Caravan Park
896	Lough Ree Caravan Park
930	Morriscastle Strand Caravan Park
938	Parsons Green Caravan Park
951	Eagle Point Caravan Park
956	Wavecrest Caravan Park
962	Flemings White Bridge
963	White Villa Farm Caravan Park

BICYCLES & MOUNTAIN BIKES

We understand that the following parks have bicycles to hire on site or can arrange for bicycles to be delivered. However, we would recommend that you contact the park to check as the situation can change.

ENGLAND

West Country
009 Trethem Mill Touring Park
011 Calloose Caravan Park
014 Penrose Farm Touring Park
025 Pentewan Sands Holiday Park
033 Killigarth Manor Caravan Park
036 Lakefield Caravan Park
069 Stowford Farm Meadows
078 Dartmoor View Holiday Park
100 Forest Glade Intl. Caravan Park
102 Oakdown Touring Park
104 Old Cotmore Farm
135 Quantock Orchard Caravan Park
141 Broadway House Caravan Park
149 Greenacres Camping
178 Freshwater Beach Caravan Park

South
205 Rowlands Wait Touring Park
210 Sandford Caravan Park
213 Grove Farm Meadow Holiday Park
214 Mount Pleasant Touring Park
225 Bashley Park
228 Lytton Lawn (Shorefield Country Park)
229 Sandy Balls Holiday Centre
258 Cotswold View Caravan Site

East Anglia
338 Clippesby Holidays
340 The Old Brick Kilns Caravan Park
356 Highfield Farm Camping Park
369 Bainland Country Park
375 Foreman's Bridge Caravan Park

Heart of England
380 Highfields Holiday Caravan Park
430 Poston Mill Caravan Park

Yorkshire
456 Golden Square Caravan Park
471 Rudding Caravan Park
472 Knight Stainforth Hall Caravan Park

North West and Cumbria
531 Pipers Height Caravan Park
555 Limefitt Park
557 Wild Rose Park

Northumbria
580 Ord House Country Park

SCOTLAND
695 Brighouse Bay Holiday Park
696 Crossburn Caravan Park
700 Strathclyde Country Park Caravan Site
723 Trossachs Holiday Park
724 Tullichewan HolidayPark
729 Craigtoun Meadows Holiday Park
786 Glendaruel Caravan Park

NORTHERN IRELAND
850 LoanEden Caravan Park
852 Share Holiday Village

IRISH REPUBLIC
874 Cong Caravan and Camping Park
879 Carra Caravan Park
901 The Shannon Cottage Caravan Park
913 Roundwood Caravan Park
923 Nore Valley Park
959 Fossa Caravan Park
959 Fossa Caravan Park
960 Glenross Caravan Park
962 Flemings White Bridge Caravan Park
963 White Villa Farm Caravan Park
964 The Flesk Muckross Caravan Park

CHANNEL ISLANDS
971 Rozel Camping Park
972 Beuvelande Camp Site
977 Vaugrat Camping
978 Fauxquets Valley Farm Campsite

There are facilities for the hire of bicycles within easy reach of many parks in this guide. When this information is available, and we have been given details, we have included this information in the individual site reports.

For the cyclist ...

Haynes Publishing's **Ride Your Bike** series of cycle guides takes you through the most scenic, traffic-free areas of Britain, including off-road rides for all abilities using numbered directions with routes clearly marked on Ordnance Survey Landranger mapping (spiral bound).

See inside cover pages for details.

GOLF

We understand that the following parks have facilities for playing golf on site. Where facilities are within easy reach and we have been given details, we have included this information in the individual site reports. However, we recommend that you contact the park to check that the facility meets your requirements.

England
022	Trevornick Holiday Park
038	Wooda Farm Caravan Park
069	Stowford Farm Meadows
072	Easewell Farm Holiday Park
101	Lady's Mile Touring Park
225	Bashley Park
367	Lakeside Park
369	Bainland Country Park
407	Somers Wood Caravan Park
430	Poston Mill Caravan Park
452	Flower of May Holiday Park
471	Rudding Caravan Park

Wales
667	The Plassey Touring Park

Scotland
691	Hoddom Castle Caravan Park
695	Brighouse Bay Holiday Park
700	Strathclyde Country Park
769	Torvean Caravan Park
780	Resipole Farm Caravan Park

Northern Ireland
831	Carnfunnock Country Park

Irish Republic
877	Parkland Caravan Park
915	River Valley Caravan Park
948	Blarney Caravan Park

HORSE RIDING

We understand that the following parks have horse riding stables on site. Where facilities are within easy reach and we have been given details, we have included this information in the individual site reports. However, we would recommend that you contact the park to check that the facility meets your requirements.

England
036	Lakefield Caravan Park
038	Wooda Farm Caravan Park
069	Stowford Farm Meadows
092	Finlake Holiday Park
137	Burrowhayes Caravan & Camping Site
178	Freshwater Beach Caravan Park
262	Wysdom Touring Park
290	Horam Manor Touring Park

Scotland
695	Brighouse Bay Holiday Park
730	Blair Castle Caravan Park

Northern Ireland
850	LoanEden Caravan Park

Irish Republic
916	Moat Farm Caravan Park

BOAT LAUNCHING

We understand that the following parks have boat slipways on site. Where facilities are within easy reach and we have been given details, we have included this information in the individual site reports. However, we would recommend that you contact the park to check that the facility meets your requirements.

England
025	Pentewan Sands Holiday Park
175	Highlands End Farm Holiday Park
269	Wellington Country Park
390	Bosworth Water Trust
421	Lickhill Manor Caravan Park
531	Pipers Height Caravan Park
532	Bridge House Marina
554	Fallbarrow Park

Scotland
695	Brighouse Bay Holiday Park
700	Strathclyde Country Park
726	Ardgartan Campsite
771	Ardmair Point Caravan Park
780	Resipole Farm Caravan Park
784	North Ledaig Caravan Park
785	Linnhe Caravan Park

Northern Ireland
831	Carnfunnock Country Park
834	Drumaheglis Caravan Park
850	LoanEden Caravan Park
852	Share Holiday Village

Irish Republic
877	Parkland Caravan & Camping Park
896	Lough Ree (East) Caravan Park
951	Eagle Point Caravan & Camping Park
956	Wavecrest Caravan & Camping Park

Gerry and Chris Bullock's Page

First of all who are Gerry and Chris, and why give them a page in this guide?

Chris and Gerry have been motorhome owners for more years than they care to remember but, in the mid seventies Chris suffered a serious back injury which has worsened over the past ten years, taking away her ability to walk any distance more than within the motorhome or around the house, and otherwise she is wheelchair bound. They have, therefore, over the years become 'experts' in finding parks with good facilities for the wheelchair bound.

We felt that it might be useful for other readers of the guide to learn something of their experiences or indeed be able to tap their experience directly. They are very happy for us to include their address and phone number at the end of this article should you wish to contact them.

As you will be aware, we always include reference to facilities provided by the parks in our Guide but have not felt ourselves qualified to assess these facilities. Below we have listed what Gerry and Chris look at when they assess a park with few examples of what they have found.

Firstly, they look at the access to the sanitary blocks:

- Are they accessible for wheelchair bound campers or walking disabled campers?
- Are door widths adequate for wheelchairs, are there steps for the walking disabled?

Secondly, what does the room offer?

- WC with handrails
- Levers on taps
- Lights with cords
- Obstructions in the room
- Handrails in the shower

- Sink accessible by wheelchair
- Handrails at the sinks
- Emergency alarm cord
- The shower and its access

Thirdly, access checks to other facilities.

- Washing up areas (even less abled persons like to help).
- Games room
- Reception (Chris likes a chance to pay the bill!)
- Bars and restaurants (why can't we all enjoy ourselves?)
- Clubs and other amenities

Fourthly, the pitches

- Where are they in relation to the facilities?
- Terraced or level?
- Conditions of paths. - gravel/tarmac/sleeping police men
- Ground - level, sloping or hilly?

For example:

One park, recently assessed by Gerry and Chris, came out well with its ramped accesses to all bars, the shop, the takeaway and reception; also for the Radar key system for the sanitary facilities. It did not score not so well with some of the paths and roadways which connect the facilities - some were unmade and difficult for wheelchair pushers (this is an area the site now hopes to address). There were also some problems with the pitches as the park is based on heathland and is consequently somewhat bumpy. Perhaps the site will be able to specially level a pitch close to the facilities. At least their attention has been drawn to some of the problems experienced by wheelchair users and the walking disabled, which they maybe able to improve. They recommend both the Caravan Club and the Camping and Caravanning Club as having good, well designed and maintained facilities.

These are the sorts of things which Gerry and Chris look at so, if you have queries concerning sites and the suitability of their facilities or would like suggestions, or have any recommendations, please contact them They would like to hear from you.

Gerry and Chris Bullock's address is:
97 Stalham Road, Hoveton, Norwich, Norfolk NR12 8EF Telephone. 01603 784152

NOTE. They advise that they are not looking at facilities for persons with special needs. They leave this to the uch people as the Sue Ryder Foundation, etc. which cater very well in this field.

Following recent visits, Gerry and Chris have made the following comments:

258 Cotswold View Caravan Park
(page 88) Excellent en-suite facilities - nice wide door, no kerbs, roadways tarmac and hardcore, woodland walk suitable for wheelchairs, nice level site.

282 Horsley C&C Club Site
(page 91) Excellent en-suite facilities , tarmac and hardcore roadways, site level.

281 Chertsey C&C Club Site
(page 90) Good en-suite facilities with ramp, tarmac roadways, level site, ground very soft when wet so can be hard to push wheelchairs.

288 Raylands Caravan Park
(page 92) Good en-suite facilities, tarmac roadways, good level site.

293 Sheepcote Valley Caravan Club Site
(page 94) Superb en-suite facilities - well laid out, all roads tarmac, kerbs lowered at all access points, walking disabled facilities in able-body block, site level and easy for wheelchairs, loose shingle on some pitches, some hardstandings.

325 Lee Valley Campsite
(page 101) Two superb en-suite units, tarmac roadways, level site, access to all areas, some hardstandings.

339 The Dower House Touring Park
(page 106) Good en-suite facilities, site bumpy for wheelchairs, roads hardcore some pot-holes.

340 The Old Brick Kilns C&C Park
(page 110) Good en-suite facilities, roadways hardcore, no kerbs, level site, quite good on site for wheelchairs.

343 Kelling Heath Holiday Park
(page 108) Excellent facilities - separate WC and shower rooms, kerbs lowered at access points, slight ramp up to facilities, site quite bumpy for wheelchairs, roadways tarmac and hardcore, access to all areas, no hardstandings.

355 Old Manor Caravan Park *(page 112)*
Toilet facilities in 'portacabin' up ramp, roadways tarmac and hardcore, site bumpy for wheelchairs, slight climb up to facilities block.

906 Green Gables C&C Park *(page 212)*
Excellent facilities, good paths around and up to the facilities block, hardcore roadways assistance needed, access to all areas including coffee bar, some hardstandings (hardcore).

915 River Valley C&C Park *(page 214)*
One of the best facilities used, all roads tarmac, slight hill out of site, access to all areas, site easy for wheelchairs, some hardstandings.

930 Morriscastle Strand C&C Park
(page 217) Good facilities, site sloping, tarmac roads, assisstance needed with wheelchairs.

mark hammerton
travel

family camping in france
we see things differently

We offer ready-erected, stylish 4 bedroom tents and 3 bedroom luxury mobile homes. They're brand new, state-of-the-art and come fully-equipped (down to the corkscrew). **Just turn up and move in!**

Our sites are small, friendly and convenient for the beaches of Brittany, the Vendee or Charentes. Most are simply not big enough for mass-market camping operators (though all are good enough to be included in this guide).

All our sites have excellent swimming pools, many with water slides, and we keep numbers low to preserve the sites' own character. But you will find mature courier couples, seasoned campers themselves, on hand to help you **enjoy your holiday.**

With incredibly low cross-Channel rates, total flexibility (depart any day of the week, visit as many sites as you like), a comprehensive Travel Pack and an experienced team it makes sense to **see things differently in 2000.**

FROM **£189**

12 nights tent holiday for 2 adults and up to 4 children starting 10th May, including return Channel crossing

See for yourself!
For full details and a virtual tour of our accommodation visit www.markhammerton.com

make it easy on yourself

For your free brochure
01892 52 54 56
Quote AR00

e-mail: enquiries@markhammerton.com

We'll organise your Channel crossing

SAVE TIME   SAVE MONEY

THE ALL NEW PITCH AND FERRY RESERVATION SERVICE FOR READERS

We'll book your preferred campsite(s)
Choose from over 100 sites featured in the Alan Rogers Guide to France (look for the Travel Service logo alongside the site descriptions).

We'll organise your Channel crossing
With direct links to all major cross-Channel operators, we have access to superb rates.

We'll provide comprehensive information
We know France. And we know camping. Our own unique Travel Pack, complete with guide book, will prove invaluable.

THE ALAN ROGERS'
travel service

SAVE MONEY
FROM
£299
12 nights pitch fees with Dover-Calais ferry for car + caravan

So don't leave it to chance - leave it to us

FOR A FREE BOOKING GUIDE CALL NOW ON

01892 61 51 41

quoting ARUK or return the coupon

☑ **Yes, I am interested in saving money!**
Please send me details about the *all new* Alan Rogers Travel Service

Name_____

Address_____
_____

THE ALAN ROGERS'
travel service

6-8 Garden Street, Tunbridge Wells TN1 2XB   travelservice@alanrogers.com   www.alanrogers.com

REPORTS BY READERS

We always welcome reports from readers concerning parks which they have visited. Generally reports provide us with invaluable feedback on parks already featured in the Guide or, in the case of those not featured in our Guide, they provide information which we can follow up with a view to adding them in future editions.

However, if you have a complaint about a site, this should be addressed to the campsite owner, preferably in person before you leave.

Please make your comments either on this form or on plain paper. It would be appreciated if you would indicate the approximate dates when you visited the park and, in the case of potential new parks, provide the correct name and address and, if possible, include a park brochure. Send your reports to:

Deneway Guides & Travel Ltd, Chesil Lodge, West Bexington, Dorchester DT2 9DG

Name of Park and Ref. No. (or address for new recommendations):

....

....

Dates of Visit: ....

Comments:

Reader's Name and Address: ....

....

....

....

TOWN and VILLAGE INDEX

ENGLAND

Abbey Wood 102
Acle 107
Adderbury 89
Allerston 136
Alnwick 157
Alsop-en-le-Dale 119
Ambergate 119
Ambleside 149
Appleby-in-Westmorland . .154
Ashbourne 118, 119
Ashburton 42-45
Ashford 97
Ashurst 81
Ashwell 102

Baldock 102
Bamburgh 157
Banbury 87, 89
Barden 141
Barmer Hall 109
Barnard Castle 159
Barnstaple 55
Bath 63, 64
Battle 95
Battlefield 130
Beaconsfield 90
Bearsted 99
Bellingham 158
Belper 119
Bere Regis 72, 73
Berrow 125
Berwick-upon-Tweed 158
Bethesda 27
Bickington 44
Birchington 97
Birmingham 124, 125
Bishop Sutton 63
Bishopdale 143
Blackawton 37
Blackpool 146, 147
Blandford Forum 74
Blue Anchor 57
Bodmin 31, 32
Boston 117
Bournemouth 77, 78
Bowness 152
Bratton Fleming 55
Bridgnorth 130
Bridlington 132
Bridport 67-69
Brighton 94
Bristol 63
Brixham 38
Brockenhurst 80
Bude 31, 33
Burford 95
Burgh Castle 105
Burnham-on-Sea 59
Burton Bradstock 67
Buxton 120

Cambridge 113
Camelford 32
Canterbury 96
Capernwray 148
Carlisle 153
Carlyon Bay 27
Carnforth 148
Carnon Downs 15

Cayton 134
Chacewater 11
Charlbury 88
Charmouth 66-69
Cheddar 61
Cheddleton 122
Cheltenham 123
Cheriton Bishop 46
Chertsey 90
Chichester 83
Chickerell 70
Chideock 68
Chingford 101
Chippenham 64, 65
Christchurch 77, 78
Chudleigh 43
Cirencester 123
Clippesby 107
Colchester 103
Colliford Lake 32
Combe Martin 55
Comberton 113
Cotherstone 159
Coventry 124
Crantock 18
Cromer 109
Croston 146
Crowcombe 58
Crows an Wra 10
Crystal Palace 100
Cullompton 51

Darley Moor 120
Dartmouth 37
Dawlish 49, 50
Densole 95
Dial Post 93
Dobbs Weir 101
Dorchester 70
Dover 95
Drewsteignton 46
Driffield 132
Dulverton 56
Dunstan 157

East Anstey 47
East Bergholt 103
East Harling 106
East Horsley 91
East Ord 158
East Runton 109
East Stoke 72
Eastbourne 93
Ellesmere 129
Emsworth 83
Epping 101
Erpingham 111
Evesham 127
Exebridge 56
Exeter 48
Exmouth 51
Eype 68

Fakenham 109, 110
Falmouth 15
Fangfoss 138
Fenny Bentley 118
Fishtoft 117
Folkestone 95
Follifoot 140
Fordingbridge 79

Fowey 26
Foxhall 104
Freshwater 86

Galmpton 38
Garstang 147
Glastonbury 60
Godmanchester 113
Godshill 79
Goonhavern 16
Gorran 25
Grafham 112
Great Bourton 87
Great Yarmouth 105
Greenbottom 13
Guildford 91

Halesowen 125
Halestown 9
Harleston 106
Harome 136
Harrogate 137, 140
Hayle 12
Helmsley 135, 136
Helston 14
Hereford 128
Hexham 158
High Hawsker 133
Hillington 110
Hoddesdon 101
Holton Heath 76
Holywell Bay 20
Honeybourne 127
Horam 93
Horsham 92, 93
Hull 131
Huntingdon 112, 113
Hurn 78

Ilfracombe 54, 55
Ipplepen 41
Ipswich 104

Kennack Sands 14
Kennford 48
Kings Lynn 110
Kingsbridge 35, 36
Kingsnorth 97
Kingsteignton 43
Kington Langley 65
Kirkby Stephen 155
Kirkbymoorside 135

Lacock 64
Landrake 30
Lanlivery 28
Lebberston 133
Leedstown 12
Leek 122
Leyburn 141, 143
Lincoln 114
Linwood 82
Little Barney 110
Littlehampton 92
London 97-99
Longleat 65
Looe 28-30
Lostwithiel 28
Louth 115, 116
Ludlow 129
Lyme Regis 66-69
Lymington 82

Town and Village Index

Lyndhurst 81
Lyneal 129

Mablethorpe 116
Maidstone 98, 99
Malvern 125
Manby 116
Marden 98
Margate 97
Market Bosworth 125
Market Rasen 114
Martin Mill 95
Martock 61
Matlock 120
Mawgan 14
Mealsgate 153
Melplash 69
Meriden 124
Mevagissey 23-26
Milford on Sea 82
Minehead 56-58
Modbury 36
Moorshop 34
Mordiford 128
Morpeth 156
Mortehoe 53

Nateby 147
Nether Heage 119
New Milton 78
Newark on Trent 121
Newbiggin 143
Newbridge 83
Newchurch 85
Newquay 17-24
Newton Abbot 41-44
North Somercotes 115
North Walsham 111
North Wootton 59
Norwich 111
Nostell 140

Okehampton 45, 46
Organford 76
Ormesby St Margaret 105
Ormskirk 145
Oswaldkirk 135
Owermoigne 70

Padstow 30
Paignton 38-40
Patterdale 151
Peel 147
Pelynt 28
Penrith 151-155
Pentewan 26
Penzance 10, 12
Perranporth 16
Peter Tavy 34
Peterborough 112
Peterchurch 128
Petham 96
Pevensey Bay 94
Pickering 136
Plymouth 35
Polperro 29
Polruan 26
Poole 73-76
Pooley Bridge 150
Porlock 57
Poughill 31
Poundstock 33

Preston 146, 147
Priddy 62
Ravenglass 150
Reading 89
Rejerrah 18
Relubbus 12
Ringwood 80-82
Ripley 137
Ripon 144
Riseley 89
Romsley 125
Ross-on-Wye 127
Rudston 132
Rugeley 122
Ryde 86

Salisbury 66
Saltash 33
Sampford Peverell 47
Sandown 84, 85
Saxmundham 104
Scarborough 133-137
Sedlescombe 95
Seer Green 90
Settle 143
Shaldon 50
Sheldon 51
Shepton Mallet 59
Sheringham 108
Shrewsbury 130
Sidmouth 52
Silverdale 148
Skegness 115
Skipsea 132
Skipton 141, 142
Slapton 36
Snainton 137
Sourton Cross 45
South Cave 131
South Cerney 123
South Muskham 121
South Petherton 61
Southbourne 83
Southwater 92
Spalding 117
Sparkford 62
St Austell 27
St Buryan 10
St Columb Major 17, 24
St Ives 9, 10
St Just-in-Roseland 24
St Leonards 80, 81
St Mabyn 31
St Martins by Looe 30
St Mawes 24
St Neot 32
Standlake 87
Stanford Bishop 126
Starcross 50
Stoke Gabriel 38
Stokenham 35
Stourport-on-Severn 126
Strensall 138
Sutton St James 117
Sutton-on-Sea 116
Sutton-on-the-Forest 139
Swaffham 111
Swanage 71
Swarland 156

Syderstone 109

Taunton 58
Tavistock 34
Tebay 155
Tedburn St Mary 48
Teignmouth 50
Telford 128
Tewkesbury 124
Thetford 106
Thornton Cleveleys 146
Threemilestone 11
Threshfield 142
Tiverton 47
Totnes 37
Truro 11-16
Tuxford 121
Tweedale 128
Two Dales 120
Two Mile Oak 42

Ulwell 71

Ventnor 85

Wakefield 140
Wareham 72, 75
Warminster 65
Washington 93
Watermillock 153
Wells 62
West Down 54
West Luccombe 57
Weston 52
Weybourne 108
Weymouth 70
Whaddon 66
Whiddon Down 46
Whitby 133
Wick 60, 92
Williton 58
Wimborne Minster 73, 75
Windermere 151, 152
Winksley 144
Winsford 56
Witney 87
Woodbury 51
Woodhall Spa 114
Wool 75
Woolacombe 53, 54
Wootton Bridge 86
Worcester 126
Worksop 121
Wortwell 106
Wrotham Heath 99
Wroxall 85
Wykeham 134

Yarmouth 83
Yeovil 62
York 138, 139

WALES

Aberaeron 168
Abergele 175
Aberystwyth 168, 169
Anglesey 174
Bala 171
Beddgelert 172
Betws Garmon 173
Brecon 167
Builth Wells 169

Town and Village Index

Caernarfon 173
Carmarthen 163
Cenarth 166
Churchstoke 170
Clarach Bay 168, 169
Colwyn Bay 174
Criccieth 172
Cwmcarn 161

Dingestow 160
Disserth 170

Eyton 176

Fishguard 165, 166

Harlech 171
Hundred House 169

Llanaber 171
Llanddulas 174
Llandeilo 163
Llandovery 162
Llandrindod Wells 170
Llanelli 162
Llangadog 163
Llangollen 175
Llanychaer 165
Llanystumdwy 172

Marianglas 174
Monmouth 160

Narberth 164
Newcastle Emlyn 166
Newport 161, 166

Pembrey 162
Pembroke 165
Pencelli 167

Rhandirmwyn 162
Ruabon 176

Saundersfoot 164
St Clears 163

Talsarnau 171

Wrexham 176

SCOTLAND

Aberfoyle 186
Aberlour 191
Acharacle 197
Achnairn 193
Alyth 187
Ardgartan 186
Ardmair Point 194
Arrochar 186
Auchterarder 187
Aviemore 192

Balloch 185
Balmacara 195
Barcaldine 197
Blair Atholl 188
Blairgowrie 187
Blairlogie 189
Borgue 180
Bothwell 184

Comrie 189
Connel 197, 198
Corpach 199
Crianlarich 185
Crieff 189
Crocketford 179

Dornoch 194
Dufftown 191
Dumfries 179

Ecclefechan 177
Edinbane 194
Edinburgh 182-184

Faichem 196
Fort William 198, 199

Glasgow 184
Glencoe 196
Glendaruel 199
Glenmore 192
Grantown-on-Spey 192

Haddington 182
Huntly 190

Invercoe 196
Invergarry 196
Inverness 191

Kirkcudbright 180

Lairg 193
Little Kildrummie 191
Lockerbie 177, 178
Luib 185

Maybole 181
Melrose 181
Mintlaw 190
Motherwell 184
Musselburgh 183

Nairn 191
Nether Coul 187

Oban 197, 198

Peebles 182
Peterhead 190
Pitlochry 188

Roslin 184

Scourie 193
Skye 193-195
St Andrews 188
Staffin 195
Stirling 189
Strachur 199
Stranraer 180
Strontian 197

Tarbet 186

Ullapool 194

NORTHERN IRELAND

Ballymoney 202
Blaney 205
Bushmills 202
Coleraine 203
Drain's Bay 201
Enniskillen 205
Gortin 204
Kesh 205
Larne 201
Lisnaskea 206
Muckross Bay 205
Newcastle 204
Omagh 204
Smith's Strand 206

REPUBLIC OF IRELAND

Achill Island 209

Annamult 216
Athlone 211
Athy 215

Ballina 208
Ballinode 207
Ballycasheen 227
Ballykeeran 211
Ballylickey 223
Ballymacoda 222
Bantry Bay 223
Belcarra 210
Bennettsbridge 216
Blarney 221

Caherdaniel 224
Cahir 219
Cahirciveen 227
Carrick-on-Suir 219
Castlebar 210
Castlegregory 224
Clogheen 220
Clonea 218
Cong 208
Connemara 208
Crookhaven 223

Donard 215
Dublin 213
Dungarvan 218

Geashill 212
Glandore 222
Glenbeigh 226

Healy Pass 225

Keel 209
Kilcornan 220
Kilkenny 217
Killarney 226-228
Kilmacanogue 214
Kilmuckridge 217
Kiltoom 211
Knock 210

Lauragh 225
Limerick 220

O'Brien's Bridge 221
Omeath 212

Portlaoise 216
Portsalon 206

Redcross Village 214
Rosses Point 207
Roundwood 213

Sligo 207

Tralee 229
Tramore 218
Tullamore 212

Warrenpoint 212
Waterville 225
Westport 209
Wicklow 213, 214

Youghal 222

CHANNEL ISLANDS

Castel 232
Herm Island 233
Sark Island 233
St Martin 231
St Sampson's 232

INDEX

map ref   page

ENGLAND

Cornwall

005 Polmanter Tourist Park . . . . .Ff . . .9
002 Cardinney Camping Park . . . . .Ff . .10
003 Ayr Holiday Park . . . . .Ff . .10
004 Trevalgan Holiday Farm . . . . .Ff . .10
001 Chacewater Park . . . . .Ff . .11
010 Leverton Place Caravan Park . . . . .Ff . .11
006 River Valley Caravan Park . . . . . . .Ff . .12
011 Calloose Caravan Park . . . . .Ff . .12
013 Liskey Touring Park . . . . .Ff . .13
007 Silver Sands Holiday Park . . . . . . .Ff . .14
039 Trelowarren Touring Park . . . . . . .Ff . .14
008 Maen Valley Holiday Park . . . . . . .Ff . .15
018 Carnon Downs Caravan Park . . . . .Ff . .15
012 Silverbow Park . . . . .Ff . .16
014 Penrose Farm Touring Park . . . . . .Ff . .16
031 Trekenning Tourist Park . . . . .Ff . .17
017 Trevella Caravan Park . . . . .Ff . .18
016 Newperran Tourist Park . . . . .Ff . .18
022 Trevornick Holiday Park . . . . .Ff . .20
021 Hendra Holiday Park . . . . .Ff . .21
020 Newquay Holiday Park . . . . .Ff . .22
025 Pentewan Sands Holiday Park . . . . .Gf . .23
041 Pengrugla Park . . . . .Ff . .23
009 Trethem Mill Touring Park . . . . . . .Ff . .24
024N Southleigh Manor Naturist Club . .Ff . .24
015 Sea View International . . . . .Ff . .25
026 Penhaven Touring Park . . . . .Gf . .26
019 Polruan Holiday Centre . . . . .Gf . .26
029 Carlyon Bay Caravan Park . . . . . . .Gf . .27
028 Powderham Castle Tourist Park . . . .Gf . .28
040 Trelay Farmpark . . . . .Gf . .28
042 Looe Valley Holiday Park . . . . . . .Gf . .29
033 Killigarth Manor Caravan Park . . . .Gf . .29
032 Polborder House Caravan Park . . . .Gf . .30
043 Trerethern Touring Park . . . . .Ff . .30
023 Glenmorris Park . . . . .Gf . .31
038 Wooda Farm Park . . . . .Gg . .31
030 Colliford Tavern Campsite . . . . . . .Gf . .32
036 Lakefield Caravan Park . . . . .Gf . .32
037 Budemeadows Touring Park . . . . . .Gg . .33
044 Dolbeare Caravan Park . . . . .Gf . .33

Devon

079 Harford Bridge Park . . . . .Gf . .34
080 Higher Longford Farm . . . . .Gf . .34
081 Riverside Caravan Park . . . . .Gf . .35
104 Old Cotmore Farm . . . . .Gf . .35
082 Moor View Touring Park, ...Gf . .36
083 C&C Club Site Slapton . . . . .Gf . .36
084 Woodlands Leisure Park . . . . .Gf . .37
085 Galmpton Touring Park . . . . .Gf . .38
086 Ramslade Touring Park . . . . .Gf . .38
087 Beverley Holidays . . . . .Gf . .39
089 Grange Court Holiday Centre . . . . .Gf . .40
090 Widdicombe Farm Tourist Park . . . .Gf . .40
091 Ross Park . . . . .Gf . .41

088 Dornafield . . . . .Gf . .42
093 Ashburton Caravan Park . . . . .Gf . .42
092 Finlake Holiday Park . . . . .Gf . .43
094 Holmans Wood Caravan Park . . . . .Gf . .43
095 The River Dart Country Park . . . . .Gf . .44
098 Lemonford Caravan Park . . . . .Gf . .44
096 Parker's Farm Holiday Park . . . . . .Gf . .45
076 Bundu Caravan Park . . . . .Gf . .45
077 Clifford Bridge Park . . . . .Gf . .46
078 Dartmoor View Holiday Park . . . . .Gf . .46
074 Zeacombe House Caravan Park . . .Gg . .47
075 Minnows Caravan Park . . . . .Hg . .47
099 Kennford Caravan Park . . . . .Gf . .48
105 Springfield Holiday Park . . . . .Gf . .48
109 Peppermint Park . . . . .Gf . .49
101 Lady's Mile Touring Park . . . . . . .Gf . .49
097 Cofton Country Holiday Park . . . . .Gf . .50
108 Coast View Holiday Park . . . . . . .Gf . .50
100 Forest Glade Int. Caravan Park . . . .Hg . .51
110 Webbers Farm Caravan Park . . . . .Hf . .51
102 Oakdown Touring Park . . . . .Hf . .52
072 Easewell Farm Holiday Park . . . . .Gg . .53
073 Twitchen Park . . . . .Gg . .53
071 Hidden Valley Touring Park . . . . . .Gg . .54
107 Woolacombe Bay Holiday Park . . .Gg . .54
069 Stowford Farm Meadows . . . . .Gg . .55
070 Greenacres Touring Caravan Park . .Gg . .55

Somerset

146 Lakeside Touring Park . . . . .Gg . .56
136 Halse Farm Caravan Park . . . . . . .Gg . .56
137 Burrowhayes Farm . . . . .Gg . .57
138 Blue Anchor Park . . . . .Hg . .57
134 Minehead & Exmoor Caravan Park Gg . .58
135 Quantock Orchard Caravan Park . .Hg . .58
148 Home Farm Holiday Park . . . . . . .Hg . .59
149 Greenacres Camping . . . . .Hg . .59
139 The Old Oaks Touring Park . . . . . .Hg . .60
140 Isle of Avalon Touring Park . . . . . .Hg . .60
141 Broadway House Holiday Park . . . .Hg . .61
142 Southfork Caravan Park . . . . .Hg . .61
150 Long Hazel Caravan Park . . . . . . .Hg . .62
143 Mendip Heights Caravan Park . . . .Hg . .62
151 Chew Valley Caravan Park . . . . . .Hg . .63
144 Baltic Wharf Caravan Club Site . . .Hg . .63
145 Bath Marina and Caravan Park . . . .Hg . .64

Wiltshire

166 Piccadilly Caravan Park . . . . .Hg . .64
168 Plough Lane Caravan Site . . . . . . .Hg . .65
169 Longleat Caravan Club Site . . . . .Hg . .65
167 Alderbury Caravan Park . . . . .Jg . .66

Dorset

181 Newlands Caravan Park . . . . .Hf . .66
176 Wood Farm Caravan Park . . . . . . .Hf . .67
173 Monkton Wylde Farm Touring Park Hf . .67
174 Golden Cap Holiday Park . . . . . . .Hf . .68

		map ref	page
175	Highlands End Holiday Park	Hf	68
178	Freshwater Beach Holiday Park	Hf	69
177	Binghams Farm Touring Park	Hf	69
180	East Fleet Farm Touring Park	Hf	70
201	Sandyholme Holiday Park	Hf	70
202	Ulwell Cottage Caravan Park	Jf	71
203	Wareham Forest Tourist Park	Hf	72
204	Manor Farm Caravan Park	Hf	72
205	Rowlands-Wait Touring Park	Hf	73
206	Wilksworth Farm Caravan Park	Jg	73
207	The Inside Park	Hg	74
208	Merley Court Touring Park	Jf	75
209	Whitemead Caravan Park	Hf	75
210	Sandford Holiday Park	Hf	76
211	Pear Tree Touring Park	Hf	76
212	Hoburne Park	Jf	77
213	Grove Farm Meadow Holiday Park	Jf	77
214	Mount Pleasant Touring Park	Jf	78

Hampshire

225	Bashley Park	Jf	78
229	Sandy Balls Holiday Centre	Jg	79
226	Camping International	Jg	80
231	Hollands Wood C&C Site	Jg	80
230	Ashurst C&C Site	Jg	81
234	Shamba Touring Park	Jg	81
235	*Red Shoot Camping Park*	Jg	82
228	Lytton Lawn Touring Park	Jf	82
232	C&C Club Site Chichester	Jg	83

Isle of Wight

245	The Orchards Holiday Park	Jf	83
244	Adgestone Camping Park	Jf	84
247	Southland Camping Park	Jf	85
248	Appuldurcombe Gardens	Jf	85
249	Kite Hill Caravan Park	Jf	86
250	Heathfield Farm Camping	Jf	86

Oxfordshire

257	Lincoln Farm Park	Jh	87
260	Barnstones Caravan Park	Jh	87
258	Cotswold View Caravan Site	Jh	88
262	Wysdom Touring Park	Jh	88
261	Bo Peep Farm Caravan Park	Jh	89

Berkshire

| 269 | Wellington Country Park | Kg | 89 |

Buckinghamshire

| 275 | Highclere Farm Touring Park | Jg | 90 |

Surrey

| 281 | C&C Club Site Chertsey | Kg | 90 |
| 282 | C&C Club Site Horsley | Kg | 91 |

Sussex

289	White Rose Touring Park	Kg	92
288	Raylands Caravan Park	Kg	92
294	*Honeybridge Park*	Kg	93

		map ref	page
295	*Washington Caravan Park*	Kg	93
290	Horam Manor Touring Park	Kf	93
293	Sheepcote Valley Caravan Club	Kg	94
292	Bay View Caravan Park	Kg	94
296	*Whydown Farm Tourist Park*	Kg	95

Kent

309	Black Horse Caravan Club Site	Lg	95
310	Hawthorn Farm C&C Site	Lg	95
306	Yew Tree Caravan Park	Lg	96
307	C&C Club Site Canterbury	Lg	96
311	*Quex Caravan Park*	Lg	97
304	Broadhembury Holiday Park	Lg	97
303	Tanner Farm Touring Park	Kg	98
305	Pine Lodge Touring Park	Kg	99
312	*Gate House Wood Touring Park*	Kg	99

London

327	*Crystal Palace Caravan Club Site*	Kg	100
321	Lee Valley Caravan Park	Kh	101
325	Lee Valley Campsite	Kg	101
322	Ashridge Farm Touring Park	Kh	102
326	Abbey Wood Caravan Club Site	Kg	102

Essex

| 330 | The Grange Country Park | Lh | 103 |

Suffolk

| 332 | Lakeside Leisure Park | Lh | 104 |
| 331 | Low House Touring Centre | Lh | 104 |

Norfolk

351	Liffens Holiday Park	Lj	105
349	The Grange Touring Park	Lj	105
339	The Dower House Touring Park	Kh	106
348	Little Lakeland Caravan Park	Lh	106
338	Clippesby Holidays	Lj	107
343	Kelling Heath Holiday Park	Lj	108
350	Woodhill Park	Lj	109
346	The Garden Caravan Site	Kj	109
340	Old Brick Kilns Caravan Park	Kj	110
344	Gatton Waters Touring Site	Kj	110
342	Two Mills Touring Park	Lj	111
345	Little Haven Caravan Park	Lj	111
347	Breckland Meadows Touring Park	Kj	111

Cambridgeshire

355	Old Manor Caravan Park	Kh	112
358	*Ferry Meadows Caravan Club Site*	Kh	112
356	Highfield Farm Camping Park	Kh	113
357	Park Lane Touring Caravan Park	Kh	113

Lincolnshire

366	Walesby Woodlands Caravan Park	Kj	114
369	Bainland Country Park	Kj	114
367	Lakeside Park	Kj	115
373	Skegness Sands Touring Site	Kj	115
365	Cherry Tree Site	Kj	116
371	Manby Caravan Park	Kj	116

map ref   page

375 Foreman's Bridge Caravan Park . . . .Kj .117
370 Pilgrims Way Caravan Park . . . . . .Kj .117

Derbyshire

380 Highfields Caravan Park . . . . .Jj .118
385 Rivendale Caravan Park . . . . .Jj .119
383 The Firs Farm . . . . .Jj .119
382 Darwin Forest Country Park . . . . . .Jj .120
384 Lime Tree Park . . . . .Jj .120

Northamptonshire

394 Smeaton's Lakes Touring Park . . . . .Jj .121
395 Orchard Park Touring Park . . . . . . .Jj .121
392 Riverside Caravan Park . . . . .Jj .121

Staffordshire

396 Silvertrees Caravan Park . . . . .Jj .122
397 Glencote Caravan Park . . . . .Hj .122

Gloucestershire

410 Cotswold Hoburne . . . . .Jg .123
412 Briarfields Caravan and Camping . .Hh .123
411 Tewkesbury Caravan Club Site . . . .Hh .124

Warwickshire

407 Somers Wood Caravan Park . . . . . .Jh .124
390 Bosworth Water Trust . . . . .Jj .125
404 C&C Club Site Clent Hills . . . . . . .Hh .125

Worcestershire

419 Kingsgreen Caravan Park . . . . . . .Hh .125
420 The Boyce Caravan Park . . . . . . .Hh .126
421 Lickhill Manor Caravan Park . . . . .Hh .126
418 Ranch Caravan Park . . . . .Jh .127

Herefordshire

432 Broadmeadow Caravan Park . . . . . .Hh .127
430 Poston Mill Park . . . . .Hh .128
431 Luck's All Caravan Park . . . . .Hh .128

Shropshire

442 Severn Gorge Caravan Park . . . . . .Hj .128
438 Fernwood Caravan Park . . . . .Hj .129
439 Westbrook Park . . . . .Hh .129
440 Stanmore Hall Touring Park . . . . . .Hh .130
441 Beaconsfield Farm Touring Park . . .Hj .130

Yorkshire

450 Waudby's Caravan Park . . . . .Jk .131
451 Thorpe Hall Caravan Site . . . . . . .Kk .132
473 Far Grange Park . . . . .Kk .132
452 Flower of May Holiday Park . . . . .Kk .133
453 Northcliffe Holiday Park . . . . .Jm .133
454 St Helens in the Park . . . . .Jk .134
455 Cayton Village Caravan Park . . . . .Kk .134
456 Golden Square Caravan Park . . . . . .Jk .135
457 Wombleton Caravan Park . . . . . . .Jk .135
458 Foxholme Touring Caravan Park . . .Jk .136

map ref   page

460 Vale of Pickering Caravan Park . . . .Jk .136
474 *Jasmine Park* . . . . .Jk .137
463 Ripley Caravan Park . . . . .Jk .137
465 Fangfoss Old Station Caravan Park .Jk .138
461 Moorside Caravan Park . . . . .Jk .138
464 Goose Wood Caravan Park . . . . . .Jk .139
462 Rawcliffe Manor Caravan Park . . . .Jk .139
471 Rudding Holiday Park . . . . .Jk .140
470 Nostell Priory Holiday Park . . . . . .Jk .140
469 Constable Burton Hall Caravan Park Jk .141
475 *Howgill Lodge Caravan Park* . . . . .Jk .141
467 Wood Nook Caravan Park . . . . . . .Hk .142
468 Street Head Caravan Park . . . . .Hk .143
472 Knight Stainforth Caravan Park . . .Hk .143
466 Woodhouse Farm Caravan Park . . . .Jk .144
476 *Riverside Meadows Country Park* . .Jk .144

Lancashire

528 Abbey Farm Caravan Park . . . . . . .Hk 145
529 Royal Umpire Caravan Park . . . . . .Hk .146
530 Kneps Farm Holiday Park . . . . . . .Hk .146
531 Pipers Height Caravan Park . . . . . .Hk .147
532 Bridge House Caravan Park . . . . . .Hk .147
534 Old Hall Caravan Park . . . . .Hk .148
535 Holgates Caravan Park . . . . .Hk .148

Cumbria

552 Skelwith Fold Caravan Park . . . . .Hm .149
553 Walls Caravan Park . . . . .Hk .150
561 Waterfoot Caravan Park . . . . .Hm .150
555 Limefitt Park . . . . .Hm .151
556 Sykeside Camping Park . . . . .Hm .151
554 Fallbarrow Park . . . . .Hk .152
562 Cove Camping Park . . . . .Hm .153
551 The Larches Caravan Park . . . . . . .Hm .153
557 Wild Rose Park . . . . .Hm .154
560 Pennine View Caravan Park . . . . . .Hm .155
559 Westmorland Caravan Site . . . . . . .Hm .155

Northumberland

576 Percy Wood Caravan Park . . . . . . .Jn .156
575 Waren Caravan Park . . . . .Jn .157
577 Dunstan Hill C&C Club Site . . . . . .Jn .157
578 Brown Rigg Caravan Park . . . . . . .Hm .158
580 Ord House Country Park . . . . .Hn 158

Co. Durham

571 Doe Park Touring Park . . . . .Jm .159
572 C&C Club Site Barnard Castle . . . .Jm .159

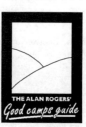

map ref *page*

WALES

South

592	The Bridge Caravan Park	Hh	.160
606	*Tredegar House Caravan Club Site*	Hg	.161
593	Cwmcarn Forest Drive Campsite	Hg	.161
594	Pembrey Caravan Club Site	Gh	.162
607	*C&C Club Site Rhandirmwyn*	Gh	.162
596	Abermarlais Caravan Park	Gh	.163
595	Afon Lodge Caravan Park	Gh	.163
597	Noble Court Holiday Park	Gh	.164
598	Moreton Farm Leisure Park	Gh	.164
599	Freshwater East Caravan Club Site	Gh	.165
600	Gwaun Vale Holiday Touring Park	Fh	.165
601	Cenarth Falls Holiday Park	Gh	.166
608	*Llwyngwair Manor Holiday Park*	Gh	.166
603	Brynich Caravan Park	Hh	.167
604	Pencelli Castle Caravan & Camping	Hh	167

Mid Wales

628	Aeron Coast Caravan Park	Gh	.168
629	Glan-y-Mor Leisure Park	Gh	.168
630	Ocean View Caravan Park	Gh	.169
632	Fforest Fields Caravan Park	Hh	.169
631	Disserth Caravan Park	Hh	.170
633	Daisy Bank Touring Park	Hh	.170
636	Pen-y-Garth Caravan Park	Gj	.171
637	*Hendre Mynach Touring Park*	Gj	.171
635	Barcdy Caravan and Camping Park	Gj	.171

North

658	C&C Club Site Llanystumdwy	Gj	.172
659	Beddgelert Caravan Site	Gj	.172
660	Bryn Gloch Caravan Park	Gj	.173
661	Cadnant Valley Caravan Park	Gj	.173
664	Home Farm Caravan Park	Gj	.174
669	Bron-Y-Wendon Touring Park	Gj	.174
665	Hunter's Hamlet Touring Park	Gj	.175
670	Ty Ucha Caravan Park	Hj	.175
667	The Plassey Touring Park	Hj	.176
668	James' Caravan Park	Hj	.176

SCOTLAND

Lowlands

692	Cressfield Caravan Park	Hm	.177
691	Hoddom Castle Caravan Park	Hm	.178
693	Park of Brandedleys	Gm	.179
694	Caldons Caravan Site	Gm	.179
695	Brighouse Bay Holiday Park	Gm	.180
702	Aird Donald Caravan Park	Gm	.180
701	C&C Club Site Culzean Castle	Gn	181
703	*Gibson Park Caravan Club Site*	Hn	.181
696	Crossburn Caravan Park	Hn	.182
697	The Monks' Muir	Hn	.182
698	Drum Mohr Caravan Park	Hn	.183
699	Mortonhall Caravan Park	Hn	.183
704	*Slatebarns Caravan Park*	Hn	.184
700	Strathclyde Country Park	Gn	.184

map ref *page*

Heart

724	Tullichewan Holiday Park	Gn	.185
725	Glen Dochart Caravan Park	Go	.185
723	Trossachs Holiday Park	Gn	.186
726	Ardgartan Caravan Site	Go	.186
727	Auchterarder Caravan Park	Go	.187
728	Nether Craig Caravan Park	Ho	.187
729	Craigtoun Meadows Holiday Park	Ho	.188
730	Blair Castle Caravan Park	Go	.188
731	Twenty Shilling Wood	Go	.189
732	Witches Craig Caravan Park	Gn	.189

Grampian

755	Huntly Castle Caravan Park	Hp	.190
753	Aden Country Caravan Park	Hp	.190
754	Aberlour Gardens Caravan Park	Hp	.191
766	Spindrift Caravan Park	Gp	.191
769	Torvean Caravan Park	Gp	.191
767	Grantown-on-Spey Caravan Park	Hp	.192
768	Glenmore Caravan & Camping	Gp	.192
773	Scourie Caravan & Camping	Gq	.193
772	Woodend Camping & Caravan	Gq	.193
770	Pitgrudy Caravan Park	Gp	.194
771	Ardmair Point Caravan Park	Gp	.194
774	Loch Greshornish Camping Site	Fp	.194
775	Staffin Caravan and Camping Site	Fp	.195
776	Reraig Caravan Site	Fp	.195
778	Faichem Park	Gp	.196
779	Invercoe Caravan Park	Go	.196
780	Resipole Farm Caravan Park	Fo	.197
781	C&C Club Site Oban	Fo	.197
782	Oban Divers Caravan Park	Fo	.197
783	Glen Nevis Caravan Park	Go	.198
784	North Ledaig Caravan Park	Fo	.198
785	Linnhe Caravan Park	Go	.199
786	Glendaruel Caravan Park	Gn	.199

NORTHERN IRELAND

Antrim

831	Carnfunnock Country Park	Dd	.201
832	Curran Court Caravan Park	Dd	.201
834	Drumaheglis Caravan Park	Dd	.202
835	Bush Caravan Park	De	.202

Londonderry

860	Bellemont Caravan Park	De	.203
859	Tullans Farm Caravan Park	De	.203

Tyrone

856	Gortin Glen Caravan Park	Cd	.204

Down

842	Tollymore Forest Caravan Park	Dc	.204

Fermanagh

850	LoanEden Caravan Park	Cd	.205
851	Blaney Caravan Park	Cd	.205
852	Share Holiday Village	Cd	.206

REPUBLIC OF IRELAND

Donegal
864 Knockalla Caravan Park ....Ce .206
869 Greenlands Caravan Park ....Cd .207
870 Gateway Caravan Park ....Cd .207

Mayo
874 Cong Caravan Park ....Bc .208
875 Belleek Caravan Park ....Bd .208
876 Keel Sandybanks Caravan Park ... .Bc .209
877 Parkland Caravan Park ....Bc .209
878 Knock Caravan Park ....Bc .210
879 Carra Caravan Park ....Bc .210

Westmeath
882 Hodson Bay Caravan Park ....Cc .211

Roscommon
896 Lough Ree East Caravan Park .....Cc .211

Louth
889 Táin Holiday Village ....Dc .212

Offaly
906 Green Gables Caravan Park ......Cb .212

Dublin
910 Camac Valley Tourist Park ....Dc 213

Wicklow
913 Roundwood Caravan Park ....Db .213
914 Valley Stopover and Caravan Park .Db .214
915 River Valley Caravan Park ....Db .214
916 Moat Farm Caravan Park ....Db .215

Kildare
908 Forest Farm Caravan Park ......Cb .215

Laois
920 Kirwans Caravan Park ....Cb .216

Kilkenny
923 Nore Valley Park ....Cb .216
924 Tree Grove Caravan Park ....Cb .217

Wexford
930 Morriscastle Strand Caravan Park . .Db .217

Waterford
933 Casey's Caravan Park ....Ca .218
934 Newtown Cove Caravan Park .....Ca .218

Tipperary
939 Carrick-on-Suir Caravan Park .....Ca .219
941 The Apple Caravan Park ....Cb .219
938 Parsons Green Caravan Park ......Ca .220

Limerick
945 Curraghchase Caravan Park ......Bb .220

Clare
901 Shannon Cottage Caravan Park ....Bb 221

Cork
948 Blarney Caravan Park ....Ba .221
949 Sonas Caravan Park ....Ca .222
950 The Meadow Camping Park ......Ba .222
951 Eagle Point Caravan Park ....Ba .223
952 Barleycove Holiday Park ....Aa .223

Kerry
955 Anchor Caravan Park ....Ab .224
956 Wave Crest Caravan Park ....Aa .224
957 Creveen Lodge Caravan Park .....Aa .225
958 Waterville Caravan Park ....Aa .225
959 Fossa Caravan and Camping Park . .Ba .226
960 Glenross Caravan & Camping Park Aa .226
961 Mannix Point Caravan Park ......Aa .227
962 Fleming's White Bridge ....Ba .227
963 White Villa Farm Caravan Park ... .Ba .228
964 The Flesk Muckross Caravan Park .Ba .228
965 Woodlands Park Touring Park ... .Bb .229

CHANNEL ISLANDS

Jersey
971 Rozel Camping Park 231
972 Beuvelande Camp Site 231

Guernsey
977 Vaugrat Camping 232
978 Fauxquets Valley Campsite 232

Herm
983 Seagull Campsite 233

Sark
987 Pomme de Chien Campsite 233

New Parks: Parks that are new to the guide this year are highlighted in bold type in this index.

Map grid system: Each grid square is identified by co-ordinates in the form of two letters - one on the horizontal axis, and a different one on the vertical axis. In the index each park is identified by two letters, indicating the map grid square in which it is located, followed by a number which identifies the actual site location within that square. We hope this will make it easier and quicker to identify the location of parks in unfamiliar areas.

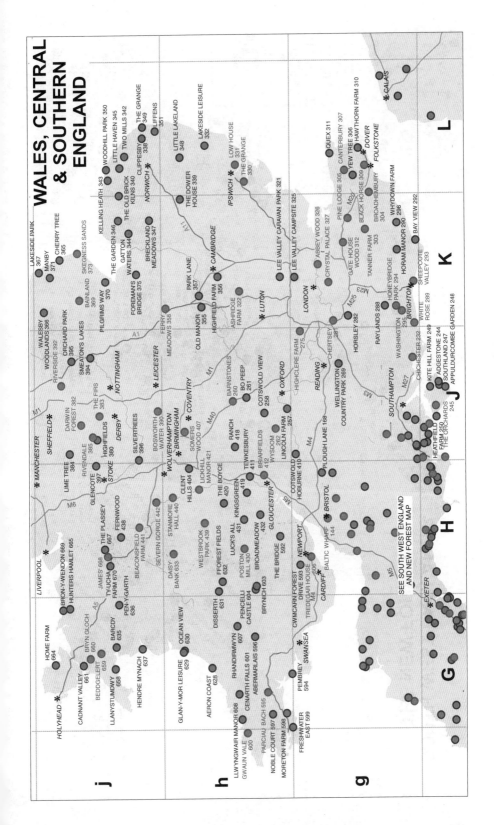

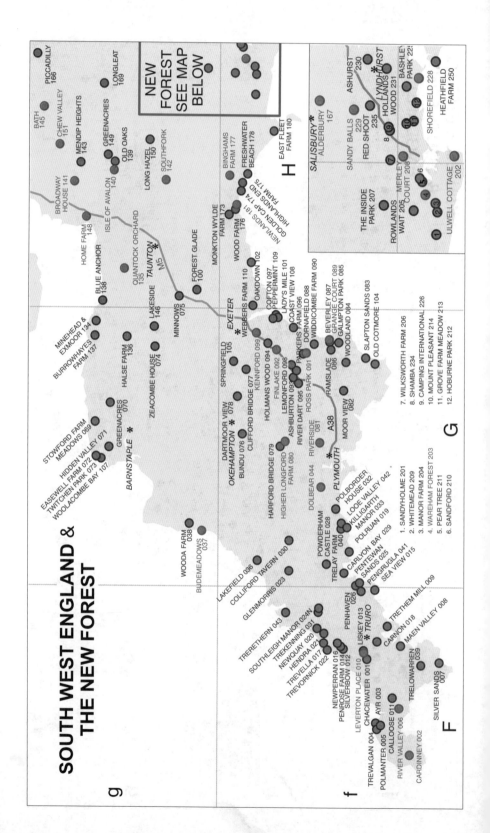

SOUTH WEST ENGLAND & THE NEW FOREST

g

f

NEW FOREST SEE MAP BELOW

PICCADILLY 166
BATH 145
CHEW VALLEY 151
LONGLEAT 169
MENDIP HEIGHTS 143
GREENACRES 149
BROADWAY HOUSE 141
ISLE OF AVALON 140
OLD OAKS 139
LONG HAZEL 150
SOUTHFORK 142
HOME FARM 148
BINGHAMS FARM 177
FRESHWATER BEACH 178
EAST FLEET FARM 180
MONKTON WYLDE FARM 176
WOOD FARM 173
HIGHLANDS END FARM 175
GOLDEN CAP 174
NEWLANDS 181
BLUE ANCHOR 138
QUANTOCK ORCHARD 135
TAUNTON *
M5
FOREST GLADE 100
MINEHEAD & EXMOOR 134
LAKESIDE 146
MINNOWS 075
BURROWHAYES FARM 137
HALSE FARM 136
ZEACOMBE HOUSE 074
MONKTON WYLDE FARM 176
WEBBERS FARM 110
OAKDOWN 102
STOWFORD FARM MEADOWS 069
GREENACRES 070
SPRINGFIELD 105
KENFORD 099
COFTON 097
PEPPERMINT 109
LADY'S MILE 101
COAST VIEW 108
HIDDEN VALLEY 071
BARNSTAPLE *
DARTMOOR VIEW 078
CLIFFORD BRIDGE 077
HOLMANS WOOD 094
FINLAKE 092
PARKERS FARM 096
DORNAFIELD 088
WIDDICOMBE FARM 090
EASEWELL FARM 072
TWITCHEN PARK 073
WOOLACOMBE BAY 107
EXETER *
LEMONFORD 098
ASHBURTON 093
BEVERLEY 087
GRANGE COURT 089
GALMPTON PARK 085
OKEHAMPTON *
BUNDU 076
RIVER DART 095
ROSS PARK 091
RAMSLADE 086
WOODLAND 084
SLAPTON SANDS 083
HARFORD BRIDGE 079
HIGHER LONGFORD FARM 080
RIVERSIDE 081
A38
MOOR VIEW 082
OLD COTMORE 104
PLYMOUTH *
WOODA FARM 038
BUDEMEADOWS 037
LAKEFIELD 036
COLLIFORD TAVERN 030
POLBORDER HOUSE 032
LOOE VALLEY 042
KILLIGARTH MANOR 033
POLRUAN 019
COLLIFORD 023
GLENMORRIS 023
POWDERHAM CASTLE 028
TRELAY FARM 040
CARLYON BAY 029
PENTEWAN SANDS 025
PENGRUGLA 041
SEA VIEW 015
TRERETHEN 043
PENHAVEN 026
SOUTHLEIGH MANOR 024N
TREKENNING 031
NEWQUAY 020
HENDRA 021
TRETHEM MILL 009
LISKEY 013
TRURO *
CARNON 018
MAEN VALLEY 008
NEWPERRAN 016
PENROSE FARM 014
SILVERBOW 012
LEVERTON PLACE 010
CHACEWATER 001
AYR 003
TRELOWARREN 039
TREVALGAN 004
POLMANTER 005
CALLOOSE 011
RIVER VALLEY 006
SILVER SANDS 007
CARDINNEY 002
TREVELLA 017
TREVORNICK 022

1. SANDYHOLME 201
2. WHITEMEAD 209
3. MANOR FARM 204
4. WAREHAM FOREST 203
5. PEAR TREE 211
6. SANDFORD 210
7. WILKSWORTH FARM 206
8. SHAMBA 234
9. CAMPING INTERNATIONAL 226
10. MOUNT PLEASANT 214
11. GROVE FARM MEADOW 213
12. HOBURNE PARK 212

H

G

F

SALISBURY* ALDERBURY 167
ASHURST 230
SANDY BALLS 229
RED SHOOT 235
LYNDHURST *
HOLLANDS WOOD 231
BASHLEY PARK 22?
SHOREFIELD 228
HEATHFIELD FARM 250
THE INSIDE PARK 207
ROWLANDS WAIT 205
MERLEY COURT 208
ULWELL COTTAGE 202
254

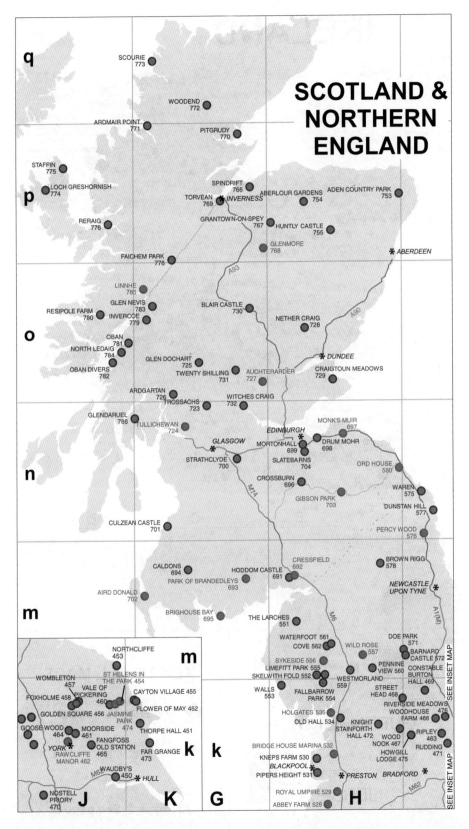

q

SCOURIE
773

WOODEND
772

**SCOTLAND &
NORTHERN
ENGLAND**

ARDMAIR POINT
771

PITGRUDY
770

STAFFIN
775

p

LOCH GRESHORNISH
774

SPINDRIFT
766

ABERLOUR GARDENS
754

ADEN COUNTRY PARK
753

TORVEAN
769 *INVERNESS

RERAIG
776

GRANTOWN-ON-SPEY
767

HUNTLY CASTLE
755

GLENMORE
768

*ABERDEEN

FAICHEM PARK
778

A93

LINNHE
785

GLEN NEVIS
783

BLAIR CASTLE
730

RESIPOLE FARM
780

INVERCOE
779

NETHER CRAIG
728

o

OBAN
781

NORTH LEDAIG
784

GLEN DOCHART
725

A90

OBAN DIVERS
782

TWENTY SHILLING
731

AUCHTERARDER
727

*DUNDEE

CRAIGTOUN MEADOWS
729

ARDGARTAN
726

TROSSACHS
723

WITCHES CRAIG
732

GLENDARUEL
786

TULLICHEWAN
724

MONK'S MUIR
697

EDINBURGH
*

n

GLASGOW
*

MORTONHALL
699

DRUM MOHR
698

STRATHCLYDE
700

SLATEBARNS
704

ORD HOUSE
580

CROSSBURN
696

WAREN
575

GIBSON PARK
703

DUNSTAN HILL
577

M74

CULZEAN CASTLE
701

PERCY WOOD
576

CRESSFIELD
692

BROWN RIGG
578

CALDONS
694

HODDOM CASTLE
691

PARK OF BRANDEDLEYS
693

NEWCASTLE
UPON TYNE *

AIRD DONALD
702

m

BRIGHOUSE BAY
695

THE LARCHES
551

M6

A1(M)

WATERFOOT 561

COVE 562

DOE PARK
571

WILD ROSE
557

BARNARD
CASTLE 572

NORTHCLIFFE
453

m

SYKESIDE 556

PENNINE
VIEW 560

CONSTABLE
BURTON
HALL 469

WOMBLETON
457

ST HELENS IN
THE PARK 454

LIMEFITT PARK 555

SKELWITH FOLD 552

WESTMORLAND
559

VALE OF
PICKERING
460

CAYTON VILLAGE 455

WALLS
553

FALLBARROW
PARK 554

STREET
HEAD 468

FOXHOLME 458

RIVERSIDE MEADOWS
WOODHOUSE
FARM 466

476

FLOWER OF MAY 452

GOLDEN SQUARE 456

JASMINE
PARK

HOLGATES 535

OLD HALL 534

KNIGHT
STAINFORTH
HALL 472

RIPLEY
463

GOOSE WOOD
464

MOORSIDE
461

474

THORPE HALL 451

WOOD
NOOK 467

RUDDING
471

YORK *

FANGFOSS
OLD STATION
465

FAR GRANGE
473

BRIDGE HOUSE MARINA 532

HOWGILL
LODGE 475

RAWCLIFFE
MANOR 462

k

k

KNEPS FARM 530

BLACKPOOL *

RIDING
REACH 471

WAUDBY'S
450 *HULL

PIPERS HEIGHT 531

*PRESTON

BRADFORD *

M62

NOSTELL
PRIORY
470

J

K

G

ROYAL UMPIRE 529

ABBEY FARM 528

H

255

IRELAND

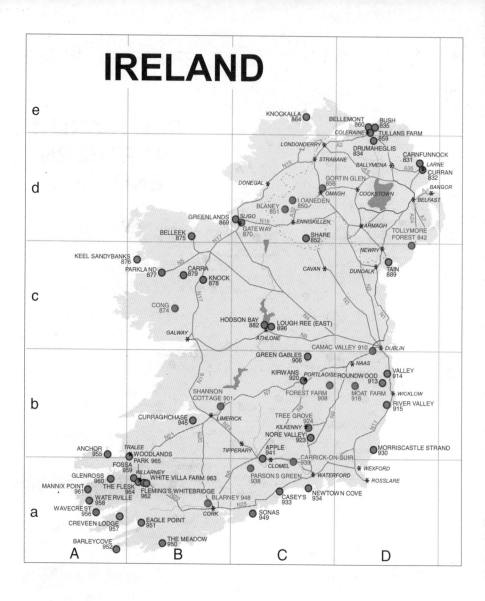

e — KNOCKALLA 864 · BELLEMONT 860 · BUSH 835 · COLERAINE * TULLANS FARM 859

LONDONDERRY * — A2 — DRUMAHEGLIS — CARNFUNNOCK 831 · LARNE

* STRABANE — BALLYMENA * — A36 — CURRAN 832

DONEGAL * — GORTIN GLEN 856 · * BANGOR

d — N15 — OMAGH * — COOKSTOWN · BELFAST

LOANEDEN 850 ·

BLANEY 851 ·

GREENLANDS 869 · SLIGO — N16 · * ENNISKILLEN · * ARMAGH · TOLLYMORE FOREST 842 ·

GATEWAY 870 ·

BELLEEK 875 · SHARE 852 · NEWRY *

N17

KEEL SANDYBANKS 876 · N5

PARKLAND 877 · CARRA 879 · CAVAN * — DUNDALK · TAIN 889 ·

KNOCK 878 ·

c — CONG 874 · N17 — N4

HODSON BAY 882 · LOUGH REE (EAST) 896 ·

GALWAY * — ATHLONE · N6

CAMAC VALLEY 910 · * DUBLIN

GREEN GABLES 906 · * NAAS

N18

KIRWANS 920 · PORTLAOISE · ROUNDWOOD 913 · VALLEY 914 ·

SHANNON COTTAGE 901 · N7 — FOREST FARM 908 · MOAT FARM 916 · * WICKLOW

b — RIVER VALLEY 915 ·

CURRAGHCHASE 945 · * LIMERICK · N24 — TREE GROVE 924 ·

N21 — N20 — KILKENNY · NORE VALLEY 923 ·

ANCHOR 955 · TRALEE · WOODLANDS PARK 965 · TIPPERARY * — APPLE 941 · CARRICK-ON-SUIR · MORRISCASTLE STRAND 930 ·

FOSSA 959 · CLOMEL · * WEXFORD

GLENROSS 960 · KILLARNEY · WHITE VILLA FARM 963 · PARSONS GREEN 938 · * WATERFORD · * ROSSLARE

MANNIX POINT 961 · THE FLESK 964 · FLEMING'S WHITEBRIDGE 962 · BLARNEY 948 · CASEY'S 933 · NEWTOWN COVE 934 ·

WATERVILLE 958 ·

WAVECREST 956 · CORK · N25 · SONAS 949 ·

a — CREVEEN LODGE 957 · EAGLE POINT 951 ·

BARLEYCOVE 952 · THE MEADOW 950 ·

A — B — C — D

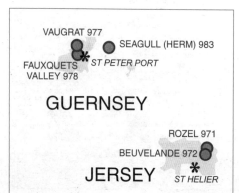

VAUGRAT 977 · SEAGULL (HERM) 983

FAUXQUETS VALLEY 978 · * ST PETER PORT

GUERNSEY

ROZEL 971

BEUVELANDE 972

JERSEY — * ST HELIER

KEY TO ALL MAPS

⬤ SITE NAME (ABBREVIATED) REFERENCE NUMBER

⬤ ALL YEAR ROUND SITE REFERENCE NUMBER

All maps © See page 2.